Higher Education

Labour Market Relevance and Outcomes of Higher Education in Four US States

OHIO, TEXAS, VIRGINIA AND WASHINGTON

OECD
BETTER POLICIES FOR BETTER LIVES

Please cite this publication as:
OECD (2020), *Labour Market Relevance and Outcomes of Higher Education in Four US States: Ohio, Texas, Virginia and Washington*, Higher Education, OECD Publishing, Paris, *https://doi.org/10.1787/38361454-en*.

ISBN 978-92-64-72873-8 (print)
ISBN 978-92-64-41149-4 (pdf)

Higher Education
ISSN 2616-9169 (print)
ISSN 2616-9177 (online)

Photo credits: Cover © elettaria/Shutterstock.com.

Corrigenda to publications may be found on line at: *www.oecd.org/about/publishing/corrigenda.htm*.

Foreword

Higher education systems play an essential role in economic growth and innovation in OECD countries. Workers with a higher education qualification continue to enjoy higher employment rates and a robust earnings advantage compared to those who have only completed upper secondary education. Today, however, many graduates have difficulty obtaining jobs that make full use of their skills and help them launch rewarding careers, while employers in some sectors of the economy lack qualified personnel. Policy makers are not only concerned about the current alignment of higher education systems to labour markets; they are increasingly uneasy about the future of work and its implications for education. Given the rising investments from students, families and governments in higher education, poor labour market outcomes for some graduates also raise concerns about the value of higher education.

Promoting alignment between higher education systems and labour market needs is an ongoing effort. Market economies are highly dynamic, and no lasting and comprehensive equilibrium between educational offerings and labour market demands can be reached. Many forces influence the supply and demand of graduate skills, from enduring trends such as globalisation, technological change or population ageing to exogenous shocks that disrupt economies and societies. The COVID-19 pandemic, which emerged as this report went into publication, exemplifies such a shock. Its ramifications for higher education systems and labour markets are deep, and it will be some time before a new – and different – alignment of labour markets and higher education systems is established in the four states we have examined, and in the wider US economy.

Initiated in 2017, the OECD project on the labour market relevance and outcomes of higher education explores how governments and institutions can improve the way higher education systems respond to labour market needs. This report, produced with the support of Lumina Foundation, is the third review in the series, following Norway (2018) and Mexico (2019). It examines four US states – Ohio, Texas, Virginia and Washington – in which the OECD team conducted interviews and workshops with over 200 stakeholder organisations in 2019.

Each state has distinctive governing institutions, higher education policies and labour market demands. Nonetheless, there are similar areas of misalignment between the labour market and higher education provision in the four states, and shared policy problems. All states struggle to meet employer demand for highly skilled graduates in fast-growing fields such as information and communications technology, as well as in high-demand fields such as teaching education, that lead to occupations that are socially important but not highly paid, such as teaching. Each of the four participating states – like other US states – has been unable to sustain public investment at levels that existed prior to the 2008-09 recession, putting at risk their ability to meet their goals for educational attainment. At the same time, the four states display a wide array of innovative policies and practices to help better align higher education and the labour market, ranging from public-private investments to significantly raise participation in work-based learning to digital tools providing up-to-date information about the skills needs of employers to students and educators. These innovations can form a rich basis for peer learning among US states and beyond.

Acknowledgements

This publication is part of the OECD project on the labour market relevance and outcomes of higher education and made possible by the support of the Lumina Foundation.

The OECD is grateful for the support of the state teams in Ohio, Texas, Virginia and Washington, led by Cheri Rice at the Ohio Department of Higher Education; Ginger Gossman, Jenna Cullinane Hege and David Gardner at the Texas Higher Education Coordinating Board; Peter Blake and Alan Edwards at the State Council of Higher Education for Virginia (SCHEV); and Isaak Kwakye, Michael Meotti and Daryl Monear at the Washington Student Achievement Council (WSAC). The state teams provided invaluable information to the OECD team, organised the team's visits across the four states, generously hosted the stakeholder workshops, and provided thoughtful comments on draft chapters. The authors are also grateful for the input of Maureen McLaughlin, Mark Schneider, Emily Slack and Diane Jones from the US Department of Education during the team's visit to Washington DC.

Our warm thanks go to the many experts and stakeholders across the four participating states and Washington, DC, who have shared their time and insights with the OECD team throughout the project. More than 200 stakeholder organisations across the four states participated in the interviews and workshops; representing government agencies, higher education institutions, employers, business associations, non-profit organisations and other organisations (a full list is available in Annex A of this report). The insights and opinions of stakeholders provided the OECD team with important contextual information that contributed to the interpretation of published data and research and to the formulation of policy recommendations.

We are grateful to Courtney Brown, Vice President of Strategic Impact, Lumina Foundation, who provided guidance and support throughout the life of the project; and to Kevin Stange, Associate Professor, University of Michigan Gerald R. Ford School of Public Policy, who shared expert guidance on the project planning and analysis and reviewed draft material at several points during the project.

The authors also wish to thank colleagues in the OECD for their input and advice, including Nora Brüning, Andrea-Rosalinde Hofer, Margarita Kalamova, Shizuka Kato and Cláudia Sarrico in the Higher Education Policy team, and Douglas Sutherland from the OECD Economics Department. We also wish to thank Shane Samuelson (Australian Government Department of Education) and Liam Lynch (Employment and Social Development Canada, Government of Canada), former members of the OECD Higher Education Policy team, for their contributions to the early development of the project.

While the report draws on data and analysis from the OECD, US and state sources, and a range of other published sources, any errors or misinterpretations remain the responsibility of the OECD team.

This report was prepared by the OECD's Higher Education Policy team in the Directorate for Education and Skills. Patricia Mangeol was the project leader responsible for co-ordinating the review. The authors of this report were: Chapter 1 (Introduction), Patricia Mangeol and Thomas Weko; Chapter 2 (United States context), Jonathan Williams, Monica Hanssen, Patricia Mangeol and Thomas Weko; Chapter 3 (Four states in a comparative perspective): Patricia Mangeol, Monica Hanssen, Simon Roy and Gillian Golden; Chapter 4 (Ohio), Simon Roy and Gillian Golden; Chapter 5 (Texas), Patricia Mangeol and Monica

Hanssen; Chapter 6 (Virginia), Simon Roy and Monica Hanssen, Chapter 7 (Washington), Patricia Mangeol and Monica Hanssen. Théodore Berut and Loris Vergolini developed the comparative context and scorecard tables presented in Chapter 3; Chloé Michaud and Carlos Moura Teixeira researched and drafted international policy examples. Théodore Berut, Maxence Castiello, Massimo Loi, and Loris Vergolini provided statistical analysis and support, with guidance from Gabriele Marconi. Thomas Weko, team leader and senior analyst of the OECD Higher Education Policy team, provided analytical guidance and advice throughout the project. Paulo Santiago, Head of the Policy Advice and Implementation Division in the Directorate of Education and Skills and Andreas Schleicher, Director of the Directorate for Education and Skills, reviewed the publication.

Cassandra Morley edited the report and provided administrative support to the project. Rachel Linden assisted with the editorial and production processes.

Table of contents

Tables

Figures

Boxes

Reader's guide

Use of "higher education" in this report

The term "higher education" in this report includes Levels 4 through 8 of the 2011 International Standard Classification of Education (ISCED) (UNESCO Institute for Statistics, 2012[1]). The correspondence between US and international higher education levels and terminology is provided in Table 1. The terms "higher education" and "post-secondary education" are used interchangeably in the report, as is commonly done in the United States.

This report focuses on sub-baccalaureate and baccalaureate levels, which include post-secondary (sub-baccalaureate) certificates, associate's degrees and bachelor's programmes, which account for the majority of entrants to the US labour market. It focuses principally on programmes offered by public higher education institutions, since state governments bear responsibility for the legal and financial bases of their operation.

Table 1. US and international educational levels

US terminology		ISCED 2011 levels and programme descriptions
Upper secondary education	High school diploma or equivalent (e.g. General Educational Development (GED) certificate)	*Upper secondary education (ISCED Level 3):* Programmes at ISCED Level 3 are typically designed to complete secondary education in preparation for tertiary education or provide skills relevant to employment, or both.
Sub-baccalaureate or sub-bachelor level	Post-secondary certificate programmes (also referred to as "certificates")*, and often delivered by higher education institutions	*Post-secondary non-tertiary education (ISCED Level 4):* Programmes at ISCED Level 4, or post-secondary non-tertiary education, are typically designed to provide individuals who completed ISCED Level 3 with non-tertiary qualifications required for progression to tertiary education or for employment when their ISCED Level 3 qualification does not grant such access. For example, graduates from general ISCED Level 3 programmes may choose to complete a non-tertiary vocational qualification; or graduates from vocational ISCED Level 3 programmes may choose to increase their level of qualifications or specialise further.
	Associate's degree programmes**	*Short-cycle tertiary education (ISCED Level 5):* Programmes at ISCED Level 5 aim to provide professional knowledge, skills and competencies. Typically, they are practically based, occupationally specific and prepare students to enter the labour market, but may also provide a pathway to other higher education programmes. Academic higher education programmes below the bachelor's level are also classified as ISCED Level 5. Programmes classified at ISCED Level 5 may be referred to as (higher) technical education, community college education, technician or advanced/higher vocational training, associate's degree or the *bac+2*.
Baccalaureate level	Bachelor's degree programmes	*Bachelor's or equivalent level (ISCED Level 6):* Programmes at ISCED Level 6 aim to provide intermediate academic and/or professional knowledge, skills and competencies, leading to a first degree or equivalent qualification. Programmes are typically theoretically based, but may include practical components and are informed by research and/or best professional practice. Programmes at this level do not necessarily involve the completion of a research project or thesis, but if they do, it is less advanced, less independent or is undertaken with more guidance than those at ISCED Levels 7 or 8. Programmes classified at ISCED Level 6 may be referred to as bachelor's programme, a *license*, or the first university cycle.

Post-baccalaureate level or post-graduate level	Master's degree programmes Post-bachelor's certificate programmes (or post-graduate certificates) Professional degree programmes (for instance, Medical Doctor (M.D.), Juris Doctor (J.D.)	*Master's or equivalent level (ISCED Level 7)*: Programmes at ISCED Level 7 are designed to provide advanced academic and/or professional knowledge, skills and competencies, leading to a second degree or equivalent qualification. Typically, programmes at this level are theoretically based, but may include practical components and are informed by state-of-the-art research and/or best professional practice. Programmes at this level may involve the completion of a research project or thesis that is more advanced than those expected at ISCED Level 6 and less advanced than those expected at ISCED Level 8. Master's programmes can be also entirely coursework-based in some countries, or there may be a differentiation between a coursework programme and a research programme. Programmes classified at ISCED Level 7 may be referred to in many ways, for example, master's programmes, magister or MPhil.
	Doctoral degree programmes	*Doctoral or equivalent level (ISCED Level 8)*: Programmes at ISCED Level 8 lead to an advanced research or qualification. Programmes at this ISCED Level are devoted to advanced study and original research, and are typically offered only by research-oriented higher education institutions, such as universities. Doctoral programmes exist in both academic and professional fields, and usually conclude with the submission and defence of a thesis, dissertation or equivalent written work of publishable quality, representing a significant contribution to knowledge in the respective field of study. In some education systems, ISCED Level 8 programmes contain very limited course work, or none at all, and individuals working towards a doctoral degree engage in research mostly independently or in small groups with varying degrees of supervision. Other countries require the completion of course work before the doctoral candidates can progress to the thesis component of the programme. Programme classified at ISCED Level 8 may be referred to in many ways, for example: PhD, DPhil, D.Lit., D.Sc., LL.D, Doctorate or similar terms.

Notes: *Post-secondary certificates vary in terms of length, from a few weeks to more than two years. They are most often less than a year or one to two years in length. They can be referred to as short or long certificates, less-than-two-year awards, and other terms. While the classroom training component of apprenticeship programme is often delivered by two-year colleges, licenses obtained by apprentices are not usually considered post-secondary qualifications. However, while not reflected in the table, apprenticeships are a pathway of growing interest in several states and are discussed in the report.

**Associate-level programmes are either academically oriented or prepare students for direct labour market entry. Academically oriented programmes are often called "transfer" programmes or stream, because students enrolled in these programmes aim to transfer the academic credits obtained through their associate's degree toward the completion of a bachelor's degree. The majority of students in associate's degree programmes in the United States are enrolled in an academically oriented, or transfer, programme. Associate-level programmes that prepare students for labour market entry are referred to in different ways, such as technical or professional programmes or streams.

Source: UNESCO Institute for Statistics (2012[1]), OECD (2019[2]).

Key terms used in the report

The report uses terminology that is specific to higher education in the United States. Some of the most commonly used terms are defined below.

- **Credit transfer:** Credit transfer refers to the process by which students are able to have the credits acquired in one post-secondary programme applied towards the completion of another, typically more advanced programme. This most often applies to the transfer of credits obtained in a programme of study at a two-year institution towards a programme of study at a four-year institution. A wide variety of processes are in place in US states to support this process, from state-wide articulation agreements that aim to indicate which academic credits obtained in two-year institutions are expected to be recognised by four-year institutions to institution- and programme-specific requirements that determine whether students' academic credits will be recognised towards a more advanced programme of study.
- **Non-resident alien:** This term refers to international students. International students are not citizens or permanent residents of the United States and are in the country on a temporary basis.
- **Open access:** Open access admissions, or non-selective admissions, are in place at most two-year colleges. They refer to a process by which students can enrol in an institution without having to demonstrate a set level of academic achievement or preparedness.

- **Post-secondary institutions:** As described in Chapter 2, a wide range of higher education institutions exists in the United States. The most commonly used criteria to differentiate institutions include:
  - Control: In the US, post-secondary institutions can be public, private not-for-profit or private for-profit. Private for-profit institutions are sometimes also referred to as "proprietary institutions". Private not-for-profit and private for-profit institutions are classified as independent private institutions (see the *OECD Handbook for Internationally Comparative Education Statistics 2018* (2018[3]) for a definition) in international statistics.
  - Educational offerings: Two-year institutions mostly deliver programmes below the bachelor's level and four-year institutions deliver programmes at bachelor's and post-graduate level.

  Two-year institutions are often referred to as community colleges, although the term used may vary both between states and within states. Four-year institutions are referred to as either "universities" or "colleges".
- **Qualifications, credentials and awards:** These terms are commonly used in US higher education policy and practice, and may have different meanings depending on the context. In general, qualifications refer to certificates and degrees obtained in a post-secondary education institution. Credentials and awards are usually broader in scope, including post-secondary qualifications and "alternative credentials" that may be delivered by other providers, such as specialised training firms or employers. Alternative credentials are very diverse, encompassing industry certifications, micro-credentials, or digital badges (see Box 3.15 in Chapter 3).
- **Race and ethnicity:** The report assesses post-secondary education participation and labour market outcomes according to several demographic variables, including race and ethnicity, which are self-reported categories available in many of the US data sources used in this report. While US data collections use several groups, those most commonly reported include Asian, Black/African American, Hispanic/Latino and White. Racial and ethnic categories are mutually exclusive. The "Black/African American" and "White" groups refer to non-Hispanic persons. For further details, readers should refer to technical documentation for the American Community Survey, compiled by IPUMS USA (n.d.[4]).
- **Skills:** The report refers to three broad levels of skills: low, medium (also referred to as middle or mid-level), and high (also referred to as advanced). These levels refer to individuals' ability to perform job tasks at different levels of complexity. While skills can be acquired in a variety of contexts, and despite limitations in associating skills and educational levels, educational qualifications are often used as a proxy for skills (OECD, 2019[5]). In addition, the US Occupation Information Network (O*NET) identifies a minimum level of education estimated to be necessary to fulfil job tasks in each occupational group. Thus, skills levels referenced in the report should be broadly understood as follows:
  - Low skills refer to the skills needed to perform a job that requires upper secondary education or less.
  - Medium (or mid-level, middle) skills refer to skills required to perform jobs usually requiring some form of post-secondary education (several months to two years).
  - High (or advanced) skills refer to skills required to perform jobs usually requiring a bachelor's degree or above.

  The report also refers to transversal skills, a term that is used interchangeably with the term "transferable skills". It refers to skills that are not job-specific but rather are used across a range of jobs and occupations. These skills can be cognitive (e.g. writing), socio-emotional (e.g. team work), or technical (e.g. programming).
- **Some college, no degree:** The US Census Bureau's American Community Survey (ACS) tracks the population of individuals who report having completed some courses at the post-secondary

level but who have not obtained a degree. This category includes both individuals who started but did not complete a post-secondary qualification and individuals who completed post-secondary qualifications shorter than associate's degrees, such as certificates. There is no separate category in the American Community Survey permitting the identification of individuals whose highest educational attainment is a post-secondary certificate.

- **Standard Occupation Classification (SOC):** The SOC system is used by US federal statistical agencies to classify workers and jobs into occupational categories. The SOC was last updated in 2018 and contains 23 major occupational groups. The report frequently refers to ten occupational groups in which jobs typically require post-secondary education based on US Bureau of Labor Statistics occupational information. These include: 11-0000 (Management), 13-0000 (Business and Financial Operations), 15-0000 (Computer and Mathematical), 17-0000 (Architecture and Engineering), 19-0000 (Life, Physical, and Social Science), 21-0000 (Community and Social Service), 23-0000 (Legal Occupations), 25-0000 (Education, Training, and Library), 27-0000 (Arts, Design, Entertainment, Sports, and Media), and 29-0000 (Healthcare Practitioners and Technical Occupations).

Sources of quantitative data

This report uses international, national and state data sources. OECD data are used for international comparisons in Chapter 1, which provides an overview of the United States labour market and higher education context, and in Chapter 3, which presents key graduate outcomes data for the United States and international jurisdictions. Colombia was not an OECD Member at the time of preparation of this publication. Accordingly, Colombia does not appear in the list of OECD Members and is not included in the zone aggregates. International data usually refers to higher education as encompassing ISCED Levels 5 to 8. When conducting international comparisons, these levels are used.

US national data sources are used throughout the report, including in state-specific chapters, as they permit comparisons between averages in the four states and the national average. The report principally uses databases from the following national sources:

- The U.S. Census Bureau's American Community Survey (2019[6])
- The National Center of Education Statistics' Integrated Postsecondary Education System (2019[7])
- The Bureau of Labor Statistics' Occupational Employment Statistics (2019[8])
- The Bureau of Labor Statistics' Current Population Survey (2019[9])

Each state chapter uses a range of state-specific data sources. These data are generally produced by government agencies responsible for higher education and workforce policies, and by other organisations, such as certain higher education sub-systems (e.g. the State Board of Community and Technical Colleges in Washington produces data for community colleges). These data are most often publicly available in reports and interactive dashboards. In some cases, indicated in the report, state agencies provided additional data not readily available via public sources to the OECD team.

Non-governmental sources are also used when relevant, including data from Lumina Foundation, the State Higher Education Executive Officers (SHEEO) association, the Education Commission for the States, or the Institute for College Access and Success (TICAS).

Detailed information on the sources and definitions used in the two comparative tables provided in Chapter 3 can be found in Annex B.

Data updates

This report makes use of the most recent data available at the time of its preparation. Data extracted from national databases were updated as of 31 December 2019, except when otherwise noted. State-specific data are based on reports that were used at the time of drafting.

Symbols for missing data

Two following symbols are used in case of missing data:

- *a* Data are not applicable (for example, certain categories used in US data do not exist in international data collections).
- *m* Data are missing.

Source of qualitative information

Extensive qualitative information was collected to prepare this report. The sources include:

- Background reports provided to the OECD by the state agencies responsible for higher education in the participating states: the Ohio Department of Higher Education (ODHE), the Texas Higher Education Coordinating Board (THECB), the State Council of Higher Education for Virginia (SCHEV), and the Washington Student Achievement Council (WSAC).
- Written and oral comments from staff at the ODHE, THECB, SCHEV and WSAC on draft chapters and documents prepared by the OECD during the course of the project.
- Interviews and workshops with stakeholders in the four participating states. These are described in Annex A of this report.

References

IPUMS USA (n.d.), *IPUMS Documentation: User's Guide*, https://usa.ipums.org/usa/doc.shtml (accessed on 15 April 2020). [4]

NCES (2019), *Integrated Postsecondary Education Data System (database)*, National Center for Education Statistics, https://nces.ed.gov/ipeds/use-the-data (accessed on 18 January 2020). [7]

OECD (2019), *Benchmarking Higher Education System Performance*, Higher Education, OECD Publishing, Paris, https://dx.doi.org/10.1787/be5514d7-en. [2]

OECD (2019), *The Survey of Adult Skills, Reader's Companion, Third Edition*, OECD Publishing, Paris, http://dx.doi.org/doi.org/10.1787/23078731. [5]

OECD (2018), *OECD Handbook for Internationally Comparative Education Statistics 2018: Concepts, Standards, Definitions and Classifications*, OECD Publishing, Paris, https://dx.doi.org/10.1787/9789264304444-en. [3]

U.S. Bureau of Labor Statistics (2019), *Labor force statistics from the current population survey*, https://www.bls.gov/cps/ (accessed on 12 March 2020). [9]

U.S. Bureau of Labor Statistics (2019), *Occupation Employment Statistics*, https://www.bls.gov/oes/home.htm (accessed on 26 August 2019). [8]

U.S. Census Bureau (2019), *American Community Survey 2018 (database)*, https://www.census.gov/programs-surveys/acs/data.html (accessed on 18 January 2020). [6]

UNESCO Institute for Statistics (2012), *International Standard Classification of Education*, http://uis.unesco.org/sites/default/files/documents/international-standard-classification-of-education-isced-2011-en.pdf (accessed on 7 April 2020). [1]

Executive summary

Economic growth and innovation in the United States rely heavily on the advanced skills of its population. More than 7 000 post-secondary institutions serve about 20 million students across the country, in programmes that range from short-term certificates to doctoral degrees. Having a higher education qualification significantly increases the chances of individuals obtaining and keeping a well-paying job – to a greater extent in the United States than in most OECD countries. Employers, for their part, look to higher education institutions to equip graduates with the skills needed to adapt to changing work demands.

This review, conducted in 2018-19 by the OECD with the support of Lumina Foundation, explores how the higher education system in four US states – Ohio, Texas, Virginia and Washington – responds to the needs of the state's labour market. This review was conducted under very different economic circumstances compared to those emerging in 2020, as the world is entering an unprecedented economic crisis resulting from the COVID-19 pandemic. However, many of the challenges it identifies may remain or deepen. Shortages in some in-demand occupations, in the health sector or digital technologies, are likely to persist. The availability of work-based learning opportunities will likely diminish due to steep declines in employment and profitability in many economic sectors. State per-student appropriations, lower in 2018 than prior to the 2008-09 recession, are likely to fall further. Policies to strengthen the responsiveness of higher education systems to changing labour market needs will be as important in the future as in the past.

Shortages in some occupations and employer concerns about transversal skills are common challenges

The four states experience labour market shortages in specific sectors and occupations, including information and communications technology jobs, health professions and education. Students appear to respond to labour market signals, with growing shares enrolling in programmes leading to well-paying jobs in science, technology, engineering and mathematics (STEM) and health fields. Recruitment challenges persist in the education sector, which is low paying across the four states. Even in high-paying occupations, the demand for workers in these fields exceeds the supply of graduates, and migration from other states and abroad is an important tool to meet skills needs. Furthermore, employers across industries and occupations met during OECD fact-finding missions to participating states highlighted certain skills gaps among graduates, including both job-specific technical skills and transversal skills such as communication or teamwork. Given their uncertainty about the skills of graduates, employers often emphasised their continued reliance on the four-year degree and institutional reputation as ways to make hiring decisions, in addition to developing tests of job applicants' skills.

Graduate numbers, in total, are insufficient to meet state needs for highly educated workers

Ohio, Texas and Washington do not set specific policy targets related to the labour market outcomes of higher education graduates, while Virginia has a specific goal on graduate wages. In contrast, all four states have established higher education attainment targets. The higher education attainment rate has grown at a moderate but steady rate in all four states over the past decade. Growth has been swiftest in states that started with higher post-secondary attainment rates, but more will need to be done if states are to meet their targets. Two ongoing challenges appear to limit progress in raising attainment. First, despite state investments and stakeholder-led initiatives to lower the cost of attending higher education, many young people choose not to pursue higher education, particularly among low-income students, and ethnic or racial minorities who are under-represented in higher education. Second, many students who start higher education do not complete their programmes, especially among under-represented populations. This share is highest in two-year public institutions, where only one-fifth to one-third of students (depending on the state) complete their two-year programme within four years. In four-year public institutions, the share of students completing their programme within six years ranges from about half to close to three-quarters. Still, this leaves an important share of students who leave post-secondary education without a credential, facing poorer labour market prospects while often carrying student debt.

The earnings advantage of higher education varies significantly by the level and field of study, and by student demographics

In each of the four states, the bachelor's degree is, on average, the undergraduate qualification associated with the largest earnings premium, while the returns on investment in certificates and associate's degrees are, on average, markedly lower. While certificates, associate's degrees, and apprenticeships in fields leading to high-demand occupations can offer initial earnings that are higher than the average starting salaries of graduates from bachelor's degree programmes, the earnings advantage of shorter qualifications does not always persist. Across all study levels, graduates in science, technology, engineering and mathematics (STEM) and information and communications technology (ICT) consistently enjoy the highest earnings advantage. Within-field earnings are also dispersed, especially in general fields of study such as business and arts and humanities, where graduates may pursue a large range of occupations. On average, women, Black/African American and Hispanic/Latino graduates experience lower rates of employment and earnings after graduation than their peers with equivalent levels of higher education. These outcomes reflect, in part, a tendency for students from these groups to pursue fields of study and occupations where subsequent employment and earnings opportunities are comparatively poor. In the case of Black/African American and Hispanic/Latino graduates, these choices and outcomes are compounded by above-average levels of underlying socio-economic disadvantage and debt accumulated during study.

State governments can improve the responsiveness of higher education to labour market needs through enhanced strategic planning and co-ordination

Across the four states, as is common in the United States, higher education institutions have a high level of autonomy, the tools of higher education agencies to link strategic policy objectives and institutional behaviour are limited, and multiple actors are engaged in activities to improve the alignment between education and workforce needs. The multiplicity of stakeholders and initiatives engaged in supporting the alignment of higher education and the labour market, while positive at a local or sectoral level, appears seldom co-ordinated, making it difficult to scale up effective practices across states' regions and economic sectors. To support better co-ordination of initiatives, potential success factors have been identified in this review that are relevant to all four states, in addition to the tailored policy recommendations provided to each state. These include:

- Processes to connect strategic policy goals for higher education and the institutional funding process, to ensure capacity exists to effectively orient the actions of the higher education system towards meeting policy goals.

- Processes to enable state agencies responsible for higher education, education and workforce development to regularly collaborate and co-ordinate efforts with each other and with key stakeholders. Sufficient human and financial resources need to be available to support such collaboration and co-ordination.
- Processes to incentivise collaboration between government agencies at the state and regional levels and to ensure stakeholders provide regular input into higher education policy and planning.

States can encourage institutions to focus on labour market relevance and promote state-wide pathways and student supports

State higher education agencies and institutions promote labour market relevant teaching and learning. However, there is wide variation across institutions and programmes in the extent to which practices shown to equip students with labour market relevant skills (such as work-based learning) are available to students. In addition, while there is widespread recognition that students need structured pathways and effective guidance to move through higher education and complete a credential, streamlining pathways and facilitating efficient transfers within the higher education system remains a challenge in the four states. To support labour market relevant offerings across programmes and facilitate state-wide pathways and student supports, potential success factors relevant to all states in addition to state-specific policy recommendations include:

- Mechanisms to provide state governments with an opportunity to identify programmes with poor labour market outcomes, the same way mechanisms exist for state-wide reviews of programme productivity or low-producing programmes, which could in turn help institutions focus their attention where it is most needed.
- Approaches to incentivise higher education institutions to encourage labour market relevant teaching and learning across all levels and fields of study. This can include supporting the recruitment of faculty in fields of study leading to high-demand occupations, the provision of high-quality work-based learning opportunities, and opportunities for faculty professional development.
- Approaches to facilitate the availability of state-wide, evidence-based student supports that effectively target students most in need, either financially or academically, for assistance in accessing and completing higher education.
- Mechanisms to streamline credential pathways and regional or state-wide transfer agreements between institutions. Information about pathways and transfers should be easy to understand and access by students and families. Examining transfer outcomes of students at two-year institutions may be important to identify ways in which to increase transfer efficiency and boost associate's and bachelor's degree attainment.

Adequate state funding is needed to support the provision of good quality and affordable study options relevant to labour market needs

The four states face an ongoing challenge with respect to higher education funding. To ensure that opportunities for study are diverse and equitable, states need to ensure the affordability of public higher education – either by providing state appropriations sufficient to contain tuition fees, or by providing robust need-based aid. At the same time, states need to take care that higher education revenues are sufficient to protect the quality of educational offerings as well as student guidance and support.

Recent state appropriation levels have not allowed real per-student funding to return to the pre-crisis levels of 2007-08 in any of the four states, and the likely impact of the COVID-19 pandemic is a further cause for concern. Potential success factors relevant to all states, in addition to state-specific policy recommendations, include:

- Sustained commitment from lawmakers to ensuring the sufficiency of state appropriations for higher education institutions. Per-student funding in the two-year sector should be a special focus of attention, given the lower per-student expenditures from which these institutions start, and the key role these institutions play in offering an entry route to higher education for under-represented populations and in meeting labour market needs in key economic sectors.
- Processes either to moderate student tuition fees across the board, while limiting negative impact on instructional quality, or to allocate additional resources to need-based student grant programmes. The latter is a more targeted and efficient way to increase post-secondary attainment than lowering tuition for all students.
- Approaches to introduce carefully designed performance-related funding that takes into account the labour market outcomes of graduates. These metrics should be used intelligently to ensure institutions are also incentivised to support disadvantaged populations. Such models should be designed in close co-operation with higher education institutions, in particular to protect institutions from financial shocks generated by sharp changes in any of the metrics used and provide institutions with adequate resources for their core instructional mission.
- Targeted funding to higher education institutions and other partners to expand the offer of opportunities for students to develop labour market relevant skills, ranging from increasing work-based learning options to incentivising students to pursue in-demand fields. Programmes to support students in choosing study fields should be designed in ways that make them easy to understand and access. They should also be developed in conjunction with broader policy efforts starting before higher education to enhance students' academic preparedness and interest in pursuing fields of study that lead to occupations with good earnings prospects.

States can enhance the provision and use of high-quality and user-friendly information about post-secondary options and labour market returns

The four states provide information about educational and career opportunities, the labour market experiences of recent graduates, and monitor the supply and demand for graduates across occupations. Much of this information is made publicly available, but it is not consistently adapted to its intended audiences. To support the provision of high-quality and user-friendly information about post-secondary education, potential success factors relevant to all states in addition to state-specific policy recommendations include:

- Mechanisms to integrate workforce information in strategic planning and forecasting processes in higher education. This can include developing state-wide supply-demand analyses and considering approaches to systematically engage employers; identifying emerging trends and granular skills needs by occupation, industry and location; assessing institutional capacity to meet changing needs; and providing state-wide access to major data resources.
- Approaches to improve the quality and availability of data on graduate outcomes in the labour market. This could include providing debt and earnings data at the programme level by sub-population, and expanding coverage to include both public and private institutions where possible. Expanding the development of metrics or tools to measure the employment outcomes of graduates, for example by developing state-wide graduate outcome or employer surveys, could be considered. Such tools could help assess the signalling value of post-secondary qualifications, help assess skills use in the workplace and help better understand in-field job placement rates.
- Mechanisms to provide integrated information to students and families about educational opportunities and pathways, costs, outcomes and supports. Information about the expected return

on investment in post-secondary education options can help students make better choices in terms of selecting their field of study and career path. However, the tailoring of information is crucial to ensure that it reaches students in a manner in which they can easily access and absorb it.

1 Introduction

This chapter outlines the purpose and scope of the report, the third in a series of OECD country reviews on the labour market relevance and outcomes of higher education. It presents the assessment framework used to examine the alignment of higher education and the labour market in the four US states participating in the review – Ohio, Texas, Virginia and Washington. Finally, it presents the structure of the report.

1.1. Purpose of the report

Higher education is a critical feature of knowledge-based economies and innovative societies. Through it, graduates acquire the knowledge, skills, and values that assist them in leading productive careers and engaged civic lives.

Policy makers look to the higher education institutions in their jurisdictions to fulfil various objectives. These include effective teaching to prepare future citizens and workers; high quality research; and engagement with enterprises, community organisations and the public sector. Students, families, employers and governments all expect that higher education equips learners with the knowledge and skills they need to lead productive and remunerative working lives, and to contribute to the economic prosperity and social well-being of the countries in which they work.

Across the OECD, workers with a higher education credential continue, on average, to enjoy robust earning premiums compared to those who complete only upper secondary education. However, many graduates have difficulty obtaining so-called "graduate jobs", or employment in fields for which they were trained. Policy makers are not only concerned about the current alignment of higher education systems to labour markets; they are increasingly uneasy about the future of work and its implications for education.

The digitalisation of the economy has created and eliminated occupations, polarised wage distributions, changed workers' tasks, and reshaped the relationships among workers, and between workers and employers. It has also changed the skills that are used in jobs, and the skills that are sought-after and rewarded by employers. The transformation of the workplace challenges higher education institutions to rethink the knowledge and skills that graduates need, while the polarisation of employment raises concerns about modest returns on investment for higher education graduates, in whose education substantial public (and often private) investments have been made.

Moreover, exogenous shocks transform the labour market in ways that cannot be predicted. The COVID-19 pandemic, which emerged as this report went into publication, is a prime example of such shock. While its profound impact on economies and labour markets is becoming apparent, the duration of the crisis and the ways in which industries and businesses may recover is unknown (Rothwell and Van Drie, 2020[1]). This leaves open questions regarding the knowledge and skills that workers will need in the aftermath of the pandemic, and reinforces the importance of strengthening the responsiveness of higher education systems.

To address these issues, the OECD's Directorate for Education and Skills launched a project on the labour market relevance and outcomes of higher education. This project involves four strands of work, outlined in Box 1.1. Through in-depth reviews of countries or sub-national jurisdictions, the OECD provides policy makers with actionable recommendations on how higher education policies and organisations linking higher education to labour markets can be oriented to promote good labour market outcomes for higher education graduates today, and promote the successful adaptation of higher education systems to the ongoing transformation of work.

This report, supported by Lumina Foundation, examines the labour market relevance and outcomes of higher education in the states of Ohio, Texas, Virginia and Washington, following the assessment framework outlined in Section 1.2.

Box 1.1. The OECD project on the labour market relevance and outcomes of higher education

Initiated in 2017, the OECD project on the labour market relevance and outcomes of higher education explores how governments and institutions can improve the way higher education responds to current and future labour needs, through various strands of work:

- In-depth reviews of the relevance and outcomes of higher education provide policy makers with actionable recommendations on how higher education policies and organisations can be oriented to promote good labour market outcomes for today's higher education graduates, and ensure that tomorrow's higher education systems are aligned to the ongoing transformation of work. In addition to this review of Ohio, Texas, Virginia and Washington, in-depth reviews were completed in Norway and Mexico in 2018 and 2019, respectively.
- Focused reviews of the relevance and outcomes of higher education adopt a similar method, with a reduced scope in the policy areas examined. Such reviews are underway in Austria, Hungary, Portugal and Slovenia, to be completed in 2021.
- Thematic Working Papers explore emerging topics of interest to improve the labour market relevance and outcomes of higher education. Working Papers to be published in 2020 will examine the emergence of alternative credentials, the use of big data to understand employer skills demand, and labour market information and student choice.
- Peer learning events, starting in 2020, will aim to stimulate exchange about policy options and institutional practices that can improve the alignment between higher education provision and labour markets.

1.2. Scope of the report

Higher education in this report refers to levels 4 through 8 of the 2011 International Standard Classification of Education (ISCED), as explained in the Reader's Guide. Given the breadth and complexity of higher education in the United States, the following choices were made to focus the analysis:

- Choice of states: While the federal government in the United States has a role in specific areas of higher education policy, as discussed in Chapter 2, state governments bear the main responsibility for the operation of higher education institutions in their state. As a result, the OECD and Lumina Foundation, in consultation with the U.S. Department of Education, jointly decided to focus the analysis at the state level, and identified four states that would offer useful insights for a broad range of states across the country. The four states were identified based on their geographic and economic diversity, their relatively large public sector of higher education, and their prior engagement with Lumina Foundation initiatives focusing on graduate outcomes and the alignment between higher education and the labour market.
- Levels of education: The report focuses on sub-baccalaureate and baccalaureate levels, which include post-secondary (sub-baccalaureate) certificates, associate's degrees and bachelor's programmes, which account for the majority of entrants to the US labour market.
- Control of institutions: The report takes note of both public and private higher education in setting the context of its analysis, but its diagnoses and recommendations focus on public higher education. Public higher education institutions enrol, on average, close to 80% of undergraduate students in the United States (NCES, 2019[2]). In addition, state governments bear responsibility for the legal and financial bases of public higher education institutions, and the policy instruments at their disposal centre principally on public institutions.

The analysis presented in this report is based upon an assessment framework with two principal features. First, it examines the labour market outcomes of graduates, primarily their employment rates and earnings, to shed light on the alignment between higher education provision and the labour market. Informed by this diagnostic, its second focus is to identify policy options that that hold promise for improving the alignment of higher education and the labour market. Each state chapter examines key state policies, ranging from institutional funding to the provision of labour market information, identifying strengths, and highlighting policy options that might strengthen labour market alignment.

1.3. Assessment framework

Overarching context

A wide set of factors influences the actions of employers, higher education institutions, students and graduates, and the labour market outcomes that their choices yield. These include contextual factors, very often outside of the control of public authorities; and policies, standards and activities put in place by public authorities or, in some cases, non-governmental bodies such as social partners or sector associations to steer labour market relevance and outcomes.

The relationships through which contextual factors and steering policies may influence the behaviours of higher education institutions, employers, students and graduates and, hence, labour market outcomes are illustrated in Figure 1.1.

Relevant contextual factors include institutional and cultural norms affecting study and employment choices, and global trends in technology and trade that affect demand for different types of skills. Such factors largely condition the policy reform capacity of governments. For instance, low rates of labour market participation among female higher education graduates of childbearing ages may result from a gendered division of responsibility for childcare, workplace practices, and low levels of social support for family responsibilities, rather than by a misalignment between their skills and the needs of the labour market.

Steering policies and factors, over which governments typically have a far greater degree of control, can be categorised into three main groups. Through higher education and skills policies, governments can provide information to institutions and learners about labour market needs, organise data systems to monitor graduate outcomes, and require that institutions disclose information about these outcomes. They can use funding methodologies that encourage institutions to adjust study places in response to labour market demands, and establish qualification frameworks and quality assurance systems that build trust in the qualifications awarded by institutions.

Co-ordinating bodies and non-governmental organisations also play an important role in influencing the behaviours of actors in the system, and in connecting education to the world of work. These organisations – professional or employer associations, rectors' conferences, and, in some systems, non-governmental accreditation bodies – can help institutions recognise career-relevant competencies; assess and validate graduates' competencies; incorporate skills standards expected by specific professions or industries in study programmes; and promote quality standards that support labour market relevance.

In addition to higher education and skills policies, a wide range of public policies can influence labour market outcomes, either directly or indirectly. For example, employment and tax policies affect hiring policies, employment conditions, and earnings, as well as social policies, may determine the level of social protections that are available to workers. Also, immigration policies govern the entry of skilled workers into the economy, and the recognition of foreign qualifications may be determined by either education or labour policies, ultimately influencing the total supply of skills.

Figure 1.1. Factors affecting outcomes for graduates and employers

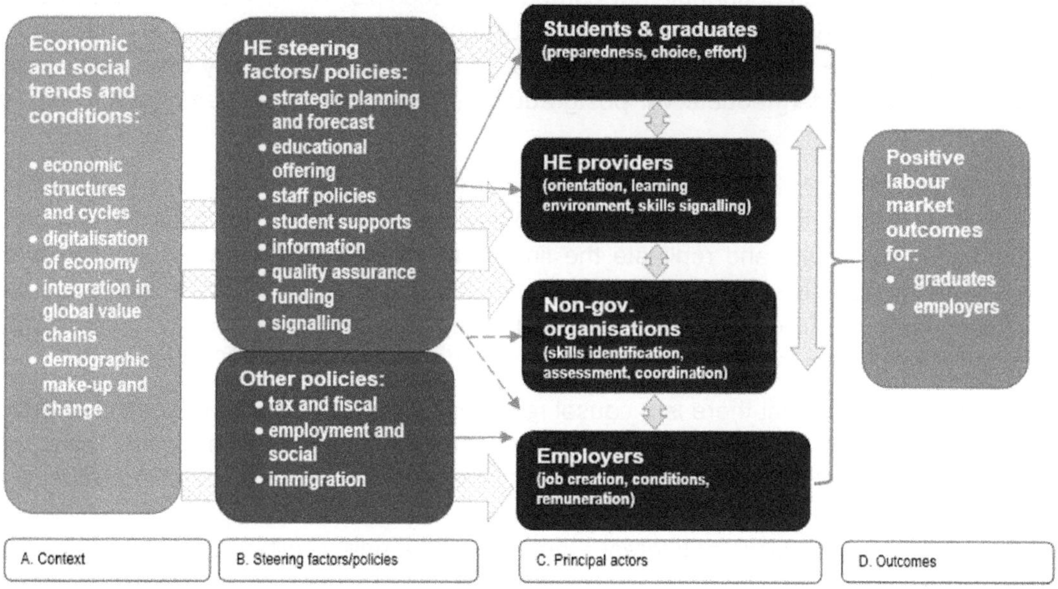

Examination of labour market outcomes

OECD reviews of labour market relevance and outcomes examine labour market outcomes experienced by higher education graduates and employers in the participating country or jurisdiction, to broadly assess the alignment between the supply and demand of graduate skills. A system where the higher education system is well articulated with the labour market allows both graduates and employers to obtain positive outcomes, as outlined in Table 1.1.

The assessment not only considers whether there is overall alignment (for example, the average outcomes experienced by graduates), but also examines where misalignment occurs (for example, poor outcomes may be concentrated among certain socio-economic groups, graduates from specific fields or types of institutions, or in specific economic sectors).

Table 1.1. Desired outcomes for graduates and employers

Graduates	Employers
• Enhanced employment prospects (compared to those without higher education) • The opportunity to use the skills acquired during higher education • A wage premium that reflects the additional skills acquired through higher education • A positive rate of return on their investment that rewards them for the costs of study (and, where necessary, service debts incurred during study) • A capacity for learning at work and adapting to the changing demands of working life	• A supply of graduates that is sufficient to meet current demand • Reliable and sufficiently transparent signalling of skills to permit employers to identify candidates fitted to their needs • Graduates with high quality skills and a developed capacity for learning and growth, responding to changing demands of work • Mechanisms to facilitate a future supply of graduates able to respond to changing technologies and skills needs, and changes in working life • Workers have good access to opportunities to refresh and update their advanced knowledge and skills

In this review, three sources of evidence are used:

- state and national data analysed using descriptive statistics;
- stakeholder input received during fact-finding visits (see Annex A for the OECD team's schedule and aggregated workshop survey results);
- academic research and published policy analysis.

Three indicators of graduate outcomes in the labour market are consistently available across OECD countries, and thus provide an opportunity for comparative analysis. These include employment, median annual earnings, and graduate earnings premiums. Graduate earnings premiums are calculated as the difference between median earnings of higher education and upper secondary graduates, and may be disaggregated by level (undergraduate vs. postgraduate), field of study, or demography (e.g. male vs. female).

In assessing the alignment of higher education systems and labour markets, we do not match the stock of graduates by study field to projected occupational openings. This would duplicate the supply-demand analyses conducted by states, and replicate the limitations of matching analysis: employers are often looking for a skills profile rather than a specific study field, and many graduates, especially bachelor's graduates, either study in a field for which a matching occupation cannot be observed, or work outside of the occupation for which they trained (see for instance Goldman and Carew (2018[3])).

Research has demonstrated that there is a causal relationship between higher education attainment and earnings, which is not just the result of the selection of high-ability students entering into higher education (Zimmerman, 2014[4]; Ost, Pan and Webber, 2018[5]). Earnings premiums are useful indicators that permit comparisons across jurisdictions (within the United States and among OECD countries), and disaggregation into key populations of interest. They are also a policy-relevant indicator: real differences in employment and earnings provide governments, students and families with important input into decision-making. Higher education graduate labour market outcomes, viewed in comparison to upper secondary graduate outcomes, are summarised and compared to the US average and that of other key OECD countries in the comparative scoreboard (see Chapter 3).

Nonetheless, descriptive analyses of employment and earnings among higher education graduates and those who have completed only upper secondary education, when based upon state-level data, are subject to four types of limitations:

1. **Wage premiums overestimate the effect of higher education on earnings due to selection bias.** On average, higher education graduates earn more than secondary graduates. Wage premiums of higher education graduates result, in part, from skills they acquire in their studies, or the educational "treatment" to which they have been exposed. However, wage premiums also result from "selection effects" – students who enter and successfully complete higher education are not a random sample of learners, but a selected group with abilities different to the population at large. Researchers who aim to estimate the unique effects of education on earnings address this issue through a variety of statistical methods, such as propensity score matching to compare individuals with similar backgrounds and academic ability. See for instance ERDC (2018[6]), Minaya and Scott-Clayton (2017[7]), Hoxby (2018[8]).
2. **Average wage premiums may underestimate earnings among graduates of flagship institutions and Science, Technology, Engineering and Mathematics (STEM) programmes.** Where graduate premiums are calculated using linked state administrative data from education and labour market information systems, they will typically fail to capture an important number of graduates who leave the state to obtain higher wage opportunities, most often graduates of flagship institutions and STEM programmes, and therefore underestimate wages for both (Foote and Stange, 2019[9]).
3. **Wage premiums do not reflect the societal or public benefits of higher education study.** Employment rates, earnings, and wage premiums measure the private benefits of higher education to graduates, but do not provide evidence of the public benefits resulting from graduate skill acquisition. For this reason, some suggest that graduate employment in "social services" (e.g. education), which have lower earnings but contribute to meeting social needs, be taken into account (Minaya and Scott-Clayton, 2017[7]).

4. **Wage premiums do not provide a full view of costs and benefits for graduates, for which calculations of private internal rates of return are required.** To fully assess the private benefits of a graduate's higher education investment, the costs of education (direct outlays and opportunity costs) and debt (and loan servicing costs) incurred must be taken into account. Because the project does not have microdata upon which to base those calculations, average debt levels are reported in the study to put wage premiums in perspective. The OECD provides international comparisons of the net private and public returns of higher education (2019, p. 96[10]). However, these calculations do not take into account the cost of loan servicing and default, which can increase costs for both graduates and governments in countries where loans play a key role in financing higher education, such as the United States.

Assessing policies that support the alignment of higher education and the labour market

While recognising the influence of contextual factors and policies in other fields, this report aims to identify where existing policies are not working as well might be expected, and to indicate policy alternatives that may yield improved alignment of higher education and the labour market.

The link between public policy choices and labour market alignment and outcomes is uncertain. Programme evaluations in higher education systems and experimental or quasi-experimental analyses of policy interventions are not systematic. Both require access to microdata and timeframes beyond the scope of this project. Nonetheless, shared experience across the higher education systems of OECD member countries and peer-reviewed research provide a useful basis for identifying policy design choices that can support a good alignment between skills supply and demand. These policy areas are outlined in Table 1.2.

The extent to which it makes sense to consider each of these policy areas individually in a given jurisdiction depends largely on the legal framework in which higher education operates, the level of institutional autonomy, and the existing policy environment.

Table 1.2. Policies and mechanisms contributing to stronger alignment between higher education and the labour market

Higher education system features/policy areas	Examples of key characteristics and mechanisms
Strategic planning and co-ordination mechanisms help ensure the higher education system delivers programmes that respond to labour market needs, both current and projected.	• Mechanisms provide state authorities with the ability to orient higher education institutions towards labour market relevant provision. • Mechanism exist to ensure ongoing co-ordination between employers, higher education institutions and relevant government agencies to ensure the current and future responsiveness of higher education to the labour market.
Educational offerings, including curricula and programme content, as well as programme duration and delivery mode, respond flexibly to current and likely future demand for knowledge and skills, including through programmes aimed at existing workers.	• The range of programmes (field, professional vs academic focus, duration) is appropriate in light of skills demands from the labour market and likely future labour market demand. • Wide access is available to labour market relevant higher education (e.g. in all geographical locations, for students of all socio-economic backgrounds, for individuals currently in the labour force). • Sufficient places are provided in programmes with high labour market demand. • Where professional and industry standards exist, curricula and assessment incorporate these into the design of programmes. • Public policies monitor/reward the development of study programmes containing high quality work-based learning opportunities, at both undergraduate and postgraduate levels. • Research or innovation funding bodies provide targeted financial assistance to support doctoral research undertaken in firms or public sector organisations.

Higher education system features/policy areas	Examples of key characteristics and mechanisms
Policies governing staff profile and time use support a focus on developing labour market relevant knowledge and skills.	• Where public policies establish standards of recruitment and qualification, staff are required to have undertaken pedagogical training (in doctoral programmes or through standalone training). • Where public policies establish standards of recruitment and qualification, staff teaching professional subjects are required/incentivized to have recent/ongoing professional experience in the sector in which they teach. • Government funding and quality assurance policies encourage higher education institutions to engage competent and relevant staff, support staff exchanges and mobility between higher education institutions and industry or non-profit and public organisations; and to adopt staff workload and performance assessment policies that reward instructor time invested in professionally-focused learning (e.g. supervision of work-based learning).
Pathways, student supports and learning environment: financial and non-financial supports encourage students to develop labour market relevant knowledge and skills and to obtain labour market relevant credentials.	• Public policies facilitate clear pathways allowing students to enter higher education and to move flexibly and efficiently between higher education sectors and institutions (e.g. through credit transfer and recognition of prior learning). • Student financial support policies help students with financial need to access and complete higher education. • Public policies encourage the design and delivery of study programmes and student services adapted to learner schedules and needs, and of student supports that promote completion of credentials and help students identify relevant career options.
Quality assurance and accreditation processes ensure that educational credentials are of good quality and trusted by employers.	• Quality assurance and accreditation processes provide a minimum guarantee of quality and the conditions for skills acquisition by students. • These processes assess steps taken by providers to ensure and enhance the labour market relevance of their provision.
Public funding to institutions of higher education takes into account the (real or projected) career prospects of graduates to encourage labour market relevant provision as part of a diversified mix of higher education study options.	• The system used to allocate public funding (and/or regulate tuition fees) supports the provision of labour market relevant skills and of sufficient places in programmes with high labour market demand. Various mechanisms exists for this purpose (incentives, requirement for disclosing graduates outcomes, linking outcomes to funding) and are designed to support improved outcomes without generating unintended effects. • Where they exist, external controls on the numbers of study places available do not lead to undersupply of certain skills to the labour market.
Reliable and accessible information is widely available about employers' skills needs, the labour market outcomes of graduates and the skills possessed by graduates from different programmes, and is effectively used for decision-making by policy makers, higher education institutions, students, graduates and employers.	• Mechanisms exist to monitor and analyse current and future knowledge and skills requirements and trends, which are used by policy makers and higher education institutions as an input to strategic planning of the educational offer. • User-friendly sources and tools provide relevant information tailored to various types of users (e.g. current students, graduates, employers, academic and administrative higher education staff, and staff involved in student counselling and career guidance). • Evidence exists of various users making use of these information sources and tools in study choice and skills development decisions.
Effective signalling mechanisms exist to help employers understand the skills that graduates from different programmes should possess, and to help graduates convey the skills they have obtained in higher education.	• Higher education institutions have tools in place that clarify the skills content of qualifications. • Wider mechanisms, such as national qualifications framework or credential inventories, facilitate the understanding of the skills conveyed by different higher education qualifications, and their relevance to labour market needs.

1.4. Structure of the report

This report is organised into seven chapters. Chapter 2 provides an overview of the labour market in the United States, and the role of the federal government in setting the policy framework within which US states and their higher education institutions operate to deliver education programmes. Chapter 3 provides a synthesis of insights generated through the state-specific analyses, and key policy examples from jurisdictions across the OECD. The four subsequent chapters provide an in-depth analysis of the higher education labour market relevance and outcomes in Ohio, Texas, Virginia and Washington, respectively. Annex A provides a summary of stakeholder engagement during the review, while Annex B provides information about the data sources used in the report's comparative tables provided in Chapter 3.

Each state chapter explores the alignment between higher education and the labour market in a similar fashion. The chapters first explore the alignment of the higher education system to labour market demands based on a set of labour market indicators. The second part of each chapter provides an examination of current higher education policies to identify ways in which they may be either contributing to or hampering the relevance of higher education provision and graduate outcomes, and what policy actions state authorities may consider to strengthen the alignment of the higher education system and the labour market. The policy areas discussed across the four states include: the strategic planning and co-ordination of higher education; higher education programmes, pathways and student supports; funding to institutions and students; and information about skills needs, the labour market outcomes of graduates and the skills content of higher education qualifications.

References

ERDC (2018), *The Earnings Premium of Washington Higher Education: Gender Deficit in Earnings among Washington College Graduates*, Washington State Education Research and Data Center, Olympia, https://erdc.wa.gov/publications/economic-returns/earnings-premium-washington-higher-education-gender-deficit-earnings (accessed on 25 July 2019). [6]

Foote, A. and K. Stange (2019), *Attrition from Administrative Data: Problems and Solutions with an Application to Higher Education*, U.S. Census Bureau, University of Michigan and NBER, https://conference.nber.org/conf_papers/f131000.pdf (accessed on 13 March 2020). [9]

Goldman, C. and D. Carew (2018), "Using workforce data to plan higher education degree programmes", in *The Handbook on the Politics of Higher Education*, Brendan Cantwell, Hamish Coate, Roger King. [3]

Hoxby, C. (2018), "The Productivity of U.S. Postsecondary Institutions", in Hoxby, C. and K. Stange (eds.), *Productivity in Higher Education*, National Bureau of Economic Research/University of Chicago Press, https://www.nber.org/chapters/c13875.pdf (accessed on 7 August 2019). [8]

Minaya, V. and J. Scott-Clayton (2017), "Labor Market Outcomes and Postsecondary Accountability: Are Imperfect Metrics Better than None?", in Hoxby, C. and K. Stange (eds.), *Productivity in Higher Education*, National Bureau of Economic Research/University of Chicago Press, https://www.nber.org/chapters/c13876.pdf (accessed on 7 August 2019). [7]

NCES (2019), *Integrated Postsecondary Education Data System (database)*, National Center for Education Statistics, https://nces.ed.gov/ipeds/use-the-data (accessed on 18 January 2020). [2]

OECD (2019), *Education at a Glance 2019: OECD Indicators*, OECD Publishing, Paris, https://www.oecd-ilibrary.org/docserver/f8d7880d-en.pdf?expires=1568316502&id=id&accname=ocid84004878&checksum=FEF13445781E06CE49671ADC97573E5B (accessed on 12 September 2019). [10]

Ost, B., W. Pan and D. Webber (2018), *The Returns to College Persistence for Marginal Students: Regression Discontinuity Evidence from University Dismissal Policies*, https://www.journals.uchicago.edu/doi/full/10.1086/696204 (accessed on 20 May 2019). [5]

Rothwell, J. and H. Van Drie (2020), *The effect of COVID-19 and disease suppression policies on labor markets: A preliminary analysis of the data*, Brookings Institution, https://www.brookings.edu/research/the-effect-of-covid-19-and-disease-suppression-policies-on-labor-markets-a-preliminary-analysis-of-the-data/?utm_campaign=Economic%20Studies&utm_medium=email&utm_content=87636981&utm_source=hs_email (accessed on 14 May 2020). [1]

Zimmerman, S. (2014), *The Returns to College Admission for Academically Marginal Students*, https://doi.org/10.1086/676661. [4]

2 The National Context

This chapter examines the national context within which state higher education systems operate. It notes key characteristics of the country's labour market and the national higher education landscape, and surveys graduate labour market outcomes nation-wide. It focuses on four areas of federal policy important to state efforts to ensure successful labour market outcomes among graduates: student financial assistance, accreditation, workforce development, and the provision of information.

This chapter provides an overview of the national conditions in which state higher education systems operate in the United States. The first three sections of the chapter highlight the labour market context in the United States, key features of US higher education, and the links between the labour market and higher education, by briefly reviewing the labour market returns to higher education and skills-matching in the labour market.

The fourth section provides a brief presentation of the role of the federal government in higher education, with a focus on policy areas most relevant to the labour market relevance and outcomes of higher education, namely student financial assistance, accreditation, workforce development, and the provision of information on higher education students and outcomes. The chapter closes by briefly highlighting the space that US states have in a federal system of higher education to orient higher education provision towards labour market relevance.

2.1. Overview of the US labour market

The US labour market is more flexible and characterised by higher average wages and greater wage dispersion than in many OECD Member countries

The United States has one of the most flexible labour markets among OECD Member countries. It has the lowest minimum wage relative to median wages in the OECD, and among the lowest legislative protections for permanent workers and levels of regulation on temporary employment. Unemployment benefits are relatively limited: in 2016, only 10.5% of unemployed workers in the United States received unemployment benefits, compared to 23.3% on average across the OECD (OECD, 2019[1]). In addition, union membership and coverage of workers by collective bargaining agreements is low: for instance, collective bargaining covered 11.6% of US workers in 2017, below the OECD average of 32.4% (OECD, 2020[2]) .

The American labour market is characterised by higher wages and a wider wage dispersion than on average across OECD countries. Average wages in the United States were USD 63 093 in 2018, well above the OECD average of USD 46 686 (OECD, 2020[3]). However, wage growth has not recovered since the 2008-09 economic recession, as it averaged 1.9% per year in the United States from 1997 to 2007, but decreased to about 0.7% per year since 2008, a figure that is close to the OECD average.

At the same time, wage disparities in the United States are considerably larger than on average in the OECD. One-quarter (24.5%) of US workers earned less than two-thirds of median annual earnings in 2017, which was the highest figure in the OECD among countries for which data was collected, with an average of 15.4% (OECD, 2020[4]). Differences by race and ethnicity, as well as by gender, are significant. Black/African American workers' median wages were 24.2% lower than those of White workers in 2018, a gap that has grown from 19.7% in 2006 and is largest among men (U.S. Bureau of Labor Statistics, 2020[5]). Hispanic or Latino workers earned even lower median wages on average in 2018 (74.2% of median White workers' wages), though they have made important gains since 2000. The gender wage gap was also notably higher in the United States (18.2%) than on average across the OECD (13.5%).

However, barriers may limit labour market flexibility in the United States. Occupational licensing has soared from 5% of workers in the late 1950s to over 20% today, a rate similar to those found in the European Union and Japan. While occupational licensing has a critical public protection role by setting standards for initial training and on-going professional development, it can result in barriers to employment and job mobility (Hermansen, 2019[6]). There are also concerns that rising industry concentration is creating labour market monopsony. For example, recent research found that 20% of all workers in 2014 had non-compete clauses in their contracts, including 12% of workers with less than college education, as well as a high prevalence of "non-poaching" agreements in franchise contracts, prohibiting franchisees from hiring workers away from each other (Starr, Prescott and Bishara, 2019[7]; Krueger and Ashenfelter, 2018[8]). At the same time, research suggests that in most industries, national-level concentration is actually increasing local-level competition (Rossi-Hansberg, Sarte and Trachter, 2018[9]).

Low labour market participation is a continuing challenge in the United States, even in periods of strong economic growth. Before the COVID-19 pandemic hit in the first quarter of 2020, the country had experienced the longest period of sustained economic growth on record and seasonally adjusted unemployment had fallen to 3.6% in October 2019, its lowest point in 50 years and well below the OECD average (OECD, 2018[10]; U.S. Bureau of Labor Statistics, 2020[11]). Employer demand has been high in recent years: the Manpower Group (2018[12]) found that 46% of American employers reported difficulty finding the right people for jobs in 2018, either due to a lack of applications or to the insufficient experience or skills of applicants. This is the highest share of employers reporting difficulties finding talent since 2012.

However, labour force participation among those aged 25-64 has not recovered in the United States since the financial crisis of 2008-09. As Figure 2.1 demonstrates, labour force participation has been in decline since 1997, falling from 80.2% to a low of 76.7% in 2015. Whereas the United States used to have much higher labour market participation than on average in the OECD and Western Europe, this is no longer the case. Gains since 2015 have been modest, amounting to a 1.1 percentage-point increase.

Figure 2.1. Labour force participation rate among individuals aged 25-64, 1970-2018

United States, OECD average and European Union-22 average

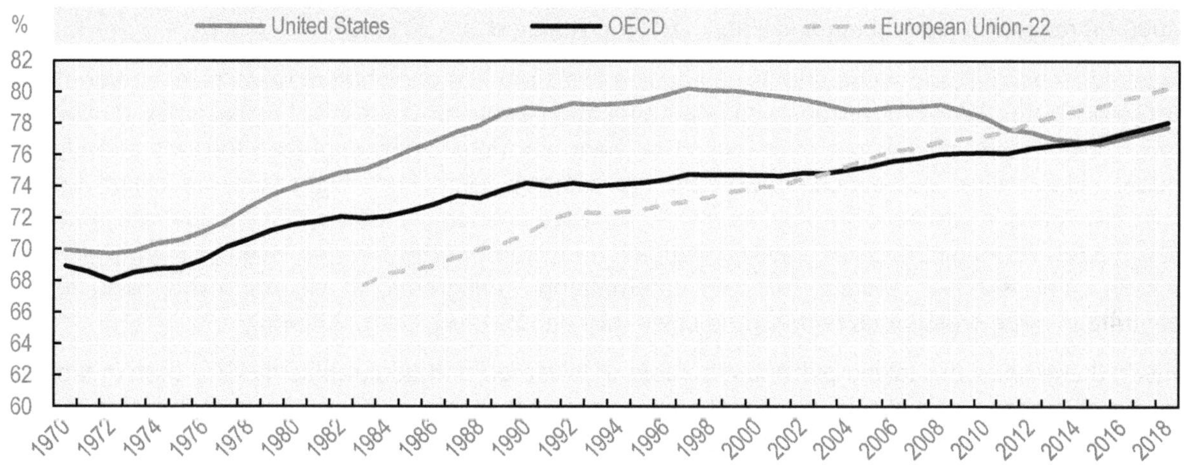

Note: European Union - 22 refers to the 22 European Union members of the OECD in 2018: Austria, Belgium, Czech Republic, Denmark, Estonia, Finland, France, Germany, Greece, Hungary, Ireland, Italy, Latvia, Luxembourg, Netherlands, Poland, Portugal, Slovak Republic, Slovenia, Spain, Sweden and United Kingdom.
Source: OECD (2018[10]), *Labour Force Survey Sex and Age Indicators*, https://stats.oecd.org/viewhtml.aspx?datasetcode=LFS_SEXAGE_I_R&lang=en#.

StatLink https://doi.org/10.1787/888934133229

The earnings advantage for high levels of skills has risen and highly skilled workers are increasingly concentrated in urban areas

Technological change and globalisation have contributed to a shift in the levels, types, and combinations of skills demanded and rewarded by employers. Two main phenomena have taken place in parallel: an increasing share of displaced workers due to automation, and a change in job tasks and the skills required to perform these tasks.

The US labour force has undergone significant transformation since the 1980s, with employment shifting from the middle level of skills towards either high- or low-skill jobs (Autor, Dorn and Hanson, 2013[13]). Much of the decline in middle-skilled employment has occurred in the manufacturing industry, which experienced a loss of approximately seven million jobs from the 1980s to 2016, even as output doubled (Carnevale, 2016[14]). While automation has displaced many routine tasks, it has begun to affect non-routine tasks as well (Acemoglu and Restrepo, 2017[15]; Deming, 2017[16]). OECD estimates using the Survey of Adult Skills (PIAAC) suggest that about 10% of US jobs are at high (greater than 70%) risk of automation, while approximately 28% are at significant risk (50%-70%) of automation (OECD, 2019[1]). This compares to OECD averages of 16.6% and 30.2% respectively, suggesting there are fewer jobs facing a high risk of automation in the United States than in other OECD countries.

The skills demanded of workers have changed significantly in the past decades. For instance, there was a strong shift in the skills profiles of workers in manufacturing, with a decline in jobs for high school graduates and a rise in jobs for post-secondary graduates. Skills requirements have risen significantly among publicly traded firms with large increases in capital stock, pointing to the complementarity between high levels of skills (Hershbein and Kahn, 2018[17]). Research also suggests that the share of US jobs "requiring high levels of social interaction" increased by 11.8 percentage points between 1980 and 2012, and that the greatest employment and wage growth was found in jobs that required both high social and mathematics skills, followed by jobs with high social skills and low mathematics skills (Deming, 2017[16]). This pattern has applied even at the bottom of the earnings distribution, in positions such as continuing care assistants, food service workers and security guards (Autor, Dorn and Hanson, 2013[13]). There is also evidence that skill requirements within occupations have been increasing in the United States since the 2008-09 recession (Hershbein and Kahn, 2018[17]; Atalay et al., 2018[18]).

Skill-biased technological change and rising housing costs are key contributors to shifts in worker mobility in the United States. While Americans with lower education levels previously had higher rates of inter-state migration, the inverse is now true: high-skilled workers are increasingly migrating towards already skill-abundant cities, while less-educated workers are moving away from higher-income cities. Leading metropolitan areas in turn benefit from dynamic "knowledge economy" clusters that concentrate innovation activity and rely on advanced skills, causing wages for educated workers to rise, even as supply increases (Giannone et al., 2017[19]; Moretti, 2012[20]). International immigrants, at all skill levels, also tend to concentrate in more prosperous regions and cities (Moretti, 2012[20]; Card, 2009[21]).

However, these shifts are taking place in a context of lower job and geographic mobility than in the past. While the US labour market has traditionally experienced high levels of job turnover, the frequency of labour market transitions has been in steady decline. In 2002, 12% of the workforce reported a change of employer within the preceding 12 months, and 6% a change of industry; in 2012, these shares were respectively 9% and 4% (Molloy, Smith and Wozniak, 2017[22]).

Globalisation has also played a role in the changing demand for skills and growing differences between geographic areas. Foreign competition has greatly affected industries concentrated in regions with lower educational attainment, and favoured skill-intensive economic sectors where the United States has a comparative advantage (Autor, Dorn and Hanson, 2013[13]; Moretti, 2012[20]). Population ageing and gradual secular shifts in demand from goods towards services are also reshaping the labour market (Abraham and Kearney, 2019[23]; Lawrence, 2018[24]).

2.2. The scope and resourcing of higher education

Higher education attainment is rising, though more slowly than in some other OECD systems

In 2018, 47% of Americans aged 25-64 had a tertiary credential, which is the fifth-highest rate of attainment in the OECD and nine percentage points above the OECD average, as shown in Figure 2.2. Tertiary education in the context of international comparisons includes the associate's degree level (ISCED 5), the bachelor's degree level (ISCED 6), and the doctoral level (ISCED 8). The United States stands out especially in terms of the highest level of degrees, ranking fourth in the attainment of doctoral degrees, behind Slovenia, Luxembourg and Switzerland.

Figure 2.2. Tertiary attainment of 25-64 year-olds, by higher education level, 2018

As compared to overall higher education attainment for 25-34 year-olds

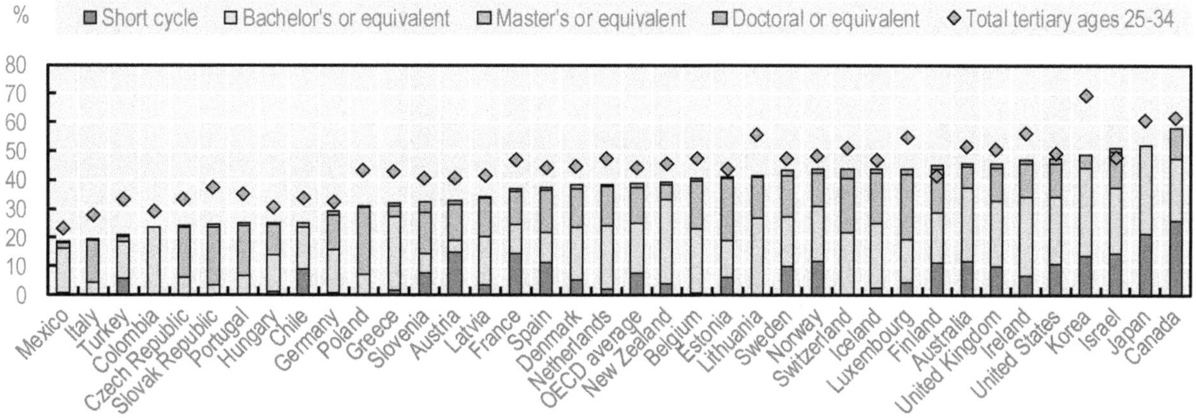

Source: OECD (2019[25]), *Education at a Glance 2019: OECD Indicators*, Tables A1.1 and A1.2, https://doi.org/10.1787/888933980792.

StatLink https://doi.org/10.1787/888934133248

Yet, America's skills advantage is driven in part by the generation of American workers currently nearing retirement (aged 55-64), who have a tertiary education attainment rate close to 43% compared to an OECD average of 27% (OECD, 2020[26]). While the higher education attainment rate for younger Americans (aged 25-34) remains above the OECD average, the United States ranks tenth for that age group, behind Canada, Australia, the United Kingdom, South Korea and Japan, among others.

Furthermore, fewer Americans are participating in higher education than a few years ago. Overall, enrolment peaked at almost 21.6 million students in 2010, and remained almost 1.3 million students below that level in 2016 (NCES, 2017[27]). Part of the decline in enrolment is driven by demographic change, namely that the youth cohort is smaller than in past generations. However, lower enrolment also reflects that the share of young high school graduates pursuing higher education has stagnated, even as an increasing number of students graduate from high school. In October 2018, the share of young high school graduates aged 16 to 24 who were enrolled in some form of higher education was 69.1%, a participation rate that is only half a percentage point higher than in 2008 (U.S. Bureau of Labour Statistics, 2019[28]).

Important differences exist in higher education attainment in the United States by socio-economic status and ethnic and racial group. For example, research suggests that among students scoring at the top of the scale in standardised exams, the rate of bachelor's degree attainment is 41% for students from low-income families compared to 74% for students from high-income families (Page and Scott-Clayton, 2016[29]). As shown in Figure 2.3, among 25-34 year-olds, in 2018, the group with highest attainment (Asians) had an attainment rate close to 2.5 times that of those with the lowest attainment (Hispanics). Between 2010 and 2018 however, gains in higher education attainment were largest for Hispanics and Black/African Americans, indicating modest progress in closing racial and ethnic attainment gaps. On the other hand, differences in attainment by socio-economic status have increased over the past few decades, according to several studies (Page and Scott-Clayton, 2016[29]).

Figure 2.3. Tertiary education attainment in the United States, by race and ethnicity, 2010 and 2018

25-34 and 25-64 year-olds

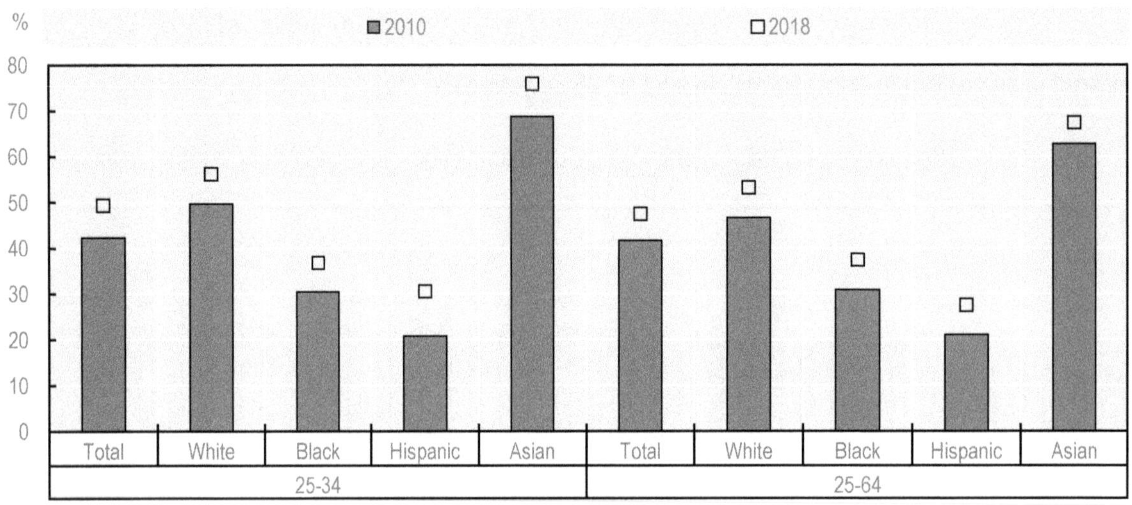

Sources: Adapted from U.S. Census Bureau (2019[30]), *Current Population Survey, 2018 Annual Social and Economic Supplement*, https://www.census.gov/data/tables/2018/demo/education-attainment/cps-detailed-tables.html and U.S. Census Bureau (2019[31]), *Current Population Survey, 2010 Annual Social and Economic Supplement*, https://www.census.gov/data/tables/2010/demo/educational-attainment/cps-detailed-tables.html.

StatLink https://doi.org/10.1787/888934133267

On average, US higher education is well resourced, with extensive private spending and a diminishing role for public spending

Spending on higher education in the United States is high. When factoring in both individual and government spending, the percentage of Gross Domestic Product (GDP) spent on higher education in the United States is second only to Chile, and per capita student expenditure is second only to Luxembourg (OECD, 2019[25]).

As indicated in Figure 2.4, in 2016, spending per student for all services in the United States was almost double the OECD average (USD 30 165 vs USD 15 556). The United States spends more than twice the OECD average on teaching ("core services"), six times the OECD average on other services to students including campus facilities ("ancillary services"), and only about 80% of the OECD average on research and development (OECD, 2019[25]).

Figure 2.4 Total expenditure on educational institutions per full-time equivalent student, by category of spending, 2016

In equivalent USD converted using PPPs.

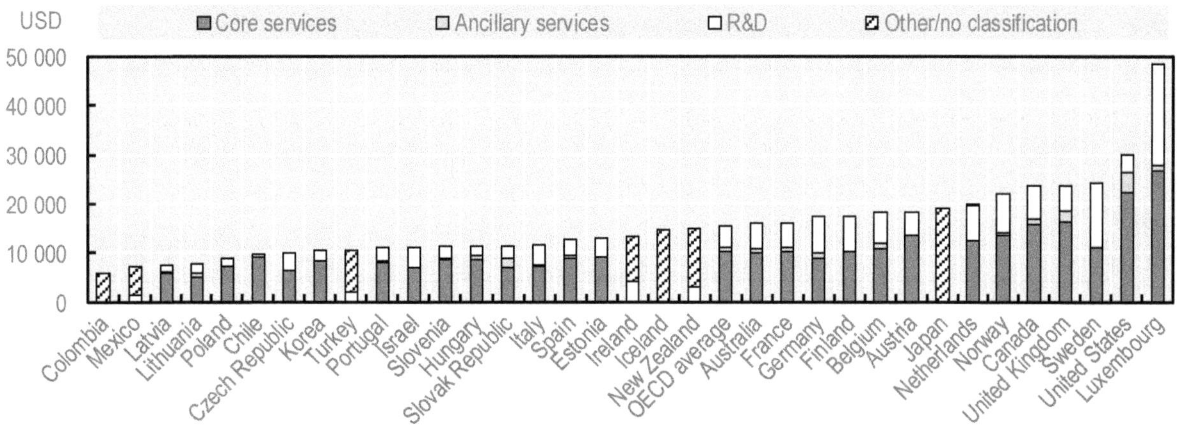

Note: Year of reference is 2017 for Chile and Colombia.
Source: OECD (2019[25]), *Education at a Glance 2019: OECD Indicators*, Table C1.2, https://doi.org/10.1787/888933978816.

StatLink https://doi.org/10.1787/888934133286

Compared to other OECD countries, the United States is characterised by a large share of private funding for higher education. Private tertiary spending relative to GDP was over three times the OECD average (1.6% versus 0.5%) in 2016, a figure equivalent to that of Chile, and well above countries such as the United Kingdom (1.2%), Canada (1.1%) or Japan (1.0%) (OECD, 2019[32]). Household expenditures account for almost half (46.2%) of tertiary funding in the US, followed by public funding (34.6%) and expenditures by other private entities (19.3%). Private not-for-profit institutions are an important feature of US higher education, as discussed in the next section.

As charitable organisations, private not-for-profit institutions supplement tuition fees with tax-favoured philanthropic gifts from individuals and business. At the end of the 2016 fiscal year, 84 universities had endowments of USD 1 billion or more (NCES, 2018[33]). These funds are more prevalent and larger in private not-for-profit institutions, but they are becoming more common in public institutions. For instance, the University of Texas system, Texas A&M University and the University of Michigan, Ann Arbor each have endowments worth at least USD 9.8 billion.

While the share of public expenditure dedicated to higher education is 15% higher in the United States than in other OECD countries, public expenditure in higher education, in aggregate, has not increased since 2008. By contrast, it has increased by 17% on average across other OECD countries (OECD, 2019[34]). This lack of increase reflects declines in state funding for higher education, driven in part by states seeking to balance their budgets in the wake of the 2008-09 economic crisis (Mitchell et al., 2018[35]).

In response to reduced state spending, public higher education institutions have resorted to increasing tuition fees and, in some cases, seeking additional international students or out-of-state students (both of whom pay higher tuition fees) to make up budget shortfalls (Ripley, 2018[36]). Between the 2007/08 and the 2015/16 academic school years, tuition and other fees at public institutions increased on average by 27%, outpacing earnings growth and inflation (NCES, 2018[37]).

This has accelerated a long-term pattern in the United States, whereby households pay a larger share of the cost of higher education. As shown in Figure 2.5, only the United Kingdom has higher tuition fees at public institutions than the United States.

Figure 2.5 Tuition fees in bachelor's or equivalent programmes, 2017/18

Annual fees charged by institutions for full-time national students, in equivalent USD using PPP

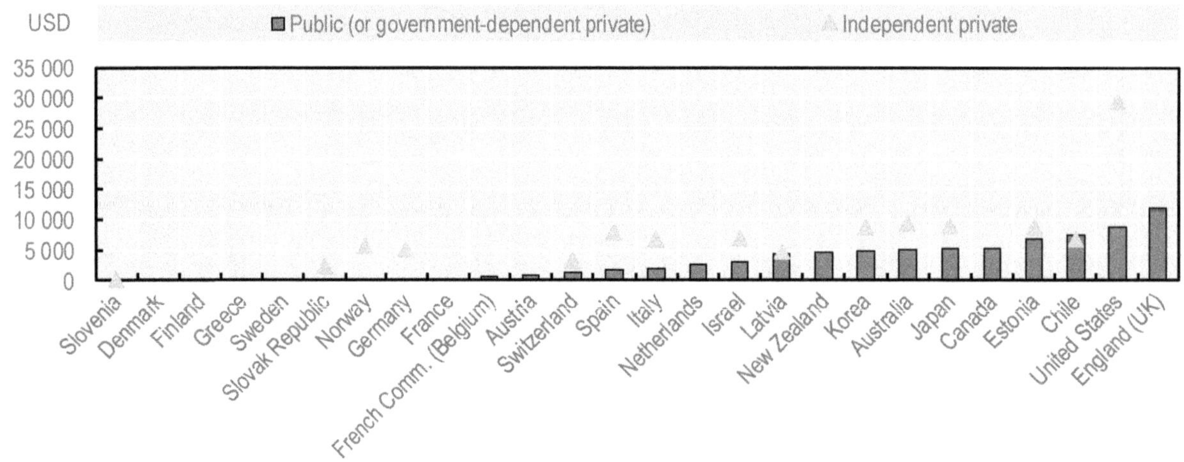

Source: OECD (2019[25]), *Education at a Glance 2019: OECD Indicators*, Table C5.2, https://doi.org/10.1787/888933979234.

StatLink https://doi.org/10.1787/888934133305

Increased private spending has led to rising student debt levels

To help offset the costs of attending post-secondary education, considerable public spending takes the form of financial aid. As indicated in Figure 2.6, in 2017/18, 89% of US bachelor's degree students received some form of public or government-guaranteed financial support, which is higher than most OECD countries and equivalent to the rate found in Australia, New Zealand, and Norway, but slightly below Sweden and England (94%) (OECD, 2019[25]). In the United States, most students (53%) receive both public/government-guaranteed private loans and public grants or scholarships, while 26% receive public grants or scholarships only, and another 10% receive public/government-guaranteed private loans only. Compared to the other countries with high student aid, the United States has a larger share of students receiving only public grants or scholarships.

At the bachelor's degree level, student loans are common. Over 70% of first-time full-time students in private for-profit four-year colleges received loan aid in 2015/16, compared to 60% of students in private not-for-profit institutions and under 50% in public institutions (McFarland et al., 2018[38]).

There are also important private sources of financial aid in the United States, financed in part by institutional endowments. The College Board (2019[39]) estimates that in 2018/19, institutional grants and private and employer grants accounted for 32% of the USD 260 billion in total financial aid provided to students that year. Additionally, private lenders also offer loans to students, which account for approximately 10% of student borrowing (Scott-Clayton, 2017[40]).

Figure 2.6 Percentage of bachelor's and master's long first degree (or equivalent) students receiving financial support, 2017/18

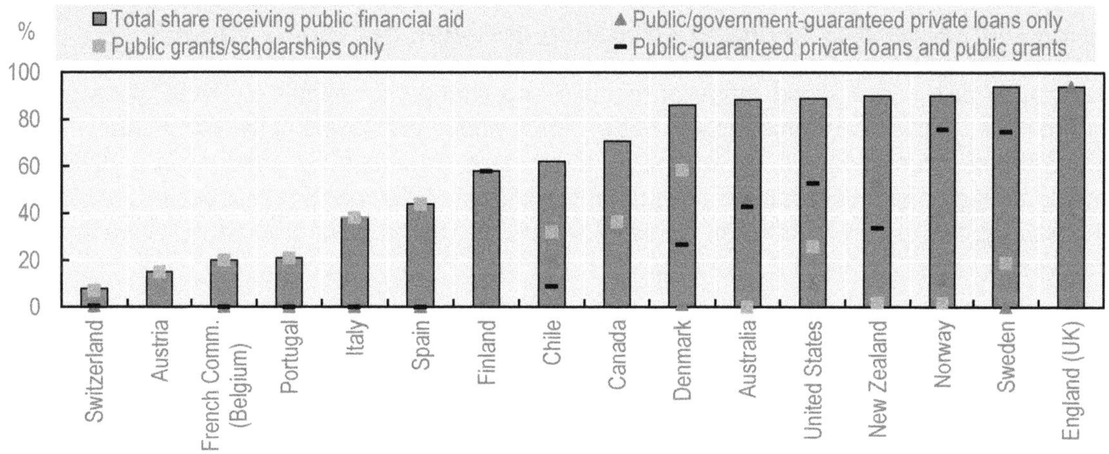

Note: Where there are no markers, data is unavailable.
Source: OECD (2019[25]), *Education at a Glance 2019: OECD Indicators*, Table C5.2, https://doi.org/10.1787/888933979234.

StatLink https://doi.org/10.1787/888934133324

Because of increased reliance on tuition fees to finance higher education, student debt has risen over the past decades. Nation-wide data indicate that for the academic year 2015/16, 61.8% of undergraduate degree and certificate completers received loans over the course of their programmes, for an average cumulative loan amount of USD 24 480 (NCES, 2018[33]). This represents a significant increase from 1999/2000, where the share was 52.5% of students for an average amount of USD 14 260 in current dollars. Spread across 43 million Americans, household student loan debt reached USD 1.5 trillion in 2018, making it the second most important form of household debt after mortgages (FRBNY, 2019[41]).

Debt loads and default rates vary substantially according to students' degree types, institution attended, and demographics. Analysis by the Urban Institute suggests that individuals in the highest income quartile hold about one-third of all student debt, as more students from higher-income background participate and complete higher education (Urban Institute, 2017[42]). Many of them also carry larger debt loads as a result of completing graduate studies (master's or doctoral programmes). While individuals in the lowest income quartile hold a smaller share of total student debt, they are more likely to carry debt than their higher-income peers: 75% of students from the lowest income quartile have debt, compared to 57% of individuals in the highest income quartile. Only 14% of Black/African American students carry no debt, and about one-third of them carry debt loads of more than USD 40 000. In contrast, 30% of Hispanic and White students carry no debt.

Students at public two-year institutions have the highest default rates (18.3% of the cohort entering repayment in 2013/14), even though they have lowest debt levels, followed by students at for-profit two-year institutions (17.5%). This is in comparison to default rates of 7.0% at private, not-for-profit four-year institutions and 7.5% at public four-year institutions (Urban Institute, 2017[42]). For-profit institutions have the highest debt levels, particularly at the four-year level. Research points to several challenges affecting graduates of these institutions including poor repayment conditions, earnings that are lower several years after attendance compared to earnings before starting the programme of study, and evidence that employers value credentials from these institutions less than credentials from public institutions (Deming et al., 2016[43]; Cellini and Turner, 2018[44]; Dynarski, 2015[45]).

2.3. Linking labour markets and higher education: Returns to higher education and skills matching

The labour market returns to higher education are high, but highly variable

Higher education provides a broad range of tangible and intangible benefits to those who complete it, ranging from better employment prospects to better health and higher levels of life satisfaction. Measuring the labour market returns on higher education attainment is of special concern to individuals and governments as they make decisions on investment in higher education. For reasons of data availability and comparability, this review focuses on the employment and earnings of graduates, as well as average debt levels (see Tables 3.1. and 3.2 in Chapter 3).

Across OECD countries, higher education graduates are more often employed and enjoy higher earnings than their peers with upper secondary education. Those who started higher education but did not complete their programme generally experience poorer outcomes, and are at higher risk of not being able to repay their student loans, compared to their peers who have obtained a qualification (Itzkowitz, 2018[46]).

According to 2017 true cohort data, the completion rate of full-time students at a bachelor's or equivalent degree programme in the United States was similar to the OECD average, at around 40% by the theoretical duration of the programme and close to 70% by the theoretical duration of the programme plus three years. However, this rate was notably below that of countries like Ireland, Israel or the United Kingdom, which ranged from 60% to 70% on the first measure, and exceeded 80% in the second (OECD, 2019[25]). The measures, however, do not take into account the much lower completion rates of students enrolled in certificates or associate's degrees programmes at two-year institutions. As discussed in the next chapters, low completion rates disproportionately affect disadvantaged students.

Among students who have graduated, employment and earnings vary significantly. The selectivity of the institution, the type (level and length of the programme), and the field of study, have all been shown to have an important effect on outcomes, after controlling for student characteristics and the particular geographic and economic context where institutions are located (Chakrabarti and Jiang, 2018[47]; Webber, 2014[48]; Andrews, Li and Lovenheim, Michael, 2016[49]).

The employment advantage of having attained a higher education degree in the United States is similar to that observed in other OECD countries. In 2018, 85% of Americans with a post-secondary qualification (ISCED 4-8) were employed, which is equivalent to the OECD average (84%). However, more young Americans with post-secondary credentials were inactive than on average in the OECD, at 13% versus 11% (OECD, 2019[50]). The earnings premium for higher education is larger in the United States than in most OECD countries. However, they are disproportionately higher for graduates with a bachelor's degree or above (ISCED 6, 7 or 8), whereas it is moderate for graduates with a two-year degree (ISCED 5). As shown in Figure 2.7, holders of master's and doctoral degrees (ISCED 7 and 8) in 2017 had an earnings advantage of 131% compared to workers with an upper secondary degree, which was 40 percentage points above the OECD average and the third highest among OECD countries, behind Chile and Mexico. In contrast, workers with associate's degrees (ISCED 5) had an earnings premium of 13% compared to upper-secondary graduates, well below the OECD average (20%).

Figure 2.7 Earnings of tertiary graduates relative to upper secondary graduates, 2017

Pre-tax annual earnings – upper secondary and post-secondary, non-tertiary graduates = 100

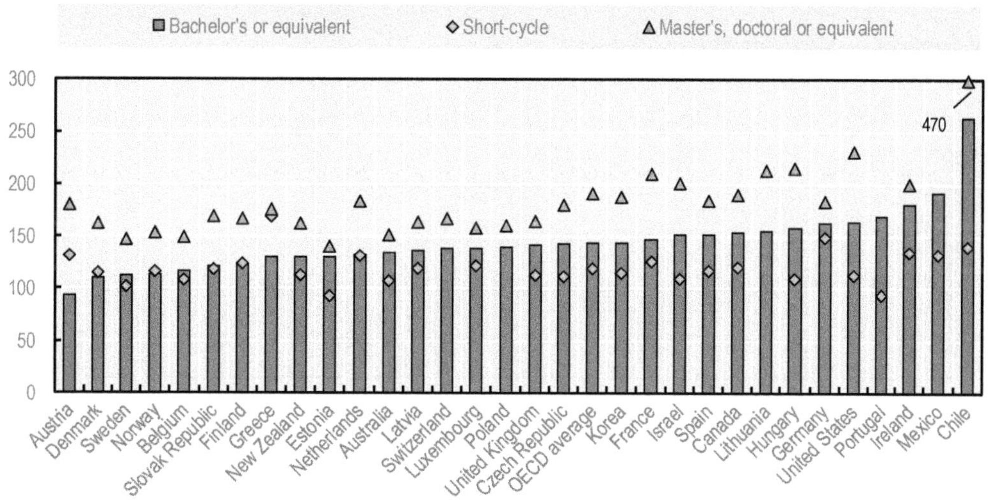

Note: Full- and part-time workers are included.
Source: OECD (2019[25]), *Education at a Glance 2019: OECD Indicators*, Table A4.1, https://doi.org/10.1787/888933976916.

StatLink https://doi.org/10.1787/888934133343

The particularly high return on investment of bachelor's and graduate-level degrees in the United States results from many factors. Research suggests that one-quarter of pay premia for higher degrees are the result of between-firm pay differences, with higher degrees associated with the best-paid firms (Engbom and Moser, 2017[51]). There is also growing evidence that differences in productivity growth are rising between American firms as some concentrate unique managerial and technological capabilities, especially in high productivity growth sectors (Autor et al., 2017[52]). The rise of "intangible capital" such as productivity-enhancing technologies, as well as branding and patent protections, is likely an important contributing factor (Crouzet and Eberly, 2019[53]). The resulting gains of the highest-performing firms are being passed along (at least in part) to their employees, creating greater firm-based differences in earnings.

Comparable data on the employment and earnings of graduates with post-secondary credentials below the associate's level, such as certificates, is scarce at the national and international level. However, there is evidence to suggest that these credentials hold value in the labour market, although this depends greatly on the field of study pursued, and whether graduates work in the field in which they obtained their certificate. Research also suggests greater benefits on average of these credentials for men (Carnevale, Rose and Hanson, 2012[54]; Strada; Gallup; Lumina Foundation, 2019[55]). States often track the employment and earnings of certificate graduates, as will be discussed in the state chapters. While these are typically lower than the returns of associate's degree, there is evidence to suggest that the returns can exceed those of longer programmes in certain high-demand occupations, and when the graduate works in the field in which they completed their certificate (Carnevale, Rose and Cheah, 2013[56]; Carruthers and Sanford, 2018[57]; Schneider, 2015[58]).

Differences in earnings by field of study are particularly large in the United States. The wide spread in earnings by field is similar to that observed in countries such as Chile, Estonia, Latvia or Germany; whereas countries such as Australia, Nordic countries and the United Kingdom combine both lower median earnings across fields and less variation in graduate earnings between fields of study. It is worth noting that the earnings premium of graduates in arts, humanities, social science, journalism and information are comparatively higher in the United States than in many OECD countries, which may result from a large proportion of these graduates pursuing graduate-level education (Figure 2.8).

Figure 2.8. Relative earnings of tertiary-educated adults by field of study, 2017

Pre-tax annual earnings – upper secondary graduates = 100

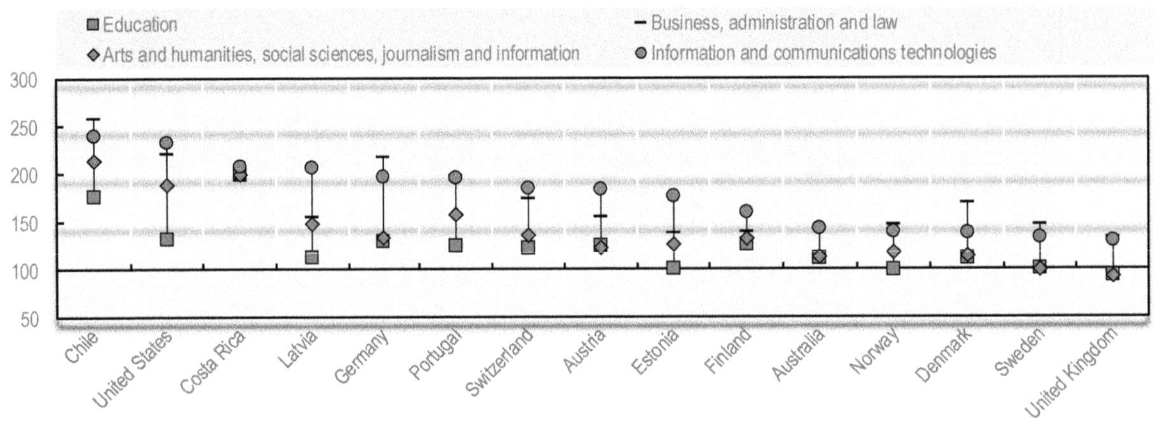

Note: Full-time and part-time workers are included.
Source: OECD (2019[25]) *Education at a Glance 2019: OECD Indicators*, figure A4.4. https://doi.org/10.1787/888933977049.

StatLink https://doi.org/10.1787/888934133362

Disparities in outcomes by institution are also important. Graduates from selective institutions have significantly higher returns than those from non-selective institutions, although there is much greater variation in returns between different non-selective institutions (Hoxby, 2018[59]). Research on public higher education institutions in Texas indicates that returns to some four-year colleges can be comparable to those from two-year colleges in some cases (Andrews, Li and Lovenheim, Michael, 2016[49]). Research by Chetty and colleagues (2017[60]) indicates that institutions vary greatly in the extent to which they facilitate students from the bottom income quintile moving up to the highest income quintile. Mid-tier public universities (e.g. City University of New York, California State University) perform the best, but the share of low-income students at these institutions fell significantly from 2000-11.

Attendance at selective institutions is uneven across demographic groups. As shown in Figure 2.9, 80.2% of post-secondary students whose family was in the highest income quintile attended a public or private not-for-profit four-year college as their first post-secondary institution. This compares to only 35.4% of students from low socio-economic backgrounds, who disproportionately attend two-year colleges, as well as private for-profit four-year colleges. Black/African American students were almost three times more likely to study at private for-profit four-year colleges than White students, while Hispanic students were 1.2 times more likely than White students to attend a public two-year institution. Black/African American and Hispanic students are underrepresented at more selective institutions, and the participation of Black/African American students in selective public institutions has fallen since the early 2000s (Carnevale et al., 2018[61]).

Figure 2.9 Enrolment in different types of higher education institutions by socio-economic status, race and ethnicity, 2018

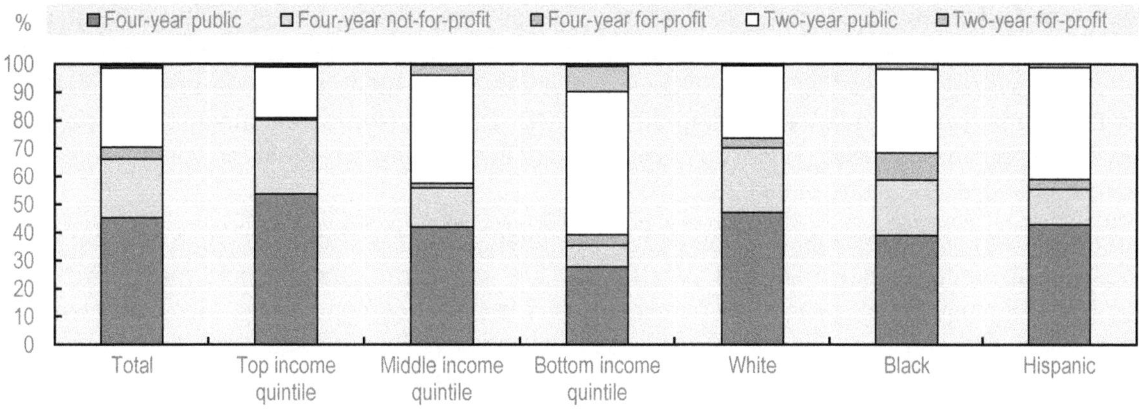

Notes: Two-year institution figures correspond to two-year or less institutions for figures by income quintile. Data by race and ethnicity are for 2018 and include all students in two-year and four-year institutions. Data by income quintile present the share of 2009 ninth graders who ever attended post-secondary by control and level of first post-secondary institution, as of 2016.
Source: Adapted from USDOE – NCES (2019[62]), *Digest of Education Statistics,* Tables 306.40 for 2019 and 302.44 for 2018 https://nces.ed.gov/programs/digest/index.asp.

StatLink https://doi.org/10.1787/888934133381

Research suggests that traditionally disadvantaged students frequently under-match, choosing institutions that are less challenging than those they would be qualified to attend, and often choose fields of study with lower completion rates and lower earnings (Blagg et al., 2017[63]; Backes, Holzer and Velez, 2015[64]). Disadvantaged students may be less responsive to wage signals because they may have less access to relevant information. Even when they graduate from high-earning fields of study, graduates from underrepresented groups face wage penalties due to the occupations in which they work, which tend to be lower-paying than those of their peers (Carnevale et al., 2017[65]).

While higher education can be a highly beneficial investment for underrepresented students (Zimmerman, 2014[66]), the lower returns they often face may dampen their incentives to participate. This can pose major challenges from an equity perspective and as public authorities aim to raise the attainment rates of their populations, as will be discussed in the next chapters.

Skills mismatches are modestly lower in the United States than in other OECD economies

The OECD Survey of Adult Skills provides information on the three different types of mismatches that can arise between workers' qualifications and skills and the requirements of the job they hold. Qualifications or skills mismatches arise when workers' educational attainment levels (or skills levels) are higher or lower than required for their jobs. Field-of-study mismatches rise when workers are employed in a different field than the field in which they have studied and are specialised (see Box 5.1 in (OECD, 2019[67]) for details on how these mismatches are defined and measured).

In the United States, skills mismatches are less prevalent than across the OECD, at 12% versus 15% (OECD, 2019, p. 118[67]). Qualification mismatches concerned around one-third of workers in the United States, in line with the OECD average. Field-of-study mismatches are the most common form of mismatch across the OECD, concerning about 40% of workers, compared to 45% of workers in the United States (Montt, 2015[68]).

While field-of-study mismatches can be a sign of saturated employment in some sectors, it can also signal high skills transferability and an ability to find better jobs in other occupations or sectors. Field-of-study mismatches alone carry a limited wage penalty: mismatched workers earn about 3% less on average than their well-matched peers. By comparison, skills mismatches carry a wage penalty of about 7% on average across OECD countries, while over-qualification is associated with a larger wage penalty for workers, of about 17% on average across the OECD. The United States is the OECD country where over-qualification carries the largest wage penalty, exceeding 30% (OECD, 2019[67]). Research suggests this penalty has risen over the past few decades (Rose, 2017[69]), and that this penalty is highest for workers who are both over-qualified and work outside of their field of study.

This can be a particular challenge for some higher education graduates. Research suggests that low initial earnings due to under-employment can persist over the long term. Under-employment affects lower-earning fields of study in particular, such as security and law enforcement; parks, recreation, leisure and fitness studies; and consumer and family sciences psychology. By contrast, graduates from Science, Technology, Engineering and Mathematics (STEM) programmes are the least likely to experience under-employment (Burning Glass Technologies and Strada Institute, 2018[70]).

At the same time, American employers report difficulty finding workers with the right skills, whether it be due to lack of experience, lack of "hard skills" or poor "soft skills" (ManpowerGroup, 2018[12]). Skills gaps have been reported in multiple employer surveys nation-wide (IHE, 2019[71]; SHRM, 2019[72]; Adecco USA, 2019[73]). In a 2018 survey conducted on behalf of the Association of American Colleges and Universities (AACU), employers indicated that recent graduates had the skills necessary to succeed in an entry-level position, but few had the skills needed for advancement or promotion within the organisation (Hart Research Associates, 2018[74]). These skills gaps likely result from a combination of factors, reflecting in part the complexity of the relationship between labour supply and demand. Aside from structural changes in the labour market, for example due to the long-term effects of technological change; an overall decline in employer-led, on-the-job training (particularly for entry-level workers) may be a contributing factor in some widely reported skills gaps (Waddoups, 2016[75]; Capelli, 2015[76]).

2.4. Higher education policy in a federal system

Federal authority in higher education is limited, as states bear the main responsibility and institutions have a high level of autonomy

In common with other federal systems of government, responsibilities for higher education in the United States are shared between the federal government and state governments. State governments have the main responsibility for public higher education in the United States. This derives from Article 10 of the US Constitution (as amended), which declares that powers not explicitly given to the federal government are the purview of state governments (Antonio, Carnoy and Nelson, 2018[77]). State governments are therefore instrumental in establishing public higher education institutions, funding the instructional missions of public higher education institutions, establishing governance structures, setting tuition policies (and often, providing financial aid), and in developing information systems, as well as articulation and credit transfer policies (Eckel and King, 2004[78]).

The federal government plays an important role in collecting and disseminating higher education data, providing oversight of accreditation agencies, and investing in basic research funding as well as student financial assistance under Title IV of the Higher Education Act. For the 2017/18 academic year, it was estimated that all forms of federal financial support for higher education students (e.g. loans, grants, tax credits, federal work-study funding) were worth over USD 240 billion (College Board, 2017[79]). The federal government has leveraged these investments to secure a role in the assurance of quality in higher education by recognising accreditation bodies, and only institutions that are accredited by a recognised accreditor are eligible for federal student financial aid.

Public funding of higher education in the United States draws from federal, state and local sources. Federal funding for instruction is provided primarily through student financial assistance, while most state and local government spending on higher education takes the form of direct transfers to institutions (Scott-Clayton, 2017[40]). As illustrated in Figure 2.10, the distribution of funding between central (federal), regional (state), and local government in the United States is characteristic of federal systems, in which a significant share of funding, sometimes the plurality or majority, is borne by regional and local governments. In 2016, the share of federal funding in tertiary education in the United States was 46%, compared with 41% state spending and 13% local spending.

Figure 2.10 Distribution across OECD countries of tertiary spending among central, regional and local government sources, 2016

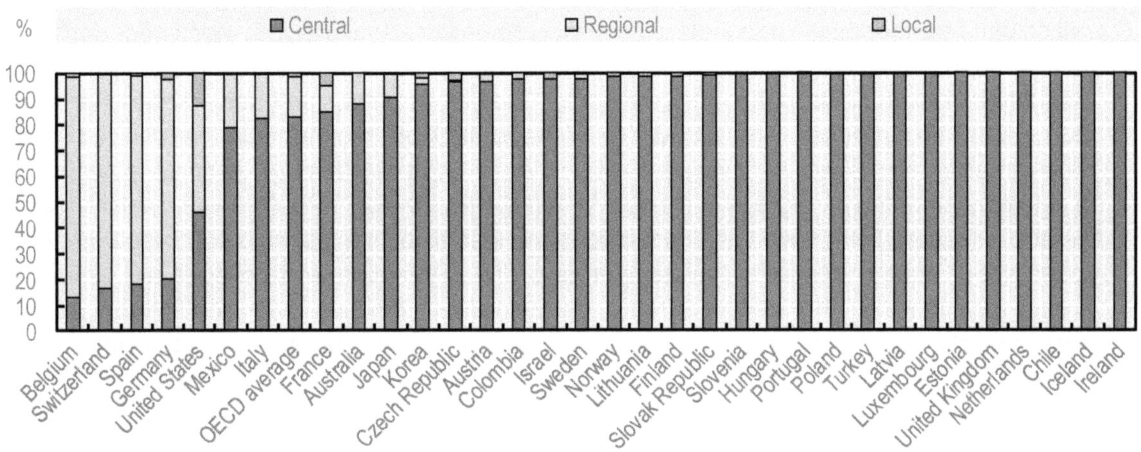

Note: Data for Canada are not available.
Source: OECD (2019a), *Education at a Glance 2019: OECD Indicators*, Table C4.2, https://doi.org/10.1787/888933981115.

StatLink https://doi.org/10.1787/888934133400

As discussed in the next chapters, the post-secondary governance system of each state determines its role in policy processes and the degree of authority it exercises over institutional decision-making. Across the United States, 25 states had at least one co-ordinating board and 25 had at least one governing board, while 14 states had multiple boards for higher education (Fulton, 2019[80]). States with a governing board for higher education generally have extensive authority over system-wide strategic planning, from setting admissions standards and credit transfer rules, to having a substantial degree of influence over academic programming and personnel decisions (Eckel and King, 2004[78]). State-wide co-ordinating boards play a less direct, but still significant, role in the state's responsibilities for public higher education and, in some cases, oversight responsibilities for independent colleges (Fulton, 2019[80]). Both governing boards and co-ordinating boards typically provide budget recommendations to the state Legislature and articulate a strategic plan for the higher education system.

Higher education institutions must be granted the right to operate in a state, a process that is often legislatively regulated, and states exercise different degrees of influence over institutional operations based on their governance structure and level of autonomy. While the governance structure determines the role of state authorities, higher education institutions across the United States have a well-established legal basis as autonomous organisations. Extensive private financing, through tuition fees, commercial activities and donations, augments this autonomy.

Box 2.1. Higher education institutions in the United States

There are over 7 000 post-secondary institutions in the United States, according to the National Center for Education Statistics (NCES). Among these, over 4 500 are entitled to award qualifications at the associate's degree level (ISCED 5) or higher, and these enrol over 98% of all higher education students tracked in national data. Most of these institutions (59%) are relatively small, enrolling less than 2 500 students each, as of fall 2018. Approximately 40% of US institutions are public, and they enrol about 75% of all students. Of the 60% that are private, institutions are either not-for-profit (43%) or for-profit (58%) (NCES, 2019[81]; NCES, 2019[62]).

- **Four-year institutions** offer programmes primarily at ISCED Levels 6, 7 and 8. The Carnegie Classification of Institutions of Higher Education identifies five sub-categories of institutions, which can be either public or private. These include doctoral universities, which offer a minimum of 20 research doctoral programmes or 30 professional practice doctoral programmes and enrol about half of all students in the four-year sector. Master's colleges and universities offer at least 50 master's programmes, and account for close to 30% of enrolments in the four-year sector. The remaining types include baccalaureate colleges and special focus institutions, which offer a high concentration of degrees in a single field (CCIHE, 2019[82]). Public universities range from selective research-intensive universities, to much less selective institutions focused on serving local labour market demand. Private, not-for-profit universities and colleges are among the oldest institutions in the United States, and are often selective, with some that are highly research-intensive and others focused on a traditional liberal arts education at the baccalaureate level.
- **Two-year institutions** offer programmes primarily at ISCED Levels 4 and 5, which include two-year associate's degrees and workforce-relevant certificates, typically ranging from six weeks to over two years in duration. Public two-year institutions, such as community and junior colleges, generally offer two main types of degree programmes: one is academically oriented and prepares students to transfer to four-year institutions to complete a baccalaureate education, and the other prepares students for direct entry into the labour market. Community colleges also serve as post-secondary providers of career and technical education (CTE), which includes industry-recognised certificates, licenses and certifications.
- **Private for-profit institutions** are a newer institutional model, predominantly classified as four-year institutions, although they often offer associate's degrees and certificates. In recent years, more for-profit college students have pursued associate's degrees or certificates than bachelor's degrees (Darolia, 2019[83]). The higher education institutions in the United States with the largest enrolment are for-profit, such as the University of Phoenix Online and Kaplan University, as are many of the country's smallest institutions (Deming, Goldin and Katz, 2012[84]). The US higher education system also includes post-secondary, non-tertiary institutions (ISCED 4), or non-degree-granting institutions, providing only certificate programmes. This segment of the system is small, accounting for just 1.6% of enrolments in post-secondary education in 2017/18. The majority of these types of institutions are private for-profit institutions.

Institutions adopt diverse approaches to their own governance, subject to state regulation where applicable. Boards of trustees, whose members often represent business and civil society, govern most US colleges and universities, both public and private. For public institutions, these boards are typically appointed by state government, though in some cases (particularly for community colleges), board members may be elected at the state level. The legal bases and revenues of institutions vary across types of higher education institutions. Box 2.1 describes principal institution types in the United States.

The federal role in higher education centres on federal grant and loan programmes aiming to widen access and promote affordability

The US federal government first took on a strong role in the student financial aid system through the 1944 GI Bill, which provided financial assistance for armed services veterans to promote access to higher education, leading to a surge in higher education participation during the post-war period (Antonio, Carnoy and Nelson, 2018[77]). With the 1965 Higher Education Act, the basic formal structure for federal student financial aid was established. Federal financial aid spending for students has grown substantially, at an estimated USD 152 billion in 2018/19 (College Board, 2019[39]). Student, programme and institutional eligibility to participate in federal grant and loan programmes has not been linked to the labour market relevance and outcomes of higher education. Rather, federal student aid programmes provide assistance based upon need (Pell Grant programme) or access to borrowing (Stafford student loan programme), as described in Box 2.2.

Box 2.2 Overview of three main federal financial aid instruments

1. Most federal student financial aid takes the form of loans. The primary student loan programme, now called the **Stafford Loan**, was launched in 1965. Initially, the federal government defined loan eligibility, made interest payments for some loans during students' studies, and guaranteed lenders against defaults, while private lenders gathered, disbursed, and collected the loan funds. In 2010, the consolidated **Federal Direct Loan Programme** became the only source of federal loans, spurred by shortfalls in private capital during the 2008-09 recession and concerns regarding private lender practices. The private sector's role has shifted towards providing services to the U.S. Department of Education in collections, record keeping, and client relations. Students with financial need can access subsidised Stafford Loans, also called **direct subsidised loans**, which are interest-free during their studies, or **unsubsidised loans** if they do not have financial need. As of 2008, dependent students can borrow up to USD 31 000 for undergraduate study and independent students up to USD 57 500.
2. The federal government provides substantial support to students in the form of grants. The **Pell Grant** is the most important need-based grant aid programme. In 2018/19, 31% of undergraduates received Pell Grants, compared to 38% in 2011/12 The average grant was USD 4 160, though the maximum amount for full-time students with full eligibility was USD 6 095. Eligibility is based on family income, and funds may be used for tuition or other needs. Over half of Pell Grant recipients are above the age of 23 and almost one-quarter are over the age of 30,
3. There are significant tax benefits in support of students enrolled in undergraduate education. The largest is the **American Opportunity Tax Credit** (AOTC), which provides up to USD 2 500 in support for education expenses. Part-time students can receive up to USD 2 000 through the **Lifelong Learning Tax Credit** (LLTC). Additional programmes support savings for education and interest payments on student loans.

Sources: Scott-Clayton (2017[40]), College Board (2019[85]).

There is one exception to the choice not to link student financial aid to labour market outcomes, which relates to vocational programmes, most often delivered by private for-profit institutions. These institutions participate in federal student aid programmes by virtue of leading to what the Higher Education Act describes as "gainful employment in a recognised occupation." For these programmes, quality assurance and federal regulations have focused on ensuring a link between student aid eligibility and labour market outcomes. In particular, in 2014, the federal government introduced the "gainful employment" (GE) rule, which required institutions delivering programmes with a focus on career preparation, enrolling about 15% of the total student population, to report on their performance using two debt-to-earnings metrics. If programmes failed to meet either one of the metrics, their eligibility for federal financial aid could be suspended (Kelchen and Liu, 2019[86]). The first GE ratings were published in 2017. While two-thirds of programmes with a focus on career preparation were delivered by private for-profit institutions, nearly all (99%) programmes that that failed the standards were delivered by private for-profit institutions (Kelchen and Liu, 2019[86]) (Jump, 2019[87]). The implementation of regulatory programme-level reporting was halted in 2017, and the regulation itself was terminated in 2019, due in part to concerns that it principally targeted institutions based on their for-profit tax status. Moreover, critics of the regulation expressed concern that it would have the effect of reducing access to higher education, most especially for disadvantaged students (Kelchen and Liu, 2019[86]).

Debates continue about whether and how to link student aid eligibility and labour market outcomes. An alternative proposal was to expand GE regulations across more programmes and institutions, removing the link to for-profit status. Though the GE rule was not in place long enough for financial aid eligibility to be withdrawn for any institutions, limited evidence of the effects of introducing the GE rule suggests that it slowed the growth of private for-profit colleges. One quasi-experimental study found that it spurred the closure of for-profit institutions (Kelchen and Liu, 2019[86]); the study also found that institutions may have responded with different strategies, including reducing debt, raising admissions standards, shortening programmes or encouraging students to enroll full-time, and hiring additional staff for student services and support to job placements.

A 2018 Government Accountability Office report found that colleges at risk of losing Title IV eligibility due to high graduate default rates were seeking to influence students' debt management decisions, often to the students' detriment (Kreighbaum, 2018[88]). Another similar policy, called "borrower-defense", currently allows students to have loans forgiven when they have attended an institution that has closed or that misrepresented itself in important ways (U.S. Department of Education - Federal Student Aid, 2020[89]). A recent policy sought to establish a more narrow definition for this misrepresentation, which the U.S. Department of Education (USDOE) estimates will save USD 11 billion over the next ten years (U.S. Department of Education, 2019[90]). One critique of the reform has concerned its short time limit for student to make claims; the USDOE indicates that less than one-third of current claims under the policy would have met the new timeline requirement (Stratford, 2019[91]).

Policy makers at federal and state levels are concerned about the protection of students as consumers of higher education. Thus, political debate continues about how best to support access to student financial aid and track graduate repayment, particularly in the context of rising student debt. Student debt levels are comparatively high by international standards, and a key challenge is the wide variability of returns among graduates. Moreover, there are concerns regarding the timing of loan repayment shortly after graduation, when graduate earnings are relatively low (Dynarski, 2015[45]). To repay federal student loans, there are multiple income-driven repayment plans available to graduates, and about one-quarter of graduates participate in some form of income-driven repayment plan (Britton et al., 2019). Participation in income-driven repayment plans has risen, but remains constrained by complexity, including variation in conditions across multiple plans. Other fee-based OECD jurisdictions such as Canada, the United Kingdom, and Australia, have much more extensive (or universal) participation in income-contingent lending (Barr et al., 2018[92]) (Dynarski, 2015[45]).

Several changes to the federal student aid system, described in Box 2.3, have been introduced in anticipation of the re-authorisation of the Higher Education Act.

Box 2.3 Higher Education Act re-authorisation proposals relating to federal financial aid

The Higher Education Act is the most important piece of federal legislation relating to higher education, dating originally to 1965. Last re-authorised in 2007, it has been due for an update since 2012 (Harris and Kelderman, 2017[93]). Various proposals have been put forward, advancing different visions for higher education and, notably, for the rules governing federal financial aid.

In 2018, Representative Virginia Foxx (R-NC) introduced the **Promoting Real Opportunity, Success and Prosperity Through Education Reform (PROSPER) Act**. The bill proposed various measures to alter the federal financial aid system, including:

- extending financial aid eligibility to programmes with fewer credit hours;
- shifting from a cohort default rate metric to a repayment rate metric for determining institutions' continuing Title IV eligibility;
- eliminating the borrower defense to repayment rules and requiring congressional approval rather than granting discretion to the Secretary of Education for similar rules in the future;
- simplifying the suite of federal repayment programmes into a choice between the current standard ten-year repayment plan or 15% of income above 150% of the federal poverty line until loans are fully repaid;
- simplifying the Free Application for Federal Student Aid (FAFSA).

Source: U.S. House Committee on Education and the Workforce (2017[94]).

In 2019, Senator Lamar Alexander (R-TN) introduced a bipartisan bill, the **Student Aid Improvement Act**, which proposes:

- increasing the maximum Pell Grant award and introducing the Short-Term Pell, which allows students to use Pell Grants for short-term skills and job training programs that lead to credentialing and employment in high-demand fields like health care or cybersecurity;
- allowing incarcerated individuals who are eligible for parole to use a Pell Grant for prison-education programmes;
- providing permanent mandatory funding, USD 255 million each year, for Historically Black Colleges and Universities and other Minority Serving Institutions;
- creating a single institutional accountability measure for student loan repayment;
- simplifying the FAFSA.

Source: U.S. Senate HELP Committee (2019[95]).

The **College Affordability Act (CAA)**, introduced by Representative Robert Scott (D-VA) in 2019, proposes:

- restoring Gainful Employment and borrower-defense regulations in legislation;
- streamlining the FAFSA and updating performance goals for the Federal Student Aid office;
- increasing the size of individual Pell Grants by up to USD 500;
- supporting a federal-state partnership to eliminate tuition fees at community colleges;
- introducing a supplemental grant for four-year college students;
- consolidating repayment assistance programmes and raising the threshold for repaying loans from 150% of the federal poverty line to 250%.

Source: U.S. House Committee on Education and Labor (2019[96]).

Quality assurance in US higher education is based on accreditation, a system of self-regulation operating independently of US states

To ensure that federal investment on higher education is well-spent, federal support to students has been linked to quality assurance processes since the 1950s, when concerns had arisen that low-quality institutions might emerge to take advantage of federal funds under the GI Bill (Kelchen, 2017[97]).

There are two main types of accreditation in the United States: institutional accreditation and programmatic accreditation. Seven regionally organised, membership-based, non-governmental bodies perform institutional accreditation, also called "regional accreditation". Regional accreditation concerns about 40% of institutions and 85% of US students, making them the most important accrediting bodies in the system (Kelchen, 2017[97]). Regional accreditation focuses on institutions' governance, financial health, academic resources and facilities, student support, and, to some extent, learning outcomes. Four of the seven US regional accrediting bodies list employment metrics as a possible way for institutions to demonstrate student success, but they do not require information on these metrics (TICAS, 2018[98]).

Seventy-nine national programmatic accrediting agencies provide accreditation for professionally oriented programmes within institutions, especially those that prepare graduates for licensed or regulated professions. These accreditors, which are often professional associations, traditionally use metrics focused on employment, such as the demonstration of a minimum pass rate on entry-to-practice examinations for regulated professions, or job placement rates. In addition, some state agencies also play an accrediting role in public post-secondary vocational education and nursing education.

While the U.S. Department of Education (USDOE) relies on independent organisations to provide accreditation, accreditors must receive recognition in order for their decisions to be considered valid. The USDOE and the Council for Higher Education Accreditation (CHEA) fulfil this role, by recognising accrediting agencies and providing guidelines, resources and relevant data regarding their work.

The recognition process entails reviews by the Department of Education's Accreditation Group and the National Advisory Committee on Institutional Quality and Integrity (NACIQI), whose members are appointed by the Secretary of Education and Congress, which provide recommendations to the Department of Education (Kelchen, 2017[97]). The NACIQI conducts reviews of accreditation bodies every five years, reviewing accrediting standards and performing site visits. Similarly, the CHEA also recognises regional, national, career and faith-related accrediting agencies, as well as programmatic accrediting agencies. A CHEA-recognised accrediting organisation will undergo a recognition review every seven years (or as approved by the Board).

There have been several debates regarding the impact of accreditation on institutional provision, and its effectiveness in ensuring minimum standards of labour market relevance and satisfactory labour market outcomes for graduates. Accreditation has been described as burdensome, limiting the capacity of higher education institutions to develop innovative programmes responding to student and labour market needs, such as competency-based programmes and micro-credentials. It is also an expensive process for institutions, with four-year institutions estimated to spend as much as USD 3 billion annually for regional institutional accreditation, and another USD 3 billion for programme accreditation (Kelchen, 2017[97]). In addition, as providers that are not institutions of higher education cannot be accredited, the accreditation process has been viewed as potentially limiting the recognition of alternative credentials.

In response, several measures have been proposed to make accreditation more flexible and less burdensome for institutions. The USDOE recently released new regulations governing accreditors and state authorisation of online education providers. These and related reform proposals are described in Box 2.4.

Box 2.4. Changes to accreditation regulations

In 2019, the federal government introduced new regulations governing accreditors and state authorisation of online education providers, to take effect in July 2020. The intent of the new regulations is to allow greater flexibility to institutions, permit innovations in programme design, and reduce administrative burdens, though there are concerns from some, including the USDOE Inspector General, that oversight will be inadequate. The new rules permit accreditors to provide approvals for colleges and for the federal government to recognise new accreditors more quickly. Accreditors will also have greater flexibility in sanctions, allowing institutions up to four years before imposing sanctions compared to two years previously – there were concerns that two years were insufficient to address problems where they occurred. Institutions will also have more flexibility to introduce new academic programmes or branch campuses without the approval of accreditors. Under earlier policies, states could waive their rules for online providers through reciprocity agreements with other states where the providers are based. The new rules maintained this approach, but without permitting states to enforce their own laws and regulations on top of these agreements.

In February 2020, Representatives Lori Trahan (D-MA), Madeleine Dean (D-PA) and Jahana Hayes (D-CT) introduced the Accreditation Reform Act. The Act would firstly require that NACIQI take part in reviews of the recognition of accrediting agencies to provide greater independence from government. The other elements of the Act focus on transparency surrounding the initial and renewal of accreditor recognition, requiring the publication of information on accreditors and documentation relating to USDOE decision-making.

Sources: U.S. House Committee on Education and Labor (2020[99]); U.S. Department of Education (2019[100]).

On the other hand, there have been critiques regarding the lack of effectiveness of accreditation, particularly in ensuring minimum standards of quality and labour market relevance. One concern is that accreditors do not focus sufficiently on student learning and labour market outcomes. As noted earlier, regional accrediting organisations do not make the reporting of labour market outcomes a compulsory feature of accreditation. National accrediting organisations characteristically require the reporting of job placement rates, but in the absence of a standard methodology for the calculation of job placement rates and infrequent validation, these measures are said to be ineffective in establishing accountability for labour market outcomes (TICAS, 2018[98]). Most failures to secure accreditation result from concerns regarding financial sustainability, rather than poor performance in education. One proposal has been for the federal government to take on the assessment of institutions' financial sustainability, allowing accrediting bodies to focus on education quality (Kelchen, 2017[97]). The GE regulations, discussed above, aimed at addressing poor graduate outcomes for some of the nation's higher education programmes

Federal workforce policy creates a workforce system that functions in parallel to higher education, in which higher education institutions play a growing role

Historically, there has been a clear distinction between the higher education and workforce development systems in the United States (Good and Strong, 2015[101]). Although community colleges and vocational schools represent a large share of workforce development training providers, mainly through provision of career and technical education (CTE), workforce development and higher education systems are not always well aligned. At the sub-baccalaureate level, education providers have traditionally been highly responsive to local labour market needs, and as countries mobilise their education and training systems to upskill and re-skill workers, strengthening the alignment between higher education and workforce development systems may become increasingly critical in addressing rapid changes in the labour market.

The public workforce development system in the United States consists of a large and highly decentralised network of local and regional workforce development agencies in each state. The federal government plays a key role in the public workforce development system through funding transfers to states, who are the primary actors in delivering programmes. The 2014 Workforce Innovation and Opportunity Act (WIOA) is the principal federal workforce development legislation. Funding under the WIOA (USD 4.8 billion in 2018) equates to approximately half of all federal Department of Labor spending on mandatory workforce development funding to states. With the Workforce Investment Act of 1998, the predecessor for WIOA, states were required to create local workforce investment boards in order to adapt policies to the needs of local communities. As a result, there is considerable variation in workforce development policies and programmes across the country, including how they interact with higher education institutions and agencies (Good and Strong, 2015[101]).

Box 2.5 The Workforce Innovation and Opportunity Act: The role of state and local workforce investment boards

Under the 2014 Workforce Innovation and Opportunity Act (WIOA) and its predecessor, the Workforce Investment Act of 1998 (WIA), each state must have a State Workforce Investment Board, which should include the Governor, members of the state Legislature and representatives of business, labour and educational organisations, economic development agencies and community-based organisations. Below this level, local jurisdictions can form Workforce Investment Areas, directed and supervised by Local Workforce Investment Boards (LWIBs), with representatives from business, labour and community organisations, and local government.

LWIBs oversee the local implementation of the public workforce development system in the United States. Their main responsibilities are setting strategic workforce development priorities that comply with federal and state regulations and are responsive to local and regional labour market needs. There are more than 560 LWIBs across the United States. LWIBs oversee federal grants through WIOA, particularly by directing the almost 3 000 American Job Centers (AJCs). AJCs are responsible for not only delivering WIOA programming, but also co-ordinating access to a much wider array of programmes. Workforce development efforts focus, in large part, on so-called core and intensive services of career planning and job search assistance, particularly for disadvantaged populations. Training is the third component of workforce development efforts.

Source: Wolff (2015[102]).

One of the key linkages between the higher education and workforce systems is information about workforce needs. Labour market information (LMI) is critical not only for the effectiveness of the workforce development system, but also as important input for strategic planning and forecasting in higher education. The U.S. Department of Labor and the Bureau of Labour Statistics are key federal actors in this area, providing current and projected occupational employment statistics. They collaborate extensively with states and local agencies, including local workforce investment boards, which assist in the development of state-wide employment statistics systems. In addition, one of the most important sources of data on the labour market outcomes of higher education graduates comes from Unemployment Insurance (UI) wage records, which are an important element of the LMI system, operated largely at the state level (Workforce Information Advisory Council, 2018[103]).

Under the Workforce Innovation and Opportunity Act, the US Secretary of Labor must “seek, review, and evaluate” recommendations from a 14-member Workforce Information Advisory Council (WIAC) on the evaluation and improvement of the workforce and labour market information system (Workforce Information Advisory Council, 2018[103]). Current reforms would seek to help state and local workforce boards better understand labour market demands, to better inform students in their career and education decisions, to improve the labour market responsiveness of education and training providers, and to facilitate evidence-based policy development. The WIAC released recommendations in 2019, which included enhancing UI wage records; investing to expand information on occupations, skills and credentials; increasing support to states for collaborative work on LMI; tackling barriers to data sharing; and strengthening the workforce LMI system through improved use of technology.

An important federal tool to support worker training is the Carl D. Perkins Career and Technical Education Act (The Perkins Act). In 2018, total federal appropriations under the Perkins Act were equal to USD 1.209 billion, almost entirely through transfers to states (Congressional Research Service, 2018[104]). Lower-income states receive relatively more funding. States can determine how to allocate the funds between secondary and post-secondary programmes, and develop their own formulae to distribute the funds between providers. The Perkins Act, originally named the Vocational Education Act, was first established in 1963. It was most recently re-authorised in 2018. Now referred to as Perkins V, the re-authorisation gave more power to states and local agencies while strengthening system alignment, seeking in particular to align performance metrics across other federal programmes such as the WIOA and the Every Student Succeeds Act (JFF, 2018[105]). Some key elements of Perkins V are described in Box 2.6.

The alignment between post-secondary education and workforce needs is well articulated through career and technical education (CTE) at the sub-baccalaureate level. The emphasis on work-based learning is an integral component of CTE and, in response to industry needs, some community and technical colleges are also beginning to offer applied bachelor's degrees, demonstrating growing demand for specific, higher-level technical skills with a direct link to the labour market. Additionally, a taskforce on workforce policy, initiated by the current administration and led by the CEOs of Apple and IBM, is launching a campaign to promote multiple post-secondary pathways to develop in-demand, career-relevant skills, including "industry-recognised stackable credentials and certifications" (U.S. Department of Commerce, n.d.[106]). Importantly, this articulation between higher education and the labour market is bolstered by alignment between education and workforce development policy. Often referred to as the "education-to-workforce pipeline", the alignment between education and workforce needs requires co-ordination between multiple actors, including the primary and secondary school (K-12) system, CTE programmes, and higher education institutions (Cushing et al., 2019[107]). Some states do better than others in connecting these parts of the education and workforce development systems, particularly in terms of strategic co-ordination. For example, in Ohio, the work of state agencies in charge of higher education and workforce development policy is co-ordinated by the Governor's Office for Workforce Transformation, which reports directly to the Lieutenant Governor. These and other comparative aspects across states are discussed in Chapter 3.

Box 2.6. Strengthening Career and Technical Education for the 21st Century Act

In 2018, the Carl D. Perkins Career and Technical Education Act was amended by the Strengthening Career and Technical Education for the 21st Century Act. Referred to as Perkins V, the legislation has increased funding for career and technical education (CTE) for the first time in 30 years. Notably, Perkins V provides states with greater flexibility to allocate funds to rural areas and for innovative programmes, as well as the discretion to set their own performance targets beyond a set of minimum thresholds, aligned with accountability metrics used under other federal laws.

Compared to its predecessor, Perkins V places greater emphasis on work-based learning, including pre-apprenticeships and apprenticeships. Work-based learning is defined as "sustained interactions with industry or community professionals in real workplace settings, to the extent practicable, or simulated environments at an educational institution that foster in depth, first-hand engagement with the tasks required in a given career field, that are aligned to curriculum and instruction" (von Zastrow, 2018[108]).

In addition, states must develop plans for co-ordinating CTE with activities under the Workforce Innovation and Opportunity Act (WIOA) and the Every Student Succeeds Act (ESSA); for example, in supporting the professional development of CTE teachers and post-secondary faculty. Local CTE providers must undertake needs assessments to ensure their study programmes are aligned to local labour market needs. Perkins V also introduces a national competitive grant programme aimed to spur evidence-based innovations in CTE.

Under Title I of Perkins V, states must:

- "provide and support equal access to at least one sequenced program of study integrating core academic and technical training, including employability skills, across secondary and post-secondary education that leads to an industry-recognized credential and meets local or state industry needs;
- contribute to attainment of higher-order reasoning and problem-solving skills, work attitudes, and employability skills;
- provide activities to prepare CTE participants (including special populations) for high-skill, high-wage, or in-demand sectors;
- provide career exploration and development activities, in collaboration with local workforce development boards, agencies, or one-stop delivery systems, including in middle grades (Cushing et al., 2019, pp. 5,15[107])."

In addition, states may use Title I funding to:

- "support local relationships among education, business, and one-stop centers, including sector partnerships, to align programs of study with industry demand;
- support work-based learning experiences for CTE students and non-academic support services for disadvantaged and/or special populations (such as child care or transportation);
- support integration of employability skills into CTE programs and programs of study;
- expand opportunities to participate in dual/concurrent coursework, early college, Advanced Placement/International Baccalaureate coursework, and CTE pathways and certification exams established through articulation agreements with post-secondary institutions" (Cushing et al., 2019, p. 15[107]).

Source: U.S. Department of Education (2020[109]).

Student and labour market information, an area of state initiative, has become an increasing focus of federal policy

Across OECD countries, governments have invested in improving the quantity and quality of information available on the labour market outcomes of higher education graduates. In the United States, the federal government plays an important role in providing information about the student population, institutional performance and graduate outcomes. The National Center for Education Statistics (NCES) collects and publishes a wealth of information about higher education, primarily through the Integrated Post-secondary Education Data System (IPEDS). All Title IV eligible institutions must complete surveys each year addressing topics such as institutional characteristics, student enrolment, and number of degrees and certificates conferred. The NCES also develops and implements several longitudinal surveys, including the Beginning Post-secondary Students Longitudinal Study (BPS) and the Baccalaureate and Beyond Longitudinal Study (B&B).

The United States has a demand-driven system of higher education, shaped by institutional autonomy and student choice. In this context, aligning the provision of higher education to labour market needs depends heavily upon students making informed choices, and institutions responding to student choices and labour market information in the design and revision of higher education programmes. In addition, as the cost of higher education continues to rise, there has been increasing public debate in the United States about the value of a college education (Federal Reserve, 2019[110]; Strada Education; Gallup, 2019[111]). This has led to renewed efforts by states and the federal government to improve information about the costs and returns to higher education and the accessibility of this information.

Information about students in public institutions, as well as earnings and employment data, have been available to states for many decades, and have been used to generate information about the labour market outcomes of graduates. By contrast, the federal role in connecting education to labour market outcomes has largely been prohibitive, as the Family Educational Rights and Privacy Act (FERPA) of 1974 barred the use of personal information that did not lead to the improvement of educational programmes. This delayed the linking of higher education and labour market information both at the state and national level. In recent decades, the federal role has expanded through a series of initiatives. These include the Statewide Longitudinal Data Systems (SLDS) programme, where the federal government has subsidised the development of state data systems, as well as the College Scorecard.

Under the SLDS and Workforce Data Quality Initiative, many states have created post-secondary longitudinal data systems and public-facing websites where students, policy makers and others can explore the earnings outcomes of higher education graduates in their state by institution, field of study and other graduate characteristics. Some states, such as Virginia, Texas and Tennessee, also collect graduate earnings data by programme level, including certificate programmes at the sub-baccalaureate level (Dorrer, 2016[112]). Post-secondary longitudinal data systems link administrative data on earnings from Unemployment Insurance (UI) wage records with data from higher education institutions on post-secondary graduates. It is estimated that administrative earnings data generally capture about 80% of the workforce (Pena, 2018[113]). Wage records do not provide information on all graduates who move out of the state, those who are self-employed, or federal civilian and uniformed military service members. These remains important gaps in state post-secondary data systems. States participating in a federal data sharing agreement are able to access wage data for graduates who live in other states to a limited extent. This system, formerly known as the Wage Record Interchange System (WRIS), has facilitated the exchange of wage data among participating states for the purpose of tracking individuals who have participated in workforce investment programmes in one state and then subsequently secured employment in another state, including employment and training programmes delivered by post-secondary education institutions. The purpose of the agreement was to assess and report on state and local employment and training program performance, and evaluate training provider performance. In 2020, the State Wage Interchange System (SWIS) Data Sharing Agreement replaced the WRIS Agreement (U.S. Department of Labor,

2019[114]). Importantly, the new data sharing agreement contains the US Department of Education, it meets the confidentiality requirements of the Family Educational Rights and Privacy Act (FERPA) for education records, and authorises record sharing for purposes other than training programme evaluation. Launched in 2013, the College Scorecard is the most prominent federal intervention specifically relating to student-oriented information on higher education and, particularly, labour market outcomes (Box 2.7).

Box 2.7. The College Scorecard

The College Scorecard is a website that publishes data on the costs of education and labour market outcomes of recipients of federal student aid at the level of individual post-secondary institutions, based on data from the National Student Loan Data System (NSLDS). The aim of the Scorecard is to improve the transparency of costs and likely outcomes of different college options to students and their families. A subset of data focusing on undergraduate study is provided through a consumer portal, while more comprehensive data are made available as file downloads or through API access. Key data available include:

- completion metrics;
- median earnings of graduates one year after graduation;
- debt and loan repayment metrics;
- average annual cost of attendance (net of grants and scholarships);
- students' average family incomes;
- characteristics of students' communities in aggregate based on ZIP codes;
- transfer student metrics.

The coverage of Scorecard data has improved over time. In 2019, new data tracked first-year earnings and debt information college graduates at the four-digit level of the Classification of Instructional Programmes. This means, for example that the Scorecard can provide data on graduates from a history programme, but not on sub-fields such as American history. Over time, programme-level income data will extend to ten years after graduation, like the institution-level Scorecard income data.

Improving how the data are communicated to students has been a priority for the U.S. Department of Education, which has used the College Scorecard as a platform for private sector firms to develop innovative tools for. For example, the USDOE has been working with Google to help direct prospective students to the data when they are searching for information on potential colleges.

Sources: Rothwell (2015[115]); Schneider (2017[116]).

Some gaps remain in the College Scorecard. For instance, it cannot distinguish earnings between campuses of multi-campus institutions (Rothwell, 2015[115]). It only tracks programme graduates, which contributes to an important gap in data regarding those who do not complete their programmes. Most importantly, the Scorecard can only track students who receive federal aid, and these students are more disadvantaged than the average college student. Since 2008, under the Higher Education Act, the federal government is prohibited from developing, implementing or maintaining a database of personally identifiable information on individuals receiving federal financial assistance, "or any other system that tracks individual students over time". The College Transparency Act proposes to revoke this restriction, as outlined in Box 2.8, as a means of improving the College Scorecard and other data.

New efforts are underway to address the limitations of state systems and the College Scorecard. For example, the U.S. Census Bureau's Post-Secondary Employment Outcomes (PSEO) pilot project matches graduate transcripts from partner institutions with the national Longitudinal Employer Household Dynamics

(LEHD) database, allowing for the outcomes of graduates to be analysed several years after graduation. Aggregate data on employment and earnings are published annually according to institution, degree level and degree major. The PSEO initiative differs from the College Scorecard programme, as the outcomes of all students are tracked, rather than federal aid recipients only, and outcomes data are tracked only for those who graduated from an in-scope institution with a certificate or degree. The PSEO project also has the important benefit of allowing graduate outcomes to be tracked out of their state of graduation, therefore overcoming a key limitation of existing state post-secondary data systems. To date, a few institutions in four states (Texas, Colorado, Michigan and Wisconsin) have participated in the initiative.

Another important challenge lies in the variety of information sources about higher education options and outcomes, which can be difficult to navigate for students. Beyond the College Scorecard, various federal platforms provide public access to institutional data from IPEDS, such as the College Navigator, the Net Price Calculator Center, and the College Affordability and Transparency List. To address this problem, there have been proposals to better co-ordinate the provision of information, for instance through the 2016 Strengthening Transparency in Higher Education Act, and to strengthen outcomes data through the 2019 College Transparency Act (see Box 2.8).

Box 2.8 Proposals to improve the quality and presentation of higher education data

The **College Transparency Act (CTA)** is a bipartisan, bicameral bill introduced in 2019 by Senator William Cassidy (R-LA). The CTA proposes eliminating the federal ban on student-level data and creating a student unit record system with more comprehensive outcomes data. Advocates for the legislation include public colleges and universities, who want to improve the data used to inform their programming and planning processes as well as the information provided to students to guide them in their educational choices. Community colleges have a particular interest in this legislation, primarily because the proposed changes would capture transfers on a more comprehensive basis and improve the data on graduation rates at community colleges (AACC, 2019[117]).

Key initiatives of the CTA include:

- creating a secure student-level data network within the NCES using strong security standards and data governance protocols;
- accurately reporting on student outcomes including enrolment, completion and post-college success across colleges and programmes, and providing information disaggregated by race, ethnicity and gender to identify inequities in students' success;
- feeding aggregate information back to states and institutions so they can develop and implement targeted, data-informed strategies aimed at supporting student success;
- requiring a user-friendly website to ensure the data are transparent, informative, and accessible to students, parents, policymakers and employers.

Sources: AACC (2019[117]); U.S. Senator Cassidy (n.d.[118]).

The **Strengthening Transparency in Higher Education Act** was introduced in 2016 by Representative Virginia Foxx (R-NC). The bill focused on improving the presentation of data to students and their families when making educational choices. It would consolidate user-oriented information into a single College Dashboard that would be user-tested to improve its design. Specifically, the College Dashboard would include completion rates of students receiving Pell Grants, students classified as having a disability, and students receiving assistance under Department of Defense tuition assistance programmes. Importantly, it would also show information for all full-time students, not just first-time students who are starting post-secondary education for the first time. The bill also required that all institutional financial aid web pages link to the results of the Net Price Calculator, providing students with information on costs of attendance, available financial aid, and the share of students at institutions receiving financial aid.

Source: U.S. House Committee on Education and Labor (2015[119]).

Despite its growing role in the provision of information on graduate outcomes, the federal government has not taken a direct role in the provision of assistance to states in how to generate accessible, usable, trusted and relevant information. This is contrast to some other federal systems, like Canada, where a new body was created, the Labour Market Information Council, with representation from the federal government and each province and territory, to assess labour market information needs and support the development of effective tools of use across the country (see Box 3.12 in Chapter 3).

States have several opportunities to strengthen the labour market relevance and outcomes of higher education

Section 2.4 has provided an overview of the role of the federal government in US higher education, which is concentrated in specific areas of policy. This suggests that the federal system of higher education in the United States empowers states to take a leading role in funding higher education institutions, and to choose whether and how to place a focus on the labour market relevance of programmes and the outcomes of graduates. States are also permitted to create student aid programmes that complement federal programmes, and may choose to take account of the labour market and outcomes of higher education in designing their programmes in a way that federal programmes are not designed to do. It also shows that states are permitted by federal law, and more recently supported by federal programmes, in playing a very substantial role in creating and disseminating labour market information for learners. However, it also shows that the nation's system of accreditation through self-regulation limits states' ability to systematically use quality assurance as a means to orient state higher education systems towards labour market outcomes.

References

AACC (2019), *College Transparency Act of 2019*, American Association of Community Colleges, https://www.aacc.nche.edu/wp-content/uploads/2019/04/College_Transparency_Act_March_2019.pdf (accessed on 2 March 2020). [117]

Abraham, K. and M. Kearney (2019), "Explaining the Decline in the U.S. Employment-to-Population Ratio: a Review of the Evidence", *NBER Working Paper No. 24333*, The National Bureau of Economic Research, https://www.nber.org/papers/w24333. [23]

Acemoglu, D. and P. Restrepo (2017), "Robots and jobs: Evidence from US labor markets.", *NBER Working Paper No. 23285*, http://dx.doi.org/10.3386/w23285. [15]

Adecco USA (2019), *The American Skills Gap is Real*, https://www.adeccousa.com/employers/resources/skills-gap-in-the-american-workforce/ (accessed on 3 February 2020). [73]

Andrews, R., J. Li and F. Lovenheim, Michael (2016), "Quantile Treatment Effects of College Quality on Earnings", *Journal of Human Resources*, Vol. 51/1, pp. 201-238, http://jhr.uwpress.org/content/51/1/200.full.pdf (accessed on 17 May 2019). [49]

Antonio, A., M. Carnoy and C. Nelson (2018), "The United States pf America: Changes and Challenges in a Highly Decentralized System", in Carnoy, M. et al. (eds.), *Higher education in federal countries : a comparative study*, SAGE Publication, Thousand Oaks, California, https://us.sagepub.com/en-us/nam/higher-education-in-federal-countries/book263092 (accessed on 3 June 2019). [77]

Atalay, E. et al. (2018), "The Evolving U.S. Occupational Structure", University of Michigan, https://ssc.wisc.edu/~eatalay/APST_task.pdf (accessed on 21 May 2019). [18]

Autor, D., D. Dorn and G. Hanson (2013), "The China syndrome: Local labor market effects of import competition in the United States", *American Economic Review*, Vol. 103/6, pp. 2121-2168, http://dx.doi.org/10.1257/aer.103.6.2121. [13]

Autor, D. et al. (2017), "The Fall of the Labor Share and the Rise of Superstar Firms", No. 10756, IZA Institute of Labour Economics, Bonn, http://www.iza.org (accessed on 12 March 2020). [52]

Backes, B., H. Holzer and E. Velez (2015), "Is it worth it? Postsecondary education and labor market outcomes for the disadvantaged", *IZA Journal of Labor Policy*, Vol. 4/1, pp. 1-30, http://dx.doi.org/10.1186/s40173-014-0027-0. [64]

Barr, N. et al. (2018), "Reflections on the US College Loans System: Lessons from Australia and England", *IZA Discussion Papers*, No. 11422, IZA - Institute of Labour Economics, http://www.iza.org (accessed on 16 March 2020). [92]

Blagg, K. et al. (2017), *Rethinking Consumer Information in Higher Education*, Urban Institute, https://www.urban.org/sites/default/files/publication/91666/rethinking_consumer_information_in_higher_education_2.pdf. [63]

Burning Glass Technologies and Strada Institute (2018), *The Permanent Detour: Underemployment's Long-Term Effects on the Careers of College Grads*, https://www.burning-glass.com/wp-content/uploads/permanent_detour_underemployment_report.pdf (accessed on 4 February 2019). [70]

Capelli, P. (2015), "Skill Gaps, Skill Shortages, and Skill Mismatches: Evidence and Arguments for the United States", *Industrial & Labor Relations Review*, Vol. 68/2, pp. 251-290, http://dx.doi.org/10.1177/0019793914564961. [76]

Card, D. (2009), "How immigration affects U.S. cities", in *Making Cities Work: Prospects and Policies for Urban America*, Princeton University Press, http://dx.doi.org/10.1515/9781400833153-010. [21]

Carnevale, A. (2016), *The New 'Good Jobs' - CityLab*, https://www.citylab.com/life/2016/12/the-new-good-jobs/509180/ (accessed on 12 March 2020). [14]

Carnevale, A. et al. (2017), *Major Matters Most. The Economic Value of Bachelor's Degrees from The University of Texas System*, Georgetown University, https://vtechworks.lib.vt.edu/bitstream/handle/10919/86951/UTSystemMajorsMatter.pdf?sequence=1&isAllowed=y (accessed on 20 May 2019). [65]

Carnevale, A., S. Rose and B. Cheah (2013), *The College Payoff: Education, Occupation, Lifetime Earnings*, Georgetown University, https://1gyhoq479ufd3yna29x7ubjn-wpengine.netdna-ssl.com/wp-content/uploads/collegepayoff-completed.pdf (accessed on 20 May 2019). [56]

Carnevale, A., S. Rose and A. Hanson (2012), "Certificates: Gateway to Gainful Employment and College Degrees", Georgetown University Center for Education and the Workforce, https://1gyhoq479ufd3yna29x7ubjn-wpengine.netdna-ssl.com/wp-content/uploads/2014/11/Certificates.FullReport.061812.pdf. [54]

Carnevale, A. et al. (2018), *Our Separate & Unequal Public Colleges: How Public Colleges Reinforce White Racial Privilege and Marginalize Black and Latino Students*, Georgetown University Center on Education and the Workforce., Washington DC, https://cew.georgetown.edu/cew-reports/sustates/#resources (accessed on 12 March 2020). [61]

Carruthers, C. and T. Sanford (2018), "Way station or launching pad? Unpacking the returns to adult technical education", *Journal of Public Economics*, Vol. 165, pp. 146-159, http://dx.doi.org/10.1016/j.jpubeco.2018.07.001. [57]

CCIHE (2019), *2018 Update Facts & Figures - Descriptive Highlights*, Center for Postsecondary Research, Indiana University School of Education, http://carnegieclassifications.iu.edu/definitions.php. (accessed on 13 January 2020). [82]

Cellini, S. and N. Turner (2018), "Gainfully Employed? Assessing the Employment and Earnings of For-Profit College Students Using Administrative Data", *NBER Working Paper No. 22287*, National Bureau of Economic Research, Massachusetts, http://www.nber.org/papers/w22287 (accessed on 30 August 2018). [44]

Chakrabarti, R. and M. Jiang (2018), *Education's Role in Earnings, Employment, and Economic Mobility*, Federal Reserve Bank of New York, New York, https://libertystreeteconomics.newyorkfed.org/2018/09/educations-role-in-earnings-employment-and-economic-mobility.html (accessed on 25 July 2019). [47]

Chetty, R. et al. (2017), "Mobility Report Cards: The Role of Colleges in Intergenerational Mobility", *NBER Working Paper No. 23618*, National Bureau of Economic Research, https://opportunityinsights.org/paper/mobilityreportcards/ (accessed on 26 July 2019). [60]

College Board (2019), *Pell grants: recipients, maximum Pell and average Pell*, https://research.collegeboard.org/trends/student-aid/figures-tables/pell-grants-recipients-maximum-pell-and-average-pell (accessed on 31 December 2019). [85]

College Board (2019), *Trends in Student Aid 2019*, Trends in higher Education Series, https://research.collegeboard.org/trends/student-aid (accessed on 12 March 2020). [39]

College Board (2017), *Trends in College Pricing 2017*, College Board, New York, https://trends.collegeboard.org/sites/default/files/2017-trends-in-college-pricing_1.pdf. [79]

Congressional Research Service (2018), *Reauthorization of the Perkins Act in the 115 th Congress: The Strengthening Career and Technical Education for the 21 st Century Act*, Congressional Research Service, Washington DC, https://fas.org/sgp/crs/misc/R45446.pdf (accessed on 16 March 2020). [104]

Crouzet, N. and J. Eberly (2019), "Understanding Weak Capital Investment: the Role of Market Concentration and Intangibles", *NBER Working Paper No. 25869*, National Bureau of Economic Research, https://www.nber.org/papers/w25869 (accessed on 12 March 2020). [53]

Cushing, E. et al. (2019), *Developing a College- and Career-Ready Workforce: An Analysis of ESSA, Perkins V, IDEA, and WIOA*, College & Career Readiness & Success Center, American Institutes for Research, https://ccrscenter.org/sites/default/files/Career-ReadyWorkforce_Brief_Workbook.pdf. [107]

Darolia, R. (2019), *What Happens to Students When the Federal Government Sanctions Colleges? – Third Way*, https://www.thirdway.org/report/what-happens-to-students-when-the-federal-government-sanctions-colleges (accessed on 18 January 2020). [83]

Deming, D. (2017), "The Growing Importance of Social Skills in the Labor Market", *The Quarterly Journal of Economics*, Vol. 132/4, pp. 1593-1640, http://www.nber.org/papers/w21473. [16]

Deming, D., C. Goldin and L. Katz (2012), "The For-Profit Postsecondary School Sector: Nimble Critters or Agile Predators?", *Journal of Economic Perspectives*, Vol. 26/1, pp. 139-164, http://dx.doi.org/10.1257/jep.26.1.139. [84]

Deming, D. et al. (2016), "The Value of Postsecondary Credentials in the Labor Market: An Experimental Study", *American Economic Review*, Vol. 106/3, pp. 778-806, http://dx.doi.org/10.1257/aer.20141757. [43]

Dorrer, J. (2016), "Using real-time labor market information to achieve better labor market outcomes", *Lumina Issue Papers*, Lumina Foundation, https://www.luminafoundation.org/files/resources/using-real-time-labor-market-information-full.pdf. [112]

Dynarski, S. (2015), "An economist's perspective on student loans in the United States.", No. 5579, Center for Economic Studies and Ifo Institute (CESifo), Munich, http://www.econstor.eu (accessed on 12 March 2020). [45]

Eckel, P. and J. King (2004), "An Overview of Higher Education in the United States: Diversity, Access, and the Role of the Marketplace", in Forest, J. and P. Altbach (eds.), *The International Handbook of Higher Education*, http://www.springeronline.com. (accessed on 3 June 2019). [78]

Engbom, N. and C. Moser (2017), "Returns to Education through Access to Higher-Paying Firms: Evidence from US Matched Employer-Employee Data", *American Economic Review: Papers & Proceedings*, Vol. 107/5, pp. 374-378, http://dx.doi.org/10.1257/aer.p20171013. [51]

Federal Reserve (2019), *Report on the Economic Well-Being of U.S. Households in 2018 - Higher Education*, https://www.federalreserve.gov/publications/2019-economic-well-being-of-us-households-in-2018-higher-education.htm (accessed on 11 March 2020). [110]

FRBNY (2019), *Quarterly Report on Household Debt and Credit - 2019:Q3. November.*, Federal Reserve Bank of New York, https://www.newyorkfed.org/medialibrary/interactives/householdcredit/data/pdf/HHDC_2019Q3.pdf (accessed on 12 March 2020). [41]

Fulton, M. (2019), *An Analysis of State Postsecondary Governance Structures*, Education Commission on the States, https://www.ecs.org/an-analysis-of-state-postsecondary-governance-structures/. [80]

Giannone, E. et al. (2017), "Skilled-Biased Technical Change and Regional Convergence", University of Chicago, https://home.uchicago.edu/~elisagiannone/files/JMP_ElisaG.pdf (accessed on 12 March 2020). [19]

Good, L. and E. Strong (2015), "Reimagining Workforce Policy in the United States", in Van Horn, C., T. Edwards and T. Greene (eds.), *Transforming U.S. Workforce Development Policies for the 21st Century*, W.E. Upjohn Institute for Employment Research, Kalamazoo, MI, https://www.kansascityfed.org/~/media/files/publicat/community/workforce/transformingworkforcedevelopment/book/transformingworkforcedevelopmentpolicies.pdf (accessed on 16 March 2020). [101]

Harris, A. and E. Kelderman (2017), *House Republicans Press for Higher-Ed Overhaul in 2018*, The Chronicle of Higher Education, https://www.chronicle.com/article/House-Republicans-Press-for/242041 (accessed on 16 January 2020). [93]

Hart Research Associates (2018), *Fulfilling the American Dream: Liberal Education and the Future of Work. Selected Findings from Online Surveys of Business Executives and Hiring Managers.*, https://www.aacu.org/sites/default/files/files/LEAP/2018EmployerResearchReport.pdf. [74]

Hermansen, M. (2019), "Occupational licensing and job mobility in the United States", *OECD Economics Department Working Papers*, No. 1585, OECD Publishing, Paris, https://dx.doi.org/10.1787/4cc19056-en. [6]

Hershbein, B. and L. Kahn (2018), “Do recessions accelerate routine-biased technological change? evidence from vacancy postings”, *American Economic Review*, Vol. 108/7, pp. 1737-1772, http://dx.doi.org/10.1257/aer.20161570. [17]

Hoxby, C. (2018), “The Productivity of U.S. Postsecondary Institutions”, in Hoxby, C. and K. Stange (eds.), *Productivity in Higher Education*, National Bureau of Economic Research/University of Chicago Press, https://www.nber.org/chapters/c13875.pdf (accessed on 7 August 2019). [59]

IHE (2019), *Survey: Employers Want 'Soft Skills' From Graduates*, Inside Higher Ed, https://www.insidehighered.com/quicktakes/2019/01/17/survey-employers-want-soft-skills-graduates (accessed on 3 February 2020). [71]

Itzkowitz, M. (2018), *Want More Students to Pay Down their Loans: Help Them Graduate*, Third Way, https://www.insidehighered.com/news/2018/08/08/link-between-college-completion-and-student-loan-repayment. [46]

JFF (2018), *Leveraging Perkins V to support college and career pathways*, Jobs for the Future, https://jfforg-prod-prime.s3.amazonaws.com/media/documents/Leveraging_Perkins_V_to_Support_College_and_Career_Pathways.pdf. [105]

Jump, J. (2019), *Ethical College Admissions: Beyond Gainful Employment*, Inside Higher Ed., https://www.insidehighered.com/admissions/views/2019/07/15/were-gainful-rules-unfair-profit-higher-education-opinion (accessed on 3 February 2020). [87]

Kelchen, R. (2017), *Higher Education Accreditation and the Federal Government*, Urban Institute , Washington, DC, https://www.urban.org/sites/default/files/publication/93306/higher-education-accreditation-and-the-federal-government_0.pdf (accessed on 10 May 2019). [97]

Kelchen, R. and Z. Liu (2019), “Did Gainful Employment Regulations Result in College and Program Closures? An Empirical Analysis”. [86]

Kreighbaum, A. (2018), *GAO: Colleges, Consultants Game Rules to Lower Default Rates*, Inside Higher Ed., https://www.insidehighered.com/news/2018/04/27/gao-finds-colleges-manipulating-loan-default-rates-keep-access-federal-aid (accessed on 19 January 2020). [88]

Krueger, A. and O. Ashenfelter (2018), *Theory and Evidence on Employer Collusion in the Franchise Sector*, IZA/ National Bureau of Economic Research, http://www.iza.org (accessed on 12 March 2020). [8]

Lawrence, R. (2018), “Recent US Manufacturing Employment: The Exception that Proves the Rule”, *18-002*, Harvard Kennedy School of Government - Faculty Research Working Paper Series, https://www.hks.harvard.edu/publications/recent-us-manufacturing-employment-exception-proves-rule (accessed on 12 March 2020). [24]

ManpowerGroup (2018), *2018 Talent Shortage Survey: United States.*, WI: ManpowerGroup, Milwaukee, https://insights.manpowergroupsolutions.com/2018-talent-shortage-survey/ (accessed on 12 March 2020). [12]

McFarland, J. et al. (2018), *The Condition of Education 2018*, US Department of Education - National Center for Education Statistics., Washington DC, https://nces.ed.gov/pubs2018/2018144.pdf (accessed on 12 March 2020). [38]

Mitchell, M. et al. (2018), *Unkept Promises: State Cuts to Higher Education Threaten Access and Equity*, http://www.cbpp.org (accessed on 12 June 2019). [35]

Molloy, R., C. Smith and A. Wozniak (2017), "Job Changing and the Decline in Long-Distance Migration in the United States", *Demography*, Vol. 54/2, pp. 631-653, http://dx.doi.org/10.1007/s13524-017-0551-9. [22]

Montt, G. (2015), "The causes and consequences of field-of-study mismatch: An analysis using PIAAC", *OECD Social, Employment and Migration Working Papers*, No. 167, OECD Publishing, Paris, https://dx.doi.org/10.1787/5jrxm4dhv9r2-en. [68]

Moretti, E. (2012), *The new geography of jobs*, Houghton Mifflin Harcourt. [20]

NCES (2019), *Digest of Education Statistics*, National Center for Education Statistics, https://nces.ed.gov/programs/digest/d18/ (accessed on 17 January 2019). [62]

NCES (2019), *Integrated Postsecondary Education Data System (IPEDS), 12-month Enrollment component 2018-19 provisional data*, National Center for Education Statistics - US Department of Education, Washington, D.C., https://nces.ed.gov/ipeds/trendgenerator/ (accessed on 5 October 2020). [81]

NCES (2018), *Digest of Education Statistics, 2018*, National Center for Education Statistics - US Department of Education, Washington, D.C., https://nces.ed.gov/programs/digest/d18/tables/dt18_330.20.asp?current=yes (accessed on 11 March 2020). [33]

NCES (2018), *Tuition costs of colleges and universities*, National Center for Education Statistics, https://nces.ed.gov/fastfacts/display.asp?id=76 (accessed on 13 June 2019). [37]

NCES (2017), *Table 303.20. Total fall enrollment in all postsecondary institutions participating in Title IV programs and annual percentage change in enrollment, by degree-granting status and control of institution: 1995 through 2016*, National Center for Education Statistics, https://nces.ed.gov/programs/digest/d17/tables/dt17_303.20.asp (accessed on 5 June 2019). [27]

OECD (2020), *Average wages* (indicator), https://dx.doi.org/10.1787/cc3e1387-en (accessed on 12 March 2020). [3]

OECD (2020), *Population with tertiary education* (indicator), https://dx.doi.org/10.1787/0b8f90e9-en (accessed on 12 March 2020). [26]

OECD (2020), *Trade Union*, https://stats.oecd.org/Index.aspx?DataSetCode=TUD (accessed on 12 March 2020). [2]

OECD (2020), *Wage levels* (indicator), https://dx.doi.org/10.1787/0a1c27bc-en (accessed on 12 March 2020). [4]

OECD (2019), *Benchmarking Higher Education System Performance*, Higher Education, OECD Publishing, Paris, https://dx.doi.org/10.1787/be5514d7-en. [34]

OECD (2019), "Employment, unemployment and inactivity rates of 25-34 year-olds, by educational attainment (2018)", in *Education at a Glance 2019: OECD Indicators*, OECD Publishing, Paris, https://dx.doi.org/10.1787/f8d7880d-en. [50]

OECD (2019), *Education at a Glance 2019: OECD Indicators*, OECD Publishing, Paris, https://dx.doi.org/10.1787/f8d7880d-en (accessed on 4 15 2020). [25]

OECD (2019), "Relative share of public, private and international expenditure on educational institutions, final source of funds (2016)", in *Education at a Glance 2019: OECD Indicators*, OECD Publishing, Paris, https://dx.doi.org/10.1787/f8d7880d-en (accessed on 10 May 2020). [32]

OECD (2019), *OECD Employment Outlook 2019: The Future of Work*, OECD Publishing, Paris, https://dx.doi.org/10.1787/9ee00155-en. [1]

OECD (2019), *Skills Matter: Additional Results from the Survey of Adult Skills*, OECD Skills Studies, OECD Publishing, Paris, https://dx.doi.org/10.1787/1f029d8f-en (accessed on 10 April 2020). [67]

OECD (2018), *Labour Force Survey by sex and age - indicators*, https://stats.oecd.org/viewhtml.aspx?datasetcode=LFS_SEXAGE_I_R&lang=en# (accessed on 12 March 2020). [10]

Page, L. and J. Scott-Clayton (2016), "Improving college access in the United States: Barriers and policy responses", *Economics of Education Review*, Vol. 51, pp. 4-22, http://dx.doi.org/10.1016/j.econedurev.2016.02.009. [29]

Pena, C. (2018), *Workforce success relies on transparent postsecondary data*, National Skills Coalition, https://m.nationalskillscoalition.org/resources/publications/file/Workforce-success-relies-on-transparent-postsecondary-data_web.pdf. [113]

Ripley, A. (2018), *Why Is College in America So Expensive?*, Emerson Collective, https://www.theatlantic.com/education/archive/2018/09/why-is-college-so-expensive-in-america/569884/. [36]

Rose, S. (2017), *Mismatch: How Many Workers with a Bachelor's Degree Are Overqualified for Their Jobs?*, Urban Institute , Washington, http://www.urban.org/sites/default/files/publication/87951/college_mismatch_final.pdf (accessed on 21 May 2019). [69]

Rossi-Hansberg, E., P. Sarte and N. Trachter (2018), "Diverging Trends in National and Local Concentration", *Federal Reserve Bank of Richmond Working Papers*, Vol. 18/15, pp. 1-39, http://dx.doi.org/10.21144/wp18-15. [9]

Rothwell, J. (2015), *Understanding the College Scorecard*, https://www.brookings.edu/opinions/understanding-the-college-scorecard/ (accessed on 16 March 2020). [115]

Schneider, M. (2017), *Reforms to Increase Transparency in Higher Education - What to do: Policy Recommendations for 2017*, American Enterprise Institute, https://www.air.org/resource/reforms-increase-transparency-higher-education (accessed on 16 March 2020). [116]

Schneider, M. (2015), *Higher Education Pays: But a Lot More for Some Graduates Than for Others*, College Measures, https://www.air.org/sites/default/files/Higher_Education_Pays_Sep_13.pdf (accessed on 20 May 2019). [58]

Scott-Clayton, J. (2017), *Undergraduate Financial Aid in the United States*, American Academy of Arts & Sciences., Washington DC, https://www.amacad.org/sites/default/files/publication/downloads/CFUE_Financial-Aid.pdf (accessed on 12 March 2020). [40]

SHRM (2019), *Employers Say Students Aren't Learning Soft Skills in College*, Society for Human Resource Management, https://www.shrm.org/resourcesandtools/hr-topics/employee-relations/pages/employers-say-students-arent-learning-soft-skills-in-college.aspx (accessed on 3 February 2020). [72]

Starr, E., J. Prescott and N. Bishara (2019), "Noncompetes in the U.S. Labor Force", *University of Michigan Law & Economics Research Paper*, Vol. 18/013, http://dx.doi.org/10.2139/ssrn.2625714. [7]

Strada Education; Gallup (2019), *From College to Life: Relevance and the Value of Higher Education*, https://go.stradaeducation.org/from-college-to-life (accessed on 11 March 2020). [111]

Strada; Gallup; Lumina Foundation (2019), *Certified Value: When do Adults without Degrees Benefit from Earning Certificates and Certifications?*, https://go.stradaeducation.org/certified-value. [55]

Stratford, M. (2019), *DeVos finalizes 'borrower defense' rules as critics plan lawsuits*, Politico, https://www.politico.com/newsletters/morning-education/2019/09/03/devos-finalizes-borrower-defense-rules-as-critics-plan-lawsuits-473901 (accessed on 31 December 2019). [91]

TICAS (2018), *Of metrics and markets: Measuring post-college employment success*, The Institute for College Access and Success, https://ticas.org/accountability/metrics-and-markets/. [98]

U.S. Bureau of Labor Statistics (2020), *Labor Force Statistics from the Current Population Survey.*, https://www.bls.gov/cps/ (accessed on 12 March 2020). [11]

U.S. Bureau of Labor Statistics (2020), *Table 3. Median usual weekly earnings by age, race, Hispanic or Latino ethnicity, and sex*, https://www.bls.gov/webapps/legacy/cpswktab3.htm (accessed on 12 March 2020). [5]

U.S. Bureau of Labour Statistics (2019), *College Enrollment and Work Activity of Recent High School and College Graduates Summary*, http://dx.doi.org/www.bls.gov/news.release/hsgec.nr0.htm (accessed on 15 April 2020). [28]

U.S. Census Bureau (2019), *Educational Attainment in the United States: 2010 - Current Population Survey, 2010 Annual Social and Economic Supplement*, https://www.census.gov/data/tables/2010/demo/educational-attainment/cps-detailed-tables.html (accessed on 12 March 2020). [31]

U.S. Census Bureau (2019), *Educational Attainment in the United States: 2018 - Current Population Survey, 2018 Annual Social and Economic Supplement.*, https://www.census.gov/data/tables/2018/demo/education-attainment/cps-detailed-tables.html (accessed on 12 March 2020). [30]

U.S. Department of Commerce (n.d.), *American Workforce Policy Advisory Board*, https://www.commerce.gov/americanworker/american-workforce-policy-advisory-board (accessed on 5 May 2020). [106]

U.S. Department of Education (2020), *Perkins V*, Perkins Collaborative Resource Network, https://cte.ed.gov/legislation/perkins-v (accessed on 2 March 2020). [109]

U.S. Department of Education (2019), *Secretary DeVos Finalizes Higher Education Regulations that Promote Innovation, Protect Students, and Reduce Regulatory Burden*, https://www.ed.gov/news/press-releases/secretary-devos-finalizes-higher-education-regulations-promote-innovation-protect-students-and-reduce-regulatory-burden (accessed on 5 May 2020). [100]

U.S. Department of Education (2019), *U.S. Department of Education Finalizes Regulations to Protect Student Borrowers, Hold Higher Education Institutions Accountable and Save Taxpayers $11.1 Billion Over 10 Years*, https://www.ed.gov/news/press-releases/us-department-education-finalizes-regulations-protect-student-borrowers-hold-higher-education-institutions-accountable-and-save-taxpayers-111-billion-over-10-years (accessed on 5 May 2020). [90]

U.S. Department of Education - Federal Student Aid (2020), *Borrower Defense*, https://borrowerdischarge.ed.gov/s/?language=en_US (accessed on 5 May 2020). [89]

U.S. Department of Labor (2019), *State Wage Interchange System (SWIS) Data Sharing Agreement*, https://www.dol.gov/sites/dolgov/files/ETA/Performance/pdfs/SWIS_Agreement_6-20-19_Accessible_PDF_Fillable_Form.pdf (accessed on 6 May 2020). [114]

U.S. House Committee on Education and Labor (2020), *H.R.5768 Accreditation Reform Act of 2020*, https://www.congress.gov/bill/116th-congress/house-bill/5768 (accessed on 5 May 2020). [99]

U.S. House Committee on Education and Labor (2019), *H.R.4674 College Affordability Act*, https://www.congress.gov/bill/116th-congress/house-bill/4674/text (accessed on 5 May 2020). [96]

U.S. House Committee on Education and Labor (2015), *H.R. 3178 Transparency Fact Sheet*, https://edlabor.house.gov/imo/media/doc/2016-06-22%20HR%203178%20Transparency%20Fact%20sheet.pdf (accessed on 18 March 2020). [119]

U.S. House Committee on Education and the Workforce (2017), *H.R.4508 PROSPER Act*, https://www.congress.gov/bill/115th-congress/house-bill/4508 (accessed on 5 May 2020). [94]

U.S. Senate HELP Committee (2019), *The Student Aid Improvement Act of 2019*, U.S. Senate Committee on Health, Education, Labor and Pensions, https://www.help.senate.gov/imo/media/doc/The%20Student%20Aid%20Improvement%20Act%20of%202019%20One%20Pager.pdf (accessed on 2 March 2020). [95]

U.S. Senator Cassidy (n.d.), *College Transparency Act: One Pager*, https://www.cassidy.senate.gov/imo/media/doc/CTA%20-%20One%20Pager.pdf (accessed on 18 March 2020). [118]

Urban Institute (2017), *Understanding College Affordability*, http://collegeaffordability.urban.org/ (accessed on 12 March 2020). [42]

von Zastrow, C. (2018), *Perkins V: Expanding Opportunities for Work-Based Learning*, Education Commission on the States: EdNote, https://ednote.ecs.org/perkins-v-expanding-opportunities-for-work-based-learning/ (accessed on 2 March 2020). [108]

Waddoups, C. (2016), "Did Employers in the United States Back Away from Skills Training during the Early 2000s?", *Industrial & Labor Relations Review*, Vol. 69/2, pp. 405-434, http://dx.doi.org/10.1177/0019793915619904. [75]

Webber, D. (2014), "The lifetime earnings premia of different majors: Correcting for selection based on cognitive, noncognitive, and unobserved factors", *Labour Economics*, Vol. 28, pp. 14-23, http://dx.doi.org/10.1016/j.labeco.2014.03.009. [48]

Wolff, K. (2015), *Governing the Public Workforce System: The Structure and Priorities of Local Workforce Investment Boards*, Social Policy Research Associates, https://wdr.doleta.gov/research/FullText_Documents/ETAOP-2016-05_Governing%20the%20Public%20Workforce%20System%20-%20The%20Structure%20and%20Priorities%20of%20Local%20Workforce%20Investment%20Boards.pdf (accessed on 2 March 2020). [102]

Workforce Information Advisory Council (2018), *Recommendations to Improve the Nation's Workforce and Labor Market Information System.*, US Department of Labor, Washington DC, https://www.dol.gov/sites/dolgov/files/ETA/wioa/pdfs/WIAC_Recommendations_Report_2018-01-25_Final_and_Signed.pdf (accessed on 16 March 2020). [103]

Zimmerman, S. (2014), *The Returns to College Admission for Academically Marginal Students*, https://doi.org/10.1086/676661. [66]

3 Four states in a comparative perspective

This chapter provides an overview of the economic and higher education characteristics of the four states participating in the review, as well as a scorecard comparing the labour market outcomes of their graduates in a national and international perspective. The chapter also summarises key policies identified in the four states that contribute to improving the alignment of higher education and the labour market. It also provides policy examples from OECD jurisdictions that offer insights on various approaches to aligning higher education and the labour market.

This chapter has two aims. First, it seeks to help policy makers and stakeholders in the four participating states compare their graduate labour market outcomes to other states and countries, and to highlight where they perform well in key areas of interest. Key outcomes are provided in a scorecard (Table 3.2) that brings together national and international comparative data on the labour market outcomes of graduates for the four participating states, the nation, and the best-performing OECD countries. Second, the chapter aims to synthesise key findings and policy options which are common to the four states in the project, augmenting this analysis with international examples. Four key areas are examined: strategic planning and co-ordination; education offerings, pathways and student supports; funding; and information.

3.1. Comparing the alignment of higher education and the labour market

Economy, population, and higher education context

Higher education graduates are, on average, rewarded for their qualifications in the labour market across the United States, as is also the case in general across OECD countries. However, a range of contextual factors influences the extent of labour market rewards for graduates in each of the four states, including their economic and social context and the resources available within their higher education systems.

Table 3.1 includes a series of indicators that shed light on each state's context. While the indicators refer to 2018 – they do not capture the drastic economic impacts of the COVID-19 pandemic – they highlight basic features of the each state's economy, population and higher education system.

Table 3.1. Economy, population and higher education in Ohio, Texas, Virginia and Washington, 2018

		Ohio	Texas	Virginia	Washington	US	US minimum	US maximum
	Economy and population							
1	Per capita real GDP, in USD	51 848	59 827	56 110	68 007	57 052	34 497	73 529
2	Employment rate, 25-64 (%)	75.2	74.4	77.8	76.0	75.1	64.9	82.7
3	Annual median earnings, 25-64, in USD	49 000	48 000	55 000	60 000	50 000	40 000	65 000
4	Total population	11 689 442	28 701 845	8 517 685	7 535 591	327 167 439	577 737	39 557 045
5	Total population under 18	2 587 952	7 399 171	1 867 261	1 659 567	73 272 939	113 412	8 981 749
6	Higher education attainment rate, associate's degrees (%)							
	25-34	9.1	7.9	9.2	10.2	9.0	6.0	17.0
	35-64	9.8	7.5	8.3	10.8	9.3	6.9	17.7
7	Higher education attainment rate, bachelor's degrees (%)							
	25-34	23.1	22.4	27.2	27.4	25.2	15.5	36.0
	35-64	18.0	19.6	22.5	22.2	20.0	13.2	25.6
8	Higher education attainment rate, associate's degrees and above (%)							
	25-34	43.0	39.1	50.8	49.8	45.3	31.1	59.6
	35-64	39.5	38.4	49.6	47.4	42.4	30.3	53.3
9	Degree holders who migrated to the state within the past year as a share of all degree holders (%)							
	25-34	5.5	6.9	9.5	11.1	6.9	3.7	17.3
	35-64	1.8	2.8	3.4	3.7	2.7	1.5	5.6
10	Share of employed bachelor's graduates by birthplace, 25-64 (%)							
	Born in the state	68.9	46.1	32.5	33.5	47.2	13.1	71.8

		Ohio	Texas	Virginia	Washington	US	US minimum	US maximum
	Born in the US, outside the state	23.9	34.0	48.8	46.9	35.4	18.8	63.8
	Born outside the US	7.2	19.9	18.8	19.7	17.4	2.5	30.7
	Higher education enrolment, completion and finance							
11	Share of the population enrolled in post-secondary education (undergraduate level) (%)							
	18-24	38.1	36.0	40.4	35.0	39.8	20.1	49.2
	25-44	4.4	5.2	4.8	5.6	5.0	2.5	7.4
12	12-month enrolment (FTE) by post-secondary sector as a share of total enrolment (%)							
	Public 4-year institutions	53.6	50.7	44.3	75.5	46.7	22.1	93.4
	Public 2-year institutions	18.4	33.0	22.2	7.7	22.2	0.0	51.2
	Private not-for-profit institutions	22.6	10.3	25.5	11.8	22.9	0.0	86.1
	Private for-profit institutions	4.5	5.9	7.9	5.0	7.9	0.8	38.4
13	Completion rate within 150% of the nominal duration by type of institution							
	Public 4-year institutions	54.1	50.7	72.8	53.6	57.0	23.5	72.8
	Public 2-year institutions	27.4	21.3	28.7	35.8	28.6	17.2	62.6
	Private not-for-profit institutions	63.2	62.4	56.0	72.7	65.8	32.2	77.8
	Private for-profit institutions	62.2	58.1	52.2	60.2	48.7	20.9	89.5
14	Completion rate within 150% of the nominal duration in public 4-year institutions, by race/ethnicity							
	White	58.2	58.8	77.6	53.1	61.0	37.0	77.6
	Black/African American	27.3	34.3	52.3	35.3	38.3	17.9	56.1
	Hispanic/Latino	45.4	44.3	71.5	45.0	49.7	25.6	71.5
15	Total educational revenue per full-time equivalent enrolment (public and private sources) in USD							
	All students (undergraduate and graduate) in public institutions							
	2008	15 158	14 305	12 701	11 457	13 695	9 144	20 987
	2018	15 473	13 187	14 577	12 403	14 566	9 901	22 508
16	Educational appropriations per full-time equivalent enrolment (public sources only) in USD							
	All students (undergraduate and graduate) in public institutions							
	2008	7 020	9 419	6 664	8 034	8 848	3 423	17 855
	2018	6 361	7 707	5 420	6 966	7 853	2 806	18 001
17	Net tuition revenue as a share of total education revenue (public post-secondary institutions)							
	All students (undergraduate and graduate) in public institutions							
	2008	53.7	34.2	47.7	29.9	35.8	13.9	81.1
	2018	58.9	41.6	63.4	43.8	46.6	17.5	87.0
18	Percentage of bachelor's degree graduates (public and private not-for-profit) with debt, 2018 (%)	60.0	56.0	57.0	48.0	a	36.0	76.0
19	Average debt of bachelor's degree graduates with loans	30 323	27 293	30 363	23 524	a	19 728	38 669
20	Degrees/certificates conferred in selected fields of study as a share of the total, all levels							
	Education	5.6	4.4	6.5	6.0	5.9	3.4	11.2
	Information and communications technology (ICT)	3.2	4.1	4.8	6.4	4.4	1.3	10.7

	Ohio	Texas	Virginia	Washington	US	US minimum	US maximum
Business and law	17.1	16.1	17.1	14.5	16.9	11.0	28.7
Arts and humanities	12.2	19.0	19.0	21.5	16.3	5.9	27.9

Notes: US minimum and maximum values correspond to the US state (excluding DC) with the lowest or highest value on each indicator. "a" means "not applicable", because the data point is not part of the OECD set of indicators, or not possible to compute with existing data. Annual median earnings are rounded in the data source and reported as such.
Sources: See Annex B for sources and definitions.

StatLink https://doi.org/10.1787/888934134654

Table 3.1 highlights important economic differences between the four states. In terms of GDP per capita, Washington tops the list (USD 68 007), while GDP per capita in Ohio and Virginia is below the US average of USD 57 052. The employment rate in all four states in 2018 was close to the national average (75.1%), with the highest rate observed in Virginia (77.8%). Annual median earnings of people aged 25-64 also vary across the states. In 2018, Ohio and Texas had earnings similar to the US average (USD 50 000), while Washington and Virginia had higher than average wage levels, particularly in Washington, where average earnings were USD 60 000, 20% higher than the national average.

While the states have been able to raise the rates of educational attainment among their adult populations over the past decade, clear differences emerge. The post-secondary attainment rate in Ohio and Texas lags behind the US average, both for the 25-34 year-old and 35-64 year-old cohorts. In Texas, the attainment rate is particularly low for associate's degrees, and for bachelor's degrees among the youngest age cohort (25-34), whereas the attainment rate of the 35-64 group is close to the US average for bachelor's degrees. Conversely, the lower overall attainment rate in Ohio is driven by lower attainment at the bachelor's degree level, as the state has similar rates to the US average for associate's degree attainment. In Virginia and Washington, where post-secondary attainment rates are above the US average, about half of the young adult population (aged 25-34) had attained at least an associate's degree in 2018.

Current enrolment and completion rates in the higher education system help to provide some indications of whether post-secondary educational attainment is likely to continue expanding in the near future, in light of the attainment goals set across all four states (see Section 3.3). In Texas and Washington, the share of 18-24 year-olds enrolled in some form of post-secondary education was below the national average in 2018, by almost four percentage points in Texas and almost five percentage points in Washington. Post-secondary enrolment rates for the same cohort are also below the national average in Ohio, but to a lesser extent (38.1% compared to the national average of 39.8%), and similar to the national average for Virginia (40.4%). Virginia has by far the highest completion rates within 150% of nominal programme duration in public institutions in the four states, reaching 72.8% in public four-year institutions, which is also the highest rate in the United States. In the other three states, completion rates are less favourable, with rates below the average for all public institutions in Ohio and Texas, and below average for public four-year institutions in Washington.

As shown in Table 3.1, the four states show diverse demographic profiles and migration patterns, which may boost or impede their efforts to increase the supply of skilled workforce. Texas is the second largest State in the United States, with a population of more than 28.7 million inhabitants; it also skews younger in age than the national average, with more than one-quarter of the population under 18 years old. On the other end of the spectrum, Virginia and Washington are less than one-third of the size of Texas, with 8.5 and 7.5 million inhabitants respectively, while Ohio has some 11.7 million inhabitants. Virginia, Washington and Ohio all show similar age profiles, with around 22% of their respective populations under the age of 18. Washington and Virginia also appear to have a greater ability to attract educated migrants to their states: in these states, 11.1% and 9.5% of 25-34 year-olds with a post-secondary education had migrated to the state within the past year, compared to a national average of 6.9%.

In the four states, and across the United States, the total educational revenue per full-time equivalent student, which includes state appropriations and tuition income, is similar in 2018 as it was in 2018 in nominal terms. As further discussed in Section 3.2, this reflects important reductions in state appropriations in the years following the 2008-09 recession, while the share of institutional revenue from tuition increased substantially over the same period, reflecting the wider national trend.

The level of financial resources for post-secondary education and the balance of funding sources varies considerably between the four states. These differences affect the states' ability to expand provision and affordability for students. The total amount of available educational revenue per student is highest in Ohio, where it reached USD 15 473 in 2018, about USD 1 000 per student higher than the national average. However, the share of educational revenue from tuition is 58.9% in Ohio, well above the national average of 46.6%. Washington has the lowest overall educational revenue per student of the four states (USD 12 403), but its public institutions are less dependent on tuition, which make up 43.8% of their revenue. Public appropriations per student are the highest in Texas compared to the three other states, although the state recorded the steepest falloff in investment among the four states, with a decline of close to 20% in appropriations per student between 2008 and 2018. In Virginia, public appropriations are the lowest among the four states (USD 5 420 per student, compared to the national average of USD 7 853) and the share of institutional revenue coming from tuition had reached 63.4% by 2018, almost 17 percentage points above the national average.

Higher expenditure on tuition has in general been accompanied by growing levels of graduate debt and a greater share of students graduating with debt, although there are signs that graduate debt levels may have levelled off in recent years as states take more concerted actions to reduce the cost of college (TICAS, 2019[11]). Among the four states, the share of bachelor's graduates with debt ranges from 48% in Washington to 60% in Ohio. Growing reliance on private financing has created concerns about the returns on investment in post-secondary education for learners, a risk that is particularly important for disadvantaged populations as discussed in the state chapters.

While the four states have placed a particular focus on raising higher education attainment, fields of study choices play an important role in meeting labour market needs. Table 3.1 shows that student choices vary significantly by state. Degrees and certificates in information and communications technology (ICT) represented 6.4% of all degrees and certificates conferred in 2018 in Washington, a share that is twice as large as that in Ohio, and notably above the US average of 4.4%. In Texas, Virginia and Washington, around 20% of students graduated in arts and humanities fields, above the national figure of 16.3%. Virginia had the highest share of degrees in education, at 6.5%, compared to 5.9% nationally and only 4.4% in Texas. While a wide range of factors shape student study choices, the four states use policies to increase awareness among students and graduates of labour market needs and to incentivise their participation in high-demand fields of study. This is further discussed in Section 3.2 and in state-specific chapters.

Scorecard on the labour market outcomes of graduates

This section uses an indicator scorecard to provide a synthetic view of the position of each of the four states within the national and (where data are available) OECD distribution on key labour market indicators. Box 3.1 provides an explanation of how the comparisons are carried out, along with some justification of the choices of indicators, while Table 3.2 presents the scorecard.

Box 3.1. A note on the labour market outcomes scorecard indicators

How to read the scorecard

The scorecard (Table 3.2) data for the US states and for the US average come from the 2018 wave of the American Community Survey, while information for the top-performing jurisdictions and the average for the OECD countries has been retrieved from the OECD.Stat data warehouse. Tests have been conducted to check consistency between US data and OECD data, and while the figures generated by both data sources for the US national average are close, some small variations exist due to differences in the indicators used (see Annex B for detailed definitions).

The data for the four US states are highlighted using different shades of brown to signal their position in the distribution of all US states (Washington DC is excluded). The dark brown indicates a position in the top 25%, while the white indicates a position in the bottom 25%. For earnings indicators by gender and race/ethnicity (#7 and #8), best performers are identified as countries where gaps were the smallest, hence when the value is closest to 100.

Choice of indicators

Many national and international indicators on the outcomes of graduates are readily available, including labour force participation, employment and earnings according to educational attainment, field of study, gender and race/ethnicity. While the scorecard focuses on employment rates and earnings, labour force participation rates are discussed alongside employment and earnings in each state chapter.

Employment and earnings are often used as proxies to assess the extent to which the supply of higher education graduates meets employer needs, both in quantity and quality. For example, the earnings of graduates by level and field of study provide some information about the extent to which employers need and value graduates with different types of qualifications. However, many factors other than employer demand affect graduates' earnings. Selection effects are important to take into account: individuals with higher earning potential more often pursue higher education. However, as noted in the previous chapter, evidence suggests that the causal relationship between degree attainment and higher earnings is not due to selection (Zimmerman, 2014[2]; Ost, Pan and Webber, 2018[3]).

Important determinants of earnings exist other than individuals' ability. For example, in fields such as education, critical shortages exist but teachers' wages across most OECD countries, including in the United States, remain low compared to those of workers with similar levels of education (OECD, 2019[4]), in part due to the manner in which they are determined by the public education system.

Beyond indicators compiled using official data sources, alternative labour market indicators are emerging. These include career path indicators based on social network data (see, for example, Box 5.10 of (OECD, 2019[5])), indicators of employer demand using real-time job postings data provided by web-scraping services (Box 3.13), or results from employer surveys (see Section 3.3). As coverage of these alternative data sources expands and comparability improves, in the future they may become integrated into national and international evidence bases on labour market supply and demand.

Sources: OECD (2019[5]; 2019[4]); Ost, Pan and Webber (2018[3]); Zimmerman (2014[2]).

Table 3.2. Scorecard: Labour market outcomes of higher education graduates, 25-34 year-olds

	Ohio	Texas	Virginia	Washington	US	OECD average	Top-performing state (excluding DC)		Top performing international jurisdictions (when available)				
									1		2		3
1. Employment rate by educational attainment (%)													
Upper secondary	72.3	70.4	73.0	75.2	71.6	77.7	North Dakota	83.9	Switzerland	85.5	Sweden	85.1	Austria
college, no degree	81.0	77.5	78.9	77.5	79.1	a	North Dakota	89.4	a	a	a	a	a
Associate's	86.0	82.0	84.3	79.9	84.1	84.5	Vermont	93.1	Greece	99.8	Luxembourg	94.9	Germany
Bachelor's	89.7	86.8	89.2	87.0	87.7	82.9	Iowa	93.5	Lithuania	91.9	Norway	91.4	United Kingdom
2. Employment rate of bachelor's degree holders by selected fields of study (%)													
, administration and law	91.3	88.5	89.8	90.7	89.4	82.6	South Dakota	100.0	Lithuania	94.5	United Kingdom	92.6	Iceland
STEM	89.0	86.2	89.9	87.0	86.6	83.8	Alaska	98.2	United Kingdom	95.5	Finland	94.0	Lithuania
ICT	84.0	83.0	91.2	87.7	86.7	88.0	Montana	100.0	Estonia	98.1	Iceland	97.6	Latvia
Education	89.0	86.3	83.9	87.3	87.5	83.6	Rhode Island	97.7	Norway	96.3	Luxembourg	95.1	Netherlands
and humanities	87.2	83.0	88.1	82.3	86.4	76.6	Delaware	97.8	Iceland	90.7	Luxembourg	89.2	Netherlands
Employment rate by gender, bachelor's degree holders (%)													
Men	91.9	90.9	93.5	91.8	91.2	86.8	North Dakota	96.6	Japan	94.2	Lithuania	94.1	United Kingdom
Women	87.8	83.4	85.0	82.4	84.6	79.9	South Dakota	94.2	Norway	92.5	Lithuania	90.0	Iceland
mployment rate by race and ethnicity, bachelor's degree holders (%)													
White	91.1	88.1	90.2	87.5	89.3	a	Delaware	94.2	a	a	a	a	a
Hispanic/Latino	86.9	88.2	86.9	89.3	87.6	a	Montana	100.0	a	a	a	a	a
frican American	87.3	88.6	90.0	93.6	88.0	a	Alaska	100.0	a	a	a	a	a
nnual median earnings (full-time full-year workers) by educational attainment (USD)													
Upper secondary	33 800	30 000	34 500	36 000	31 000	a	Massachusetts	38 600	a	a	a	a	a
ome college, no degree	34 000	34 600	36 000	40 000	35 000	a	North Dakota	42 000	a	a	a	a	a
Associate's	39 000	40 000	40 000	40 000	38 900	a	Delaware	48 000	a	a	a	a	a
Bachelor's	50 000	52 000	55 000	60 000	51 000	a	California	65 000	a	a	a	a	a
r secondary=100													
ome college, no degree	100.6	115.3	104.3	111.1	112.9	a	North Dakota	120.0	a	a	a	a	a
Associate's	115.4	133.3	115.9	111.1	125.5	109.9	Montana	142.9	Ireland	139.6	Netherlands	124.7	Chile
Bachelor's	147.9	173.3	159.4	166.7	164.5	132.5	California	187.5	Chile	213.7	Ireland	183.2	Mexico

	Ohio	Texas	Virginia	Washington	US	OECD average	Top-performing state (excluding DC)		Top performing international jurisdictions (when available)				
									1		2		3
6. Annual median earnings (full-time full-year workers) of bachelor's degree holders by selected fields of study (USD)													
, administration and law	54 000	56 000	55 000	62 000	56 000	a	Connecticut	69 000	a	a	a	a	a
STEM	60 000	63 000	70 000	79 000	65 000	a	Washington	79 000	a	a	a	a	a
ICT	63 000	64 000	75 000	95 000	69 000	a	Alaska	175 000	a	a	a	a	a
Education	40 000	48 000	43 000	45 000	40 000	a	Alaska	69 000	a	a	a	a	a
and humanities	40 000	46 000	45 000	48 000	45 000	a	Hawaii	60 000	a	a	a	a	a
Upper secondary=100													
, administration and law	159.8	186.7	159.4	172.2	180.6	a	Illinois	206.7	a	a	a	a	a
STEM	177.5	210.0	202.9	219.4	209.7	a	California	234.4	a	a	a	a	a
ICT	186.4	213.3	217.4	263.9	222.6	a	Alaska	500.0	a	a	a	a	a
Education	118.3	160.0	124.6	125.0	129.0	a	Alaska	197.1	a	a	a	a	a
and humanities	118.3	153.3	130.4	133.3	145.2	a	California	168.8	a	a	a	a	a
nnual median earnings (full-time full-year workers) by gender, bachelor's degree holders (USD)													
Men	55 000	58 000	63 000	68 000	58 000	a	Alaska	70 000	a	a	a	a	a
Women	45 000	50 000	50 000	51 000	48 000	a	California	60 000	a	a	a	a	a
Women	81.8	86.2	79.4	75.0	82.8	80.6	North Dakota	128.6	Belgium	94.1	Spain	90.5	Netherlands
nnual median earnings (full-time full-year workers) by race and ethnicity, bachelor's degree holders (USD)													
White	50 000	55 000	56 000	60 000	52 000	a	California	68 000	a	a	a	a	a
Hispanic/Latino	46 800	48 000	57 000	50 000	47 700	a	North Dakota	130 000	a	a	a	a	a
frican.American	40 000	45 000	45 000	45 000	42 000	a	Hawaii	70 000	a	a	a	a	a
Hispanic/Latino	93.6	87.3	101.8	83.3	91.7	a	Louisiana	265.3	a	a	a	a	a
frican.American	80.0	81.8	80.4	75.0	88.1	a	New Mexico	161.5	a	a	a	a	a
of the population with a degree (associate's and above) earning above the median wage for the 25-64 year-old population (all earners) (%)													
25-34 year-olds	86.8	87.2	86.6	85.1	88.5	a	New Mexico	88.5	a	a	a	a	a
25-64 year-olds	64.9	68.0	65.5	64.2	70.6	68.3	California	68.8	Mexico	83.9	Portugal	82.5	Hungary

Notes: The ranking of "top-performing states" excludes Washington, DC. The dark brown indicates a position in the top 25%, while the white indicates a position in the bottom 25%. For earnings indicators by gender and race/ethnicity (#7 and #8), best performers are identified as countries where gaps were the smallest, hence when the value is closest to 100. "a" means "not applicable", because the data point is not part of the OECD set of indicators, or not possible to compute with existing data. Annual median earnings are rounded in the data source and reported as such.
Sources: See Annex B for sources and definitions.

StatLink https://doi.org/10.1787/888934134673

The scorecard (Table 3.2) shows that on average, completion of post-secondary education confers benefits to learners across the four states, both in terms of reducing the incidence of unemployment and increasing earnings relative to those without post-secondary education. In Ohio, Texas and Virginia, having only an upper secondary qualification results in an employment penalty of more than 16 percentage points compared to those with a bachelor's degree; while in Washington, the gap is about 12 percentage points, according to 2018 data. Among the four states, employment rates for all levels of post-secondary education were highest in Ohio in 2018, reflecting the tight labour market in the state for post-secondary education graduates (see Chapter 4).

The median earnings data presented in the scorecard confirm the advantage for those with post-secondary education, compared to people with an upper secondary qualification only or who have completed "some college but no degree". Importantly, individuals who have completed post-secondary credentials other than degrees, such as certificates, are categorised as having "some college but no degree" in the American Community Survey. The "some college, no degree" category thus includes both people who have taken some college courses but not completed a credential, and those who hold a post-secondary credential other than a degree. Among the four states, the financial value of achieving "some college but no degree" is highest in Texas and Washington, where the average wage premium over upper secondary education is USD 4 000 or greater. The lowest earnings premium for some college education without a degree is in Ohio, where earnings for full-time, full-year workers are essentially the same as for those with only upper secondary education. However, there is a substantial additional premium for obtaining an associate's degree in Ohio (of USD 5 200). In Texas, the average earnings premium for an associate's degree amounts to USD 10 000, the highest of the four states in review. The share of 25-34 year-olds with post-secondary education earning above the median salary of all earners (aged 25-64) is also above 85% in all four states, even if the values are slightly below the US average (88.5%).

Wage premia and private returns on post-secondary education in the United States tend to be relatively large compared to many other OECD countries (OECD, 2019[5]). The average gap in employment premium between upper secondary school and a bachelor's degree in the OECD amounts to just under 5 percentage points (77.7% vs. 82.9%), notably lower than the same employment premium in all the four states. Similarly, the earnings gain from a bachelor's degree in the United States and in all the four states is higher than the OECD average (32.5%), and reaches 73.3% in Texas.

At the same time, employment prospects and earnings in the four states vary by field of study and demographic characteristics. As in other OECD countries, business and some STEM fields show the most favourable outcomes. Employment rates surpass 90% for business and law graduates in Ohio and Washington, and ICT graduates in Virginia. Comparing earnings advantages across different fields of study with those from upper secondary only, STEM and ICT emerge as the fields with the clearest earnings advantage in the four states. Washington workers experience the largest gaps in return by field of study, where workers with a bachelor's degree in ICT earn almost double the salary of those with a degree in liberal arts and humanities.

Other important differences in the outcomes of higher education graduates are also evident in the four states. For example, the gender gap in employment rates is larger than the national average (6.6 percentage points) in all states except Ohio, and reaches more than nine percentage points in Washington. The scorecard also shows sizeable differences in earnings across different subgroups of the population. The gender gap in median earnings for full-time full-year workers is particularly wide in Washington state, where the median salary for women is approximately 75% of the median salary for men; while it is smallest in Texas, where the median female earnings reaches about 86% of the median male earnings. Beyond gender, the scorecard shows the persistent disparities in median earnings between different racial and ethnic groups. Annual median earnings for Black/African American workers are at least USD 10 000 lower than those of White workers in all four states. The gap in median earnings between White and Hispanic workers in general tends to be narrower, but Hispanic workers still earn less on average in all states except

Virginia, and the size of the disparity exceeds the national average in Texas and Washington (about USD 7 000 and USD 10 000 respectively).

The dispersion of graduate outcomes shown in the scorecard raise a variety of policy implications for states, from improving the attractiveness of occupations that currently have insufficient labour supply but high societal value, to ensuring that students are able to make well-informed decisions about education pathways, having some understanding of future employment prospects. States also face the challenge of improving equity of access and outcomes for different groups of the population, and continuing to grow the pipeline of available talent to meet current and future labour market needs. The remainder of this chapter discusses the different policy levers for improving the articulation between higher education and the labour market, and compares the policy actions that states are taking to improve strategic planning and co-ordination, enhance educational offerings, develop more effective information channels and use funding effectively.

3.2. Comparative policy overview

The labour market outcomes of higher education graduates, like the ability of employers to hire skilled workers, result from many contextual factors outside the remit of higher education authorities, such as demographic trends, migration patterns, macroeconomic conditions, employment law and labour market institutions, as well as economic policies and taxation. However, across the OECD and the United States, public officials aim to use the policy instruments at their disposal to help higher education graduates experience successful labour market outcomes and meet employers' skills demand.

The socio-economic and demographic characteristics of Ohio, Texas, Virginia and Washington vary widely, as do the characteristics of their higher education systems and graduate outcomes. Consequently, each state faces distinct challenges that may be addressed through different policy approaches and tools. Chapters 4-7 of this report highlight the specificity of each state's economic context and higher education system, provide a tailored assessment of the extent to which higher education is aligned with the state's labour market needs, and offer policy recommendations for each state to help improve alignment.

At the same time, the state chapters show that certain broad challenges are common to all states. These range from the difficulty in supplying sufficient numbers of qualified workers to the state economy, persistent shortages in specific – and often similar – industries and occupations, and wide dispersion in the returns to higher education. While the mix of policies adopted by each state is distinctive, there are also common policy choices and challenges they share.

Across the four states participating in the review, policies in four areas have been identified as most consistently used to help better align higher education and the labour market. These areas are:

- **Strategic planning and co-ordination:** The processes by which states develop a common understanding of policy problems and develop strategies to tackle them. States can use strategic planning and co-ordination mechanisms to orient the actions of higher education institutions and other stakeholders towards improving the alignment of higher education and the labour market. They can also use these mechanisms to improve co-operation among government agencies with responsibilities for education and the workforce policy.
- **Educational offerings, pathways and student supports:** States can develop policies and programmes that ensure certain quality standards in higher education and incentivise institutions to enhance the labour market relevance of the programmes they offer. States can also create clear pathways for students between different types of programmes and institutions, and seek to ensure students receive sufficient guidance and support services to help them navigate and complete higher education successfully.

- **Funding:** States can use public funding and the financial rules applying to higher education institutions to support the labour market relevance of their higher education system. This includes using public funding and regulation to make higher education more affordable for students, in turn helping to increase post-secondary participation and attainment. They can also direct public funding to stimulate the supply and quality of labour market relevant programmes. They can also design institutional funding and student financial assistance programmes in ways that incentivise the supply and take-up of programmes in areas of high labour market demand.
- **Information:** Information about occupational demand and the skills employers require is a key input into higher education policy and institutional planning. For students, information on the expected returns of higher education programmes and the cost of attending these programmes can contribute to study choices that align with labour market needs. For employers, information about the skills that students develop through different higher education programmes can support better hiring and training decisions.

The following section reviews policies across the four states, and provides insights from international policy and practice. Each sub-section ends with potential success factors that states could consider alongside the state-specific recommendations provided in Chapters 4-7.

Strategic planning and co-ordination

What is the role of strategic planning and co-ordination?

As discussed in the previous chapter, state authorities are responsible for the governance of higher education. An organisational and governance structure exists in each state to co-ordinate and govern the higher education system, which is composed of public and private higher education institutions operating in their state. According to the powers conferred to them by law, state agencies responsible for higher education govern the higher education system through a range of policies in the four areas highlighted earlier: strategic planning and co-ordination; educational offerings, pathways and student supports; funding; and information.

Strategic planning refers to the stage of policy making through which public authorities set high-level priorities and goals concerning the higher education workforce. State-wide strategic planning processes can help establish a common understanding of problems, a shared vision of how to tackle these problems, and a framework within which actors inside of government and stakeholders outside of government co-ordinate with one another. While these processes are common across OECD countries, certain factors may contribute to their effectiveness as a policy tool to help align higher education and the labour market. These include:

- the extent to which targets emphasise the labour market relevance of higher education as a priority;
- the scope of the steering authority of higher education agencies and departments to direct actions of higher education institutions;
- the capacity of higher education authorities to work across government actors with a responsibility for skills development and with broader stakeholder groups with a role in the alignment of education and the workforce.

The four states have established system-level goals for higher education with a strong focus on raising post-secondary attainment

In the four participating states, government agencies have placed a strong focus on increasing post-secondary educational attainment among the working age population. As in most US states (42 in 2019), quantitative targets for post-secondary attainment exist in all four states (Lumina Foundation, 2019[6]). As shown in Table 3.3, these targets vary in terms of the population targeted, the types of post-secondary credentials and the timeline to reach these targets.

Table 3.3. Higher education attainment targets

	Ohio	Texas	Virginia	Washington
Target	65%	60%	60-70%	70%
Population	25-64	25-34	25-64	25-44
Credential type	Degree, certificate or other post-secondary credential	Certificate or degree	60% with an associate's degree or higher, another 10% with a workforce credential (post-secondary certificate), industry certification, state licensure or apprenticeship	Post-secondary credential
Timeline	By 2025	By 2030	By 2030	By 2023

Sources: Ohio Department of Higher Education (ODHE) (n.d.[7]), *Attainment Goal 2025*, https://www.ohiohighered.org/attainment; Texas Higher Education Coordinating Board (THECB) (2015[8]), *60x30TX: Texas Higher Education Strategic Plan 2015-2030*, http://reportcenter.thecb.state.tx.us/agency-publication/miscellaneous/60x30tx-strategic-plan-for-higher-education/; State Council of Higher Education for Virginia (SCHEV) (2019[9]), *The Virginia Plan for Higher Education: Annual Report 2018*, https://www.schev.edu/docs/default-source/virginia-plan/Reports-and-Updates/the-virginia-plan-annual-report-2018.pdf; Washington Student Achievement Council (WSAC) (2013[10]), *The 2013 Roadmap*, https://www.wsac.wa.gov/the-2013-roadmap.

StatLink https://doi.org/10.1787/888934134692

The four states differ in the extent to which state-wide targets relate to the labour market outcomes of graduates. One of the goals of the *Virginia Plan for Higher Education* is to ensure that 75% of graduates earn a sustainable wage – defined as a wage at or above 200% of the federal poverty level – three years after graduation (SCHEV, 2019[9]). In Texas, no quantitative targets are set for labour market outcomes, but all public higher education institutions are required to develop and implement a process to identify "marketable skills" provided to students in each programme of study by 2020. In Washington and Ohio, the key state-wide targets focus on increasing post-secondary attainment but do not include targets related to graduate labour market outcomes.

In all four states, multi-year strategies are in place to achieve these targets that contain a series of directions or required actions to help meet them, as well as requirements to monitor progress. However, these strategies differ in scope. In Texas and Virginia, the *60x30TX* plan (2015-30) and the *Virginia Plan for Higher Education* (2014-20) strictly focus on higher education. Washington's *Ten-Year Roadmap* (2013-23) applies to the secondary and post-secondary level; whereas in Ohio, the state's post-secondary attainment target is part of Ohio's *Workforce Transformation Strategy*, created in 2018, which emphasises the need for a highly skilled workforce to meet the demands of Ohio businesses.

In all states, approaches exist to monitor progress towards the targets. These approaches help ensure that public authorities and stakeholders place continuous attention on key priorities, constitute an accountability mechanism to legislative bodies, and inform the wider public about the state's progress in meeting its higher education policy objectives. The monitoring approaches used are relatively similar across states, including the publication of reports on an annual or biennial basis to the Legislature. Some states have also developed public-facing tools with data that enable further analysis. For example, the Washington Student Achievement Council (WSAC) monitors progress on the state's Roadmap by publishing a Strategic Action Plan every two years providing progress updates and maintaining a Roadmap dashboard on its website, which offers information on a range of issues from graduate labour market outcomes to enrolment, completion, affordability and equity gaps. In Texas, monitoring of progress against higher education plans involves annual and final reporting. For instance, the final report for the 2000-15 Closing the Gap plan suggests a majority of targets were met (THECB, 2016[11]). The current *60x30TX* higher education plan also provides an interactive online tool with updated information on its four targets alongside regular progress reports (see Chapter 5).

Thus, in all four states, selecting state-wide targets and monitoring outcomes are key mechanisms used to identify challenges that policy – alongside other initiatives – needs to remedy, and to justify the need for public investment. However, publicly funded policies and programmes supporting state-wide objectives do not appear to be systematically evaluated in any of the four states. Policy evaluations tend to occur on an ad hoc basis, often at the request of the state Legislature, and may be conducted by a legislative oversight or audit body. In Virginia, for example, the Joint Legislative Audit and Review Commission conducts programme evaluations and policy analyses on behalf of the Virginia General Assembly. In some cases, research institutes dedicated to specific policy areas may conduct policy evaluations, as with the Washington State Institute for Public Policy and the Ohio Education Research Center. The existence of dedicated bodies to conduct such evaluations may lead to more frequent and larger-scale evaluations. In some jurisdictions like Ontario, Canada, a dedicated government agency is in charge of conducting research and policy evaluation on higher education, providing a regular mechanism to assess the effectiveness of policies and promote their improvement or change (see Box 3.2).

Box 3.2. Evaluating policy: The Higher Education Quality Council of Ontario (Canada)

Created in 2005, Higher Education Quality Council of Ontario (HEQCO) is an agency of the Government of Ontario with a mandate to evaluate the post-secondary sector and provide policy recommendations to the Ministry of Colleges and Universities to enhance the access, quality and accountability of Ontario's colleges and universities.

HEQCO's work is based on a Multi-Year Business Plan, with the latest plan spanning 2017-20. The plan identifies three long-term goals to which the activities of the Council aim to contribute:

- By 2025, every Ontario student has an equal opportunity to attend and succeed in post-secondary education. Participation and graduation rates for under-represented groups will equal those of the most advantaged groups currently well represented within colleges and universities.
- By 2025, every Ontario post-secondary institution annually identifies, evaluates and publicly reports on the skills and competencies its students acquired as a result of their post-secondary education.
- By 2025, all Ontario post-secondary are financially sustainable and capable of delivering on their distinctive missions.

The Council's recent research publications include for instance: *Immigrant Labour Market Outcomes and Skills Differences in Canada*; *Gendered Returns to Cognitive Skills in Canada*; and *Government's Role in Digital Learning: Review and Recommendations for the Ministry of Colleges and Universities*.

HEQCO includes a team of about fifteen researchers and policy analysts and receives funding from the provincial government of about CAD 5 million annually. Each year, the Council prepares an annual report on its activities, which it submits to the Minister of Colleges and Universities for tabling in the Legislative Assembly of Ontario.

Source: Higher Education Quality Council of Ontario (2020[12]).

Based on the information available to the OECD team, it was not possible to determine the extent to which state agencies in charge of higher education requested or initiated policy or programme evaluations. This includes internal programme evaluations, which may be conducted by the state agency responsible for implementing the programme.

Despite a similar governance structure, the capacity of state government to steer the higher education system varies across the four states

The ability of governments to steer higher education depends on the legal framework that organises the relationships between public authorities and institutions. Across the OECD, the level of government influence on higher education varies considerably. As outlined in the previous chapter, the US higher education system is characterised by a high degree of institutional autonomy and generally less government steering than in many European or Asian countries. Important differences also exist between US states. As shown in Table 3.4, only 28 states have some type of state-wide entity governing higher education, which is the case in Ohio, Texas, Virginia and Washington.

Table 3.4. Post-secondary governance structure by state

Number of states that have at least one board of each type

Structure	Count	States
Single, state-wide co-ordinating board	20	Alabama, Arkansas, Colorado, Illinois, Indiana, Kentucky, Louisiana, Maryland, Massachusetts, Missouri, Nebraska, New Mexico, **Ohio**, Oklahoma, Oregon, South Carolina, Tennessee, **Texas, Virginia, Washington**
One or more major system-wide co-ordinating board	2	West Virginia (2), Wyoming
Single, state-wide governing board	8	Alaska, Hawaii, Idaho, Kansas, Montana, Nevada, North Dakota, Rhode Island
One or more major system-wide governing board	14	Arizona, California (3), Connecticut, Florida (2), Georgia (2), Iowa (2), Maine (2), Minnesota (2), New Hampshire (2), New York (2), North Carolina (2), Pennsylvania, Utah (2), Vermont
One or more, major system-wide co-ordinating and governing board	3	Mississippi (2), South Dakota (2), Wisconsin (2)
Administrative/service agencies	11 and DC	Alaska, Arizona, Connecticut, Delaware, District of Columbia, Florida, Iowa, Minnesota, New Hampshire, New Jersey, New York, Pennsylvania

Note: Michigan does not have a state-level board or agency.
Source: Education Commission of the States (2019[13]), *High-Level Analysis of State Postsecondary Governance Structures*, https://www.ecs.org/wp-content/uploads/PS-Gov-Structures-50_State-Analysis_Compacts_Other-States_May2019.pdf.

StatLink https://doi.org/10.1787/888934134711

Among the 28 US states with a single, state-wide entity governing higher education, 20 US states – including the four states in this review – have a single state-wide co-ordinating board; the eight other states have a governing board. States with a governing board generally have extensive authority over system-wide strategic planning, from setting admissions standards and credit transfer rules, to having a substantial degree of influence over academic programming and personnel decisions (Eckel and King, 2004[14]). State-wide co-ordinating boards play a less direct, but still significant, role in the state's responsibilities for public higher education and, in some cases, oversight responsibilities for independent colleges (Fulton, 2019[15]). Both governing boards and co-ordinating boards typically provide budget recommendations to the state Legislature and articulate a strategic plan for the higher education system.

Within this similar governance framework, the ability of states to steer the actions of higher education institutions varies. Institutional plans are a tool used by governments to assess the extent to which institutional actions contribute to state-wide goals. These plans can include state-wide targets, institution-specific targets, involve requirements for regular updates, and may or not be tied to funding to reward institutions that meet their targets. Across the OECD, various jurisdictions have developed such mechanisms, such as Austria, Denmark, Ireland, the Netherlands or Ontario (Canada). In Ireland, as shown in Box 3.3, these plans served as a tool to develop a sustained and open dialogue between government and institutions.

Box 3.3. Ireland's Institutional Compacts

Objective and approach

Performance compacts, defined through strategic dialogue between the Higher Education Authority (HEA) of Ireland and institutions, are a key instrument to help meet government policy goals in higher education policy, and improve both the accountability and autonomy of higher education institutions (HEIs). Compacts are designed within a broader System Performance Framework, which lays out key system goals and metrics since 2013. One of these key goals for 2020 relates to improving the labour market relevance of higher education. The System Performance Framework includes indicators for each system objective, with an emphasis on labour market-oriented indicators, including employee engagement and collaboration, student employment, and the alignment between the flow of graduates by field and level of study with national, regional and/or local needs.

The first cycle of performance compacts and strategic dialogue started in 2014 and was used to establish strategic engagement between HEIs and the HEA, facilitated by international peers. The first cycle included an aspect of performance funding which penalised insufficient performance and was applied to those with poor planning processes or who exhibited governance and/or financial issues. In the second cycle (2018-21), the government aims to increase the connection between compacts and national policy objectives and to step up the assessment of institutional performance. In this cycle, institutions set out more specific targets and objectives, based on the framework as well as their own strategies and strengths.

The current performance review process will provide a progress report on the institutions' selected priorities and identify best practices that show how institutional strategic initiatives can address key national objectives. Institutions selected as having best practices, based on impact case studies they provide, were granted additional funding rewarding their performance. In 2019, EUR 5 million were allocated for this purpose.

Institutions are then categorised according to a "traffic light system" introduced to monitor progress, performance and compliance. This allows the HEA, together with the higher education institution, to take relevant action. Funding penalties in the range of 3-5% can be enacted in the case of poor performance, although these have not so far been implemented.

Lessons learnt

The compact and strategic dialogue process has enabled a better level of understanding and co-operation between HEIs and the HEA, and increased the higher education sector's focus on meeting national strategies and objectives. The process has also become very useful in terms of identifying potential strategic initiatives implemented by individual HEIs that could be amplified as part of the development of new national strategies and policies.

Sources: Department of Education and Skills (2018[16]); HEA (2017[17]); HEA (2019[18]); Neavyn (2019[19]); OECD/European Union (2017[20]).

In both Virginia and Ohio, there is an annual planning process whereby each institution defines priorities and targets against which they are held accountable. These vary in scope and purpose. In Virginia, the

Top Jobs Act requires institutions to develop six-year plans identifying specific institutional initiatives that contribute to state-wide goals, prioritise these initiatives and indicate funding needs for each initiative for the coming biennium. The Act requires institutions to submit these plans to the State Council of Higher Education for Virginia (SCHEV), which facilitates review by state policy makers. These plans are complemented by Institutional Performance Standards (IPS) establishing standard institutional targets for enrolment; total degree awards; degree awards in science, technology, engineering, mathematics and health-related fields (STEM-H); awards to under-represented groups; and two-year to four-year transfers. Institutions meeting these standards are eligible for additional funds, albeit the funds available remain small in scale.

Since 2014-15, the Ohio Department of Higher Education (ODHE) requires institutions to establish "Campus Completion Plans", which must be updated every two years. In contrast to Virginia, no financial incentives are attached to these plans.

Texas and Washington do not use institutional plans. However, in Texas, the Texas Higher Education Coordinating Board (THECB) seeks information from institutions to monitor certain aspects of its 60x30TX plan, for instance by surveying public institutions regarding their design and implementation of a process to identify "marketable skills" across study programmes. In Washington, the co-ordination between the state agency (WSAC) and institutions differs across sectors –while no formal co-ordination mechanisms are in place between government and public four-year institutions, the State Board for Community and Technical Colleges, a Governor-appointed body, provides general oversight of the college system, allocates state operating and capital funds, and oversees policy development.

The four states differ in their capacity to join up policy efforts across education and workforce agencies, and in how they engage stakeholders in policy making

A whole-of-government approach is important to improve the alignment of higher education and the labour market, as different government agencies typically deal with primary and secondary education, post-secondary education, and workforce policies.

In some states, higher education plans and targets are developed as part of a broader state efforts to develop a strong skills pipeline, or to promote the alignment of education and the workforce. Washington's *Ten-Year Roadmap* (2013-23) applies to the secondary and post-secondary levels and contains attainment targets for both. In Ohio, the state's post-secondary attainment target is part of Ohio's *Workforce Transformation Strategy*, created in 2018, which emphasises the need for a highly skilled workforce to meet the demands of Ohio businesses. This is in contrast to Texas and Virginia, where the *60x30TX* plan (2015-30) and the *Virginia Plan for Higher Education* (2014-20) respectively strictly focus on higher education.

The way bodies responsible for higher education policy are structured also influences the opportunities and incentives for education and workforce agencies to work together. In Ohio, co-operation between the state agencies in charge of higher education and workforce policy is co-ordinated by the Governor's Office for Workforce Transformation, which reports directly to the Lieutenant Governor. In Texas, the Tri-Agency Workforce Initiative sets shared goals for the three state agencies responsible for K-12, post-secondary education and the workforce development. A new set of objectives was announced in early 2020 by the Governor of Texas, increasing the focus of the three agencies on the labour market relevance of education (see Chapter 5). In Washington, the biennial production of a publicly available report describing current and projected gaps between the educational supply and labour market needs state-wide generates collaboration between the respective government agencies and facilitates the establishment of a common understanding of areas where improvement is needed to meet the needs of the state's economy. In Virginia, the current Governor created the cabinet-level post of Chief Workforce Development Advisor to increase co-ordination between state agencies involved in education, training and labour market development.

Supporting the alignment of higher education and workforce needs may also require policy action across a broader range of areas than just education and the workforce. As outlined in the assessment framework of the project (see Chapter 1), various policies may have an effect on states' ability to meet their objectives to raise post-secondary attainment and enhance the alignment of higher education with workforce needs. Policy action in areas ranging from childcare, transportation, housing or taxes can have an influence on individuals' choices to pursue higher education, and of what type of higher education to pursue. For example, a lack of affordable childcare may motivate some students to favour flexible programmes over programmes that offer better labour market prospects. A lack of co-ordinated action across these policy areas may limit states' success in meeting their higher education policy goals.

The alignment of higher education and the labour market requires close co-ordination with employers and other labour market stakeholders. As discussed in the state-specific chapters, higher education institutions in the four states often engage with employers in their local area to develop educational programmes, particularly in vocational and professional programmes than in general programmes. The extent to which state authorities engage with stakeholders when developing higher education policy is also critical to ensure labour market needs are identified and addressed. The regular involvement of a broad range of stakeholders can also increase the continuity of policy efforts, which can otherwise be subject to frequent changes as the state's political landscape evolves.

In this area, the four states have an array of localised or specific partnerships between institutions and employers, often involving public agencies at different levels, as described in the state-specific chapters of this report. At the state level, board members of the State Council of Higher Education for Virginia (SCHEV), which include representatives of the business community, appear to play an active role in representing the employer perspective in higher education policy. In Ohio, the Governor's Workforce Board brings together representatives of employers, education and training institutions and workforce development bodies to provide advice on workforce skills needs. In Washington, the development of the Washington Career Connect initiative is an example of policy development conducted through a multi-stakeholder engagement process, while the STEM Education Innovation Alliance, a multi-stakeholder partnership, advises the Governor and Legislature on policies related to STEM education on an ongoing basis (see Chapter 7). In Texas, the Tri-Agency initiative began with a stakeholder consultation process throughout the state, which resulted in a set of prime recommendations. The three state agencies reported to the Governor in early 2020, outlining actions taken to address both the initial goals of the initiatives, set by the Governor, as well as the prime recommendations made by stakeholders.

Some European countries have established bodies or mechanisms to develop and sustain strong relationships between government and stakeholders in the formulation and implementation of education and skills policies. As described in Box 3.4, Norway engages a wide range of stakeholders in a Skills Policy Council, while Germany has developed broad agreements between government and employers to significantly expand the availability of work-based learning.

Box 3.4. Co-ordination between government agencies and employers in Norway and Germany

Norway's Skills Strategy, Committee on Skills Needs, and Skills Norway

Norway launched a National Skills Strategy for 2017-21 to improve the development and use of skills in the Norwegian workforce. As a result of this strategy, Norway established a number of co-ordinating bodies to improve the responsiveness of skills policies to the country's labour market needs. A multi-stakeholder Skills Policy Council was created to oversee the Strategy's implementation and provide input on new skills policies. The Council is headed by the Minister of Research and Higher Education, and involves a range of government members across different economic and social policy areas and the eight main social partners (including labour unions and employer associations), including a representative for regional authorities, and a representative from the voluntary sector and adult-learning associations.

The Committee on Skills Needs was established to provide the best possible assessment of Norway's future skills needs, in order to improve the evidence base for national and regional planning and to guide individual educational choices. It gathers evidence on skills needs and skills availability in the labour market, including quantitative forecasts of supply for and demand of skills for the upcoming years. The Committee also plays a key role in co-ordinating Norwegian ministries and agencies involved in assessing and responding to skills needs, as well as in contributing to public dialogue. While the Committee was established by the government, it is not political and works independently from the government. Its secretariat is placed in Skills Norway.

Skills Norway is the directorate for lifelong learning under the purview of the Norwegian Ministry of Education and Research. It is responsible for co-ordinating priority areas highlighted in the National Skills Strategy and promoting international co-operation on skills policies. Skills Norway is currently the national representative for the European Agenda for Adult Learning. The directorate also encourages active citizenship and employability through work on recognition of prior learning, adult basic skills training, and training for adult refugees and immigrants.

Germany's whole-of-government collaboration on skills

In 2004, the German government established the "Pact for Vocational Education and Training". The Pact falls within Germany's tradition of corporatist decision-making in the field of vocational education and training. After previous unfruitful attempts to establish a training levy, due to employer opposition, the Pact was designed as a new type of alliance between government and employer associations. It requires employers and government to work together to expand learning opportunities for youth in firm-based traineeships, which should eventually lead to regular apprenticeship training. However, the voluntary character of the Pact was heavily criticised by unions, which refrained from participating.

The Pact was replaced in 2014 by the national "Alliance for Initial and Further Education", which differs mainly in that it involves unions as co-operation partners. The Alliance brings together a larger set of stakeholders to achieve consensual co-ordination. Stakeholders involved include the Federal Employment Agency, the *Kultusminister Konferenz* (the standing conference of the Ministers of Education and Cultural Affairs), and the federal ministries for labour affairs, business and education, as well as representatives of the *Länder* ministries for labour and social affairs. While the previous pacts were mainly voluntary, the Alliance passed binding decisions. For instance, the Alliance committed employers to increase the number of apprenticeship places by 30 000 on a yearly basis.

Sources: Eurydice (2019[21]); Ministry of Education and Research (2017[22]); OECD (2019[23]); Norwegian Committee on Skills Need (n.d.[24]).

Potential success factors for strategic planning and co-ordination

In the four states participating in the review, higher education institutions have a large degree of autonomy. At the same time, state authorities have established clear targets and strategies to raise higher education attainment and meet the needs of their economies and labour markets. While specific targets or goals related to the labour market relevance of higher education or graduate outcomes are less frequent, the states' strategies for higher education and the workforce recognise the importance of better aligning education and the labour market. These plans can be powerful tools to focus the actions of government and institutions.

Despite clear targets, significant co-ordination challenges exist, at various levels: between government and institutions; within government; and between government, institutions, employers and other stakeholders engaged in activities to align education and the workforce. Across the four states, stakeholders described this lack of co-ordination as an obstacle to policy effectiveness, by limiting the opportunity to scale up effective practices across the various regions and economic sectors of their state.

Thus, a balance must be found between the highly autonomous institutions and other actors with state-wide mechanisms that can facilitate the design, implementation and monitoring of larger-scale initiatives. Effective stakeholder engagement mechanisms can ensure that higher education policy is meeting the needs of business and society, create a sense of joint ownership of policy initiatives and strengthen trust in government (OECD, 2019[25]; Burns, Köster and Fuster, 2016[26]). Based on the analysis conducted in the four states and international examples, potential success factors to improve the effectiveness of their policies in the area of strategic planning and co-ordination of higher education include the following:

- Processes to enable the connection between strategic policy that establishes key goals for higher education and the funding process to ensure capacity exists to effectively orient the actions of the higher education system towards meeting key policy goals. Approaches have been suggested for such processes, that should be carefully designed and would need a legislative basis to be sustainable (McGuinness, 2016[27]).
- Processes to enable higher education agencies to regularly collaborate with agencies in charge of K-12 education and workforce development to co-ordinate with each other and with key stakeholders. Key stakeholders include higher education institutions, workforce boards, and other intermediary organisations such as non-profits, industry or professional associations that play a role in the alignment of education and workforce at the state, regional or local level. Alongside a mandate emphasising cross-agency collaboration, sufficient human and financial resources need to be available to agencies to support such collaboration.
- Processes to incentivise collaboration between government agencies at the state and regional levels. For agencies working directly on education-workforce alignment, these mechanisms could include the creation of cross-agency objectives, activities and staffing positions (Federal Reserve Bank of Dallas; Center for Public Policy Priorities, 2016[28]). For example, states could consider cross-agency work to develop a single state-wide pathways framework that would make it easier for students to identify the education and training needed to pursue careers in sectors and occupations with growth potential. For agencies working on broader policy areas (e.g. housing, social supports, infrastructure), mechanisms could include regular cross-agency interactions at key points in the strategic policy process (e.g. before the adoption of a new strategic plan).
- Mechanisms to ensure stakeholders can provide regular input into higher education policy and planning (OECD, 2015[29]). Approaches to promote stakeholder engagement in policy are diverse. They include, for example, multi-agency co-ordination and government-institution co-ordination to streamline consultation processes and maximise the use of stakeholder time and input; the use of financial incentives for small and medium enterprises to organise in consortia and more easily participate in consultative processes; and utilising sector partnerships as a channel to provide feedback on state-wide policy.

Educational offerings, pathways and student supports

How can policy affect educational offerings, pathways and student supports?

The delivery and content of educational programmes in all four states are primarily the responsibility of higher education institutions and their academic and teaching faculty, as institutions generally enjoy substantial autonomy in organisational, academic and staffing decisions. This is reflected in institutional initiatives to enhance curriculum design, exploit online learning, and offer guidance and co-curricular activities to students. Public policy can influence the programmes offered by higher education institutions and ensure certain quality standards; incentivise institutions to enhance the labour market relevance of programmes; create clear pathways for students between different types of programmes and institutions; and seek to ensure students receive guidance and support services to help them manoeuvre smoothly into and through the post-secondary education system (OECD, 2019[5]). By influencing the post-secondary educational offerings available, students' ability to progress and transfer, and the level of support available to students at risk of not pursuing post-secondary education or of dropping out, these policies are all relevant in states' efforts to strengthen the alignment between higher education and the labour market.

Programme offerings are shaped by a range of regulatory processes

Programme offerings are shaped by a range of regulatory processes, arising both from institution and programme accreditation, as discussed in the previous chapter, and from state regulatory processes.

State regulations are of two main types. States authorities often have a process to authorise new institutions, usually private or out-of-state, to operate in their state. They typically require new institutions to meet minimum standards of operation, which relate to the institution's financial stability, institutional infrastructure, academic programmes, faculty and staff qualifications, student services, accreditation, and business practices. These mechanisms focus primarily on basic aspects of adequate provision, rather than on the labour market prospects, or outcomes, of graduates. Many states have also established programme approval processes, requiring public institutions to demonstrate that a proposed programme meets requirements regarding the programme's focus, resources and need. The focus of programme approval is generally to ensure an effective use of public funds, in part through avoiding unnecessary programme duplication. Requirements sometimes include the demonstration of current or future labour market need.

Taken together, the processes of institution and programme accreditation and state authorisation and programme approval influence higher education offerings. However, they do not form a strategic and integrated steering process that orients the provision of higher education towards labour market outcomes. This is because they usually do not focus on labour market relevance – except in the case of programme approval – and are not co-ordinated.

Across the participating states, the Ohio Department of Higher Education (ODHE), Texas Higher Education Coordinating Board (THECB) and State Council of Higher Education for Virginia (SCHEV) all play a role in the approval of new programmes proposed by public higher education institutions. By contrast, the Washington Student Achievement Council (WSAC) does not have a role in approving programmes offered by public four-year institutions, although the State Board for Community and Technical Colleges does co-ordinate the approval of new programmes developed by two-year institutions (see Chapter 7).

Where the state has a programme approval process in place, it requires institutions to demonstrate that there is a current and projected labour market need for graduates of the proposed programme. However, none of the states participating in the review had a process in place to evaluate the continued labour market relevance of programmes once established. Whereas Ohio, Texas and Virginia have a process to regularly monitor "low-producing" programmes with low student enrolment, this process is not concerned with the labour market outcomes of graduates and no equivalent process exists to assess labour market relevance.

Across the four states, programme approval could be an important mechanism for state authorities to monitor the labour market relevance of new programmes. However, the way in which these processes are implemented, and their perceived effectiveness and usefulness, vary. In Virginia, for example, stakeholders have noted concerns about the length of time required by the state approval process, which SCHEV is currently reviewing with a view to streamlining it. In Texas, there are different programme approval processes in place depending on whether the new programme is offered by a two-year institution or a four-year institution. There is also a different, more comprehensive, programme approval process for doctoral degrees, bachelor's degrees offered by two-year institutions, and select programmes with high operating costs.

The length of time and complexity of accreditation was viewed differently across the four states. In Texas and Virginia, stakeholders interviewed by the OECD review team voiced concerns about the delays involved in accreditation and a perceived lack of relevance of some accreditation criteria. In Washington and Ohio, stakeholders noted an evolution in their regional accreditor's practices, with an increased focus on recognising the specific missions of institutions and of workplace success as an important metric. In all states however, institutional representatives reported responding to new labour market needs in various ways, such as creating new course concentrations (e.g. minors, micro-credentials) or expanding their offer of non-credit programmes.

In some OECD countries, regulatory processes have been used to orient institutions towards delivering labour market relevant programmes. Denmark in particular has developed a set of policies to support relevance, as outlined in Box 3.5.

Box 3.5. Promoting labour market relevance through quality assurance in Denmark

Denmark has introduced comprehensive policy reforms since the early 2000s to improve the labour market relevance of higher education programmes. In the 2000s, government efforts focused on taking labour market relevance into account in quality assurance processes. This included the introduction of legislation in 2004 requiring universities to impose enrolment caps on programmes according to their labour market relevance. In 2006, the government made the inclusion of labour market relevance indicators in the accreditation processes mandatory, and included employment goals in universities' "strategic contracts" signed between institutions and government in 2006. A legal requirement that all universities have employer panels to inform the design of programmes was further introduced in 2007.

In 2014, after Denmark went through a period of excess supply of graduates from certain programmes such as humanities and biology, intake caps were set by government based on employment rates of graduates assessed between 2 and 12 years after graduation. Institutions have, however, some autonomy on how to distribute their intake cap (up to 15%) across study programmes. This policy was accompanied by significant efforts to increase the transparency of higher education returns for prospective students, through the publication of information on earnings and unemployment as well as evaluations from alumni about their experience through a guidance tool. An evaluation of study caps concluded that the model had effectively re-oriented student choice towards high employment study fields. Between 2013 and 2016, programmes with good labour market outcomes saw applications and enrolments grow by approximately 11% and 7% respectively.

In 2017, the Danish government also implemented limits to second degree enrolment. It restricted the ability of graduates to pursue an additional fully-funded degree within six years after graduation to students pursuing fields with very low unemployment or experiencing a shortage in the labour market. In parallel, the government reformed its approach to strategic contracts with universities, shifting from numeric targets to the fostering of concrete actions for improvement aligned with institutional missions. It also introduced a portion of performance-based funding into the university funding model (7.5% of funding is allocated according to metrics such as time-to-completion, the employment rate of graduates, and educational quality).

Sources: European Training Foundation (2018[30]); Steen Roesdahl (2017[31]); *Uddannelses- og Forskningsministeriet* (Danish Ministry of Education and Research) (2018[32]; 2018[33]; 2019[34]).

States can use various tools to support the labour market responsiveness of higher education programmes

Higher education institutions in the United States are responsible for the development of educational programmes and the recruitment, professional development and promotion of academic faculty. Institutions, academic departments and individual faculty members thus have the largest influence on curriculum design and teaching practices. However, state authorities can use a range of policies to encourage institutions to develop programmes that are relevant to current and future labour market needs. This is done typically through block grant funding to institutions, which allows them to flexibly allocate funding in response to student and workforce demand, as well as targeted funding, notably for capital and staffing, to address need in high-demand fields. State authorities also support responsive offerings by providing a flexible framework of operation that allows them to develop innovative labour market-oriented education such as non-credit workforce and continuing education on a fee-per-service basis; innovative minors and course concentrations; or the provision of graduate certificates or digital badges.

Supply and take-up of programmes leading to high-demand occupations

The provision of labour market relevant higher education requires first an adequate supply of programmes at the levels and in the fields corresponding to occupations that are currently or projected to require a large supply of workers. It also requires that the full range of higher education programmes, whether or not they are connected to high-demand occupations, equips students with labour market relevant skills, in turn helping these graduates identify and succeed in a career that may or may not relate to their initial field of study. Labour market relevant skills involve a combination of discipline-specific (or job-specific) skills alongside a range of transversal skills, which are both cognitive and socio-emotional.

In the four states participating in this review, the supply of higher education programmes to meet labour market needs appears to be adequate, except in a small number of fields of study leading to high-demand occupations such as engineering, medicine and nursing, and ICT. Institutions across the four states reported two main types of challenges in expanding the supply of programmes in these fields: attracting faculty due to competitive salaries outside of academia and relatively high equipment and facility costs. This echoes recent research that shows that some of the highest-earning fields of study are also the most costly to deliver (Hemelt et al., 2018[35]). This creates a challenge for public authorities as they aim to support more students in enrolling in Science, Technology, Engineering, Mathematics and Health (STEM-H) programmes.

In response to faculty shortages in high-demand fields, both Virginia and Washington have recently passed legislation to increase faculty salaries. In Virginia, the Governor and General Assembly authorised in 2019 a 3% increase in general fund appropriations for college and university faculty recruitment and retention. However, this increase has been applied across all faculty and staff, rather than being targeted specifically to those fields where competition for staff is greatest. Given constraints on core institutional funding from limited increases in state appropriates and tuition moderation, the State Council of Higher Education for Virginia has invited lawmakers to consider a targeted salaries fund (SCHEV, 2018[36]). In Washington, the *Workforce Education Investment Act 2019* commits over USD 40 million over two years to increase high-demand programme faculty salaries including (but not limited to) nursing educators, other health-related professions, information technology, computer science, and trades including welding.

In Virginia, the "Tech-Talent Pipeline" initiative includes state investments of up to USD 1.1 billion to increase the supply of graduates in computer science and closely related fields. For higher education institutions to be eligible for a grant from the state, each institution is required to enter into a memorandum of understanding that sets criteria for eligible degrees, degree production goals and graduation rates. Additionally, Virginia's six-year plans with institutions are complemented by institutional performance standards that include targets for increasing degrees awarded in STEM-H fields. Institutions meeting the standards can be eligible for additional, though modest, funding.

Some OECD countries have taken steps to expand the offer of post-secondary programmes in fields of study leading to high-demand occupations and industries, often by aligning the curriculum with employer needs and incorporating a work-based learning component. While institutions are responsible for the development of these types of programmes, public funding and employer contributions often enables their expansion and quality. France and the United Kingdom offer examples of the expansion, and creation, of such post-secondary vocationally oriented programmes (Box 3.6).

Box 3.6. Vocationally oriented higher education programmes in France and the United Kingdom

The *Brevet de Technicien Supérieur* (BTS) and *Diplôme Universitaire de Technologie* (DUT)

In France, students enrolled in two-year programmes called BTS (Advanced Technician's Certificate) and DUT (Technology University Diploma) accounted for about 14% of all students enrolled in higher education institutions in 2016/17. These programmes are attractive for both students and employers, and generally lead to quality outcomes in terms of further education and labour market opportunities. These selective short-cycle tertiary (ISCED Level 5) programmes are available in a range of study fields, combine theoretical and practical components, usually involve work-based learning as part of the curriculum, and can be completed through an apprenticeship in some cases.

DUT are delivered by University Institutes of Technology (IUT), which are part of public universities, and deliver a more general training than BTS, which are delivered in high schools. The majority of BTS holders enter the labour market after graduation, while almost all DUT holders pursue further education.

In 2018, about 61% of students enrolled in a short-cycle tertiary programme graduated within the theoretical duration of the programme, which is about 16 percentage points above the OECD average. The completion rate is higher in DUT, with over 75% of students enrolled from 2015 graduated within three years. Thirteen per cent of students who started a bachelor's degree programme transfer to a short-cycle tertiary programme by the beginning of their second year of study.

However, the attractiveness of these short-cycle tertiary education programmes for students, universities and employers has had drawbacks. Their selectivity has increased, which hinders the participation of students from vocational and technical high school streams, as more students from the general stream of high school choose these programmes over bachelor's degree programmes. In response, the French government revised and extended the apprenticeship and vocational education systems in 2018, and plans further reforms in the coming years.

Sources: Calmand and Lemistre (2019[37]); Eurydice (2019[38]); INSEE (2018[39]); Ministère de l'Enseignement Supérieur, de la Recherche et de l'Innovation (MESRI-SIES) (French Ministry of Higher Education, Research and Innovation) (2017[40]; 2018[41]; 2019[42]; 2019[43]; 2020[44]); Ministère de l'Éducation Nationale et de la Jeunesse (French Ministry of Education) (2019[45]); OECD (2019[4]).

Degree apprenticeships in the United Kingdom

The degree apprenticeship allows students to work part-time while studying towards a bachelor's or master's degree. Degree apprenticeships correspond to the highest-level apprenticeship in the United Kingdom. They represented around 3% of all apprenticeships in 2018/19. The employer and the institution providing training can make their own arrangements regarding the structure of the apprenticeship, which may take up to 6 years to complete and includes distance and blended learning options.

Government covers most tuition-related costs through an apprenticeship levy, which is paid by employers with revenue above GBP 3 million (0.5% of revenue). The amount available for employers in this category to finance apprentice training and assessment depends on the value of the levy, and a 10% top-up from the government on this amount. For smaller non-levy-paying businesses, the government finances 95% of the cost of their apprentices training, and 5% is supported by the employer. By 2020, through the levy, GBP 2.5 billion will be available to invest in degree apprenticeships.

While a job is not guaranteed upon completion, in 2018, approximately 80% of apprentices at levels 5 or higher were hired by their employer after graduation.

Sources: Department for Education (2018[46]; 2019[47]); Knowles (2020[48]); Kuczera and Field (2013[49]); National Collaborative Outreach Programme (2018[50]); Office for Students (2019[51]; 2019[52]; 2019[53]); UCAS (2019[54]; 2019[55]).

Fostering labour market relevance through work-based learning

While many higher education institutions are committed to improving the labour market relevance of their educational offerings, a frequently cited concern among stakeholders in all four states was a general lack of workplace readiness among recent graduates, in part due to weak transversal skills such as communication and teamwork. This mirrors a common sentiment among employers nation-wide and across a range of industries, as reflected in multiple employer surveys (IHE, 2019[56]; SHRM, 2019[57]; Adecco USA, 2019[58]; Manpower Group, 2018[59]). In a 2018 survey conducted on behalf of the Association of American Colleges and Universities (AACU), employers indicated that recent graduates had the skills necessary to succeed in an entry-level position, but few had the skills needed for advancement or promotion within the organisation (Hart Research Associates, 2018[60]).

These skills gaps likely result from a combination of factors, reflecting in part the complexity of the relationship between labour supply and demand. Aside from structural changes in the labour market, for example due to the long-term effects of technological change, an overall decline in employer-led on-the-job training, particularly for entry-level workers, may be a contributing factor in some widely reported skills gaps (Waddoups, 2016[61]; Capelli, 2015[62]). The implications for higher education are significant, as institutions of higher education increasingly represent the primary vehicle for the education and training of most American workers (Carnevale, Smith and Strohl, 2013[63]). To better prepare graduates for the world of work, stakeholders often called for pedagogical practices that equip graduates with labour market relevant skills and for more widely accessible work-based learning opportunities for students that offer relevant learning. Such forms of work-based learning would thus go beyond traditional student employment, in which about two-thirds of undergraduate students engage, but that is not often linked to learning (Carnevale and Smith, 2018[64]).

Stakeholders also expressed a desire for higher education institutions not only to integrate more transversal skills in technical fields, but also to integrate foundational digital skills in non-technical fields. In this regard, stakeholder feedback across the four states suggests that there is great variation in the extent to which higher education institutions, their academic departments and individual faculty members emphasise the labour market relevance of programmes. It was often identified as a greater concern and focus for action among faculty in fields of study that have clear connections to occupations, such as engineering, business, and health-related fields. In those fields, work-based learning in particular is common, often as requirement for programme accreditation. In more general fields of study, and despite the fact that employment and earnings for these graduates are generally lower compared to their peers in professional fields of study, work-based learning and other practices to enhance the labour market relevance of programmes appeared less widespread.

State authorities in Texas have encouraged higher education institutions to ensure programmes equip graduates with knowledge and skills relevant in the labour market. The Texas higher education plan, *60x30TX,* requires public higher education institutions to identify and document "marketable skills" across all of their programmes. Texas also provides guidelines for several aspects of educational content at the sub-baccalaureate and baccalaureate levels, with the aim of ensuring a minimum level of knowledge, skills and competencies are developed through public higher education (see Chapter 5).

Fostering labour market relevant skills also implies that teaching faculty are well aware of skills requirements in the world of work, and are supported and incentivised to continuously update their own knowledge and skills. The hiring, training and performance management of academic faculty is the responsibility of higher education institutions, and an area where state action appeared to be limited across the four states. Institutional stakeholders met by the OECD team indicated that many faculty members express interest in regularly updating their knowledge and skills in line with labour market and industry demands, but pointed out the challenge of balancing teaching and research responsibilities with professional development. They also suggested that academic career structures often do not facilitate or incentivise a focus on building professional skills and knowledge. In this context, governments can play a role in requiring, incentivising or promoting a greater focus of faculty on the labour market relevance of their curriculum and teaching practices. Washington provides an example in this area: the State Board for Community and Technical Colleges requires faculty in the professional and technical stream to update their skills on a regular basis to maintain their status as certified faculty. In Texas, stakeholder-led programmes such as the Texas Regional STEM Degree Accelerator, an initiative that ran from 2015-18 in five regions to develop STEM degree programmes, supported faculty professional development as one of its actions (see Chapter 5). Other countries have invested in this area to foster a focus on professional development across the higher education system. Ireland, for instance, has developed a system to recognise the participation of academic faculty in professional development, and begun linking professional development to institutional performance, as shown in Box 3.7.

Box 3.7. Supporting improved teaching and learning in Ireland

Ireland has placed a strong focus on enhancing the quality of teaching in higher education. Ireland's *National Strategy for Higher Education 2030* identifies teaching and learning as a core role of higher education institutions. To foster this role, the Higher Education Authority (HEA), which is the statutory funding authority and policy development body for higher education in Ireland, provided funding beginning in 2012 to launch the National Forum for the Enhancement of Teaching and Learning (the National Forum). The National Forum pursues activities in five areas: professional development; learning impact awards; scholarship in teaching and learning; building digital capacity; and partnership and collaboration.

An important activity of the National Forum has been to develop the Professional Development Framework (PDF). The PDF was established through a multi-year process of consultation, drafting and roll-out, including with various pilots. The PDF describes five domains of professional development activity:

- the self (core area, relating to professional and personal values that the individual brings to their teaching);
- professional identity, values and development;
- professional communication and dialogue;
- professional knowledge and skills;
- personal and professional digital capacity.

The PDF also establishes elements of teaching performance and five associated values: inclusivity, authenticity, collaboration, scholarship and learner centeredness. The PDF aims to help instructors to set objectives and chart progress, thereby helping faculty to better determine their continuing learning needs and how they can integrate innovations in their practices. Following roll-out, the National Forum introduced an independent Expert Advisory Group to help HEIs develop their capacity to support the PDF, and also funded 22 pilot studies to explore how faculty members used the PDF. Pilot participants could develop a professional development portfolio to explore the framework domains and reflect on their practices. The evaluation of these pilots found strong support among participants with regards to short-term and, to a lesser extent, long-term impact.

Additionally, the National Forum has led the development of 15 open access 25-hour professional development programmes in teaching and learning. Subject expert teams collaborated in the design and development of these programmes, which cover an array of topics relating to reflective practice, teaching skills, specialist expertise, curriculum design and student-focused approaches. Those who complete the programmes are eligible for a National Forum digital badge.

Under the Higher Education Performance Framework 2018-20, the HEA identified implementation of the continuous PDF and the number of staff with continuous professional development digital badges by academic year as indicators of performance regarding staff capability. Another effort has focused on the development of learning awards for disciplines, building on the National Forum's prizes for individual teachers.

Sources: Caroll et al. (2018[65]); Department of Education and Skills (2018[66]); Donnelly et al. (2018[67]); Hénard and Roseveare (2012[68]); Learning Avenue (2017[69]); National Forum for the Enhancement of Teaching and Learning in Higher Education (2019[70]).

All four states have work-study programmes that provide students with paid employment on- or off-campus to help them cover the costs of attending higher education. These programmes are modelled on the Federal Work-Study programme, a financial aid programme that is not traditionally envisioned as a skill development programme. However, some states are using work-study programmes to provide relevant work-based learning opportunities, particularly to low-income students who are traditionally targeted through the Work-Study programme. For instance, in Texas, legislation was passed in 2017 (through Senate Bill 1119) which requires annual reporting of data on the employment positions provided to students through the programme. Over time, this could help assess the extent to which the Texas Work Study programme helps provide relevant work-based learning to students. In addition, the Texas Legislature established a new internship programme in 2019 – the Texas Reinforcing Knowledge and Skills (TXWORKS) programme – to provide partly state-funded jobs that enable students to develop and strengthen marketable skills.

In Ohio, the General Assembly provided a total of almost USD 20 million from 2014-17 to support the expansion of co-operative education and other forms of work-based learning through the Ohio Means Internships and Co-ops (OMIC) programme. The available funds were allocated by the ODHE through requests for proposals, initially to individual higher education institutions and, from 2015, to consortia of institutions across the six JobsOhio regions. While in operation, the OMIC funded almost 6 500 internships and co-operatives across the state. The programme was discontinued in 2017, which the OECD team has recommended be re-evaluated (see Chapter 4).

In Virginia, the "Innovative Internship Fund and Program", expanded in 2019 and administered by the state higher education agency, provides grants on a competitive basis to public higher education institutions to expand internship opportunities for undergraduate students through partnerships with business and public sector employers (VEDP, 2017[71]).

In Washington, Career Connect Washington (CCW) is a multi-stakeholder initiative established in 2019 that aims to significantly expand the scale of career-connected learning opportunities in the state through a system-wide approach. The initiative will received close to USD 40 million in the period 2019-21, which will support the creation of new career-connected learning opportunities, increased enrolment, supports for low-income students and those in under-served areas to participate, including for transportation, as well as start-up and capital funding (see Chapter 7). CCW has two key objectives to prepare youth for success in the labour market. By 2030, 100% of young Washingtonians under the age of 29 are expected to have completed career awareness or exploration activities (such as career fairs) or career preparation activities (such as work-based learning for credit), and 60% are expected to have completed high-quality paid work-based learning opportunities. Furthermore, by making apprentices eligible for the main state student aid programme, the Washington College Grant, Washington further promotes career-connected learning and improves access to alternative pathways such as apprenticeships.

Policies and practices promoting clear credential pathways, credit transfers and student supports can improve graduate completions and lead to better labour market outcomes

Clear and structured pathways serve to guide students efficiently into and through higher education, relying on a system of credits that can build on each other and transfer between institutions, to ensure a sufficient degree of "stackability" and mobility within the higher education system. An important mechanism to facilitate transferability are inter-institutional articulation agreements, either between individual higher education institutions, between institutions within a particular region, or state-wide. Efficient transfer processes are essential to improve students' chances of completing a credential (Bailey et al., 2017[72]; Xu et al., 2017[73]). Improving transfer opportunities, particularly from two-year to four-year institutions, is a policy priority in all four states participating in the review.

Many states have developed a supporting infrastructure to help students and educators identify which courses can be counted towards a credential in public higher education institutions. Washington has created a set of collaborative bodies that bring the public and private sectors together, through the Joint Transfer Council and the Intercollege Relations Commission. In Ohio, the Ohio Articulation and Transfer Network co-ordinates the work of faculty in public higher education institutions in developing and applying standards for curriculum requirements, advising, credit recognition, and guaranteed transfer pathways. In a large state like Texas, regional partnerships and transfer collaboratives are common, which are based on articulation agreements between institutions within the partnership or collaborative that establish a set of pathways and transitions between secondary school districts and higher education institutions, and among higher education institutions (Bailey et al., 2017[72]). In Virginia, state authorities have used institutional planning and performance standards to incentivise greater take-up of two-year to four-year transfer opportunities, but left the development of transfer standards and pathways to institutions.

Public two-year institutions in Virginia and Washington have associate's degree programmes – transfer associate's degrees – that are specifically designed for transfer to a bachelor's degree programme. These are typically part of state-wide articulation agreements that provide guaranteed transfer pathways to four-year institutions, and thus are tailored to students who have earned a transfer associate's degree. In Virginia, transfer students who have earned an associate's degree prior to transfer are more likely to complete a bachelor's degree (SCHEV, 2016[74]). Though measuring transfer outcomes can be challenging, national data suggest that Washington's transfer-out rate is relatively low, while bachelor's completion rates for transfer students are comparatively high (Jenkins and Fink, 2016[75]). In Texas, approximately 35% of degree-seeking transfer students typically transfer out of community college to a four-year institution (Bailey et al., 2017[72]), which is not far from the national average. Because lower-income transfer students typically have poorer outcomes than high-income students, this is often an important group to target for policy intervention.

Virginia established a transfer grant programme in 2007, the Two-year College Transfer Grant, which can provide students who have earned a transfer associate's degree with up to USD 3000 annually to be applied towards tuition at a public or private four-year institution. In addition, maintaining or increasing transfer-out rates is one of six institutional performance standards that the state has set for all public higher education institutions in Virginia. Legislation passed in 2018 requires four-year institutions to develop "transfer maps" to improve the legibility of transfer pathways for students (JLARC, 2019[76]), and a recently launched initiative in Virginia's community college system aims to simplify the transfer process with clearer pathways and more systematic guidance to students (VCCS, 2019[77]).

Ohio has developed guaranteed transfer pathways, in which a set of courses at a public two-year college are guaranteed to transfer into specific majors a public four-year university. Discipline-specific guides specify the content and combination of courses that students need to take to be able to transfer efficiently to public four-year institutions. Similarly, in Texas, "fields of study curricula" have been developed as a framework for grouping courses that are guaranteed to transfer between any public Texas institution as part of the same field of study. Courses in career and technical education (CTE), at the sub-baccalaureate level, are typically treated separately, with their own set of guidelines and clustering of courses.

One of the challenges in ensuring clear pathways and efficient transfer processes is the potential to create confusion for students and faculty trying to navigate a complex system of credential pathways and individual transfer agreements, often based on a variety of approaches to clustering courses into broader fields of study. Thus, finding ways to streamline credential pathways within the higher education system is a challenge for all four states participating in the review. In addition, states may face challenges in enforcing guaranteed transfers. In Texas, the Legislature recently passed a bill requiring institutions to report on transfer credits that do not transfer, and why, to help monitor activity and compliance with the guaranteed transfer policy.

Structured, guided pathways through higher education are particularly important for first-generation and economically disadvantaged students who typically face additional barriers to completion and are at higher risk of incurring debt (Holzer and Baum, 2017[78]). Additional student support services, for example in the form of informational tools, guidance and counselling initiatives, can further improve the likelihood of completion, which is an important policy priority in all four states given state-wide goals to increase post-secondary attainment levels.

While the availability and quality of student support services vary across institutions, some state-level initiatives exist to encourage higher education institutions to increase their focus on non-financial student supports. Notably, the Texas Legislature recently passed House Bill 3808 requiring all public higher education institutions to designate a "liaison officer" who provides current or incoming students with information about available support services and other resources (Texas Legislature, 2019[79]). Washington is one of the leading states to implement the Guided Pathways model, a national initiative rooted in research that has identified critical factors supporting student success primarily at two-year institutions (Bailey, 2017[80]). By funding the expansion of Guided Pathways programmes to all community and technical colleges, Washington is taking a step towards a more systematic student support system. In Texas, Guided Pathways are also gaining traction across public two-year institutions at the initiative of individual institutions and with the guidance of the Texas Association of Community Colleges.

Across the OECD, several jurisdictions have taken steps to develop broad support systems that help students access and complete higher education, such as the Accelerated Study in Associate Programs implemented in several US states, which is described in Box 3.8. Some have focused on student supports to help students choose courses and programmes suited to their career goals.

Box 3.8. The Accelerated Study in Associate Programs (ASAP) at the City University of New York (CUNY)

ASAP was established in 2007 to address CUNY's low completion rates and time to graduation for associate's degree students; at the time, approximately 22% of students were graduating within three years, and about 32% within six years. ASAP's main goal is to have at least 50% of enrolled students graduate within three years, by providing comprehensive interconnected financial, social and academic support. Participants benefit from financial aid (including fee waivers, transportation passes and free access to books) and are required to meet regularly with academic tutors, social advisors and employment specialists. The programme also encompasses a structured education pathway. This includes schedules designed to facilitate family or work obligations, capped classes, as well as mandatory attendance. The nine CUNY community colleges offering ASAP enrolled over 25 000 students in the 2019/20 academic year.

An external evaluation conducted by MDRC, using random assignment, compared the outcomes of 896 ASAP students to a comparable control group over a period of three years. The share of students graduating within three years was twice as high for ASAP students (about 40%, versus 22% for control group students). ASAP students also experienced positive outcomes in terms of transition to four-year colleges (about 25%, versus 17% for the control group), number of credits earned, and full-time enrolment rates. The evaluation shows that the ASAP model can generate positive impacts, particularly for educationally and economically disadvantaged populations (Scrivener et al., 2015[81]). A cost-benefit analysis commissioned by CUNY further highlighted that while offering ASAP requires additional expenditures, the higher completion rates and lower time to graduation result in a lower overall cost per degree than without the programme (Levin and Garcia, 2017[82]).

The ASAP model is being expanded and replicated to reach an increasing share of students. CUNY opened a programme similar to ASAP for students at the bachelor's level, and launched a campus-wide extension of ASAP in the Bronx Community College (BCC) in 2019. BCC's ASAP now enrols all 5 000 eligible students, representing 50% of BCC associate's degree students. ASAP has also extended beyond CUNY – Ohio replicated CUNY's model in three community colleges in 2015. An impact evaluation by MRDC highlighted that the programme significantly increased the graduation rate within three years (19% of students enrolled in the programme, against 8% for the control group), as well as the persistence (programme students have a higher enrolment and accumulate more credits) (Sommo et al., 2018[83]). Ohio plans to extend the programme to enrol most eligible students.

Sources: City of New York (2020[84]), Cormier et al. (2019[85]), CUNY (2020[86]; 2020[87]), Levin and Garcia (2017[82]), Scrivener et al. (2015[81]), Sommo et al. (2018[83]), Strumbos, Kolenovic and Tavres (2016[88]).

Potential success factors for effective policies related to educational offerings, pathways and student supports

Across the four states, there is widespread recognition that students need structured, guided pathways to move efficiently through the higher education system towards credential attainment. However, finding ways to streamline credential pathways and facilitate efficient transfers within the higher education system is a challenge for all four states. The level of guidance and student support varies across institutions.

Based on the analysis conducted in the four states and international examples, potential success factors to improve the effectiveness of their policies in the area of educational offerings, pathways and student supports could include:

- Mechanisms to provide state authorities with an opportunity to identify programmes with poor labour market outcomes, the same way mechanisms currently exist for state-wide reviews of programme productivity or low-producing programmes. Outcomes data provided at the programme level could be utilised to identify programmes with persistently poor graduate outcomes, in turn helping institutions focus their attention where it is most needed.
- Approaches to incentivise higher education institutions to encourage labour market relevant teaching and learning across all levels and fields of study. This can include supporting the recruitment of faculty in fields of study leading to high-demand occupations, the provision of high-quality work-based learning opportunities, and opportunities for faculty professional development.
- Approaches to facilitate the availability of state-wide student supports that effectively target students most in need, either financially or academically, for assistance in accessing and completing higher education. There is evidence from evaluations of Accelerated Study in Associate

Programs, which provide wrap-around academic and student support services to community college students, that this has doubled graduation rates in states like New York and Ohio (MDRC, 2016[89]). Some research suggests that effective student supports can reduce the public cost per degree, as the cost of intervention is offset by an increase in number of degrees produced (Scrivener et al., 2015[81]).

- Mechanisms to streamline credential pathways and regional or state-wide transfer agreements between institutions. Information about pathways and transfers should be easy to understand and made available in one place for students and families to consult as they make educational and career choices. Examining transfer outcomes of community college students may be important to identify ways in which to increase transfer efficiency and boost associate's and bachelor's degree attainment.

Funding higher education institutions and students

How can public funding for higher education institutions and students influence the alignment between higher education systems and the labour market?

Governments can use public funding and the financial rules applying to higher education providers to support the workforce relevance of higher education systems in different ways:

- They can use public funds and regulation to make higher education more *affordable* for students, making study more attractive to a larger proportion of the population, and thus helping to increase the supply of skilled workers. This can be achieved, for example, through subsidies to higher education institutions (allowing them to charge lower fees to students, or no fees at all), controls on cost of tuition or financial aid programmes for students in financial need.
- They can also direct public funding to stimulate the *supply and quality of specific programmes* relevant to workforce needs that would not be provided at all, or might be provided only at a lower scale or quality in a purely market-driven system.
- They can design institutional subsidies and student aid programmes to *incentivise institutions and students* to behave in ways that are likely to increase the supply of relevant skills. Performance-based allocation mechanisms can incentivise institutions to focus on producing more graduates or specific skills sets. Earmarked funding can require institutions to invest in capital and activities that support the development of workforce-relevant skills. Targeted student aid programmes can incentivise students to choose specific study options relevant for high-demand occupations.

Across all four states, the level of state budget appropriations to higher education institutions, the level of tuition and mandatory fees charged to students, and state student aid programmes emerge as central issues in policy discussions about college affordability and its impact on access, credential completion and the overall supply of workforce-relevant skills. At the same time, the design of public funding allocation mechanisms has been a major concern for lawmakers and policy makers seeking to promote the quality, relevance and efficiency of higher education systems in their states. Output and outcome-based allocation of institutional funding, as well as targeted funding programmes for institutions and students have been introduced – or are being considered – in the states covered by this review.

Decisions about public investment in higher education institutions and student aid over the last decade have contributed to making higher education less affordable

Public higher education institutions across the United States rely primarily on state appropriations and tuition revenue to cover the costs of their instructional activities. As shown in Figure 3.1, the average total amount of funding per full-time equivalent (FTE) student from state appropriations and tuition in public two-year and four-year institutions varies between the four states. For public two-year institutions, total per-student revenue in the financial year 2018 ranged from around 80% of the US average in Texas and Washington to 95% in Ohio. For public four-year institutions, the equivalent revenue figures vary from 85% of the nation-wide average in Ohio to just above the national average in Texas and Virginia.

Across the four states, public higher education institutions rely on different revenue sources to varying extents. Public two-year colleges in Texas, Ohio and Washington receive 70% or more of their educational revenue from public funds (state and local), while the proportion is only around 50% in Virginia. In the four-year sector, Texas also invests the most public funds per student, in dollar terms and as a proportion of institutions' educational revenue. Whereas public funds account for 60% of institutions' educational revenue in Texas, the equivalent proportion is around 45% in Washington and around one-third in Ohio and Virginia.

Figure 3.1. Total revenue of public higher education institutions by source, 2018

State appropriations, local taxation and research, agricultural and medical (RAM) appropriations and net tuition revenue per full-time equivalent student (FTE) in 2018 USD

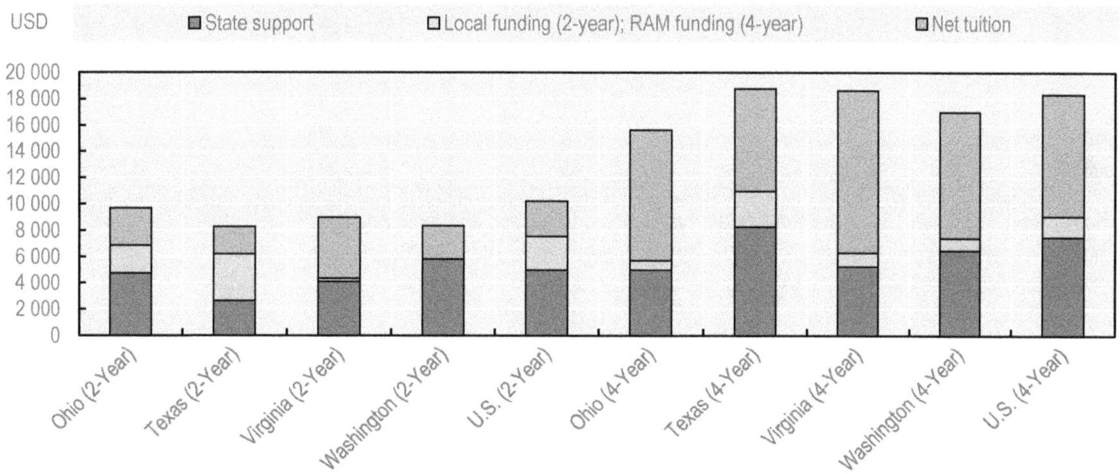

Notes: State support and local funding consist of state tax appropriations, local tax support, additional non-tax funds like lottery revenue that support higher education, and funds appropriated to other state entities for specific higher education expenditures or benefits (e.g., employee fringe benefits). Net tuition revenue is the total amount of tuition and fees minus state financial aid, institutional tuition waivers or discounts, and medical student tuition and fees. This includes revenue from in-state and out-of-state students as well as undergraduate and graduate students. While net tuition revenue reflects the share of instructional support received from students and their families, it does not consider many factors that contribute to a student's net price and does not directly measure tuition rate increases.
Source: State Higher Education Executive Officers (SHEEO) (2019[90]), *SHEF: FY 2018 State Higher Education Finance*, Tables 4 and 6, https://sheeo.org/project/state-higher-education-finance/.

StatLink https://doi.org/10.1787/888934133419

State educational appropriations per FTE student in public higher education institutions fell between 2008 and 2012 in all four review states, in the wake of the Great Recession and the concomitant budgetary retrenchment at state level. Over the four years from 2008, Washington saw a real-terms fall of 33% in state funding per FTE to public institutions (four-year and two-year combined), while the equivalent fall was 28% in Virginia, 25% in Ohio and 23% in Texas. From 2013-18, as a result of increasing state budgetary allocations, appropriations per student increased again, by about 30% in Washington, 20% in Ohio, 14% in Virginia and 7% in Texas, leading the levels shown in Figure 3.1.

The level of public funding per student that public higher education institutions receive in the four states is closely correlated with the level of tuition they charge students. As state appropriations declined sharply after 2008, tuition fees increased significantly. Between 2008 and 2013, the net tuition revenue per FTE student in public institutions increased in real terms by 56% in Washington, 31% in Virginia, 14% in Ohio and less than 2% in Texas, as institutions sought – to varying extents – to compensate for lost state funding. This compares with a nation-wide average increase of 26%. Between 2013 and 2018, as state funding began to rise again, net tuition revenue per FTE student in public institutions still increased in real terms by 17% in Virginia, 10% in Texas and 2% in Washington, while it actually fell by 2% in real terms in Ohio as a result of tuition moderation policy.

In 2017/18, as shown in Table 3.5, tuition and mandatory fees charged to in-state students in public four-year institutions were the lowest in Texas and Washington – the states with the highest state appropriations per student - and the highest in Ohio and Virginia. For public two-year colleges, fees for in-state students were highest, by some margin, in Virginia, followed in order by Washington, Ohio and Texas.

Table 3.5. Average undergraduate tuition and mandatory fees charged for full-time students in public degree-granting post-secondary institutions, 2018, in USD

	Public four-year in-state	Public four-year out of state	Public two-year in-state	Public two-year out of state
Ohio	10 026	24 098	3 672	7 456
Texas	8 645	24 937	2 209	6 418
Virginia	12 637	33 428	5 118	11 275
Washington	6 830	28 263	4 078	5 976
US average	9 037	25 657	3 243	7 971

Source: Adapted from NCES (2018[91]), *Average undergraduate tuition and fees and room and board rates charged for full-time students in degree-granting postsecondary institutions, by control and level of institution and state or jurisdiction: 2017-18*, https://nces.ed.gov/programs/digest/d18/tables/dt18_330.20.asp?current=yes.

StatLink https://doi.org/10.1787/888934134730

In the four-year sector, institutional governing boards have tuition-setting authority in Ohio, Virginia and Washington. This authority is shared in Texas between institutional governing boards and the Legislature (see Chapter 5). In the two-year sector, individual college governing boards set tuition in Ohio and Texas. In Washington and Virginia, the system-wide governing boards, respectively the State Board of Community and Technical Colleges (SBCTC) and the State Board for Community Colleges (SBCC) set tuition levels. Washington and Ohio have legislated to limit increases in tuition (for undergraduate residents in Washington, and applying to all students in Ohio). No tuition caps are currently in place in Virginia, although the General Assembly has previously made increases in state appropriations conditional on tuition moderation by institutions (WSIPP, 2019, p. 57[92]).

Discussions are taking place across the United States about establishing "free college" policies in the two-year sector. These include policies to eliminate fees in public two-year institutions or "promise programmes" aiming to bridge the gap between the student aid available and students' costs to attend higher education (the Dallas Promise programme is an example of this). Among the four states in the review, the Governor of Virginia introduced the "Get Skilled, Get a Job, Give Back" Initiative, which would make tuition-free community college available to low- and middle-income students who pursue jobs in high-demand fields (Northam Administration, 2019[93]). Rather than a policy to eliminate or moderate fees in the Virginia Community College System (VCCS), this is effectively a proposal for an additional needs-based student support programme, complementing existing programmes, discussed below.

A majority of other OECD countries have either long-standing policies for free or very low tuition or, where substantial tuition has been introduced, as in England (United Kingdom) and Australia, comprehensive systems of income-contingent loans that effectively make studying free to students at the time of studying. As such, policy debates relating to affordability in much of the OECD take place in a very different context to those in the United States. One country that does share many similarities with the American system, but has gone further than the United States in providing public funding to its two-year colleges, is Canada (Box 3.9).

Box 3.9. Canada's model for funding community colleges

The Canadian higher education system is among the most similar to that in the United States among OECD countries, in terms of its predominantly binary structure of four-year ("universities") and two-year institutions ("colleges"), and its funding model. Canada ranked fifth in the OECD in terms of tertiary education spending (including R&D) per student in 2016, a figure 21% lower than in the United States. Spending was equal to 2.3% of GDP that year, just behind the United States (2.5% of GDP). In Canada, provinces and territories (the equivalent of states) have exclusive jurisdiction over education and are responsible for direct transfers to higher education institutions, while the federal government provides a portion for research funding. In the majority of provinces and territories, student financial aid is funded through a mix of federal and provincial/territorial funding.

Most higher education spending in Canada comes from public sources (about 53%), compared to just over one-third (35%) in the United States (these figures include all categories of expenditure). However, there are considerable differences between provinces. Ontario (the most populous province in Canada) is more similar to the United States in its funding profile: in 2016/17, public sources accounted for about 37% of revenue to public higher education institutions. Tuition fees are significantly higher in Ontario than in any of the other large provinces (Quebec, British Columbia and Alberta).

An important difference in public funding in Canada relative to the United States is how much is spent per student on four-year versus two-year institutions. In 2016, state spending per student in the United States was approximately twice as high for public four-year degree-granting institutions as for public two-year degree-granting institutions (see above). In Canada, provincial/territorial spending per full-time equivalent student was about 12% lower for two-year institutions than for four-year institutions. In Alberta, Nova Scotia and New Brunswick, public spending per student is actually higher in two-year institutions. Canada is the world leader in attainment of two-year level diplomas, at a level almost double that in the United States, while returns to these credentials relative to high school graduates and bachelor's graduates are stronger in Canada than in the United States.

Sources: HESA (2019[94]), Hicks and Jonker (2016[95]), Howard and Edge (2014[96]), NCES (2017[97]), OECD (2019[4]).

To compensate for the impact of (rising) tuition on the affordability of higher education for students, all four states in the review provide financial aid to students, complementing the Pell Grants provided by the federal government. The State Higher Education Executive Officers Association (SHEEO) collects comparable data from all states on state funds allocated to student financial aid. As shown in Figure 3.2, Washington has consistently invested more per student than the other states in student aid since the financial crisis. In 2018, the state spent USD 1 180 per FTE student on student aid programmes, compared to an average of US states of USD 750, around USD 710 in Virginia, USD 250 in Texas and just USD 220 in Ohio. In Texas, it should be noted that two of the programmes targeting financial need, the Texas Public Educational Grant (TPEG) and Financial Assistance Funded by Designated Tuition Set-Asides (resulting from House Bill 3015 that deregulated tuition in 2003), are categorised as "state financial aid" (THECB, 2018[98]) but are funded from institutional resources (see Chapter 5).

Figure 3.2. Real-terms change in public student aid per FTE student in 2018 USD, 2008-18

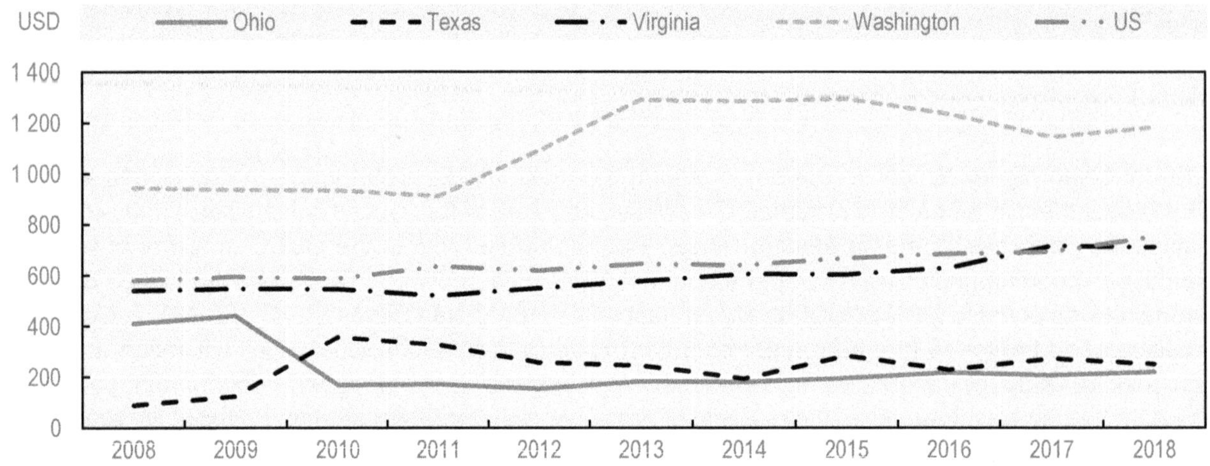

Note: Adjusted for inflation using Higher Education Cost Adjustment (HECA).
Source: SHEEO (2019[99]), *Data Downloads, Tableau Visualization Data*, https://sheeo.org/project/state-higher-education-finance/.

StatLink https://doi.org/10.1787/888934133438

The majority of state funding for student financial aid is allocated through means-tested student support programmes. These programmes target degree-seeking, in-state students, who must first apply for federal Pell Grant funding through the Free Application for Federal Student Aid (FAFSA). Table 3.6 highlights main student aid programmes in the four states. Virginia and Texas restrict state financial aid to students attending public institutions, whereas Ohio and Washington include students in private institutions. While Ohio and Texas have set maximum amounts, which is high in the case of the TEXAS grant, the Virginia and Washington programmes cover up to the full tuition fee levels for in-state students. In Washington, recent changes were made to the Washington College Grant to transform the programme into a guarantee, whereby all eligible students are guaranteed to obtain funding, unlike in the previous programme, where some eligible students were unfunded due to the programme's budget limitations.

Table 3.6. Main means-tested student aid programmes in the four states: eligibility and allocation

	Ohio	Texas	Virginia	Washington
Main programme	Ohio College Opportunity Grant (OCOG)	Toward EXcellence, Access and Success (TEXAS) Grant	Virginia Student Financial Assistance Program (VSFAP)	Washington College Grant
Budget latest financial year	USD 122 million	USD 433 million	USD 250 million	USD 120 million***
Students in four-year public institutions eligible	✓	✓	✓	✓
Students in two-year public institutions eligible			✓	✓
Students in private not-for-profit institutions eligible	✓		*	✓
Students in private for-profit institutions eligible	✓			✓

	Ohio	Texas	Virginia	Washington
Eligibility established through the FAFSA	✓	✓**	✓	✓**
Allocated by state coordinating board to institutions	✓	✓	✓	✓
Fixed state-wide award amounts	✓	✓		
Maximum annual award for full-time student in 4-year public college	USD 2 000	USD 14 688	Up to level of in-state tuition and mandatory fees (amount determined by each institution)	Full tuition amount at any approved/eligible in-state public college or university, and comparable amount towards tuition and other education-related costs at an approved private college or career-training program

Notes: Cells with tick marks indicate features of the state's main means-tested grant programme. Empty cells mean the programme does not have these features. For Texas, only student financial programme with highest annual expenditure is included in the table; several other programmes exist, as described in Chapter 5. *Students at accredited not-for-profit institutions in Virginia can receive funding through the separate Tuition Assistance Grant program (TAG), which is awarded to students by institutions without a requirement to use income-based criteria. **Students who are not eligible to complete the FAFSA due to their immigration status can use the Washington Application for State Financial Aid or the Texas Application for State Financial Aid. ***This is the planned investment for fiscal year ending June 2021 in the Washington Education Investment Act, including about USD 99 million to cover previously unfunded students and expand maximum award, and USD 21 million to fund expanded income eligibility (see Chapter 7 for further details).

Sources: ODHE (2019[100]), *Financial Aid Guidance Memo - Ohio College Opportunity Grant (OCOG)*, https://www.ohiohighered.org/sites/default/files/uploads/sgs/guidance-memos/FA%2020-002.pdf; THECB (2019[101]), *Operating Budget: Fiscal Year 2020*, http://www.thecb.state.tx.us/DocID/PDF/12963.PDF; THECB (2019[102]), *2019-20 Program Guidelines Toward EXcellence, Access, & Success Grant (TEXAS Grant)*, http://reportcenter.thecb.state.tx.us/agency-publication/miscellaneous/texas-grant-fy-2020-program-guidelines/; SCHEV (2019[103]), *2020-22 Systemwide Operating and Financial Aid Budget Recommendations for Higher Education in Virginia State Council of Higher Education for Virginia*; https://www.schev.edu/docs/default-source/Reports-and-Studies/2019/soc2020-22budgetrecommendations.pdf; Washington Legislature (2019[104]), *Washington Education Investment Act*, https://app.leg.wa.gov/billsummary?BillNumber=2158&Initiative=false&Year=2019; WSAC (n.d.[105]), *The New Washington College Grant*, https://wsac.wa.gov/wcg.

StatLink https://doi.org/10.1787/888934134749

While states have invested in student financial assistance to complement federal programmes, many students continue to face "unmet need" (see Box 3.10). This has prompted new initiatives to further reduce the cost of higher education, ranging from expanding financial aid programmes, as in Washington, or considering free tuition programmes, as described above.

Box 3.10. The concept of "unmet need"

Unmet financial need is calculated as follows:

- cost of attendance (COA) – expected family contribution (EFC) = financial need;
- financial need – financial aid received = unmet financial need.

The **COA** is calculated by institutions and typically includes:

- tuition and fees;
- the cost of "room and board" (or housing/living expenses for students who do not contract with the school for housing);
- the cost of books, supplies, transportation, loan fees and miscellaneous expenses (including a reasonable amount for the documented cost of a personal computer);

- an allowance for child care or other dependent care;
- costs related to a disability; and/or
- reasonable costs for eligible study-abroad programmes.

The **EFC** is calculated according to a formula set in law and that is reported on the Free Application for Federal Student Aid (FAFSA) form.

Several limitations of the concept have been identified:

- A similar unmet need for different students can have different implications. For instance, an unmet need of USD 10 000 is different if a student is in a high-cost, selective institution with high expected earnings after graduation, or if a student attends a two-year institution with low costs and lower expected returns.
- Concerns exist about the proper reporting of the EFC, and that the calculation may overstate families' abilities to cover higher education costs, especially those with low income.
- The COA, calculated by institutions, may underestimate the cost of living off-campus, which largely affects students at two-year institution institutions. Additionally, some stakeholders suggested costs such as childcare and transportation continue to be barriers, even though they are theoretically taken into account into the COA.

Sources: CLASP (2018[106]), NASFAA (n.d.[107]), U.S. Department of Education (n.d.[108]).

Other countries have explored different approaches to providing financial assistance to students, including through providing loans instead of the grants typical in state-level student support in the United States. As noted, the United Kingdom and Australia operate formal income-contingent loan (ICL) programmes, where students repay government-sponsored loans after graduation, once they reach a certain earnings threshold. The earnings threshold and arrangements for forgiveness after a specific period provide significant safeguards for students.

In Canada, several measures exist to keep federal student debt manageable, for which provincial equivalents generally exist. This includes charging no interest during and six months after studies, charging only the prime lending rate thereafter, providing tax credits on the interest portion of repayments and making low-income borrowers eligible to a repayment assistance plan, which covers the portion of their payments that is deemed unaffordable. In addition, student loan borrowers with a permanent disability can have their student loan repayments limited to what they can reasonably afford based on their family income, family size, and disability-related expenses.

Performance-based funding models are increasingly used to encourage completions, but have a lesser focus on labour market outcomes

In addition to the variation in overall level of state funding for higher education, the four states use different approaches to allocate state operating funding to higher education institutions. The main differences lie in the role of formula-based as opposed to historical allocation models and, where formulae do exist, the use of output or outcome measures, such as course completions, credentials awarded and employment outcomes, as opposed to input or process measures, such as student enrolment.

Across the United States, recent analysis shows that 47 of the 50 states have some form of performance-based formula in place for allocating at least a proportion of operating funding to two-year institutions; and 43 states use output measures in allocating funds to four-year institutions (Li, 2018[109]). While all four states in the review use some form of performance-based funding in the allocation of funds to two-year colleges, Texas, Virginia and Washington are among the seven states that do not currently have any output-based element in their university funding model. Virginian authorities are, however, currently considering a new output-based model (SCHEV, 2019[103]).

Ohio uses distinct performance-based funding formulae to allocate 100% of available state operating funds to its two-year and four-year institutions, as well as the vocationally focused Ohio Technical Centers (OTCs). By comparison, the other three states only use output measures in allocating a proportion of funds to two-year institutions and technical colleges, as outlined in Table 3.7.

Table 3.7. Output measures used in allocation of educational appropriations to public institutions

Share of state educational appropriations awarded to two- or four-year institutions based on output measures

	Ohio	Texas	Virginia	Washington
Two-year institutions (% of state funding)	**(100%)**	**(10.6%)***	**(20%)****	**(5%)**
College-readiness: e.g. students completing English and mathematics courses successfully	✓	✓	✓	✓
Retention in same and next academic year			✓	✓
Progression based on credits/GPA	✓	✓	✓	✓
Course completion	✓			✓
Transfer: students transferring to senior/other institutions	✓	✓	✓	
Credentials: total and under-served population students gaining awards	✓	✓	✓	✓
Credentials in "critical" or in-demand fields		✓		
Extra weighting for "at-risk" or "under-served" students***	✓			✓
Four-year institutions (% of state funding)	**(100%)**	**a**	**a**	**a**
Course completions	Approx. 30%	a	a	a
Degree completions	50%	a	a	a
Reserved for doctoral training and medical studies	Approx. 20%	a	a	a
Extra weighting for "at-risk" students	✓	a	a	a

Notes: Cells with tick marks indicate output measures that are used in the allocation of educational appropriations to public institutions. Empty cells mean the output measure is not used in the allocation of appropriations. In Texas, Virginia and Washington, no output measures are used in the allocation of educational appropriations to public institutions. *Public two-year institutions in Texas receive only a third of their operational funding from state funds, with another third coming from local taxation. **The Virginia Community College Board uses these performance metrics to allocate 20% of the educational appropriations for the Virginia Community College System among the constituent colleges. ***At-risk students in Ohio include students from low-income backgrounds, minority communities and – for community colleges – older learners. Under-served students in Washington include Basic Skills students, low-income students, and students of colour.

Sources: ODHE (2019[110]), *State Share of Instruction Handbook for Use by University Regional and Main Campuses 2019/20*; DHE (2019[111]), *State Share of Instruction Handbook for use by Community and Technical Colleges 2019/20*; Legislative Budget Board (2019[112]), Financing Public Higher Education in Texas: Legislative Primer, https://www.lbb.state.tx.us/Documents/Publications/Primer/4909_Financing_Public_Higher_Ed.pdf; VCCS (2017[113]), *VCCS E&G Outcomes-Based Funding Model*, https://www.ccleague.org/sites/default/files/images/overview_vccs_outcomes_based_funding_model.pdf; SBCTC (n.d.[114]), *Student Achievement Initiative*, https://www.sbctc.edu/about/agency/initiatives-projects/student-achievement-initiative.aspx.

StatLink https://doi.org/10.1787/888934134768

The metrics used by the four states all include a focus on course and credential completion. In Ohio, progression and course completion metrics are given greater weight in the formula for two-year institutions than for four-year institutions, to allow for the fact many students in these institutions are not "degree-seeking". The formula for all institution types gives greater weight (and thus funding) for each course or credential completed by students from "at-risk" groups, including those from low-income backgrounds, minority communities and – for community colleges - older learners. This weighting is designed to incentivise institutions to support student populations facing greater obstacles to progression and completion; evaluation shows that institutional focus on this has increased since the model's introduction.

In the other states, the use of an output-based funding formula is restricted to a minority share of state funding to two-year institutions and technical colleges. In Texas, for instance, while 10.6% of state funding is allocated based on performance, state funding represents approximately one-third of community college funding (see Chapter 5). Texas is the only of the four states that includes a metric directly related to workforce needs, by including points for completion of credentials in "critical fields" of study, which include STEM or allied health programmes.

Both Ohio and Texas have introduced output-based funding allocation mechanisms for their vocationally oriented technical college sectors that explicitly reward colleges for the labour market outcomes achieved by their graduates. In Ohio, half of available state operating funds for OTCs is awarded based on the number of graduates successfully transitioning to employment, military service of further post-secondary study after graduation. In Texas, a "returned value" funding formula is used to determine the amount of state general revenues provided to the Texas State Technical College System (TSTCS) for instruction and administration expenditure. This uses the amount each graduate earns above the minimum wage during a fixed period after graduation to calculate an added value score for each graduate, which is then used to distribute funds between institutions. This is the most explicit attempt to link graduate employment outcomes to funding found in the four states under review.

There are risks attached to the use of performance-based funding models, including the risk that institutions seek out students with higher academic ability (a practice known as "cream-skimming"), which may result in limiting access for under-represented populations. States such as Ohio and Washington respond to this challenge by allocating points to at-risk or under-served students. None of the four states under review currently uses indicators of graduate labour market outcomes in their allocation formulae for two and four-year colleges, although the Ohio General Assembly has tasked the Ohio Department of Higher Education with exploring the feasibility of introducing such metrics (Ohio General Assembly, 2019[115]). Seven states in the United States do currently use labour market outcome metrics in their allocation formulae (TICAS, 2018[116]).

Box 3.11 provides examples from one of these states – Tennessee – as well as details of the funding allocation system used in Korea. Depending on the metrics used, linking funding to employment outcomes may create the risk that institutions seek to cut programmes that are socially important but do not lead to high earnings or focus on employment placement, irrespective of suitability of available jobs for the students in question. Ensuring that approaches are in place to mitigate these risks – including by understanding the type of employment graduates obtain – are thus important.

Box 3.11. Funding models to support labour market relevance

Performance funding in Tennessee

Tennessee was the first US state to introduce a performance-based formula for allocating funding to its public higher education institutions. The formula includes variables reflecting strategic objectives for higher education outlined in the state's Master Plan. Between 80% and 90% of the overall state funding is delivered through the outcome-based formula.

University-oriented metrics	Community college-oriented metrics
Students accumulating 30/60/90 credit hours	Students accumulating 12/24/36 credit hours
Bachelor's & associate's degrees completed	Dual enrolment
Master's/Ed. specialist degrees completed	Associate's degrees completed
Doctoral/law degrees completed	1-2 year certificates
Research, service and sponsored programmes	<1-year certificates
Degrees per 100 FTE	Job placements
Six-year graduation rate	Transfers out with 12 credit hours
	Workforce training (contact hours)
	Awards per 100 FTE

Institutions that show above-average performance on the metrics for under-represented populations, such as Pell Grant recipients, adults over age 25, and academically under-prepared students (only for community colleges) can receive additional funding. An analysis of student-level outcomes between 2005 and 2013 illustrates significant changes in certificate completion, credit accumulation and, in some cases, degree completion in Tennessee – but causal links cannot be firmly established.

Sources: Dougherty et al. (2011[117]), Research for Action (2017[118]), Tennessee Higher Education Commission (2016[119]).

Competitive funding in Korea

Education is a national priority in Korea, with about 6% of GDP devoted to educational institutions (all levels and types of funding combined), a rate that is among the highest in OECD countries. This includes one of the highest shares of private funding in the OECD. Governance of the education system is shared between central and local authorities.

In tertiary education, government focuses on labour market relevance to address the high shares of tertiary graduates who are not employed, in education or training (NEET). Special funding is provided to the 50 universities with the best performance regarding graduate employment, the share of teachers with industry experience, and the share of students who took part in internships or fieldwork. In addition, scholarships are provided to encourage the take-up of sciences, engineering and the humanities. Tuition fees are high in Korea, and affordability is a key concern to maintain equity. In 2012, the government introduced income-contingent financial aid through the Half-Tuition Policy of the National Scholarship System. Between 2011 and 2013, the government increased its budget for scholarships by 480%. The Half-Tuition Policy allows all students to apply for and receive scholarships. It funds full scholarships for students from low-income families, and progressive subsidies for higher-income families. The policy ultimately aims to reduce total tuition fees paid by households by 50%.

Sources: Dejardins (2017[120]), OECD (2017[121]; 2017[122]; 2019[4]).

States have used targeted funding for institutions and students to incentivise institutional activities and student choices that align with workforce needs

The performance-based funding models discussed above reward institutions for the results they achieve, leaving institutions largely free to decide how they allocate resources and design activities internally to achieve these results. Targeted state funding for institutions, in contrast, earmarks specific funds for specific activities or types of activity. The four participating states have used different forms of targeted funding to support investments in activities and facilities that support workforce-relevant skills development.

Supply side: Targeted funding to increase institutional supply

Some states provide top-up funding for increasing the supply of labour market relevant programmes. In Virginia, public higher education institutions can obtain additional funding for initiatives they prioritise in every biennial update of their institutional six-year plans (SCHEV, 2018[123]). A dedicated committee, including representatives from the state Legislature, the executive branch and staff of the State Council of Higher Education for Virginia, reviews the proposed initiatives and has the ability to award a modest level of funding for the highest ranked proposals. However, the Virginia General Assembly has not always made funds available for this component of institutional funding in recent biennial budgets, which, combined with the low levels of funding involved in other years, has limited the initiative's influence on institutional behaviour.

Ohio has used targeted funding programmes for institutions, with requests for proposals, for a number of workforce-related initiatives. The Regionally Aligned Priorities in Developing Skills (RAPIDS) programme, for example, provides targeted funding to regional consortia of public higher education institutions to invest in equipment to educate students in in-demand occupations. It requires those submitting bids to demonstrate how investments in specific items of equipment will allow students to acquire career-relevant skills that meet demonstrated need in specific industries, with a focus on the growth sectors of advanced manufacturing, robotics and cybersecurity (see Chapter 4). The Ohio Means Internships and Co-ops (OMIC) program, referenced earlier in the chapter, provided funding to enhance the capacity of campuses to build links with businesses offering internships and organise and follow up internship placements.

In Texas, targeted institutional funding is also available to enhance enrolment capacity in fields of study leading to shortage professions, though this comprises a small share of public funding. For instance, the Graduate Medical Education Expansion Grant (USD 78.6 million in 2019) provides funding to public medical schools to increase first-year residency positions, a commonly referenced barrier to the expansion of the medical workforce. The state also provides some targeted funding to institutions to provide support to students in in-demand fields. For instance, the Texas Science, Technology, Engineering, and Math (T-STEM) Challenge Scholarship Program provides funding to community and technical colleges, which allows them, in turn, to offer merit-based scholarships to high-achieving students in STEM and related fields. Participating colleges collaborate with local businesses and industry to identify local employment needs in STEM occupations and develop part-time employment opportunities for scholarship recipients.

In Washington, the Career Connect initiative outlined earlier in the chapter provides an example of an infusion of funding dedicated to expand career awareness and exploration activities, as well as work-based learning opportunities for secondary and post-secondary students under the age of 29. The funding provided includes competitive funding for organisations at the regional level to create new opportunities, funding provided to organisations that are currently delivering work-based learning, and funding to provide student supports, such as transportation, for individuals who face barriers to participating in work-based learning.

Demand side: Targeted funding to boost student awareness, choice and success

States also direct targeted funding to students to promote credential acquisition in high-demand skills fields. In Ohio, for example, the "Choose Ohio First" scholarship programme, initiated in 2008, provides scholarship funding for students studying Science, Technology, Engineering and Mathematics and Medical (STEMM) subjects in public and private universities in the state. Institutions request funding from the Ohio Department of Higher Education and are required to use allocated resources for financial assistance to students, which ranges from USD 1 500 to USD 7 995 per year. Historically, Choose Ohio First only provided funding for degree programmes, but the 2020/21 state budget extended the scope of the initiative to include funding for students in certificate programmes in STEM fields, medicine and dentistry. Ohio has also just introduced the *TechCred* programme to provide refunds to employers who pay for existing or prospective employees to acquire short-term certificates related to high-demand technology fields.

Virginia has also introduced a targeted student support initiative – the New Economy Workforce Credential Grant Program, branded as *FastForward* – to help Virginia residents gain long or short-term certificates in specified high-demand fields, provided by public two-year colleges. Students must pay one-third of the cost of the certificate programme, with state then contributing the second third if students complete the coursework for the programme and the final third on award of the certificate. The maximum award is USD 3 000 per student.

In Texas, a range of programmes channel funding directly to prospective students in fields of high labour market demand, from medicine, nursing and teaching to peace operations. The loan repayment for certain physicians is a long-standing programme and the largest of the programmes targeting occupations in shortage fields, with an investment of about USD 15 million for fiscal year 2020. Biennial surveys of physicians are conducted to determine how many continue to serve in a health shortage area. Results suggest an initially high rate of retention that steadily declines over time, from more than 90% retention in the first of the programme to about 70% during the fourth (and last) year of the programme. Retention decreases to around 40-50% three to four years after programme completion (THECB, 2018[98]). The THECB also indicated that a review of the Nursing Shortage Reduction Programme, in place since 2005, is underway.

Washington has similarly introduced several programmes to help students cover the cost of higher education programmes in fields leading to high-demand occupations, such as medicine and teaching. In addition, the state has recently placed a focus on leveraging funding from industry alongside public support. For instance, the Washington State Opportunity Scholarship, created in 2011, is funded through funds provided by industry and philanthropic organisations and matched dollar for dollar by the state. The programme supports students enrolling in aerospace, engineering, technology and health care, and focuses on low- and middle-income students. This initiative has served close to 20 000 students to date, with a large proportion of women, students of colour and first-generation college students, and positive employment and earnings outcomes for participants (see Chapter 7).

Evidence on state-specific programmes that aim to assist with loan repayment in fields facing labour market shortages is limited and evaluations are not conducted systematically. National evidence suggests that aid programmes designed to encourage entry into occupations, such as the Teacher Education Assistance for College and Higher Education (TEACH) grant programme, may not produce the results that were anticipated, due to complexity in their design and administration that leads to confusion, non-compliance and loss of eligibility among programme participants (GAO, 2015[124]). In addition, it is unclear whether programmes aimed at promoting STEM or other high-demand fields are successful in persuading students and potential students to change their choice of subject or major. For STEM subjects in particular, students' ability to enrol in STEM programmes is highly dependent on the classes they took during high school as well as individual aptitude. Targeted scholarship funding alone cannot influence the profiles of prospective students, and must be part of a broader strategy to increase student interest in in-demand fields early in their educational experience.

Potential success factors for funding policies to support alignment between higher education and the labour market

Against a backdrop of significant cuts to state funding to institutions following the Great Recession, all four states are working to increase the number of affordable study options for students to gain post-secondary credentials, with a particular focus on the public two-year college sector. There is an increased emphasis on workforce-relevant certificate programmes, supported by targeted student funding schemes, which have the potential to be an effective way to bring under-served groups into higher education and equip them with valuable skills. In implementing strategy to increase post-secondary attainment, law and policy makers nevertheless will need to keep in mind the limits of certificate qualifications in terms of breadth of skills and long-term impact on earnings. At the same time, there are proposals in some states to further reduce the costs of attending a two-year college for low- and middle-income students in a bid to support more people to gain associate's degrees and lower costs of transfer-based routes to gaining a bachelor qualification.

These recent or planned efforts to reduce the costs of attending a two-year college are occurring in a context where state funding per student for public higher education institutions is still well below its pre-crisis level in real terms in all four states and budgets for need-based student aid remain modest. There are no easy solutions to the challenge of increasing affordability while ensuring high levels of quality in provision. Nevertheless, potential success factors for using public funding of higher education institutions and students to support workforce alignment include the following:

- Sustained commitment from law makers to ensuring the sufficiency of state appropriations for higher education institutions. Per-student funding in the two-year sector should be a special focus of attention, given the lower per-student expenditures from which these institutions start, and the key role these institutions plays in offering an entry route to higher education for under-represented populations and in meeting labour market needs in key economic sectors. Price is a factor in students' decisions to enter higher education and affordability must be a concern for policy makers (Urban Institute, 2017[125]; Kelchen, 2017[126]; Dearden et al., 2011[127]). However, evidence shows a correlation between per-student funding and student completion (Carnevale and Strohl, 2013[128]; Goolsbee, Hubbard and Ganz, 2019[129]), and suggests that public investment in higher education institutions, allowing additional resources to be allocated to student advising and guidance, can be more effective for increasing enrolment and completion than imposing tuition cuts (Deming and Walters, 2017[130]).
- Processes either to moderate student tuition across the board, while limiting negative impact on instructional quality, or to allocate additional resources to need-based student grant programmes. The latter is a more targeted and efficient way to increase post-secondary attainment than lowering tuition for all students.
- Approaches to introduce carefully designed performance-related funding that use metrics intelligently to ensure institutions are also incentivised to support disadvantaged populations (Minaya and Scott-Clayton, 2017[131]). Such models should be designed in close co-operation with higher education institutions, in particular to protect institutions from financial shocks generated by sharp changes in enrolment and provide institutions with adequate resources for their core instructional mission.
- Targeted funding to higher education institutions and other partners to expand the offer of opportunities for students to develop labour market relevant skills, ranging from increasing work-based learning options to incentivising students to pursue in-demand fields. Programmes to support students in choosing study fields should be designed in ways that make them easy to understand and access. They should also be developed in conjunction with broader policy efforts starting before higher education to enhance students' academic preparedness and interest in pursuing fields of study that lead to occupations with good earnings prospects.

Information

How do data and information support alignment between higher education and labour market needs?

Providing targeted information to policy makers, educators, students, employers and other stakeholders is important to ensure transparent and accurate information about educational and occupational opportunities (OECD, 2004[132]; Musset and Mytna Kurekova, 2018[133]). Information about the skills requirements of the labour market, now and in the future, allows policy makers to ensure they have well-targeted policies in place and helps educational providers plan and adapt their educational offerings. At the same time, information about the labour market outcomes of past higher education graduates can provide an indication of the labour market demand for graduates from specific programmes or fields. Alongside information about the costs of attending higher education programmes, such information can help prospective and current students make informed choices about what to study (although it does not guarantee that they will make rational choices). As graduate labour market outcomes also depend on personal choices, economic and labour market conditions and wage levels in specific sectors, care is always needed in interpreting such data. In addition, information about the skills that students develop through different higher education programmes allows employers to make better decisions about hiring and training needs.

States are developing tools for policy makers to better understand skills supply and demand and support strategic forecasting in higher education

In the context of changing skills demand, state governments are developing approaches to monitor the state's ability to meet the demand for skilled workers and inform strategic planning processes, often at both regional and state levels. Many states have developed interactive dashboard tools to observe and predict potential gaps in workforce supply and demand by occupation (Prince et al., 2015[134]; Wilson, 2014[135]). These tools can support policy making, but can also aid higher education institutions in the development of new programmes. While many higher education institutions engage directly with employers and conduct their own labour market analyses to inform programming and curriculum design, they also rely on public workforce data and labour market information, which underscores the importance of ensuring accurate and easily accessible information about the labour market and state-wide workforce needs.

All four states participating in this review have made higher education data publicly available through interactive data platforms or dashboards and have attempted to connect these data to information on workforce needs to provide an indication of potential gaps in skills supply and demand. Basic workforce supply-demand analyses may, for example, match records of credential production by field of study to occupational projections in order to indicate future gaps in supply and demand (Wilson, 2014[135]). In Texas, a labour gap analysis tool estimates current and anticipated labour gaps for major occupational groups and career clusters. Estimates of anticipated labour gaps are based on average projected annual job openings by occupation (demand side) and higher education data of annual graduates by programme of study (supply side). Ohio received support from the National Skills Coalition to create its workforce supply tool, which was developed as a "one-stop-shop" for information about workforce needs for educators, businesses, career counsellors and job seekers. Information is provided for the state as a whole and by region. In Virginia, the State Council of Higher Education for Virginia recently launched an initiative to identify data needs related to workforce supply and demand. In addition, the state's employment agency is developing a methodology for linking the production of credentialed graduates from Virginia's higher education institutions to projected employment demand, as well as injecting known in-migration patterns, by occupation.

In Washington, a workforce supply-demand analysis is conducted every two years as a joint agency initiative, using both national- and state-level data (WSAC, SBCTC and WTECB, 2018[136]; Hershbein and Hollenbeck, 2015[137]). To estimate future gaps, Washington considers that a proportion of completers will not enter the labour market and that some post-secondary completers are upskilling and not available for new jobs. Washington's supply-demand analysis also permits the identification of "high-demand fields", which are occupational groupings mapped to broader fields of study. Occupational groups are considered to be in high demand when the gap between the supply of graduates and projected annual openings is equal to or exceeds 15% of the total number of projected annual openings.

However, there are important limitations to using these tools to inform policy and programme planning. There is not always a one-to-one relationship between fields of study and occupations or jobs, particularly in fields such as the social sciences, humanities and liberal arts. While forecasting the number of nursing graduates required to meet state needs is closely tied to current and projected occupational demand, graduates of a large range of programmes – from business to social sciences– may enter a wide range of occupations (Coffey, Sentz and Saleh, 2019[138]). This kind of flexibility in the labour market is desirable, but makes it difficult to assess the adequacy of the supply of graduates in general fields of study compared to employer demand. In addition, these tools do not always consider migration of skilled workers into and out of different occupational groups, which affects the supply of labour.

Another limitation relates to the occupational information as the main source of data for skills demand, which does not necessarily capture a sufficient level of detail to understand variations in skills demanded by employers. This could include, for example, differences in skills demanded for different jobs within the same occupation, or changes in skills demanded in the same occupation across different geographic areas. The need for increased data granularity is discussed in the next section.

Thus, supply-demand models and gap analyses can provide an indication of where there is likely to be considerable misalignment between labour market demand and the supply of credentialed graduates. To inform policy, however, these models should be supplemented with other qualitative and quantitative information (Goldman et al., 2015[139]). Governments across OECD countries have taken different approaches to improve their ability to understand labour market needs. The Labour Market Information Council (LMIC) in Canada, created in 2017, exemplifies efforts of the federal and provincial governments to develop higher quality information on labour markets and evaluate the ways in which different groups can most effectively use labour market information in their decision making (see Box 3.12).

Box 3.12. Canada's Labour Market Information Council (LMIC)

The LMIC is a non-profit organisation that conducts and communicates research on the Canadian labour market to better understand what kind of labour market information is most relevant to users. The LMIC has identified criteria for good quality labour market information, which include the availability of information at the local level, its granularity, frequency and timeliness. The LMIC platform includes a LMI Interactive Dashboard, which examines how seven different stakeholder groups (students, parents, employed, unemployed, persons with disabilities, recent immigrants and recent graduates) perceive the access, readability and impact of labour market information. It also includes a LMI employer dashboard, which provides information about how over 3 000 employers in Canada obtain, perceive and use labour market information in their recruitment processes.

The Council's Board of Directors includes fifteen government officials, representing each province and territory, the federal government and the national statistical body (Statistics Canada), with the support of a National Stakeholder Advisory Panel, which includes non-government representatives, and a Labour Market Information Experts Panel, which provides methodological advice.

Sources: Labour Market Information Council (2019[140]), OECD (2018[141]).

Increased data granularity is needed to help policy makers and educators understand the skills demanded by employers

Many OECD countries and US states are exploring alternative approaches to understand the rapidly changing skills demand in their labour markets and complement supply-demand tools based on occupational projections. The use of unstructured data sources is of increasing interest to policy makers, higher education institutions and other actors with an interest in better understanding skills demand. Virginia and Washington both received support from the National Center for Higher Education Management Systems to develop a dashboard system based on graduate (supply side) data from the Integrated Post-secondary Data System (IPEDS) matched with real-time data from job advertisements (demand side) provided by Burning Glass Technologies (BGT).

Real-time labour market data may capture more granular information about the types of skills, certifications and qualifications that employers seek. (See Box 3.13 for a preliminary analysis of changing skills demand in the four states.) State higher education, workforce or economic development agencies may contract with commercial services such as BGT or Economic Modeling Specialists International (EMSI) to use their data for labour market and skills needs analyses, either systematically or on an ad hoc basis (Goldman et al., 2015[139]). Moreover, applying this kind of data to skills need analyses may also help educators to align curriculum more closely with the skills that employers are seeking, contributing to improved labour market outcomes for both graduates and employers (Dorrer, 2016[142]).

Box 3.13. Skills demand for higher education graduates in Ohio, Texas, Virginia and Washington: An analysis of online job postings data

Employers increasingly use online platforms to disseminate job postings, particularly for jobs requiring a higher education qualification. The availability of millions of online job postings thus constitutes a new source of data that has the advantage of providing information in real-time and at a high level of detail. This type of data also involves limitations; for instance, when job postings imply information, such as a higher education requirement for a medical doctor, inferring the demand for higher education graduates directly from the data will yield biased results. Moreover, the job postings do not directly represent labour demand as they provide hiring information but no information on job separations. Despite its drawbacks, this type of data can offer valuable insights on employer demand when used alongside traditional, representative survey data.

The OECD has begun undertaking analysis using data provided by Burning Glass Technologies, which collects and categorises information daily from job postings taken from over 40 000 online sources using machine-learning techniques, after excluding duplicate postings that appear on multiple websites.

In an ongoing OECD analysis, the skills requirements for job postings with a higher education requirement are examined for Ohio, Texas, Virginia and Washington. The skills information provided in job postings is classified in four categories: cognitive skills; socio-emotional skills; technical, transferable skills; and technical, job-specific skills. The first three categories are considered transferable skills that are valued across a range of occupations, whereas technical, job-specific skills are particular to certain occupations. The analysis comprises three parts: i) a study of skill variation across occupations and states, with a particular focus on transferable skills; ii) an examination of the occupational and skills demand for graduates from more general fields of study; iii) an exploration of the qualifications and skills required for jobs in ICT occupations. The results will be published in Q2 2020.

Source: Brüning and Mangeol (forthcoming[143]).

In some jurisdictions, employer surveys are used to obtain employer input on the skills they need, and their perspectives on the skills of higher education graduates. In Washington and Texas, state-wide graduate outcomes surveys have been conducted on an ad hoc basis, for example for a particular sector (public two-year institutions) or for a particular purpose. However, systematic, state-wide graduate or employer surveys are not currently conducted in any of the four states. The General Assembly of Virginia recently granted funding for the development of a graduate outcomes survey that aims to collect information on whether or not graduates have secured employment related to their degree. The survey is currently designed to be a one-off activity and will be developed by the State Council of Higher Education for Virginia in collaboration with the Virginia Economic Development Partnership. This will obtain more detailed information on graduates' post-graduation employment trajectories and their engagement in "civic life" (SCHEV, 2019[144]).

As outlined in Box 3.14, Australia and the United Kingdom have developed nation-wide employer and graduate surveys. These surveys can provide valuable insights into the planning of education and skills policies and programmes. For instance, a stakeholder consultation held in 2017 in the United Kingdom indicated that national, regional and local skills and economic development agencies leveraged the insights from the employer skills survey in their work. It also highlighted some limitations, such as the reliance on employer perceptions, the lack of common job tasks definitions, and challenges in obtaining information on items such as training costs (London Economics, 2017[145]).

Box 3.14. Nation-wide employer and graduate surveys in the United Kingdom and Australia

Australia's Employer Satisfaction Survey

Since 2016, the Australian government has funded an annual survey of higher education graduates and their employers. The Employer Satisfaction Survey (ESS) is the first national survey that directly links the experiences of graduates to the views of their direct supervisors. The ESS is conducted on a systematic basis by asking employed graduates who participated in the Graduate Outcomes Survey (GOS) four months after graduation to provide the contact details of their supervisor for follow-up. In 2019, the survey gathered responses of 4 500 employers.

The survey provides information about employer satisfaction with the graduate's skills overall and broken down by specific skills. These include foundational skills (e.g. literacy, numeracy, communication, and the ability to investigate and integrate knowledge), adaptive skills (e.g. the ability to apply skills/knowledge and work independently), collaborative skills such as teamwork, technical skills, and employability skills, such as the ability to perform and innovate in the workplace. The survey permits an analysis of employer satisfaction by institution and field of study, and offers insights about graduate and employer perceptions of the importance of the graduate's higher education qualification for their current job.

The United Kingdom's Employer Skills Survey

The United Kingdom has a long tradition of surveying employers. The Employer Skills Survey has been conducted nation-wide every two years since 2011 and is designed to ensure a balanced representation of employers, in terms of size, sector, geography, training provided, and across the private, public and non-profit sectors. It is conducted at the establishment level, and covered 87 000 establishments in 2017. The questionnaire takes 20 minutes to fill and is administered by research firms contracted by the government, which collect the responses through telephone calls.

The survey covers a range of questions regarding recruitment and vacancies, qualifications and skills of employees (including mismatch between qualifications and skills and job requirements), skills gaps, employee training, and the prevalence of high-performing practices in the work place. The survey provides information on the incidence and density of particular challenges; for instance, it allows for the analysis of the proportion of establishments reporting at least one hard-to-fill vacancy (incidence) and for hard-to-fill vacancies as a proportion of all vacancies.

Sources: Australian Department of Education and Training (2018[146]); IFF Research - Department for Education (2018[147]; 2018[148]); QILT (2019[149]).

Accurate and user-friendly data on graduates' return on investment is important to inform the educational choices of students and families

Providing accurate information on graduate outcomes including employment, earnings and debt levels

While several factors such as individual choice and local labour market conditions influence the outcomes of graduates in the labour market, graduate earnings and employment outcomes provide an important indication of how graduates are valued in the labour market through the skills they bring to the workplace. Along with information about the cost of study, options for financial aid and expected debt levels, information about labour market outcomes is important for students and families to assess the potential returns on investing in higher education.

To develop information about graduate outcomes, many states have invested heavily in building linked education and employment information systems, and platforms displaying the information they yield. Ohio, Texas, Virginia and Washington all have state-wide longitudinal data systems that link administrative data on earnings from Unemployment Insurance (UI) wage records with student-level data from higher education institutions. It is estimated that administrative earnings data generally capture about 80% of the workforce (Pena, 2018[150]). Wage records do not provide information on all graduates who move out of the state, those who are self-employed, or federal civilian and uniformed military service members. These remain important gaps in state post-secondary data systems. As discussed in Chapter 2 (Section 2.4), the federal State Wage Interchange System (SWIS) Data Sharing Agreement provides some access to wage data for graduates who live in other states, to a limited extent. In addition, the degree of coverage by institution type and level of disaggregation of the data varies across the states. The most recent survey of state post-secondary data systems conducted by SHEEO shows that many states provide coverage of both public and private not-for-profit higher education institutions in their post-secondary data systems (Whitfield, Armstrong and Weeden, 2019[151]). In Virginia, for example, earnings data are provided across all public and private not-for-profit institutions at the programme level; whereas in Washington, earnings data are made available by major or field of study only for graduates from public institutions. Similarly, in Texas, longitudinal graduate earnings data are available mainly for graduates of public institutions.

Obtaining accurate and informative data on the employment outcomes of graduates – for example, whether they are working in their field of study or in a job commensurate with their qualification level – is often more challenging (TICAS, 2018[116]). At the national level, graduate employment outcomes are surveyed through the National Association of Colleges and Employers (NACE) First-Destination survey, which is designed to obtain information about whether or not graduates have found full-time employment, are seeking continuing education or still looking for work six months after graduation. It does not attempt to measure over-qualification or underemployment. At the state level, Unemployment Insurance (UI) wage records used to obtain graduate earnings information typically indicate the industry in which an individual is employed, but do not provide information on their occupation or field of work. Thus, it is difficult to assess whether or not a graduate is employed in an occupation that matches his or her field of study. In order to obtain more detailed information on in-field job placements, higher education institutions typically use alumni surveys. However, these data can be unreliable due to low response rates.

Texas tracks graduate outcomes for both public and private institutions one year post-completion to monitor whether graduates are working or enrolled in further study (within the state). The University of Texas system is also participating in the Post-Secondary Employment Outcomes (PSEO) project, a partnership between the US Census Bureau and several states and post-secondary institutions. This project sheds light on graduate trajectories after graduation for the period 2001-16 and aims to fill key information gaps by tracking students who work outside of the state in which they studied, and by providing information about the firm's industry sector and geographic location (Foote et al., 2019[152]).

Furthermore, because of rising student debt levels and growing public concern over the cost of higher education in the United States, reporting accurate information on student debt alongside earnings data is critical. Students can benefit from access to reliable data about tuition and fees, average debt and loan repayment levels, earnings, and employment outcomes in order to increase their awareness of the expected rates of return on post-secondary education. Thus, information on graduates' return on investment is an important labour market metric that should be included in post-secondary longitudinal data systems (TICAS, 2018[116]). For example, information about student debt levels and loan repayment is not always easily accessible or available by programme level in the four states participating in this review. According to the SHEEO, many states struggle to find ways to report accurate information on student debt and loan repayment. SHEEO suggests strengthening state agency capacity to collect this kind of information, by acknowledging gaps in student financial indicators and publicising plans to collect and report this data (Whitfield, Armstrong and Weeden, 2019[151]).

Easily accessible and user-friendly information

Despite the availability of a wide array of information sources on labour market outcomes, tuition and fees, financial aid options, and sometimes debt and loan repayment information, it is not always easy for users to access or understand, which may limit its use by students and families. There have been attempts to enhance the transparency of higher education outcomes and costs, notably through the College Scorecard, a tool funded by the US Department of Education (see Chapter 2). The Scorecard connects institutional-level data about higher education requirements, costs and labour market outcomes. Programme-level data on earnings and debt have also been made available in 2019 through the Scorecard. While this new information holds significant promise for students and families to better understand and compare the returns on investment of different programmes, this information is currently only available in a downloadable "test" version.

Across the four states, student-oriented information about educational opportunities is not always linked in an easily accessible way to data on graduate labour market outcomes or information about employment prospects (for example, occupational projections and in-demand fields). While the resources made available through the states' post-secondary data systems are comprehensive, they often appear to be mainly targeted towards educators and policy makers. These data often include relevant information about labour market outcomes that could be made available to students in an easy-to-access manner as part of the information they consider when exploring educational opportunities. For example, Washington's Roadmap dashboard, which includes information about projected supply and demand, is a tool targeted mainly to policy makers and educators and does not appear to be connected to information about educational options that is targeted to students. In Texas, an attempt to combine resources on one site is under development, and multiple sites exist that are targeted to different users with various sources of information.

There are also challenges with respect to the choice of measures in the information to present on public-facing websites. For instance, while short-term measures such as the earnings of recent graduates may be of most interest to students, the long-term earnings may be a more reliable measure to understand the career prospects of a certain programme. Another challenge relates to the selection effect that skews the outcomes of graduates in high-earning fields of study. The raw earnings difference between programmes should thus be interpreted with caution, as they are not necessarily the earnings all students can expect.

In this respect, providing information on the academic requirements alongside earnings data is important to contextualise this data.

The provision of accessible and user-oriented information has been a widely shared priority among OECD countries, often in partnership with the private sector. In some countries, governments have funded innovative approaches to provide targeted information to students. In the Netherlands, a combination of measures are used to try to help students choose the right programme, as outlined in Box 3.15.

Box 3.15. Supporting student choice in the Netherlands

Study Choice 123: Providing information on educational pathways and labour market outcomes

Studiekeuze 123 (Study Choice 123) is an independent, publicly funded tool launched in 2006. It supports student choice by providing web-based tools to compare study programmes and educational pathways, based on specific indicators. The website targets prospective students in the process of making educational or career choices, and presents information that is tailored to user needs through customisation tools (including personality tests and "select-and-compare" tools).

At the programme level, comparable indicators on courses comprise information on programme availability, requirements, content and completion rates. Labour market information is provided at the study level (by study field), and includes results of alumni surveys (gross earnings, most chosen occupation, unemployment rates, labour market prospects) and employment forecasts. These forecasts include five-year employment prospects, sensitivity of the occupations in the field to economic change, and potential pathways to different jobs and positions.

The Study Choice Check: Assessing students' interests and abilities

The *Studiekeuzecheck* (Study Choice Check) was established by the 2013 Law on Higher Education in the Netherlands. It requires higher education institutions to offer a package of activities enabling prospective students to assess whether their skills and interests fit with the programme to which they are applying. The Study Choice Check intends to decrease the time to graduation and address dropout rates by supporting students in their decision-making process, ultimately facilitating their path to a career that matches their chosen field of study. Some programmes require students to complete the Study Choice Check before enrolment.

Students can benefit from at least three checks (i.e. for three programmes), taking place after high school graduation. The Study Choice Check can include activities such as an initial questionnaire about the student's study plans, motivation and skills, or a homework assignment. For each institution of interest, students can benefit from talking with representatives of the university, meeting fellow students, or experiencing, for at least a full day, the programme of their choice.

Students are provided with an individualised report resulting from participation in these activities. This report highlights how the student's interests and abilities fit the content and requirements of the programme they have pre-selected, and what skills the student should develop within and/or outside the programme, to be successful in the programme and secure good labour market outcomes. The decision to accept or reject the institution's advice on one's suitability with the programme remains with the student and does not breach the Dutch open access policy; except for capacity-constrained programmes, students can enter higher education upon the completion of secondary education.

Sources: OECD (2019[5]); Studiekeuze123 (2020[153]).

Developing effective approaches to skills signalling is becoming increasingly prevalent

Signalling skills content of higher education qualifications to employers

In all four states, stakeholders highlighted the importance of helping graduates effectively communicate the labour market value and skills content of their credentials to employers. In Texas, the state's current higher education plan requires all public institutions to identify and document the "marketable skills" that each degree programme will provide to students, enabling them to market themselves effectively to employers. The Texas Higher Education Coordinating Board (THECB) monitors institutional progress on the creation and implementation of these processes, and facilitates discussions on practices. The THECB has defined marketable skills as "those skills valued by employers that can be applied in a variety of work settings, including interpersonal, cognitive, and applied skill areas. These skills can be either primary or complementary to a major and are acquired by students through education, including curricular, co-curricular, and extracurricular activities" (THECB, 2015, p. 22[8])

Many higher education institutions in the United States have developed innovative approaches to skills signalling by using digital student records, skills inventories and other tools to engage employers and help students connect with them. For example, comprehensive learner records (CLR) enable students to share a verifiable record of their academic achievements. With consent, the CLR gathers data about a student's performance beyond just grades, with the ultimate goal of communicating the student's entire learning experience (Educause, 2019[154]). Some states have tried to facilitate or support this activity by establishing state-wide credential or skills inventories, which seek to standardise and harmonise different types of qualifications and skills. In Washington, the Workforce Training and Education Coordinating Board launched the development of a credential inventory that will include a registry of degrees, certificates, licenses, apprenticeships and micro-credentials. In Texas, the Texas Workforce Commission supported the development of a skills inventory for the Texas State Technical College System with skills that are validated by employers and can help educators align curriculum content with labour market needs.

Demand for specific, often ICT-related, skills may also be contributing to intensifying interest in so-called "alternative credentials", both within and outside the post-secondary environment. Alternative credentials, such as micro-credentials, digital badges and industry-recognised certificates, have been touted as a way to fill a gap between the programmes that higher education institutions provide and the skills that employers seek; as a way of increasing the efficiency of higher education systems by offering more highly targeted training than traditional degree programmes. Many higher education institutions interviewed by the OECD team reported they are responding to this need by offering additional specialisation tracks, badges or certificates – for example, in data science or artificial intelligence – for degree-seeking students across multiple fields of study.

According to a study conducted by the Corporation for a Skilled Workforce and the Lumina Foundation, professional certificates across more than 16 industry sectors, such as health care, ICT and manufacturing, have been embedded into study programmes offered by higher education institutions in the United States (Zanville, Porter and Ganzglass, 2017[155]). A Pearson VUE survey also shows that one-quarter of the respondents with at least one IT certificate pursued their certificate as a result of an academic programme or course in which they were enrolled (Pearson VUE, 2019[156]). To date, these types of micro-credentials serve mainly to supplement other degrees or credentials and are valued by employers as such (Gallagher, 2018[157]), as outlined in a recent OECD study (2020[158]), although they have the potential to serve as a substitute for some higher education qualifications in certain circumstances (see Box 3.16).

Box 3.16. The development of alternative credentials and credential inventories

The emergence of alternative credentials

So-called "alternative credentials" – such as micro-credentials, digital badges and industrial certifications – have proliferated as a consequence of a rising demand for upskilling and reskilling, as well as a sharp reduction in the unit cost of education and training provision made possible by digitalisation. According to a recent OECD study on alternative credentials, these new credentials do not yet serve as an "alternative" to a formal higher education qualification; rather, they serve to complement prior education, training and experience. However, factors that may limit the labour market relevance of these credentials include employers' unfamiliarity with these credentials, confusing signals caused by lack of standardisation, the frequent absence of validation procedures, and the lower signalling value of these credentials compared to other factors, such as professional experience.

However, alternative credentials may have a near-term potential to become a substitute for some formal higher education qualifications in selected sectors where alternative credentials are well recognised, and are successful at attracting non-traditional learners, such as the ICT sector. Similarly, micro-credentials that attempt to substitute for substantial parts of formal higher education programmes (e.g. MicroBachelors and MicroMasters programmes offered through an online learning platform, EdX) may be able to provide learners with skills and quality signals faster and at lower prices than traditional higher education programmes.

The development of credential inventories and criteria

In 2013, a non-profit organisation, Credential Engine, started developing an online registry with information about post-secondary credentials, including alternative credentials. It aims to help learners find post-secondary credentials that match their needs, by allowing them to compare information about credentials, including learning content, requirements, estimated time to earn, estimated costs and graduates' labour market outcomes.

With funding from Lumina Foundation, Rutgers' School of Management and Labor Relations developed a conceptual model of non-degree credential quality in 2019. The conceptual model identifies four steps in the provision of non-degree credentials, with set indicators in each step: 1) designing credentials, 2) developing competencies, 3) being exposed to the labour market, and 4) leading to economic and social outcomes.

The Council for Higher Education Accreditation has listed possible quality criteria for alternative credentials in their 2019 publication. Additionally, the International Organization for Standardization has been working on setting minimum requirements for learning provided outside of formal education (such as the ISO 29991:2014 and the ISO 29993:2017).

Sources: Credential Engine (2019[159]); International Organization for Standardization (2017[160]); Kato, Galán-Muros and Weko (2020[158]); Van Noy, McKay and Michael (2019[161]).

Signalling skills to higher education institutions based on prior learning and alternative credentials

While less frequently discussed during OECD interviews with US states, recognising individuals' existing skills and competencies for the purpose of pursuing higher education has been a long-standing effort in some OECD countries. In Europe, in particular, governments have actively supported the development of tools that aim to encourage individuals to pursue higher education through the recognition of prior learning, whether formal or informal. The prevalence of national qualifications frameworks, which are used to classify a country's qualifications at different levels, alongside the learning outcomes expected at each level, has facilitated processes of prior learning recognition and assessment. Box 3.17 describes examples in France and Quebec, a Canadian jurisdiction that has developed mechanisms of prior learning recognition in a context where no national framework of qualifications is in place. In the United States, national actors such as Lumina Foundation have been paying increasing attention to the challenges posed by the absence of such frameworks, particularly in a context where the provision of alternative credentials is expanding rapidly, and more often outside of higher education. This challenge also highlights opportunities to leverage technology to develop such tools in the American context (Travers et al., 2019[162]).

Box 3.17. Prior learning assessment in France and Quebec (Canada)

Prior Learning Assessment (PLA) involves the review and formal recognition of knowledge, skills and competencies obtained through previous formal, and especially informal and non-formal learning. The basic purpose of PLA is to improve the accessibility and efficiency of education delivery by ensuring learners do not have to take courses on what they already know, and often to tackle inequities in supporting those with less formal schooling who still have skills and knowledge that they should be able to certify to become more successful in the labour market.

France has a system of PLA known as *validation des acquis de l'expérience* (VAE), helping learners to achieve vocational or professionally oriented credentials. The basis for the system is set out in legislation (the labour code). France has defined VAE as an individual right, although it can be pursued on behalf of groups of workers in concert with employers and businesses. All qualifications in the national directory of qualifications (*répertoire national des certifications professionnelles* – RNCP) must be accessible through VAE unless they are a regulated profession where activity without a formal qualification is illegal. As of 2014, companies are legally required to review employees' professional development and inform them of VAE, and significant leave and funding support are available for learners to fill any gaps. VAE has been a focus of steady policy evolution in recent years, for instance in connection with the skills investment plan (*plan d'investissement dans les compétences*) that aims to invest EUR 13 billion in the period 2019-22.

The Quebec model allows learners to obtain their full college (CÉGEP) diploma through Recognition of Acquired Competencies (RAC); and where gaps are identified in students' learning it permits learners to fill these gaps through whatever form of learning they choose to complete their credential, including self-study, apprenticeship, classroom instruction or distance education. As in France, Quebec does not distinguish between credentials obtained through RAC or other avenues. The Government of Quebec is the primary source of funding for RAC undertaken in school boards and colleges, making the service free for all of the province's residents.

Sources: Bohlinger (2017[163]); Cedefop (2018[164]); Mathou (2019[165]); Moss (2011[166]); Werquin (2010[167]).

Potential success factors for information policies to support alignment between higher education and the labour market

Multiple tools are in place in Ohio, Texas, Virginia and Washington to provide information about educational and career opportunities, graduate outcomes in the labour market, and the alignment between skills supply and demand. Across the four states, information on graduate earnings by programme or major/field of study are available for several years post-graduation through post-secondary longitudinal data systems. However, understanding graduates' employment trajectories, field of study match, and the quality and degree of skills use in the workplace continues to be a challenge. While systematic, state-wide graduate surveys have been attempted, these have often been discontinued and are conducted only on an ad hoc basis.

Across all four states, public authorities maintain a wealth of information that is made available to students and families, educators, policy makers, employers and other stakeholders. However, it is challenging to ensure that the information provided is both sufficiently comprehensive and easy to navigate for different users. State efforts to develop credential inventories to help students, employers and institutions understand the value of different credentials are still in their early stages, and would benefit from more effective co-ordination between state agencies, institutions, employers and other industry/professional associations.

Based on international examples and the analysis conducted in the four states, potential success factors to improve the effectiveness of information policies to improve the alignment between higher education and workforce needs could include:

- Mechanisms to integrate workforce information in strategic planning and forecasting processes in higher education. This can include developing state-wide supply-demand analyses and considering approaches to systematically engage employers, identify emerging trends and more granular skills needs, assessing institutional capacity to meet changing needs and providing state-wide access to major data resources (Goldman et al., 2015[139]).
- Approaches to improve the quality and availability of data on graduate outcomes in the labour market by providing debt and earnings data at the programme level and expanding coverage to include both public and private institutions, where possible. Make use of data that enable outcomes to be disaggregated for different student groups and sub-populations, for example low-income and minority students. Explore the development of metrics or tools to measure the employment outcomes of graduates, for example by developing state-wide graduate outcomes or employer surveys to assess the signalling value of post-secondary qualifications and skills use in the workplace as well as in-field job placement rates.
- Mechanisms to provide integrated information to students and families about educational opportunities and pathways, costs, outcomes and supports. Information about the expected return on investment of post-secondary education options can help students make better choices in terms of selecting field of study and career path. However, the tailoring of information is crucial to ensure that it reaches students in a manner in which they can easily access and absorb it (Lavecchia, Liu and Oreopoulos, 2015[168]). In order to make it easier for users to navigate and access all the information that is available, it may be beneficial to consolidate existing and relevant tools into a single information platform that differentiates between different types of users.

References

Adecco USA (2019), *The American Skills Gap is Real*, https://www.adeccousa.com/employers/resources/skills-gap-in-the-american-workforce/ (accessed on 3 February 2020). [58]

Australian Department of Education and Training (2018), *QILT - Quality Indicators for Learning and Teaching*, QILT, http://www.qilt.edu.au/ (accessed on 27 March 2018). [146]

Authority, H. (ed.) (2019), *Funding, Governance and Performance - Process*, Higher Education Authority, https://hea.ie/funding-governance-performance/process/ (accessed on 5 February 2020). [18]

Bailey, T. (2017), "Guided Pathways at Community Colleges: From Theory to Practice", *Diversity and Democracy*, Vol. 20/4, https://www.aacu.org/diversitydemocracy/2017/fall/bailey (accessed on 28 August 2019). [80]

Bailey, T. et al. (2017), "Policy Levers to Strengthen Community College Transfer Student Success in Texas", Community College Research Center, https://ccrc.tc.columbia.edu/media/k2/attachments/policy-levers-to-strengthen-community-college-transfer-student-success-in-texas.pdf. [72]

Bohlinger, S. (2017), "Comparing recognition of prior learning (RPL) across countries", in Mulder, M. (ed.), *Technical and Vocational Education and Training*, Springer Nature, http://dx.doi.org/10.1007/978-3-319-41713-4_27. [163]

Brüning, N. and P. Mangeol (forthcoming), "What skills do employers seek in higher education graduates? An analysis using Burning Glass Technologies job posting data", *OECD Education Working Papers*, OECD, Paris, https://doi.org/10.1787/19939019. [143]

Burns, T., F. Köster and M. Fuster (2016), *Education Governance in Action: Lessons from Case Studies*, Educational Research and Innovation, OECD Publishing, Paris, https://dx.doi.org/10.1787/9789264262829-en. [26]

Calmand, J. and P. Lemistre (2019), "Effet du parcours à diplôme donné sur l'insertion professionnelle Groupe de travail sur l'enseignement supérieur", *Céreq Echanges*, Vol. 11, pp. 1-168, https://www.cereq.fr/effet-du-parcours-diplome-donne-sur-linsertion-professionnelle (accessed on 24 February 2020). [37]

Capelli, P. (2015), "Skill Gaps, Skill Shortages, and Skill Mismatches: Evidence and Arguments for the United States", *Industrial & Labor Relations Review*, Vol. 68/2, pp. 251-290, http://dx.doi.org/10.1177/0019793914564961. [62]

Carnevale, A. and N. Smith (2018), *Balancing Work and Learning: Implications for Low-Income Students*, Georgetown University Center on Education and the Workforce, https://1gyhoq479ufd3yna29x7ubjn-wpengine.netdna-ssl.com/wp-content/uploads/Low-Income-Working-Learners-FR.pdf (accessed on 12 March 2020). [64]

Carnevale, A., N. Smith and J. Strohl (2013), *Recovery: Job Growth and Education Requirements through 2020*, Georgetown University Center on Education and the Workforce, Washington, DC, https://1gyhoq479ufd3yna29x7ubjn-wpengine.netdna-ssl.com/wp-content/uploads/2014/11/Recovery2020.FR_.Web_.pdf (accessed on 10 May 2019). [63]

Carnevale, A. and J. Strohl (2013), *Separate and Unequal: How Higher Education Reinforces the Intergenerational Reproduction of White Racial Privilege*, Georgetown Public Policy Institute; Center on Education and the Workforce, Washington D.C., https://cew.georgetown.edu/wp-content/uploads/SeparateUnequal.FR_.pdf (accessed on 22 July 2019). [128]

Caroll, A. et al. (2018), *Higher Education Learning Framework Matrix - An Evidence Informed Model for University Learning*, Science of Learning Research Centre , Brisbane: The University of Queensland, https://www.slrc.org.au/wp-content/uploads/2018/05/HELF-isbn.pdf (accessed on 27 February 2020). [65]

Cedefop (2018), *European Inventory on validation of non-formal and informal learning - European Inventory on Validation: 2018 update*, https://www.cedefop.europa.eu/en/events-and-projects/projects/validation-non-formal-and-informal-learning/european-inventory#Country (accessed on 27 February 2020). [164]

City of New York (2020), *Accelerated Study in Associate Programs - Growing Up NYC*, https://growingupnyc.cityofnewyork.us/programs/cuny-asap/#section-summary (accessed on 12 March 2020). [84]

CLASP (2018), *When Financial Aid Falls Short: New Data Reveal Students Face Thousands in Unmet Need*, The Center for Law and Social Policy, Washington, DC, https://www.clasp.org/sites/default/files/publications/2018/12/2018whenfinancialaidfallsshort.pdf. [106]

Coffey, C., R. Sentz and Y. Saleh (2019), *Degrees at Work: Examining the serendipitous outcomes of diverse degrees*, EMSI, https://www.economicmodeling.com/wp-content/uploads/2019/08/Emsi_Degrees-at-Work_Full-Report-1.pdf (accessed on 6 March 2020). [138]

Cormier, M. et al. (2019), *Scaling Success: Lessons From the ASAP Expansion at Bronx Community College*, CCRC Research, https://ccrc.tc.columbia.edu/publications/scaling-success-cuny-asap-bcc.html (accessed on 12 March 2020). [85]

Credential Engine (2019), *Credential Engine*, https://credentialengine.org/ (accessed on 1 December 2019). [159]

CUNY (2020), *CUNY ASAP*, http://www1.cuny.edu/sites/asap/ (accessed on 12 March 2020). [86]

CUNY (2020), *Significant Increases in Associate Degree Graduation Rates: CUNY Accelerated Study in Associate Programs (ASAP)*, http://www.mdrc.org/publication/doubling-graduation-rates (accessed on 12 March 2020). [87]

Dearden, L. et al. (2011), *The Impact of Tuition Fees and Support on University Participation in the UK*, Institute of Fiscal Studies, London, https://www.ifs.org.uk/wps/wp1117.pdf (accessed on 5 February 2020). [127]

Deming, D. and C. Walters (2017), *The Impact of Price Caps and Spending Cuts on U.S. Postsecondary Attainment*, Harvard University, UC Berkeley, NBER, https://scholar.harvard.edu/files/ddeming/files/DW_Aug2017.pdf (accessed on 28 August 2019). [130]

Department for Education (2019), *Apprenticeship funding in England*, https://www.gov.uk/government/publications/apprenticeship-funding (accessed on 24 February 2020). [47]

Department of Education and Skills (2018), *Higher Education System Performance Framework 2018-2020*, http://www.education.ie/en/Publications/Corporate-Reports/Strategy-Statement/Department-of-Education-and-Skills-Strategy- (accessed on 27 February 2020). [66]

Department of Education and Skills (2018), *Key System Objectives for the Higher Education System 2018-2020*, https://www.education.ie/en/Publications/Corporate-Reports/Strategy-Statement/Department-of-Education-and-Skills-Strategy- (accessed on 5 February 2020). [16]

Desjardins, R. (2017), *Political economy of adult learning systems : comparative study of strategies, policies and constraints*, https://www.bloomsbury.com/uk/political-economy-of-adult-learning-systems-9781474273664/. [120]

Donnelly, R. et al. (2018), *Ireland's Higher Education Teachers Have a National Professional Development Framework, Now What?*, https://arrow.tudublin.ie/ltccon (accessed on 27 February 2020). [67]

Dorrer, J. (2016), "Using real-time labor market information to achieve better labor market outcomes"*, Lumina Issue Papers*, Lumina Foundation, https://www.luminafoundation.org/files/resources/using-real-time-labor-market-information-full.pdf. [142]

Dougherty, K. et al. (2011), *The Politics of Performance Funding in Eight States: Origins, Demise, and Change - Final Report to Lumina Foundation for Education*, Community College Research Center, http://ccrc.tc.columbia.edu (accessed on 27 February 2020). [117]

Eckel, P. and J. King (2004), "An Overview of Higher Education in the United States: Diversity, Access, and the Role of the Marketplace", in Forest, J. and P. Altbach (eds.), *The International Handbook of Higher Education*, http://www.springeronline.com. (accessed on 3 June 2019). [14]

Educause (2019), *7 things you should know about the comprehensive learner record*, Educause Learning Initiative, https://credentialengine.org/wp-content/uploads/2019/01/Educause_Comprehensive-Learner-Record.pdf (accessed on 14 February 2020). [154]

European Training Foundation (2018), *Support to VET - Financing Policy guidance note; Formula Funding*, https://www.etf.europa.eu/sites/default/files/2018-11/Policy%20guidance%20note_Formula%20%20funding_0.pdf (accessed on 4 March 2020). [30]

Eurydice (2019), *National Reforms in Vocational Education and Training and Adult Learning | France*, https://eacea.ec.europa.eu/national-policies/eurydice/content/national-reforms-vocational-education-and-training-and-adult-learning-23_en (accessed on 24 February 2020). [38]

Eurydice (2019), *National Reforms related to Transversal Skills and Employability | Norway*, https://eacea.ec.europa.eu/national-policies/eurydice/content/national-reforms-related-transversal-skills-and-employability-48_en (accessed on 24 February 2020). [21]

Federal Reserve Bank of Dallas; Center for Public Policy Priorities (2016), *Regional Talent Pipelines: Collaborating with Industry to Build Opportunities in Texas*, https://www.dallasfed.org/-/media/Documents/cd/pubs/pipelines.pdf?la=en, https://www.dallasfed.org/-/media/Documents/cd/pubs/pipelines.pdf. [28]

Foote, A. et al. (2019), *Post-Secondary Employment Outcomes (PSEO)*, United States Census Bureau, https://lehd.ces.census.gov/doc/PSEOTechnicalDocumentation.pdf (accessed on 19 November 2019). [152]

Fulton, M. (2019), *An Analysis of State Postsecondary Governance Structures*, Education Commission on the States, https://www.ecs.org/an-analysis-of-state-postsecondary-governance-structures/. [15]

Gallagher, S. (2018), *Educational Credentials Come of Age: A Survey on the Use and Value of Educational Credentials in Hiring*, Northeastern University, Center for the Future of Higher Education and Talent Strategy, https://www.northeastern.edu/cfhets/wp-content/uploads/2018/12/Educational_Credentials_Come_of_Age_2018.pdf (accessed on 20 July 2019). [157]

GAO (2015), *Better Management of Federal Grant and Loan Forgiveness Programs for Teachers Needed to Improve Participant Outcomes*, United States Government Accountability Office, https://www.gao.gov/assets/670/668634.pdf (accessed on 18 March 2020). [124]

Goldman, C. et al. (2015), *Using Workforce Information for Degree Program Planning in Texas*, RAND Corporation, https://doi.org/10.7249/RR1011. [139]

Goolsbee, A., G. Hubbard and A. Ganz (2019), "A Policy Agenda to Develop Human Capital for the Modern Economy", in Kearney, M. and A. Ganz (eds.), *Expanding Economic Opportunity for More Americans: Bipartisan Policies to Increase Work, Wage and Skills*, https://www.aspeninstitute.org/longform/expanding-economic-opportunity-for-more-americans/a-policy-agenda-to-develop-human-capital-for-the-modern-economy/ (accessed on 12 August 2019). [129]

Hart Research Associates (2018), *Fulfilling the American Dream: Liberal Education and the Future of Work. Selected Findings from Online Surveys of Business Executives and Hiring Managers.*, https://www.aacu.org/sites/default/files/files/LEAP/2018EmployerResearchReport.pdf. [60]

HEA (2017), *Higher Education System Performance 2014-2017 - Third Report of the Higher Education Authority to the Minister for Education and Skills Higher Education System*, Higher Education Authority, https://hea.ie/assets/uploads/2018/01/Higher-Education-System-Performance-2014-17-report-1.pdf (accessed on 5 February 2020). [17]

Hemelt, S. et al. (2018), "Why is Math Cheaper than English: Understanding Cost Differences in Higher Education", *Discussion Paper Series*, No. 11968, IZA Institute of Labor Economics, http://ftp.iza.org/dp11968.pdf. [35]

Hénard, F. and D. Roseveare (2012), *Fostering Quality Teaching in Higher Education: Policies and Practices*, OECD/ IMHE, http://www.oecd.org/edu/imhe (accessed on 27 February 2020). [68]

Hershbein, B. and K. Hollenbeck (2015), *Refining Workforce Education Supply and Demand Analysis: Final Report*, W.E. Upjohn Institute for Employment Research, https://research.upjohn.org/cgi/viewcontent.cgi?article=1034&context=up_technicalreports. [137]

HESA (2019), *The State of Post Secondary Education in Canada*, Higher Education Strategy Associates, http://www.higheredstrategy.com (accessed on 27 February 2020). [94]

Hicks, M. and L. Jonker (2016), *The Differentiation of the Ontario University System: Where are we now and where should we go?*, Higher Education Quality Council of Ontario (HEQCO), http://www.heqco.ca (accessed on 27 February 2020). [95]

Higher Education Quality Council of Ontario (2020), *HEQCO*, http://www.heqco.ca/en-CA/Pages/Home.aspx. [12]

Holzer, H. and S. Baum (2017), *Making College Work: Pathways to Success for Disadvantaged Students*, Brookings Institution Press, https://www.brookings.edu/book/making-college-work/. [78]

Howard, A. and J. Edge (2014), *Policies, Laws, and Regulations - Governing Post-Secondary Education and Skills in Canada*, The Conference Board of Canada - Centre for Skills and Post-Secondary Education. [96]

IFF Research - Department for Education (2018), *Employer skills survey 2017*, IFF Research and Department for Education, https://assets.publishing.service.gov.uk/government/uploads/system/uploads/attachment_data/file/746493/ESS_2017_UK_Report_Controlled_v06.00.pdf. [46]

IFF Research - Department for Education (2018), *Employer skills survey 2017: Research report*, IFF Research and Department for Education, https://assets.publishing.service.gov.uk/government/uploads/system/uploads/attachment_data/file/746493/ESS_2017_UK_Report_Controlled_v06.00.pdf. [147]

IFF Research - Department for Education (2018), *Employer skills survey 2017: Technical report*, https://assets.publishing.service.gov.uk/government/uploads/system/uploads/attachment_data/file/733999/Employer_Skills_Survey-Technical_report.pdf. [148]

IHE (2019), *Survey: Employers Want 'Soft Skills' From Graduates*, Inside Higher Ed, https://www.insidehighered.com/quicktakes/2019/01/17/survey-employers-want-soft-skills-graduates (accessed on 3 February 2020). [56]

INSEE (2018), "L'école et ses sortants [Education and its aftermath]", *Formation et emploi - Insee Références*, pp. 68-81, https://www.insee.fr/fr/statistiques/fichier/3526077/Formemp18f_F1_ecole.pdf (accessed on 24 February 2020). [39]

International Organization for Standardization (2017), *ISO 29993:2017(en) Learning services outside formal education - Service requirements*, https://www.iso.org/obp/ui/#iso:std:iso:29993:ed-1:v1:en (accessed on 2 October 2019). [160]

Jenkins, D. and J. Fink (2016), *Tracking Transfer - New Measures of Institutional and State Effectiveness in Helping Community College Students Attain Bachelor's Degrees*, Community College Research Center, Columbia University; The Aspen Institute; National Student Clearinghouse Research Center, https://ccrc.tc.columbia.edu/media/k2/attachments/tracking-transfer-institutional-state-effectiveness.pdf (accessed on 7 February 2020). [75]

JLARC (2019), *JLARC Impacts - Actions taken on report recommendations 2015-2018*, Joint Legislative Audit and Review Commission , Richmond, http://jlarc.virginia.gov/pdfs/reports/Rpt517-3.pdf (accessed on 21 September 2019). [76]

Kato, S., V. Galán-Muros and T. Weko (2020), "The emergence of alternative credentials", *OECD Education Working Papers*, No. 216, OECD Publishing, Paris, https://doi.org/10.1787/b741f39e-en (accessed on 8 April 2020). [158]

Kelchen, R. (2017), *MHEC POLICY BRIEF Tuition Control Policies: A Challenging Approach to College Affordability*, Midwestern Higher Education Compact (MHEC), http://dx.doi.org/10.1016/j.econedurev.2017.07.007. [126]

Knowles, E. (2020), *Degree apprenticeships*, Prospects, https://www.prospects.ac.uk/jobs-and-work-experience/apprenticeships/degree-apprenticeships (accessed on 24 February 2020). [48]

Kuczera, M. and S. Field (2013), "A Skills beyond School Review of the United States", *OECD Reviews of Vocational Education and Training*, OECD Publishing, Paris, https://doi.org/10.1787/9789264202153-en (accessed on 24 June 2019). [49]

Labour Market Information Council (2019), *Public Opinion Research Project*, https://lmic-cimt.ca/public-opinion-research-project/. [140]

Lavecchia, A., H. Liu and P. Oreopoulos (2015), "Behavioral Economics of Education: Progress and Possibilities", *NBER Working Paper No. 20609*, http://www.nber.org/papers/w20609. [168]

Learning Avenue (2017), *Review of the National Forum for the Enhancement of Teaching and Learning*, https://hea.ie/assets/uploads/2017/04/Review-of-the-National-Forum-for-the-Enhancement-of-Teaching-and-Learning-2.pdf (accessed on 27 February 2020). [69]

Legislative Budget Board (2019), *Financing Public Higher Education in Texas: Legislative Primer*, The State of Texas, https://www.lbb.state.tx.us/Documents/Publications/Primer/4909_Financing_Public_Higher_Ed.pdf. [112]

Levin, H. and E. Garcia (2017), "Accelerating Community College Graduation Rates: A Benefit–Cost Analysis", *The Journal of Higher Education*, Vol. 89/1, pp. 1-27, http://dx.doi.org/10.7916/D8ST82BS. [82]

Li, A. (2018), *Lessons Learned: A Case Study of Performance Funding in Higher Education*, https://www.researchgate.net/publication/328615362_Lessons_Learned_A_Case_Study_of_Performance_Funding_in_Higher_Education (accessed on 30 January 2020). [109]

London Economics (2017), *Review of the Employer Skills and Employer Perspectives surveys: A synthesis of stakeholder views*, https://assets.publishing.service.gov.uk/government/uploads/system/uploads/attachment_data/file/622310/Review_of_EPS_and_ESS.pdf. [145]

Lumina Foundation (2019), *A Stronger Nation: National Report 2019*, http://blob:http://strongernation.luminafoundation.org/0e7dea0c-7a70-4ac4-a43f-389fa705b1ac. [6]

Manpower Group (2018), *2018 Talent Shortage Survey: United States.*, WI: ManpowerGroup, Milwaukee, https://www.manpower.com/wcm/connect/ManpowerUSA/eb76e7d3-637a-4982-aea3-8693256aa6a8/manpower-2020-talent-shortage-candidate-infographic.pdf?MOD=AJPERES&CVID=n0gDg20 (accessed on 12 March 2020). [59]

Mathou, C. (2019), *European inventory on validation of non-formal and informal learning 2018 update - Country report: France*, Cedefop/ETF/ European Commission, http://libserver.cedefop.europa.eu/vetelib/2019/european_inventory_validation_2018_France.pdf (accessed on 27 February 2020). [165]

McGuinness, A. (2016), *State Policy Leadership for the Future: History of state coordination and governance and alternatives for the future*, Education Commission of the States, Denver, https://www.ecs.org/wp-content/uploads/051616-State-Policy-Leadership-for-the-Future-KL-final4-1.pdf (accessed on 10 September 2019). [27]

MDRC (2016), *Accelerated Study in Associate Programs*, https://www.mdrc.org/sites/default/files/ASAP%202-pager%2002.09.16.pdf (accessed on 9 March 2020). [89]

MESRI-SIES (French Ministry of Higher Education, Research and Innovation) (2020), *Note Flash n°03- Les étudiants en sections de technicien supérieur en 2019-2020 [Students in higher vocational education in 2019-2020]*, Systèmes d'Information et d'Etudes Statistiques (SIES), Ministère de l'Enseignement Supérieur, de la Recherche et de l'Innovation (MESRI), https://cache.media.enseignementsup-recherche.gouv.fr/file/2020/19/7/NF_2020_03_sts_1241197.pdf (accessed on 24 February 2020). [44]

MESRI-SIES (French Ministry of Higher Education, Research and Innovation) (2019), *Note Flash n°25- Parcours et réussite en DUT: les résultats de la session 2018 [Pathways and success in DUT: results of the 2018 session]*, Systèmes d'Information et d'Etudes Statistiques (SIES), Ministère de l'Enseignement Supérieur, de la Recherche et de l'Innovation (MESRI), https://cache.media.enseignementsup-recherche.gouv.fr/file/2019/04/5/NF_Reussite_IUT_1214045.pdf (accessed on 24 February 2020). [42]

MESRI-SIES (French Ministry of Higher Education, Research and Innovation) (2019), *Note Flash n°29- Les indicateurs d'insertion des diplômés de DUT à 18 et 30 mois s'améliorent [Indicators of DUT graduates' employability 18 and 30 months after graduation are improving]*, Systèmes d'Information et d'Etudes Statistiques (SIES), Ministère de l'Enseignement Supérieur, de la Recherche et de l'Innovation (MESRI), https://data.enseignementsup-recherche.gouv.fr/pages/insertion_professionnelle/ (accessed on 24 February 2020). [43]

MESRI-SIES (French Ministry of Higher Education, Research and Innovation) (2018), *Note Flash n°17- Parcoursup 2018: Propositions d'admission dans l'enseignement supérieur et réponses des bacheliers [Parcoursup 2018: Higher education admission proposals and responses from high school graduates]*, Systèmes d'Information et d'Etudes Statistiques (SIES), Ministère de l'Enseignement Supérieur, de la Recherche et de l'Innovation, http://www.enseignementsup-recherche.gouv.fr/pid30617/notes-flash.html (accessed on 24 February 2020). [41]

MESRI-SIES (French Ministry of Higher Education, Research and Innovation) (2017), *Note Flash n°11- Les effectifs dans l'enseignement supérieur en 2016-2017 [2016-2017 Enrolments in higher education]*, Systèmes d'Information et d'Etudes Statistiques (SIES), Ministère de l'Enseignement Supérieur, de la Recherche et de l'Innovation (MESRI), https://cache.media.enseignementsup-recherche.gouv.fr/file/2017/29/0/NF_2017-11_Synthese_effectifs_etudiants_2016-2017_num_802290.pdf (accessed on 24 February 2020). [40]

Minaya, V. and J. Scott-Clayton (2017), "Labor Market Outcomes and Postsecondary Accountability: Are Imperfect Metrics Better than None?", in Hoxby, C. and K. Stange (eds.), *Productivity in Higher Education*, National Bureau of Economic Research/University of Chicago Press, https://www.nber.org/chapters/c13876.pdf (accessed on 7 August 2019). [131]

Ministère de l'Education Nationale et de la Jeunesse (French Ministry of Education and Youth) (2019), *Résultats de la session de juin du baccalauréat 2019 [Results of the June session of the 2019 Baccalaureate]*, https://www.education.gouv.fr/resultats-de-la-session-de-juin-du-baccalaureat-2019-7385 (accessed on 24 February 2020). [45]

Ministry of Education and Research (2017), *Norwegian Strategy for Skills Policy 2017-2021*, https://www.regjeringen.no/en/topics/education/voksnes-laring-og-kompetanse/artikler/National-Skills-Policy-Strategy-2017-2021/id2516169/ (accessed on 17 December 2017). [22]

Moss, L. (2011), "The Recognition of Prior Learning in Quebec: Current Practices", *McGill Journal of Education*, Vol. 46/3, pp. 395-406, https://mje.mcgill.ca/article/view/5783 (accessed on 27 February 2020). [166]

Musset, P. and L. Mytna Kurekova (2018), "Working it out: Career Guidance and Employer Engagement", *OECD Education Working Papers*, No. 175, OECD Publishing, Paris, https://dx.doi.org/10.1787/51c9d18d-en. [133]

NASFAA (n.d.), *Glossary of Terms for Financial Aid Offers*, National Association of Student Financial Aid Administrators, https://www.nasfaa.org/glossary#efc (accessed on 18 March 2020). [107]

National Collaborative Outreach Programme (2018), *A Student's Guide to Higher and Degree Apprenticeships*, https://www.pathwaystohe.ac.uk/wp-content/uploads/2018/05/Pathways-Higher-and-Degree-Apprenticeships-Guide.pdf (accessed on 24 February 2020). [50]

National Forum for the Enhancement of Teaching and Learning in Higher Education (2019), *National Professional Development Framework for all Staff Who Teach in Higher Education*, https://www.teachingandlearning.ie/publication/national-professional-development-framework-for-all-staff-who-teach-in-higher-education/ (accessed on 27 February 2020). [70]

NCES (2018), *Digest of Education Statistics, 2018*, National Center for Education Statistics, Washington, DC, https://nces.ed.gov/programs/digest/d18/tables/dt18_330.20.asp?current=yes (accessed on 11 March 2020). [91]

NCES (2017), *Digest of Education Statistics-Advance Release of Selected 2017 Digest tables*, https://nces.ed.gov/programs/digest/2017menu_tables.asp (accessed on 27 February 2020). [97]

Neavyn, R. (2019), *Higher Education Authority, Presentation to the 17th OECD Informal Working Group on Higher Education*. [19]

Northam Administration (2019), *Governor Northam Unveils Tuition-Free Community College Program for Low- and Middle-Income Students*, Webpage of the Virginia Governor, https://www.governor.virginia.gov/newsroom/all-releases/2019/december/headline-849869-en.html (accessed on 26 February 2020). [93]

Norwegian Committee on Skill Needs (n.d.), *Official Committee on Skill Needs*, https://kompetansebehovsutvalget.no/mandate-of-official-norwegian-committee-on-skill-needs/ (accessed on 10 March 2020). [24]

ODHE (2019), *Financial Aid Guidance Memo - Ohio College Opportunity Grant (OCOG)*, Ohio Department of Higher Education, Columbus, https://www.ohiohighered.org/sites/default/files/uploads/sgs/guidance-memos/FA%2020-002.pdf (accessed on 9 February 2020). [100]

ODHE (2019), *State Share of Instruction Handbook for use by Community and Technical Colleges*, Ohio Department of Higher Education, Columbus. [111]

ODHE (2019), *State Share of Instruction Handbook for use by University Regional and Main Campuses*, Ohio Department of Higher Education, Columbus. [110]

OECD (2019), *Benchmarking Higher Education System Performance*, Higher Education, OECD Publishing, Paris, https://dx.doi.org/10.1787/be5514d7-en. [5]

OECD (2019), *Education at a Glance 2019: OECD Indicators*, OECD Publishing, Paris, https://dx.doi.org/10.1787/f8d7880d-en. [4]

OECD (2019), *Government at a Glance 2019*, https://www.oecd-ilibrary.org/governance/government-at-a-glance-2019_8ccf5c38-en (accessed on 10 March 2020). [25]

OECD (2019), *OECD Skills Strategy 2019: Skills to Shape a Better Future*, OECD Publishing, Paris, https://doi.org/10.1787/9789264313835-en. [23]

OECD (2018), *OECD Economic Surveys: Canada 2018*, OECD Publishing, Paris, https://dx.doi.org/10.1787/eco_surveys-can-2018-en. [141]

OECD (2017), *Education at a Glance 2017: OECD Indicators*, OECD Publishing, Paris, https://dx.doi.org/10.1787/eag-2017-en. [121]

OECD (2017), *Financial Incentives for Steering Education and Training*, Getting Skills Right, OECD Publishing, Paris, https://dx.doi.org/10.1787/9789264272415-en. [122]

OECD (2015), *Education Policy Outlook 2015: Making Reforms Happen*, OECD Publishing, Paris, https://dx.doi.org/10.1787/9789264225442-en. [29]

OECD (2004), *Career Guidance and Public Policy : Bridging the Gap*, OECD Publishing, https://doi.org/10.1787/9789264105669-en (accessed on 10 March 2020). [132]

OECD/European Union (2017), *Supporting Entrepreneurship and Innovation in Higher Education in Ireland*, OECD Skills Studies, OECD Publishing, Paris/European Union, Brussels, https://dx.doi.org/10.1787/9789264270893-en. [20]

Office for Students (2019), *Analysis of degree apprenticeships*, https://www.officeforstudents.org.uk/data-and-analysis/analysis-of-degree-apprenticeships/disadvantage/ (accessed on 24 February 2020). [51]

Office for Students (2019), *Degree apprenticeships - guide for apprentices*, https://www.officeforstudents.org.uk/advice-and-guidance/skills-and-employment/degree-apprenticeships/degree-apprenticeships-guide-for-apprentices/. [52]

Office for Students (2019), *Degree apprenticeships: a viable alternative?*, https://www.officeforstudents.org.uk/media/c791216f-a1f1-4196-83c4-1449dbd013f0/insight-2-degree-apprenticeships.pdf. [53]

Ohio Department of Higher Education (n.d.), *Attainment*, https://www.ohiohighered.org/attainment (accessed on 20 April 2020). [7]

Ohio General Assembly (2019), *House Bill 166 - Creates FY 2020-2021 operating budget*, https://www.legislature.ohio.gov/legislation/legislation-summary?id=GA133-HB-166 (accessed on 8 February 2020). [115]

Ost, B., W. Pan and D. Webber (2018), *The Returns to College Persistence for Marginal Students: Regression Discontinuity Evidence from University Dismissal Policies*, http://www.journals.uchicago.edu/t-and-c (accessed on 20 May 2019). [3]

Pearson VUE (2019), *2018 Value of IT Certification*, Pearson Education, London, https://home.pearsonvue.com/voc (accessed on 24 July 2019). [156]

Pena, C. (2018), *Workforce success relies on transparent postsecondary data*, National Skills Coalition, https://m.nationalskillscoalition.org/resources/publications/file/Workforce-success-relies-on-transparent-postsecondary-data_web.pdf. [150]

Prince, H. et al. (2015), *Are people getting credentials that lead to jobs? Using dashboards for state workforce planning*, National Skills Coalition, State Workforce and Education Alignment Project, https://www.nationalskillscoalition.org/resources/publications/file/SWEAP_Using_Dashboards_for_State_Workforce_Planning.pdf. [134]

QILT (2019), *2018 Employer Satisfaction Survey: National Report*, Quality indicators for learning and teaching, https://www.qilt.edu.au/docs/default-source/ess/ess-2018/2018-ess-national-report.pdf?sfvrsn=9d2ae33c_8. [149]

Research for Action (2017), *Implementation and Impact of Outcomes-Based Funding in Tennessee*, https://8rri53pm0cs22jk3vvqna1ub-wpengine.netdna-ssl.com/wp-content/uploads/2017/07/RFA-OBF-in-Tennessee-Full-Brief_updated-July-2017.pdf (accessed on 27 February 2020). [118]

SBCTC (n.d.), *Student Achievement Initiative*, Washington State Board for Community and Technical Colleges, https://www.sbctc.edu/about/agency/initiatives-projects/student-achievement-initiative.aspx (accessed on 12 March 2020). [114]

SCHEV (2019), *2020-22 Systemwide Operating and Financial Aid Budget Recommendations for Higher Education in Virginia State Council of Higher Education for Virginia*, State Council of Higher Education for Virginia, Richmond, https://www.schev.edu/docs/default-source/Reports-and-Studies/2019/soc2020-22budgetrecommendations.pdf (accessed on 22 February 2020). [103]

SCHEV (2019), *Agenda Book - September 16-17, 2019*, State Council of Higher Education for Virginia, Richmond, https://www.schev.edu/docs/default-source/about-section/council-files/2019-council-meetings/september-2019/rev-agenda-book-pdf-(w-page-numbers-for-posting).pdf (accessed on 21 September 2019). [144]

SCHEV (2019), *The Virginia Plan for Higher Education - Annual Report 2018*, State Council of Higher Education for Virginia, Richmond, https://www.schev.edu/docs/default-source/virginia-plan/Reports-and-Updates/the-virginia-plan-annual-report-2018.pdf (accessed on 27 June 2019). [9]

SCHEV (2018), *Current Six-Year Plans - 2018*, State Council of Higher Education for Virginia, Richmond, https://www.schev.edu/index/institutional/planning-and-performance/currentsixyearplans (accessed on 30 June 2019). [123]

SCHEV (2018), *FY 2020 Budget and Policy Recommendations for Higher Education in Virginia*, State Council of Higher Education for Virginia, Richmond, https://www.schev.edu/docs/default-source/Reports-and-Studies/2018-reports/fy2020budget-recommendations11918.pdf (accessed on 29 June 2019). [36]

SCHEV (2016), *Aspects of Student Transfer and Post-Transfer Success at Virginia Public Institutions*, State Council of Higher Education for Virginia, Richmond, https://www.schev.edu/docs/default-source/Reports-and-Studies/2016-reports/transferreport2016.pdf. [74]

Scrivener, S. et al. (2015), *Doubling Graduation Rates*, MDRC, New York, https://files.eric.ed.gov/fulltext/ED558511.pdf (accessed on 28 August 2019). [81]

SHEEO (2019), *SHEF: FY 2018 State Higher Education Finance*, State Higher Education Executive Officers Association, http://www.sheeo.org/shef (accessed on 30 July 2019). [90]

SHEEO (2019), *SHEF: State Higher Education Finance*, State Higher Education Executive Officers Association, https://sheeo.org/project/state-higher-education-finance/ (accessed on 23 September 2019). [99]

SHRM (2019), *Employers Say Students Aren't Learning Soft Skills in College*, Society for Human Resource Management, https://www.shrm.org/resourcesandtools/hr-topics/employee-relations/pages/employers-say-students-arent-learning-soft-skills-in-college.aspx (accessed on 3 February 2020). [57]

Sommo, C. et al. (2018), *Doubling graduation rates in a new state: Two-year findings from the ASAP demonstration in Ohio.*, MDRC, https://www.mdrc.org/sites/default/files/ASAP_brief_2018_Final.pdf (accessed on 12 March 2020). [83]

States, E. (2019), *High-Level Analysis of State Postsecondary Governance Structures*, Education Commission of the States, https://www.ecs.org/wp-content/uploads/PS-Gov-Structures-50_State-Analysis_Compacts_Other-States_May2019.pdf. [13]

Steen Roesdahl, M. (2017), *Initiatives to Promote Labour Market Match and Relevance in Danish Higher Education*. [31]

Strumbos, D., Z. Kolenovic and A. Tavares (2016), “CUNY Accelerated Study in Associate Programs (ASAP): Evidence from six cohorts and lessons for expansion.”, in *Proceedings of the 12th National Symposium on Student Retention, Norfolk, Virginia*, http://csrde.ou.edu (accessed on 12 March 2020). [88]

Studiekeuze123 (2020), *Studiekeuze123 (Study Choice 123)*, https://www.studiekeuze123.nl/ (accessed on 12 March 2020). [153]

Tennessee Higher Education Commission (2016), *Outcomes-Based Formula Model Data Definitions - Revised 08-15-2016*, https://www.tn.gov/content/dam/tn/thec/bureau/fiscal_admin/fiscal_pol/obff/Detailed_Outcomes_Formula_Definitions_08-2016.pdf (accessed on 27 February 2020). [119]

Texas Legislature (2019), *H.B. No. 3808: An act relating to measures to facilitate the timely graduation of and attainment of marketable skills by students in public higher education.*, https://capitol.texas.gov/tlodocs/86R/billtext/pdf/HB03808F.pdf#navpanes=0 (accessed on 26 January 2020). [79]

THECB (2019), *2019-20 Program Guidelines Toward EXcellence, Access, & Success Grant (TEXAS Grant)*, Texas Higher Education Coordinating Board, http://reportcenter.thecb.state.tx.us/agency-publication/miscellaneous/texas-grant-fy-2020-program-guidelines/ (accessed on 12 March 2020). [102]

THECB (2019), *Operating Budget: Fiscal Year 2020*, Texas Higher Education Coordinating Board, http://www.thecb.state.tx.us/DocID/PDF/12963.PDF (accessed on 12 March 2020). [101]

THECB (2018), *Report on Student Financial Aid in Texas Higher Education: Fiscal Year 2017*, http://www.60x30tx.com/media/1412/student-fin-aid-in-texas-report.pdf (accessed on 12 April 2020). [98]

THECB (2016), *Closing the Gaps Final Progress Report*, Texas HIgher Education Coordinating Board, http://www.thecb.state.tx.us/DocID/PDF/8138.PDF (accessed on 9 December 2019). [11]

THECB (2015), *60x30TX: Texas Higher Education Strategic Plan 2015-2030*, http://reportcenter.thecb.state.tx.us/agency-publication/miscellaneous/60x30tx-strategic-plan-for-higher-education/ (accessed on 12 April 2020). [8]

TICAS (2019), *Student Debt and the Class of 2018*, The Institute for College Access and Success, https://ticas.org/interactive-map/. (accessed on 23 October 2019). [1]

TICAS (2018), *Of metrics and markets: Measuring post-college employment success*, The Institute for College Access and Success, https://ticas.org/accountability/metrics-and-markets/ (accessed on 10 March 2020). [116]

Travers, N. et al. (2019), *Learning Frameworks: Tools for Building a Better Educational Experience*, Lumina Foundation, https://www.uschamberfoundation.org/workforce-development/JDX (accessed on 9 March 2020). [162]

U.S. Department of Education (n.d.), *Federal Student Aid Handbook*, https://ifap.ed.gov/ilibrary/document-types/federal-student-aid-handbook (accessed on 18 March 2020). [108]

UCAS (2019), *Degree apprenticeships*, https://www.ucas.com/alternatives/apprenticeships/apprenticeships-england/what-apprenticeships-are-available/degree-apprenticeships (accessed on 10 May 2020). [54]

UCAS (2019), *Entry requirements for apprenticeships in England*, https://www.ucas.com/alternatives/apprenticeships/apprenticeships-england/entry-requirements-apprenticeships-england (accessed on 10 April 2020). [55]

Uddannelses- og Forskningsministeriet (Danish Ministry of Education and Research) (2019), *Bevillingssystemet for de videregående uddannelser (The higher education grant system)*, https://ufm.dk/uddannelse/videregaende-uddannelse/institutionstilskud/nyt-bevillingssystem-for-de-videregaende-uddannelser (accessed on 4 March 2020). [34]

Uddannelses- og Forskningsministeriet (Danish Ministry of Education and Research) (2018), *Dobbeltuddannelse: Uddannelsesloftet fjernes [The Education Ceiling is repealed]*, https://ufm.dk/uddannelse/videregaende-uddannelse/dobbeltuddannelse (accessed on 4 March 2020). [33]

Uddannelses- og Forskningsministeriet (Danish Ministry of Education and Research) (2018), *Evaluering - Af den ledighedsbaserede dimensioneringsmodel [Evaluation of the unemployment-based dimensioning model]*, http://www.ufm.dk (accessed on 4 March 2020). [32]

Urban Institute (2017), *Understanding College Affordability*, http://collegeaffordability.urban.org/ (accessed on 12 March 2020). [125]

Van Noy, M., H. McKay and S. Michael (2019), *Non-Degree Credential Quality: A Conceptual Framework to Guide Measurement*, Rutgers' School of Management and Labor Relations, New Jersey, https://smlr.rutgers.edu/sites/default/files/rutgerseerc_ndcquality_framework_full_paper_final.pdf. [161]

VCCS (2019), *Transfer Virginia launches*, http://www.vccs.edu/vccsblog_post/transfer-virginia-launches-goal-is-to-ensure-that-students-are-able-to-make-the-jump-from-community-college-to-the-states-four-year-universities-more-efficiently/ (accessed on 21 September 2019). [77]

VCCS (2017), *VCCS E&G Outcomes-Based Funding Model*, Virginia Community College System, Richmond, https://www.ccleague.org/sites/default/files/images/overview_vccs_outcomes_based_funding_model.pdf (accessed on 19 February 2020). [113]

VEDP (2017), *Amazon HQ2 Submission: Partnership Proposal*, Virginia Economic Development Partnership, https://issuu.com/teamsubjectmatter/docs/nova_r1_proposal_full_doc_single_pa?e=35488011/65733964. [71]

Waddoups, C. (2016), "Did Employers in the United States Back Away from Skills Training during the Early 2000s?", *Industrial & Labor Relations Review*, Vol. 69/2, pp. 405-434, http://dx.doi.org/10.1177/0019793915619904. [61]

Washington Legislature (2019), *Washington Education Invesment Act*, https://app.leg.wa.gov/billsummary?BillNumber=2158&Initiative=false&Year=2019 (accessed on 7 August 2019). [104]

Werquin, P. (2010), *Recognising Non-Formal and Informal Learning: Outcomes, Policies and Practices*, OECD Publishing, Paris, https://doi.org/10.1787/9789264063853-en (accessed on 30 August 2018). [167]

Whitfield, C., J. Armstrong and D. Weeden (2019), *The State of State Postsecondary Data Systems: Strong Foundations 2018*, SHEEO, https://postsecondarydata.sheeo.org/wp-content/uploads/2019/04/SHEEO_StrongFoundations_18.pdf (accessed on 26 August 2019). [151]

Wilson, B. (2014), *How many more skilled workers do we need? Using supply and demand reports for state workforce planning*, National Skills Coalition, State workforce and education alignment project, https://www.nationalskillscoalition.org/resources/publications/file/how-many-more-skilled-workers.pdf. [135]

WSAC (2013), *The 2013 Roadmap*, Washington Student Achievement Council, Olympia, https://www.wsac.wa.gov/the-2013-roadmap (accessed on 15 July 2019). [10]

WSAC (n.d.), *The New Washington College Grant*, Washington Student Achievement Council, https://wsac.wa.gov/wcg (accessed on 12 March 2020). [105]

WSAC, SBCTC and WTECB (2018), *A Skilled and Educated Workforce 2017 Update: An analysis of postsecondary education, workforce preparation, and employer demand in Washington*, Washington Student Achievement Council/State Board for Community and Technical Colleges/ Workforce Training and Education Coordinating Board / Workforce Training and Education Coordinating Board, Olympia, https://wsac.wa.gov/sites/default/files/2017.ASkilledAndEducatedWorkforce.pdf (accessed on 31 May 2019). [136]

WSIPP (2019), *Higher Education Funding: Models Used in Washington and Similar States*, Washington State Institute for Public Policy, Olympia, https://www.wsipp.wa.gov/ReportFile/1702/Wsipp_Higher-Education-Funding-Models-Used-in-Washington-and-Similar-States_Report.pdf. [92]

Xu, D. et al. (2017), *Strengthening Transfer Paths to a Bachelor's Degree: Identifying Effective Two-Year to Four-Year College Partnerships*, https://ccrc.tc.columbia.edu/media/k2/attachments/strengthening-transfer-paths-bachelors-degree.pdf (accessed on 31 October 2018). [73]

Zanville, H., K. Porter and E. Ganzglass (2017), *Report on Phase I Study: Embedding Industry and Professional Certifications within Higher Education*, Corporation for a Skilled Workforce, Lumina Foundation, https://www.luminafoundation.org/files/resources/report-on-phase-i-study-embedding-industry-professional-certifications-within-higher-education-january-2017.pdf. [155]

Zimmerman, S. (2014), *The Returns to College Admission for Academically Marginal Students*, https://doi.org/10.1086/676661. [2]

4 Ohio

This chapter provides an overview of the labour market and higher education system in the state of Ohio, an assessment of the labour market outcomes of graduates, and a discussion of state policies that contribute to aligning higher education and the labour market. The policy discussion focuses on four policy areas – strategic planning and co-ordination of higher education; educational offerings, student supports and pathways; funding; and information – and includes policy recommendations in each area.

4.1. The labour market and higher education in Ohio

The economy and labour market

Ohio's economy is transforming, but manufacturing remains a vital industry

Ohio is the 7th largest economy in the United States, and the 36th largest economy in the world, with a Gross Domestic Product (GDP) of almost USD 676 billion in 2018 (U.S. Bureau of Economic Analysis (BEA), 2020[1]; Ohio Development Services Agency, 2019[2]). In the context of the wider OECD, Ohio's productivity is at a similar level to that of Germany and Sweden. However, Ohio lags behind many other parts of the United States on some indicators of productivity. For example, GDP per capita is slightly below the average level of the United States as a whole, and below that of the Great Lakes area (U.S. Bureau of Economic Analysis, 2019[3]).

Ohio is located in the Great Lakes industrial region in the Midwest of the United States, and is well connected by road and waterway to many of the region's largest population centres. Manufacturing and other forms of heavy industry, including automotive manufacturing and the production of rubber and fabricated metals, have traditionally been leading economic sectors in the state. Mining, agriculture and construction are also important industries in the state, though compared to manufacturing they provide a relatively small contribution to the overall economy.

Following the 2008-09 economic recession, Ohio's GDP recovered quickly, and increased by 40% in the period from 2009 to 2018 (U.S. Bureau of Economic Analysis, 2019[4]). The state has been undergoing a period of de-industrialisation for many decades, in tandem with other nearby areas that make up the United States' "rust belt". As in other rust-belt areas, much of the economic growth of recent years has been driven by growth in the service economy, which contributed 65% of the overall growth in GDP between 2009 and 2018 in Ohio. Over the same period, the GDP of the goods-producing sector increased by 53% and the sector has maintained its share of the overall Ohio economy – at about 22% – over the past decade (U.S. Bureau of Economic Analysis, 2019[5]). Manufacturing remains a vital industry in Ohio; the state is the third largest producer of manufactured goods in the United States, after California and Texas (Ohio Development Services Agency, 2019[2]). Nevertheless, evidence indicates that the nature of many manufacturing jobs is changing rapidly (Box 4.1).

Efforts have been made at the state level to diversify the economy as traditional industries decline. In particular, through its long-established Third Frontier initiative, Ohio has invested heavily in enhancing capabilities for research and development and entrepreneurship in technology (Ohio Development Services Agency, n.d.[6]). In recent decades, Ohio has become one of the leading US states for technological research and development in areas such as fuel cell development, biomedical instrumentation, aerospace, defence and biotechnology. As of 2018, the information and communications technology (ICT) industry made up around 6% of Ohio's economy, and employed 7% of the workforce (COMPTIA, 2019[7]). Some start-up clusters have also developed in Ohio in recent years, particularly in Cincinnati and Columbus, which both perform well nationally in measures of start-up growth and activity (Ewing Marion Kauffman Foundation, 2017[8]).

As in other states and jurisdictions, macro-level indicator values mask important internal variations. Ohio is among the US states that suffer from marked regional inequality, in the context of decline in the traditional industrial and coal mining industries in some areas of the state. Half of the 88 counties of Ohio have poverty rates greater than the US national average, with the highest poverty rates in the Appalachian region (Ohio Development Services Agency, 2019[9]).

Ensuring a sufficient volume of skilled workers to meet current and future economic needs is an ongoing concern in Ohio. The state is ageing; in the year 2000, Ohio had 3.2 million people under the age of 20, compared to 1.9 million over the age of 60. By 2017, the estimated population under 20 was 2.9 million, compared to 2.7 million people over 60 (U.S. Census Bureau, 2018[10]).The changing demographic profile could lead to more pronounced labour market shortages in the coming years, as much of the incumbent workforce reaches retirement age. Indeed, by 2030 it is estimated that 20% of the Ohio population will be aged 65 years or over, and in nine counties the share is likely to be above 25% (Scripps Gerontology Center, 2019[11]).

Table 4.1 presents an overview of some key contextual indicators for Ohio.

Table 4.1. Ohio at a glance

	Ohio	United States	Source
Population			
Population estimate as of July 2019	11 689 100	327 167 434	U.S. Census
Projected population estimate in 2030	11 678 452	357 975 719	U.S. Census Bureau, Ohio Development Services Agency
Percentage of individuals under the age of 18	22.2%	22.4%	U.S. Census
Percentage of individuals aged 65 and over	17.1%	16.0%	U.S. Census
Dependency ratio (% 65+ over population aged 15-64)	26.4%	24.5%	OECD regional statistics
Percentage of Black or African American individuals	13.0%	13.4%	U.S. Census
Percentage of Hispanic or Latino individuals	3.9%	18.3%	U.S. Census
Percentage of Asian individuals	2.5%	5.9%	U.S. Census
Percentage of American Indian or Alaska Native individuals	0.3%	1.3%	U.S. Census
Percentage of White (non-Hispanic) individuals	78.7%	60.4%	U.S. Census
Economy and labour market			
GDP per capita	USD 51 848	USD 57 052	U.S. Bureau of Economic Analysis
Labour force participation rate (out of civilian population aged 16+)	62.7%	62.9%	U.S. Bureau of Labor Statistics
Unemployment rate (seasonally adjusted)	4.5%	3.9%	U.S. Bureau of Labor Statistics
Median annual earnings for working-age population aged 25-64	USD 49 000	USD 50 000	American Community Survey
Estimated annual wage needed to cover basic expenses for a working adult	USD 22 588	USD 25 297	MIT Living Wage Calculator
Percentage of population aged 25-64 with an associate's degree or higher	40.4%	42.5%	American Community Survey

Notes: All numbers are for 2018 unless otherwise noted. Racial and ethnic categories are mutually exclusive. MIT Living Wage annual calculations are based on full-time working hours (2 080 hours per year).

StatLink https://doi.org/10.1787/888934134787

Box 4.1. The changing face of manufacturing globally and in Ohio

Across OECD countries, major changes in goods production and distribution processes are taking place. In addition to automation and increasing use of software and data in the manufacturing process, new production technologies, such as 3D printing, synthetic biology and nanotechnology, are making manufacturing processes more efficient and reliable while also reducing cost. (OECD, 2018[12]) This evolution of manufacturing is also evident in Ohio, where regions of the state with a strong manufacturing tradition have shifted focus from low-tech to high-tech industries (Bacher, 2012[13]).

As in the wider United States, the number of manufacturing jobs in Ohio has increased in the last decade, while wages have also increased (Figure 4.1). New manufacturing facilities have also been established; the volume of new site selections for businesses in Ohio was second-highest in the United States in 2017, with over half of new sites earmarked for manufacturing (Ohio Manufacturers' Association, 2018[14]).

Figure 4.1. Index of change in manufacturing employment and earnings, 2010-19

December 2010 = 100

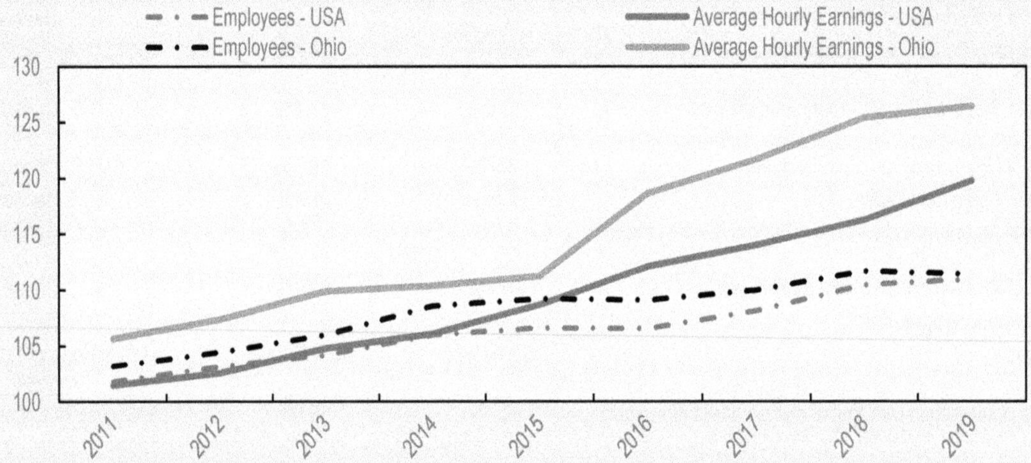

Note: Employment and earnings data are as at December of each year, and seasonally adjusted.
Source: U.S. Bureau of Labor Statistics (2019[15]), *State and Metro Area Employment, Hours and Earnings* (database), https://www.bls.gov/sae/data/home.htm.

StatLink https://doi.org/10.1787/888934133457

Between 2000 and 2016, some sectors within the manufacturing industry in Ohio have grown rapidly, while others have diminished. By 2016, output in manufacturing of motor vehicles, trailers and cars had halved from 2000 levels (from USD 24.4 billion to USD 12.1 billion), while chemical manufacturing is now the largest manufacturing industry in Ohio, contributing USD 16 billion to the economy in 2016.

The required skillset of manufacturing employees has also evolved rapidly. Beyond traditional manufacturing-related competencies, employers in the United States are increasingly searching for people who have strong competence with computer-aided technologies, quality control, or engineering process improvement (Emsi, 2019[16]). The changing nature of manufacturing jobs and industries therefore creates a strong imperative for employers, policy makers and education institutions to upskill workforce in sufficient numbers to align with industry needs.

Sources: Bacher (2012[13]), Emsi (2019[16]), OECD (2018[12]), Ohio Manufacturers' Association (2018[14]), U.S. Bureau of Labor Statistics (2019[15]).

In Ohio's tight labour market, demand for skilled workforce is high, and likely to increase further in the future

The labour market in Ohio has been steadily adding jobs in the years following the 2008-09 economic and financial crisis. Non-farm employment has increased by almost 6% in the five years from 2014-19, with almost all sectors of the economy recording jobs growth in this period. Trade, transportation and utilities is the largest single sector of employment, accounting for more than 18% of non-farm employees in the state in January 2019. A further 17% of employees work in the education and health services sector. Other major sectors include the government sector (14% of employees) and professional and business services sector (13% of employees) (U.S. Bureau of Labor Statistics, 2019[15]).

Despite the changes in the manufacturing industry in Ohio in the most recent decade, the long-term labour market trend has been a steady shift towards service-providing industries. While the overall numbers in non-farm employment in Ohio at the beginning of 2019 were similar to the levels in 2000 (approximately 5.6 million people) the share employed in goods-producing jobs declined from 23% in 2000 to less than 17% in 2019 (U.S. Bureau of Labor Statistics, 2019[15]).

The labour market in Ohio has become tighter in recent years. The unemployment rate has steadily declined from a peak of 11.1% in January 2010 to 4.1% in November 2019, though it remains slightly higher than the national average. Over the same period the employment rate increased by more than two percentage points from a low point of 58.2% at the beginning of 2010. While some level of underemployment will always exist (as some graduates choose to work in non-graduate jobs and transition between education and graduate employment or between graduate jobs) in the tight labour market in Ohio, there is limited evidence of underemployment of higher education graduates. At the same time, as in other states, labour force participation has declined over the past decade, even as the number of available jobs has increased (Figure 4.2). The labour force participation rate in Ohio in November 2019 was just under 63%, similar to the national average level, and has remained close to this level since 2014. Many contributing factors to declining labour force participation have been identified, including changes in job quality, required skills and job location since the recession, as well as addiction problems and the ageing population (Hanauer and Mcgowan, 2019[17]).

As in many other states, a geographic mismatch is evident in Ohio, with larger metropolitan areas experiencing labour market shortages, while workers in many rural areas have difficulty finding jobs (OWT, 2018[18]). The highest unemployment rates are in Ohio's Appalachian regions, where around 15% of Ohio's labour force is located. Unemployment is above the state average in 30 of the 32 counties that comprise the Appalachian region, and surpasses 7% in three counties in the region (Monroe, Meigs and Adams). In other parts of the state, such as in Mercer Country, Delaware County and Wyandot County, the unemployment rate is below 3.5% (U.S. Bureau of Labor Statistics, 2019[19]).

The underlying demographic situation also indicates a likelihood of increasing demand for workers for many occupations into the future, as the number of jobs becoming vacant due to retirements continues to grow. Data from the Ohio Department of Jobs and Family Services indicate that the labour market is likely to add approximately 250 000 jobs between 2016 and 2026, putting even greater pressure on workforce supply (Ohio Department of Jobs and Family Services, 2018[20]).

Figure 4.2. Trends in the key labour market indicators in Ohio, 2009-19

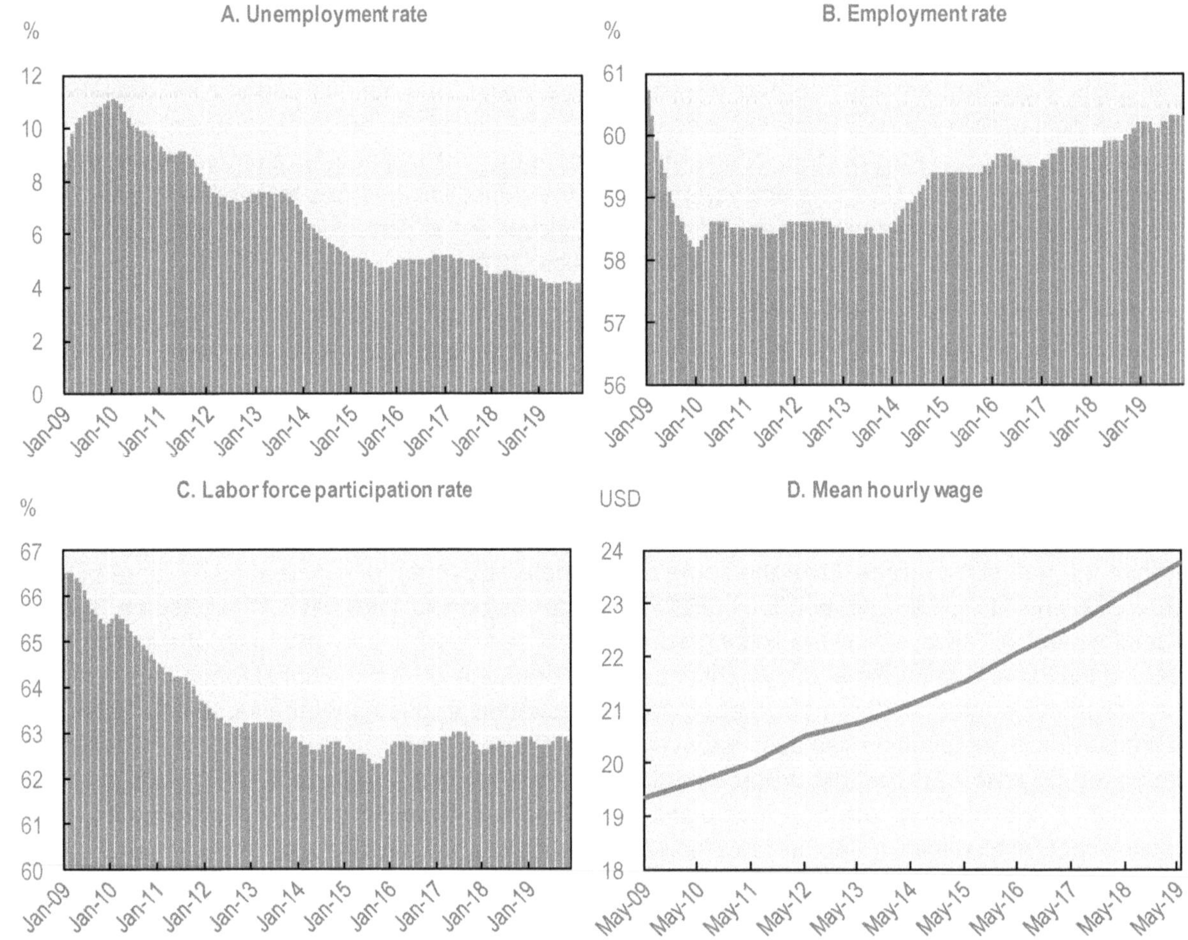

Notes: Data in panels A, B and C are seasonally adjusted. The labour force participation rate is defined as the percentage of people who are either employed or unemployed (but looking for jobs) out of the total civilian non-institutional population, which includes all individuals over the age of 16 who are potentially available for work. The employment rate is the percentage of people who are employed out of the total civilian non-institutional population. The unemployment rate is the percentage of people who are unemployed (but looking for jobs) out of all individuals in the labour force (employed or unemployed but looking for jobs). The mean hourly wage is not adjusted for inflation.

Sources: Panels A, B and C: U.S. Bureau of Labor Statistics (2019[21]), *Labor Force Statistics from the Current Population Survey* (database), https://www.bls.gov/cps/tables.htm; Panel D: U.S. Bureau of Labor Statistics (2019[22]), *Occupation Employment Statistics* (database), https://www.bls.gov/oes/home.htm.

StatLink https://doi.org/10.1787/888934133476

In 2018, around 43% of the young adult population (aged 25-34) had attained a post-secondary degree, while a further 22% had some college education but had not attained a degree[1] (Figure 4.3). These shares are slightly higher than the education levels in the population aged 25-64, where just over 40% have at least an associate's degree. Going forward, a key policy goal in Ohio is to raise educational attainment levels in the overall population substantially, to help ensure an adequate supply of workforce for existing middle- and high-skilled jobs, and emerging jobs of the future in the state (see Section 4.3). In general, higher levels of education also can help to insulate graduates against the effects of economic downturns: in the most recent economic crisis, beginning in 2008-09, unemployment in the OECD rose to more than 12% for those without upper secondary education, while remaining below 5% for higher education graduates (OECD, 2016[23]). Higher education graduates are also more likely to perform the non-routine jobs most resistant to automation, and are in a stronger position to pivot to new job profiles and keep pace with technological developments in the workplace (OECD, 2016[24]; OECD, 2019[25]).

Figure 4.3. Level of educational attainment for Ohio residents aged 25-34, 2018

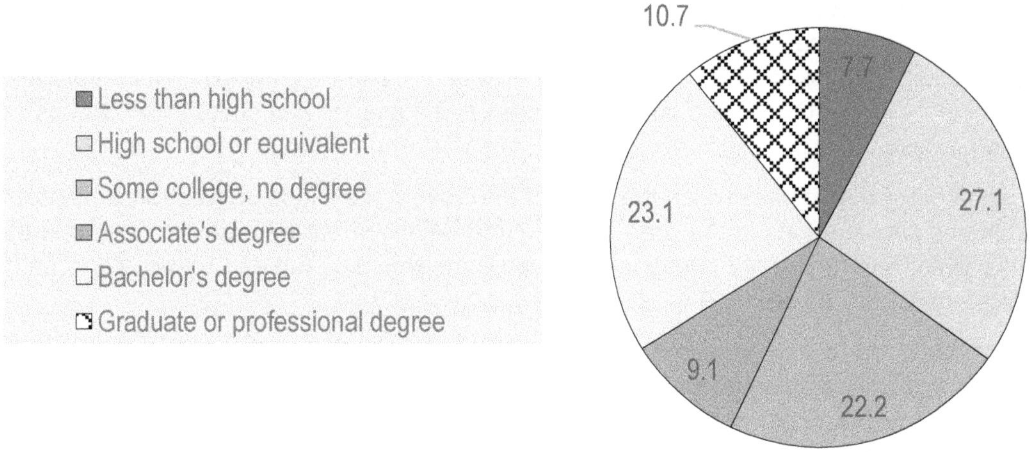

Source: U.S. Census Bureau (2019[26]), *American Community Survey 2018* (database), https://www.census.gov/programs-surveys/acs/data.html.

StatLink https://doi.org/10.1787/888934133495

The higher education system

The Ohio Department of Higher Education co-ordinates and oversees higher education in the state

The Ohio Department of Higher Education (ODHE), formerly known as the Ohio Board of Regents, is the cabinet-level agency that oversees higher education in Ohio. Originally created in 1963, the ODHE is led by the Chancellor of Higher Education, who is appointed by the Governor. The current Chancellor, Randy Gardner, was a long-standing member of the Ohio Legislature before being appointed by Governor DeWine in January 2019 to head the ODHE. With a permanent staff of around 80 people, the agency's main responsibilities include approving new degree programmes in public and private higher education institutions, managing the allocation of state funds to public higher education institutions, co-ordinating state-funded financial aid programmes, and supporting the state Legislature in policy making and budget planning. The ODHE operates under the direction of the Chancellor and Governor, and implements policy adopted by the General Assembly. Four permanent staff, including one of the Vice Chancellors, work specifically on higher education and workforce alignment.

Each of Ohio's 14 public universities and 23 community colleges is autonomously governed by its own board of trustees. Each institution has considerable autonomy in relation to designing its educational offerings, managing staffing and compensation levels, setting admission criteria, and determining internal quality assurance processes. Exceptions to institutional autonomy are set forth in the Ohio Revised Code and include, notably, compliance with state rules relating to programme approval, transfer and articulation, and tuition increases. As elsewhere in the United States, public and private institutions in Ohio have to comply with federal regulations relating to external accreditation in order to be eligible to receive federal student aid funding.

The Governor's Office of Workforce Transformation plays a central role in co-ordinating Ohio's skills and workforce policies

The Ohio General Assembly is the main driver of higher education policy in the state. Higher education objectives and initiatives are set forth in the biennial state operating budget, adopted every odd-numbered year, while any capital investments relating to higher education are included in the biennial capital budget adopted every even-numbered year. The Legislature also leads on the development of any specific higher education legislation or amendments to the Ohio Revised Code relating to higher education. The Legislature consults with the ODHE and other state executive agencies and stakeholder groups as part of its law-making process.

Higher education policy also comes within the remit of the Governor's Office of Workforce Transformation, which co-ordinates Ohio's efforts in the area of workforce development through direct co-operation with the ODHE, the Ohio Department of Education, the Ohio Department of Job and Family Services (ODJFS) and other state agencies (see Box 4.2).

Associations of higher education providers and employers also contribute to policy making in the field of higher education and workforce development. The Inter-University Council (IUC), for example, represents four-year public state universities, while the Ohio Association of Community Colleges (OACC) represents two-year public community colleges and the Association of Independent Colleges and Universities (AICUO) represents 51 major private universities and colleges in the state. The Ohio Chamber of Commerce, local chambers, and the Ohio Business Roundtable (Ohio BRT), representing the interests of major companies in Ohio, are among the employer organisations routinely involved in higher education and workforce policy.

Box 4.2. Governor's Office of Workforce Transformation in Ohio

Under the direct responsibility of the Lieutenant Governor, the Governor's Office of Workforce Transformation (OWT) seeks to co-ordinate Ohio's skills and workforce policies. Established in 2012, the Office acts as a dedicated co-ordination point between 17 state agencies, including the Departments of Education (ODE) and Higher Education (ODHE), Jobs and Family Services (ODJFS), Rehabilitation and Corrections (DRC), and the Governor's Office of Appalachia, responsible for regional development in the south east of the state.

Advised by the Governor's Executive Workforce Board, composed of leaders in business, education, and workforce development, the OWT's stated objective is to identify the needs of Ohio businesses and align workers' skills with those needs "to close the skills gap and get more people into rewarding careers". The OWT seeks to do this primarily though established priorities in the state workforce development plan (see Section 4.3) and by connecting Ohio's business, training and education communities to support skills development and workforce alignment.

Source: OWT (2020[27]).

The majority of students in Ohio attend public institutions, and there is an increasing focus on shorter-duration programmes of study

Post-secondary education in Ohio is provided by a diverse range of institutions. In addition to public and private four-year universities, there is an extensive network of public two-year community colleges and some private institutions delivering shorter-duration qualifications. In addition, the Ohio Technical Center (OTC) network delivers a range of courses leading to industry-recognised and vocational qualifications, and high school graduates can also pursue federal apprenticeships.

All public higher education institutions and some private institutions in Ohio are accredited by the Higher Learning Commission (HLC), one of six regional bodies responsible for institutional accreditation in the United States. The OTCs are accredited by a national agency, the Accrediting Commission of Career Schools and Colleges (Accrediting Commission of Career Schools and Colleges, 2020[28]), while other national agencies accredit the remainder of institutions. In total, there are about 250 institutions offering post-secondary education programmes based in the state, in the public and private sectors (Table 4.2).

Table 4.2. Post-secondary institutions in Ohio, 2019

	Public	Private	
		Not-for-profit	For-profit
Four-year institutions/Universities	14	68	11
Two-year institutions	23	8	49
Less than two-year institutions	53	5	23

Note: Only post-secondary institutions listed in the Integrated Postsecondary Education Data System (IPEDS) as being located in the state of Ohio are included in this table. Each institution is counted only once in the table, regardless of the number of campuses it operates.
Sources: ODHE (n.d.[29]), *Public Institution Profiles*, https://www.ohiohighered.org/campuses/map; NCES (2019[30]), *Integrated Postsecondary Education Data System* (database), https://nces.ed.gov/ipeds/use-the-data.

StatLink https://doi.org/10.1787/888934134806

In 2018, Ohio post-secondary institutions had more than 800 000 enrolled students across all institution types, making the state the seventh largest post-secondary education system in the United States in terms of enrolments (NCES, 2018[31]). Approximately half of the student body was enrolled in the 14 public four-year institutions, and more than one-quarter of students were enrolled in public two-year colleges (Figure 4.4). The majority of the private sector is made up of not-for-profit institutions, while enrolment in private for-profit colleges makes up about 4% of overall enrolment.

Figure 4.4. Annual enrolment in selected types of post-secondary education institutions, 2001-18

As a share of the total number of enrolled students

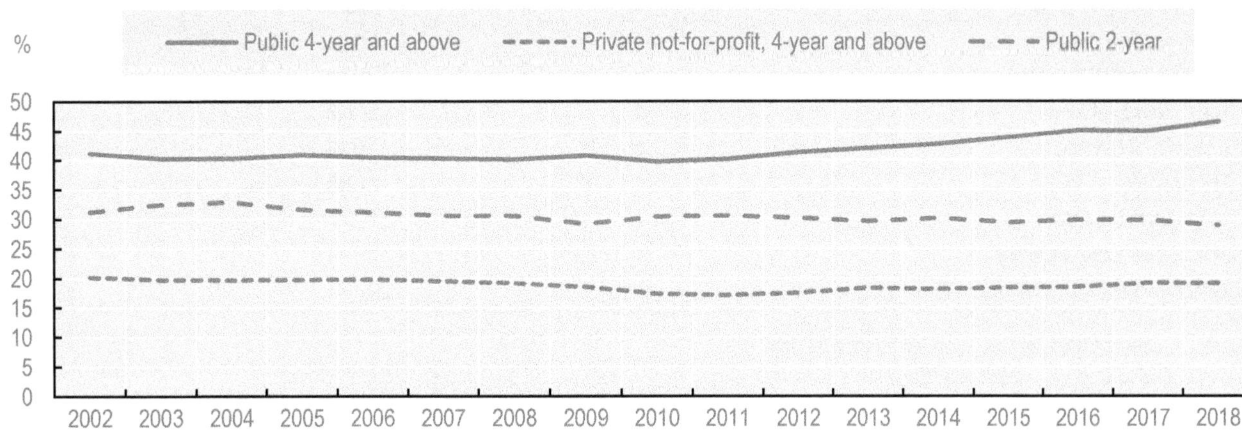

Source: NCES (2019[30]), *Integrated Postsecondary Education Data System* (database), https://nces.ed.gov/ipeds/use-the-data.

StatLink https://doi.org/10.1787/888934133514

While absolute numbers remain relatively small, an increasing number of young people in Ohio are availing themselves of federal apprenticeships, as an alternative to more traditional post-secondary options. In 2018, there were 28 000 apprentices enrolled in Ohio, double the 2011 level. This reflects the national trend of renewed interest in apprenticeships among young people; the number of new apprentices across the United States has increased steadily since 2011 (U.S. Department of Labor, 2019[32]).

Public four-year institutions

Ohio's 14 public four-year institutions educate the majority of post-secondary students in the state, awarding bachelor's (ISCED 6) and master's (ISCED 7) degrees, and providing doctoral-level training (ISCED 8). The public four-year sector in Ohio is also a major contributor to national research and development activity. Public universities in Ohio range from "open access" institutions, such as Central State University, Shawnee State University or Youngstown State University, to highly selective institutions such as Miami University and The Ohio State University. Six Ohioan public universities ranked in the top 200 institutions nationally in 2017 for expenditure on research and development (R&D), including The Ohio State University and the University of Cincinnati, which ranked 22nd and 54th respectively (National Science Foundation, n.d.[33]).

Many of the public state universities have regional branch campuses in addition to their main campus, which enhances accessibility to the public university system throughout the state. In total, about 17% of all public university students were attending branch campuses in 2018 (Table 4.3).

Table 4.3. Public university campuses and enrolment in Ohio, 2018

University	Number of campuses (main and regional)	Enrolment (main campus)	Enrolment (regional campuses)
Bowling Green State University	2	17 557	1 990
Central State University	1	2 066	a
Cleveland State University	1	16 298	a
Kent State University	8	28 318	16 303
Miami University	3	19 992	7 346
Northeast Ohio Medical University	1	944	a
Ohio University	6	29 026	10 091
The Ohio State University	6	61 610	7 301
Shawnee State University	1	3 289	a
The University of Akron	2	19 108	2 242
University of Cincinnati	3	38 988	11 399
The University of Toledo	1	20 258	a
Wright State University	2	14 276	1 534
Youngstown State University	1	12 614	a
Total enrolment	38	284 344	58 206

Note: Enrolment totals are based on fall headcount data.
Source: ODHE (n.d.[34]), *Headcount Enrollment Statistics*, https://www.ohiohighered.org/data-reports/enrollment.

StatLink https://doi.org/10.1787/888934134825

All of Ohio's public universities have arrangements that allow students to begin their studies at either a community college or a branch campus. This can help to defray costs substantially for students, by allowing them to continue to live with family or in their local region while beginning their post-secondary studies. For example, at community colleges, students who complete the Ohio Transfer Module and achieve an associate's degree with a designated transfer pathway become eligible to transfer to a main university campus (see Box 4.6). Students studying at regional university campuses can become eligible for transfer to the main campus after meeting a designated set of criteria, which can differ across institutions, but generally requires the completion of a minimum number of credit hours or attaining a minimum grade point average in college coursework.

At the same time, students can also complete their entire degree programmes at regional university campuses. Many of the branch campuses are specialised in particular fields of education, such as the Ohio State Agricultural and Technical Institute in Wooster or the Heritage Medical Clinic in the Cleveland campus of Ohio University.

Public sub-baccalaureate institutions

Public sub-baccalaureate institutions in Ohio comprise community colleges and Ohio Technical Centers. Ohio has 23 community colleges across the state, offering a range of sub-baccalaureate qualifications, including associate's degrees and certificates. As is the case in other US states, community colleges play an important role in improving access to post-secondary education in Ohio, and tend to serve a broader cross-section of the population than the public university sector. Under-represented populations represent a much larger share of enrolment in community colleges than in public or private four-year colleges (Table 4.4).

While the share of overall student enrolments at community colleges has remained reasonably steady in the past 10 years, in absolute numbers, enrolment in Ohio's community colleges has been in decline in the last decade, falling from a peak of about 315 000 in 2010/11 to just under 247 000 in 2017/18. This reflects, to some extent, the current high labour market demand in Ohio; in general, demand for community college education across the United States tends to fluctuate depending on prevailing local labour market conditions (Hillman and Orians, 2013[35]).

The OTC network, funded through the Ohio Department of Higher Education and located throughout the state, delivers a range of career and technical education. Programmes offered by the OTCs generally take between six and eighteen months to complete, and lead to the award of a vocationally-oriented industry certification or licence. In some cases, credits earned from completed OTC programmes are transferable to a degree programme at a two-year or four-year institution. During the 2016/17 academic year, just over 11 800 credentials were awarded by OTCs, an increase from the 9 657 awarded during 2012/13 (ODHE, 2019[36]). Community colleges are also increasingly offering students the opportunity to earn industry-recognised credentials, which can be in addition to, or integrated into, their more traditional offerings of associate's degrees or post-secondary certificates. These trends reflect the recent state-wide push to incentivise and improve "certificate productivity" in colleges and OTCs (Box 4.3).

Box 4.3. Improving certificate productivity in Ohio

In the last decade, Ohio state authorities have taken a number of steps to improve non-degree certificate productivity in career and technical education. Key actions have been as follows:

- In 2014, the state adopted new requirements on institutions for reporting certificates, and a new classification of certificates into technical certificates and general certificates, with a premium subsequently placed on technical certificates.
- A new process was developed to designate certificates as having labour market value, by ascertaining whether the certificate is specifically requested by employers in job advertisements, or by other means of demonstrating labour market value. The state maintains a public list of technical certificates that have achieved the labour market value criteria.
- Since 2016/17, state funding for Ohio Technical Centres is based completely on certificate productivity.
- Ohio has developed clear transfer pathways to degree programmes from many certificate programmes (see Section 4.3).

Source: ODHE (n.d.[37]).

Performance monitoring mechanisms for publicly funded career and technical education cover both community colleges and Career and Technical Centers. Under the Carl D. Perkins Career and Technical Education Act, introduced by the federal government in the 1980s and last re-authorised in 2018, states are required to develop accountability mechanisms for career and technical education providers, and report on key performance indicators, including non-traditional participation and completion, student retention and placement, and credential attainment. State performance targets for each of the indicators are negotiated with the U.S. Department of Education, and local performance targets are in turn agreed between the state and the institutions. Institutions that do not reach 90% of their target are required to submit a performance improvement plan to the state (Ohio Board of Regents, 2015[38]).

Private higher education institutions

The majority of students enrolled in private post-secondary institutions are in the not-for-profit sector, at four-year institutions, which is the third largest post-secondary sector in the state (Table 4.4). Institutions in this sector offer a range of undergraduate and graduate programmes across the state and vary in mission and orientation, encompassing comprehensive and research-active universities, religious colleges, liberal arts colleges and specialist institutions.

About 4% of students in Ohio attend private for-profit institutions. In general, the number of for-profit institutions across the United States has been in decline in recent years, following tightening of federal restrictions on eligibility for student financial aid at many institutions in this sector as part of the Gainful Employment regulations (National Student Clearinghouse Research Center, 2019[39]).

Table 4.4 provides a profile of public and private not-for-profit higher education institutions in Ohio.

Table 4.4. Profile of public and private not-for-profit higher education institutions in Ohio

	Public four-year institutions	Public two-year institutions	Private not-for-profit four-year institutions
Total student population (12 month enrolment, 2018)	389 550	257 646	165 929
Undergraduate students as a percentage of total enrolment (12 month enrolment, 2018)	80.2%	100%	75.5%
Percentage of total enrolments that are part-time (2018)	24.5%	71.0%	22.5%
Percentage of undergraduate students who are adult age (25 -64)	11.8%	14.1%	23.0%
Percentage of students who are from minority ethnic or racial groups (fall enrolment, 2018)	28.6%	32.0%	31.9%
Total number of post-secondary credentials awarded (2017)	78 395	33 356	34 670
Percentage of certificates awarded, out of total awarded credentials	2.2%	42.3%	1.5%
Percentage of associate's degrees awarded, out of total awarded credentials	7.5%	57.8%	8.2%
Percentage of bachelor's degrees awarded, out of total awarded credentials	62.9%	a	62.4%
Percentage of professional or master's degrees and above, total awarded credentials	27.4%	a	27.9%
First-year retention rate for first-time, full-time undergraduate students (fall 2018)	81.2%	62.6%	81.2%
Average tuition and mandatory fees for full-time in-state undergraduate students, (2017/18)	USD 10 026	USD 3 672	USD 31 242
Percentage of full-time first-time students availing of a federal student loan (2016/17)	56.5%	43.7%	71.1%

Notes: These figures are based on information from Ohio-based higher education institutions that are eligible for federal (Title IV) funding and that are required to report student-level data to state and federal authorities. Colleges and universities that do not receive some forms of federal or state-funded student assistance, are therefore not included. The 150% graduation rate refers to the percentage of graduates who completed their degree within one and a half times the normal completion time; that is, 6 years for a four-year degree and 3 years for a two-year degree. The completion rate for four-year institutions is based on the 2012/13 graduate cohort and the completion rate for two-year institutions is based on the 2011/12 graduate cohort.

Sources: NCES (2019[30]), *Integrated Postsecondary Education Data System* (database), https://nces.ed.gov/ipeds/use-the-data; NCES (2018[31]), *Digest of Educational Statistics 2018*, https://nces.ed.gov/programs/digest/.

StatLink https://doi.org/10.1787/888934134844

4.2. Assessment of labour market outcomes: The alignment between supply and demand of graduate skills in Ohio

Alignment of supply and demand

The share of jobs requiring a post-secondary credential in Ohio is expected to increase rapidly in the coming years

Public authorities in Ohio use projections of labour market needs to inform workforce planning. The Bureau of Labour Market Information in the Ohio Department of Jobs and Family Services (ODJFS) produces projections of jobs by occupation and type of qualification required, which are updated at regular intervals. A "Short-term Outlook" provides a near-term indication based on current trends, while longer-term projections anticipate employment needs over the coming decade. The Department of Jobs and Family Services also periodically publishes a list of in-demand occupations, compiled using statistics on job openings, labour market outcomes, a survey of employers and recent employment trends. In addition to informing potential students about career areas with the best employment prospects, the in-demand jobs list is used to prioritise the allocation of funding towards producing new credentials. For example, the state requires that at least 85% of federal funding allocated under the Workforce Innovation and Opportunity (WIOA) Program is invested in programmes related to in-demand occupations.

The Bureau of Labour Market Information classifies occupations according to the typical experience and education required for entry to the occupation, as assigned by staff in the U.S. Bureau of Labor Statistics (U.S. Bureau of Labor Statistics, 2019[40]). According to the latest long-term occupational projections, overall, about 40% of jobs in Ohio in 2026 will require a post-secondary credential as a minimum standard for entry (Ohio Department of Jobs and Family Services, 2018[20]). Demand for workforce with post-secondary credentials is expected to increase particularly strongly in certain occupational groups, including healthcare and technical practitioners, education and training, management, and business and financial operations. However, most occupational groups are likely to either maintain current demand levels, or surpass them by 2026 (

Figure 4.5).

Figure 4.5. Projected employment growth in occupations that typically require post-secondary education, 2016-26

Total number of jobs, based on long-term occupational projections for Ohio

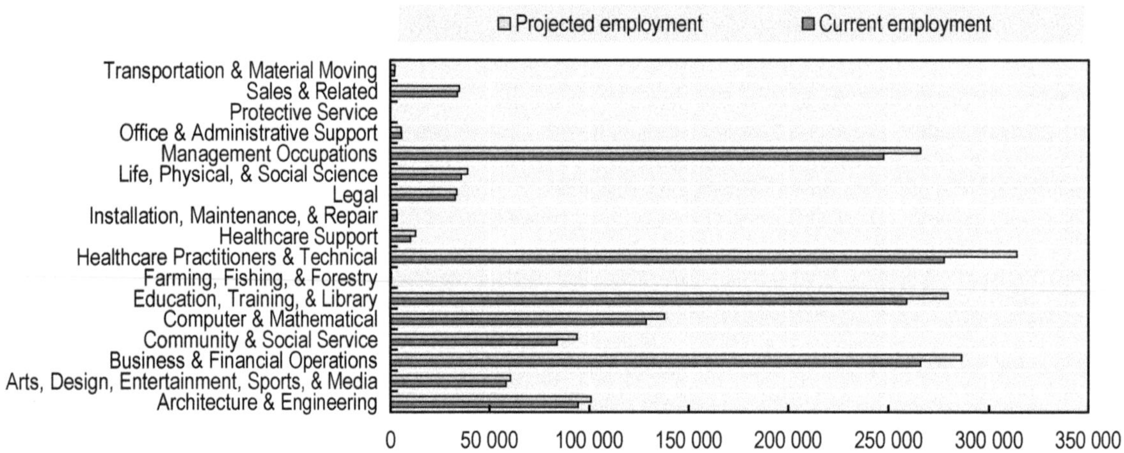

Note: Occupational groupings are based on the Bureau of Labour Statistics Standard Occupational Classification. See the Reader's Guide for more details.
Source: Ohio Department of Jobs and Family Services (2018[41]), *Ohio Job Outlook*, http://www.ohiolmi.com/proj/OhioJobOutlook.htm.

StatLink https://doi.org/10.1787/888934133533

The projection by the ODJFS of 40% of jobs requiring a post-secondary qualification by 2026 is likely to be overly conservative, as it is based on the minimum educational requirements for entry into an occupation, assumes that educational requirements will not change over time, and may not adequately capture emerging jobs in rapidly evolving fields. Analysis by the Georgetown Center on Education and the Workforce (CEW) showed that, in 2010, actual education levels of those employed in various occupations were substantially higher than the minimum level indicated by the U.S. Bureau of Labor Statistics. Alternative projections of educational demand by CEW, based on these actual education levels across occupation, and employment growth rates by industry, indicated that by 2020, 65% of all jobs nationally would require at least some post-secondary education (Carnevale, Smith and Strohl, 2013[42]). Within this 65%, 18% of jobs are expected to require a level of "some college or post-secondary certificate", while the remaining 47% of jobs are projected to require at least an associate's degree. Ohio policy makers have adopted this higher projection of 65% of workers requiring post-secondary education as the most likely scenario (Demaria, Carey and Burgess, 2018[43]).

The higher level of actual qualifications among staff across various occupations may, to some extent, reflect a trend of "credential inflation" observed across the United States and other economies, with employers demanding higher credentials for jobs that traditionally would have required a high school diploma only (Fuller and Raman, 2017[44]). At the same time, it is evident that the world of work is changing rapidly, as more routine jobs become vulnerable to automation, new job types emerge, and the nature of many existing jobs is evolving as technology becomes more embedded across occupations (OECD, 2019[25]). Research by Burning Glass Technologies on employer needs indicates a new set of skills is rapidly becoming foundational in today's digitalised economy: digital building block skills, such as data management and programming; business enabling skills (such as project management and business process); and "human skills" (such as critical thinking, collaboration and problem solving) (Burning Glass Technologies, 2019[45]). In this context, public authorities across the United States have identified high-quality post-secondary education credentials as the best means to develop and demonstrate the broad range of skills and competencies demanded in the contemporary labour market.

Many of the jobs on the most recent list of in-demand jobs compiled by the Ohio Department of Jobs and Family Services do not necessarily require a post-secondary qualification, or even a high school qualification. For example, the highest identified demand is for labourers, customer service representatives and office clerks, none of which specify a post-secondary credential as a necessary minimum level of education (Table 4.5). At the same time, 56% of all of the occupations on the list require post-secondary attainment as a minimum level (Ohio Department of Jobs and Family Services, 2018[20]). This reflects the wider trend across the United States of job growth concentrating in areas where post-secondary credentials are required; national employment projections show that 15 of the 20 fastest-growing occupations require some post-secondary education (U.S. Bureau of Labor Statistics, 2019[46]).

Table 4.5. The top ten in-demand jobs in Ohio and typical education required, 2019

Job title	Typical Education Required	Employment	Annual Job openings
Laborers/Freight/Stock/Material Movers, Hand	No formal educational credential	111 616	16 347
Customer Service Representatives	High school diploma or equivalent	90 387	11 757
Office Clerks, General	High school diploma or equivalent	94 521	10 498
Registered Nurses	Bachelor's degree	129 954	8 848
Truck Drivers, Heavy and Tractor-Trailer	Post-secondary non-degree award	76 084	8 465
Nursing Assistants	Post-secondary non-degree award	68 537	8 184
Secretaries, except Legal, Medical, and Executive	High school diploma or equivalent	83 502	7 758
Bookkeeping, Accounting and Auditing Clerks	Some college, no degree	66 288	6 928
Landscaping and Grounds-keeping Workers	No formal educational credential	45 531	5 908
Maintenance and Repair Workers, General	High school diploma or equivalent	56 262	5 895

Note: Job titles are based on the Bureau of Labor Statistics Standard Occupational Classification; see the Reader's Guide for more details.
Source: OhioMeansJobs (2019[47]), *In-demand occupations list*, http://omj.ohio.gov/OMJResources/In-DemandOccupations.stm.

StatLink https://doi.org/10.1787/888934134863

Unmet demand for post-secondary education is already evident in many sectors of the economy in Ohio. Shortages of graduates with a post-secondary credential have become acute in many occupations (see the next section), and are likely to increase in the future. It has been estimated that the greatest shortages across the state are likely to occur in middle-skill jobs: those that require some post-secondary education but not a bachelor's degree (National Skills Coalition, 2017[48]; JP Morgan Chase and Co, 2015[49]). As a result, there is a collective focus within both the higher education system and wider workforce development policy on increasing the output of graduates with certificates and other shorter-term post-secondary credentials, such as industry certifications, as discussed in the next section.

Credential awards are increasing, particularly for short-term certificates, but Ohio will not reach its attainment goal at current levels of output

Given evidence of widespread and deepening shortages of workers with post-secondary education, states across the United States are responding by putting greater emphasis on workforce development (see Chapter 2). Ohio is 1 of 42 states that has placed quantifiable and ambitious post-secondary attainment goals at the centre of its workforce development strategy (Lumina Foundation, 2019[50]). In 2018, the Governor's Office of Workforce Transformation, the Ohio Department of Education and the Ohio Department of Higher Education jointly endorsed a state-wide goal for post-secondary attainment: by 2025 65% of Ohioans aged 25-64 should have a post-secondary credential of value in the workplace (Demaria, Carey and Burgess, 2018[43]; Ohio Board of Regents, 2015[51]).

State authorities have estimated that, in order to achieve the 2025 attainment goal, Ohio will need to produce almost one million additional credentials in total between 2017 and 2025 (Ohio Board of Regents, 2015[51]). The establishment of the numerical goal provides a common focus for all organisations and agencies in the state with a role to play in workforce development. Ohio has also taken steps to monitor advancement towards the goal at the state level, by tracking levels of post-secondary attainment in the state and producing regular progress reports.

Ohio has made notable gains in the past decade on post-secondary attainment, even as overall enrolments in post-secondary education have fallen. By 2017, an estimated 45% of adults aged 25-64 had a degree or workforce-relevant post-secondary certificate, compared to 35% in 2008[2] (ODHE, 2020[52]). Within the 45%, around 5% hold post-secondary certificates, while the remaining 40% hold a degree. The overall volume of credentials awarded has also gradually risen in the last decade, with increases recorded in awards at all levels (Figure 4.6). As discussed in Section 4.3, the introduction of a performance-based award formula for the State Share of Instruction in 2012, which allocates funding to post-secondary institutions based on completion of qualifications and courses, incentivises institutions to increase the volume of credentials awarded annually.

Figure 4.6. Trends in the production of degrees by education level, 2009-18

Number of degrees awarded annually

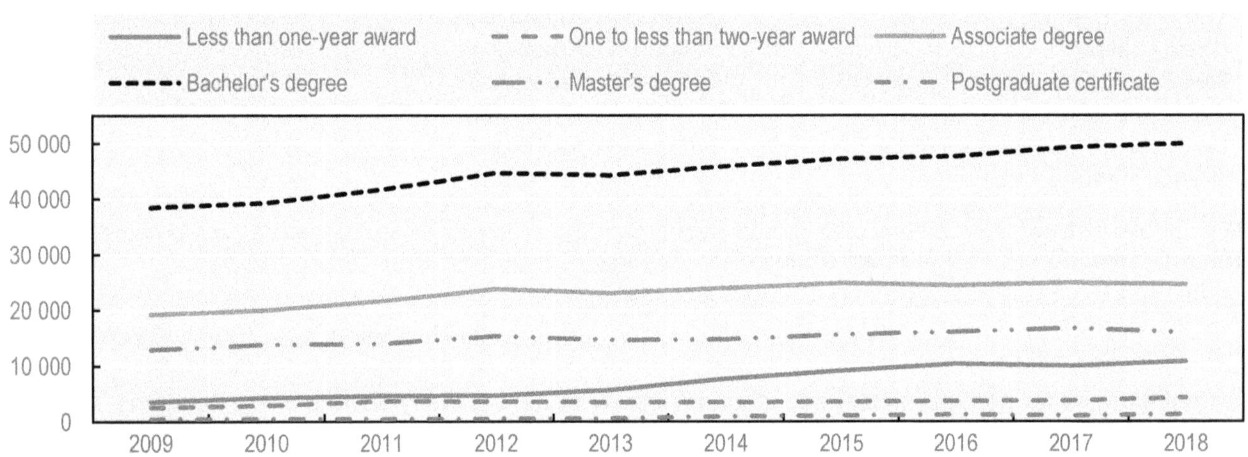

Note: See Reader's Guide for further information on credential education levels.
Source: ODHE (2019[36]), *Degrees & Certificates Awarded at Ohio Institutions* (database), https://www.ohiohighered.org/data-reports/degrees.

StatLink https://doi.org/10.1787/888934133552

In absolute numbers, the greatest increase in awards has been at the bachelor's level, where annual degrees awarded increased from 38 483 in 2009 to 49 963 in 2018. However, credential output has expanded most substantially at the less-than-one-year award level, where credential output has more than tripled since 2009 and reached an annual level of 10 800 awards in 2018 (Figure 4.6). This category of credentials are defined in Ohio as awards for completion of organised programmes of less than 30 semester credit hours, or less than 900 clock hours, that are designed for an occupation or specific employment opportunities (for technical certificates) and completion of an organised programme of study at sub-baccalaureate level of less than one year (for general certificates). These awards made up 14% of all qualifications awarded in 2018, compared to 7% in 2009, reflecting Ohio's focus in recent years on non-degree employment-oriented credentials as a cost-effective way to upskill the population (ODHE, n.d.[37]).

Despite increases in output at all levels of post-secondary credentials, current trends indicate that the increases in awards at all levels are not at the scale needed to reach the attainment goal in 2025. An extra one million credentials between 2017 and 2025, achieved linearly over time, indicate that annual award production would need to be more than double its 2018 level of around 105 000 awards. Latest projections from Lumina Foundation, based on the rates of increase in credential completions in recent years, show that the post-secondary attainment rate among adults is unlikely to surpass 50% by 2025 if current trends continue (Lumina Foundation, 2019[53]).This highlights the challenge ahead for Ohio.

Skills shortages are evident in many fields and industries, creating risks for Ohio's economy

Across Ohio, many economic sectors are experiencing an ongoing struggle to fill open positions. A 2015 analysis by the National Skills Coalition found that shortages were most severe in the middle-skill jobs category, where 55% of jobs in the economy are concentrated, but only 47% of total workers are qualified at the appropriate level (National Skills Coalition, 2017[48]). However, across the state, shortages of workers at all skill levels are evident. In the Northeast, for example, there is a severe shortage of manufacturing and construction professionals; health professionals and technicians; architects; finance and business professionals; and supervisors of skilled workers (Team NEO, 2019[54]).

Skills shortages create both economic and social risks across Ohio. During the Ohio fact-finding mission, the OECD review team heard from business leaders that shortages of qualified workers in some industries are resulting in a "rush to automate" to support continued business growth in the face of a lack of qualified workers. In the manufacturing industry, employers rank the lack of qualified workers as the number one challenge hampering growth. In 2019, 53% of employers in the sector reported that worker shortages would directly affect profits in their company, an increase from 45% in 2017 (MAGNET, 2019[55]).

The social impact of skills shortages can also be acute. Healthcare practitioner coverage is identified as insufficient in 59 geographic areas across Ohio (Health Resources and Services Administration, 2020[56]). In Appalachia, there are shortages of paediatric primary care providers, dentists and mental health providers, as well as early childhood education and care providers. This creates risks for the healthy growth and development of children in the region (Children's Defense Fund, 2016[57]). As in many other states, Ohio is also dealing with a shortage of education professionals, including arts and science teachers, Teaching English as a Second Language (TESOL) teachers, teachers for special educational needs and school psychologists (Office of Postsecondary Education, 2017[58]).

At the same time, there are indications that the supply of new credentials to the labour market in many high-demand areas is stagnant or decreasing. While overall, the volume of credentials awarded is on an upward trajectory in Ohio, the share of qualifications in many fields experiencing labour market shortages has declined in the past decade (Figure 4.7). For example, despite acute labour market shortages, the share of credentials of all types awarded in the field of education has declined from 2008 to 2018, with annual output of more advanced qualifications falling sharply (by more than 25% for bachelor's degrees and more than 45% for master's degrees). In health, while the overall volume of qualifications awarded increased by about 25% between 2008 and 2018, certificate and associate's degree production has decreased over the same period (Figure 4.7).

Figure 4.7. Qualifications awarded in selected fields of education, 2008-18

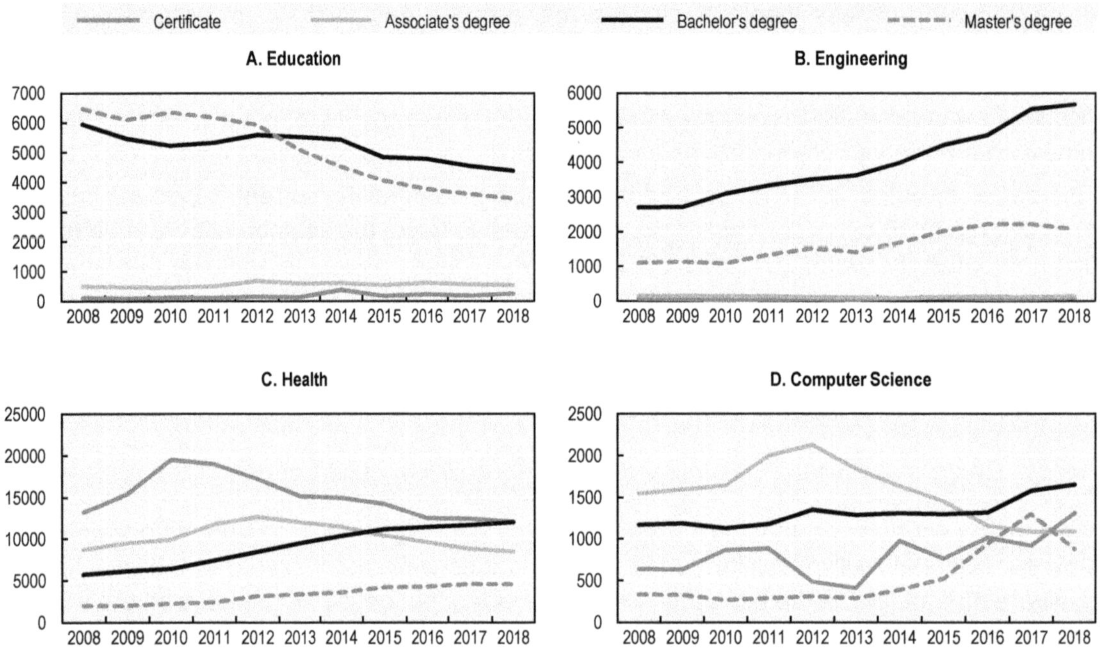

Source: Adapted from NCES (2019[30]), *Integrated Postsecondary Education Data System* (database), https://nces.ed.gov/ipeds/use-the-data.

StatLink https://doi.org/10.1787/888934133571

Outside of increasing its own production of skilled workforce, there appear to be limited opportunities for Ohio to mitigate the economic risks created by skills shortages. Across the OECD, many jurisdictions have taken measures to encourage migration of skilled workers, as a means to shore up local labour supply and address acute skills shortages, including expanding existing programmes and the range of occupations eligible for award of a visa (OECD, 2019[59]). Immigrants accounted for 8% of the high-skilled workforce in Ohio in the period 2009-13, double the share of immigrants in the overall Ohio population, and were less likely to be subject to underemployment than elsewhere in the United States (Batalova, Fix and Bachmeier, 2016[60]). However, declines in immigration across the United States and restrictions in scope to the main skilled labour visa programme (H1-B)[3] limit the potential to fill acute skills needs through immigration. This puts an even greater onus on the workforce development system in Ohio to meet its future labour market needs by upskilling a larger share of its incumbent population.

Some notable differences also exist in attainment between racial and ethnic groups and gender across different fields of study (Figure 4.8). For example, Black/African American graduates are less likely to be awarded a degree or certificate in some fields that are highly valued in the labour market such as mathematics and statistics, engineering and computer and information services; about 4% of all degrees awarded to Black/African American graduates are in these fields, compared to more than 7% of all degrees awarded to Whites, and about 13% of all degrees awarded to Asians.

These differences shown in Figure 4.8 indicate that some high-value fields of study or those with labour market shortages appear to be currently less accessible to certain population groups. Drivers of these differences can be linked to underlying socio-economic patterns, or reflect wider stereotypical or cultural beliefs related to fields of study. Regardless, their impact is to reduce the overall size of the available talent pool for these fields in Ohio. Identifying and tackling the underlying reasons for variations in field of study choice by gender or race/ethnicity is therefore likely to be an ongoing policy concern in the future in Ohio, as in other jurisdictions.

Figure 4.8. Certificates/degrees awarded by race/ethnicity, gender and field of study, 2018

As a percentage of all certificates/degrees awarded to each demographic group

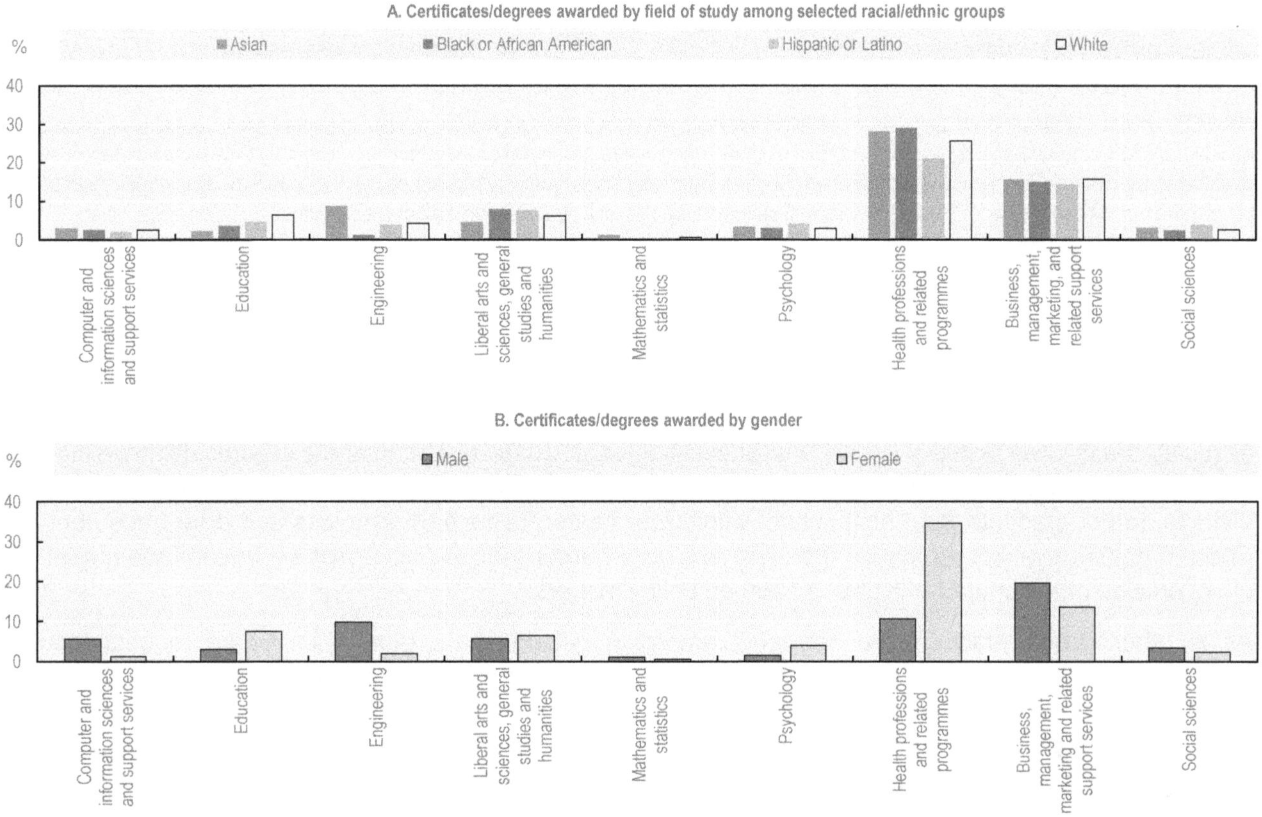

Note: The figure includes all credentials awarded from certificate to doctoral level.
Source: Adapted from NCES (2019[30]), *Integrated Postsecondary Education Data System* (database), https://nces.ed.gov/ipeds/use-the-data.

StatLink https://doi.org/10.1787/888934133590

Bottlenecks and barriers in the pipeline

Addressing imbalances in post-secondary attainment between different population groups is vital to meeting Ohio's state-wide attainment goal

As discussed above, at current rates of enrolment and completion in post-secondary education programmes, Ohio is unlikely to meet its ambitious target for post-secondary education attainment. A number of supply-side factors create leaks in the talent pipeline and impede progress towards the goal. Firstly, the overall volume of students passing through the high school system has been decreasing in Ohio in recent years. In addition, a sizeable share of the young student population does not make it to high school graduation, or graduates without the necessary knowledge and skills for college-level study (Table 4.6).

Table 4.6. Indicators on upper secondary education imbalances in Ohio

Indicator	Value	Indicator	Value
Change in enrolment in Ohio public schools, 2006 to 2018	-6%	Share of Ohio students meeting college readiness standards across all four benchmarks (reading, science, math and English),2018	25%
Share of economically disadvantaged students, 2018	50%	Share of Ohio students meeting college readiness standards in reading, 2018	43%
Share of students living in poverty, 2017	20%	Four-year high school graduation rates, state-wide, 2018	84%
Share of students in urban, high or very high poverty school districts, 2018	29%	Four-year high school graduation rates, urban school districts, 2018	72%

Note: Students are generally identified as economically disadvantaged via federal meal programs, open to pupils from households with incomes at or below 185% of federal poverty levels. Through a recently enacted program known as the Community Eligibility Provision, a certain number of students are deemed economically disadvantaged even though they come from households above 185% poverty. In contrast, children in poverty are from households at or below 100% federal poverty; they also include some non-school-aged children.
Source: Adapted from Thomas B Fordham Institute (2019[61]), *Ohio education by the numbers: 2019 statistics*, http://ohiobythenumbers.com/.

StatLink https://doi.org/10.1787/888934134882

Other barriers to increasing the availability of skilled workforce are also evident. One in two Ohio school students is classified as economically disadvantaged, and one in five students lives in poverty, both factors associated with lower levels of educational success (OECD, 2018[62]). Urban areas in particular have higher poverty rates and lower high school graduation rates in Ohio; almost 30% of high school students in urban districts do not graduate from high school within four years (Table 4.6). The loss and disengagement of talent in earlier levels of education therefore is a core barrier to increasing post-secondary attainment in Ohio, outside of the control of higher education policy makers.

As in other states, stark imbalances exist among population subgroups with regard to educational achievement, and ability to access the enhanced labour market prospects that post-secondary education brings. For example, while about 40% of the White population had at least a post-secondary certificate in Ohio in 2018, the share of the Black and Hispanic population with post-secondary education reached only 27%, a gap of more than 13 percentage points (Lumina Foundation, 2019[50]).

There is also a widening gender gap in post-secondary attainment – the female post-secondary attainment rate reached almost 49% in 2018, compared to just under 41% for males (ODHE, 2020[52]). The size of the gender gap has increased in recent years, mirroring the trend across the OECD of women pulling ahead on educational attainment (OECD, 2019[63]). Furthermore, gender gaps in achievement are more pronounced for some already lower-achieving groups, such as Black and Hispanic students and those from lower-income backgrounds. The intersection of group inequalities further increases the educational barriers faced by some subgroups and creates more extreme gaps in achievement.

State projection models of future attainment levels indicate that a range of adjustments to tackle the leaky pipeline would be required to increase the volume of credentials over current levels to the extent needed to approach Ohio's goal of almost 1 million additional credentials by 2025. Table 4.7 shows the projected numbers of additional credentials that could be obtained under a number of different conditions related to individual variables, as calculated by the Ohio Department of Higher Education attainment goal projection model (ODHE, 2018[64]). For example, if the state managed to boost both high school graduation rates and post-secondary enrolment rates to the same levels as the top three states in the United States, it would contribute about 5% of the additional credentials required to meet the goal (Table 4.7). This reflects the demographic situation in Ohio, where the additional credentials gained by increasing high school completion and post-secondary enrolment would be offset, to some extent, by smaller cohorts of young people in the education system. Increasing the enrolment of adult learners to the levels of the top three states would also contribute an additional 5% of credentials to the goal.

Table 4.7. Projected additional credentials produced during 2017-25 under different scenarios

Scenario	Projected additional credentials 2017-25	Percentage of overall required additional credentials (966 000)
The high school graduation rate raised to the average level of the top three states in the U.S. (90%)	7 430	<1.0%
The post-secondary enrolment rate raised to the average level of the top three states in the U.S. (67%)	44 517	4.6%
First time enrolment of adult learners raised to the average level of the top three states in the U.S. (22% for 20-24 year-olds and 4.4% for 25-44 year-olds)	47 921	5.0%
Converging the attainment levels among different under-represented minority groups to the expected 2025 level for the White non-Hispanic population (51%)	136 090	14.1%
Converging male attainment levels to the expected 2025 attainment level for the female population (54%)	328 835	34.0%

Note: Projected additional credentials refer to potential additional credentials produced under the given change in conditions alone, compared to the continuation of 2016 enrolment and completion rates. Projections also aim to consider future demographic change.
Source: ODHE (2018[64]), *Attainment Goal Projection Tool,* https://www.ohiohighered.org/attainment/projection-tool.

StatLink https://doi.org/10.1787/888934134901

However, the projections indicate that closing gaps in attainment is by far the most promising pathway for Ohio to meet its attainment goal. Table 4.7 shows that addressing existing attainment imbalances between different population subgroups is likely to yield the most dramatic increases in attainment, compared to increasing overall high school completion, post-secondary enrolment rates, or enrolment in the adult population. The most promising avenues for increasing attainment may therefore be to strongly target attainment gaps between different sub-populations. For example, elevating the attainment rate of Black/African American, Hispanic, Native American and Alaska Native adults to the same level as the expected attainment rate of White adults by 2025 would contribute approximately 14% of the additional qualifications required to reach the goal. Raising the attainment rate of males to match the expected rate of females by 2025 would contribute about 34% of the required credentials to meet the goal (Table 4.7).

Much is already being done at the school level in Ohio to close achievement gaps between different groups of the population, and targeting increased achievement in particularly vulnerable subgroups. For example, schools are regularly evaluated on their ability to improve the achievement of students with disabilities, from lower-income backgrounds, and from disadvantaged minority groups (Ohio Department of Education, n.d.[65]). However, the underlying trends and future projections imply that Ohio will need to step up policy actions to close gaps, in order to achieve the attainment goal. Ohio could also consider defining more granular targets to support the goal that prioritise increasing throughput in areas with the most pressing need, or closing gaps between different subgroups.

Brain drain, economic imbalances across the state, and wider social issues slow down progress towards the goal

Across the OECD, regional inequalities have been compounded in the years following the 2008-09 economic crisis, as urbanisation continues to progress and regional differences in productivity and economic growth persist (OECD, 2019[66]). In the United States, employment growth rates in larger cities have far surpassed that of smaller cities and non-metro areas. While employment grew by over 14% in metro areas with a population of 1 million or more between 2010 and 2016, the growth rate in non-metro areas over the same period was at just over 2% (Muro and Whitman, 2018[67]). Intra-state economic inequalities are also pronounced within Ohio, where 10 of the 88 counties were responsible for more than

60% of Ohio's overall GDP in 2018, and the bottom 40 counties combined contributed less than 10% of the state's GDP (U.S. Bureau of Economic Analysis, 2019[68]).

Overall, Ohio is one of the US states that has experienced a net "brain drain" in the last decades, as highly educated young adults migrate to other states in greater numbers than those choosing to relocate from out-of-state to Ohio (United States Joint Economic Committee, 2019[69]). However, the economic imbalances within the state also create additional regional brain drain and contribute to differences in educational achievement across Ohio, as highly educated workers are attracted to areas of the state with better labour market prospects, contributing further to brain drain in certain regions of the state. As Figure 4.9 shows, in 17 out of Ohio's 88 counties, less than one in four adults has an associate's degree or higher, while in 8 counties around half of adults have a degree (Figure 4.9).

The geographic spread of attainment across the state reflects the difficulty in ensuring that employers in some regions can access an adequate pipeline of the skills they need. Concentration of talent in dynamic areas such as Columbus and Cincinnati can create some of the new economic activity the state needs, and help to achieve the attainment goal by providing attractive environments that encourage graduates to remain in the state. However, this also presents economic risks to areas of the state that may lose vital talent to major urban regions. The review team heard about the difficulties that employers faced in a number of regions to attract and retain suitably qualified workforce. Hence, it is important to ensure that workforce policy and regional development policy are closely aligned and complementary to each other (see Section 4.3).

Figure 4.9. Attainment rate of adults (25-64) in Ohio counties, 2017

Share of adults in the county with at least an associate's degree

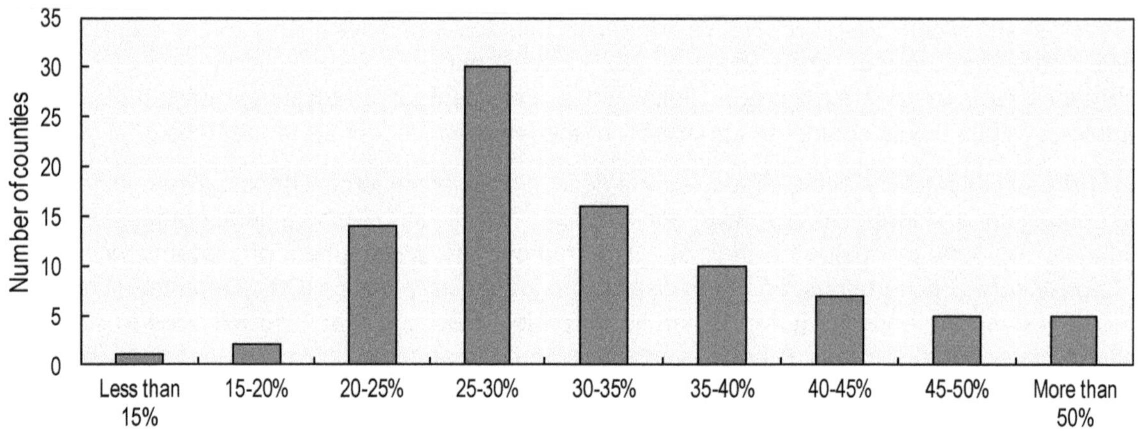

Source: U.S. Census Bureau (2019[26]), *American Community Survey 5-year Estimates (2013-2017)*, https://www.census.gov/programs-surveys/acs/data.html.

StatLink https://doi.org/10.1787/888934133609

Economic stagnation and population decline also limit labour market opportunities and rewards in some areas of Ohio, and reduce the incentives for the local population to pursue post-secondary education. This is further compounded by the difficulty that the population in some disadvantaged rural areas can face to physically access post-secondary educational opportunities and improve their skills, as a result of being located in "education deserts" (Hillman and Weichman, 2016[70]). Indeed, the OECD review team in Ohio heard a number of times during their review visit that lack of transportation was a significant impediment to accessing both education and the labour market in some areas of the state.

At the same time, while talent tends to flow from rural to urban areas and physical access to education in rural areas is more difficult, a sizeable share of urban populations in the state face obstacles of their own to accessing post-secondary education. As discussed in the previous section, students in urban school districts across the state have lower high school completion rates, and lower rates of transfer to post-secondary education than suburban or rural students (Table 4.6). Urban poverty rates have also been on the increase in recent years (Ohio Development Services Agency, 2019[9]). Improving educational success in high-poverty urban areas of Ohio can increase the available pool of talent to meet labour market needs, as well as reduce overall economic inequality. The state-wide introduction of a new rating system and a wider suite of data and indicators for public schools in 2017 has the potential to allow policy makers to more systematically identify the greatest areas of difficulty, and highlight practices of schools that are successful despite adverse socio-economic conditions (Churchill, 2019[71]).

Given its ageing population and labour market shortages, Ohio more than many other US states needs to remove social barriers for access to and completion of post-secondary educational offerings. This arguably puts greater pressure on policy makers to work together to overcome social issues and contextual challenges that are not directly related to post-secondary education, but have an impact on the supply of available workforce, such as poverty, transportation, and problems of addiction.

Output from workforce programs related to post-secondary education has been flat in recent years, and there is some evidence of bottlenecks in selected fields

Ohio has put a heavy focus on workforce development in recent years, particularly following the establishment of the Governor's Office of Workforce Transformation in 2012 (Box 4.2). The Office co-ordinates many innovative state-level initiatives to upskill the population, as well as Ohio's participation in federal workforce development programmes. While workforce programmes make up a relatively minor component of overall education provision in the state, most programmes have at least some objectives that relate to post-secondary attainment. Workforce programmes also play an important role in improving access to education for under-represented and disadvantaged groups. For example, two key state-led policies are the Choose Ohio First Scholarship Program (see Section 4.3) and the Aspire Program for adult learners needing additional support to earn a post-secondary qualification (ODHE, n.d.[72]). The federal Workforce Innovation and Opportunity Act (WIOA) also provides funding for education and training to unemployed and under-employed young people in Ohio; one of its objectives is to increase post-secondary attainment (Ohio Department of Jobs and Family Services, 2017[73]).

Available data on workforce development initiatives indicate that the scale of provision in many of the state's core workforce alignment programmes is likely to make only a modest impact on overall post-secondary attainment. Furthermore, in some programmes, completions have decreased since monitoring of the programmes began in 2012. For example, completions in the Choose Ohio First initiative peaked at 1 257 in 2014/15, and reduced to 731 by 2016/17 (Figure 4.10). Completions in apprenticeships also remained flat, at around 1 500 annually, over the period 2012/13 to 2016/17.

Figure 4.10. Completion trends in key workforce initiatives in Ohio, 2013-17

Total number of individuals completing a key workforce initiative

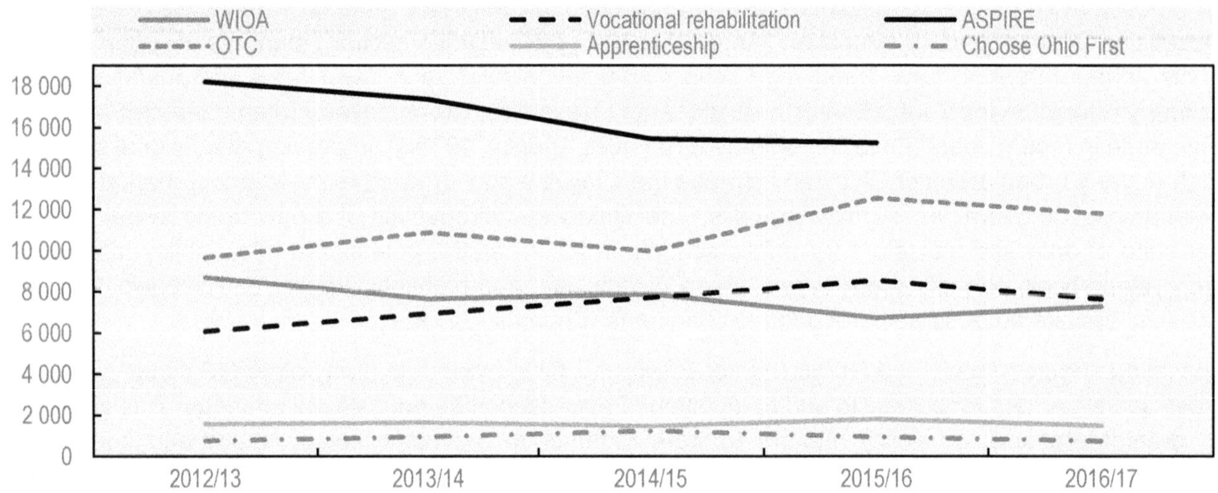

Note: Data on completions for the ASPIRE Program in 2016/17 are not currently available.
Source: OWT (n.d.[74]), *Workforce Success Measures*, https://workforcesuccess.chrr.ohio-state.edu/home.

StatLink https://doi.org/10.1787/888934133628

Decreasing or even stable trends in completion across workforce programmes linked to post-secondary education provision is a potential cause for concern, given the current state-wide focus on workforce development, and on post-secondary attainment. It could indicate that despite the existence of well-designed initiatives and the multi-dimensional approach to workforce development in Ohio (as outlined in (Governor's Office of Workforce Transformation, 2019[75])), workforce programmes may not currently have the capacity needed to increase their contribution to meeting current and future skills needs in Ohio. It appears that completion rates in programmes targeting populations with traditionally lower levels of educational success (such as the ASPIRE Program) may also not be scaling up over time, although future growth in labour market supply in Ohio depends partially on the ability of the state to harness talent from these population groups.

Other types of bottlenecks also may restrict growth in attainment. For example, there is some evidence that individual institutions are not always in a position to add capacity to their educational offerings, even when there is demand by qualified students and the labour market. In nursing, an occupation in current and future high demand, and experiencing shortages, the OECD review team heard from institutional representatives that qualified candidates are not able to access places in some programmes in public institutions, because of faculty shortages and a lack of available placement spots in hospitals. Faculty shortages are likely to become more acute in high-demand fields in future years, as the current workforce ages and higher education institutions have to compete to a greater extent with industry for staff (Pritchard et al., 2019[76]). Relatively low general public funding levels to institutions may also limit their ability to expand capacity (see Section 4.3).

The long-term value of post-secondary credentials

Most graduates in Ohio enjoy a positive return on attaining post-secondary education, even when taking above-average student debt levels into account

US and international evidence show a strong relationship between higher education attainment and enhanced rates of labour market participation (OECD, 2019[63]; U.S. Census Bureau, 2019[26]). This is also the case in Ohio, where higher education graduates have considerably better employment prospects than those with upper secondary education, and better integration into the labour market than the US average. Labour force participation rates for both the workforce as a whole and for younger adults rise progressively for each level of post-secondary credential achieved. Participation in Ohio is particularly strong for graduates with a bachelor's degree; 92% of bachelor's graduates aged 25-34 participated in the labour force in 2018, higher than the U.S. average (90%) and far above the OECD average (88%) (U.S. Census Bureau, 2019[26]).

Employment rates for graduates with all types of post-secondary education are above the US average in Ohio, and above the rates of the other three states participating in the review. The employment benefits of attaining an associate's degree also appear to be stronger in Ohio than in most other US states; the employment premium gained by those with an associate's degree is higher than the US average. The gap in labour force participation rates between graduates with associate's degrees and those with bachelor's degrees is also smaller in Ohio than in the other three states in the review. This underlines the generally favourable outlook for post-secondary graduates in the tight labour market in Ohio.

Earnings for graduates with post-secondary education in Ohio also increase with each successive level of education achieved, compared to those without a post-secondary education. The median salary of 25-64 year-olds in Ohio with some college is USD 2 000 higher than that of high school graduates, while the median salary premium is USD 5 000 for achieving an associate's degree, and USD 20 000 for achieving a bachelor's degree (Figure 4.11).

Figure 4.11. Median annual pre-tax earnings by level of education and age group, 2018

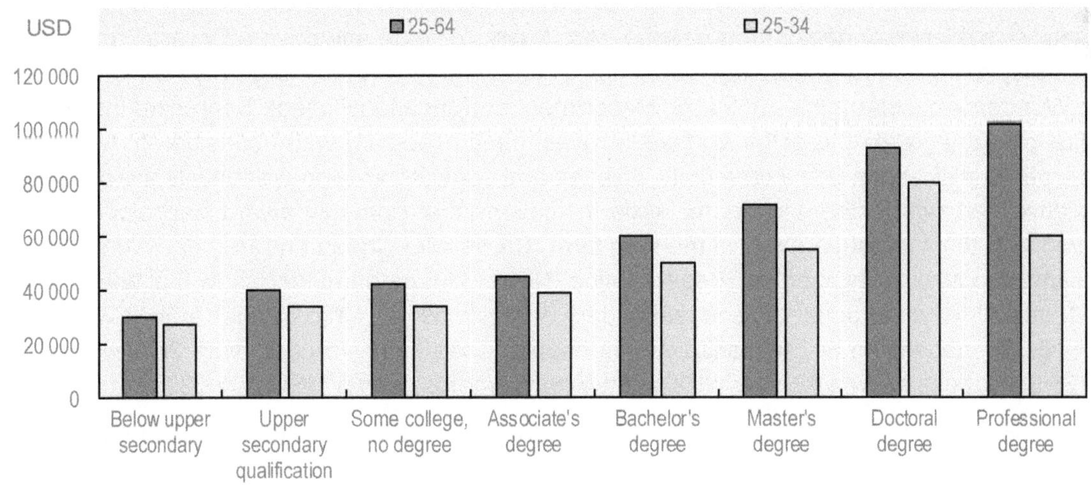

Note: Data refer to the earnings of full-time employees.
Source: U.S. Census Bureau (2019[26]), *American Community Survey 2018* (database), https://www.census.gov/programs-surveys/acs/data.html.

StatLink https://doi.org/10.1787/888934133647

For the younger population aged 25-34, Figure 4.11 shows that the financial benefit of achieving "some college" is less evident in the data. This reflects national trends, where cumulative additional earnings of those with some college (net of foregone earnings and costs of attending college), only begin to exceed the earnings of high school graduates on average once a graduate reaches their mid-30s (Ma, Pender and Welch, 2019[77]). However, young Ohioan graduates in this age group with degrees are generally already earning a substantial wage premium compared to peers with high school education, starting with a median wage USD 5 000 higher for those that have achieved an associate's degree, rising to more than USD 16 000 higher for those with a bachelor's degree (Figure 4.11).

Additional employment and earnings gains from post-secondary education need to be considered with respect to the cost of higher education and the impact of individual student debt accrued during study, important factors to take into account when assessing the overall returns to post-secondary education. Although state regulation has imposed caps in tuition fee increases in public higher education institutions, tuition fees in public 2-year and 4-year institutions in Ohio remain above the US average. In 2017/18 tuition fees in public four-year colleges were USD 10 026 (16th highest in the US) while tuition fees in public 2-year colleges were USD 3 672, slightly above the national average of USD 3 243, though below the US median of USD 3 891 (SHEEO, 2019[78]). Graduates are also more indebted in Ohio than on average in the United States. Average student debt at public and private not-for-profit 4-year institutions in 2018 was USD 30 323, slightly above the national average (USD 29 200) and 18th highest in the United States. Ohio also had the 16th highest share of students graduating with debt in the United States in 2018 (60%) (TICAS, 2019[79]).

U.S. Department of Education College Scorecard data for institutions in Ohio show that, as expected, both debt and returns on attending college vary by type of institution. In general, graduates from institutions that predominantly award certificates have lower debt levels and lower median earnings 10 years after enrolment, while graduates from institutions that predominantly award bachelor's degrees have higher median 10-year earnings along with higher levels of debt (Figure 4.12). These two sets of institutions form distinct clusters, while the group of institutions that predominantly award associate's degrees show a more varied set of outcomes, with some having debt and earnings levels similar to certificate-awarding institutions, and others showing 10-year earnings similar to some predominantly bachelor's institutions, with generally lower levels of debt.

Nevertheless, evidence suggests that despite debt levels, college still pays off overall for a majority of students, despite the variety of earnings outcomes. A 2019 report by the Georgetown Center for Education and the Workforce based on the 2019 U.S. Department of Education College Scorecard indicates that, in general, a college education is still a worthwhile investment, especially when considered over a long-term time horizon. Qualifications from community colleges and some short-term credentials are associated with good relative earnings in the short-term, while institutions that primarily award bachelor's degrees are associated with the highest earnings in the long term (Carnevale, Cheah and Van der Werf, 2019[80]). For Ohio, estimates using a metric of Net Present Value (NPV) of future earnings[4] show that potential earnings over 40 years for graduates of post-secondary institutions in Ohio range from USD 343 000 to USD 1 519 000, depending on the institution (Carnevale, Cheah and Van der Werf, 2019[80]). In total, 163 of the 225 institutions show a 40-year NPV of their programmes of over USD 600 000[5].

It is also important to take into account the wider benefits of higher education, beyond financial returns. Across the OECD, graduates with a higher education degree on average tend to enjoy a range of more positive social outcomes, compared to their peers without a degree (OECD, 2019[81]). While no specific studies on social benefits of higher levels of education appear to have been carried out in Ohio, in the United States as a whole, college graduates are more likely to vote, take on voluntary work, exercise regularly and engage in educational activities with their children (Ma, Pender and Welch, 2019[77]).

Figure 4.12. Median earnings and median debt of graduates of Ohio post-secondary institutions, by type of institution

Type of institution according to most common degree type awarded to graduates

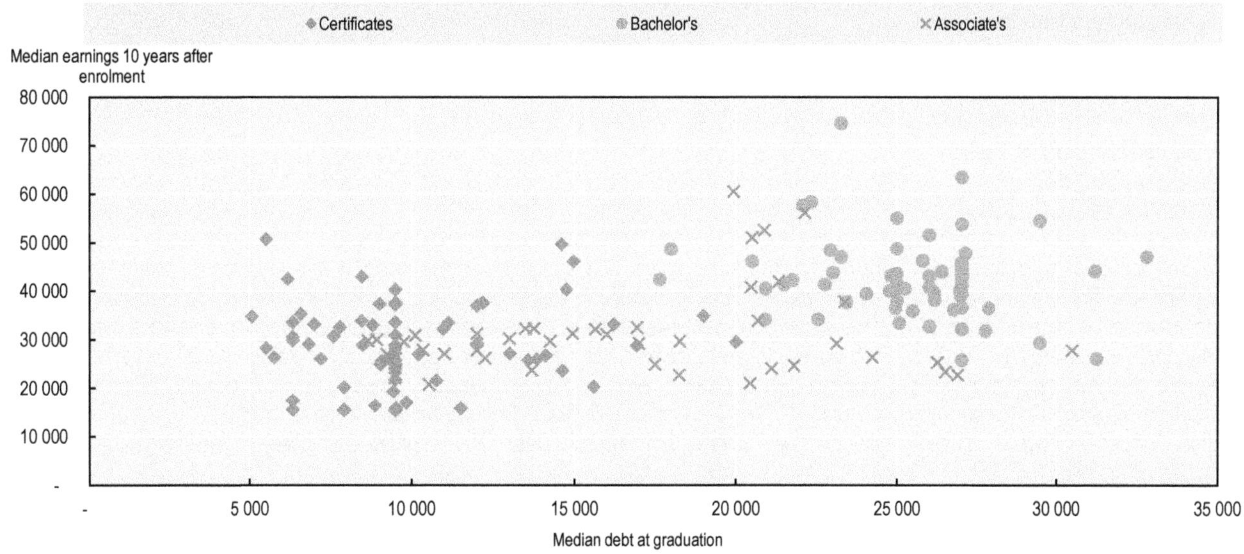

Notes: Earnings and median debt are in USD. Only institutions with available data on both median earnings 10 years after enrolment and median debt at graduation are included in the figure. Institutions whose data is suppressed for either of these variables for privacy reasons were excluded. In total, 222 of the 317 institutions contained in the 2019 College Scorecard are included in the figure. The debt figure used covers only the debt of those who graduated with a qualification and does not include the debt of those who did not complete their course of study.
Source: Adapted from U.S. Department of Education (2019[82]), *College Scorecard* (database), https://collegescorecard.ed.gov/data/.

StatLink https://doi.org/10.1787/888934133666

Some groups of graduates achieve less favourable labour market outcomes and face a more uncertain future

As discussed in previous sections, overall returns on investment in post-secondary education in Ohio remain positive, and the skills shortage and tight labour market mean that job prospects are generally favourable for those who invest in post-secondary education. Nevertheless, a large body of evidence demonstrates that post-secondary credentials in Ohio differ vastly in terms of their value to employers and ability to produce favourable labour market outcomes, depending on the type of institution and credential awarded, the field of study, and the industry of employment.

Labour market outcomes data show that some types of institutions and credentials produce poorer labour market outcomes on average. For example, the vast landscape of non-degree credentials encompasses credentials with sizeable labour market returns, as well as those that employers either do not value or do not recognise (ExcelinEd and Burning Glass Technologies, 2019[83]). US Gainful Employment data for non-degree credentials in public and not-for-profits in Ohio, and all credentials in for-profit institutions, illustrate the wide spectrum of possible returns on these credentials. Annual earnings rates are in general most favourable for public and private not-for-profit institutions, while for-profit institutions have the highest ratios of debt-to-earnings (Table 4.8). In particular, the average ratio of debt-to-earnings across for-profit 4-year institutions was just above 9%, the "pass" benchmark set by the Gainful Employment legislation[6].

Table 4.8. Average debt-to-earnings annual rate for non-degree credentials, by type of institution

Type of Institution	Average of debt-to-earnings annual rate (%)
Public 2-3 years	1.8
Public 4 or more years	2.0
Private, not-for-profit less than 2 years	2.3
Public less than 2 years	2.4
Private, not-for-profit 2-3 years	4.0
Private, not-for-profit 4 or more years	4.8
Private, for-profit less than 2 years	6.2
Private, for-profit 2-3 years	8.9
Private, for-profit 4 or more years	9.1

Note: The debt-to-earnings annual rate is the ratio of the median annual Title IV loan payment amount, for all student loans, incurred by students who completed the Gainful Employment (GE) Program compared to those former students' average annual earnings. The median annual loan payment amount is based on the median of the student loan debt incurred by students who completed the GE program, amortized over 10 years for certificate and associate's degree GE Programs, 15 years for bachelor's and master's degree GE Programs, and 20 years for graduate doctoral and first-professional degree GE Programs. Earnings are based on actual average earnings using the most recently available data from programme completers in the previous three academic years, based on U.S. Social Security Administration records.
Source: Office of Federal Student Aid (2017[84]), *Gainful Employment Data: 2015 cohort* (database), https://studentaid.gov/data-center/school/ge/data.

StatLink https://doi.org/10.1787/888934134920

The share of post-secondary students in private for-profit institutions across the United States has been on a downward trend since 2010, and the share in Ohio is less than 5%. Evidence suggests that for the average student, for-profit education does not pay off (Cellini and Turner, 2019[85]) and can contribute to the persistence of socio-economic disadvantage (Gelbgiser, 2018[86]). Previous studies have shown credentials from private for-profit institutions in the United States appear to be valued less by employers than credentials from public or private not-for-profit institutions (Deming et al., 2016[87]). The generally poor outcomes in Ohio for graduates from for-profit institutions even in the tight Ohio labour market also indicate that qualifications from these institutions are not meeting employer needs (Halbert, 2017[88]). State authorities therefore have a role to play in ensuring that clear and accessible information is available to students on labour market outcomes, particularly for this sector of provision (see Section 4.3).

The extent to which graduates use the skills they acquire in the labour market also varies according to their field of study and the industry they enter after graduation. At the bachelor's level, graduates from some fields are less likely to be employed following graduation. For example, employment rates of liberal arts bachelor's graduates are below the average employment rates for bachelor's graduates in Ohio (see Chapter 3). Liberal arts graduates also have lower earnings than the median levels overall for bachelor's graduates in Ohio (USD 40 000 compared to the average of USD 50 000). However, a recent national-level study also indicates that while short-term returns to liberal arts degrees are relatively low, the long-term returns for liberal arts colleges are higher than those of many other types of four-year institutions in the United States (Carnevale, Cheah and Van Der Werf, 2020[89]).

For other types of credential, labour market returns and the earnings premium provided by each successive level of education can vary substantially by both field of study and industry of employment. As discussed in Section 4.2, from 2009-18 the largest rate of growth in post-secondary education awards has been in certificates of less than one year of duration. Studies carried out across the United States provide a mixed view of whether certificates in general provide positive labour market returns over and above a high school diploma (Dadgar and Trimble, 2015[90]). Nevertheless, many openings in high-demand fields require certificates. Shorter-term programmes leading to a certificate can also broaden access to post-secondary education and provide pathways to higher levels of post-secondary education.

The returns to certificates and associate's degree are linked heavily to the field of study, given that these qualifications are often heavily oriented toward specific occupations (Georgetown Center on Education and the Workforce, 2020[91]). State-level data show that for some fields of study and industry combinations, certificates appear to be associated with similar earnings to associate's degrees in the years after graduation, while for other fields an associate's degree achieves superior earnings. For example, the earnings level and trajectory of those with business-related credentials entering the retail industry are similar for certificates and associate's degrees, while those with associate's degrees in health professions earn a considerable premium over those with a certificate (Figure 4.13).

Figure 4.13. Median pre-tax salary of post-secondary graduates by selected field of study and industry in the six years after graduation

Annual earnings in 2016 USD (adjusted for inflation), based on the cohort of students graduating from postsecondary education in 2011

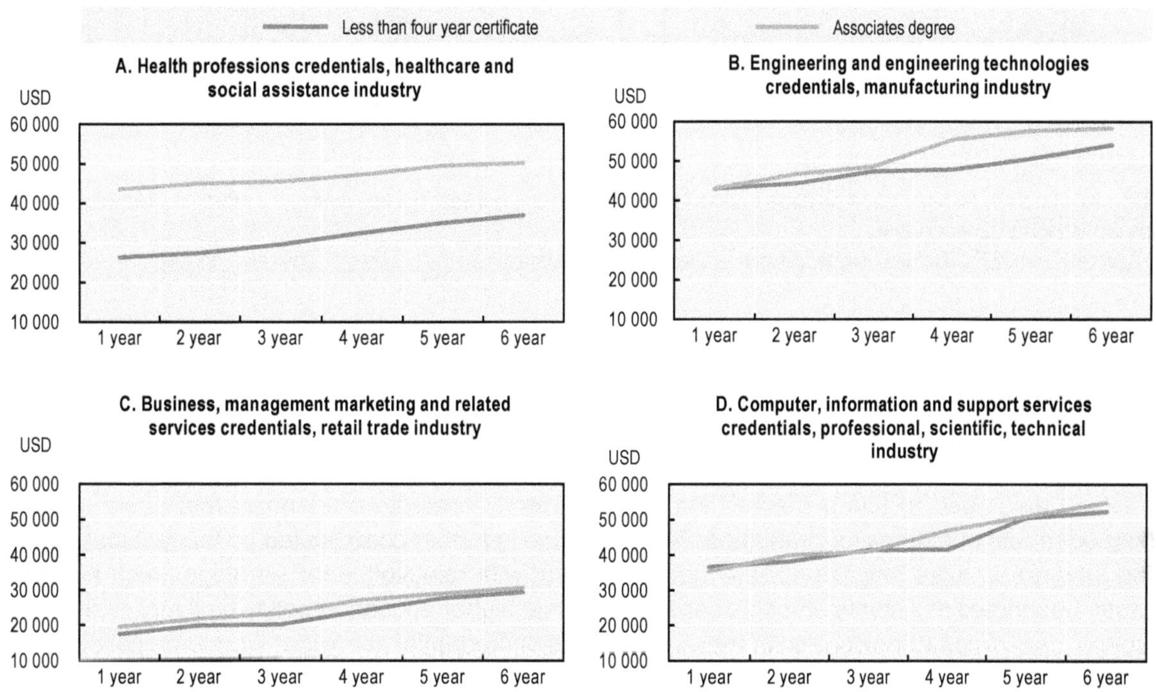

Source: Adapted from Ohio Education Research Center (OERC) (2020[92]), *Higher Education Outcomes Dashboard*, https://oerc.osu.edu/higher-ed-outcomes.

StatLink https://doi.org/10.1787/888934133685

At the same time, even graduates with qualifications in the same broad field show steadily poorer labour market outcomes in certain industries of employment. Figure 4.14 shows that graduates with business-related credentials appear to have consistently poorer earnings when they enter the accommodation and food service industry, and, for certificate graduates, the retail trade and administrative support industries. In each of these cases, even at six years after graduation, the median earnings of the 2011 cohort were far below the median earnings for Ohio high school graduates in 2018. On the other hand, the median salary for graduates entering the manufacturing industry immediately after achieving a credential is at least 20% higher than the median high school salary. Many certificate qualifications in this field also appear highly valued in some industries; the highest earnings overall for graduates with business-related sub-baccalaureate qualifications are for those with certificates working in either the professional, scientific and technical industry (USD 46 900) or the finance and insurance industry (USD 50 700).

Figure 4.14. Earnings by industry for graduates with qualifications in business, management, marketing and related services, one and six years after graduation

Pre-tax annual earnings in 2016 USD (adjusted for inflation), based on the cohort of students graduating from postsecondary education in 2011

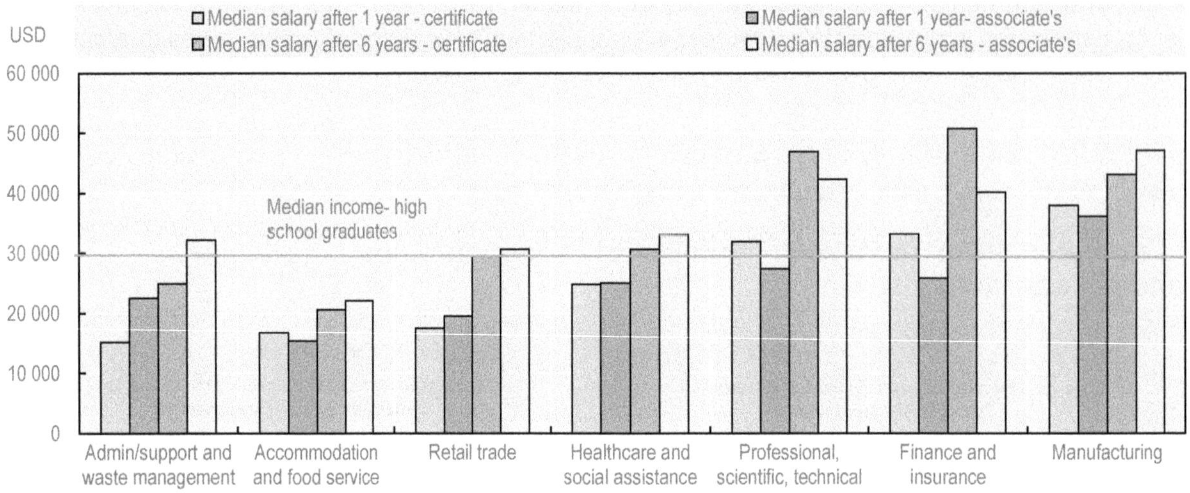

Note: The median income for high school graduates refers to the 2018 full-time full-year pre-tax earnings of adults in Ohio with high school education as the highest level achieved.
Source: Adapted from OERC (2020[92]), *Higher Education Outcomes Dashboard*, https://oerc.osu.edu/higher-ed-outcomes.

StatLink https://doi.org/10.1787/888934133704

Further investigation would be required to ascertain whether less valuable subfields within the broader field, local labour market conditions or study programme quality are the determinants of poorer outcomes. As Ohio works to accelerate expansion of the output of credentials of all types to meet the attainment goal, the state will also need to find a mechanism to concurrently evaluate credentials and ensure they are providing adequate outcomes for graduates. The challenge is further complicated by the fact that many in-demand jobs are in roles that are socially necessary, but with relatively poor earnings (such as nursing assistants, healthcare assistants and childcare staff). While higher education policy has very limited scope to influence labour market outcomes for these categories of credential, the wider workforce policy network in the state will need to ensure that appropriate incentives are in place to create a steady pipeline of workforce for these jobs into the future.

4.3. Policies to improve the alignment of the higher education system and the labour market in Ohio

The three key challenges relating to the supply of high-level skills and graduate outcomes in Ohio identified in the previous section have implications for the design of policy in the state. In particular, Ohio law makers and policy makers would be well advised to take steps to:

1. **Increase the overall volume of graduates in high-demand fields**, including through ensuring accessible, relevant, high-quality study options aligned to skills requirements are in place, communicating about and incentivising access to higher education, and ensuring students are supported to complete credentials.
2. **Address the specific needs of non-traditional student populations** through high-quality and joined-up services to support first generation and disadvantaged student groups (non-traditional

learners) to access and progress through higher education. This includes making study affordable and physically accessible.

3. **Help students to make good choices** by providing clear information and advice to allow individuals to make decisions based on knowledge of likely labour market outcomes when choosing programmes, courses and majors.

In reality, these three policy priorities are strongly related and will need to be addressed with a combination of distinct policies. This section of the chapter assesses how well the current policy environment in Ohio is responding to the priorities identified and provides recommendations on how policies might be strengthened. It first considers the way in which overall strategy is set and policies co-ordinated. It then assesses specific state policies governing the educational programmes offered in Ohio, pathways for students between programmes and non-financial support to help students enter and complete higher education. The final sections of the chapter look at higher education funding – and the impact this has on affordability and relevance – as well as policies on the collection, dissemination and use of data on skills production and labour market outcomes.

Strategic planning and co-ordination

Strategic goals and strategies can provide a vision of how higher education should contribute to workforce needs and the kinds of actions that are needed to achieve this objective. Overarching goals and state-wide strategies have the potential to focus the efforts of the multiple actors involved in aligning higher education and workforce needs, including higher education institutions, state agencies and employers. Alongside statements of intent, leadership is needed to drive actions forward and practical mechanisms are required to co-ordinate the activities of different bodies involved in policy development and implementation.

Current and past Ohio administrations have prioritised workforce development and created structures to co-ordinate policy across state agencies

Ohio's current Governor has identified workforce development as a key priority, building on an established tradition of strongly developed workforce policy in the state. At the centre of state government, under the direct responsibility of the Lieutenant Governor, the Governor's Office for Workforce Transformation (OWT) seeks to co-ordinate Ohio's skills and workforce policies (see Box 4.2). Advised by the Governor's Executive Workforce Board, composed of leaders in business, education, and workforce development, and under the leadership of the Governor and Lieutenant Governor, the OWT establishes overall strategy for workforce development in Ohio and co-ordinates with Ohio's state agencies involved in workforce policy.

The state's commitment to workforce development is also reflected in the organisational structure of the Ohio Department of Higher Education (ODHE), which has a specific Vice Chancellor post and staff team for workforce alignment. This is unique among the four states taking part in the current project. ODHE's workforce alignment team co-operates directly with the Governor's Office for Workforce Transformation, which helps to create coherence in policy making at the operational level. Moreover, as will be discussed in Section 4.3, Ohio has created mechanisms to share and pool administrative data from different state agencies dealing with education, employment and workforce policies, creating a shared information resource across the related policy areas.

Ohio's Workforce Transformation Strategy establishes overarching priorities for skills development, although focuses relatively little on post-secondary education

In 2018, under the previous governorship, the Governor's Office of Workforce Transformation, working with the Governor's Executive Workforce Board, co-ordinated the development of a state workforce development strategy entitled "Workforce 2.0" (OWT, 2018[18]). As summarised in Box 4.4, this strategy established broad goals for workforce development, each linked to specific actions, with a strong focus on promoting co-operation between education and employers.

Box 4.4. "Workforce 2.0" – Ohio's Workforce Transformation Strategy

Against a backdrop of an ageing population, regional disparities in employment opportunities and stagnant population growth, Ohio's Workforce Transformation Strategy sets out to help "connect Ohio's business, training, and education communities" and "to attract and build a dynamically skilled, productive, and purposeful workforce that can compete globally to meet the needs of Ohio's businesses and diverse economies". The specific goals of the strategy, each associated with actions, are:

1. "**Connect Business and Education**" by supporting community-based partnerships, aligning education and business priorities to meet workforce demand and developing methods to determine and meet workforce supply and demand.
2. "**Create a Culture of Continuous Learning**" by leveraging Ohio's public library system for workforce development and increasing educational attainment "in alignment with in-demand jobs" (this includes contributing to the 65% post-secondary attainment target).
3. "**Build Career Pathways**" by working with the business community to strengthen vocational training, increasing opportunities for those with disabilities and ex-offenders, and allowing students to earn credit for work, competency, and career-based experiences.
4. "**Leverage Data for Accountability**" by exploiting data for policy making, enabling more efficient data sharing and evaluating results of programmes "to ensure continuous improvement".
5. "**Coordinate Workforce Efforts**" by aligning workforce-related efforts with other state entities and with federal workforce efforts, and by creating awareness of best practices.

Source: OWT (2018[18]).

Workforce 2.0 includes a commitment for all state agencies to contribute to the goal established by the Ohio Board of Regents in 2015 of achieving 65% of Ohio's adult-age workers with a degree, certificate, or other "credential of value" by 2025 (Ohio Board of Regents, 2015[51]). As discussed earlier, this attainment goal, adopted in recognition of the need to increase the supply of qualified graduates to the Ohio labour market, has guided policy making in higher education in Ohio in recent years.

Despite the inclusion of this reference to the 65% goal, it is striking that Ohio's Workforce Transformation Strategy contains relatively limited reference to post-secondary education and few specific actions in the sector. Specific actions in the area of higher education relate to certificate programmes, including focusing the now-discontinued OhioMeansJobs revolving loan fund on certificate programmes that align with in-demand jobs, conducting an inventory of such programmes, and taking action to create more career and technical education (CTE) programmes at the post-secondary (and secondary) level. Most other specific actions target those seeking secondary-level qualifications and/or participating in workforce programmes.

The priorities and actions included in Ohio's workforce strategy do respond to the pressing need to ensure a higher proportion of the population gains good quality secondary-level education and training. The actions in the current strategy are those most closely associated with traditional "workforce policy" in Ohio and the United States more generally. However, given the demand for post-secondary qualifications outlined in the previous sections, there is scope to include a greater focus on boosting post-secondary attainment aligned with workforce needs in future iterations of the strategy.

There have been numerous state-level initiatives to support post-secondary attainment, but some have lacked scale or continuity, and evaluation of effectiveness is limited

Notwithstanding the limited references to actions to promote post-secondary attainment in "Workforce 2.0", Ohio has implemented a wide range of policies and programmes to encourage more people to enter and complete higher education and to encourage credential acquisition in high-demand fields. Current initiatives are discussed in the next sections of this chapter. Nevertheless, two general points about the design and implementation of policies in the area of higher education-workforce alignment emerge from discussions with stakeholders in Ohio and analysis of current policy.

First, policy activity in the area of workforce transformation in Ohio in recent years, often at the initiative of the Legislature, has yielded a large number of distinct initiatives of varying duration. While the targeted student scholarship programme Choose Ohio First (see below) has existed since 2008, other initiatives such as the Ohio Means Internships and Co-ops (OMIC) programme received funding support for four years and appears to have lacked the critical mass of resources to achieve scale and widespread impact. While some degree of experimentation is welcome, frequent changes in policy programmes risk creating administrative burden and "reform fatigue" at the level of institutions. Each new reform effort requires extensive investment of resources by state authorities to raise awareness among institutions and the general public about the programme, and among institutions to learn about the parameters of new programmes and make applications for resources. As a general principle, it would be advisable to adopt a more long-term approach to policy making, aimed to ensuring stability, effectiveness and efficiency. This would be in line with the principle expressed in "Workforce 2.0" of "creating sustainability and longevity of best practices through future administrations" (OWT, 2018[18]).

Second, there is no evidence of systematic evaluation of policy and spending programmes to assess effectiveness and inform design of future initiatives and reforms. This is also a challenge highlighted explicitly in "Workforce 2.0". More specifically, programmes appear to be established without a clear explanation of how they relate to other state initiatives, while independent evaluations of funding initiatives are not generally conducted. Developing evaluation plans as part of policy development and more systematic monitoring and evaluation would provide a stronger evidence base for law makers and policy makers to use to guide future decisions.

Higher education institutions have developed Campus Completion Plans to help reach state workforce goals, but these are less comprehensive than in other states

At the same time, as the adoption of the 65% post-secondary attainment goal, in the operating budget for the 2014/15 biennium, the General Assembly included a requirement for public higher education institutions to adopt "Campus Completion Plans" and submit these to the ODHE (ODHE, 2019[93]). These plans were conceived as a means to provide a continuous improvement framework to allow campuses to identify and implement strategies to increase the number and proportion of students earning post-secondary credentials. Public institutions were further required to update these plans every two years.

The detail and scope of Campus Completion Plans appear to vary widely. While all plans appear to focus on completion rates, some also report on efforts to align programme offerings more closely to workforce demand. Although the submission of updated plans every two years is a legal requirement, it is not clear how the plans are assessed or their implementation monitored by the ODHE. Furthermore, no financial resources are explicitly attached to the development of the plan or the implementation of the strategies in them. This contrasts with the situation in some other states, such as Virginia, where such institutional plans are used more actively as a means to align institutional and state strategies, and funding (albeit limited) is awarded to institutions for specific initiatives within the plans.

Recommendations for strategic planning and co-ordination

1. Ensure the 65% post-secondary attainment goal is strongly emphasised in the implementation of Ohio's broader workforce strategy and in any potential future revisions to "Workforce 2.0". Given projected demand for advanced skill sets in the state, Ohio's overall skills strategy will need to create and promote as many opportunities as possible for different population groups to transition to post-secondary study options. Ensuring opportunities to access relevant industry certificates and cost-effective associate degrees will be particularly important in reaching first generation and disadvantaged student populations.
2. Ohio law makers should base decisions on future policies and programmes to support workforce alignment in post-secondary education on careful analysis of potential impact, and aim to ensure the continuity of successful initiatives. While small-scale interventions may be justified to test new concepts or innovative approaches, careful consideration should be given to the level of resourcing required to achieve impact and the administrative burden of each new initiative for higher education institutions, employers or other beneficiaries.
3. State authorities should build more detailed evaluation strategies into the design of policy initiatives and commission independent evaluations of existing policies and programmes.
4. Ohio law makers could consider introducing a requirement for more comprehensive institutional development plans for public institutions, integrating existing reporting on labour market outcomes of graduates and campus efforts to promote alignment with labour market needs (in addition to the actions already reported on attainment). Institutional initiatives in Campus Completion Plans could potentially be linked to small-scale targeted state funding to complement the core, performance-based funding model (see Section 4.3).

Student supports and pathways

In higher education systems with a strong tradition of institutional autonomy, such as those in the United States, higher education institutions and faculty make most of the crucial decisions on which educational programmes to offer and how they are offered. Public authorities nevertheless take actions that influence the provision, design and delivery of post-secondary educational programmes, the way different programmes relate to one another and the way students are encouraged to enter and move through the post-secondary system. The way they do this can have an impact on the ability of the system to meet the students' needs for knowledge and skills, and to respond effectively to workforce demand.

In Ohio, as elsewhere in the United States, higher education institutions must comply with the standards of recognised regional or national accrediting bodies to receive funds from the federal student aid budget. As elsewhere, Ohioan state authorities have no direct role in accreditation, but do implement a rigorous system of authorisation of private providers and approval of new degree programmes in all higher education institutions in the state. They also enact rules and standards governing the co-ordination between different programmes and the options students have to transfer between them. Targeted state initiatives have also been used in Ohio to promote work-based learning opportunities for post-secondary students and to provide additional personal support for prospective students, who are deciding whether and what to study, and existing students, who may need help in navigating through higher education.

This section considers these various aspects of state policy and their potential to support alignment between higher education and workforce needs.

State authorities take into account evidence of workforce alignment in approval of new academic programmes, but have few mechanisms to monitor existing provision

The Chancellor of the Ohio Department of Higher Education is responsible for authorising independent (not-for-profit and for-profit) and out-of-state institutions to provide academic credit in the state, as well as for approving all new academic programmes and majors in public and private institutions. Institutions are also required to gain approval for substantial changes to existing programmes, although these "change requests" are usually handled at an administrative level by ODHE staff. This system of authorisation and approval means Ohioan public authorities have a direct say in steering the development of the academic post-secondary educational offerings in the state, even if primary responsibility for programme design and delivery rests with each institution. The state-level authorisation and approval processes required all institutions submitting proposals to be accredited by Ohio's regional accrediting body (the Higher Learning Commission (HLC)) or national accrediting agencies.

Box 4.5. Workforce relevance criteria in academic programme approval in Ohio

Ohio's general standards for approval of academic programmes include general requirements relating to the broad institutional environment for the programme, including external accreditation; mission and governance; resources and facilities; student support services; and faculty. Specific standards relating to the programme to be approved examine the coherence and content of the proposed curriculum, assessment, online learning and the programme budget, resources and facilities. As part of the consideration of the curriculum, the programme approval examines, where appropriate, if programmes include capstone experiences or culminating projects related to the needs of the workforce, internships or co-op opportunities and experience with technologies relevant to specific professions.

In addition, the general standards require institutions to demonstrate evidence of "workforce relevance, need and student interest". Proposals or change requests must present evidence of: collaboration with employers, students' potential for employment on graduation, and the competitive advantage of the submitting institution in providing the programme. In addition, public institutions must demonstrate that the proposed programme is not unreasonably duplicative of other programmes in the state and is aligned with state policy initiatives. Evidence may include local, state and national labour market research, demographic analysis, evidence of partnerships with business and industry (such as secured opportunities for co-ops and internships, or provision of adjunct faculty or mentors for students) or pilot courses or certificate programmes with a history of success, demonstrating the need and opportunity for a full degree.

Source: ODHE (2016[94]).

Detailed General Standards for Academic Programs (ODHE, 2016[94]) have been established, which are used to guide programme approval processes. These standards include consideration of the proposed programme curriculum and, as set out in Box 4.5, a requirement for institutions submitting proposals to demonstrate the labour market need for the programme. For the approval of new programmes and majors, following initial contacts with the ODHE, public institutions submit proposals to the ODHE, which are subsequently subject to a peer review by content experts from Ohioan public universities and colleges. The ODHE then works with proposing institutions to resolve concerns identified and makes a decision on whether to refer the proposal to the Chancellor for approval. Proposals that are recommended for approval are subject to a period of public comment before final approval by the Chancellor. For private for-profit private institutions and non-for-profit institutions that have been continuously accredited for less than 20 years, the approval process for new programmes additionally involves a site-visit to the proposing institution by reviewers appointed by the ODHE. Not-for-profit institutions that have been continuously accredited for over 20 years follow essentially the same procedure as public institutions.

The current Ohio system for evaluating the workforce relevance of new programme proposals incentivises higher education institutions to pay close attention to skills demand and workforce development issues in planning and implementing new educational programmes, or in making major revisions to existing programmes. As such, it is likely to contribute positively to the state's overall higher education attainment and workforce alignment goals.

It is also noteworthy that the Higher Learning Commission, the regional accreditation body covering Ohio, has recently changed the language in their criteria for accreditation and now calls for institutions to demonstrate that their curricular and co-curricular activities prepare students for "informed citizenship and workplace success" (HLC, 2019[95]). Although the emphasis on the workforce-relevance of programmes and institutional procedures within HLC accreditation procedures remains modest and renewal of HLC institutional accreditation is generally required only every 10 years, HLC staff consulted by the OECD argued there was a shift towards greater focus on these issues within the accreditor and accreditation teams. This is likely to complement state-level efforts to increase emphasis on skills needs and workforce relevance through programme approval.

Despite the focus on workforce issues in the up-front authorisation and approval process and – to a limited extent – accreditation, there is no systematic monitoring of the labour market outcomes achieved by graduates from established programmes. State-level monitoring of the performance of existing programmes is restricted to analysis of basic efficiency measures and ongoing monitoring of the accreditation status of institutions. In common with states such as Virginia, public institutions in Ohio are required to report regularly on programmes that have low enrolment or duplicate others in the public system. Where enrolment in a programme falls below certain levels (with thresholds determined by each institution) or programmes are found to replicate others in the same region, public institutions are required to propose solutions, such as sharing courses across different campuses (Ohio General Assembly, 2017[96]).

The ODHE procedures for programme approval do set out requirements for maintaining approval, but for public and long-established not-for-profit institutions, these simply call for institutions to report on the results of accreditation processes by the HLC or other accrediting bodies (ODHE, 2016, p. 47[94]). The standard periodicity for HLC accreditation is every 10 years. In the case of for-profit and newer not-for-profit private institutions, the ODHE may nominate a representative to accompany the institutional site visit by the HLC or other accrediting body. As in other states examined in this review, the question arise as to whether more can or should be done to monitor the workforce-relevance of established post-secondary programmes.

Ohio has enacted a particularly comprehensive set of policies to promote articulation and transfer between levels of education and programmes

Ohio has implemented a range of credit accumulation and recognition policies to help students transition between different levels of education and programmes. The state's "Articulation and Transfer Policy" (ODHE, 2019[97]), encompasses initiatives to allow students in secondary and technical education to gain credits that count towards post-secondary qualifications, as well as rules governing transfer of students between public higher education institutions.

As in other states, Ohio has a system of Advanced Placement (AP) in high schools, which allows students to gain learning credits that can subsequently count towards college-level general education requirements. Similarly, like other states, it also has a system for dual enrolment – College Credit Plus (CCP) – which allows students to enrol in college and take college-level courses while simultaneously completing their high school education. In addition, Ohio policy promotes articulation between specific courses in high school and technical colleges and related college-level programmes. Bilateral articulation agreements between certain schools and partner colleges and universities provide written assurance that courses completed in a secondary programme will count for credit at a particular college or university that offers a programme in the same field. For students in Career and Technical Education (CTE), state authorities have adopted Career-Technical Assurance Guides (CTAGs), which define guidelines for specific CTE programmes for which, by law, all public colleges and universities are required to award post-secondary credit (ODHE, 2020[98]; Poiner, 2018[99]).

Articulation and transfer policy within the higher education sector has focused on transfer between two-year and four-year institutions. Ohio introduced the first elements of a systematic articulation and transfer policy in 1990, with the development of the Ohio Transfer Module (Box 4.6). Since then, policy in this area has been further developed and strengthened, with a strong focus on guaranteeing credit recognition and transfer pathways. State legislation adopted in 2015 required the Chancellor of Higher Education to establish state-wide guaranteed transfer pathways from two-year to four-year degree programmes in public institutions in an equivalent field (Ohio General Assembly, 2015[100]). A new system of guaranteed transfer pathways is currently being implemented across the public college and university system, under the co-ordination of the Ohio Department of Higher Education (Box 4.6).

Box 4.6. Ohio's policies for articulation and transfer within higher education

The Ohio Articulation and Transfer Network (OATN), a dedicated team of staff within the ODHE, co-ordinate the development and implementation of Ohio's post-secondary articulation and transfer policy across Ohio's public university and college system. Under the supervision of an oversight board composed of senior representatives from higher education institutions, the OATN co-ordinates the work of faculty in public higher education institutions in developing and applying standards for curriculum requirements, advising, credit recognition and guaranteed pathways. Key components in the articulation and transfer system include:

- The **Ohio Transfer Module (OTM):** a standard set of general education learning outcomes corresponding to core elements of the general education component of associate's and bachelor's degree programmes. Each public institution has an OTM specified according to state-wide guidelines, and OTMs completed in all public institutions are recognised as equivalent and automatically accepted for credit accumulation on transfer between institutions.
- **Transfer Assurance Guides (TAGs):** discipline-specific guides that specify the content and combination of courses (called "TAG courses") that students need to take to be able to transfer efficiently to specific majors in public four-year institutions. Career-Technical Assurance Guides (CTAGs), designed on the same principle, perform a similar role for transfer between Career and Technical Education (CTE) to college-level credit programmes.
- **Ohio Guaranteed Transfer Pathways (OGTPs):** a more recent initiative, building on the OTM and TAGs, to create coherent, pre-defined sets of courses in two-year colleges that lead to associate's degrees that are automatically recognised for transfer into specific majors in four-year public universities. OGTPs are being developed by faculty in public institutions in eight main disciplinary areas, and institutions are stepping up student advising activities to help more students decide on learning goals early and select the right course combination to allow efficient transfer to bachelor's-level study.

Sources: ODHE (2019[97]; 2020[101]).

It is clear that Ohio has developed a highly sophisticated system of policies and initiatives to promote articulation and transfer between the state's public colleges and universities. The state Legislature has taken a keen interest in the issue and has legislated to require articulation and transfer to a greater extent than in other states involved in the United States labour market relevance project. The modular, flexible nature of higher education in the United States, which allows students more freedom to choose pathways than in many other OECD higher education systems, inevitably leads to students following more complex pathways. The articulation and transfer policy is an attempt to reduce this complexity by building clearer pathways, backed up with stronger steering and guidance for students. It is nevertheless evident, as illustrated in Box 4.6, that the highly developed nature of articulation and transfer policies in Ohio has itself created a complex system of distinct, but related components, which has the potential to create confusion for faculty, staff and students trying to navigate the system. There may be scope to streamline the system and reduce the number of distinct elements used as the new guaranteed pathways initiative is implemented.

It is challenging to assess the impact of Ohio's articulation and transfer policies to date because of limitations in the publicly available data, the absence of a counterfactual situation with which to compare, and the wide range of external factors that influence individual students' decisions to transfer between institutions. Data on the proportion of all enrolled students in public two-year colleges in Ohio who transfer each year to public four-year main campus show an increase in the transfer rate from 3.4% in 2012 to 4.0% in 2018 (Mustafa, 2018, p. 16[102]). In addition, about 2% of two-year students transfer to other public two-year colleges of regional campuses of public universities. In the same period, the average transfer rate from regional campuses – which have similar enrolment profiles to community colleges – to main public four-year campuses increased from 9.8% to 12.9%.

These low rates of transfer in part reflect the fact that only a minority of students enrol in community college and university main campuses with the intention of transferring to another institution. A cross-state analysis of two-year to four-year transfer rates restricted to degree-seeking students and using data from the National Student Clearinghouse found that 21% of such students from Ohio community colleges in the studied cohort transferred to a four-year institution with a completed associate's degree (Jenkins and Fink, 2016, p. 20[103]). This rate of "transfer with award" is lower than the US average of 29% and the equivalent rates in states such as Florida, Virginia or Washington. Although the specific configuration of Ohio's public higher education system, with its network of university regional campuses, may have affected the analysis, the study shows the importance of developing robust metrics for measuring transfer and of carefully monitoring the effects of articulation and transfer policy.

Despite past initiatives, state authorities currently provide limited support for work-based learning opportunities for students and workforce engagement by faculty

Ohio has a strong history of provision of co-operative education, particularly in fields related to the state's historically dominant industries. The University of Cincinnati, in particular, was a pioneer in providing co-operative education for its students. In the state operating budgets covering 2014-17, the General Assembly provided a total of almost USD 20 million to support the expansion of co-operative education and other forms of work-based learning through the Ohio Means Internships and Co-ops Program. The available funds were allocated by the ODHE through requests for proposals, initially to individual higher education institutions and, from 2015, to consortia of institutions across the six JobsOhio regions. The funds were to be used to incentivise more students to pursue co-ops and internships in majors other than STEM (Science, Technology, Mathematics and Engineering), incentivise more businesses to hire student co-ops and interns, and enhance the capacity of campuses to organise and follow up internship placements.

The OMIC funded almost 6 500 internships and co-operatives across the state, and the grants are reported to have "catalyzed and accelerated efforts by campuses across Ohio to make work-based and experiential learning a priority" (ODHE, 2018[104]). Overall, the investment programme appears to have addressed a reality confirmed in interviews by the OECD that operating co-op and internship programmes effectively takes considerable time and effort on the part of faculty and staff. In particular, the process of identifying and working with employers to develop the ability to offer high-quality internships, interaction with businesses during internships, and follow-up and evaluation all require resources.

The OMIC programme did not receive further funding after the financial year 2017, so has effectively been wound up. Although the programme was most successful in promoting uptake of internships and co-ops in universities and employment sectors where internships were already common (ODHE, 2018[104]), it provided potentially valuable support to institutions and employers across the state. The OECD team does not know the exact reasons for the discontinuance of the programme. However, given the potential of internships and co-ops to strengthen students' workforce-relevant skills and the strong support for internships heard from stakeholders during the OECD visit, there is a case for reintroducing state funding for initiatives in this area.

At the same time, institutional representatives consulted by the OECD team highlighted an increasing commitment on the part of academic staff to ensuring the relevance of programmes to workplace skills needs, and an increased focus on advising students about career choices and work-based learning opportunities. While there is variation between institutions and departments, there is a risk that academic staff become detached from industry practice and wider developments in the world of work outside of academia. Staff have limited opportunities to engage in their own experiential learning in organisations outside of their institutions to update their knowledge and build networks. Support for staff practice-oriented sabbaticals in organisations and businesses working in their fields could potentially be integrated into future state support for higher education-employer co-operation.

Supporting more people from disadvantaged backgrounds into and through higher education is a priority for Ohio, but the challenges are considerable

As discussed earlier in this chapter, Ohio is characterised by substantial regional disparities in household income and educational levels, with many comparatively deprived localities where college attendance rates remain low. Reaching the state's ambitious 65% post-secondary attainment target implies bringing a large numbers of individuals from less advantaged backgrounds and communities with a limited tradition of college-going into higher education, and supporting them in acquiring qualifications. The barriers faced by these populations in entering and completing higher education in the United States, as elsewhere in the OECD, are well documented. They include inadequate academic preparation, limited information and parental support, an absence of role models, financial constraints, a lack of transport options and problems related to substance addiction.

Many local and regional initiatives led by higher education institutions, schools, community groups and municipalities seek to tackle the different barriers to higher education attendance. State agencies involved in regional and local development, such as the Governor's Office of Appalachia, have a strong focus on skills development (GOA, 2020[105]). In the 2020-21 biennium, the ODHE has secured around USD 6.5 million from the U.S. Department of Education's Gaining Early Awareness and Readiness for Undergraduate Program (GEAR UP) to develop "college-going culture" in targeted schools and communities. The programme is funding consortia of educational institutions, bodies involved in college access and business partners to develop guidance and supports for students from low-income families. Four consortia are currently supported (ODHE, 2020[106]), with further funding planned. At the same time, the state has committed funds to the OhioCorps pilot project to help address the opioid crisis in low-income communities. Current higher education students will be trained and supported financially to mentor at-risk middle and high school students and help at-risk students' parents as part of a service learning component in their degrees (ODHE, 2020[107]).

Within higher education institutions, many stakeholders consulted during the OECD visit highlighted the considerable efforts being made to enhance student advising and entrust academic staff with greater responsibility for guiding students in study choice. Provision for student support and advising is considered in the programme approval system discussed above. As noted in the next section, the formulae for the state's output-based institutional funding systems for public universities and community colleges incentivise institutions to support students at risk of non-completion. Moreover, the latest Ohio state budget calls on the Chancellor of higher education to establish a "community college acceleration program" to enhance financial, academic and personal support services to students in need of support from local social service agencies and help them access educational opportunities in the state's public two-year colleges.

The OECD team was struck by the commitment of many of those involved in increasing engagement with prospective students and students from disadvantaged backgrounds; the various activities noted above involve many innovative and promising approaches. In light of the challenges the state faces, Ohio could expand its targeted efforts to reach out to non-traditional student groups through greater co-ordination and investments in larger-scale initiatives.

Recommendations on programmes, pathways and non-financial student support

1. ODHE should complement its up-front processes for approval of new academic programmes with monitoring and review of the outcomes achieved by graduates from each programme in terms of; a) employment in the one to five years following graduation or b) transition to further study. Ideally, such a system should take into account graduate earnings as a proxy indicator of job quality, while taking into account low average earnings in certain socially valuable graduate occupations. It is likely to be most efficient for this monitoring to occur centrally, using existing administrative and educational data sources. Such a review process could potentially occur on a three-year cycle, with higher education institutions called upon to justify or improve programmes with persistently poor graduate outcomes.
2. ODHE should maintain close working relations with HLC to ensure that Ohio's priorities and concerns in relation to the labour market alignment of higher education are adequately heard in policy making and practice in the regional accrediting body.
3. Building on existing efforts by the Ohio Articulation and Transfer Network (OATN), ODHE should explore ways to streamline and simplify the existing landscape of articulation and transfer policies to ensure it is readable for students, faculty and staff. ODHE should also take steps to improve the evidence base for future policy making on articulation and transfer in the states. The Department should consider how more transparent reporting could be achieved on the effectiveness of existing policies in promoting transfer into and within higher education. In particular, it would be valuable to provide clear information on the proportion of students successfully transferring and gaining credit recognition and, where problems are detected, to analyse remaining barriers to transfer and credit recognition.
4. Building on the experience gained in the OMIC program, Ohio law makers should consider allocating new resources to develop the capacity of higher education institutions and employers to organise high-quality internship and co-op experiences for students. It will be important to consider how funds can be targeted more equitably across regions, to promote greater take-up in institutions, fields of study and parts of the state where such work-based learning experiences are less well established.
5. Potentially as part of a programme to support broader regional co-operation projects between higher education institutions and employers, Ohio law makers should consider making funding available to allow academic staff to spend time working or contributing to projects within organisations outside of their institutions (businesses, public sector agencies, cultural bodies, etc.) to develop their knowledge of contemporary working environments. An exchange model,

where employers of the host organisations teach or otherwise contribute to academic programmes, could be envisaged.

6. Potentially under the co-ordination of the Governor's Office for Workforce Transformation, ODHE and state agencies responsible for education, jobs and family services, and regional development should analyse how existing policies to increase uptake and completion of higher education among disadvantaged population groups can be streamlined, co-ordinated and funded. The objective should be to eliminate unnecessary fragmentation and put in place "joined-up" services for these population groups, with a view to reaching the state's 65% attainment target.

Funding

From a theoretical perspective, the ability of higher education institutions to satisfy the knowledge and skills needs of students and the economy is likely to be influenced by funding levels and arrangements in three main ways:

1. The overall level of funds – from public and private sources – available to institutions for educating each student inevitably has an impact on the design, potential quality and likely relevance of provision, even if there is no universal and straightforward relationship between "more money" and "better" education. It is reasonable to assume that institutions with adequate funds will be better able to attract and keep qualified staff, deploy more resource-intensive instructional practices, provide higher quality facilities and equipment and devote more resources to student advising. If used effectively, these factors all have the potential for positive impact on students' skills acquisition, preparation for the labour market and chance of graduating successfully. Determining the actual level of resources needed to ensure high-quality provision efficiently is, of course, notoriously difficult, and a challenge with which educational policy makers across the OECD struggle continuously.
2. The level of public funding available to institutions and students will affect the cost and affordability of study for students. This, in turn, is likely to influence the flow of students into (and through) the higher education system, and the ability of systems to meet attainment targets and skills demand. Institutional subsidies that allow institutions to charge lower tuition and fees and student financial aid to cover the costs of tuition, fees and living expenses all reduce the upfront cost of study for individuals. Studies from different OECD countries, including the United States, show that students and potential students from low- and middle-income backgrounds are particularly price sensitive and that higher study costs tend to reduce their likelihood of entering and completing higher education (Gallet, 2007[108]; Attanasio et al., 2011[109]; Dearden et al., 2011[110]).
3. The design of the mechanisms used to allocate funds to higher education institutions and students is likely to influence the behaviour of those receiving the funds. Higher financial awards for particular study options can influence students in their choice of study and institutions in their educational programming, potentially increasing the supply of graduates in high-demand fields. Earmarked funding streams and outcomes-based allocation formulae for universities and colleges can force or encourage institutions to devote resources and efforts to achieving specific goals related to labour market alignment.

The following section assesses the current situation in Ohio in relation to these three issues.

Total revenue per student in public higher education institutions in Ohio is around the US average and has held stable in real terms since the Great Recession

As elsewhere in the United States, Ohio's public higher education institutions rely primarily on a combination of student charges (tuition) and appropriations from the state budget to fund their educational activities. Public institutions are not subject to specific enrolment caps imposed by public authorities and have some flexibility in determining the tuition and non-educational fees they charge students.

Data from the State Higher Education Executive Officers Association (SHEEO) show that the average educational revenue per full-time equivalent student (FTE) in public institutions in Ohio remained broadly stable between 2008 and 2018, at a level just below the average of all 50 states. Average educational revenue across all types of public institution rose by 2.1% in real terms over the 10-year period to almost USD 13 900 per FTE, compared to a 2018 US average of almost USD 14 600. The relative stability in revenue levels in Ohio in recent years contrasts with more dramatic changes in FTE revenue in public institutions in other states in the decade to 2018, ranging from increases of over 30% in Illinois and Colorado and decreases of over 10% in Louisiana, Nevada and Missouri (SHEEO, 2019[111]).

State spending on public higher education institutions in Ohio has historically been low compared to other states, and the net tuition paid by students comparatively high. For the financial year 2020, the State Share of Instruction (SSI) allocated to Ohio's public institutions in the state budget amounted to just over USD 2 billion (Ohio General Assembly, 2019[112]). SHEEO's comparative data for the financial year 2018, which also take into account specific allocations for medical studies and doctoral institutions, show an average state appropriation to public institutions of USD 5 700 per FTE. This is equivalent to around 73% of the 2018 nation-wide average, placing Ohio in bottom fifth of states in terms of state financial support to institutions. Between 2008 and 2018, state appropriations in Ohio fell by 9.4% in real terms, but this is a smaller fall than in many others states and below the nation-wide average of an 11.2% reduction (SHEEO, 2019[111]). As shown in Figure 4.15 below, educational appropriations to public institutions have recovered in recent years after reaching a low point during the financial year 2013, when, after adjusting for inflation, they were 25% below their 2008 level and 45% below the level seen in 2000.

As also illustrated in Figure 4.15, the fall in state appropriations after 2008 was compensated over time by an increase in average net tuition paid by students, in particular through a substantial rise in revenues from student contributions in 2012. Since then, however, average fee revenue has remained relatively stable, largely as a result of explicit tuition fee caps incorporated into biennial operating budgets by the Ohio General Assembly. In the current budget (2020/21), annual increases in tuition and general fees are limited to two percent for universities and regional campuses and five dollars per credit hour in community and technical colleges (Ohio General Assembly, 2019[112]).

The use of such fee caps in recent years marks a return to a long-standing policy of legislative fee moderation implemented before the 2008 crisis, and has allowed Ohio to limit tuition inflation comparatively effectively. Whereas average net tuition revenue in public universities and colleges nation-wide increased by almost 40% between 2008 and 2018, the equivalent figure for Ohio was around 12%. Despite this, average net annual tuition revenue in Ohioan public universities and colleges, at USD 8 160 in 2018, remains around 20% above the average of U.S. states (SHEEO, 2019[111]). The SHEEO data on net tuition revenue include income from graduate and out-of-state tuition and fees. Ohio's own data show average annual "sticker price" tuition and general fees for in-state students for 2020 of around USD 4 800 in community colleges; USD 6 100 in university regional campuses; and USD 9 950 in university main campuses (ODHE, 2019[113]).

Figure 4.15. State appropriations and tuition revenue in public higher education institutions, 1994-2018

Educational appropriations per FTE and net tuition revenue per FTE in public higher education institutions in 2018 USD (adjusted for inflation)

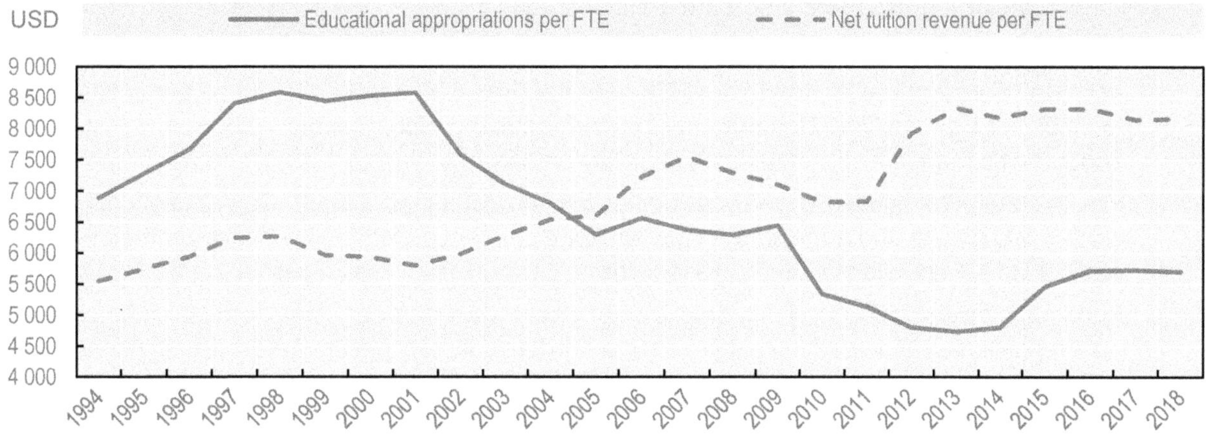

Notes: Based on average appropriations and net tuition revenue for all public higher education institutions. Net tuition revenue refers to the published tuition fee minus student financial aid provided by the institution. Amounts adjusted for inflation using the Higher Education Cost Adjustment (HECA).
Source: Adapted from SHEEO (2019[78]), *SHEF: State Higher Education Finance*, https://sheeo.org/project/state-higher-education-finance/.

StatLink https://doi.org/10.1787/888934133723

Public spending on student financial aid in Ohio is lower than in comparable states and many students are ineligible for state support

Alongside institutional subsidies to public institutions (the SSI) and the policy of capping rises in tuition and fees discussed above, Ohio seeks to make attending higher education more affordable for state residents by providing state student aid to complement the system of Pell Grants administered by the federal government. The main source of state-level financial aid for students is currently the Ohio College Opportunity Grant (OCOG), which, in 2020, had an annual budget allocation of just over USD 122 million. As explained in Box 4.7, OCOG is a "Pell first" grant system, awarded to institutions for Pell-eligible degree-seeking students who meet specific financial need criteria.

OCOG was created in the wake of the Great Recession, when Ohio public finances were under considerable strain. In common with other states across the country at the time, Ohio law makers sought to reduce public spending. In the field of higher education, the funding reductions were focused proportionally more on state grant aid to students than on state operating subsidy to institutions, which, as discussed above, was less severely impacted than in some other states. As illustrated in Figure 4.16, Ohio's average state spending per FTE student fell by over 60% between the financial years 2009 and 2010. In the same year, state appropriations to institutions per FTE student also fell, but only by around 16%. As a result, as also illustrated in Figure 4.16, state spending on student aid per FTE student declined as a percentage of educational appropriations per FTE from 7% in 2009 to 3% in 2010. The level of state spending per FTE on student aid has subsequently been increased (by around 30% in real terms between 2010 and 2018), but remains comparatively low in comparison to other states. In 2018, the level of annual state student aid spending per FTE student in Ohio was only around 30% of the average of 47 states for which data are available, at USD 218 compared to USD 752 (SHEEO, 2019[111]).

Box 4.7. The Ohio College Opportunity Grant (OCOG)

The Ohio College Opportunity Grant (OCOG) was introduced in 2010, replacing an earlier system of state financial aid, to provide financial support to Ohio residents attending higher education in the state. The key characteristics of the grant programme are:

- OCOG is a "Pell first" student grant programme: students must apply for federal financial aid using the Free Application for Federal Student Aid (FAFSA), with OCOG funds being allocated to institutions by the Ohio Department of Higher Education for students in receipt of Pell Grant support who meet specific state-level eligibility criteria.
- For the 2019/20 academic year, students with an Expected Family Contribution (EPC) of USD 2 190 or less and a maximum household income of USD 96 000 – based on their FAFSA application – were eligible for OCOG awards.
- Funding is available for students studying for associate's degrees, first bachelor's degrees or nursing diplomas in accredited public, private not-for-profit and private for-profit institutions, with different standardised maximum award amounts established for different institutional types. Pro-rata award amounts are calculated for part-time students.
- OCOG is designed to cover only instructional and general fees charged to students, which are the only costs included in the "state cost of attendance". The maximum awards for each institutional type take into account only fee levels that exceed USD 6 095, which is the standard combination of maximum Pell Grant and EPC fixed by the federal student aid system.

Source: ODHE (2019[114]).

Figure 4.16. Spending on state public student aid since 2008

State public student aid per FTE student in 2018 USD (adjusted for inflation) and spending on public student aid as a percentage of educational appropriations to institutions 2008-18

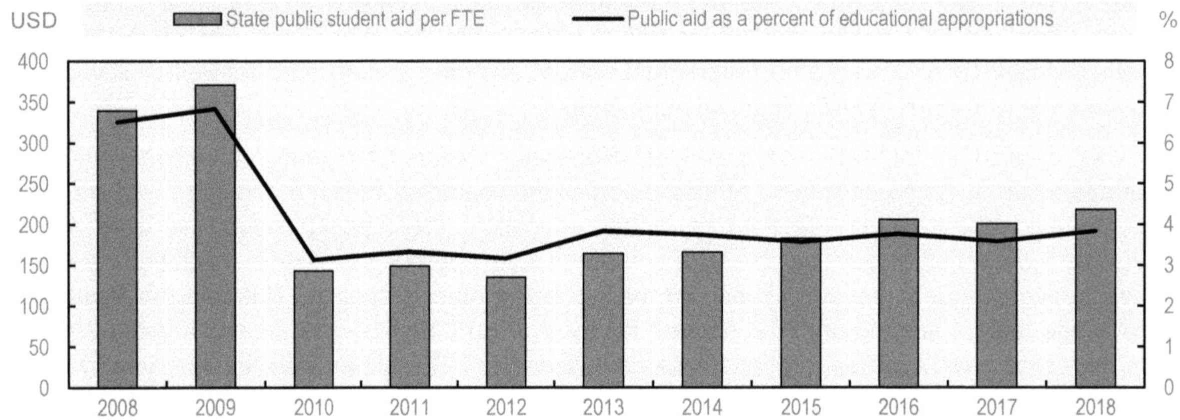

Note: Left axis shows student aid per FTE in 2018 dollars, adjusted for inflation using the Higher Education Cost Adjustment (HECA). Right axis shows public aid as a percent of educational appropriations

Source: Adapted from SHEEO (2019[78]), *SHEF: State Higher Education Finance*, https://sheeo.org/project/state-higher-education-finance/.

StatLink https://doi.org/10.1787/888934133742

OCOG's comparatively limited overall budget has made it necessary to target the available resources. A key choice has been to focus OCOG funds exclusively on helping students to cover tuition and fees. Whereas the definition of "cost of attendance" used by the federal student aid system includes housing and living costs as well as the costs of books, equipment and transport (FSA, 2019[115]), the "state cost of attendance" used by Ohio authorities to calculate OCOG award levels includes only instructional and general fees charged to the students (ODHE, 2019[114]). Using this concept of cost of attendance, OCOG is targeted at covering tuition and fees for eligible students where these costs are not already covered by a combination of Pell Grants and the federally determined Expected Family Contribution (EFC). As the current maximum annual combination of Pell Grant and EPC is USD 6 095, and annual tuition and general fees in community colleges and university regional campuses are lower than this, students at community colleges and university regional campuses are not eligible for OCOG. Similarly, Pell-eligible students at public universities with lower tuition and fees – including the Historically Black institution Central State University – are eligible for lower OCOG awards.

The current system is transparent and equitable. It assumes the first duty of the state is to help students from low- and middle-income backgrounds cover the unavoidable costs of tuition and fees, putting more expensive study options more easily within reach of these groups. Based on "sticker price" rates (ODHE, 2019[113]), even with a full Pell Grant (USD 6 095) and maximum OCOG award of USD 2 000, a student at a public doctoral university in Ohio in 2019 will have to "cover" at least an additional USD 2 000 a year from other sources for tuition and education fees. Although, in practice, many such students will benefit from institutional funding awards and tuition waivers to cover fees, they will still need to cover housing, equipment and living costs that come on top. With a maximum Pell Grant, full-time students on degree programmes at public community colleges (where average "sticker price" tuition in 2020 was USD 4 828 and no OCOG is available), would receive around USD 1 250 per year towards other costs. In university regional campuses, where costs are higher (ODHE, 2019[113]), Pell funding would be fully absorbed by full tuition and fees.

While other more targeted state-level student funding streams exist (see below), it is clear that mainstream federal and state student aid programmes provide limited or no financial support to help low-income students in Ohio with costs beyond core tuition and fees. It is also striking that the state's main financial aid programme offers no support to students in the open access institutions (community colleges and university regional campuses) that concentrate the largest numbers of low-income and Black/African American students in the state. State financial support systems in comparable states tend to offer at least some support in such cases. A 2016 nation-wide analysis by University of Pennsylvania's Institute for Research on Higher Education ranked Ohio 45th of the 50 states in terms college affordability, based on the percentage of income required to pay for the net price of college, including living costs (Institute for Research on Higher Education, 2016[116]). Given the influence of cost on college entry and completion and Ohio's ambitious attainment target, leveraging additional investment for student support is likely to be an important priority for Ohio law makers. The state operating budget for the 2020/21 biennium includes a 20% increase in OCOG funding for 2021 (Ohio General Assembly, 2019[112]). It is likely further increases will be needed to support achievement of Ohio's 65% attainment goal.

Ohio uses a strongly output-focused system to allocate state funding to public higher education institutions

If the overall level of funding directed to higher education institutions and students affects the ability of higher education systems to meet societal skills demands, so (in theory) do the ways in which this funding is allocated and targeted. Ohio has used both its main institutional funding mechanism and targeted student funding programmes to support state goals related to skills supply and workforce development.

The State Share of Instruction (SSI) that provides core state funding for instructional activity to public colleges and universities is allocated entirely based on the outputs achieved by institutions. As explained in Box 4.8, distinct output-based formulae are used to allocate the available SSI funding for each sector to universities and community colleges, while a separate budget line and allocation formula exists for Ohio Technical Centers (OTCs). The key metrics used – course completion, success points (in community colleges) and degrees awarded – all promote credit and credential completion. Additional weighting is given for "at-risk" students from low-income and disadvantaged backgrounds, which means institutions receive additional money when such students attain success points and complete courses and programmes. This provides incentives for institutions to support progression and completion for students in these groups.

Box 4.8. Allocation of the State Share of Instruction (SSI) in Ohio

The Ohio General Assembly establishes the budget envelope available for educational appropriations to universities, colleges and Ohio Technical Centers (OTCs) in Ohio in the biennial state operating budget. The budget for the biennium 2020/21 allocates around USD 2 billion annually for universities and colleges (the State Share of Instruction – SSI) and USD 20 million annually for OTCs (Ohio General Assembly, 2019[112]).

These funds are allocated to individual institutions using three distinct output-based formulae:

4. For **universities and their regional campuses**: around 30% of total SSI funds earmarked for universities are allocated for course completions by FTE students; 50% for degree completions by FTE students; and the remaining 20% to eligible institutions for medical and doctoral training (referred to as "set-asides").
5. For **community and technical colleges**: 50% of SSI funds earmarked for colleges are allocated for course completions; 25% allocated on the basis of "success points" (credits and development programmes completed); and 25% on the basis of specific completion metrics (associate's degrees, long-term certificates and transfers to four-year institutions).
6. For **OTCs**: 25% is allocated for programme completion; 20% for retention (students completing 50% of programme); 5% for industry-recognised third-party credentials; and 50% for each FTE student who moves to employment, military service or further post-secondary study.

In the allocation process, the first step for universities and colleges is to determine cost of courses and degrees. All courses are assigned to 1 of 26 cost categories depending on subject area and level of instruction, with cost per FTE student updated each year based on reported cost and enrolment data for previous years. STEM subjects are protected from potential reductions in FTE costs.

The second step is to calculate the numbers of FTE students completing courses and degrees and obtaining success points, using a rolling three-year average of the relevant data for each institution. "At-risk" students are given additional weighting in the formulae (so institutions receive additional funding for each of these students who completes courses or programmes). In universities, students from low-income backgrounds, with low ACT scores at entry, or doing developmental coursework are counted as "at-risk". For colleges, extra weighting is given for "access students", which, in addition to the criteria similar to those used in universities, includes students over 25 and from under-represented ethnic groups.

The SSI allocation received by each institution is essentially a function of: a) the total funds available for the sector; b) the number of relevant outputs they achieve in different course cost categories; and c) the demographic profile of their successful students (proportion of "at-risk" or "access" students).

Sources: ODHE (2019[117]), ODHE (2019[118]), Ohio General Assembly (2019, p. 2448[112]).

Since the new system was introduced in 2012, completion rates have been rising (ODHE, 2020[119]), and institutions and stakeholders consulted by the OECD team generally view the system to have been successful. In particular, institutional representatives praised the decision of the then Ohio Board of Regents to delegate the detailed development and design of the new funding allocation system to a working group composed of representatives of public higher education institutions. This helped to ensure the new system took into account the specificities of the different sectors, contained safeguards to prevent very radical changes in funding from one year to the next, and was widely accepted by faculty and staff within institutions.

Independent research has examined the impact of performance-based institutional funding systems in the United States, including the SSI in Ohio (Hillman, Tandberg and Fryar, 2015[120]; Dougherty and Reddy, 2013[121]; Li, 2018[122]; Hillman, Hicklin Fryar and Crespín-Trujillo, 2018[123]). These different analyses provide mixed findings on the real effectiveness of performance-based funding systems in general, and in Ohio in particular. The available evidence does not point to a strong relationship between the introduction of output-based systems and improved progression and completion rates. Several of the authors point to the wide range of factors that influence students' progress through higher education, including disadvantaged backgrounds, financial pressures and other challenges in their life beyond college, as well as the limits of the actions higher education institutions can take to help students overcome these external challenges. At the same time, the research suggests that the introduction of output-based funding, including the SSI, has influenced institutional and faculty behaviour, increasing focus on helping students to progress and complete their studies.

Although the evidence on the effectiveness of output-based funding is inconclusive, there have been calls within Ohio to include a stronger focus on graduate employability in the metrics used to calculate the SSI. It is true that the current SSI model provides strong incentives for institutions to support completion in general, but does not specifically reward efforts to address specific workforce skills shortages or ensure a strong focus within programmes on preparing graduates for the labour market. The current state budget calls on the ODHE to undertake a study into how post-graduation employment measures could be used in the distribution of state funding (Ohio General Assembly, 2019, p. 2463[112]). Possible metrics suggested in the legislation include the relevance of graduates' degrees to job placement, employment in Ohio versus employment out-of-state, placement in high-demand fields, and other qualitative factors. Although some other states do use employment metrics in their funding allocation formulae, the evidence to support such a move outside very specific career-oriented programmes is weak. In particular, it is questionable whether the influence institutions have on graduate employment is sufficient for them to be held directly accountable for employment outcomes in a funding formula. Ohio authorities and law makers will need to take this into account in future decision-making on this matter.

Other targeted funding programmes seek to promote workforce-relevant objectives, although the sums involved are comparatively small

Ohio authorities have used several targeted funding programmes to promote the workforce relevance of higher education provision in Ohio, complementing the core institutional funding and student support mechanisms discussed above.

The Regionally Aligned Priorities in Developing Skills (RAPIDS) Program, for example, focuses on capital investment. It provides targeted funding to regional consortia of public higher education institutions for equipment to educate students in in-demand occupations. The programme has a budget allocation of USD 16 million for the 2020/21 biennium (Ohio General Assembly, 2019[112]). The ODHE administers the programme through open requests for proposals. It requires those submitting bids to demonstrate how investments in specific items of equipment will allow students to acquire career-relevant skills that meet demonstrated need in specific industries, with a focus on the growth sectors of advanced manufacturing, robotics and cybersecurity. All funding requests must include letters of support for the project and equipment investment from at least seven businesses in the target industry (ODHE, 2019[124]). Once in place, the equipment purchased with RAPIDS funding is accessible to all the institutions in the regional partnership.

In common with other states, Ohio has also used targeted funding for student financial aid to incentivise students to pursue study options that correspond to identified areas of skills demand in the state. The "Choose Ohio First" scholarship programme, initiated in 2008, provides scholarships to students studying Science, Technology, Engineering, Mathematics and Medical subjects (STEMM). The programme is open to public and private institutions. To secure funding, institutions must submit proposals to the Ohio Department of Higher Education. Programmes that are successful are required to use the funds awarded to provide financial assistance to students of between USD 1 500 (required minimum) to USD 7 995 (maximum) annually, based on current tuition levels. Students from under-represented groups are prioritised, although detailed award criteria are established by each institution. Evidence from elsewhere in the United States suggests that targeted funding programmes, such as Choose Ohio First, can be an effective means to increase uptake and completion of STEM programmes (Castleman, Long and Mabel, 2017[125]).

Historically, Choose Ohio First only provided funding for degree programmes, but the 2020/21 state budget extended the scope of the initiative to include funding for students on certificate programmes in STEMM fields. The biennial budget also allocates increased resources to the programme, with total annual funding planned to increase from around USD 28 million in 2020 to USD 40 million in 2021 (Ohio General Assembly, 2019[112]). In late 2019, the ODHE launched a special request for proposals for eligible degree and certificate programmes in the field of computer science (ODHE, 2019[126]).

The most recent targeted funding initiative to support post-secondary skills development aligned to workforce needs is the TechCred programme (Box 4.9). This initiative, launched in summer 2019, is innovative in Ohio in that it provides funding to employers to support the upskilling of existing or prospective employees in high-demand technology fields (ODHE, 2019[127]).

Box 4.9. Ohio's TechCred program for existing and prospective employees

With an annual budget of USD 15 million for the 2020/21 biennium, the TechCred programme will award funding to businesses that invest in training their existing staff or new recruits in approved technology-focused programmes that lead to an industry-recognised credential. Businesses that submit successful applications will be reimbursed up to USD 2 000 for each current or prospective employee who successfully completes a credential. Employers are eligible to receive up to USD 30 000 per funding round.

The TechCred eligible credential list includes only short-term, industry-recognised certificates and certifications in approved technology-focused fields. Credentials are added to the list through employer applications which are reviewed by a panel of stakeholders. Employers must identify specific technology-related skills needs in their workforce and partner with a credential provider before applying online. If their proposal is approved, the proposed training can proceed and, on production of the valid credential certificates, the Ohio Development Services Agency (DSA) reimburses the employer for training costs up to the fixed ceiling per employee and per funding round. At the time of writing, the first funding round was ongoing.

Sources: ODHE (2019[127]), Ohio General Assembly (2019[128]).

Ohio's main targeted funding programmes to promote workforce skills development at the post-secondary level each has a well-defined and complementary focus. The programmes have been carefully designed to create incentives for higher education institutions and employers to focus on workforce skill issues and co-operate across traditional institutional boundaries. The Choose Ohio First scholarship initiative and, more recently, the RAPIDS programme have secured a high-level of engagement from higher education institutions and employers over a number of years. The ODHE collects performance and financial data from grantees on a regular basis, which allow the Department to assess the effectiveness and efficiency of the programme. However, to the knowledge of the OECD team, none of these targeted programmes has been subject to an external evaluation of the results and potential impacts received. Evaluations would be valuable as an input for Ohio law makers making decisions about the future development of these programmes and the potential scale of state investment, as well as for policy makers involved in the day-to-day implementation of the programmes.

Recommendations on funding

1. In recognition of the importance of financial barriers to participation in higher education among low- and middle-income groups, Ohio law makers should continue to prioritise increases to the budget envelope allocated to the OCOG student aid programme, which is currently funded at a lower level than its equivalents in other states.
2. To help increase the supply of graduates in support of the state's 65% post-secondary attainment goal, future iterations of OCOG should seek to increase the availability of public student aid to students from disadvantaged backgrounds who are most in need of financial support for living expenses, transport, books and equipment. One way to do this would be to make OCOG awards available to students at university regional campuses and community colleges, which concentrate a large proportion of low-income students in the state, but are currently excluded from OCOG. Ohio authorities should also adopt the federal definition of "cost of attendance", which includes the full range of costs associated with study, as a reference for assessing financial need and policy making.
3. Ohio authorities should analyse the impact that output-based formulae used to allocate the State Share of Instruction (SSI) have had to date on student progress, completion and credential acquisition to develop a clear picture of the effects of the policy. In considering the inclusion of labour market outcome indicators in the formula (as requested by the Ohio General Assembly), policy makers should take into account evidence on the effectiveness of using such measures from states that have already used them in performance funding models. Florida and Louisiana are the only states known to have has used labour market outcome measures for funding allocations to four-year institutions. A wider set of states, including New York, North Carolina, Tennessee and Virginia have used such measures in funding two-year institutions (Li, 2018[122]). Internationally, Denmark has experimented with using employment outcome measures in institutional funding allocations (see Chapter 3).
4. The ODHE should consider using the additional resources made available for the Choose Ohio First programme to expand the availability of scholarship funding for high-quality, industry-recognised certificate programmes in high-demand fields (building on the experience of the current request for proposals for STEMM-related programmes).
5. The full payment of the scholarship funding under Choose Ohio First could be made conditional on successful acquisition of a degree or industry-recognised credential, potentially drawing inspiration from Virginia's FastForward programme (see Chapter 6).
6. To improve the evidence base for decision makers, the ODHE should consider commissioning independent evaluations of its targeted funding programmes to support the workforce alignment of higher education, including RAPIDS, Choose Ohio First and (once implementation is well underway) the newly launched TechCred programme. The results of such evaluations would

inform decisions about the continuation and appropriate funding of these programmes (including whether scaling up would be appropriate), as well as possible changes to their detailed design and implementation.

Information

For those working to achieve a good alignment between higher education and the needs of the labour market – whether student advisers, educators, employers or policy makers – good quality information on skills demand and the outcomes of current graduates is important. It is inherently challenging to measure labour market skills demand, as individual "skills" can be understood in different ways and it is not always easy to define the exact skill sets needed for each distinct occupation. Similarly, care is needed in interpreting graduate labour market outcomes, as a wide range of factors, from personal choice to macro-economic conditions, can affect the employment rate, occupation and earnings of graduates. In common with other states across the United States, Ohio has exploited state-level administrative data to develop information tools in the areas of skills demand, skills supply and graduate outcomes.

Ohio has a co-ordinated approach to collecting, collating and making public data on labour market skills demand and the outcomes of higher education graduates

The Ohio Education Research Center (OERC), a unit within Ohio State University's college of public affairs, co-ordinates the analysis and publication of educational outcome and workforce data in Ohio on behalf of relevant state agencies. The OERC is member of Ohio Analytics, an administrative data partnership that centralises state administrative data into a single data repository, the Ohio Longitudinal Data Archive (OLDA), for education and workforce research. As summarised in Box 4.10, the OERC has exploited this data source to develop several data "dashboards" relating to skills supply and demand and graduate outcomes (OERC, 2020[92]).

JobsOhio regional forecasts and employer survey data on job openings, as well as data on median earnings by occupation, are used to generate an annual "in-demand jobs list" for Ohio. This list currently contains 229 occupations, with in-demand occupations categorised by the education level typically required for entry (OhioMeansJobs, 2019[47]).

Box 4.10. Data resources produced by the Ohio Education Research Center (OERC)

The OERC co-ordinates Ohio's state-wide data resources on labour market demand and the outcomes of post-secondary education graduates. It has produced public data "dashboards" using this data, as well as a tool to monitor the outcomes achieved by individuals who have participated in-state workforce programmes:

- **OhioMeansJobs Workforce Data Tools**: First, a workforce supply tool that provides information about graduates from educational programmes that support in-demand occupations in Ohio, to inform users about the pipeline of supply of workers to industry. Second, an employment projections tool that provides information about the growth in job openings over time by occupation, as well as the number of job openings and median wages. Both tools are hosted on the OhioMeansJobs website, the web presence of Ohio's public employment service.
- **Ohio Higher Education Outcomes**: Longitudinal data showing employment outcomes of graduates who stay in Ohio after earning a degree. The first visualisations show the industry in which a graduate works for each major (field of study), as well as earnings for up to six years after graduation. Additional earnings outcomes visualisations are in development.

- **Workforce Success Measures**: With the Governor's Office of Workforce Transformation (OWT), OERC has used historical Ohio administrative data to provide employment and related outcomes of individuals who have completed (federally funded) workforce development programmes in the state. These data are designed to enable workforce programme administrators and policy makers to understand and improve the effectiveness of Ohio's workforce development programmes.

Source: OERC (2020[92]).

Existing data resources are not always well targeted to the needs of specific user groups, and there is limited evidence on how data are used

The data resources developed by OERC provide valuable information and potential user groups and uses for each dashboard are clearly identified on the relevant web pages. Dashboards are designed to make complex data sets more accessible by presenting them in a simple, interactive way. There is a risk, however, that in attempting to serve multiple user groups that the dashboards serve no one particularly well. Policy makers, analysts and higher education institutions may simply want access to the underlying data sets to perform their own analyses, but these data sets are not easily downloadable. At the same time, the dashboards may not be sufficiently accessible and intuitive for prospective students, current students and jobseekers. In their current form, the dashboards seem most likely to be of use for those involved in student advising, who can use the tools in their work.

Together, the OERC, the Ohio Department of Jobs and Family Services, and the Governor's Office of Workforce Transformation make large amounts of labour market information available through various means, including programme-level workforce success measures, as well as employment rates earnings at the individual programme level. However, the existing state information sources suffer from a number of limitations. Firstly, graduate outcomes data relate only to those who remain working in Ohio after graduation, and therefore provide only a partial picture of employment and earnings outcomes. For example, even though employment rates for bachelor's graduates living in Ohio surpassed 90%, between 2010 and 2015, only about 65% of bachelor's graduates from Ohio institutions were found working in the state in the fourth quarter after graduation, illustrating that information on labour market outcomes for a large share of graduates is not available.

Secondly, in the absence of any defined performance targets or benchmarks related to the information on labour market outcomes, the available data do not provide any guidance on how to interpret and assign a value judgement to it. For example, while comprehensive data on completions, employment and earnings are provided in the Governor's Office of Workforce Transformation's "workforce success measures" dashboard, without associated targets, and a counterfactual or reference group, it is not possible to ascertain whether the existing workforce programmes are judged to be meeting their objectives and effectively contributing to the state attainment goal.

The absence of benchmarking also limits the interpretability of published labour market outcomes data by users. In particular, earnings data are difficult for prospective students to interpret without corresponding information on completion rates and student indebtedness at graduation. It is particularly important to make this information readily available to those considering studying in programmes and institutions that have demonstrably poor labour market outcomes, to ensure students can make informed choices (see Section 4.2). Data at the federal level from the period of implementation of the Gainful Employment regulations and the Department of Education College Scorecard can potentially provide information that is more comprehensive and meaningful to prospective students. The newly implemented "report-card" system for public schools in Ohio also offers an example of how information can be synthesised in an accessible manner for the benefit of diverse users.

It is also important to ensure that students from lower socio-economic backgrounds and minority groups have suitable channels of access to information, both on labour market outcomes and the educational supports available to them. Evidence indicates that these cohorts are often disadvantaged in terms of their ability to locate and interpret information and advice on going to college, and attach weight to choice factors differently (e.g. (Perna, 2006[129]), (Thomsen et al., 2013[130]) (Hofer, forthcoming[131])).

Recommendations on information

1. Introduce a regular publication schedule for labour market outcomes data and promote it to user groups, including data aimed at students deciding upon their post-secondary education options.
2. Consider relating labour market outcomes data to a set of benchmark metrics in order to give some additional guidance to users. For example, earnings data could be related to the Ohio minimum wage or general sectoral wages for workers without post-secondary credentials, in order to give some indication of the value of obtaining additional credentials in the field. Earnings data could also be shown in conjunction with data on student debt and completion, to help prospective students better contextualise the figures.
3. Consider implementing dedicated information channels tailored for potential students without a family background in post-secondary education, those with lower financial literacy or those who may be unable to easily access information online.

References

Accrediting Commission of Career Schools and Colleges (2020), *Directory of Accredited Institutions*, http://www.accsc.org/directory/ (accessed on 9 February 2020). [28]

Attanasio, O. et al. (2011), *Education Choices and Returns on the Labour and Marriage Markets: Subjective Expectations, Gender and Decision Making*, http://www.homepages.ucl.ac.uk/~uctpjrt/Files/Attanasio%20Kaufmann_270911.pdf. [109]

Bacher, T. (2012), *Under the Rust Belt: Revealing Innovation in Northeast Ohio*, https://muse.jhu.edu/book/39144. [13]

Batalova, J., M. Fix and J. Bachmeier (2016), *The Costs of Brain Waste among Highly Skilled Immigrants in the United States*, https://files.eric.ed.gov/fulltext/ED586143.pdf (accessed on 9 February 2020). [60]

Burning Glass Technologies (2019), *The New Foundational Skills of the Digital Economy Developing the Professionals of the Future*, https://www.burning-glass.com/wp-content/uploads/New_Foundational_Skills.pdf (accessed on 5 February 2020). [45]

Carnevale, A., B. Cheah and M. Van Der Werf (2020), *ROI of Liberal Arts Colleges - Value Adds Up Over Time*, Center on Education and the Workforce - McCourt School of Public Policy, https://vtechworks.lib.vt.edu/bitstream/handle/10919/97782/LiberalArtsROI.pdf?sequence=1 (accessed on 21 February 2020). [89]

Carnevale, A., B. Cheah and M. Van der Werf (2019), *A First Try at ROI: Ranking 4,500 Colleges*, https://cew.georgetown.edu/cew-reports/collegeroi/ (accessed on 19 February 2020). [80]

Carnevale, A., N. Smith and J. Strohl (2013), *Recovery: Job Growth and Education Requirements through 2020*, Georgetown University Center on Education and the Workforce, Washington, DC, https://1gyhoq479ufd3yna29x7ubjn-wpengine.netdna-ssl.com/wp-content/uploads/2014/11/Recovery2020.FR_.Web_.pdf (accessed on 10 May 2019). [42]

Castleman, B., B. Long and Z. Mabel (2017), *Can Financial Aid Help to Address the Growing Need for STEM Education?*, https://scholar.harvard.edu/files/zmabel/files/fsag_stem_manuscript_9-15-17.pdf (accessed on 11 March 2020). [125]

Cellini, S. and N. Turner (2019), "Gainfully employed?: Assessing the employment and earnings of for-profit college students using administrative data", *Journal of Human Resources*, Vol. 54/2, pp. 342-370, http://dx.doi.org/10.3368/jhr.54.2.1016.8302R1. [85]

Children's Defense Fund (2016), *Ohio's Appalachian Children at a Crossroads: A Roadmap for Action*, https://www.cdfohio.org/wp-content/uploads/sites/6/2018/10/Ohios-Appalachian-Children-at-a-Crossroads-1.pdf (accessed on 9 February 2020). [57]

Churchill, A. (2019), *Poverty Isn't Destiny: An analysis of Ohio's 2018-19 school report cards An analysis of Ohio's 2018-19 school report cards*, http://www.fordhaminstitute.org (accessed on 23 February 2020). [71]

COMPTIA (2019), *2019 Tech Industry Job Market & Salary Trends Analysis | Cyberstates*, https://www.cyberstates.org/index.html#keyfindings (accessed on 9 February 2020). [7]

Dadgar, M. and M. Trimble (2015), "Labor Market Returns to Sub-Baccalaureate Credentials", *Educational Evaluation and Policy Analysis*, Vol. 37/4, pp. 399-418, http://dx.doi.org/10.3102/0162373714553814. [90]

Dearden, L. et al. (2011), *The Impact of Tuition Fees and Support on University Participation in the UK*, Institute of Fiscal Studies, London, https://www.ifs.org.uk/wps/wp1117.pdf (accessed on 5 February 2020). [110]

Demaria, P., J. Carey and R. Burgess (2018), *Joint statement on OHIO ATTAINMENT GOAL 2025*, https://www.ohiohighered.org/sites/ohiohighered.org/files/uploads/Link/Attainment-Joint-Statement-odhe_owt_ode.pdf (accessed on 7 February 2020). [43]

Deming, D. et al. (2016), "The Value of Postsecondary Credentials in the Labor Market: An Experimental Study", *American Economic Review*, Vol. 106/3, pp. 778-806, http://dx.doi.org/10.1257/aer.20141757. [87]

Dougherty, K. and V. Reddy (2013), "Performance Funding for Higher Education: What Are the Mechanisms? What Are the Impacts?", Community College Research Center, Teacher's College, Columbia University, https://ccrc.tc.columbia.edu/publications/performance-funding-mechanisms-impacts.html (accessed on 7 August 2019). [121]

Emsi (2019), *Manufacturing Is Not Dead - the Rise of High-Skill High-Wage Production Jobs*, https://www.economicmodeling.com/manufacturing-is-not-dead/ (accessed on 4 February 2020). [16]

Ewing Marion Kauffman Foundation (2017), *2017 Kauffman Index of Startup activity-Metropolitan area and city trends*, https://www.kauffman.org/kauffman-index/reporting/startup-activity/~/media/9f685e8c214248f0884fa21416f6b03e.ashx (accessed on 3 February 2020). [8]

ExcelinEd and Burning Glass Technologies (2019), *Credentials Matter Report 1: A National Landscape of High School Student Credential Attainment Compared to Workforce Demand*, https://www.excelined.org/wp-content/uploads/2019/05/ExcelinEdBurningGlassTechnologies.CredentialsMatterNationalLandscapeofHighSchoolCredentialAttainmentComparedtoWorkforceDemand.May2019.pdf (accessed on 2 July 2019). [83]

FSA (2019), *2018-19 Federal Student Aid Handbook Volume 3, Chapter 1, Cost of Attendance*, Federal Student Aid, Washington, D.C., https://ifap.ed.gov/fsahandbook/attachments/1920FSAHbkVol3Ch2.pdf (accessed on 6 February 2020). [115]

Fuller, J. and M. Raman (2017), *Dismissed by Degrees: How degree inflation is undermining U.S. competitiveness and hurting America's middle class*, https://www.hbs.edu/managing-the-future-of-work/Documents/dismissed-by-degrees.pdf (accessed on 5 February 2020). [44]

Gallet, C. (2007), "A comparative analysis of the demand for higher education: results from a meta-analysis of elasticities", *Economics Bulletin*, Vol. 9/7, pp. 1-14, http://economicsbulletin.vanderbilt.edu/2007/volume9/EB-07I20002A.pdf (accessed on 5 February 2020). [108]

Gelbgiser, D. (2018), "College for All, Degrees for Few: For-Profit Colleges and Socioeconomic Differences in Degree Attainment", *Social Forces*, Vol. 96/4, pp. 1785-1824, http://dx.doi.org/10.1093/sf/soy022. [86]

Georgetown Center on Education and the Workforce (2020), *The Overlooked Value of Certificates and Associate's Degrees: What Students Need to Know Before They Go to College*, https://cew.georgetown.edu/cew-reports/subba/ (accessed on 23 February 2020). [91]

GOA (2020), *Governor's Office of Appalachia*, Ohio Development Services Agency, https://development.ohio.gov/cs/cs_goa.htm (accessed on 12 February 2020). [105]

Governor's Office of Workforce Transformation (2019), *Workforce 2.0: Ohio's Workforce Transformation Strategy for 2018 and Beyond*, https://workforce.ohio.gov/wps/portal/gov/workforce/initiatives/reports/workforce-2point (accessed on 19 February 2020). [75]

Halbert, H. (2017), *Risky business: For-profit career colleges bad bet for public investment Workforce and higher education*, https://files.eric.ed.gov/fulltext/ED591115.pdf (accessed on 19 February 2020). [88]

Hanauer, A. and J. Mcgowan (2019), *State of Working Ohio 2019 Realities and Remedies Work & Wages*, https://www.policymattersohio.org/files/research/sowo2019-final.pdf (accessed on 15 January 2020). [17]

Health Resources and Services Administration (2020), *Health Professional Shortage Area Find tool*, https://data.hrsa.gov/tools/shortage-area/hpsa-find (accessed on 9 February 2020). [56]

Hillman, N., A. Hicklin Fryar and V. Crespín-Trujillo (2018), "Evaluating the Impact of Performance Funding in Ohio and Tennessee", *American Educational Research Journal*, Vol. 55/1, pp. 144-170, http://dx.doi.org/10.3102/0002831217732951. [123]

Hillman, N. and E. Orians (2013), *Community Colleges and Labor Market Conditions: How Does Enrollment Demand Change Relative to Local Unemployment Rates?*, Springer, http://dx.doi.org/10.2307/24571744. [35]

Hillman, N., D. Tandberg and A. Fryar (2015), "Evaluating the Impacts of "New" Performance Funding in Higher Education", *Educational Evaluation and Policy Analysis*, Vol. 37/4, pp. 501-519, http://dx.doi.org/10.3102/0162373714560224. [120]

Hillman, N. and T. Weichman (2016), *Education Deserts: The Continued Significance of "Place" in the Twenty-First Century*, American Council on Education, Washington, DC, https://www.acenet.edu/news-room/Pages/CPRS-Viewpoints-Education-Deserts.aspx. [70]

HLC (2019), *Criteria for Accreditation Policy Change Adopted on Second Reading*, Higher Learning Commission, Chicago, http://hlcommission.org/criteria (accessed on 28 November 2019). [95]

Hofer, A. (forthcoming), *The role of labour market information in guiding student choice*, OECD Publishing Paris. [131]

Institute for Research on Higher Education (2016), *College Affordability Diagnosis: Ohio*, https://www.gse.upenn.edu/pdf/irhe/affordability_diagnosis/Ohio_Affordability2016.pdf (accessed on 6 December 2019). [116]

Jenkins, D. and J. Fink (2016), *Tracking Transfer - New Measures of Institutional and State Effectiveness in Helping Community College Students Attain Bachelor's Degrees*, Community College Research Center, Columbia University; The Aspen Institute; National Student Clearinghouse Research Center, https://ccrc.tc.columbia.edu/media/k2/attachments/tracking-transfer-institutional-state-effectiveness.pdf (accessed on 7 February 2020). [103]

JP Morgan Chase and Co (2015), *Skills in demand in building a middle-skill workforce to grow the Columbus economy*, http://www.burning-glass.com (accessed on 4 February 2020). [49]

Li, A. (2018), *Lessons Learned: A Case Study of Performance Funding in Higher Education*, https://www.researchgate.net/publication/328615362_Lessons_Learned_A_Case_Study_of_Performance_Funding_in_Higher_Education (accessed on 30 January 2020). [122]

Lumina Foundation (2019), *A Stronger Nation - Goal exploration tool*, http://strongernation.luminafoundation.org/report/2019/#predictive. [53]

Lumina Foundation (2019), *A Stronger Nation: Ohio Report 2019*, http://strongernation.luminafoundation.org/report/2020/#state/OH. [50]

MAGNET (2019), *2019 State of Northeast Ohio Manufacturing Report*, https://www.manufacturingsuccess.org/2019-state-of-neo-manufacturing-report (accessed on 9 February 2020). [55]

Ma, J., M. Pender and M. Welch (2019), "Education Pays 2019: The Benefits of Higher Education for Individuals and Society. Trends in Higher Education Series.", *College Board*, https://research.collegeboard.org/pdf/education-pays-2019-full-report.pdf (accessed on 21 October 2018). [77]

Muro, M. and J. Whitman (2018), *Geographic gaps are widening while U.S. economic growth increases*, https://www.brookings.edu/blog/the-avenue/2018/01/22/uneven-growth/ (accessed on 18 February 2020). [67]

Mustafa, S. (2018), *Transfer Numbers and Transfer Ratios Explanations for Current Trends*, Ohio Department of Higher Education, Columbus, https://www.ohiohighered.org/transfer/research (accessed on 7 February 2020). [102]

National Science Foundation (n.d.), *Academic Institution Profiles – Rankings by total R&D expenditures*, https://ncsesdata.nsf.gov/profiles/site?method=rankingBySource&ds=herd (accessed on 24 February 2020). [33]

National Skills Coalition (2017), *Ohio's Forgotten Middle*, https://www.nationalskillscoalition.org/resources/publications/2017-middle-skills-fact-sheets/file/Ohio-MiddleSkills.pdf (accessed on 4 February 2020). [48]

National Student Clearinghouse (2019), *Some College, No Degree - 2019*, https://nscresearchcenter.org/some-college-no-degree-2019/ (accessed on 11 May 2020). [132]

National Student Clearinghouse Research Center (2019), *Term Enrollment Estimates Spring 2018*, http://nscresearchcenter.org/wp-content/uploads/CurrentTermEnrollment-Spring2018.pdf (accessed on 5 February 2020). [39]

NCES (2019), *Integrated Postsecondary Education Data System (database)*, National Center for Education Statistics, https://nces.ed.gov/ipeds/use-the-data (accessed on 15 May 2020). [30]

NCES (2018), *Digest of Education Statistics, 2018*, National Center for Education Statistics - US Department of Education, Washington, D.C., https://nces.ed.gov/programs/digest/d18/tables/dt18_330.20.asp?current=yes (accessed on 11 March 2020). [31]

ODHE (2020), *Career-Technical Credit Transfer (CT)²*, Ohio Department of Higher Education, https://www.ohiohighered.org/transfer/ct2 (accessed on 10 February 2020). [98]

ODHE (2020), *GEAR UP Ohio*, https://www.ohiohighered.org/gearup (accessed on 5 February 2020). [106]

ODHE (2020), *Graduation & Retention Rates*, Ohio Department of Higher Education, https://www.ohiohighered.org/data-reports/graduation-retention (accessed on 9 February 2020). [119]

ODHE (2020), *Ohio Attainment Goal 2025 - 2019 Annual Report*, https://www.ohiohighered.org/sites/default/files/uploads/attainment/Attainment-Report-2019_FINAL_012220.pdf (accessed on 1 December 2019). [52]

ODHE (2020), *Ohio Guaranteed Transfer Pathways*, Ohio Department of Higher Education, https://www.ohiohighered.org/OGTP (accessed on 11 February 2020). [101]

ODHE (2020), *OhioCorps Pilot Project*, Ohio Department of Higher Education, https://www.ohiohighered.org/ohiocorps (accessed on 12 February 2020). [107]

ODHE (2019), *Annual Survey of Student Charges - Fall 2019*, Ohio Department of Higher Education, https://www.ohiohighered.org/data-reports/tuition-financial-aid (accessed on 8 February 2020). [113]

ODHE (2019), *Campus Completion Plans*, https://www.ohiohighered.org/campus-completion-plans (accessed on 1 December 2019). [93]

ODHE (2019), *Data & Reports:Degrees*, https://www.ohiohighered.org/data-reports/degrees (accessed on 20 April 2020). [36]

ODHE (2019), *Financial Aid Guidance Memo - Ohio College Opportunity Grant (OCOG)*, Ohio Department of Higher Education, Columbus, https://www.ohiohighered.org/sites/default/files/uploads/sgs/guidance-memos/FA%2020-002.pdf (accessed on 9 February 2020). [114]

ODHE (2019), *Regionally Aligned Priorities in Delivering Skills (RAPIDS) Request for Proposals Submission September 20 - October 4, 2019*, https://www.ohiohighered.org/content/rapids_home. (accessed on 10 February 2020). [124]

ODHE (2019), *Special Request for Choose Ohio First (COF) Proposals in Computer Science and Related Areas*, Ohio Department of Higher Education, https://www.ohiohighered.org/grants-rfps#COF2019 (accessed on 10 February 2020). [126]

ODHE (2019), *State Share of Instruction Handbook for use by Community and Technical Colleges*, Ohio Department of Higher Education, Columbus, https://www.ohiohighered.org/sites/default/files/hei/FY20_FY21_College_SSI.pdf (accessed on 4 December 2019). [118]

ODHE (2019), *State Share of Instruction Handbook for use by University Regional and Main Campuses*, Ohio Department of Higher Education, Columbus, https://www.ohiohighered.org/sites/default/files/hei/FY20_FY21_University_SSI.pdf (accessed on 28 November 2019). [117]

ODHE (2019), *TechCred*, Ohio Department of Higher Education website, https://techcred.ohio.gov/wps/portal/gov/techcred/home (accessed on 1 December 2019). [127]

ODHE (2019), *The Ohio Articulation and Transfer Policy*, Ohio Department of Higher Education, Columbus, https://www.ohiohighered.org/sites/default/files/uploads/transfer/policy/OATN%20Policy%20Update%20COMPLETE%2010.28.19%20Updated%20%28FINAL%29.pdf (accessed on 7 February 2020). [97]

ODHE (2018), *Attainment goal projection tool*, https://www.ohiohighered.org/attainment/projection-tool. [64]

ODHE (2018), *Ohio Means Internships and Co-ops Program Annual Report*, Ohio Department of Higher Education, Columbus, https://www.ohiohighered.org/sites/default/files/uploads/omi/2018-OMIC-Annual-Report.pdf (accessed on 5 December 2019). [104]

ODHE (2016), *Guidelines and Procedures for Academic Program Review*, Ohio Department of Higher Education, Columbus, https://www.ohiohighered.org/sites/ohiohighered.org/files/uploads/program-approval/Academic-Program-Review-Guidelines_070516.pdf (accessed on 28 November 2019). [94]

ODHE (n.d.), *Aspire: Learn More, Earn More*, https://www.ohiohighered.org/aspire (accessed on 18 February 2020). [72]

ODHE (n.d.), *Data & Reports | Enrollment*, https://www.ohiohighered.org/data-reports/enrollment (accessed on 24 February 2020). [34]

ODHE (n.d.), *Making Certificates Count: An Update on Ohio's Efforts to Identify, Strengthen, Promote and Increase Certificates of Value in the Workplace*, https://www.ohiohighered.org/sites/ohiohighered.org/files/uploads/trustees/2017/Making-Certificates-Count_FINAL.pdf (accessed on 7 February 2020). [37]

ODHE (n.d.), *Ohio Colleges & Universities Map & Profiles*, https://www.ohiohighered.org/campuses/map (accessed on 20 April 2020). [29]

OECD (2019), *Benchmarking Higher Education System Performance*, Higher Education, OECD Publishing, Paris, https://dx.doi.org/10.1787/be5514d7-en. [81]

OECD (2019), *Education at a Glance 2019: OECD Indicators*, OECD Publishing, Paris, https://doi.org/10.1787/f8d7880d-en (accessed on 12 September 2019). [63]

OECD (2019), *International Migration Outlook 2019*, OECD Publishing, Paris, https://doi.org/10.1787/1999124x (accessed on 9 February 2020). [59]

OECD (2019), *OECD Employment Outlook 2019: The Future of Work*, OECD Publishing, Paris, https://doi.org/10.1787/9ee00155-en (accessed on 5 February 2020). [25]

OECD (2019), *OECD Regional Outlook 2019: Leveraging Megatrends for Cities and Rural Areas*, OECD Publishing, Paris, https://dx.doi.org/10.1787/9789264312838-en. [66]

OECD (2018), *Enabling the next production revolution: the future of manufacturing and services - interim report*, http://www.oecd.orgTel.:+33 (accessed on 6 January 2020). [12]

OECD (2018), *Equity in Education: Breaking Down Barriers to Social Mobility*, PISA, OECD Publishing, Paris, https://dx.doi.org/10.1787/9789264073234-en. [62]

OECD (2016), *Education at a Glance 2016: OECD Indicators*, OECD Publishing, Paris, https://dx.doi.org/10.1787/eag-2016-en. [23]

OECD (2016), *Skills matter : further results from the survey of adult skills.*, https://doi.org/10.1787/9789264258051-en (accessed on 31 January 2018). [24]

OERC (2020), *Ohio Education Research Center - Dashboards*, Ohio Education Research Center, https://oerc.osu.edu/dashboards (accessed on 13 February 2020). [92]

Office of Federal Student Aid (2017), *Gainful Employment Data: 2015 cohort (database)*, https://studentaid.gov/data-center/school/ge/data (accessed on 20 April 2020). [84]

Office of Postsecondary Education (2017), *TSA Nationwide Listing Comprehensive Compendium*, http://www2.ed.gov/about/offices/list/ope/pol/tsa.doc (accessed on 9 February 2020). [58]

Ohio Board of Regents (2015), *Ohio Board of Regents Resolution for Attainment Goal 2025*, Ohio Board of Regents, Columbus, https://www.ohiohighered.org/sites/ohiohighered.org/files/uploads/Link/Attainment%20Resolution%20-%20signed%20by%205%20of%205.pdf (accessed on 1 December 2019). [51]

Ohio Board of Regents (2015), *PERKINS IV Performance Improvement Plan (PIP) Policy for Postsecondary Institutions*, http://www.ohiohighered.org/Perkins/Performance. (accessed on 25 February 2020). [38]

Ohio Department of Education (n.d.), *Gap Closing Component*, http://education.ohio.gov/Topics/Data/Report-Card-Resources/Gap-Closing-Component (accessed on 18 February 2020). [65]

Ohio Department of Jobs and Family Services (2018), *Ohio Job Outlook 2026*, https://ohiolmi.com/Portals/206/proj/ohio/Ohio_Job_Outlook_2016-2026.pdf (accessed on 20 April 2020). [41]

Ohio Department of Jobs and Family Services (2018), *Projections - Ohio Job Outlook*, Ohio Job Outlook, http://www.ohiolmi.com/proj/OhioJobOutlook.htm (accessed on 7 February 2020). [20]

Ohio Department of Jobs and Family Services (2017), *Fact sheet: Workforce Innovation and Opportunity Act*, http://jfs.ohio.gov/factsheets/WIOA-factSheet.stm (accessed on 18 February 2020). [73]

Ohio Development Services Agency (2019), *Economic Overview: Ohio*, https://development.ohio.gov/files/research/E1000.pdf (accessed on 3 February 2020). [2]

Ohio Development Services Agency (2019), *The Ohio Poverty Report*, https://www.development.ohio.gov/files/research/p7005.pdf (accessed on 26 February 2020). [9]

Ohio Development Services Agency (n.d.), *Ohio Third Frontier*, https://development.ohio.gov/bs_thirdfrontier/ (accessed on 3 February 2020). [6]

Ohio General Assembly (2019), *House Bill 166 - Creates FY 2020-2021 operating budget*, https://www.legislature.ohio.gov/legislation/legislation-summary?id=GA133-HB-166 (accessed on 8 February 2020). [112]

Ohio General Assembly (2019), *House Bill 2 - Create TechCred and Microcredential Assistance Programs*, https://www.legislature.ohio.gov/legislation/legislation-summary?id=GA133-HB-2 (accessed on 9 February 2020). [128]

Ohio General Assembly (2017), *Ohio Revised Code: Chapter 3345.35 Course evaluation based on enrollment and duplication with other institutions*, http://codes.ohio.gov/orc/3345.35 (accessed on 11 February 2020). [96]

Ohio General Assembly (2015), *Ohio Revised Code: Chapter 3333.16 Universal course equivalency classification system for state institutions of higher education*, http://codes.ohio.gov/orc/3333.16 (accessed on 7 February 2020). [100]

Ohio Manufacturers' Association (2018), *Ohio Manufacturing Counts*, https://ohiomfg.com/OMA_Manufacturing_Counts_2018-19.pdf. [14]

OhioMeansJobs (2019), *In-Demand Occupations*, Ohio Means Jobs, http://omj.ohio.gov/OMJResources/In-DemandOccupations.stm (accessed on 13 February 2020). [47]

OWT (2020), *Governor's Office of Workforce Transformation*, Governor's Office of Workforce Transformation, https://workforce.ohio.gov/wps/portal/gov/workforce/ (accessed on 14 February 2020). [27]

OWT (2018), *Workforce 2.0 - Ohio's Workforce Transformation Strategy for 2018 and Beyond*, Ohio Governor's Office for Workforce Transformation, Columbus, https://workforce.ohio.gov/wps/portal/gov/workforce/initiatives/reports/workforce-2point (accessed on 1 December 2019). [18]

OWT (n.d.), *Workforce Success Measures*, Governor's Office of Workforce Transformation, https://workforcesuccess.chrr.ohio-state.edu/home (accessed on 20 April 2020). [74]

Perna, L. (2006), "Understanding the relationship between information about college prices and financial aid and students' college-related behaviors", *American Behavioral Scientist*, http://dx.doi.org/10.1177/0002764206289144. [129]

Poiner, J. (2018), *Ohio's dual credit landscape: A primer*, The Thomas B. Fordham Institute, https://fordhaminstitute.org/ohio/commentary/ohios-dual-credit-landscape-primer (accessed on 10 February 2020). [99]

Pritchard, A. et al. (2019), *The Challenges of an Aging Higher Ed Workforce*, https://www.cupahr.org/surveys/research-briefs/. (accessed on 19 February 2020). [76]

Scripps Gerontology Center (2019), *Ohio Population Research State and County Reports - Miami University*, https://www.miamioh.edu/cas/academics/centers/scripps/research/ohio-population/reports/index.html (accessed on 3 February 2020). [11]

SHEEO (2019), *SHEF: FY 2018 State Higher Education Finance*, State Higher Education Executive Officers Association, http://www.sheeo.org/shef (accessed on 30 July 2019). [78]

SHEEO (2019), *SHEF: State Higher Education Finance - State Changes Since Recession*, State Higher Education Executive Officers Association, https://sheeo.org/project/state-higher-education-finance/ (accessed on 8 February 2020). [111]

Team NEO (2019), *Aligning Opportunities in Northeast Ohio*, https://teamneo.org/wp-content/uploads/2019/07/aligning-opportunities-executive-summary.pdf (accessed on 4 February 2020). [54]

Thomas B. Fordham Institute (2019), *Ohio Education by the Numbers : 2019 Statistics*, http://www.ohiobythenumbers.com/#student-enrollment (accessed on 18 February 2020). [61]

Thomsen, J. et al. (2013), "The Educational Strategies of Danish University Students from Professional and Working-Class Backgrounds", *Comparative Education Review*, Vol. 57/3, http://dx.doi.org/10.1086/670806. [130]

TICAS (2019), *Student Debt and the Class of 2018*, The Institute for College Access and Success, https://ticas.org/interactive-map/. (accessed on 23 October 2019). [79]

U.S. Bureau of Economic Analysis (2019), *GDP by County, Metro, and Other Areas |*, https://www.bea.gov/data/gdp/gdp-county-metro-and-other-areas (accessed on 18 February 2020). [68]

U.S. Bureau of Economic Analysis (2019), *GDP by Industry (database)*, https://www.bea.gov/data/gdp/gdp-industry (accessed on 20 April 2020). [5]

U.S. Bureau of Economic Analysis (2019), *GDP by State (database)*, https://www.bea.gov/data/gdp/gdp-state (accessed on 20 April 2020). [4]

U.S. Bureau of Economic Analysis (2019), *Gross Domestic Product by State, First Quarter 2019*, https://www.bea.gov/data/gdp/gdp-state (accessed on 2 August 2019). [3]

U.S. Bureau of Economic Analysis (BEA) (2020), *Gross Domestic Product by State, Third Quarter 2019*, https://www.bea.gov/data/gdp/gdp-state (accessed on 3 February 2020). [1]

U.S. Bureau of Labor Statistics (2019), *Fastest growing occupations: 20 occupations with the highest percent change of employment between 2016-26*, https://www.bls.gov/ooh/fastest-growing.htm (accessed on 23 August 2019). [46]

U.S. Bureau of Labor Statistics (2019), *Labor force statistics from the current population survey*, https://www.bls.gov/cps/ (accessed on 12 March 2020). [21]

U.S. Bureau of Labor Statistics (2019), *Local Area Unemployment Statistics*, https://www.bls.gov/lau/ (accessed on 10 May 2020). [19]

U.S. Bureau of Labor Statistics (2019), *Measures of education and training*, https://www.bls.gov/emp/documentation/education/tech.htm (accessed on 7 February 2020). [40]

U.S. Bureau of Labor Statistics (2019), *Occupation Employment Statistics*, https://www.bls.gov/oes/home.htm (accessed on 26 August 2019). [22]

U.S. Bureau of Labor Statistics (2019), *State and Metro Area Employment, Hours and Earnings*, https://www.bls.gov/sae/data/home.htm (accessed on 8 August 2019). [15]

U.S. Census Bureau (2019), *American Community Survey 2018 (database)*, https://www.census.gov/programs-surveys/acs/data.html (accessed on 18 January 2020). [26]

U.S. Census Bureau (2018), *Population Statistics*, https://www.census.gov/topics/population/age-and-sex.html (accessed on 14 March 2020). [10]

U.S. Department of Education (2019), *College Scorecard (database)*, https://collegescorecard.ed.gov/data/ (accessed on 12 April 2020). [82]

U.S. Department of Labor (2019), *Apprenticeship Data and Statistics*, https://www.doleta.gov/oa/data_statistics2018.cfm (accessed on 5 February 2020). [32]

United States Joint Economic Committee (2019), *Losing Our Minds: Brain Drain across the United States*, https://www.jec.senate.gov/public/index.cfm/republicans/2019/4/losing-our-minds-brain-drain-across-the-united-states (accessed on 18 February 2020). [69]

Notes

[1] This category includes college graduates who have received a post-secondary level certificate, as well as those who did not complete a college programme. See (National Student Clearinghouse, 2019[132]) and Section 4.2 for more details.

[2] The 2008 and 2018 figures are not directly comparable, as Ohio began to include workforce-relevant certificates in the progress statistics only in 2014.

[3] Limited to workers with bachelor's degrees or above in specific occupations, who are sponsored by an employer, and annual places are capped at 85 000 nation-wide.

[4] Using a 2% discount rate. See Appendix A of (Carnevale, Cheah and Van der Werf, 2019[80]) for more details.

[5] The calculations do not benchmark against the returns on not attending post-secondary education. For reference, (Carnevale, Cheah and Van der Werf, 2019[80]) estimates the 40-year NPV of the federal minimum hourly wage of USD 7.25 as USD 347 000 and a worker earning USD 10 per hour, as USD 547 000.

[6] In order to be eligible for federal funding under the United States Higher Education Act Title IV student assistance programmes, an educational programme must lead to a degree at a not-for-profit or public institution, or it must prepare students for "gainful employment in a recognized occupation." Gainful employment regulations introduced in 2014 removed access to federal financial aid for programmes where graduates' debt repayments made up more than 8% of their annual income, or 20% of their discretionary income, on average. The Gainful Employment regulations were repealed by the US government in 2019.

5 Texas

This chapter provides an overview of the labour market and higher education system in the state of Texas, an assessment of the labour market outcomes of graduates, and a discussion of state policies that contribute to aligning higher education and the labour market. The policy discussion focuses on four policy areas – strategic planning and co-ordination of higher education; funding; educational offerings, student supports and pathways; and information – and includes policy recommendations in each area.

5.1. The labour market and higher education in Texas

The economy and labour market

The economy of Texas is the second largest in the United States, with consistently high growth over the last ten years

In 2018, the Gross Domestic Product (GDP) of Texas was USD 1.8 trillion, which constitutes the tenth largest economy in the world (Perry, 2019[1]). The compound annual growth rate for Texas between 2008 and 2018 was 3%, compared to an annual growth rate of 1.8% for the United States as a whole (U.S. Bureau of Economic Analysis, 2019[2]). Texas is known for its abundance of resources, accounting for about 24% of natural gas production and 37% of production of crude oil in the United States (TXEDC, n.d.[3]). As such, Texas is responsible for about 20% of total exports from the United States (Dallas Federal Reserve, 2020[4]). The United States recently became a net energy exporter due to reduced domestic consumption coupled with continued growth in petroleum and natural gas production. This growth in production was largely driven by the development of tight oil and shale gas resources, led by extraction in the Permian Basin region of Texas (EIA, 2020[5]).

Texas is a key manufacturing hub for the United States, producing 10% of US manufactured goods (Dallas Federal Reserve, 2020[4]). Though petroleum and coal products account for a large portion of the state's manufactured goods, computer and electronic products, chemicals, and transportation equipment also contribute a substantial share of production and exports (Canas and Gullo, 2019[6]). Because the Texas economy did not contract during the recession of 2008-09, unlike many other states, it has often been referred to as the "Texas Miracle". However, reliance on the oil and gas sector subjects the economy to a boom and bust cycle triggered by fluctuations in the price of oil. As a result, Texas has continued to diversify its economy by supporting the growth of other industries, including biotechnology and life sciences, aerospace and aviation, as well as wind, solar and other renewable energies (TXEDC, n.d.[3]). Texas also has a well-established automotive manufacturing sector that has continued to grow despite shrinking automotive sectors in many states (TXEDC, n.d.[3]).

With a relatively low cost of living, a competitive tax environment, and over 13 million workers, Texas attracts businesses from around the world and across the United States (CNBC, 2019[7]; TXEDC, n.d.[3]; Dallas Federal Reserve, 2020[4]). Moreover, Texas is a "right-to-work" state, which means that employers can hire non-unionised workers. Texas has a population of over 28 million and is expected to gain 5 million new residents by 2028 (TWC, 2019[8]). Some of the fastest-growing cities in the United States are located in Texas, and part of this growth is fuelled by substantial net in-migration from other states. As described in Box 5.1, population growth in Texas is largest in metropolitan areas and, given current trends, 95% of the state's future growth is expected to occur in urban, metropolitan counties (White et al., 2017[9]). The six largest metropolitan areas are Dallas-Fort Worth-Arlington, Houston-the Woodlands-Sugar Land, San Antonio-New Braunfels, Austin-Round Rock, McAllen-Edinburg-Mission, and El Paso. Though economic growth tends to be more uneven throughout areas of El Paso and McAllen-Edinburg-Mission, all six metropolitan areas are expected to see overall growth in employment and GDP across a wide range of industries through 2023 (The Perryman Group, 2019[10]).

Box 5.1. Texas metropolitan areas

Migration drives population growth in the state's largest metropolitan areas. In metropolitan areas such as Brownsville-Harlingen, El Paso, McAllen-Edinburg-Mission, and Laredo, which are located along the border between Texas and Mexico, urban growth is primarily due to natural increase (greater births than deaths). Other areas, including Longview, Odessa, and Wichita Falls, have been experiencing zero growth or negative growth. Migration tends to favour urban over rural population growth, and population growth in Texas is increasingly linked to urbanisation. Current patterns suggest that "migration is transforming the state's largest metropolitan areas into urban growth hubs", while more rural areas see low or negative growth (White et al., 2017, p. 4[9]).

Metropolitan and non-metropolitan counties in Texas, 2018

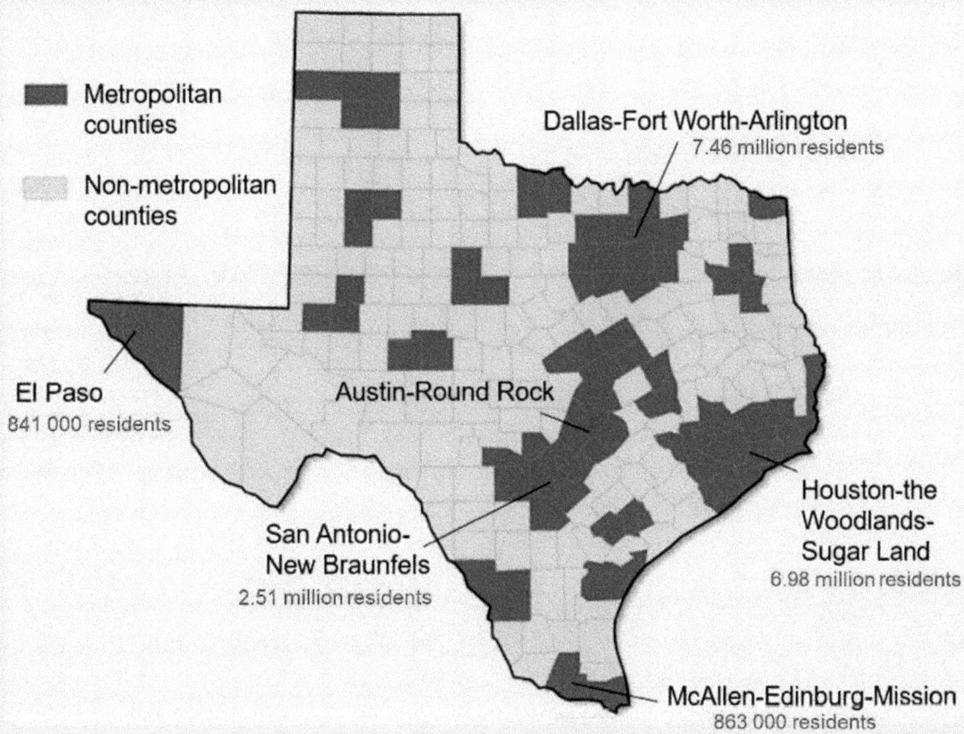

Sources: Map: Texas DSHS (n.d.[11]), *Texas Metropolitan Status by County*, https://www.dshs.texas.gov/chs/info/current-msa.shtm; Population estimates: Federal Reserve of St. Louis (n.d.[12]), *Resident Population by MSAs, 2018* (data from U.S. Census Bureau), https://fred.stlouisfed.org/categories/30907.

The population of Texas is relatively young, which is promising for the state's future workforce supply. As shown in Table 5.1, the dependency ratio, which represents the share of individuals age 65 and older over the 15-64 population, is 19% in Texas, which is well below both the US (24.5%) and OECD (26.5%) averages. The share of individuals in the population under the age of 18 is comparatively high at 26%. Approximately 61% of the population are Texans from minority backgrounds. Hispanic or Latino individuals comprise the largest minority group in Texas, making up approximately 39% of the state's population.

Table 5.1 presents an overview of some key contextual indicators for Texas.

Table 5.1. Texas at a glance

	Texas	United States	Source
Population			
Population estimate	28 701 845	327 167 434	U.S. Census Bureau
Dependency ratio (% 65+ over population aged 15-64)	19.0%	24.5%	U.S Census Bureau
Percentage of individuals under the age of 18, 2017	26.0%	22.4%	U.S. Census
Percentage of individuals aged 65 and over, 2017	12.2%	16.0%	U.S. Census
Percentage of Black or African American individuals, 2017	11.8%	13.4%	U.S. Census
Percentage of Hispanic or Latino individuals, 2017	39.4%	18.3%	U.S. Census
Percentage of Asian individuals, 2017	4.8%	5.9%	U.S. Census
Percentage of American Indian or Alaska Native individuals, 2017	0.3%	1.3%	U.S. Census
Percentage of White individuals, 2017	41.9%	60.4%	U.S. Census
Economy and labour market			
GDP per capita	USD 59 827	USD 57 052	U.S. Bureau of Economic Analysis
Labour force participation rate (out of civilian population aged 16+)	64.0%	62.9%	U.S. Bureau of Labor Statistics
Unemployment rate (seasonally adjusted)	3.9%	3.9%	U.S. Bureau of Labor Statistics
Median annual earnings for working-age population aged 25-64	USD 48 000	USD 50 000	American Community Survey
Estimated annual wage needed to cover basic expenses for a full-time working adult	USD 24 416	USD 25 297	MIT Living Wage Calculator
Percentage of population aged 25-64 with an associate's degree or higher	38.6%	42.5%	American Community Survey

Notes: All numbers are for 2018 unless otherwise noted. Racial and ethnic categories are mutually exclusive. MIT Living Wage annual calculations are based on full-time working hours (2 080 hours per year).

StatLink https://doi.org/10.1787/888934134939

Employment growth has been strong across a range of sectors, but post-secondary educational attainment may be insufficient to meet the state's changing skills needs

In 2019, job growth in Texas outpaced growth overall in the United States (Dallas Federal Reserve, 2020[4]). Total nonagricultural employment in Texas grew by almost 11% between 2014 and 2019, compared to 9% for the United States overall, and annual job growth has increased almost continuously since 2016 (TWC, 2019[8]). Employment growth has been widespread across most industries in Texas during the five-year period from 2014-19. The construction industry saw the highest growth during this period (20%), while the mining and logging industry contracted by 18% due to a downward trend in West Texas Intermediate crude oil prices since 2017 (TWC, 2019[8]). Services industries employ the most workers in Texas, including professional and business services, education and health services, and leisure and hospitality, collectively accounting for almost 50% of total nonfarm employment in Texas (TWC, 2019[8]). The government sector represents about 15% of total employment. It is estimated that 2.1 million new jobs will be added to the Texas economy by 2026, and services industries will likely drive the majority of job gains (TWC, 2019[8]; The Perryman Group, 2019[10]).

Prior to the economic crisis unfolding in 2020 as a result of the COVID-19 pandemic, Texas had experienced particularly low rates of unemployment. At 3.9% in January 2019, the unemployment rate in Texas was at its lowest level in several decades, though slightly higher than the national unemployment rate. In 2009, the unemployment rate for Texas ranged between 6.1% in January and 8.3% in December;

thus, Texas has seen a significant reduction in unemployment since the recession of 2008-09. In the working-age population, however, the unemployment rate is highest among 25-34 year-olds (TWC, 2019[8]). Unemployment rates also vary widely by region; in the large metropolitan areas, unemployment is typically higher in the San Antonio and Houston areas compared to the areas around Austin and Dallas-Fort Worth. Similar to the rest of the country, the labour force participation in Texas has been in decline since the recession (U.S. Bureau of Labor Statistics, 2016[13]). Figure 5.1 shows the labour force participation rate, wage growth, employment and unemployment rates in a ten-year perspective for Texas.

Figure 5.1. Trends in key labour market indicators in Texas, 2009-19

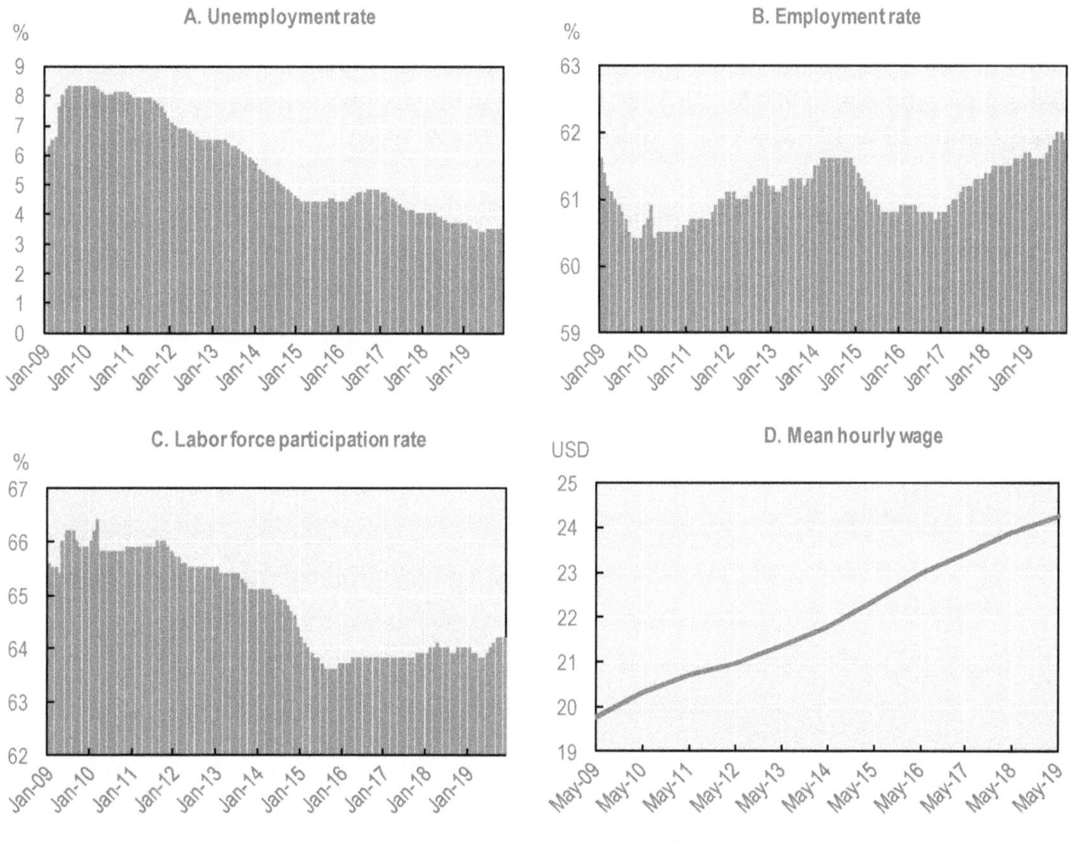

Notes: Data in panels A, B and C are seasonally adjusted. The labour force participation rate is defined as the percentage of people who are either employed or unemployed (but looking for jobs) out of the total civilian non-institutional population, which includes all individuals over the age of 16 who are potentially available for work. The employment rate is the percentage of people who are employed out of the total civilian non-institutional population. The unemployment rate is the percentage of people who are unemployed (but looking for jobs) out of all individuals in the labour force (employed or unemployed but looking for jobs). The mean hourly wage is not adjusted for inflation.
Sources: Panels A, B and C: U.S. Bureau of Labor Force Statistics (2019[14]), *Labor Force Statistics from the Current Population Survey* (database), https://www.bls.gov/cps/tables.htm; Panel D: U.S. Bureau of Labor Statistics (2019[15]), *Occupation Employment Statistics* (database), https://www.bls.gov/oes/home.htm.

StatLink https://doi.org/10.1787/888934133761

Texas has also seen a growing polarisation of jobs in the last four decades. Between 1979 and 2014, Texas experienced a 13% increase in lowest wage jobs and a 6% increase in its highest wage jobs (Blum and Groves, 2016[16]). At the same time, Texas saw a 10% decrease in lower middle-wage jobs and an 11% decrease in upper middle-wage jobs (Blum and Groves, 2016[16]). As in the United States as a whole, the decline of middle-wage jobs involving routine tasks and the growing demand for creative task aptitudes and critical thinking skills have occurred at the same time as a rise in post-secondary attainment in Texas

(Blum and Groves, 2016[16]; Carnevale, Smith and Strohl, 2013[17]). Thus, in order to qualify for higher wage jobs and achieve a sustainable quality of life, there is a growing need for workers to increase their value in the labour market and seek educational and training opportunities beyond a high school diploma (Blum and Groves, 2016[16]).

However, post-secondary educational attainment levels in Texas are below the national average, and progress is lower than anticipated, as further discussed in Section 5.2. As shown in Figure 5.2, 38.6% of the working-age population (aged 25-64) earned an associate's degree or higher in 2018, with a relatively low proportion of adults having earned an associate's degree. The share of adults who have not completed high school is large, which signals challenges early in the education system in Texas. With the inclusion of workforce-relevant certificates, the post-secondary attainment level rises to 43.6% for the working-age population, below the US average of 48.4% (Lumina Foundation, 2019[18]). A potential challenge facing Texas in light of demographic trends is the lower educational attainment of Hispanic students compared to their peers. For example, in 2018, 115 735 Hispanic/Latino students completed certificates or degree programmes, compared to 131 324 White students (THECB, 2019[19]).

Figure 5.2. Levels of educational attainment for Texas residents aged 25-64, 2018

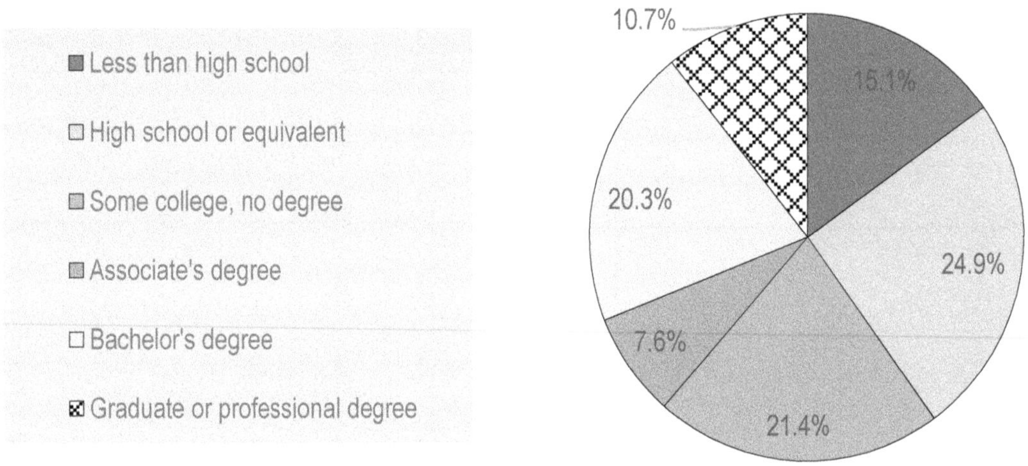

Source: U.S. Census Bureau (2019[20]), *American Community Survey 2018* (database), https://www.census.gov/programs-surveys/acs/data.html.

StatLink https://doi.org/10.1787/888934133780

The higher education system

The Texas Higher Education Coordinating Board serves as a regulatory co-ordinating body providing strategic direction for higher education in Texas

The Texas Higher Education Coordinating Board (THECB) serves as a single state-wide co-ordinating body for higher education in Texas. Established in 1965, the Board has nine voting members nominated by the Governor and approved by the State Senate who sit for staggered six-year terms, plus one non-voting student member with a one-year term; the Chair is elected from among the members of the Board. The Board also selects a Commissioner of Higher Education who functions as the organisation's executive head.

The state Legislature approves appropriations for higher education on a biennial basis. The THECB is responsible for recommending formulas for use by the Governor and Legislative Budget Board in determining legislative appropriations to public higher education institutions, administering state financial assistance programmes for students, setting standards for public community colleges, and authorising elections to create districts that provide funding for public community colleges through property taxes. The THECB also has a statutory mandate to approve all new degree programmes and off-campus activities for public universities as well as community and technical colleges. Institutions defined as private or independent institutions of higher education are exempt from the THECB's oversight. The THECB authorises other private post-secondary degree-granting institutions to operate in Texas through an application and oversight process.

Higher education governance is shared among the Legislature, Governor, the THECB, higher education systems and institutions, in accordance with the Texas Education Code. Texas has six university systems, governed by boards of regents, and four stand-alone public universities. Public four-year institutions in Texas have shared autonomy with the state government. Since the deregulation of tuition in 2003, the governing boards of universities have been authorised to set their own tuition above an established base tuition level set by the state Legislature. Public universities in Texas have substantial academic autonomy in the development of curricula, but at the same time, the state Legislature can enact policy with respect to admissions, credit transfer and other managerial matters that institutions are required to follow. Quality assurance rests primarily with the regional accrediting body, the Southern Association of Colleges and Schools Commission on Colleges (SACSCOC).

Two-year institutions include the three Lamar State colleges, which are part of the Texas State University System, the Texas State Technical College system, and 50 community college districts with more than 80 sites across the state. Several local district boards govern community colleges in Texas, though the THECB has a role in oversight and capital allocations. Each district board has its own governance system, with many overseeing just a single campus, while six community colleges have five or more campuses. The only exception is the Texas State Technical College System, which is governed by a board of regents as a single state-wide institution with multiple campuses (ECS, 2019[21]).

Higher education and workforce development policy in Texas involves multiple agencies and stakeholder groups across state, regional and local levels

Agencies and stakeholders across both education and workforce policy environments play a role in supporting the alignment between higher education and the labour market in Texas. Numerous associations represent different sectors of higher education in Texas, including the Texas Association of Community Colleges, the Council of Public University Presidents and Chancellors, the Independent Colleges and Universities of Texas (ICUT) and Career Schools and Colleges of Texas (CCST). These organisations support policy advocacy as well as information curation and dissemination to legislative and other audiences. They also serve as convening fora for their members and other stakeholders.

In addition, the Texas Success Center, a member of the national Student Success Center Network, supports the 50 community college districts in the state as they align their work to promote student success. The Texas Success Center supports community colleges in building capacity to implement and scale practices, for example in increasing completions, supporting transfers without loss of credit, and encouraging employment in careers valued in the labour market.

The Texas Workforce Commission (TWC) is the state agency responsible for workforce development. The Commission has three members appointed by the Governor, representing employers, labour and the public, and these commissioners together appoint the Executive Director. The TWC co-ordinates the Texas Workforce Solutions network, which includes the state's 28 local Workforce Development Boards (WDBs). The WDBs are located in various regions across Texas and act as important intermediaries between educational providers, employers and other stakeholders. They help develop and fund education and training programmes, often in partnership with institutions of higher education. While the TWC is publicly funded, the WDBs are comprised of local business stakeholders. Funding from the federal Workforce

Innovation and Opportunity Act (WIOA) accounts for most public workforce development spending in Texas.

The Texas Workforce Investment Council (TWIC) is the state's Workforce Development Board under the WIOA. The TWIC plays an advisory role on behalf of the Governor and Legislature, assisting in strategic planning and performance evaluation for the workforce development system. Fourteen of the TWIC's nineteen members are appointed by the Governor to represent various stakeholder groups (business, labour, education and community-based organisations), and the balance are ex-officio representatives from relevant state agencies. Recently, workforce development has provided an organising principle for a number of education-related initiatives. In 2016, Texas established the Tri-Agency Workforce Initiative bringing together three separate agencies: the TWC, the THECB and the Texas Education Agency (TEA), which is responsible for the public K-12 school system. Both the TWC and the TEA also have a strong regional presence, with the 28 regional Workforce Development Boards operating under the authority of the TWC and 20 regional Education Service Centers, which provide assistance to school districts. The Tri-Agency Workforce Initiative, and other related policy initiatives, are discussed in more depth in Section 5.3.

Education Workforce Partnerships aim to improve educational and workforce alignment through programmes such as the Texas Regional STEM Degree Accelerator, Pathways to Prosperity, and Pathways in Technology Early College High Schools (P-TECH). These partnerships are convened by Educate Texas, an initiative of Communities Foundation of Texas, working with multiple stakeholders regionally and state-wide in education and workforce communities. Education Workforce Partnerships also provide a forum for identifying and meeting the needs of industry and engaging with experts. In addition, there are a number of non-profit intermediary organisations at the state and regional levels, such as the Center for Public Policy Priorities, the Texas Association of Institutional Researchers, Educate Texas, Texas Public Policy Foundation, Commit Dallas, and P-16 Councils. These organisations complement the formal responsibilities of the Legislature and the THECB, for example by providing funding to institutions and oversight of programmes, administering state financial aid to students, maintaining state-wide systems for applications, and collecting data.

Texas has a large and diversified system of higher education, characterised by several large sub-systems within the public sector and many small private institutions

The Texas post-secondary education system is large and diverse, enrolling approximately 1.6 million students in 2018 (total headcount). Of these students, the vast majority (88%) were enrolled in public institutions, 8% in private or independent institutions of higher education (which are all not-for-profit institutions), and 4% in private post-secondary institutions, which include both not-for-profit and for-profit institutions operating degree programs under the oversight of the THECB (THECB, n.d.[22]).

Figure 5.3 provides data from the National Center for Education Statistics (NCES) that show enrolment trends for full-time, first-time students over a 15-year period across different institution types in Texas, allowing for comparisons with other states in the study (see Chapters 4, 6 and 7 for Ohio, Virginia and Washington enrolment trends, respectively). The figure shows that enrolments in public four-year and private, not-for-profit institutions have seen a steady increase over time. The trend lines show a decline in enrolment at public two-year institutions since 2012, which is not unusual given that enrolments in community colleges tend to closely mirror trends in the labour market; when the labour market conditions are tight, enrolments typically decline (Hillman and Orians, 2013[23]). However, enrolments at two-year public institutions have resumed growing in recent years, albeit at a slower pace compared to growth in four-year public institutions. Enrolments at private, for-profit institutions in Texas increased substantially during the recession of 2008-09 and have continued to increase, with enrolment growth tapering off in the last five years but remaining at a level that is close to triple the number of enrolments in 2003.

Figure 5.3. Fall higher education enrolment in Texas, 2003-18

Total number of first-time, full-time equivalent (FTE) students, by institution type

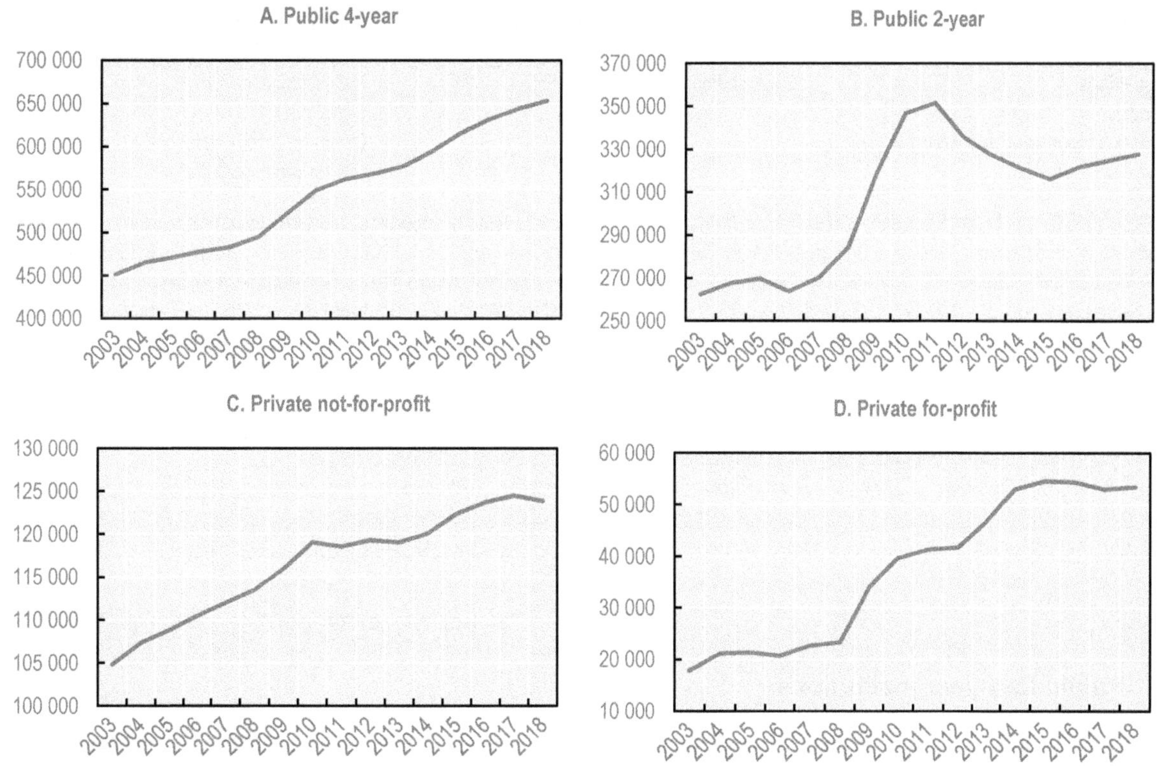

Note: Data for 2018 are provisional.

Source: NCES (2019[24]), *Integrated Post-secondary Education Data System* (database), https://nces.ed.gov/ipeds/use-the-data.

StatLink https://doi.org/10.1787/888934133799

All public institutions have statutory authority to operate and are accredited by SACSCOC. There are various types of private institutions in Texas, with different legal status and requirements to operate. Private or independent institutions of higher education are not-for-profit institutions that hold accreditation recognised by the THECB and are exempt from obtaining THECB approval to operate. Private post-secondary educational institutions include in-state and out-of-state institutions that offer clinical placements or internships in Texas. These institutions can be not-for-profit or for-profit, and are accredited by recognised accreditors, but need to obtain a Certificate of Authorization from the THECB to operate.

Table 5.2 provides an overview of accredited higher education institutions operating in Texas. In addition, a small number of institutions that are unaccredited are working towards accreditation are permitted to operate in Texas under a Certificate of Authority delivered by the THECB.

Table 5.2. Accredited, degree-granting institutions of higher education in Texas

Public institutions of higher education	Private or independent institutions of higher education (not-for-profit institutions)	Private post-secondary educational institutions (both not-for-profit and for-profit institutions under a Certificate of Authorization)
120 institutions Including: 37 institutions four-year institutions 83 two-year institutions	39 institutions	193 institutions Including: 88 not-for-profit institutions 105 for-profit institutions

Notes: According to the Texas Education Code (TEC) provision 61.003(15), a "private or independent institution of higher education" includes only a private or independent college or university that is: (a) organized under the Texas Non-Profit Corporation Act (Article 1396-1.01 et seq., Vernon's Texas Civil Statutes); (b) exempt from taxation under Article VIII, Section 2, of the Texas Constitution and Section 501(c)(3) of the Internal Revenue Code of 1986 (26 U.S.C. Section 501); and (c) accredited by: (i) the Southern Association of Colleges and Schools Commission on Colleges; (ii) the Liaison Committee on Medical Education; or (iii) the American Bar Association.
According to TEC 31.302(2), "private postsecondary educational institution" means an educational institution which: (a) is not an institution of higher education as defined by Section 61.003; (b) is incorporated under the laws of Texas, maintains a place of business in Texas, has a representative present in Texas, or solicits business in Texas; and (c) furnishes or offers to furnish courses of instruction in person, by electronic media, or by correspondence leading to a degree or providing credits alleged to be applicable to a degree.
Sources: THECB (2019[25]), *2019 Texas Public Higher Education Almanac*, http://reportcenter.thecb.state.tx.us/agency-publication/almanac/2019-texas-public-higher-education-almanac; THECB (2020[26]), *Private Postsecondary Institutions Authorized to Operate in Texas*, http://reportcenter.thecb.state.tx.us/agency-publication/miscellaneous/private-postsecondary-institutions-operating-in-texas/.

StatLink https://doi.org/10.1787/888934134958

Public four-year institutions

Four-year institutions are those that offer at least a bachelor's degree (International Standard Classification of Education (ISCED) Level 6). This category of higher education institutions includes research universities, comprehensive universities and colleges offering post-secondary education from ISCED Level 5 to ISCED Level 8 (associate's degrees, bachelor's degrees, master's degrees and doctoral degrees).

There are 37 public four-year institutions in Texas, including four independent institutions and 33 institutions that are part of one of the state's six multi-campus university systems. These include the Texas A&M System, the Texas Tech University System, the Texas State University System, the University of Texas System, the University of Houston System and the University of North Texas System. Each institution is governed by a Board of Regents that includes nine voting members and a single non-voting student representative.

The University of Texas (UT) system has a total fall enrolment of close to 240 000 students across eight university campuses and six health-related institutions, while the Texas A&M system enrols about 151 000 students across eleven universities and a health science centre (UT System, 2020[27]; TAMUS, n.d.[28]). The main campuses of university systems are typically the largest, as illustrated in Table 5.3

The University of Texas at Austin and Texas A&M College Station are research-intensive universities. While selective and highly ranked nationally, some of the state's leading universities remain relatively accessible, not only because of their large size, but also because of state policies requiring top institutions to accept top students from every high school. This policy, referred as the "Top 10% law", was established in 1997 and guarantees admission to any Texas public university to students who graduate in the top decile of their class. This law has been shown to facilitate the entry of Hispanic students and students from high schools where disadvantaged students predominate into the state's flagship institutions, in particular the University of Texas at Austin and Texas A&M University (Niu and Tienda, 2010[29]). In 2018, about 26% of undergraduate students who enrolled for the first time in a public four-year institution, also called first-time-in-college students, had entered higher education via the Top 10% law (THECB, 2019[25]).

Table 5.3. Ten largest Texas public institutions by enrolment, 2018

	Enrolment	Acceptance rate
Texas A&M – College Station	63 694	66.6%
The University of Texas at Austin	51 684	42.1%
The University of Houston, Houston	46 324	62.8%
The University of Texas at Arlington	42 496	79.5%
Texas State University, San Marcos	38 644	79.2%
University of North Texas, Denton	38 087	79.0%
Texas Tech University, Lubbock	37 845	64.4%
The University of Texas at San Antonio	32 101	79%
The University of Texas at Dallas	28 755	80.8%
The University of Texas Rio Grande Valley	28 489	81.0%

Note: The acceptance rate refers to the number of admitted students divided by the number of applicants.
Source: Background information provided by the THECB (2019[25]), *2019 Public Higher Education Almanac*, http://reportcenter.thecb.state.tx.us/agency-publication/almanac/2019-texas-public-higher-education-almanac.

StatLink https://doi.org/10.1787/888934134977

Public two-year institutions

Public two-year institutions offer post-secondary education primarily at ISCED Levels 4 and 5, awarding associate's degrees and short- and long-term certificates. The associate's degree normally requires two years of full-time college work and is designed either to prepare learners for a career (technical programmes), or to transfer to a four-year institution in order to pursue a bachelor's degree (academic programmes).

A number of districts contain multiple colleges with large total fall enrolments. Both the Dallas County Community College District and the Lone Star College System District (suburban Houston) enrolled more than 60 000 students each in 2018, while the Alamo Community College District (San Antonio), the Houston Community College System and the Tarrant County College District (Fort Worth) enrolled around 50 000 students each. The Austin Community College, the Collin County Community College District (suburban Dallas), the South Texas College, and the San Jacinto College district (north of Houston) each enrolled between 30 000 and 40 000 students. The three Lamar State Colleges enrolled about 7 500 students, and the six campuses of the Technical State College System enrolled more than 12 000 students.

Public two-year institutions provide an entry point to higher education for many students, as more than 70% of all Texas bachelor's graduates take at least one college course at a public two-year college (THECB, 2019[25]). As shown in Table 5.4, the majority of students in two-year colleges study part-time (almost 77%), a proportion that is the inverse in four-year institutions. About 75% of students in two-year institutions study in academic programmes preparing them for transfer to a four-year institution, while the remaining 25% study in technical programmes preparing them for labour market entry. While the large majority of students in two-year institutions intend to transfer, a minority of them do so successfully: about 23% of the cohort entering public two-year colleges in 2012 had transferred to a university by 2018 (THECB, 2019[25]).

Table 5.4. Profile of public higher education institutions in Texas, 2018

	Public four-year institutions	Public two-year institutions
Total student population (total headcount, fall enrolment 2018)	658 219	758 133
Undergraduate students as a percentage of total enrolment (fall enrolment, 2018)	80%	100%
Percentage of undergraduate students who are Black/African American	12.2%	12.9%
Percentage of undergraduate students who are Hispanic/Latino	37.5%	45.2%
Percentage of undergraduate students who are White	36.3%	31.1%
Percentage of undergraduate students who are Pell Grant recipients	39.4%	30.3%
Percentage of undergraduate students who study full-time	77.2%	23.3%
150% completion rate (full-time, undergraduate students)	61.6%	30.5%
Average tuition and mandatory fees for in-state undergraduate students (USD, 2019/20 academic year)	USD 8 375	USD 2 099
Percentage of undergraduate students graduating with debt in 2017	58.5%	30.6%
Average student debt for undergraduates in 2017 (USD)	USD 30 825	USD 16 414

Note: The 150% graduation rate refers to the percentage of graduates who completed their degree within one and a half times the normal completion time; that is, six years for a four-year degree and three years for a two-year degree.
Source: THECB (2019[25]), *2019 Texas Public Higher Education Almanac*, http://reportcenter.thecb.state.tx.us/agency-publication/almanac/2019-texas-public-higher-education-almanac.

StatLink https://doi.org/10.1787/888934134996

Private institutions

While there are many private institutions in Texas, they constitute a relatively small share of total enrolments in Texas, with about 12% of all students attending a private institution in 2018, or about 192 000 students in total (THECB, n.d.[22]; ICUT, 2018[30]).

Of students in private institutions, about two-thirds were enrolled in four-year private independent institutions of higher education represented by the Independent Colleges and Universities of Texas Association (ICUT). Many of these institutions were originally religious establishments, the largest including Baylor University in Waco, Texas and Southern Methodist University in University Park, Dallas. The only significant non-denominational private, not-for-profit institution is Rice University in Houston. These institutions are very diverse in size, with enrolments ranging from less than 200 undergraduate students to about 14 000, and have seen a large increase in enrolments of students from racial and ethnic minorities over the past decades. Five of these institutions are currently classified as Historically Black Colleges and Universities and sixteen qualify as Hispanic-serving Institutions, with at least 25% Hispanic undergraduate enrolment. While no information is available on the average tuition for this group of institutions, about 30% of undergraduate students receive Pell Grants, and 80% of them receive some form of grant aid. About 48% of students are White in these institutions, while Black/African American and Hispanic students are less represented than in public higher education. Four-year independent institutions have six-year graduate rates that are slightly higher than the average in public four-year institutions, at 64.4% for the cohort entering in 2011 (ICUT, 2018[30]).

The remaining one-third of students in private institutions, approximately 63 000 in 2018, were enrolled in private post-secondary education institutions, which can be either not-for-profit or for-profit and must obtain a Certificate of Authorization from the THECB to operate. Some of these institutions are out-of-state institutions that offer clinical placements or internships in Texas. The majority of these students (about 39 000) were enrolled in four-year institutions. Data from the THECB shows that enrolments in these institutions has declined in recent years, with fall headcount falling by about 19% in four-year institutions between 2017 and 2019, and about 16% in two-year institutions. Black and African American students were overrepresented in these institutions compared to their share in other institution types, representing about 26% of enrolments in four-year institutions and about 21% in two-year institutions. Average tuition is high in these institutions, at USD 15 322 and USD 13 728 in 2018 in four- and two-year institutions respectively, and a large share of students receive Pell Grants (56% and 63% in the four- and two-year sectors respectively). The share of students who graduate within 150% of their programme's nominal time is high in two-year institutions (close to 63% in 2019), but low in four-year institutions, at 27% (THECB, n.d.[22]).

There are also non-degree private institutions operating under licensure by the Texas Workforce Commission; these institutions do not need accreditation, although some have been accredited.

5.2. Assessment of labour market outcomes: The alignment between supply and demand of graduate skills in Texas

Alignment of supply and demand

Employment in post-secondary-intensive occupations continues to grow, with strong demand for middle and advanced skills

At the national level, research indicates that the skills intensity within occupations is growing, and that a majority of the new jobs created since the recession of 2008-09 have required post-secondary education (Carnevale, Smith and Strohl, 2013[17]; Deming and Kahn, 2018[31]). Detailed occupational projections conducted by the Georgetown Center on Education and the Workforce indicated that 59% of jobs in Texas would require some form of post-secondary education or training by 2020 (Carnevale and Smith, 2012[32]). While Texas has a lower proportion of post-secondary-intensive jobs compared to the national average, this share has been steadily growing.

As discussed in the previous section, the labour market in Texas has continued to expand since the end of the 2008-09 recession, and long-term projections suggest that employment growth is expected in almost every major sector of the economy, with 2.1 million new jobs to be added by 2026 (TWC, 2019[8]). The professional and business services, educational services, and health care and social services sectors are the fastest-growing industries in Texas – industries which include a substantial share of occupations and jobs that require some form of post-secondary education. Indeed, the 2019 Texas Workforce Report states that, "Texas remains driven by a continued economic shift towards high-skilled jobs in the professional and business services sector, while the state's rapid population growth and aging baby-boomer population increases demand for service sector jobs, primarily in education and health services" (TWC, 2019, p. 26[8]).

Figure 5.4 shows long-term employment projections in Texas for occupations that require a post-secondary degree. As shown, employment of post-secondary graduates in education and health care occupations is high and expected to continue growing. High-demand, high-wage professions within these occupational groups include nurse practitioners, registered nurses, physical therapists, post-secondary teachers in health specialities, and education and health care management. Other high-demand, high-wage professions include software developers, civil engineers, and management analysts (TWC, 2019[8]). The largest growth in employment requiring post-secondary education is expected in community and social services occupations, which are projected to double by 2026 compared to 2018.

Figure 5.4. Projected employment growth in occupations that typically require some form of post-secondary education, 2018-26

Total number of jobs, based on long-term occupational projections for Texas

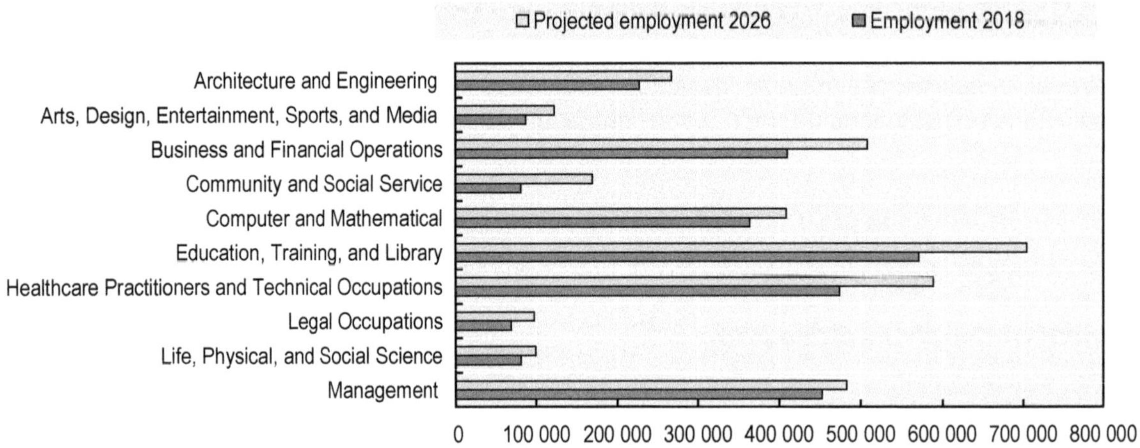

Note: Occupational groups correspond to major groups 11-0000 to 29-0000 of the Standard Occupation Classification (SOC) system. The educational requirement for each occupation is the minimum level of education needed for entry into an occupation, based on U.S. Bureau of Labor Statistics occupational information.
Source: Adapted from TWC (2019[33]), *Texas Labor Analysis*, https://texaslaboranalysis.com/GapAnalysis.

StatLink https://doi.org/10.1787/888934133818

In Texas, jobs requiring education and training in science, technology, engineering and mathematics (STEM) fields are primarily concentrated in engineering, computer, and mathematical occupations. While STEM jobs do not represent a large proportion of jobs in Texas, they are expected to grow as a proportion of total employment (Carnevale and Smith, 2012[32]). Moreover, STEM skills are in high demand across different fields and occupations, and are often associated with higher earnings.

Middle-skill jobs – defined as those that require some post-secondary education but less than a bachelor's degree – make up a relatively large proportion of employment in Texas. According to an analysis by the National Skills Coalition (NSC), about 56% of all jobs in Texas were defined as middle-skill jobs in 2015 (National Skills Coalition, 2017[34]). Good jobs at the middle skill level are becoming less attainable for workers with only a high school diploma, thus increasing the importance of the associate's degree and other post-secondary training, including certificates (Carnevale et al., 2018[35]; Carnevale, Smith and Strohl, 2013[17]). The Georgetown University Center on Education and the Workforce (CEW) has defined good jobs as those with minimum annual earnings of USD 35 000 for individuals under the age of 45 and USD 45 000 for those above 45. In Texas, the CEW has estimated that the share of good jobs held by workers with associate's degrees increased by 10 percentage points between 1991 and 2015. In the same time period, the share of good jobs held by workers with only a high school diploma decreased by five percentage points (Carnevale, Strohl and Ridley, 2017[36]).

The NSC has pointed to a middle-skills gap in Texas because the supply of middle-skill workers has not been keeping pace with middle-skill job openings, partly due to the fact that many jobs previously requiring a high school degree now require some post-secondary education or training. The NSC argues further that that many low-skilled individuals may not be participating in the labour force despite low unemployment due to the gap between their skills and the requirements of middle-skilled jobs (National Skills Coalition, 2018[37]). Based on projections for the period 2014-24, the NSC estimates that the demand for middle skills in Texas will remain strong, with about half of all job openings requiring middle skills (National Skills Coalition, 2017[34]).

Skills misalignment is observed in certain fields and in some regions

Labour gap analyses in Texas point to state-wide shortages in some healthcare and education professions (TWC, 2019[33]). Shortages have been reported specifically in nursing, teaching (including post-secondary faculty in healthcare fields), engineering, and information and communications technology (ICT) fields. According to the Texas Workforce Commission, there is a critical shortage of elementary school teachers and teacher assistants. Five teacher shortage areas were identified for the 2019/20 school year to receive federal support for loan forgiveness programmes (TEA, 2019[38]). Furthermore, shortages in regulated professions such as nursing and other healthcare specialties may be exacerbated by a complex system of third-party licensing and certification requirements, creating additional barriers to employment or career progression (OECD, 2018[39]).

Domestic and international migration of skilled workers into key occupations or fields can alleviate labour shortages. However, current statistical tools at the state level do not allow for labour gap analyses that take into account migration patterns, thus making it difficult to estimate the impact of migration on the supply of skilled workers state-wide and by occupational group. In recent years, Texas has attracted skilled workers from out of state and around the world. Between 2014 and 2017, Texas experienced net domestic in-migration from other states; however, out-migration of young degree holders (aged 25-34) has steadily increased while international in-migration has remained stagnant, thus reducing net total in-migration (THECB, 2019[19]).

At the regional level, migration patterns differ. Based on data from LinkedIn, the Austin area gained the most workers between 2018 and 2019, compared to the Dallas and Houston metropolitan areas (LinkedIn, 2019[40]). However, the most migration activity was observed between (to and from) these three metro areas, indicating strong competition for skilled workers between these regional economies (LinkedIn, 2019[41]; LinkedIn, 2019[42]). Graduates typically gravitate towards cities and regions with higher earnings and better career opportunities, but individual mobility depends on multiple factors. Furthermore, labour market needs may change rapidly due to entry or exit of different industries in a particular region.

The THECB previously set a state-wide goal to increase the number of degrees produced in STEM fields. The goal was to increase the number of baccalaureate and sub-baccalaureate STEM degrees conferred by public higher education institutions to a total of 29 000 degrees in 2015 (THECB, 2016[43]). However, at 23 679 total STEM degrees in 2015, this goal was not met, with the slowest growth in computer science fields. Similarly, the state-wide goal for completions of teacher education certifications fell short, and the number of initial teacher certifications in 2015 only reached about 50% of the state-wide target. According to data from the National Center for Education Statistics (NCES), the number of bachelor's degrees conferred in education declined between 2008 and 2017 in Texas, while the number of master's degrees increased. The growth in master's degree completions may be associated with the rise in dual credit delivery, as high school teachers are required to have a master's degree to teach dual credit courses. State-wide targets for degree completion in allied health and nursing fields were met in 2015, but have evidently not been enough to meet nursing shortages in the state.

At a more granular level, data from LinkedIn allow for a rudimentary skills gap analysis using self-reported information from individual profiles and comparing this to skill demand extracted from online job postings. The top reported skill shortages between 2018 and 2019 were remarkably similar in Austin, Houston and Dallas-Fort Worth (LinkedIn, 2019[40]; LinkedIn, 2019[41]; LinkedIn, 2019[42]). About half of the top ten skills reported as shortages in all three regions were so-called "soft" skills (typically transversal skills), including oral communication, leadership and people management. Technical skills such as business management, data storage technologies and data science were also reported as top skill shortages. OECD interviews with employers in Texas confirmed that, while the quality of the skills of Texas graduates were generally seen to be positive, employers saw a need for stronger social and emotional skills such as communication, punctuality and resilience.

At the same time, employers' skills needs and hiring choices are complex and vary over time. During OECD interviews, some employers in Texas reported a reluctance to hire graduates with associate's degrees even when a job does not strictly require a baccalaureate degree. Employers met by the study team often reported a preference for candidates with bachelor's degrees, also for middle-skill jobs, reflecting a stronger signalling effect of the baccalaureate degree, which may be based on either the real or perceived quality of skills associated with bachelor's degree graduates. While national research has shown that good jobs are becoming increasingly unattainable for workers without some form of post-secondary education or training (Carnevale, Smith and Strohl, 2013[17]), there is also some evidence of over-qualification or so-called "credential inflation", particularly at the sub-baccalaureate level (Fuller et al., 2017[44]; Rose, 2017[45]). This may result in fewer opportunities for workers with less than a bachelor's degree, and others being employed in jobs for which they are over-qualified.

Without further data on in-field job placement rates for Texas graduates, it is difficult to ascertain the extent, if any, of mismatch or over-qualification. It is clear that the baccalaureate degree holds significant value for employers in the Texas labour market; however, on average, associate's degree holders in Texas do reasonably well in terms of labour market outcomes, which are on par with the US average. This will be explored further in the next section.

Post-secondary attainment rates are below the national average and degree completions per year are not increasing rapidly enough to reach state-wide targets

As of 2017, 38% of Texas residents aged 25-64 have an associate's degree or higher. In addition, an estimated 5% of Texans have earned a workforce-relevant certificate, bringing the average total attainment rate for the state to 43% (Lumina Foundation, 2019[18]). This is lower than the national average of 47.6%. Because Texas is such a large and diverse state, educational attainment rates vary widely across counties and regions, reflecting, to some extent, differing labour market and economic needs across the state. Of the six largest metropolitan areas in Texas, the Austin-Round Rock region has the highest post-secondary attainment rate of 50.4% (Lumina Foundation, 2018[46]). As seen in Table 5.5, the largest region, Dallas-Fort Worth-Arlington – with a population of about 7.4 million – has an attainment rate of 41.6%. Out of the 100 most populous metropolitan areas in the United States, the Dallas-Fort Worth-Arlington region ranks 59th in terms of post-secondary attainment, despite being the fourth largest metropolitan area in the country. As the fifth largest metropolitan area in the country, the Houston-Woodlands-Sugar Land region ranks only 76th in terms of post-secondary attainment.

Table 5.5. Degree attainment rates in Texas by metropolitan area, 2017

Share of adults aged 25-64 with at least an associate's degree in the six largest metropolitan areas (MSAs) in Texas, relative to population size and rank among the 100 most populous MSAs in the United States

Metropolitan Statistical Area (MSA)	Population estimate	Degree attainment rate	Population rank (of 100 MSAs nationwide)	Attainment rank (of 100 MSAs nationwide)
Dallas-Fort Worth-Arlington	7 399 662	41.6%	4	59
Houston-The Woodlands-Sugar Land	6 892 427	39.4%	5	76
San Antonio-New Braunfels	2 473 974	36.4%	24	86
Austin-Round Rock	2 115 827	50.4%	31	14
McAllen-Edinburg-Mission	860 661	24.2%	66	99
El Paso	844 818	32.4%	69	93

Source: Lumina Foundation (2019[18]), *A Stronger Nation: Texas Report 2019*, https://luminafoundation.org/stronger-nation/report/2020/#nation.

StatLink https://doi.org/10.1787/888934135015

Attainment rates in Texas also vary widely by race and ethnic group. Despite representing around 40% of the state's population, only 20% of Hispanic adults in Texas have an associate's degree or higher, which is also lower than the average post-secondary attainment rate for Hispanics nation-wide (Lumina Foundation, 2019[18]). This represents an untapped potential in the workforce. While Texas attracts skilled workers from around the country and the world, boosting the supply of skilled workers through the Texas higher education system can serve to fill shortages in certain fields and strengthen Texas residents' capacity for re-skilling and up-skilling, especially in certain regions and for under-represented populations. In order to keep pace with the growing demand for middle and advanced skills, the Texas Higher Education Coordinating Board (THECB) has set a state-wide goal to achieve 60% post-secondary attainment by 2030 among young adults aged 25-34. In 2018, 43.7% of 25-34 year-olds in Texas had a post-secondary degree or certificate. Because this is at the same level of attainment as for the working-age population as a whole, this could pose a problem in ensuring a sufficiently skilled workforce in the future.

Post-secondary attainment rates for 25-34 year-olds in Texas have been steadily increasing since 2014. The THECB had expected that the state would reach its attainment goal by 2030. However, most recent data indicate that attainment in 2018 has increased by 0.1 percentage point from the previous year, far below the annual increase needed to stay on track (THECB, 2019[19]). Progress on higher education attainment depends on a number of factors, including a sufficient number of high school students transitioning into higher education, improved completion rates within higher education, and a continued flow of skilled workers from out of state and internationally. More importantly, increasing the supply of graduates from Texas higher education institutions will be critical in order to boost overall attainment rates. When it comes to the number of credentials completed, however, the rate of progress in completions from 2015-17 has been much slower compared to the increasing attainment rate for the population, which may have indicated a strong reliance on out-of-state workers. In Texas' current higher education plan, the THECB aims to increase completions (up to and including master's degrees) by 3.9% per year.

Figure 5.5 shows the number of credentials completed at Texas post-secondary institutions between 2015 and 2019 (THECB, 2019[19]). The number of completions increased by an average of 3.1% annually between 2015 and 2018, and by 1.9% between 2018 and 2019. Recent data show the number of certificates, associate's, bachelor's and master's degrees dropping from 341 307 in 2018 to 322 800 in 2019 (THECB, n.d.[22]). This appears to be largely driven by a decrease in production of certificates and associate's degrees. Reaching the state-wide target for 2020 requires a 16% increase in degree production from 2019, which is much higher than current rates of production. Even without a decline in completions in 2019, yearly rates of increase in the past five years have not been high enough to meet the state's goals.

Figure 5.5. Certificate and degree completions in Texas, 2015-19

Total numbers for 2015-19 and targeted numbers for 2020, 2025 and 2030

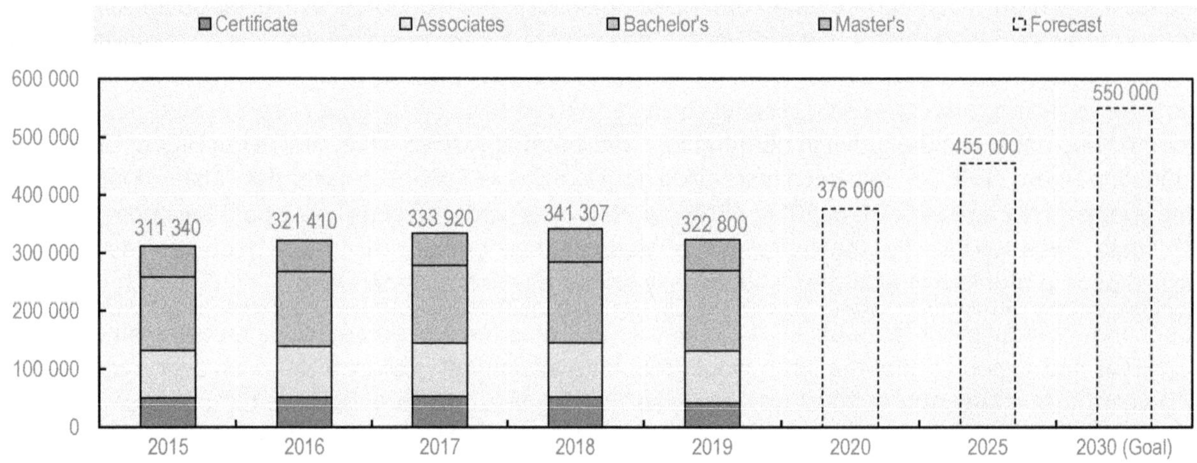

Notes: Figures for 2015-19 include certificate and degree completions at public, private independent, and private career institutions in Texas. Figures for 2020, 2025 and 2030 are targets. Certificates in Texas are formal awards granted by an institution of higher education and are of different levels. Certificates counted by the THECB includes Level I (15-42 hours of instruction), Level II (30-51 hours) and Advanced Technical Certificates (16-50 hours). Advanced Technical Certificates also require the previous award of an associate's degree, a bachelor's degree, or "junior status" towards a baccalaureate (meaning having completed 60-89 credit hours). Shorter certificates and industry certifications are excluded from the count (for further detail on certificates in Texas, see TEA, THECB and TWC (n.d.[47])).
Source: THECB (2019[19]), *60x30TX Progress Report*, http://www.60x30tx.com/media/1518/2019-60x30tx-progress-report.pdf.

StatLink https://doi.org/10.1787/888934133837

Post-secondary enrolment and completion rates

Texas' population growth is contributing to increased higher education participation, but the share of the population enrolled in higher education has remained stable in past decades

Texas has experienced significant growth in higher education enrolments over the past two decades. The number of students enrolled in higher education has grown by 40% in public four-year institutions, and by 55% in public two-year institutions over 2002-18 (THECB, 2019[25]). Total enrolments peaked in 2012 after the financial crisis, declining slightly for two-year institutions in the following years, but overall higher than pre-crisis due to growth in enrolments at four-year institutions. This absolute increase in enrolments represents a major success according to the key participation target set in Texas' 2000-15 *Closing the Gaps* higher education plan.

However, this growth has been uneven among population groups; the state fell short on the post-secondary enrolment targets for Whites and Hispanics, as well as for men, set in the *Closing the Gaps* plan (THECB, 2016[43]). The gender gap remains important, with men being under-represented, especially among African Americans. In addition, this strong post-secondary enrolment growth largely reflects demographic trends in Texas, the population of which is younger and faster-growing than most states in the country. When looking at post-secondary enrolments in public institutions as a share of the total population, the enrolment rate has remained stable over time, as shown in Figure 5.6.

Figure 5.6. Annual enrolment in public higher education institutions, 2001-18

Individuals enrolled (12-month enrolment) as a share of the total Texas population

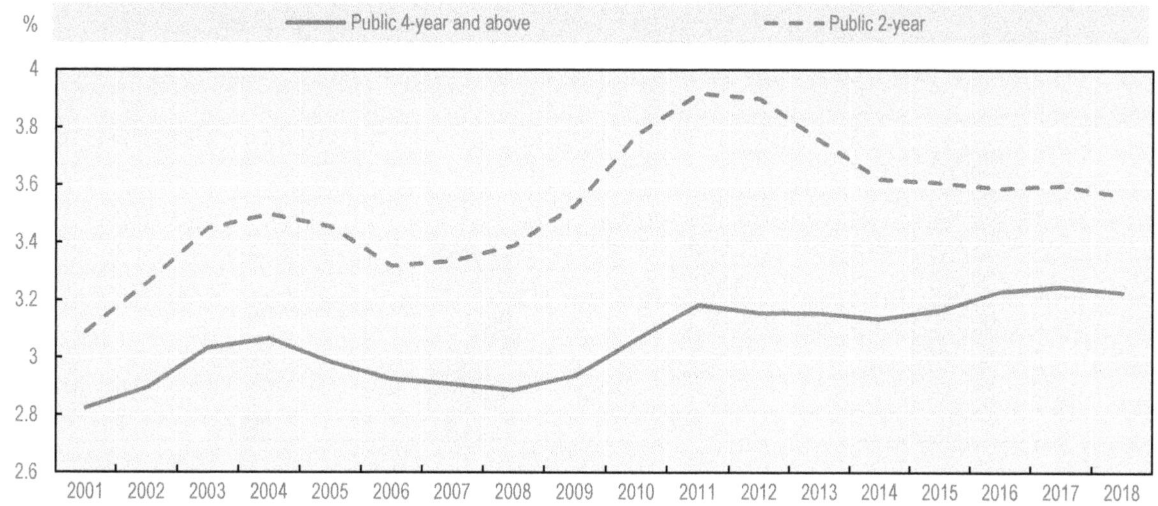

Note: 12-month enrolment includes all individuals enrolled in post-secondary education for a 12-month period regardless of their age.
Sources: Enrolment: NCES (2019[24]), *Integrated Post-secondary Education Data System* (database), https://nces.ed.gov/ipeds/use-the-data (Public 2-year and Public 4-year institutions); Population: Texas Demographic Center (2018[48]), *Texas Population Estimates Program (TPEP)*, https://demographics.texas.gov/Data/TPEPP/estimates.

StatLink https://doi.org/10.1787/888934133856

Ensuring access to higher education for all Texans regardless of their ethnic, racial or socio-economic background is a key concern in Texas. Despite efforts to ensure affordable higher education, especially in the two-year sector, the transition rate to post-secondary education within one year of high school graduation has not increased over the past 16 years. Instead, the transition rate has decreased slightly from 52.2% in 2002 to 51.6% in 2018, with variations in the intervening years and a high point of 56.3% in 2009 (THECB, 2016[43]; THECB, 2019[25]).

Recent cohort data show large gaps between students of differing socio-economic status in Texas. Of all high school students who completed 8th grade in 2002, about 64% of the economically advantaged had enrolled in higher education in 2013, but only 37% of students from a disadvantaged background had done so (THECB, 2013[49]). Most recent data suggest the gap has reduced, although it remains substantial: of all high school students who completed 8th grade in 2007, about 65% of economically advantaged students entered higher education in 2018, compared to 44% of those who were economically disadvantaged (Figure 5.7).

A range of factors underpins these divergent trajectories. Insufficient academic readiness is one key factor identified by the THECB as requiring joint work with the K-12 education system (THECB, 2019[25]). While Texas has relatively affordable tuition and fees in the public higher education sector, particularly at the two-year level, other financial and non-financial barriers appear to limit the ability and motivation of high school graduates to pursue higher education. Understanding what those barriers may be – such as insufficient or ineffective information, or a lack of "wrap-around" supports for disadvantaged students – will be important to address this challenge.

Figure 5.7. Progression within the education system of students enrolled in 8th grade in fall 2007

Total number of students and shares of students enrolled in 8th grade in 2007

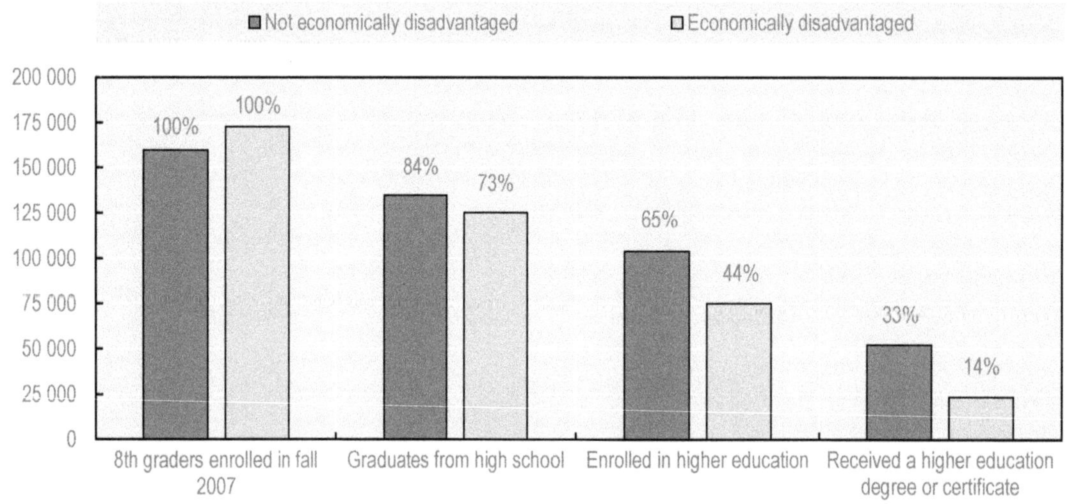

Notes: The left axis indicates the total number of students in each group (not economically disadvantaged and economically disadvantaged). Economically disadvantaged students are students who qualify for free or reduced-price lunch. The percentages indicate the share of students in each group who were enrolled in grade 8 in 2007 (100% of both groups), who then graduated from high school, enrolled in higher education and received a higher education degree or certificate. Data are based on a longitudinal study tracking 8th grade students into higher education.
Source: THECB (2019[25]), *Texas Public Higher Education Almanac*, http://reportcenter.thecb.state.tx.us/agency-publication/almanac/2019-texas-public-higher-education-almanac.

StatLink https://doi.org/10.1787/888934133875

Non-completion and low graduation rates continue to be a challenge

In Texas, as across the United States, a large share of post-secondary education entrants drop out before completing their programme. This population, along with individuals who hold a post-secondary certificate, is typically identified in census surveys such as the American Community Survey as having "some college, no degree". The size of this population is large in Texas. According to 2018 estimates from the American Community Survey, there were 3.9 million Texans aged 25 and older with some college and no degree.

Importantly, a sizeable share of individuals with "some college, no degree" hold a post-secondary certificate. Estimates suggest that about 735 000 Texans aged 25-64 hold a high-quality post-secondary certificate, defined as providing an earnings premium of at least 20% compared to having only completed high school (Lumina Foundation, 2019[18]; CEW, 2019[50]). However, the majority of individuals with some college and no degree are non-completers, who face penalties in the labour market, often compounded by student debt they incurred before dropping out, as discussed later in this section. From the employer perspective, non-completers represent a population whose skills are viewed are either insufficient or difficult to ascertain. Thus, the non-completion challenge remains critical in Texas.

Four-year graduation rates at Texas institutions remain relatively low in a national perspective. For the cohort entering in 2012, 53.7% of first-time, full-time degree-seeking students enrolled in four-year institutions graduated within six years in Texas, below the national average of 60.2% (NCES, 2019[24]). However, in public four-year institutions, state data suggest that graduation rates have improved by close to three percentage points for the cohort graduating in 2019, compared to the cohort graduating in 2017 (THECB, n.d.[51]). As elsewhere in the country, graduation rates are lower at two-year colleges in Texas than they are at four-year institutions. The 150% completion rate at public two-year colleges in Texas was 21.3% in 2017, compared to 27.4 in Ohio, 28.7% in Virginia and 35.8% in Washington (see Chapter 3). It should be noted, however, that national graduation rates exclude students who have transferred between institutions, study part-time or complete credentials that are not degrees. Texas data take into account part-time students in two-year institutions and measures the graduation rates over a six-year period (200% of a two-year programme's normal length). These data show that six-year graduation rates in public two-year institutions have remained around or slightly above 30% over the past decade, with little improvement over time (THECB, 2016[43]; THECB, 2019[25]).

College-ready students are significantly more likely to graduate than those who are not. For the entering cohort of 2012, 44.2% of college-ready students graduated within six years at Texas public two-year institutions, which is double the share of those who were not ready. While a much smaller share of non-ready students enrol in four-year institutions, a similar graduation gap exists between ready and non-ready students. This is a particular challenge in Texas given the lower-than-average student performance at the end of high school. The scores of high school students on standardised tests widely used in the United States as part of the higher education admissions process, the ACT and SAT, illustrate this challenge. Texas ranks around the middle of the 50-state distribution on ACT scores, and 42nd in the SAT writing and math mean. About 40% of students entering public post-secondary education in Texas do not meet state readiness standards, with the large majority of unprepared students attending two-year institutions (THECB, 2019[25]).

Data on the "some college no degree" population in Texas suggest a relatively large proportion of individuals who have completed some post-secondary credits then re-enrol in an educational programme. Following on the status of individuals found to have some college but no degree in 2013, 16% had re-enrolled in post-secondary education in 2018, compared to 13% on average in the country, and 4% had completed, compared to a national average of about 3% (National Student Clearinghouse, 2019[52]). This suggests that efforts to re-engage adults with some post-secondary credits may contribute to raising the state's attainment levels.

An increasing number of post-secondary students choose programmes linked to high-demand, high-earning occupations

Over the past decade, Texas students appear to have responded to the labour market signals, shifting increasingly towards high-demand, high-earning study fields. Figure 5.8 relies on national data, which allow comparison of the enrolment in high-demand fields in the states participating in the study (see Chapter 3). The figure shows that, between 2008 and 2018, the total number of bachelor's degrees awarded in engineering and computer and information science quadrupled in Texas, whereas it increased more slowly in health-related professions, and remained stable in education. With respect to shorter credentials, there has been a limited but steady growth in the production of associate's degrees across the four fields, though it has been much larger in computer and information science. The number of certificates awarded has been robust in computer and information science, but stable in the three other fields.

Changes in student choices are particularly visible when considering, at different levels of study, which field they choose to pursue. At the bachelor's level, degrees awarded in STEM fields, namely those related to biological and physical sciences, mathematics, computer and information sciences and engineering, represented 14.7% in 2007/08, growing to 20.1% of all bachelor's degrees awarded in 2017/18. The share of bachelor's degrees awarded in health fields has grown faster, from 6.5% to 12.6%, over the same period. By contrast, in the field of education, bachelor's degrees awarded declined from 2.2% to 1.1% of all bachelor's degrees awarded.

Figure 5.8. Trends in the production of certificates and degrees in high-demand fields, 2008-18

Number of certificates and degrees awarded annually

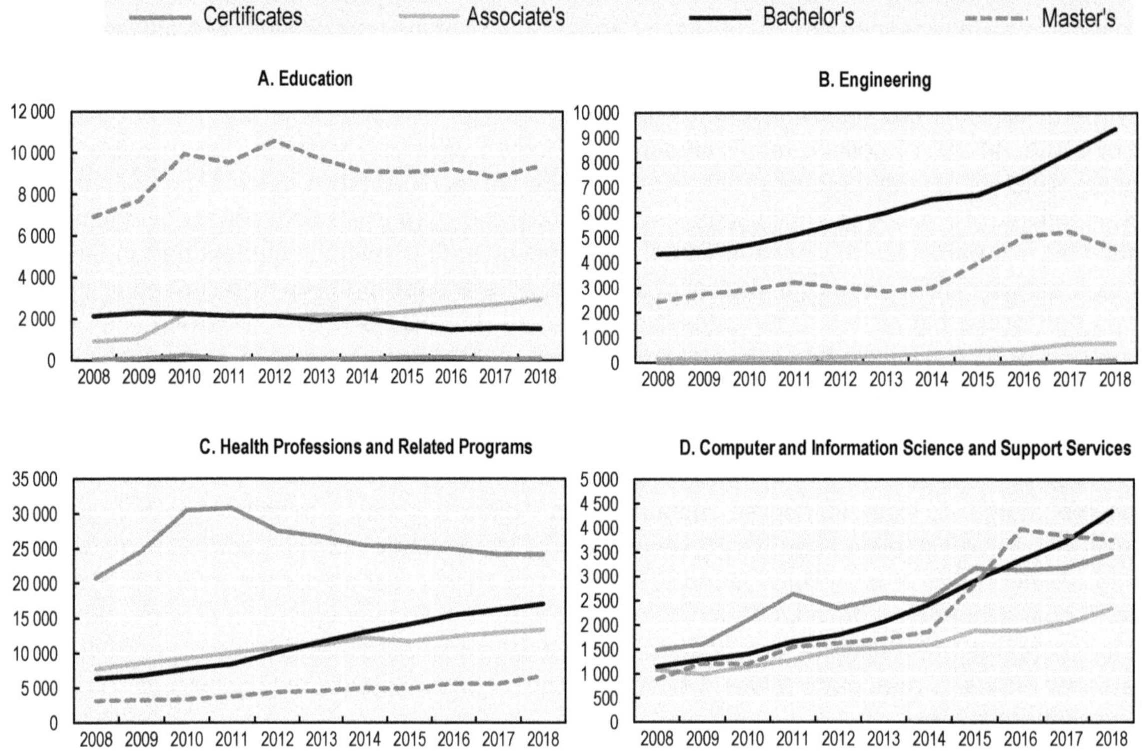

Source: NCES (2019[24]), *Integrated Post-secondary Education Data System* (database), https://nces.ed.gov/ipeds/use-the-data.

StatLink https://doi.org/10.1787/888934133894

Regarding short programmes such as certificates, trends differ by fields. For instance, certificates of less than one year in length awarded in computer science have grown from 4.6% to 6.8% of all certificates awarded of that duration from 2007/08 to 2017/18. By contrast, short certificates of less than one year awarded in health-related fields have fallen as a share of total certificates of less than one year, from 59.0% to 24.1% over the same period (NCES, 2019[24]). As will be discussed further, expected earnings may explain these choices, which may be less connected to the length of the certificate, but rather to the field of study, whether the certificate holder works in their field of study after graduation, and gender

While Texas students have, on average, shown strong responsiveness to labour market signals, not all students pursue high-earning fields or attend selective institutions whose graduates generally enjoy stronger labour market outcomes. Figure 5.9 shows degrees awarded in select fields of study in 2018 as a share of total degrees awarded to key ethnic and racial groups and to each gender. The figure illustrates that Asian students receive a larger share of degrees in high-earning fields – close to 16% of all degrees awarded to this group were in engineering, engineering technologies, computer science or mathematics, compared to about 9% for Whites, 8% for Hispanics and 5% for Black/African Americans. It is also noteworthy that almost half of international students in Texas institutions have obtained degrees in these high-earning fields. By contrast, degrees awarded in lower-earning fields, including social sciences, liberal arts, education and psychology, represented around 34% of all degrees awarded to Black/African Americans and Hispanics, compared to 27% of degrees awarded to Whites and 23% of degrees awarded to Asian students.

Figure 5.9. Degrees awarded by race/ethnicity or gender and field in Texas, 2018

As a share of all degrees awarded to each demographic group

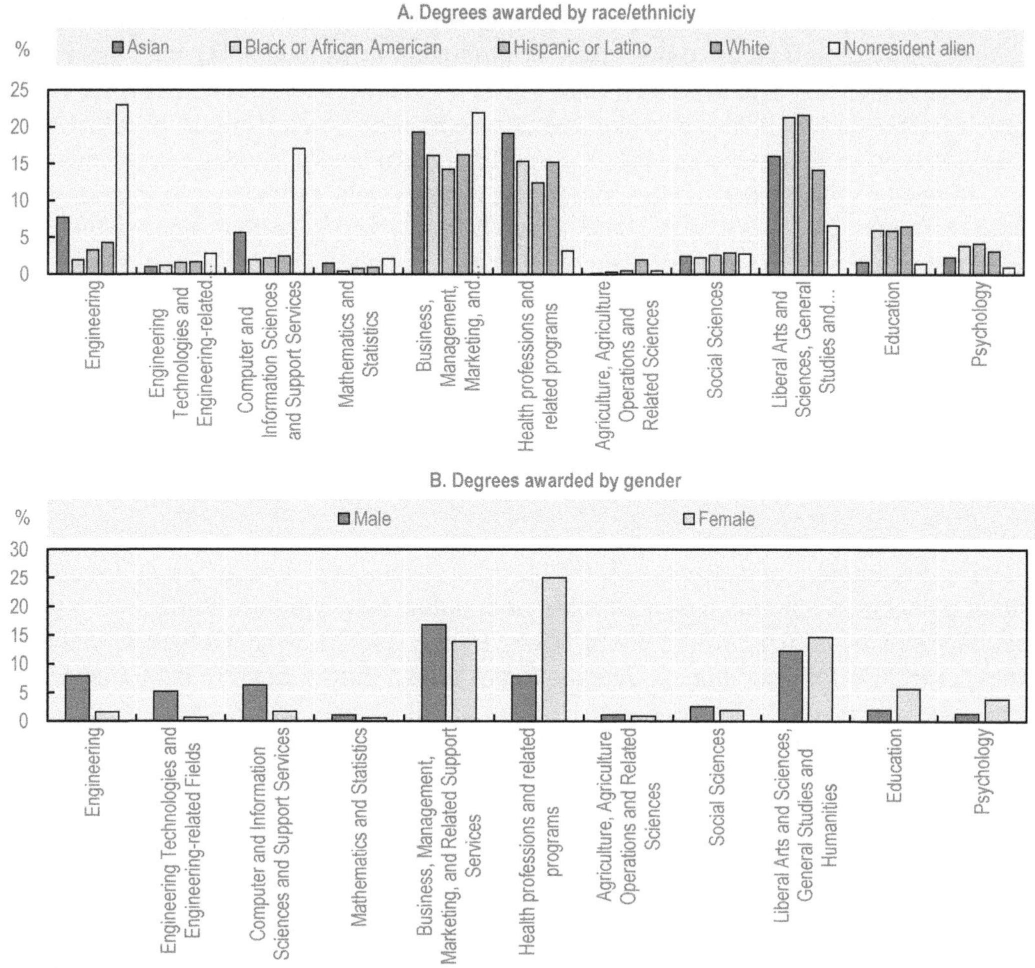

Notes: Fields of study are ordered from highest- to lowest-earning. The figure shows for each racial/ethnic group and for each gender the share of degrees awarded in each field as a share of all degrees received by that ethnic/racial group or gender. For example, more than 5% of all degrees awarded to Asian students were in engineering, and 25% of all degrees awarded to women were in health professions and related programmes. The field of study reflected is that of the degree awarded during the year considered: a student with a bachelor's degree in engineering, who is then awarded a PhD in computer sciences is recorded as "computer sciences".
Source: NCES (2019[24]), *Integrated Post-secondary Education Data System* (database), https://nces.ed.gov/ipeds/use-the-data.

StatLink https://doi.org/10.1787/888934133913

From a gender perspective, a similar imbalance exists. Close to 20% of degrees awarded to men in 2018 were in engineering, engineering technologies, computer science, or mathematics; whereas fewer than 4% of degrees awarded to women were in these high-earning fields. By contrast, 25% of all degrees awarded to women were in health professions and related programmes, an area which includes both high- and lower-earning professions, and 15% were in liberal arts and sciences or general studies and humanities, which command lower earnings compared to other study fields.

Enrolments according to institution type also show some notable differences in ethnic and racial profile as noted in Section 5.1. While approximately 48.7% of Asians and 44.4% of Whites were enrolled in public four-year institutions, this figure was only 39.7% and 33.3% among Hispanics and African Americans, respectively. By contrast, while the share of Hispanics and Africans Americans enrolled in private two-year institutions, which are largely for-profit institutions, remains small overall, at 2.2% and 3.2% respectively, it is much larger than that of Whites or Asians, at 1.1% and 0.6% respectively (NCES, 2019[24]).

Students' choices in terms of fields of study raise two issues. One relates to areas of critical shortages such as teaching and some health-related professions, which command low earnings and often difficult working conditions. Another relates to the ability of graduates in various fields, and especially in highly technical and specialised fields, to develop transversal skills that will allow them to adapt to new demands. For instance, as short-term certificates in high-earning fields may be an increasingly attractive option for some students looking to secure income within a short period of time and low financial investment, these students would need to have opportunities to add to their skill sets as they move through their careers. Ensuring that graduates can continue to obtain the skills they need over time requires the provision of a solid foundation of both specific and transversal skills across levels and fields of post-secondary study, discussed in Section 5.3. It also requires a transparent and flexible higher education system with effective pathways between programmes to allow individuals at various points in their careers to upgrade their skills.

Return on investment of higher education

Despite very low unemployment across the state, the share of graduates employed in Texas within one year of graduation has declined in recent years

As elsewhere in the country and across the OECD, higher education graduates in Texas enjoy higher labour market participation and employment rates and higher earnings than those who have completed upper secondary education. A smaller share of Texas adults aged 25-34 with a high school diploma were either working or looking for work than on average in the United States, at around 74% versus 77%. Their employment rates are also slightly lower on average, at 69% versus 71%, respectively (U.S. Census Bureau, 2019[20]). Thus, the advantage provided by completing a degree in terms of labour market participation and employment is greater in Texas than on average in the United States.

However, when compared to their peers with a degree nationally, the labour market participation and employment rates of Texas graduates could be better. While graduates with a bachelor's degree have similar, albeit slightly lower, participation and employment rates as their peers nationally, associate's degree holders experience poorer outcomes than on average in the United States. Their labour market participation rate is two percentage points below the national average, at 85.1%, and their employment rates are 2.5 percentage points below the national average, at 81.1% (U.S. Census Bureau, 2019[20]) (see comparative scorecard in Chapter 3).

State data matching higher education and Unemployment Insurance (UI) records permit the tracking of graduates employed in Texas within one year of graduation. It should be noted that UI records exclude self-employed individuals, or federal or military employees, and that Texas has a high share of federal employees compared to other states (U.S. Office of Personnel Management, 2017[53]). These data show that between 2007 and 2018, the share of Texas higher education graduates who were found working in the state within one year of graduation has declined (Figure 5.10). The share of graduates found working, whether they are also enrolled in further study or not, declined for university graduates by 4.2 percentage points for undergraduates and by 5.9 percentage points for post-graduates. Similarly, in the community and technical college sector, the share of graduates found working over the period has declined by 4.3 percentage points for academic stream graduates and by 2.9 percentage points in the technical stream.

Figure 5.10. Share of graduates who are employed in Texas within one year of graduation, 2007-18

Including graduates who are still enrolled in education

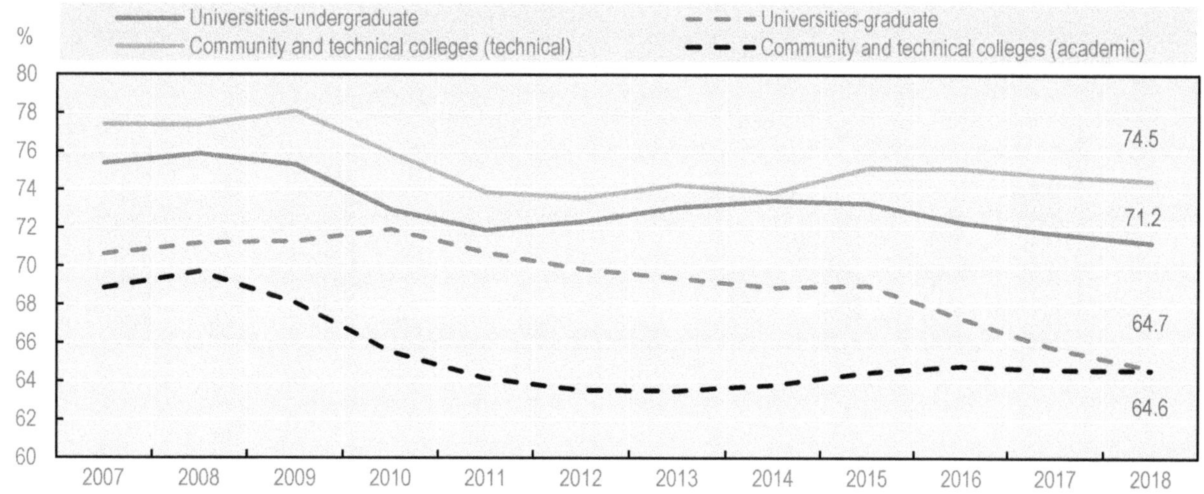

Notes: The horizontal axis represents the year in which graduates were found working in Texas (the 2018 figures correspond to the 2017 exit cohort). The data include graduates who are working only, or who are working and enrolled. It does not include graduates who are enrolled only.
Source: THECB and TWC (2019[54]), *Exit Cohort Reports CBM001 and CBM009* http://www.txhighereddata.org/reports/performance/ctcasalf/exitcohorts/

StatLink https://doi.org/10.1787/888934133932

Importantly, there has been a steady increase over the past decade in the share of graduates from community and technical colleges who choose to enrol in further study within one year of graduation. In the academic stream – the stream designed to prepare students to transfer to universities – the share of students enrolled in further study within one year after graduation increased from 19.7% to 23.9% between 2006 and 2017. Interestingly, those graduating from the technical stream have also been a larger share to enrol after graduation, from 7.5% in 2006 to 10.9% in 2017 (THECB and TWC, 2019[54]). This may point to a perception by graduates that a two-year degree, even if designed for labour market entry, may not be sufficient to find good employment. By contrast, the share of university graduates found enrolled within one year of graduation has stayed stable since 2006.

The factors behind the decline in the share of graduates found working in Texas have not been investigated to date. However, they are of interest particularly in a context of very low unemployment, combined with recruitment challenges in some sectors – from engineering to health or finance – which lead employers to recruit nationally or internationally. The competition for talent across US states may provide one explanation: while Texas continues to be a net importer of degree holders (see Section 5.2), the share of Texans aged 25-34 with a degree who have left the state has increased by more than 30% over the period 2014-18 (U.S. Census Bureau, 2019[20]). Figure 5.11 shows that in areas of important labour market demand, such as healthcare and education, both in- and out-migration flows are substantial. Further, research suggests that outward mobility is skewed towards those with the highest levels of qualifications, which can perpetuate shortages for highly qualified or specialised workers (Foote and Stange, 2019[55]).

Figure 5.11. Net domestic migration by occupation, Texas, 2017

Difference between the number of degree holders in Texas who reported residing in another US state in 2016 and the number of US degree holders outside of Texas who reported residing in Texas in 2016

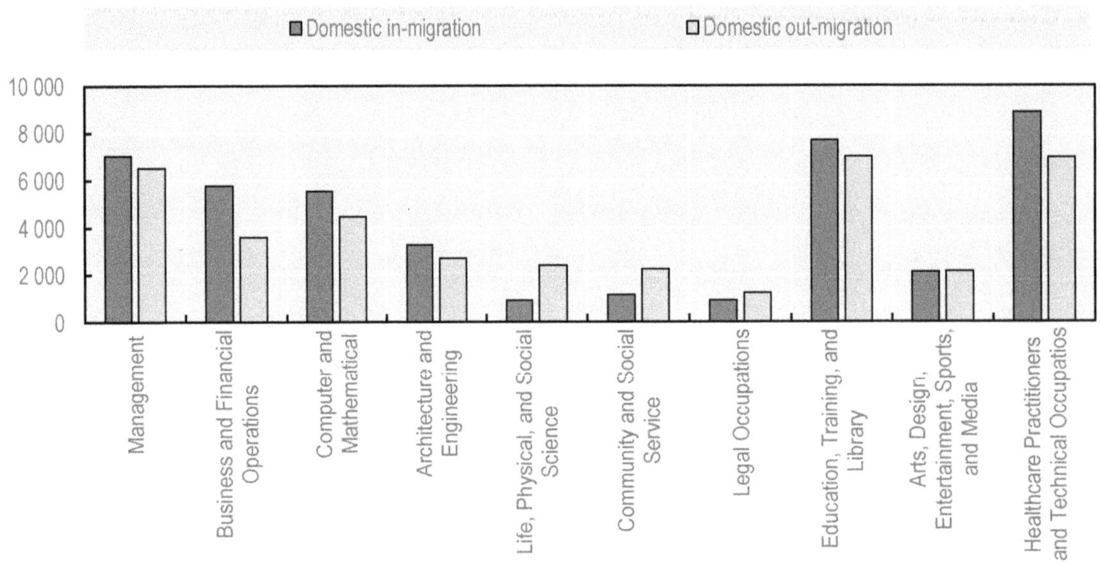

Notes: The figure was computed using data from the American Community Survey and following the approach to estimate net migration used by the THECB (2019[19]). The ten occupational groups correspond to major groups 11-0000 to 29-0000 of the Standard Occupation Classification (SOC) system, which typically require post-secondary qualifications.
Source: U.S. Census Bureau (2019[20]), *American Community Survey* (database), https://www.census.gov/programs-surveys/acs/data.html.

StatLink https://doi.org/10.1787/888934133951

Data produced by the Post-Secondary Employment Outcomes project, a partnership between the U.S. Census Bureau and several states and post-secondary institutions, also underscore the importance of outward mobility. This project sheds light on graduates' trajectories after graduation for the period 2001-16 and aims to fill key information gaps by tracking students who work outside of the state in which they study, and by providing information about the employer's industry sector and geographic location (Foote et al., 2019[56]). For Texas, data are only available at this time for institutions that compose the University of Texas (UT) system, and suggest that a large share of students leave Texas to work in other states at various points post-graduation. Looking at all cohorts for whom data is available, the share of UT graduates who leave the state was 38% within one year of graduation, 44% after 5 years and 42% after 10 years (U.S. Census Bureau, 2019[57]).

On average, the bachelor's degree remains the entry point to higher earnings in Texas, but shorter credentials in some fields of study also deliver good outcomes

Completing higher education in Texas is associated with a strong earnings advantage at the bachelor's and graduate level. For the 25-34 age group, the annual median earnings of bachelor's degree holders in Texas are USD 2 000 higher than the national average. By comparison, associate's degree holders earn slightly more (USD 400) than the national average (U.S. Census Bureau, 2019[20]) (see comparative scorecard in Chapter 3), and the median wage of upper secondary graduates in Texas is the same as on average in the United States.

State data on the earnings trajectories of graduates from 1-10 years post-graduation suggest that these differences grow over time (Figure 5.12). While graduates with a certificate or associate's degree experience slower earnings growth at year 5 post-graduation, and relatively flat earnings from years 5-10, the earnings of bachelor's degree holders continue to grow, albeit slower after year 5, which is more in line with the patterns observed for holders of advanced degrees.

Figure 5.12. Earnings trajectory of the 2008 cohort of higher education graduates in Texas, 1-10 years after graduation

Pre-tax annual earnings in current USD (not adjusted for inflation), by education level

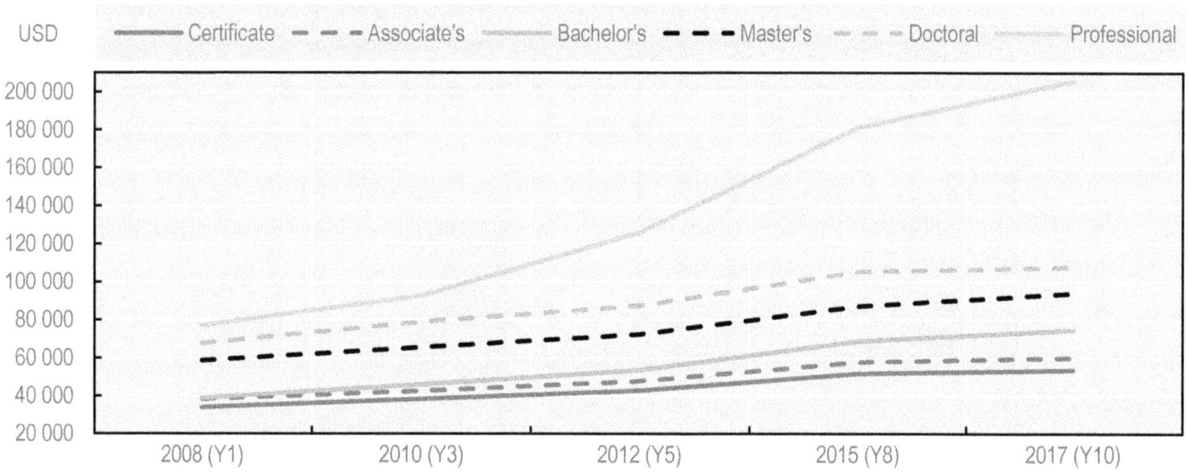

Note: Public institutions only.
Source: THECB (2019[25]), *Texas Public Higher Education Almanac*, http://reportcenter.thecb.state.tx.us/agency-publication/almanac/2019-texas-public-higher-education-almanac.

StatLink https://doi.org/10.1787/888934133970

These general patterns are consistent with research that shows the long-term benefits of general education compared to vocational education (Hanushek et al., 2017[58]) and with research suggesting the premium for advanced levels of higher education has accelerated in the past two decades (Baum, 2014[59]). However, the relatively low performance of associate's degree holders is somewhat surprising given the dynamism and diversity of Texas' economy, and the high number of "good jobs" that do not require education at the bachelor's level or above, as defined by the Georgetown University Center on Education and the Workforce (see Section 5.2).

This points to the particular importance of the field of study pursued by students choosing to complete sub-baccalaureate credentials. In certain study fields, including health (especially registered nursing, health care administration and some health technician specialties), information, engineering- and manufacturing-related technology, as well as certain protective services (policing, firefighting), certificates and associate's degrees can command higher earnings than bachelor's degrees in general fields of study (Schneider, 2015[60]; Carnevale, Rose and Cheah, 2013[61]). Research further suggests that certificate holders who enjoy the greatest benefits are men, and those working in the field in which they obtained their certificate (Carnevale, Rose and Hanson, 2012[62]; Strada, Gallup and Lumina Foundation, 2019[63]).

Field of study differences also matter at the bachelor's degree level. However, the variation in earnings by field is lower than it is on average in the United States, as shown in Figure 5.13. For instance, whereas high-earning fields such as information and communications technology command lower earnings in Texas than on average in the country, graduates from lower-paying fields such as education enjoy notably higher earnings than elsewhere in the country. Despite lower differences in a national perspective, field of study differences do affect long-term earning trajectories. While some general fields of study, such as biological sciences, offer good salary growth, others, such as psychology and English majors, face low starting salaries and lower-than-average salary growth, in line with findings elsewhere in the country.

Figure 5.13. Annual median earnings of bachelor's degree graduates in Texas and the United States

Annual gross earnings in current USD (not adjusted for inflation)

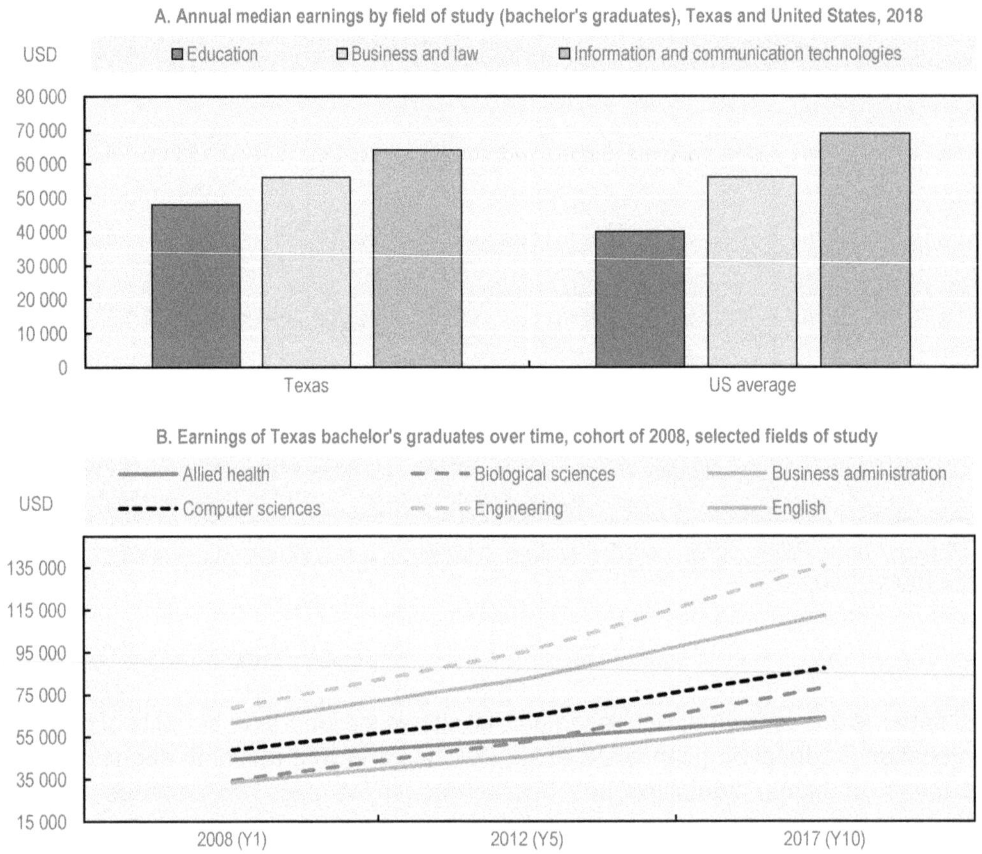

Note: A. Public and private institutions; B. Public institutions only.
Sources: A. Adapted from U.S. Census Bureau (2019[20]), *American Community Survey 2018* (database), https://www.census.gov/programs-surveys/acs/data.html; B. THECB (2019[25]) *Texas Public Higher Education Almanac*, http://reportcenter.thecb.state.tx.us/agency-publication/almanac/2019-texas-public-higher-education-almanac.

StatLink https://doi.org/10.1787/888934133989

From a gender and demographic perspective, the difference in earnings by race and ethnicity follow similar patterns as those observed elsewhere in the country. However, as shown in the comparative table in Chapter 3, while Whites and African Americans who hold an associate's or bachelor's degree in Texas earn notably more than their peers on average across the country (USD 2 000 annual earnings advantage for Whites and USD 5 000 annual earnings advantages for African Americans), this is not the case for Hispanics (USD 500 earnings advantage) (U.S. Census Bureau, 2019[20]).

The rising costs of education and debt burdens limit graduates' return on investment

The cost of higher education has increasingly shifted from state sources to individuals over the past decades, as discussed in the policy section of the report. The deregulation of tuition fees at Texas public universities in 2003 was a major policy change, which has resulted in sharp tuition fee increases, in particular in selective institutions and high-demand or costly fields of study such as business or engineering. Research suggests that the higher cost of study has not had a damaging effect on disadvantaged students accessing high-earning, high-cost programmes, in part because the tuition rises have allowed increased needs-based institutional aid (Andrews and Stange, 2016[64]).

However, the rising cost of study has an impact on graduates' return on investment. Compared to the rest of the country, tuition and fees of public higher education are moderate in Texas at four-year universities (23rd most affordable out of the 50 states) and low at two-year colleges (2nd most affordable) (NCES, 2019[24]). However, the costs of higher education go beyond tuition and fees and can diminish the benefits of attainment. Two groups appear to face particular challenges in Texas: non-completers and those who have graduated but whose debt represents a large share of their starting salaries. Economically disadvantaged students and students who are not adequately prepared for college are more likely to drop out and thus face a double challenge in the labour market, as they carry debt but will not benefit from the advantage of a completed credential. A large number of Texans aged 25-64 have completed some college but no degree. This group also faces the risk of poor return on investment if they have incurred debt for the post-secondary courses they have taken. However, as discussed earlier, individuals in this group may wish to re-engage with post-secondary education, and a slightly greater share re-enrols in Texas compared to the US average. This pattern suggests an opportunity to support individuals without a credential but some experience in post-secondary study to return and complete a credential valued in the labour market.

Regarding completers with debt, African American and White students graduating from four-year public institutions are most at risk of facing heavy debt burdens, with debt burdens of 101% and 70% respectively of their first-year wage in 2017 (debt data for 2016), well above the state target of 60%. Debt loads as a share of first-year wages are lower at two-year public institutions, but remain high (54%) for African American students (THECB, 2019[25]). No information is currently available on debt loads over a longer time period post-graduation.

5.3. Policies to improve the alignment of the higher education system and the labour market in Texas

The assessment of labour market outcomes in the previous section suggests that, to achieve a good alignment between the supply and demand of skills in Texas, the state would benefit from focusing on the following four policy areas to improve the articulation between higher education and the labour market:

- **strategic planning and co-ordination** to support alignment between higher education and workforce needs;
- **funding** to address issues of access, equity and attainment;
- **educational offerings** responsive to labour market needs, and **student supports and pathways** to promote completion and good labour market outcomes;
- **targeted information for students, families, educators and policy makers** about educational opportunities and labour market needs to support student choices and guide institutional practices and policy.

This section of the chapter identifies current strengths and areas for improvement in each of these four policy areas, and provides recommendations to help improve the articulation between higher education and the labour market in Texas.

Strategic planning and co-ordination

With the current higher education plan and Tri-Agency Workforce Initiative, Texas' higher education policy has increased its focus on labour market relevance in recent years

The Texas Higher Education Coordinating Board (THECB) provides leadership for and co-ordination of Texas higher education through 15-year strategic higher education plans, which set state-wide policy objectives and targets to monitor progress and results. The current *Texas Higher Education Strategic Plan: 2015-2030*, or *60x30TX*, focuses on raising the attainment of post-secondary certificates and degrees to 60% among 25-34 year-olds by 2030. As outlined in Box 5.2 , the plan includes four broad goals. The THECB promotes progress towards the plan's goals in two main ways: guidance for institutions, students and employers; and the monitoring and publication of key targets identified in the plan to measure progress against the 60x30TX goals. Guidance includes, for instance, the Career Readiness Handbook, which offers definitions and concrete examples of "marketable skills", or the 60x30 and Internships Toolkit, which provides guidance to employers on creating or expanding high-quality, paid internships for post-secondary students (THECB, 2018[65]; THECB, 2019[66]).

Box 5.2. *Texas Higher Education Strategic Plan: 2015-2030: 60x30TX*

Launched in 2015, the *60x30TX* higher education plan has four goals with specific targets:

- **Educated population**: By 2030, at least 60% of Texans aged 25-34 will have a certificate or degree.
- **Completion**: By 2030, at least 550 000 students graduating in that year will complete a certificate, associate's, bachelor's or master's from an institution of higher education in Texas.
- **Marketable skills**: By 2030, all graduates from Texas public institutions of higher education will have completed programmes with identified marketable skills.
- **Student debt**: By 2030, undergraduate student loan debt will not exceed 60% of first-year wages for graduates of Texas public institutions.

Source: THECB (n.d.[67]).

The THECB monitors progress against the goals and associated targets at the state level but also provides publicly available information on the progress of regions and individual institutions on the dedicated *60x30TX* website and through regular progress reports. OECD interviews indicated that higher education institutions perceived the plan, along with the actions it required, as a useful catalyst for action at the institutional level. For instance, the plan calls for institutions to create and implement a process to identify and update marketable skills for each programme in collaboration with employers and other stakeholders by 2020. As of spring 2018, 41% of institutions had created and implemented such a process. (This is described further in Section 5.3.) While greater progress is still needed, institutions interviewed by the OECD who had created and implemented a marketable skills process highlighted its value in engaging key parties within the institution, including faculty members, in a dialogue about labour market relevant skills and ways to convey those skills (THECB, 2019[19]).

In Texas, as in many other states, separate government agencies oversee primary and secondary education, higher education, and workforce development. While efforts in all three areas are critical to develop a skilled workforce, co-ordination and integration between them is often challenging. In 2016, the Governor of Texas created the Tri-Agency Workforce Initiative, establishing a shared set of goals for three state agencies: the Texas Education Agency (TEA), which oversees the public education system, the Texas Higher Education Coordinating Board (THECB), and the Texas Workforce Commission (TWC), which produces labour market information and oversees workforce development efforts in the state. These goals, called "charges", were assigned to the Commissioners of the three agencies and designed to align with *60x30TX,* which had been launched the previous year, in 2015. Two of the five charges laid out by the Governor had a clear focus on the labour market relevance of post-secondary education: the first charge referenced the need to equip post-secondary students with marketable skills, and the third charge required the Commissioners to "evaluate current agency efforts, as well as state and local web-based education and career awareness systems, in an effort to better link students, parents, and educators to the broad array of high-demand jobs in this state and the educational requirements to secure those opportunities" (TEA, THECB and TWC, 2020, p. 2[68]).

The initiative began with the organisation of eight regional meetings with stakeholders throughout the state, resulting in four prime recommendations, supported by a range of initiatives and additional recommendations. The prime recommendations focused on identifying initiatives to boost the state's economic competitiveness, strengthening instruction from early childhood through high school, building a proactive partnership between the three agencies, and advancing education and employment opportunities for veterans (TEA, THECB and TWC, 2016[69]). In February 2020, the three agencies submitted a progress report to the Governor's Office, outlining a large number of initiatives taken across the state by educators, employers, government officials and community stakeholders to meet the initial charges set out in 2015 and the prime recommendations of 2016 (TEA, THECB and TWC, 2020[68]).

In February 2020, the Governor of Texas announced new charges for the Tri-Agency initiative, outlined in Box 5.3. The new set of charges builds on the previous focus on the labour market relevance of post-secondary education. They also sharpen this focus, making it more specific by tasking Commissioners with identifying strategies to streamline educational pathways to high-wage, high-demand careers, increase the state's capacity to produce credentials of value, and increase entry into the teaching profession.

Box 5.3. Tri-Agency charges to promote access to high-quality education and workforce training

The Governor of Texas tasked the TEA, THECB and TWC with a set of charges in seven areas:

- **Readiness:** The Commissioners should recommend strategies to ensure students are prepared for future growth at each stage in the educational pipeline.
- **Completion:** The Commissioners should recommend strategies to ensure students who pursue higher education and workforce educational programs can complete those programmes in a cost-efficient and timely manner.
- **Transitions:** The Commissioners should analyse and make recommendations regarding strategies to streamline educational pathways, ensuring students can seamlessly transition into high-wage and high-demand careers.
- **Upskilling:** The Commissioners should recommend strategies for improving the state's capacity to produce credentials of value aligned with the needs of high-wage and high-demand occupations.
- **Educational pipeline:** The Commissioners should analyse and make recommendations to increase the supply of highly qualified and well-trained individuals entering the teaching profession across the state.
- **Partnerships:** The Commissioners should explore and recommend options for increasing economic activity in rural Texas, including innovative collaborations among employers, institutions, and rural communities; and easing of regulatory burdens that may inhibit economic growth and collaboration. The Commissioners should also explore ways for

businesses, school districts, and institutions of higher education to partner together to offer expanded educational options to employees and their children, and to strengthen educational and workforce programmes across the state.

- **Infrastructure:** The Commissioners should identify strategies to align agency operations, increase programme efficiency, improve data analysis and capacity, and to refine 60x30TX, if necessary, to ensure the state's goals continue to reflect the state's needs.

Source: Office of the Texas Governor (n.d.[70]).

Partnership initiatives and intermediary organisations play an important role in supporting the alignment between higher education and labour market needs in Texas

A wide array of state-wide, regional and local partnerships exist in Texas, aiming to tackle key issues facing students and employers. The stakeholders involved in these partnerships are diverse, spanning the public, private and non-profit sectors, and focusing on issues from education at all levels to workforce and economic development. For example, Texas benefits from a dense network of non-profit organisations that facilitate alignment between secondary and post-secondary education. In addition, there are a number of higher education associations representing different sectors, such as the Texas Association of Community Colleges, Council of Public University Presidents and Chancellors, and Independent Colleges and Universities of Texas. These organisations advocate for policy changes to the Legislature and citizens at large, provide convening fora for members and other stakeholders, and design initiatives to serve their students and member institutions.

Some of these partnerships have a broad geographic remit, attempting to serve various regions across the state. Educate Texas, an educational initiative of the philanthropic organisation Communities Foundation of Texas, supports various collective impact programmes, including supporting higher education success and the alignment between education and workforce needs. Examples of such programmes include the Texas Regional STEM Degree Accelerator, an initiative that ran from 2015-18 in five regions to develop STEM degree programmes aligned with high-demand regional workforce needs. Actions included professional development of faculty, aligning mathematics pathways from K-12 to higher education and workforce, and developing next-generation sector partnerships (Educate Texas, 2019[71]).

Frequently, partnerships identified by stakeholders during the OECD visit had a regional or local scope. These were active in both densely populated urban areas and in rural areas, such as West Texas or along the southern border, where more efforts are needed to grow talent locally due to greater difficulty in importing skilled workers. The Greater Houston Partnership is an example of a business-led partnership that promotes economic development in the Greater Houston area. As outlined in Box 5.4 , the UpSkill Houston initiative is targeted to businesses, higher education institutions and job-seekers in the Houston area to meet labour market needs. Shortages of qualified workers in particular industries and regions are also an important trigger for the development of sector partnerships. In the Houston area, examples of industry-led partnerships include the East Harris County Manufacturers Association (EHCMA), which represents 130 large and small companies in the region's petrochemical industry, and worked with post-secondary partners in the region to tackle the lack of student awareness of job opportunities with the aim of raising enrolments.

In several regions of the state, partnerships exist between institutions and employers that facilitate the development of labour market relevant programmes. These are most prevalent in sectors, industries and occupations that face shortages (e.g. nursing, engineering, advanced manufacturing, information and communications technology). These partnerships often take the form of employer participation on programmes' advisory committees and other channels that facilitate employer input on the content of programmes. They can also take the form of direct funding from industry to institutions to support the expansion of particular in-demand programmes, as evidenced, for example, by the relationship between Texas Instruments and the University of Texas in Dallas as well as Texas A&M engineering programmes.

Box 5.4. The Greater Houston Partnership – UpSkill Houston initiative

The Greater Houston Partnership brings together industry leaders, educational institutions, and community organisations in an employer-led initiative that works to develop the talent pipeline to meet the needs of Greater Houston's economy. UpSkill Houston has received national recognition for its work, including from the U.S. Chamber of Commerce Foundation's Talent Pipeline Management Initiative, the Aspen Institute, the Global Cities Initiative of the Brookings Institution, JP Morgan Chase, and United Way Worldwide.

UpSkill Houston provides resources for career-seekers, educators, and industry partners to help fill the need for middle-skill workers (requiring less than a four-year degree) in the Greater Houston area. In addition, UpSkill Houston conducts analyses to gain a deeper understanding of student choices in both education and employment, public perception of middle skills jobs, and alignment with industry and labour market needs.

Sources: Greater Houston Partnership (n.d.[72]); UpSkill Houston (n.d.[73]).

Stakeholders have pointed to the need for deeper alignment between higher education and workforce development actors in Texas

The decentralised higher education system in Texas, and its large scale in terms of geography and population, pose a number of co-ordination challenges. The OECD has identified three general types of co-ordination challenges: co-ordination within government, departments or agencies whose actions need alignment to achieve policy goals; co-ordination between government and stakeholders; and co-ordination among stakeholders (OECD, 2019[74]). These three types of co-ordination challenges exist to some extent in Texas and may limit the effectiveness of efforts to align higher education and labour market needs.

Co-ordination within government is particularly important when achieving a policy objective depends on the actions of several departments or agencies, as is the case for improving the alignment between higher education and the labour market. As described earlier, the Tri-Agency Workforce Initiative offers an important opportunity to improve student preparedness, foster access and success in higher education, and successful transition to gainful employment. However, a challenge that emerged through the OECD team's discussions with stakeholders in Texas is that each agency has legislatively mandated functions and targets to meet, requiring staff to focus on their own agency goals. By comparison, no legislative charges exist that relate to Tri-Agency Work. Thus, the impact of the Tri-Agency initiative on the work of each agency is not yet clear. Alignment of work across government agencies is a common challenge in OECD countries, especially as more countries move towards integrated policies on skills development that enable a more effective skills pipeline from childhood to adulthood and that also allow for adults to upskill and reskill. Some countries have developed mechanisms to pursue whole-of-government work to improve the skills pipeline, which may be of interest as Texas seeks to ensure higher education supports good labour market opportunities for all Texans (see Chapter 3).

While it is important to encourage local, bottom-up approaches, strengthening linkages between higher education and labour market actors at the regional level can benefit both employers and graduates in achieving good labour market outcomes. For example, stakeholders in Texas noted that because institutions often partner individually with employers at the programme or field of study level, this may lead to an over-solicitation of employers from multiple institutions and risk an overly narrow focus on one specific employer's talent pipeline. Thus, streamlining points of contact between higher education and employer or industry groups at the regional level may be beneficial. Stakeholders in Texas also highlighted the importance of partnerships between higher education institutions and Workforce Development Boards, underlining a greater need for higher education institutions, particularly four-year institutions, to view Workforce Development Boards as a partner and intermediary body.

Stakeholders also noted additional administrative barriers to co-ordination between the tri-agencies at the regional level. For example, while the Texas Education Agency and the Texas Workforce Commission have regional-level offices or contact points, the Texas Higher Education Coordinating Board (THECB) does not have corresponding regional contact points. In addition, each agency uses different regional catchment areas, as there are 10 higher education regions, 28 workforce regions and 20 education service centres. Thus, the three main state agencies involved in broader workforce and skills development in Texas all operate in different regions, with varying degrees of authority for action. This may complicate co-ordinated action at the regional level. For example, the THECB places emphasis on the importance of regional context in increasing post-secondary attainment levels, setting regional targets to accompany the state-wide targets for *60x30TX*. However, there do not seem to be mechanisms facilitating engagement of the THECB with other state agencies to help regions reach these targets.

Moreover, part of the rationale for the Tri-Agency model was to avoid duplication of efforts and strengthen cross-agency collaboration. Agency Commissioners were charged with evaluating current agency efforts to better link education and workforce opportunities. However, to date, it is unclear whether efforts have been made to implement a review or evaluation process of policies and programmes across agencies that would allow for a broader examination of potentially overlapping, contradictory or incoherent policies in terms of aligning with the goals of the Tri-Agency Workforce Initiative.

Box 5.5. Improving regional workforce development through state agency alignment

One of the recommendations in a 2016 report by the Federal Reserve Bank of Dallas to improve regional workforce development in Texas was to increase state agency alignment. The report states that, "Workforce alignment and collaboration must be modeled at the state level. Beyond collaborating on strategic planning efforts, state agencies in Texas have modeled effective collaboration by partnering on several joint initiatives, most prominently the Tri-Agency initiative. There are several options to increase state agencies' co-ordination to accomplish the goals and objectives of the Tri-Agency initiative". (Blum and Groves, 2016, p. 41[16]).

The report provides examples of recommended state actions such as creating joint staffing positions that report to multiple agencies, increasing the number of cross-agency initiatives that produce services or products used by partners at the regional level, or creating inter-agency councils or leadership committees responsible for cross-agency initiatives or strategies.

Source: Blum and Groves (2016[16]).

Recommendations for strategic planning and co-ordination

1. Texas can benefit from deepening Tri-Agency collaboration in support of long-term employability goals common to the three agencies. This could be done by agreeing on a set of metrics to monitor goals common to the three agencies. This exercise could serve to ensure alignment between the three agencies and translate the top-level co-operation that is currently in place to the policy and operational level. As the new Tri-Agency charges established by the Governor of Texas in 2020 include a focus on the production of credentials of value for all Texans and on supporting entry to the teaching profession, consideration could be given to establishing quantitative state-wide targets that support these objectives. Such targets could help provide a clear focus for stakeholder efforts and facilitate the reporting of progress to the public.
2. Consider ways to align, strengthen and scale up local initiatives to align education programmes to labour market needs. This could include strengthening the regional presence of the Texas Higher Education Coordinating Board. In addition, following models that exist in other US states, the three agencies (TEA, THECB, and TWC) could identify ways to create regional networks, and identify appropriate lead organisations to co-ordinate efforts in improving the alignment between education and the labour market. The lead organisations could report annually on progress in regional co-ordination to improve the alignment of education and workforce needs, providing other regions and state-level policy makers with mappings of collaborative practices and policy initiatives. Available funding could cover administrative costs, and to help foster and scale up promising practices and partnerships among educational providers (both secondary and post-secondary), between education and labour market actors, and among employers.
3. As part of its role as co-ordinating body for higher education, particularly in monitoring progress towards state-wide goals for higher education, the THECB could consider implementing a regular review process for evaluating policies and programmes with a direct impact on higher education-labour market alignment. The process could involve key stakeholders, including representatives from the higher education sector, employers and others who work on the alignment of education and workforce needs, to help identify policies and procedures that hamper alignment or could improve it.

Funding

Texas supports a large public higher education system with relatively low tuition and a range of financial aid programmes

Institutional funding model

The state of Texas supports a large public higher education sector, which enrols about 90% of all students. State data suggest that private institutions have experienced a decrease in enrolments since the financial crisis of 2008-09, whereas public institutions have experienced a surge in enrolments. Since the financial crisis, total enrolments in public higher education in Texas increased by 30.8%, whereas the average growth in the United States was 7.1%. This places Texas as the top state in terms of growing public higher education enrolments, far ahead of other comparable states. The next states with large enrolment growth are Arizona, Idaho and Utah, ranging from 24.7% to 21.5%, but those states have much smaller higher education systems (SHEEO, 2019[75]).

The total amount of public expenditure dedicated to higher education has decreased over the past decade, both in absolute terms and as a share of total state expenditure in Texas. However, Texas allocates a substantial amount of public funding to higher education compared to other states, dedicating about 7.9% of public expenditure in 2017 compared to 5.8% on average in the United States (SHEEO, 2019[75]).

Another feature of the Texas system is that an important share of community college funding comes from local appropriations, although the share vary significantly by college. On average, about one-third (33.5%) of community colleges' funding comes from local property tax, with another 33.5% coming from state appropriations, and the remainder split between federal funds (17.5%) and net tuition and fees (15.4%) (Legislative Budget Board, 2019[76]). Owing to wide differences in the fiscal capacities of local governments, there is wide variation in local revenues per FTE student. For example, Austin Community College had revenues from local appropriations of USD 8 286 per full-time equivalent student in 2018, while this figure was USD 5 623 for Houston Community College and USD 3 343 for El Paso Community College (NCES, 2019[24]).

The state has taken steps to use funding provided to institutions to promote student success and help address key labour market shortages. Starting in 2014/15, the state introduced outcomes-based funding in public community colleges, which enrol the large majority of students in the two-year sector (over 730 000 students in 2018), and changed the funding model for the Texas State Technical College (TSTC) system. While the outcomes-based funding approach in community colleges focuses on student retention and completion, this comprises only about 10% of the funding coming from the state. By contrast, all state funding for instruction and administration for the TSTC is based on graduates' labour market outcomes. Both approaches are described in Box 5.6. Despite some initial opposition, the inclusion of some performance funding in the funding model for public community colleges is now well established. In the TSTC system, stakeholders who met with the OECD team described the model as effective in improving student employment and earnings as well as in motivating changes in institutional behaviours, such as greater efforts to increase the labour market relevance of the curriculum and to strengthen partnerships with employers.

In the four-year sector, while the THECB recommended a Graduation Supplement programme to incentivise universities for completions to the 85th Texas Legislature, it did not become law. The proposal was to provide USD 150 million for the biennium to incentivise universities with USD 500 for each "not at risk" student awarded a bachelor's degree and USD 1 000 for each "at risk" student awarded a bachelor's degree. At risk students were defined as Pell Grant eligible or scoring below average ACT or SAT scores (TACC, 2018[77]). Some targeted institutional funding is also available to four-year institutions to enhance capacity in fields of study leading to shortage professions, though this comprises a small share of public funding. For instance, the Graduate Medical Education Expansion Grant (USD 78.6 million in 2019) provides funding to public medical schools to increase first-year residency positions.

Box 5.6. The Success Point Model for Texas public community colleges

Outcomes-based funding in community colleges

The funding formula for public community colleges allocates 10.6% of state funding to community colleges through a Success Point model that rewards students' progression and completion. State funds represent about one-third of total community college funding. The remainder of the community college state formula funding is allocated based on contact hours. Success Points are awarded based on milestones achieved, so multiple points can be awarded for an individual student. Points are awarded for students who enrol in a current year and:

- became college-ready;
- successfully completed the first college-level math course;
- successfully completed the first college-level reading/writing course;
- successfully completed their first 15 semester credit hours;
- successfully completed their first 30 semester credit hours;
- earned a degree or certificate (not in a critical field);
- earned a degree or certificate in a critical field (2.25 points);
- transferred to a senior institution after having successfully completed 15 semester credit hours.

Funding is determined based on the three-year average performance on these metrics.

Returned value formula in the Texas State Technical College System (TSTCS)

A "returned value" funding formula is used to determine the amount of state general revenues provided to the TSTCS for instruction and administration expenditure. Other sources of funding also exist, including tuition fees. The method, reviewed every two years, involves several steps:

1. identify cohort of students who have completed a minimum amount of training in the TSTCS (9 semester credit hours) and left the system for at least two years and calculate their wages;
2. calculate TSTCS value-add by comparing student wages to the minimum wage;
3. calculate worker's additional impact on the state of Texas by applying a standard tax rate and economic multiplier;
4. allocate funding amongst TSTCS colleges by determining their share in the total value-add.

Sources: Legislative Budget Board (2019[76]); THECB (2013[78]), background information provided by the THECB (2019).

Tuition levels

The responsibility for tuition fee setting is shared between the Legislature and institutions for all public four-year institutions, public health-related institutions, and two types of two-year institutions, the Lamar Colleges (which are lower-division institutions of higher education within the Texas State University System) and the colleges of the Texas State Technical College System (TSTCS). The Legislature sets statutory tuition, institutions set board authorised tuition (within legislative limits), and institutions set designated tuition, which makes up the largest part of tuition revenue (WSIPP, 2019[79]). In the public four-year sector, which enrols about 40% of students in Texas, average tuition and fees were slightly below the national average, at USD 8 375 per year versus USD 8 804, placing Texas in the middle of the 50-state distribution (THECB, 2019[25]). As will be discussed in the next section, tuition and fees in the four-year sector have increased significantly since the deregulation of tuition in 2003.

Texans have access to affordable higher education due to the large network of two-year community colleges across the state, which enrols about 45% of all higher education students. In this sector, average tuition and fees for domestic students were USD 2099 per year in 2016/17. This was the third lowest tuition amount in the two-year public sector among the US states, after California and New Mexico.

Financial aid

The financial aid available to Texas students from federal, state and institutional sources provided more than USD 10 billion in grant and loan assistance to Texas students in 2017 (THECB, 2018[80]).

A large range of programmes is available at the state level, aiming to achieve different goals. The largest programmes focus on supporting students with financial need: in 2017, four programmes, including the TEXAS grant, Texas Public Educational Grant (TPEG), the Texas Educational Opportunity Grant (TEOG) and the Texas College Work-Study (TCWS) programme served over 232 000 students (although students may be double counted in the case of multiple awards). Students in receipt of this aid had an average family income below USD 35 000. Two of the programmes targeting financial need, the Texas Public Educational Grant (TPEG) and financial assistance funded by designated tuition set-asides (resulting from House Bill 3015 that deregulated tuition fees in 2003), are funded from institutional resources and institutions are free to set specific eligibility criteria. These two programmes are only applicable in the public higher education sector. Other programmes are also available for students who have higher family incomes, including the College Access Loan (CAL) programme that provides one of the lowest-cost non-federal student loan options in the United States with a fixed annual interest rate of 5.2%.

In addition, a range of small-scale programmes ranging from USD 100 000 to 15 million channel funding directly to prospective students in fields of high labour market demand, from medicine, nursing and teaching to policing and public safety. As shown in Table 5.6, the scale of these programmes is small compared to needs-based programmes; for example, the three largest needs-based programmes combined amount to approximately USD 785 million. The loan repayment for certain physicians is the largest of the programmes targeting occupations in shortage fields, with an investment of about USD 15 million for fiscal year 2020 to encourage physicians to practice in areas facing shortages of health professionals. In place for more than 30 years, this programme has seen its funding expand in recent years, yet it enrols relatively low numbers of participants, namely around 100 on average over the seven most recent cohorts. Biennial surveys of physicians are conducted to determine how many continue to serve in a health shortage area. Results suggest an initially high rate of retention that steadily declines over time, from more than 90% retention in the first of the programme to about 70% during the fourth (and last) year of the programme. Retention decreases to around 40-50% three to four years after programme completion (THECB, 2018[80]). The THECB also indicated that a review of the Nursing Shortage Reduction Program, in place since 2005, is underway. However, there is no systematic information available to assess whether the scale and design of these types of programmes are effective in achieving the state's goal of expanding the available workforce in shortage occupations.

Table 5.6. Overview of state financial assistance programmes

Main need-based programmes in fiscal years (FY) 2017 and 2020 and programmes for students in high-demand fields of study in FY 2020

	FY 2020	FY 2017			
	Total awarded (USD)	Total awarded (USD)	Number of recipients	Average award (USD)	Average family income (USD)
Need-based programmes					
Toward EXcellence, Access, and Success (TEXAS) Grant	422 222 737	357 662 758	72 144	4 949	31 465
Financial assistance funded by designated tuition set-asides (HB 3015)	m	252 029 316	107 943	2 332	38 904
Texas Public Educational Grant (TPEG)	m	176 135 596	133 156	1 318	32 166
College Access Loan (CAL)	m	166 215 488	11 429	14 454	92 300
Tuition Equalization Grant (TEG)	89 305 147	96 081 753	27 374	3 507	47 240
Texas Educational Opportunity Grant (TEOG)	47 996 150	46 963 354	23 039	4 210 PSC 3 840 PTC 1 959 PCC	23 422
Texas B-On-Time (BOT)*	a	28 844 731	3 866	7 443	89 658
Texas College Work-Study (TCWS) (including Work-Study Mentorship programme)	8 404 639	9 016 128	4 102	2 197	32 601
Top 10%**	a	7 207 826	3 631	1 985	55 715
Texas Armed Services Scholarship Program (TASSP)	3 420 000	1 758 369	246	7 147	113 100
Texas WORKS internship programme	1 000 000				
Programmes for students in high-demand fields of study					
Repayment of certain physician education loans	15 345 078				
Joint Admissions Medical Program (guaranteed admissions, financial and non-financial supports)	10 206 794				
Nursing Shortage Reduction Program	9 940 024 (2019)				
Family Medicine Residency Program	5 000 000 (2019)				
Peace Officer Loan Repayment Program (starts in FY 2021)	4 000 000***				
Nursing Faculty Loan Repayment Assistance Program	1 500 000				
Texas Statewide Preceptorship Programs in Family Practice, Internal Medicine, and Pediatrics	1 500 000 (2019)				
Teach for Texas Loan Repayment Assistance Program	1 337 500				
Math and Science Scholars Loan Repayment Program	1 287 500				
Repayment of certain mental health professional education loans	1 062 500				
Programmes to encourage certification to teach bilingual education, English as a second language, or Spanish	750 000				
Rural Rotations Program (family medicine in rural and underserved areas)	102 500 (2018)				

Notes: *FY 2020 was the final year of issuing loans through this programme. **FY 2018 was the final year of issuing grants through this programme. ***The figure refers to the FY 2021 budget for this programme. Other programmes targeting students in fields leading to shortage occupations exist but have not been funded for 2020 and are excluded from the table. With respect to programmes for students in high-demand fields of study, cells for 2017 are empty because this information is based on background information provided by the THECB, which focused on recent years.
Sources: FY 2017: THECB (2018[80]), *Report on Student Financial Aid in Texas Higher Education: Fiscal Year 2017*, http://www.60x30tx.com/media/1412/student-fin-aid-in-texas-report.pdf. FY 2020: Background information provided by the THECB (2019).

StatLink https://doi.org/10.1787/888934135034

Declining state funding to institutions and limited financial aid may hinder the state's efforts to develop a skilled workforce and meet labour market needs

State appropriations

The overall level of state funding for higher education institutions is important to ensure the quality of provision while maintaining affordability; achieving this balance is critical. Low quality of provision can result in insufficient knowledge and skills among graduates, leading to poor outcomes for both graduates and employers, but also to high drop-out rates (TCF, 2019[81]; Deming and Walters, 2017[82]). The lack of affordability limits access to higher education, particularly for disadvantaged students, which both hinders equity and reduces the pool of future highly skilled workers available to meet labour market needs.

Most states have experienced a reduction in higher education spending since the global financial crisis of 2008. As the US economy returned to expansion, fiscal capacities have increased again, although they differ across states. According to a research report that calculated the revenue capacity and expenditure need of US states, Texas presents a relatively high fiscal capacity, ranking 18th in the country for total taxable resources, behind Virginia (11th) and Washington (12th), but close to California (15th), and ahead of Ohio (32nd). In higher education, the report suggests that Texas ranks 13th in terms of higher education spending need, but 20th in terms of higher education expenditure (Gordon, Auxier and Iselin, 2016[83]).

Total public higher education appropriations in Texas decreased from USD 19 462 million in 2008/09 to a budgeted amount of USD 17 687 million in 2018/19. As a share of total state expenditure, this represents a reduction in the state budget allocated to higher education, from 11.3% to 8.5% (Legislative Budget Board, 2019[76]). A portion of this decrease is due to the reduction in one component of state appropriations for higher education, referred to as "other funds". Other funds decreased from USD 7 890 million for the 2012-13 biennium to USD 1 881 million for the 2014-15 biennium, due to the exclusion of an estimated USD 6 100 million in patient income from the appropriations to health-related institutions of higher education in the 2014-15 appropriations process. The receipt of these funds was not limited by the Legislature and institutions continued to receive this revenue (Legislative Budget Board, 2013[84]).

Given rapidly growing enrolments, Texas has experienced a greater decline in per full-time equivalent (FTE) student state spending since the economic recession than on average in the country (-18.2% compared to -11.2% nationally between 2008 and 2018). While the economic recovery has led to increases in higher education spending across the United States, the increase was modest in Texas, with 6.5% over 2013-2018 in Texas, compared to a US average of 15.2%.

Public higher education appropriations per FTE student in Texas in 2018 was USD 7 707, very close to the US average of USD 7 853, but below California for instance, at USD 8 553. Compared to the other states examined in this report, state spending per FTE student in public higher education is higher in Texas than in Virginia (USD 5 420), Ohio (USD 6 361) and Washington (USD 6 966) (SHEEO, 2019[75]). However, when looking at the split between the four-year and the two-year sector, higher education appropriations per FTE are notably higher than average in the four-year sector in Texas, but well below average in the two-year sector.

Table 5.7. Public higher education appropriations, four-year and two-year sector, 2018

Per full-time equivalent (FTE) student, USD

	State support	Local support (two-year) or research, agricultural and medical (RAM) (four-year)	Total
Two-year sector			
Ohio	4 728	2 114	6 843
Texas	**2 621**	**3 594**	**6 215**
Virginia	4 108	231	4 338
Washington	5 811	-	5 811
United States	**4 988**	**2 553**	**7 541**
Four-year sector			
Ohio	4 975	752	5 727
Texas	**8 258**	**2 723**	**10 981**
Virginia	5 257	1 053	6 310
Washington	6 471	943	7 414
United States	**7 482**	**1 602**	**9 083**

Source: SHEEO (2019[75]), *SHEEO State Higher Education Finance (SHEF) Tableau Data*, https://sheeo.org/project/state-higher-education-finance.

StatLink https://doi.org/10.1787/888934135053

Texas faces particular challenges that require ensuring adequate state funding in the public two-year sector. The post-secondary population in Texas is large and growing; and about 45% of post-secondary students attend community colleges. The state's students are less prepared academically and have lower completion rates than on average in the United States, and a growing share of incoming students come from minority and low-income families. As discussed below, students with the highest unmet financial need in Texas are those studying at community colleges. In addition, Texas relies more heavily than other states on local taxes for funding community colleges, as noted in Chapter 3.

Financial aid

Texas has significantly increased the amount of need-based aid provided per total fall enrolment over the past three decades. However, it remains below the investments of various states, as shown in Figure 5.14. While Texas investments grew fast between 1980 and 2010, reaching the level of California, they stagnated after 2010.

Figure 5.14. State undergraduate financial aid per total fall enrolment (1980, 2000, 2010, 2013 and 2016)

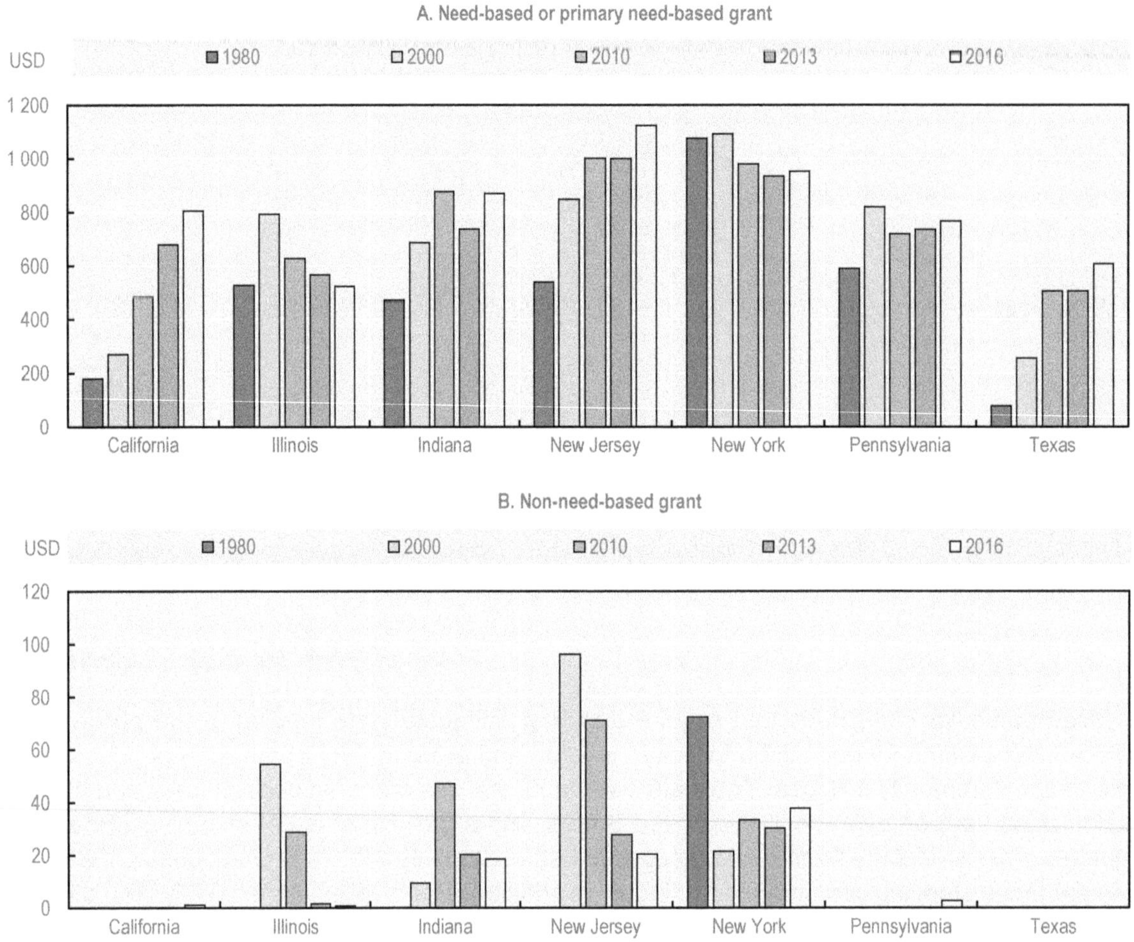

Note: All figures are in 2018 USD (inflation-adjusted).
Sources : Financial aid data: NASSGAP (n.d.[85]), *NASSGAP Annual Surveys for academic years 1979-1980, 1999-2000, 2009-2010, 2012-2013 and 2015-2016*, https://www.nassgapsurvey.com. Total fall enrolment: NCES (2019[24]), *Integrated Post-secondary Education Data System* (database), https://nces.ed.gov/ipeds/use-the-data.

StatLink https://doi.org/10.1787/888934134008

Limitations in the financial aid system are apparent when considering the large number of students enrolled in higher education institutions in Texas who demonstrate substantial "unmet need". Unmet need refers to the difference between the "cost of attendance" (COA), which includes tuition and other study and living costs for one year, and the funds available to cover these costs, namely the student or family contribution (the "expected family contribution", or EFC) as well as financial aid in the form of grants (see Box 3.10 in Chapter 3 for further information).

In Texas, in 2017, the unmet need was highest for students attending public two-year institutions, at USD 6 495, and was USD 7 002 for students attending public universities and health-related institutions (THECB, 2018[80]). By comparison, a recent study using data from the U.S. Department of Education for the academic year 2015/16 suggests that, nationally, the unmet need is greater among students attending four-year not-for-profit and for-profit institutions. The report also finds that at public two-year institutions, 71% of students had some unmet need, averaging USD 4 920, a figure that is well below that in Texas

(CLASP, 2018[86]). In Washington, where two-year students are, like in Texas, those with the highest unmet need, that unmet need was still lower than in Texas, at USD 5 346 on average, according to a study that followed students who graduated in 2008 and 2009 (ERDC, 2018[87]). This indicates that, despite Texas' affordable public two-year sector by national standards and the existence of several student aid programmes, students attending two-year institutions continue to face important financial barriers. As noted in Section 5.2, and in line with national research, students who are low-income and Black/African American or Hispanic are more likely to attend two-year institutions (Chetty et al., 2017[88]; Carnevale and Rose, 2003[89]).

One consequence of high unmet need is that students may incur heavy debt loads to cover the cost of attending higher education and related costs. Black/African American and White students graduating from four-year institutions are most at risk of facing heavy debt burdens in proportion to their starting wages; in 2017, student loan debt represented 101% of the first-year wages of African American graduates from four-year institutions, whereas the *60x30TX* target is 60% (THECB, 2019[25]). High debt loads may deter some students from entering higher education, depress graduates' return on investment, and dissuade graduates from entering professions that are societally important but that have relatively low starting salaries, such as teaching, social work and nursing.

Financial assistance can also be a tool to promote and incentivise the participation of low-income students in educational opportunities that they may not otherwise engage in. The Texas College Work-Study (TWCS) programme, which includes both placements and mentorships, and the recently introduced Texas WORKS internship programme, provide opportunities for work-based learning. In addition, the recently passed HB 3808 allows for work-study students to do internships off campus and centralises the application process through the THECB. However, both the placement and mentorship streams of the Work-Study programme served a limited number of students: 4 102 students benefitted from these opportunities in fiscal year 2017, as shown in Table 5.6. The new Texas WORKS internship programme is small in scale, with USD 1 million in funding for 2020.

Community and regional initiatives to respond to the challenge of affordability are numerous. In recent years, various College Promise programmes have been launched in Texas with strong support from local and regional leaders (see Box 5.11 on the Dallas County Promise). These programmes are designed to eliminate tuition and fees by ensuring that federal student aid eligibility is fully used, and by providing "last dollar" student financial assistance from local funds to eliminate tuition fees for (eligible) entering students.

Recommendations on funding higher education

Institutional funding

1. Raise state community college funding to improve student completion and attainment. Consider new approaches to raise funds for post-secondary education, taking into account examples of other states with a high need for skilled workers. See, for example, Washington's legislation requiring contributions from industries and firms employing highly skilled workers (Chapter 7).
2. Consider the incorporation of student employment outcomes in institutional funding at both public two-year and four-year institutions, taking into account experiences from other states (see Chapter 3).
3. Consider dedicated funding to strengthen institutional capacity to develop new programmes/opportunities to respond to labour market needs. This funding could support dedicated staff at institutions to promote and oversee processes to develop new learning opportunities (courses, programmes, minors, micro-credentials, etc.) responding to labour market needs across departments. Such dedicated staff could also serve as a point of contact for the programmes, from state agencies and non-profit partners that promote partnerships between institutions, employers and other stakeholders to develop accelerated programmes to meet labour market needs.

Student funding

4. Consider expanding the coverage and award levels of state grant programmes to reduce the number of students with unmet need and the level of unmet need in both the four-year and two-year sectors.
5. Monitor the impact of local and regional College Promise initiatives in Texas, by assessing the extent to which they are effective at facilitating completions for low-income students. Consider ways to expand the scope of these programmes, for instance by providing matching funds designated for non-tuition expenses that may not be covered by these programmes.
6. Review the availability of financial supports to meet basic needs (e.g. transportation, childcare) for economically disadvantaged students facing barriers to participation in educational and work-based learning opportunities. Monitor the development of funding recently made available for support services through the Texas WORKS initiative. Consider examples of countries with programmes combining financial and non-financial supports with a demonstrated positive impact on student success.
7. Conduct an independent and comprehensive evaluation of the existing programmes to address shortages in fields such as nursing and teaching to: i) ascertain whether or not they have achieved their intended effect, and ii) if not, identify ways to redirect the investment. The programmes to be reviewed include shortage reduction programmes, loan forgiveness/repayment programmes, and other financial assistance programmes intended to increase enrolment in critical and high-demand fields of study.

Educational offerings, student supports and pathways

The state's "marketable skills" goal aims to increase institutional focus on labour market relevance and outcomes

The higher education system in Texas encompasses a wide range of programme and credential types, from certificates lasting less than one year to doctoral degrees. The delivery and content of educational programmes in Texas are primarily the responsibility of higher education institutions and their academic and teaching faculty, as institutions in Texas enjoy substantial autonomy in organisational, academic and staffing decisions.

The state provides guidelines for several aspects of educational content at the sub-baccalaureate and baccalaureate levels with the aim of ensuring a minimum level of knowledge, skills and competencies are developed through public higher education in Texas. The Texas Core Curriculum provides a framework for the general education component of all academic associate's and bachelor's degree offerings at public institutions. A revised Texas Core Curriculum was implemented in 2014 and incorporated "21st century competencies". Each Texas public institution of higher education has its own unique listing of core courses and provides annual updates and revisions to the THECB. In addition, the Texas Higher Education Coordinating Board (THECB) provides guidelines for instructional programmes for workforce education, including certificates and applied associate's degrees, which were last updated in 2015 (THECB, 2015[90]).

The concept of "marketable skills" was a key component of the state's higher education plan, *60x30TX*, for the period from 2015-30. The higher education plan emphasised the importance of embedding marketable skills in all educational programmes in order to strengthen signalling of the skills content of credentials to employers, thus facilitating the transition of graduates into the workforce. By encouraging the development of a "marketable skills" language which reflects the labour market value of educational programmes, the marketable skills goal may serve to increase institutional focus on labour market relevance (see Box 5.7). In addition, the marketable skills goal is accompanied by a state-wide target to have 80% of graduates from all public institutions working or enrolled one year after graduation. The state calls this a "maintenance goal", as outcomes over the last few years are very close to the goal, with 78.5% of graduates working or enrolled one year after graduation in 2017 (THECB, 2019[19]).

Box 5.7. Communicating labour market value through "marketable skills"

Marketable skills have been defined as "skills valued by employers that can be applied in a variety of work settings, including interpersonal, cognitive, and applied skill areas. These skills can be either primary or complementary to a major and are acquired by students through education, including curricular, co-curricular, and extracurricular activities" (THECB, 2015, p. 22[91]).

The *60x30TX* plan requires public two-year and four-year higher education institutions to identify and document the marketable skills that each degree programme confers to students, enabling them to market themselves effectively to employers. Though not a requirement, private higher education institutions are also encouraged to participate in the goal. The Texas Higher Education Coordinating Board (THECB) monitors institutional progress on the creation and implementation of these processes, and facilitates discussions on practices.

An intermediate term goal in the *60x30TX* plan is that, by 2020, higher education institutions will have created and implemented a process to identify and regularly update marketable skills for each of their programmes. This requires creating an effective process for "continually updating the skills that are in demand and in development" (THECB, 2018, p. 4[92]) In order to facilitate this process, the THECB has established implementation guidelines for higher education institutions.

The marketable skills implementation guidelines suggest that institutions:

- work with career services and engage with industry and other stakeholders, including regional and workforce partners;
- draw on national resources for information about competencies and skills, such as the National Association of Colleges and Employers (NACE) Competencies, the Degree Qualifications Profile (DQP), and Liberal Education and America's Promise (LEAP);

- consider the NACE First Destination survey or Gallup-Purdue Index as survey examples if conducting an annual survey of recent graduates;
- use labour market information, including data from O*NET, the U.S. Bureau of Labor Statistics, and the US Census, for information about employment and skills requirements for different occupations;
- consult international sources on transferable and employability skills from the United Kingdom, Ireland and Canada.

As of 2018, 41% of higher education institutions had reported creating and implementing a process for identifying marketable skills in their programmes (THECB, 2019[19]).

Targeted to students, the recently published Career Readiness Handbook aims to provide students with information on how to prepare for their careers and how to communicate with employers about their skills. The handbook explains that both hard skills (such as building websites or performing statistical analysis) and soft skills (for example, listening and reasoning) are important in the workplace. In addition, students are encouraged to use a digital tool, Match your Skills to Career, provided by the Virtual Career Network. The handbook is published by the THECB in collaboration with the Texas Workforce Commission.

Sources: THECB (2015[91]; 2018[92]; 2019[19]).

Texas higher education institutions are aware of the need for greater labour market alignment, but workplace readiness among recent graduates is a concern among employers

OECD interviews with institutional leaders in Texas demonstrated a commitment at both two-year and four-year institutions across Texas to ensure graduates are equipped with the relevant knowledge and skills to meet the changing demands of the labour market. This is generally reflected in institutional practices including systematically reviewing programme offerings and curriculum content, providing professional development opportunities for faculty, engaging industry representatives through the use of advisory boards or practitioner-faculty, and providing career services and counselling to guide students towards viable jobs and careers. It also includes facilitating access to adult and part-time learners by ensuring that the delivery of programmes meets their needs, and providing relevant educational offerings for workers who need to update their skills.

In OECD interviews, some institutions also pointed to increased use of data on graduate labour market outcomes in programme review and curriculum-planning processes. This includes using alumni surveys to understand how graduates have fared in the labour market, particularly in terms of skills use in the workplace. The University of Texas (UT) system is also participating in a US Census study on Post-Secondary Employment Outcomes (PSEO), which will allow for more detailed analyses of the employment outcomes of UT graduates. Other institutions also conduct their own labour market analyses and engage systematically with employers to better understand emerging skills needs.

Many higher education institutions in Texas have developed innovative approaches to skills development and labour market alignment by using comprehensive learner records, skills inventories and other digital tools to engage employers and help students connect with them. Some examples of these approaches are outlined in Box 5.8.

Box 5.8. Innovative tools to facilitate skills-based labour market alignment in Texas

Texas State Technical College System: SkillsEngine

The Texas State Technical College has developed a Shared Skills Language Platform that standardises skills and competencies with the aim of facilitating alignment of curricula with labour market needs and across institutions. The platform and skills library forms the basis of several digital applications, including SkillsEngine API, which translates text from resumes and curricula into skills data, and Calibrate, which allows educators to validate and align curriculum content with employer needs.

Dallas County Community College District: GreenLight Credentials

The Dallas County Community College District partnered with GreenLight Credentials to create a platform where students could gain ownership of their complete transcript history, thereby initiating a digital lifelong learning record. The platform uses blockchain technology to securely store and share credentials. Sharing credentials through the platform also allows employers to verify applicants' credentials and identify qualified candidates by matching skills and education history to open positions.

Sources: C4EO (n.d.[93]); DCCCD (2019[94]); GreenLight Credentials (n.d.[95]); SkillsEngine (n.d.[96]).

While Texas institutions are demonstrating commitment to improving the labour market relevance of their educational offerings, a frequently cited concern among stakeholders was a general lack of workplace readiness among recent graduates, mainly due to weak "soft skills" such as interpersonal and professional skills, including team work, persistence and communication. This challenge is not unique to Texas, and the general desire for stronger soft skills among graduates mirrors a common sentiment among employers nation-wide and across a range of industries, as reflected in multiple employer surveys (IHE, 2019[97]; SHRM, 2019[98]; Adecco USA, 2019[99]). To better prepare graduates for the world of work, stakeholders in Texas called for deeper higher education-industry partnerships and more widely accessible work-based learning opportunities for students. This echoes some of the recommendations in the state's Tri-Agency Workforce Initiative, which also calls for a substantial increase in paid internships, apprenticeships, externships, and other applied workplace learning opportunities (TEA, THECB and TWC, 2016[69]).

State-funded initiatives such as the Texas College Work-Study programme may not be providing a sufficient diversity of work-based learning opportunities for students, due to the programme's requirement for campus-related work. The funding allocated to the Texas College Work-Study programme has declined by almost 40% between 2017 and 2020; and in 2017, the programme only served 4 102 students. By contrast, the Washington State Work-Study programme served approximately 4 000 students in a higher education system enrolling about one-fifth of the number of students in Texas. Through House Bill 3808, the Texas Legislature recently provided funding for a new programme, the Texas WORKS internship programme, which will allow work-study students to take internships off campus. The intention of the new Texas WORKS internship programme is promising, but is currently small in scale, with USD 1 million in funding for 2020.

While labour market relevance is a criterion for approving new degree programmes, it is not considered in any ex-post review process at the state level

General quality assurance and accreditation of higher education in Texas falls under the purview of the regional accrediting body for all public and private not-for-profit degree-granting institutions in the southern states, the Southern Association of Colleges and Schools Commission on Colleges (SACSCOC). The institutional accreditation standards and processes used by SACSCOC verify a wide range of institutional characteristics and policies, and provide a basic guarantee of academic quality (SACSCOC, 2018[100]).

However, the institutional standards make no explicit reference to institutional policies and practices to align skills development with labour market needs and do not take into account the labour market outcomes of graduates in the accreditation process.

At the state level, public higher education institutions in Texas are required to seek approval from the Texas Higher Education Coordinating Board (THECB) for the opening of new degree programmes as well as "substantive changes" to existing programmes. The programme approval process requires institutions to provide labour market data to substantiate the job market need for the programme. For most new programmes at the certificate, associate's, bachelor's and master's levels, institutions must submit information demonstrating that a series of criteria are met and that local institutions have raised no objections during a public notice period to receive approval from the Board. The criteria are wide-ranging, from demonstrating student demand and workforce need, to sufficient faculty resources, administrative capacity and equipment. The criteria generally differ to some extent between two- and four-year institutions. The criteria pertaining to workforce need are highlighted in Box 5.9.

Box 5.9. Workforce need and the labour market relevance of new programmes

The Texas Administrative Code outlines a series of criteria public institutions must meet when submitting a request for a new programme to the Texas Higher Education Coordinating Board. These include criteria related to workforce need and labour market relevance.

Bachelor's and master's degree programmes delivered by public four-year institutions (TAC, § 5.45)

- Workforce need: There should be a demonstrated or well-documented need for the programme in terms of meeting present and future workforce needs of the state and nation. There should be a ready job market for graduates of the programme, or alternatively, it should produce students for master's or doctoral-level programmes in fields in which there is a demonstrated need for professionals.
- Marketable Skills: There must be a list of the marketable skills associated with the proposed programme, in keeping with the state strategic plan, *60x30TX*, and a plan for how students will be informed of the marketable skills.

Certificates and associate's degree programmes delivered by public two-year institutions (TAC, § 9.93)

- The institution has researched and documented current job market need for the programme and/or that the programme would lead to opportunities for further education.
- Basic and career technical/workforce skills have been integrated into the curriculum.
- Representatives from private sector business and industry have been involved in the creation of the programme through participation in an advisory committee.
- The institution has an improvement plan in place for all career technical/workforce programmes that do not currently meet Board standards for both graduation and placement.
- Skill standards recognized by the Texas Skill Standards Board, if they exist for the discipline, have been reviewed and considered for inclusion in the curriculum for the programme.

Sources: Texas Administrative Code (2003[101]; 2004[102]).

For some programmes, a specific and detailed programme approval process is required. In the four-year sector, institutions must provide a "planning notification" if they plan to develop new doctoral programmes in any discipline, engineering programmes, or programmes with new costs likely to exceed USD 2 million during the first five years. In the public two-year sector, colleges seeking approval for applied bachelor's programmes must also undergo this process. In these cases, detailed labour market data to substantiate need are requested of the institution. This includes providing evidence of labour market demand in Texas and nationally for the occupations for which the programme aims to prepare students, as well as a state and national supply-demand analysis to demonstrate present and future gaps that justify the creation of the programme.

While the above process ensures that the creation of programmes takes account of labour market demand, there is no state requirement or process enabling the THECB to review the labour market relevance of existing programmes. In other words, the state requires an explicit labour market need to establish new programmes (ex-ante), but does not assess labour market relevance in programmes once established (ex-post). As labour market needs change rapidly, such a mechanism would be useful to encourage institutions to adapt their programmes on an ongoing basis. The THECB conducts an annual review of low-producing programmes (LPP), but this is primarily with the objective of consolidating or closing programmes with few degree completions. THECB may recommend to an institution's governing board the consolidation or closure of any non-exempt degree programme that has been on the annual list of low-producing programmes for three or more consecutive reviews. New degree programmes are exempt from LPP review for the first five years of operation. Programme reviews do not consider graduate outcomes in the labour market; thus programmes that are producing a sufficient number of graduates, but resulting in poor outcomes for their graduates, are not considered for re-design or closure.

Different jurisdictions approach the challenge of preserving and enhancing the labour market relevance of higher education in various ways, utilising tools that range from funding, information, and strategic planning and co-ordination tools. Some countries utilise various mechanisms to ensure an ongoing dialogue between public authorities and institutions on the labour market relevance and outcomes of higher education. For instance, jurisdictions as diverse as Austria, Denmark, Ireland, the Netherlands and the province of Ontario in Canada have established "compacts" and "strategic mandate agreements" with each public institution (see Chapter 3).

Multiple initiatives are in place to increase college access and preparedness in Texas, but sufficient supports are critical for student success

With rapid population growth and a demographic makeup that is relatively young and diverse, ensuring adequate access to and preparedness for higher education are important concerns for higher education policy in Texas. This is important not only to ensure that more Texans benefit from the value of a post-secondary credential, but also to bolster the supply of highly skilled workers in the state's economy. The state grants automatic admission to all public universities for students who reach the top 10% in class rank during their penultimate year of high school, but many students in Texas schools struggle to transition from secondary to post-secondary education. As seen in Section 5.2, only 52% of Texas secondary school students enrol in higher education, compared to a national average of 67% (THECB, 2019[25]). Notably, a majority (59%) of public secondary school students in Texas are considered to be economically disadvantaged (TEA, 2019[103]), and these students are less likely to be adequately prepared for college, which in turn reduces their likelihood of completing a post-secondary credential. This is particularly prevalent in under-represented populations, such as the African American and Hispanic communities, and in economically distressed regions such as West Texas and the Rio Grande Valley.

An important public policy tool to facilitate access to higher education is through means-tested financial aid programmes to help students cover the costs of attending higher education, including living costs. In Texas, state-funded programmes targeted to economically disadvantaged students include various programmes, such as the Toward Excellence Access and Success (TEXAS) and the Texas Educational Opportunity Grant (TEOG), which have been described in the preceding section, along with a recommendation to examine current policy tools to reduce the number of students in Texas with substantial unmet financial need. Informational tools and counselling initiatives have also been developed to reach out to high school students throughout the state. *Generation TX* and *Advise TX* are two examples of state-wide initiatives that are targeted to first-generation and low-income students to encourage and guide their transition from high school to higher education. State-wide initiatives often supplement the work that is conducted through local partnerships between school districts, higher education institutions and local workforce boards, in addition to programmes initiated by private companies, non-profit organisations and advocacy groups.

Ensuring students are adequately prepared for college improves the likelihood of completion, which is an important policy priority for Texas, given the state's goals to increase post-secondary attainment levels among 25-34 year-olds. Thus, strengthening the pipeline not only into higher education, but also within and through higher education, is critical to improving graduation rates and completions. However, according to the 2019 Texas Public Higher Education Almanac, 40% of incoming undergraduates in Texas are not deemed to be "college-ready" by state standards (THECB, 2019[25]). These statistics are based on outcomes from the state-wide Texas Success Initiative (TSI) assessment, which determines college readiness and eligibility for developmental education or remedial coursework. While there are certain exemptions, in principle all incoming students to Texas higher education institutions are required to take the TSI assessment, which examines skills in reading, writing and mathematics. If a student does not pass one or any of the content areas, the student is required to enrol in developmental education courses either prior to or at the same time as enrolling in college-level courses.

However, practices regarding developmental education differ across institutions, with varying degrees of success in improving students' preparedness for college-level courses, as evidenced by the proportion of students who fail or withdraw from first-year courses (THECB, 2018[104]). In 2017, House Bill 2223 was passed by the Texas Legislature to standardise the use of assessment instruments across institutions and set standards for designing developmental coursework (Texas Legislature, 2017[105]). The legislation requires, among other things, the use of "co-requisite models" for a share of students enrolled in developmental or remedial courses. This allows a student to enrol simultaneously in a college course as well as a "support course" or intervention that is designed specifically to encourage successful completion of college coursework, for example through student counselling. The state's strategy for increasing college preparedness is articulated through the *2018-2023 Statewide Plan for Supporting Underprepared Students*. In this strategy, the THECB has set a goal for public higher education institutions to deliver developmental education through co-requisite models by 2023.

Once successfully enrolled in college-level courses, however, students may face additional barriers to completion. In order to facilitate student success in higher education, students often need non-financial supports (Holzer and Baum, 2017[106]; Angrist, Lang and Oreopoulos, 2009[107]). This is particularly important for students from disadvantaged backgrounds. Some research suggests that effective student supports can reduce the public cost per degree, as the cost of intervention is offset by an increase in number of degrees produced (Scrivener et al., 2015[108]). As highlighted in the Texas *Statewide Plan for Supporting Underprepared Students*, students entering their first year of higher education who are struggling to pass their courses may be struggling due to the need for so-called "wrap-around" supports in the form of housing, child care and additional financial support. State funding was approved by the 85th Texas Legislature to expand grant eligibility for institutions to provide student support programmes for all students, not just for those who are deemed under-prepared through the TSI assessment (Texas Legislature, 2017[105]). This includes funding for support services such as supplemental instructors and targeted tutoring, adaptive courseware, and advising. Furthermore, the Texas Legislature recently passed House Bill 3808 requiring all public higher education institutions to designate a "liaison officer" who provides current or incoming students with information about available support services and other resources, as described in Box 5.10 (Texas Legislature, 2019[109]).

Box 5.10. Designation of a support services liaison officer to assist students in higher education

Texas House Bill 3808, passed in 2019, requires public higher education institutions to designate at least one employee to act as liaison officer for students at each institution. The liaison officer would be responsible for providing students with information and resources about:

- medical and behavioural health coverage;
- public benefit programmes, including those related to housing and food security, as well as case management assistance and counselling;
- parenting and child care resources;
- employment assistance;
- financial counselling and tax assistance;
- student academic success strategies.

Source: Texas Legislature (2019[109]).

Stakeholders highlighted the need for clearer credential pathways, more efficient transfers, and guidance to identify the routes to in-demand careers

Pathways into and across higher education

The Texas higher education landscape is large and complex, with several sub-systems in the public higher education sector and a diverse range of private colleges and universities. One of the most consistent findings to emerge from the OECD team's discussions with stakeholders was the need for higher education pathways that are clearer to learners. The need for streamlined pathways has been highlighted in the state's Tri-Agency Workforce Initiative, which also emphasises more industry-aligned career pathways, credentials with marketable skills, and efficient stackable programme opportunities (TEA, THECB and TWC, 2016[69]).

As in many other states, Texas promotes multiple pathways to give students a range of options to obtain a post-secondary credential. Dual credit programmes have continued to expand in the United States over the last two decades, facilitating the pathway to sub-baccalaureate and baccalaureate degree programmes (Troutman et al., 2018[110]; Miller et al., 2018[111]). In Texas, participation in dual credit courses increased by 753% between 2000 and 2017, representing 10% of public higher education enrolments in 2017 (THECB, 2018[112]). Research suggests that while dual credit participation increases college enrolment and completion, there are important racial disparities in outcomes among Texas students (Miller et al., 2017[113]).

In addition to dual credit programmes and similar models such as early college high schools, alternative pathways such as apprenticeships are gaining traction in Texas. In some apprenticeship programmes, credits can be applied towards associate's degrees. This and other models are outlined in Box 5.11.

Clear and structured pathways serve to guide students efficiently into and through higher education, relying on a system of credits that can build on each other and transfer between institutions, to ensure a sufficient degree of "stackability" and mobility within the higher education system. Efficient transfer processes are essential to improve students' chances of completing a credential (Bailey et al., 2017[114]; Xu et al., 2017[115]). Important mechanisms to facilitate transferability are articulation agreements between institutions, not only from two-year to four-year institutions, but also between two-year institutions. Regional partnerships and transfer collaborations can be especially effective in creating clear pathways and transitions between secondary school and higher education, and within higher education (Bailey et al., 2017[114]).

Box 5.11. Alternative pathways and education models facilitating the transition from high school to post-secondary education or training and into the workforce

Apprenticeship programmes – Example of Houston Community College

Apprenticeships combine paid on-the-job training under the supervision of experienced journey workers with related classroom instruction. Registered apprenticeship training programmes typically have a duration of 3-5 years, determined by industry standards. To qualify for public funds, apprenticeship training programmes and apprentices must be registered with the U.S. Department of Labor Office of Apprenticeship.

Houston Community College (HCC) works with local employers to provide apprenticeship training opportunities in high-demand fields, where students complete classroom instruction through the college. Successful completers of registered apprenticeship programmes can receive up to 36 college credits towards their associate's degree in applied science and construction management as a HCC student.

Early college high schools – Example of P-TECH (Pathways in Technology)

P-TECH is a public-private education model and form of "early college high school", which encourages students to obtain a post-secondary credential while in high school. As of the 2019/20 school year, Texas had 63 designated P-TECH schools. According to the Texas Education Agency, P-TECH programmes:

- enable students to earn a high school diploma, an associate's degree, and a two-year post-secondary certificate or industry certification, within six years;
- allow students to gain work experience through internships, apprenticeships, or other job training programmes;
- partner with higher education institutions (typically through articulation agreements) and regional businesses and industries in Texas.

'Promise' initiatives – Example of Dallas County Promise

Dallas County Promise is a public-private partnership that has the dual objective of improving equity in access to post-secondary education as well as aligning post-secondary education with labour market needs. Key features include:

- a "last dollar" scholarship to bridge the gap between the cost of attending post-secondary education and available resources;
- individual success coaches and career mentoring with a focus on middle-skill, high-demand careers in Dallas county, such as health professions and the skilled trades;
- partnerships between institutions to track student progress through education and workforce pathways, using real-time reporting.

Sources: TWC (n.d.[116]); HCC (n.d.[117]); TEA (n.d.[118]); Dallas County Promise (2019[119]).

In addition to the Texas Core Curriculum and the College and Career Readiness Standards, the Texas Higher Education Coordinating Board (THECB) has developed "fields of study curricula" as a framework for grouping lower-division undergraduate courses that are guaranteed to transfer between any public

Texas institution as part of the same field of study (THECB, 2019[120]). A related initiative is the framework for "programs of study", which is similar to fields of study, but specific to career and technical education (CTE). A third framework is the concept of "meta majors", which is a grouping of academic disciplines or "programs of study" that share common foundational skills (Texas Legislature, 2019[121]). In a recent Senate Bill (SB 25) proposed to facilitate transfers between Texas higher education institutions, the Texas Legislature tasked the THECB with conducting a study on the feasibility of implementing "meta majors" for eight discipline areas state-wide (Texas Legislature, 2019[121]). As part of this study, and to support more efficient transfers at the undergraduate level, the Legislature has requested that an advisory committee make recommendations on the effectiveness of requirements regarding transfer of credits between institutions for courses in the core curriculum. The bill goes on to state that:

> *The study and recommendations must include an analysis of: 1) The efficacy of dividing the recommended core curriculum for each meta major into a general academic core curriculum and an academic discipline core curriculum and, if determined to be efficacious, the recommended number of semester credit hours for each component of the recommended core curriculum for each meta major; 2) Methods to ensure that courses completed in the general academic core curriculum and academic discipline core curriculum transfer between institutions of higher education for course credit applied toward a student's major at the receiving institution; 3) The potential inclusion of courses in the field of study curricula adopted by the board under Section 61.823 in the recommended core curriculum adopted by the board under Section 61.822.*
>
> *(Texas Legislature, 2019, p. 12[121])*

While efforts to facilitate transferability are necessary and positive, the existence of multiple frameworks and pathway initiatives may in fact interfere with students' ability to efficiently complete a credential, particularly in cases of transfers between two-year and four-year institutions. If institutions use different typologies to cluster courses and define pathways, this may present a hindrance to students' ability to understand their opportunities to "stack" credentials across institutions and within a similar field. In particular, stakeholders in Texas highlighted the need to do more to ensure that those who attain lower-level credentials have opportunities to achieve higher-level qualifications later in life. This includes potential returners to higher education, in need of re-skilling or up-skilling, and the "some college, no degree" population that needs a clear pathway towards credential attainment. Moreover, it is unclear to what extent institutions actually accept credits from transfer students towards a particular field of study or major, as required by law. Thus, it is important that the state monitors and follows up on transfer credits to ensure that institutions comply with this requirement (Texas Legislature, 2019[121]).

Guidance for students

In a system that encourages a great deal of student choice, providing sufficient student support and guidance towards a credential that leads to a viable career path is important for improving the labour market outcomes of graduates. Based on a growing concern over students taking excess credits that do not count towards a credential, and the gap in completion between low-income and high-income transfer students, a 2017 paper written by the Community College Research Center in collaboration with the Greater Texas Foundation suggested several policy recommendations to improve transfer processes in Texas (Bailey et al., 2017[114]). One of the most important policy levers highlighted in the paper was to help students select and enter a transfer pathway through clear guidance and better support for transfer students.

Structured, guided pathways through higher education are particularly important for first-generation and economically disadvantaged students who typically face additional barriers to completion and are at higher risk of incurring debt (Holzer and Baum, 2017[106]). *Guided Pathways* is an example of a national initiative that has developed and expanded to a large number of two-year institutions across the United States, rooted in research that has identified critical factors supporting student success (Bailey, 2017[122]). Box 5.12 describes the Guided Pathways model and a number of colleges in Texas that are involved in implementation initiatives. One example is the Dallas County Community College District (DCCCD), where faculty and staff have designed approximately 200 pathways that fall into seven main "career paths": Arts, Humanities, Communications & Design; Business; Education; Health Sciences; Industry, Manufacturing & Construction, Social Sciences & Public Service; and STEM. The DCCCD has developed standardised one-page, mobile-friendly documents for each pathway, providing information about the career path to which each pathway leads, the specific college(s) offering the pathway, the courses necessary to complete either a degree or a certification, and key milestones to stay on track with course progression/completion.

Box 5.12. Implementing the Guided Pathways model at community colleges in Texas

Thirty community colleges across the United States were selected to participate in a project co-ordinated by the American Association of Community Colleges (AACC) to implement the Guided Pathways model at their institutions over a period of three years. Among these, four community colleges in Texas were selected: Alamo Community College, El Paso Community College, Paris Junior College, and San Jacinto College. Tarrant County College is also participating in a separate but related project, the so-called Pathways 2.0 Project, where institutions can receive customised assistance.

The Texas Pathways Project has been developed to support community colleges in Texas who want to implement the Guided Pathways model. This project is co-ordinated by the Texas Success Center and the Texas Association of Community Colleges (TACC), and funded by the Greater Texas Foundation. Biannual conferences gather participants to discuss pathways implementation at their institutions and to learn from participating colleges in the AACC Pathways Project. Texas Pathways participants include: Amarillo College, Brazosport College, Dallas County Community College District, Grayson College, Houston Community College System, Lone Star College District, McLennan Community College, Midland College, South Texas College, Southwest Texas Junior College, and Temple College.

The Guided Pathways model is based on developing broad "programs of study" that are explicitly aligned with requirements for successful employment and further education, and where student supports and instructional approaches are fully integrated and aligned with each programme of study.

Key features of Guided Pathways include:

- programme "maps" that show clear pathways to completion, further education, and employment in key fields;
- transfer pathways that align pathway courses and expected learning outcomes with transfer institutions;
- remedial or developmental education designed for entry into a programme of study;
- academic and non-academic student supports and a strong advising process;
- programme-level learning outcomes aligned with the requirements for successful employment and further education in a given field;
- learning outcomes assessments to improve the effectiveness of instruction;
- integrated applied learning experiences for students.

Sources: AACC (n.d.[123]); TACC (n.d.[124]).

Recommendations on educational offerings, pathways and student supports

1. Consider ways to expand work-based learning opportunities for undergraduate students both on and off campus, for example through programmes like Texas College Work-Study and Texas WORKS. Monitor student participation in relevant work-based learning opportunities through the newly initiated Texas WORKS programme.
2. Consider implementing a process to review labour market outcomes of graduates by programme, signalling the importance of monitoring the labour market outcomes of higher education graduates. This could be conducted in conjunction with the low-producing programme (LPP) review process, or as a stand-alone exercise. For example, data on employment and earnings by programme up to ten years post-graduation could form the basis for identifying which programmes have consistently low labour market outcomes and should be reviewed in priority.
3. Monitor the implementation of "student support liaison officers" at higher education institutions to provide information and resources about student support services. Review, and consider expanding, funding for "wrap-around supports" (see recommendation in funding section).
4. Develop clear and consistent formats and resources for presenting information about credential pathways that facilitate student transfers and promote consistency between institutions and across institution types.
5. Continue work to improve the measurement and monitoring of transfers and non-transfers between institutions, following from Senate Bill 25, 86(R) Legislature, which requires institutions to report on the credits that are not transferring.
6. Consider following up on specific policy recommendations in the Community College Center, Columbia University (Bailey et al., 2017[114]), to support and strengthen transfers from two-year to four-year institutions.
7. Strengthen regional articulation agreements between two-year and four-year institutions within a region or metro area, following the model from the Dallas County Community College District or the University of Houston's Joint Admissions initiative.
8. Ensure that dual credit programmes benefit all students, particularly those who face barriers to access and completion in higher education.

Information

Texas maintains a wealth of information about educational opportunities, institutional performance and graduate outcomes

Texas has a well-established system for collecting longitudinal post-secondary data, as well as multiple sources of publicly available information about post-secondary education and career opportunities. The Educational Data Center at the Texas Higher Education Coordinating Board (THECB) co-ordinates the collection of data from public higher education institutions in Texas. Private institutions report data related to certain performance measures as required by the state Legislature. The Texas Higher Education Accountability System, targeted mainly to educators and policy makers, was established in 2004 and provides data for 38 public universities, nine health-related institutions, four Texas State Technical Colleges, and three two-year Lamar State Colleges. Data from the state's 50 public two-year community colleges were added to the Accountability System in 2005. In addition, longitudinal data across several agencies are made available in a data repository through the Texas Education Research Centers to enable policy research.

The Texas Public Higher Education Almanac is published every year with detailed information about the student population and graduate outcomes of public two-year and four-year institutions of higher education. This includes institutional comparisons of graduate outcomes such as the number of degrees awarded, graduation rates and graduate debt levels. While the Almanac also contains a state-wide overview of graduate earnings and debt profiles, only debt information is provided at the individual institutional level. Average earnings by field of study and institution can be found on the Texas Consumer Resource for Education and Workforce Statistics (CREWS) dashboard, which is targeted primarily to students and families in order to explore average wage outcomes and loan levels for specific majors and by institution.

While Texas collects data on whether graduates are found working or enrolled in further education one year after graduating, obtaining information on in-field job placements is more challenging. State-level post-secondary data systems that collect data on earnings through Unemployment Insurance (UI) wage records typically cannot obtain information on the specific occupation of graduates. While UI records often indicate the industry in which an individual is employed, this does not include information on their occupational group and is thus insufficient to assess qualification or field mismatch. The US Census study on Post-Secondary Employment Outcomes (PSEO) is intended to allow for more detailed analyses of graduate employment outcomes, but currently only the University of Texas System is participating in the study.

Information on labour market outcomes is not clearly targeted to prospective and current higher education students

Studies on the intergenerational persistence in educational attainment and occupational choice have shown that young people often take the educational level of their parents as a reference point for their own aspired educational attainment (Page, Levy Garboua and Montmarquette, 2007[125]). When learning about the economic returns on education, young people also rely substantively on what they know about their parental earnings. As a result, youth with higher socio-economic status are more likely to opt for a higher education degree and aim for higher salary jobs than youth with lower socio-economic status. Thus, information about the costs and benefits of post-secondary education can help students to make better choices in terms of selecting a field of study and career path that leads to good labour market outcomes.

Moreover, some studies suggest that a significant share of students do not fully understand the costs of higher education or how much debt they are accumulating (Akers and Chingos, 2014[126]). For first-generation students, the costs of attending higher education are often more salient than future benefits. Ideally, information on graduates' return on investment should be a labour market metric that is included in post-secondary longitudinal data systems (TICAS, 2018[127]). According to the State Higher Education Executive Officers Association (SHEEO), many states struggle to find ways to report accurate information on student debt and loan repayment. SHEEO suggests strengthening state agency capacity to collect this kind of information, by acknowledging gaps in student financial indicators and publicising plans to collect and report this data (Whitfield, Armstrong and Weeden, 2019[128]).

Texas offers various websites that contain information on the labour market outcomes of higher education programmes, but these do not appear to be well-connected to other resources dedicated to prospective and current higher education students. At present, users interested in labour market outcomes are left to find their way between various national, state and institutional data sources, which may use different sources and measures, running the risk of providing inconsistent information. Students in Texas currently lack easily accessible information on the average return on investment from different study programmes. In order to increase student awareness about the labour market outcomes of post-secondary education, it is important that this information is made available – and is easy to find – on the same sites where students find information about educational opportunities and pathways.

While the resources made available through the Texas Higher Education Data website are comprehensive, they appear to be mainly targeted towards educators and policy makers. These data include detailed information about earnings and debt that could be made available to students in an easy-to-access manner as part of the information they consider when exploring educational opportunities. Similarly, while information about average earnings and loan amounts is presented at the programme level in the Texas Consumer Resource for Education and Workforce Statistics (CREWS) dashboard, this tool appears somewhat disconnected from other student-oriented sites on post-secondary opportunities, and thus it is unclear if the intended users are prospective students, educators or policy makers. By contrast, websites clearly targeted to prospective students, such as *ApplyTX* and *College for all Texans*, do not appear to include information on either labour market outcomes or employment prospects based on changing labour market needs. *Texas OnCourse* aims to combine tools and links to various websites for students and families, as well as educators. However, while the site contains a wealth of information, it may be difficult for the ordinary user to identify which of the tools are most relevant.

Table 5.8 provides an overview of some commonly referenced sources of information about post-secondary educational opportunities and graduate labour market outcomes or opportunities.

Table 5.8. Common sources of information about post-secondary education and labour market outcomes or opportunities in Texas

Website, publication or platform	Description	Co-ordinator
Texas Higher Education Accountability System	Provides data on high-priority measures of higher education performance in Texas, organised around the goals and targets of the state's *60x30TX* higher education plan.	THECB
Higher Education Almanac	Provides an annual summary of key features and performance of Texas public higher education institutions. This includes a state-wide overview of graduate earnings and debt levels, as well as percentage of students working or enrolled one year after graduation.	THECB
Texas Higher Education Regional Portal	The portal includes information and data on occupational growth, population growth, graduate completions, enrolments and other education information. Regional links provide data about each of the state's 10 higher education regions.	THECB
Texas Labor Analysis	Uses data on graduate completions from the THECB, online job postings, and TWC unemployment insurance data to compare labour demand and supply by industry or occupational career cluster.	TWC
Texas P-16 Public Education Information Resource	Provides information about Texas public school students from pre-K through college and into the workforce, including wage comparison by educational attainment level for high school graduates.	TEA
Texas Consumer Resource for Education and Workforce Statistics (CREWS)	An interactive dashboard tool that provides comparative information about graduate earnings of Texas public two-year and four-year post-secondary institutions. Each allows a comparison of degree programmes and career choices.	THECB, TWC
Texas OnCourse	Serves as a college and career planning guide for educators, students and their families through the planning process from high school and into the workforce. Provides links to multiple other sites, such as MapMyGrad, Share Your Road, and College Scorecard.	UT Austin
Texas Career Check	Shows 25 top occupations with earnings above the Texas median wage, ranked by the highest projected number of annual openings for a ten-year period. Also provides links to sites such as Texas Reality Check, which provides estimates of monthly expenses per city to compare with salaries in each occupation.	TWC

Note: The table is not meant to provide a comprehensive overview of all websites, publications or platforms that provide information on post-secondary education or labour market opportunities in Texas.

There is considerable potential for improvement in the quality and use of labour market information in higher education in Texas

Many higher education institutions engage directly with employers and conduct their own labour market analyses to understand changing skills needs, inform programming and curriculum design, and obtain approval for new programmes. As part of these efforts, they also rely on public workforce data and labour market information, which underscores the importance of ensuring transparent, consistent and easily accessible information about the labour market and state-wide workforce needs. Labour market and career information for Texas, including employment statistics and occupational projections, is provided by the Texas Workforce Commission (TWC).

Texas has several tools that combine higher education data with labour market information, primarily for policy planning purposes. The Texas Higher Education Regional Portal is a useful site that presents information about occupational projections and population growth estimates with relevant information on graduate enrolments, completions and labour market outcomes for ten higher education regions (THECB, n.d.[129]). This regional context data is used as a basis for the so-called Regional Target Starter Kits that the THECB has created to help regions develop strategies to reach the attainment targets of the *60x30TX* plan. One of the tools developed by the TWC is a labour gap analysis tool, which can be applied either state-wide or by region (TWC, 2019[33]). The tool utilises different sources of data to estimate current and anticipated labour gaps for major occupational groups and career clusters. Estimates of anticipated gaps rely on a crosswalk between fields of study and occupations, but it is not clear how this was developed. As limited feedback was received about this tool during OECD interviews, the extent to which it is used in higher education planning or workforce development is not clear.

In some states, gap analyses are conducted systematically at the state level, using diverse methodologies. In Washington, for example, a workforce supply-demand analysis is conducted every two years as a joint agency initiative, using both national and state level data (WSAC, SBCTC and WTECB, 2018[130]; Hershbein and Hollenbeck, 2015[131]) Many states have developed dashboard tools to estimate gaps in workforce supply and demand (Prince et al., 2015[132]). As data-scraping methods improve and data from online job postings can be used to obtain more granular information about skills needs, supply and demand models using real-time labour market information may also become increasingly useful for strategic planning and forecasting in higher education (Dorrer, 2016[133]). Regional economic development agencies and state workforce or higher education agencies sometimes contract with commercial services such as Burning Glass Technologies or Economic Modeling Specialists International (EMSI) to conduct skills gap analyses based on data from online job postings (Goldman et al., 2015[134]). Generally, as a basis for policy, supply and demand models should also be supplemented with both quantitative and qualitative information from employers, workforce boards and other stakeholders to provide a comprehensive picture of labour market demand.

There are opportunities for Texas to improve the use of workforce data for strategic planning purposes in higher education. A recent report by the RAND Corporation provides a guide for educators and policy makers in Texas on how to use workforce information for programme planning (Goldman et al., 2015[134]). The report was commissioned by the THECB after the Texas Legislature passed a bill (HB 1296) in 2013 requiring the THECB and the TWC to collaborate to provide a broad supply-demand analysis based on five-year projections of state workforce needs and the educational attainment and training levels of individuals projected to enter the workforce (Texas Legislature, 2013[135]). The bill states that the THECB "shall identify the types and levels of education, training, and skills that are needed to meet the state's future workforce needs and shall make recommendations concerning the expansion of existing programs or the development of new programs at public and private post-secondary educational institutions in this state as necessary to meet the projected workforce needs" (Texas Legislature, 2013, p. 3[135]). The RAND report suggests that workforce data should be more systematically integrated into higher education planning, noting that this has not been common practice among state agencies. In addition, the report recommends designing a website with relevant data sources that can help guide institutions on how to apply the information for their own programme and curriculum-planning purposes.

Recommendations on information

1. Review the portfolio of informational tools and websites on Texas post-secondary and career opportunities, with the aim of consolidating and streamlining sites tailored to specific user groups. Consolidated information on likely future employment prospects and return on investment for higher education should be part of the state's future communication and awareness-raising activities targeted to prospective and current students. In particular, for sites targeted to students and their families, information about graduate outcomes in the labour market and career opportunities should be easily accessible along with information about post-secondary educational opportunities and credential pathways. This can build on an existing source or platform such as Texas OnCourse, for example.
2. As a joint initiative between the Texas Higher Education Coordinating Board and the Texas Workforce Commission, follow up on the recommendations of the RAND report (Goldman et al., 2015[134]) and conduct regular skills supply and demand analyses in order to achieve a comprehensive picture of the demand for and supply of both middle and high-level skills at the state level. A skills gap analysis can be supplemented with both quantitative and qualitative information from employers, workforce boards, educators and other stakeholders. Mechanisms to ensure regular stakeholder engagement on skills forecasting could be considered, for example by drawing on mechanisms in place in Ireland and Finland (see Chapter 3).
3. Develop tools to generate information about graduate employment trajectories and employer perspectives on graduate skills. This could include the development of a state-wide graduate outcomes survey, in collaboration with higher education institutions, to complement other data sources, and to provide information on rates of in-field job placement, capturing graduates who left the state as well as those who are self-employed. In the longer term, the graduate outcomes survey could be combined with an employer survey to gather systematic employer views on the quality and relevance of graduate skills, as is current practice in Australia and the United Kingdom (see Chapter 3). It can also include the use of real-time labour market information through online job postings to obtain a better understanding of changing skills demand.

References

AACC (n.d.), *AACC Pathways Project*, American Association of Community Colleges, https://www.aacc.nche.edu/programs/aacc-pathways-project/ (accessed on 6 February 2020). [123]

Adecco USA (2019), *The American Skills Gap is Real*, https://www.adeccousa.com/employers/resources/skills-gap-in-the-american-workforce/ (accessed on 3 February 2020). [99]

Akers, E. and M. Chingos (2014), *Are College Students Borrowing Blindly?*, Brooking Institution, https://www.brookings.edu/wp-content/uploads/2016/06/Are-College-Students-Borrowing-Blindly_Dec-2014.pdf. [126]

Andrews, R. and K. Stange (2016), "Price Regulation, Price Discrimination, and Equality of Opportunity in Higher Education: Evidence from Texas", *NBER Working Paper No. 22901*, National Bureau of Economic Research, Cambridge, http://www.nber.org/papers/w22901 (accessed on 29 October 2019). [64]

Angrist, J., D. Lang and P. Oreopoulos (2009), "Incentives and Services for College Achievement: Evidence from a Randomized Trial", *American Economic Journal: Applied Economics*, Vol. 1/1, pp. 136-163, http://dx.doi.org/10.1257/app.1.1.136. [107]

Bailey, T. (2017), "Guided Pathways at Community Colleges: From Theory to Practice", *Diversity and Democracy*, Vol. 20/4, https://www.aacu.org/diversitydemocracy/2017/fall/bailey (accessed on 28 August 2019). [122]

Bailey, T. et al. (2017), "Policy Levers to Strengthen Community College Transfer Student Success in Texas", Community College Research Center, https://ccrc.tc.columbia.edu/media/k2/attachments/policy-levers-to-strengthen-community-college-transfer-student-success-in-texas.pdf. [114]

Baum, S. (2014), *Higher Education Earnings Premium: Value, Variation, and Trends*, Urban Institute, https://files.eric.ed.gov/fulltext/ED544781.pdf (accessed on 20 May 2019). [59]

Blum, E. and G. Groves (2016), *Regional Talent Pipelines: Collaborating with Industry to Build Opportunities in Texas*, Federal Reserve Bank of Dallas, https://www.dallasfed.org/-/media/Documents/cd/pubs/pipelines.pdf?la=en. [16]

C4EO (n.d.), *Shared Skills Language Platform*, Center for Employability Outcomes, https://www.c4eo.org/skills-platform (accessed on 3 February 2020). [93]

Canas, J. and S. Gullo (2019), "Position as Top Exporting State Exposes Texas to Shifting Trade Policy", Federal Reserve Bank of Dallas, https://www.dallasfed.org/~/media/documents/research/swe/2019/swe1901b.pdf. [6]

Carnevale, A. and S. Rose (2003), *Socioeconomic Status, Race/Ethnicity, and Selective College Admissions.*, The Century Foundation, New York, https://eric.ed.gov/?id=ED482419 (accessed on 26 July 2019). [89]

Carnevale, A., S. Rose and B. Cheah (2013), *The College Payoff: Education, Occupation, Lifetime Earnings*, Georgetown University, https://1gyhoq479ufd3yna29x7ubjn-wpengine.netdna-ssl.com/wp-content/uploads/collegepayoff-completed.pdf (accessed on 20 May 2019). [61]

Carnevale, A., S. Rose and A. Hanson (2012), "Certificates: Gateway to Gainful Employment and College Degrees", Georgetown University Center for Education and the Workforce, https://1gyhoq479ufd3yna29x7ubjn-wpengine.netdna-ssl.com/wp-content/uploads/2014/11/Certificates.FullReport.061812.pdf. [62]

Carnevale, A. and N. Smith (2012), *A Decade Behind: Breaking out of the Low-Skill Trap in the Southern Economy*, https://1gyhoq479ufd3yna29x7ubjn-wpengine.netdna-ssl.com/wp-content/uploads/2014/11/DecadeBehind.FullReport.073112.pdf. [32]

Carnevale, A., N. Smith and J. Strohl (2013), *Recovery: Job Growth and Education Requirements through 2020*, Georgetown University Center on Education and the Workforce, Washington, DC, https://1gyhoq479ufd3yna29x7ubjn-wpengine.netdna-ssl.com/wp-content/uploads/2014/11/Recovery2020.FR_.Web_.pdf (accessed on 10 May 2019). [17]

Carnevale, A., J. Strohl and N. Ridley (2017), *Good jobs that pay without a BA: A state by state analysis*, https://1gyhoq479ufd3yna29x7ubjn-wpengine.netdna-ssl.com/wp-content/uploads/Good-Jobs-States.pdf. [36]

Carnevale, A. et al. (2018), *Three educational pathways to good jobs: High school, middle skills and bachelor's degree*, Georgetown Center on Education and the Workforce, https://1gyhoq479ufd3yna29x7ubjn-wpengine.netdna-ssl.com/wp-content/uploads/3ways-FR.pdf. [35]

CEW (2019), *Methodology: Certificates Estimates for Lumina Foundation's A Stronger Nation*, Georgetown University Center on Education and the Workforce, https://cew.georgetown.edu/wp-content/uploads/CEW-CertficatesMethodology_StrongerNation_2019.pdf. [50]

Chetty, R. et al. (2017), "Mobility Report Cards: The Role of Colleges in Intergenerational Mobility", *NBER Working Paper No. 23618*, National Bureau of Economic Research, https://opportunityinsights.org/paper/mobilityreportcards/ (accessed on 26 July 2019). [88]

CLASP (2018), *When Financial Aid Falls Short: New Data Reveal Students Face Thousands in Unmet Need*, The Center for Law and Social Policy, Washington, DC. [86]

CNBC (2019), *America's Top States for Business in 2019*, https://www.cnbc.com/2019/07/10/americas-top-states-for-business-2019.html (accessed on 2 August 2019). [7]

Dallas County Promise (2019), *Fulfilling the Promise of Talent: the Dallas County Promise Talent Report*, http://dallascountypromise.org/uploads/images/2019-Dallas-County-Promise-Talent-Report.pdf. [119]

Dallas Federal Reserve (2020), *Overview of Texas Economy*, Federal Reserve Bank of Dallas, https://www.dallasfed.org/-/media/Documents/research/econdata/texaseconomy.pdf (accessed on 12 March 2020). [4]

DCCCD (2019), *Dallas County Community College District Students Receive 'GreenLight' Toward Ownership, Lifelong Access to Academic Records*, Dallas County Community College District, https://www.dcccd.edu/news/2019/pages/viewnewsitem.aspx?NewsItem=38 (accessed on 3 February 2020). [94]

Deming, D. and L. Kahn (2018), *Skill Requirements across Firms and Labor Markets: Evidence from Job Postings for Professionals*, University of Chicago, https://www.journals.uchicago.edu/doi/pdfplus/10.1086/694106 (accessed on 16 May 2019). [31]

Deming, D. and C. Walters (2017), *The Impact of Price Caps and Spending Cuts on U.S. Postsecondary Attainment*, Harvard University, UC Berkeley, NBER, https://scholar.harvard.edu/files/ddeming/files/DW_Aug2017.pdf (accessed on 28 August 2019). [82]

Dorrer, J. (2016), "Using real-time labor market information to achieve better labor market outcomes", *Lumina Issue Papers*, Lumina Foundation, https://www.luminafoundation.org/files/resources/using-real-time-labor-market-information-full.pdf. [133]

ECS (2019), *Postsecondary Governance Structures: Texas State Profile*, Education Commission for the States, http://www.ecs.org|@EdCommission (accessed on 23 April 2020). [21]

Educate Texas (2019), *Texas Regional STEM Degree Accelerator*, https://www.edtx.org/our-impact-areas/higher-education/texas-regional-stem-degree-accelerator. [71]

EIA (2020), *Annual Energy Outlook 2020*, U.S. Energy Information Administration, https://www.eia.gov/outlooks/aeo/pdf/AEO2020%20Full%20Report.pdf. [5]

ERDC (2018), *Unmet Need among Financially Needy College Students in the State of Washington*, Washington State Education Research and Data Center, Olympia, https://erdc.wa.gov/publications/student-outcomes/unmet-need-among-financially-needy-college-students-state-washington (accessed on 30 July 2019). [87]

Federal Reserve Bank of St. Louis (n.d.), *FRED Economic Research, MSAs*, https://fred.stlouisfed.org/categories/30907 (accessed on 23 April 2020). [12]

Foote, A. et al. (2019), *Post-Secondary Employment Outcomes (PSEO)*, United States Census Bureau, https://lehd.ces.census.gov/doc/PSEOTechnicalDocumentation.pdf (accessed on 19 November 2019). [56]

Foote, A. and K. Stange (2019), *Attrition from Administrative Data: Problems and Solutions with an Application to Higher Education*, U.S. Census Bureau, University of Michigan and NBER, https://conference.nber.org/conf_papers/f131000.pdf (accessed on 13 March 2020). [55]

Fuller, J. et al. (2017), *Dismissed by degrees: How degree inflation is undermining US competitiveness and hurting America's middle class*, Accenture, Grads of Life, Harvard Business School, https://www.hbs.edu/managing-the-future-of-work/Documents/dismissed-by-degrees.pdf. [44]

Goldman, C. et al. (2015), *Using Workforce Information for Degree Program Planning in Texas*, RAND Corporation, https://doi.org/10.7249/RR1011. [134]

Gordon, T., R. Auxier and J. Iselin (2016), *Assessing Fiscal Capacities of States: A Representative Revenue System–Representative Expenditure System Approach, Fiscal Year 2012*, Urban Institute, https://www.taxpolicycenter.org/sites/default/files/publication/140136/2000646-assessing-fiscal-capacities-of-states-a-representative-revenue-system-representative-expenditure-system-approach-fiscal-year-2012.pdf. [83]

Greater Houston Partnership (n.d.), *UpSkill Houston Initiative*, https://www.houston.org/upskillhouston (accessed on 4 February 2020). [72]

GreenLight Credentials (n.d.), *A platform that helps students succeed*, https://greenlightlocker.com/ (accessed on 3 February 2020). [95]

Hanushek, E. et al. (2017), "General Education, Vocational Education, and Labor-Market Outcomes over the Lifecycle", *The Journal of Human Resources*, Vol. 52/1, pp. 52-87, http://dx.doi.org/10.3368/jhr.52.1.0415-7074R. [58]

HCC (n.d.), *HCC Apprenticeship Program*, Houston Community College, https://www.hccs.edu/continuing-education/departments/apprenticeship/ (accessed on 4 February 2020). [117]

Hershbein, B. and K. Hollenbeck (2015), *Refining Workforce Education Supply and Demand Analysis: Final Report*, W.E. Upjohn Institute for Employment Research, https://research.upjohn.org/cgi/viewcontent.cgi?article=1034&context=up_technicalreports. [131]

Hillman, N. and E. Orians (2013), "Community Colleges and Labor Market Conditions: How Does Enrollment Demand Change Relative to Local Unemployment Rates?", *Springer*, http://dx.doi.org/10.2307/24571744. [23]

Holzer, H. and S. Baum (2017), *Making College Work: Pathways to Success for Disadvantaged Students*, Brookings Institution Press, https://www.brookings.edu/book/making-college-work/. [106]

ICUT (2018), *2018 Impact Report: Independent Higher Education in Texas*, Independent Colleges and Universities of Texas, Inc., https://icut.org/uploads/cms/nav-58-5c33850dce335.pdf. [30]

IHE (2019), *Survey: Employers Want 'Soft Skills' From Graduates*, Inside Higher Ed, https://www.insidehighered.com/quicktakes/2019/01/17/survey-employers-want-soft-skills-graduates (accessed on 3 February 2020). [97]

Legislative Budget Board (2019), *Financing Public Higher Education in Texas: Legislative Primer*, The State of Texas, https://www.lbb.state.tx.us/Documents/Publications/Primer/4909_Financing_Public_Higher_Ed.pdf. [76]

Legislative Budget Board (2013), *Summary of Senate Bill 1 Conference Committee Report: Appropriations for the 2014-15 Biennium*, http://www.lbb.state.tx.us/Documents/Appropriations_Bills/83/849_Summary_SB1_CCR_6-17-13_430PM_web.pdf (accessed on 2 May 2020). [84]

LinkedIn (2019), *LinkedIn Workforce Report: Austin July 2019*, https://www.linkedin.com/jobs/blog/linkedin-workforce-report-july-2019-austin-tx (accessed on 16 December 2019). [40]

LinkedIn (2019), *LinkedIn Workforce Report: Dallas-Ft. Worth August 2019*, https://www.linkedin.com/jobs/blog/linkedin-workforce-report-august-2019-dallas-tx (accessed on 16 December 2019). [41]

LinkedIn (2019), *LinkedIn Workforce Report: Houston August 2019*, https://www.linkedin.com/jobs/blog/linkedin-workforce-report-august-2019-houston-tx (accessed on 16 December 2019). [42]

Lumina Foundation (2019), *A Stronger Nation: Texas Report 2019*, https://luminafoundation.org/stronger-nation/report/2020/#nation. [18]

Lumina Foundation (2018), *A Stronger Nation*, https://www.luminafoundation.org/resources/a-stronger-nation-report (accessed on 19 June 2019). [46]

Miller, T. et al. (2018), *Dual Credit Education Programs in Texas: Phase II*, American Institutes for Research, Washington, DC, http://reportcenter.thecb.state.tx.us/reports/data/dual-credit-education-programs-in-texas-phase-ii1/. [111]

Miller, T. et al. (2017), *Dual Credit Education in Texas: Interim Report*, RAND Corporation, https://www.rand.org/pubs/research_reports/RR2043.html. [113]

NASSGAP (n.d.), *NASSGAP Annual Survey*, National Association of State Student Grant and Aid Programs, https://www.nassgapsurvey.com/ (accessed on 2 May 2020). [85]

National Skills Coalition (2018), *Building a skilled workforce for a stronger southern economy*, https://www.nationalskillscoalition.org/resources/publications/file/Building-a-Skilled-Workforce-for-a-Stronger-Southern-Economy.pdf. [37]

National Skills Coalition (2017), *Middle skill jobs state by state: Texas' forgotten middle*, https://www.nationalskillscoalition.org/resources/publications/2017-middle-skills-fact-sheets/file/Texas-MiddleSkills.pdf. [34]

National Student Clearinghouse (2019), *Some College, No Degree: A 2019 Snapshot for the Nation and 50 States*, https://nscresearchcenter.org/some-college-no-degree-2019/. [52]

NCES (2019), *Integrated Postsecondary Education Data System (database)*, National Center for Education Statistics, https://nces.ed.gov/ipeds/use-the-data (accessed on 18 January 2020). [24]

Niu, S. and M. Tienda (2010), "The Impact of the Texas Top 10 Percent Law on College Enrollment: A Regression Discontinuity Approach", *Journal of Policy Analysis and Management*, Vol. 29/1, pp. 84-110, http://dx.doi.org/10.1002/pam.20480. [29]

OECD (2019), *OECD Skills Strategy 2019: Skills to Shape a Better Future*, OECD Publishing, Paris, https://doi.org/10.1787/9789264313835-en. [74]

OECD (2018), *OECD Economic Surveys: United States 2018*, OECD Publishing, Paris, https://dx.doi.org/10.1787/eco_surveys-usa-2018-en. [39]

Office of the Texas Governor (n.d.), *Tri-Agency 2020: Empowering all Texans to reach their full potential*, https://gov.texas.gov/uploads/files/press/Tri-Agency_2020_One_Pager.pdf (accessed on 2 May 2020). [70]

Page, L., L. Levy Garboua and C. Montmarquette (2007), "Aspiration levels and educational choices: An experimental study", *Economics of Education Review*, Vol. 26/6, pp. 747-757, http://dx.doi.org/10.1016/J.ECONEDUREV.2007.06.001. [125]

Perry, M. (2019), *Putting America's huge $20.5T economy into perspective by comparing US state GDPs to entire countries*, American Enterprise Institute - Blog Post, https://www.aei.org/carpe-diem/putting-americas-enormous-20-5t-economy-into-perspective-by-comparing-us-state-gdps-to-entire-countries-2/ (accessed on 22 April 2020). [1]

Prince, H. et al. (2015), *Are people getting credentials that lead to jobs? Using dashboards for state workforce planning*, National Skills Coalition, State Workforce and Education Alignment Project, https://www.nationalskillscoalition.org/resources/publications/file/SWEAP_Using_Dashboards_for_State_Workforce_Planning.pdf. [132]

Rose, S. (2017), *Mismatch: How Many Workers with a Bachelor's Degree Are Overqualified for Their Jobs?*, Urban Institute , Washington, http://www.urban.org/sites/default/files/publication/87951/college_mismatch_final.pdf (accessed on 21 May 2019). [45]

SACSCOC (2018), *Resource Manual for The Principles of Accreditation: Foundations for Quality Enhancement*, Southern Association of Colleges and Schools Commission on Colleges, Atlanta, http://www.sacscoc.org (accessed on 1 July 2019). [100]

Schneider, M. (2015), *Higher Education Pays: But a Lot More for Some Graduates Than for Others*, College Measures, https://www.air.org/sites/default/files/Higher_Education_Pays_Sep_13.pdf (accessed on 20 May 2019). [60]

Scrivener, S. et al. (2015), *Doubling Graduation Rates*, MDRC, New York, https://files.eric.ed.gov/fulltext/ED558511.pdf (accessed on 28 August 2019). [108]

SHEEO (2019), *SHEF: FY 2018 State Higher Education Finance*, State Higher Education Executive Officers Association, http://www.sheeo.org/shef (accessed on 30 July 2019). [75]

SHRM (2019), *Employers Say Students Aren't Learning Soft Skills in College*, Society for Human Resource Management, https://www.shrm.org/resourcesandtools/hr-topics/employee-relations/pages/employers-say-students-arent-learning-soft-skills-in-college.aspx (accessed on 3 February 2020). [98]

SkillsEngine (n.d.), *Calibrate: Teach What Matters*, https://skillsengine.com/calibrate (accessed on 3 February 2020). [96]

Strada, Gallup and Lumina Foundation (2019), *Certified Value: When do Adults without Degrees Benefit from Earning Certificates and Certifications?*, https://go.stradaeducation.org/certified-value. [63]

TACC (2018), *Outcomes Based Funding in Texas: A Policy History*, Texas Association of Community Colleges, https://tacc.org/sites/default/files/documents/2018-08/outcomes_based_funding_in_texas.pdf. [77]

TACC (n.d.), *Texas Pathways*, Texas Association of Community Colleges, https://tacc.org/tsc/what-we-do (accessed on 6 February 2020). [124]

TAMUS (n.d.), *About the University of Texas System*, https://www.tamus.edu/system/about/ (accessed on 26 April 2020). [28]

TCF (2019), *Recommendations for Providing Community Colleges with the Resources They Need*, The Century Foundation Working Group on Community College Financial Resources, https://tacc.org/sites/default/files/documents/2019-04/recommendations_cc_resources.pdf. [81]

TEA (2019), *2018 Annual Report*, Texas Education Agency, https://tea.texas.gov/sites/default/files/TEA_Annual_Report_2018.pdf. [103]

TEA (2019), *Student Loan Forgiveness for Teachers*, Texas Education Agency, https://tea.texas.gov/Texas_Educators/Educator_Initiatives/Student_Loan_Forgiveness_for_Teachers (accessed on 12 November 2019). [38]

TEA (n.d.), *Pathways in Technology Early College High School (P-TECH)*, Texas Education Agency, https://tea.texas.gov/Academics/College%2C_Career%2C_and_Military_Prep/Pathways_in_Technology_Early_College_High_School_%28P-TECH%29 (accessed on 21 January 2020). [118]

TEA, THECB and TWC (2020), *Prosperity Requires Being Bold: A Progress Report*, Texas Education Agency, Texas Higher Education Coordinating Board, Texas Workforce Commission, https://gov.texas.gov/uploads/files/press/Tri_Agency_Report_FINAL_SUBMITTED_TO_GOVERNOR_02.2020.pdf (accessed on 2 May 2020). [68]

TEA, THECB and TWC (2016), *Prosperity Requires Being Bold: Integrating Education and the Workforce for a Bright Texas Future. The Tri-Agency Report to the Office of the Governor*, Texas Education Agency/ Texas Higher Education Coordinating Board/ Texas Workforce Commission, https://www.txcte.org/sites/default/files/2016%20Tri_Agency%20Report_0.pdf. [69]

TEA, THECB and TWC (n.d.), *Understanding Credentials in Texas: Certificates and Certifications*, Texas Education Agency, Texas Higher Education Coordinating Board, Texas Workforce Commission, https://reportcenter.thecb.state.tx.us/reports/data/understanding-credentials-in-texas-certificates-certifications/. [47]

Texas Administrative Code (2004), *19 Tex. Admin. Code §9.93 Presentation of Requests and Steps for Implementation of New Degree and Certificate Programs in Career Technical/Workforce Education*, https://texreg.sos.state.tx.us/public/readtac$ext.ViewTAC?tac_view=3&ti=19&pt=1. [102]

Texas Administrative Code (2003), *19 Tex. Admin. Code §5.45 Criteria for New Baccalaureate and Master's Degree Programs*, https://texreg.sos.state.tx.us/public/readtac$ext.ViewTAC?tac_view=3&ti=19&pt=1. [101]

Texas Demographic Center (2018), *Texas Population Estimates Program*, https://demographics.texas.gov/Data/TPEPP/Estimates/ (accessed on 3 November 2019). [48]

Texas DSHS (n.d.), *Texas Metropolitan Status by County*, Texas Department of State Health Services, https://www.dshs.texas.gov/chs/info/current-msa.shtm (accessed on 17 March 2020). [11]

Texas Legislature (2019), *H.B. No. 3808: An act relating to measures to facilitate the timely graduation of and attainment of marketable skills by students in public higher education.*, https://capitol.texas.gov/tlodocs/86R/billtext/pdf/HB03808F.pdf#navpanes=0 (accessed on 26 January 2020). [109]

Texas Legislature (2019), *S.B. No. 25: An act relating to measures to facilitate the transfer, academic progress, and timely graduation of students in public higher education.*, https://capitol.texas.gov/tlodocs/86R/billtext/html/SB00025S.htm (accessed on 26 January 2020). [121]

Texas Legislature (2017), *H.B. No. 2223: An act relating to developmental coursework offered by public institutions of higher education under the Texas Success Initiative*, https://capitol.texas.gov/tlodocs/85R/billtext/pdf/HB02223F.pdf#navpanes=0 (accessed on 26 January 2020). [105]

Texas Legislature (2013), *H.B. No. 1296: An act relating to information regarding postsecondary education and career opportunities and workforce needs in this state.*, https://capitol.texas.gov/tlodocs/83R/billtext/pdf/HB01296F.pdf#navpanes=0 (accessed on 29 January 2020). [135]

The Perryman Group (2019), *The 2019 Perryman Economic Forecast*, https://www.perrymangroup.com/publications/. [10]

THECB (2020), *Private postsecondary institutions authorized to operate in Texas*, Texas Higher Education Coordinating Board, http://reportcenter.thecb.state.tx.us/agency-publication/miscellaneous/private-postsecondary-institutions-operating-in-texas/ (accessed on 24 April 2020). [26]

THECB (2019), *60x30TX and Internships: A toolkit for integrating the goals and targets of 60x30TX into employer internship programs*, Texas Higher Education Coordinating Board, http://www.60x30tx.com/media/1516/internshiptoolkit.pdf. [66]

THECB (2019), *60x30TX Progress Report*, Texas Higher Education Coordinating Board, http://www.60x30tx.com/media/1518/2019-60x30tx-progress-report.pdf. [19]

THECB (2019), *Implementing Fields of Study*, http://reportcenter.thecb.state.tx.us/agency-publication/miscellaneous/implementing-fields-of-study/ (accessed on 4 February 2020). [120]

THECB (2019), *Texas Public Higher Education Almanac*, Texas Higher Education Coordinating Board, Austin, http://www.thecb.state.tx.us/data-reports/texas-public-higher-education-almanac/ (accessed on 3 November 2019). [25]

THECB (2018), *Career Readiness*, Texas Higher Education Coordinating Board, http://www.60x30tx.com/media/1409/thecb-career-readiness-handbook.pdf. [65]

THECB (2018), *Developmental Education Update and 2018-2023 Statewide Plan for Supporting Underprepared Students*, Texas Higher Education Coordinating Board, http://reportcenter.thecb.state.tx.us/agency-publication/miscellaneous/developmental-education-update-and-2018-2023-statewide-plan-for-supporting-underprepared-students/. [104]

THECB (2018), "Marketable Skills Goal Implementation Guidelines", Texas Higher Education Coordinating Board, http://board.thecb.state.tx.us/reports/PDF/10796.PDF?CFID=75920892&CFTOKEN=79194126. [92]

THECB (2018), *Overview: Dual Credit*, http://www.thecb.state.tx.us/institutional-resources-programs/public-community-technical-state-colleges/transfer-resources/dual-credit-initiatives/. [112]

THECB (2018), *Report on Student Financial Aid in Texas Higher Education: Fiscal Year 2017*, http://www.60x30tx.com/media/1412/student-fin-aid-in-texas-report.pdf. [80]

THECB (2016), *Closing the Gaps Final Progress Report*, Texas HIgher Education Coordinating Board, http://www.thecb.state.tx.us/DocID/PDF/8138.PDF (accessed on 9 December 2019). [43]

THECB (2015), *60x30TX: Texas Higher Education Strategic Plan 2015-2030*, http://reportcenter.thecb.state.tx.us/agency-publication/miscellaneous/60x30tx-strategic-plan-for-higher-education/. [91]

THECB (2015), *Guidelines for Instructional Programs in Workforce Education*, http://www.thecb.state.tx.us/institutional-resources-programs/public-community-technical-state-colleges/career-technical-education-workforce-initiatives/guidelines-for-instructional-programs-in-workforce-education-gipwe/2015. [90]

THECB (2013), *Texas Public Higher Education Almanac*, Texas Higher Education Coordinating Board, Austin, http://www.lee.edu/irep/files/2016/03/THECB-2013-Public-Higher-Education-Almanac.pdf. [49]

THECB (2013), *Texas State Technical College System Returned Value Funding Model Methodology*, Texas Higher Education Coordinating Board, http://reportcenter.thecb.state.tx.us/reports/data/texas-state-technical-college-system-value-add-formula-methodology/. [78]

THECB (n.d.), *60x30TX: Goals*, Texas Higher Education Coordinating Board, http://www.60x30tx.com/goals/ (accessed on 2 May 2020). [67]

THECB (n.d.), *Graduation Rates*, Texas Higher Education Accountability System, http://www.txhigheredaccountability.org/AcctPublic/InteractiveReport/Predefined (accessed on 1 May 2020). [51]

THECB (n.d.), *Texas Higher Education Accountability System: Interactive data report*, http://www.txhigheredaccountability.org/AcctPublic/InteractiveReport/AddReport (accessed on 4 February 2020). [22]

THECB (n.d.), *Texas Higher Education Regional Portal*, http://www.txhighereddata.org/reports/performance/regions/ (accessed on 31 January 2020). [129]

THECB and TWC (2019), *Exit Cohort Reports CBM001 and CBM009*, Texas Higher Education Coordinating Board, http://www.txhighereddata.org/reports/performance/ctcasalf/exitcohorts/. [54]

TICAS (2018), *Of metrics and markets: Measuring post-college employment success*, The Institute for College Access and Success, https://ticas.org/accountability/metrics-and-markets/. [127]

Troutman, D. et al. (2018), *Dual Credit and Success in College*, The University of Texas System Dual Credit Study, https://www.utsystem.edu/sites/default/files/documents/ut-system-reports/2018/dual-credit-and-success-college/utsystem-dualcreditstudy.pdf. [110]

TWC (2019), *Texas Labor Analysis - Gap Analysis*, Texas Workforce Commission, https://texaslaboranalysis.com/GapAnalysis (accessed on 8 November 2019). [33]

TWC (2019), *Texas Workforce Report 2018-2019*, Texas Workforce Commission, https://lmci.state.tx.us/shared/PDFs/Workforce_Report.pdf. [8]

TWC (n.d.), *Apprenticeship - Program Overview*, https://twc.texas.gov/programs/apprenticeship-program-overview (accessed on 22 January 2020). [116]

TXEDC (n.d.), *Business in Texas*, Texas Economic Development Corporation, https://businessintexas.com/resources/texas-snapshots (accessed on 11 March 2020). [3]

U.S. Bureau of Economic Analysis (2019), *Regional BEARFacts: Texas*, https://apps.bea.gov/regional/bearfacts/pdf.cfm?fips=48000&areatype=48000&geotype=3 (accessed on 10 March 2020). [2]

U.S. Bureau of Labor Statistics (2019), *Labor force statistics from the current population survey*, https://www.bls.gov/cps/ (accessed on 12 March 2020). [14]

U.S. Bureau of Labor Statistics (2019), *Occupation Employment Statistics*, https://www.bls.gov/oes/home.htm (accessed on 26 August 2019). [15]

U.S. Bureau of Labor Statistics (2016), *Labor force participation: what has happened since the peak?*, Monthly Labor Review, https://www.bls.gov/opub/mlr/2016/article/pdf/labor-force-participation-what-has-happened-since-the-peak.pdf. [13]

U.S. Census Bureau (2019), *American Community Survey 2018 (database)*, https://www.census.gov/programs-surveys/acs/data.html (accessed on 18 January 2020). [20]

U.S. Census Bureau (2019), *Post-Secondary Employment Outcomes - Longitudinal Employer-Household Dynamics*, https://lehd.ces.census.gov/data/pseo_experimental.html (accessed on 19 November 2019). [57]

U.S. Office of Personnel Management (2017), *Federal Civilian Employment*, https://www.opm.gov/policy-data-oversight/data-analysis-documentation/federal-employment-reports/reports-publications/federal-civilian-employment (accessed on 1 May 2020). [53]

UpSkill Houston (n.d.), *Your Path to a Great Career Starts Here*, http://www.upskillhouston.org/?_ga=2.81200478.898218766.1580813805-509735731.1580813805 (accessed on 4 February 2020). [73]

UT System (2020), *University of Texas System Smartbook*, University of Texas System, https://www.utsystem.edu/sites/default/files/documents/publication/2020/ut-system-smartbook/smartbook-2020-withlinks.pdf (accessed on 26 April 2020). [27]

White, S. et al. (2017), *Components of Population Change in Urban Texas*, Texas Demographic Center, https://demographics.texas.gov/Resources/publications/2017/2017_09_14_UrbanTexas.pdf. [9]

Whitfield, C., J. Armstrong and D. Weeden (2019), *The State of State Postsecondary Data Systems: Strong Foundations 2018*, SHEEO, https://postsecondarydata.sheeo.org/wp-content/uploads/2019/04/SHEEO_StrongFoundations_18.pdf (accessed on 26 August 2019). [128]

WSAC, SBCTC and WTECB (2018), *A Skilled and Educated Workforce 2017 Update: An analysis of postsecondary education, workforce preparation, and employer demand in Washington*, Washington Student Achievement Council/State Board for Community and Technical Colleges/ Workforce Training and Education Coordinating Board / Workforce Training and Education Coordinating Board, Olympia, https://wsac.wa.gov/sites/default/files/2017.ASkilledAndEducatedWorkforce.pdf (accessed on 31 May 2019). [130]

WSIPP (2019), *Higher Education Funding: Models Used in Washington and Similar States*, Washington State Institute for Public Policy, Olympia, https://www.wsipp.wa.gov/ReportFile/1702/Wsipp_Higher-Education-Funding-Models-Used-in-Washington-and-Similar-States_Report.pdf. [79]

Xu, D. et al. (2017), *Strengthening Transfer Paths to a Bachelor's Degree: Identifying Effective Two-Year to Four-Year College Partnerships*, https://ccrc.tc.columbia.edu/media/k2/attachments/strengthening-transfer-paths-bachelors-degree.pdf (accessed on 31 October 2018). [115]

6 Virginia

This chapter provides an overview of the labour market and higher education system in the state of Virginia, an assessment of the labour market outcomes of graduates, and a discussion of state policies that contribute to aligning higher education and the labour market. The policy discussion focuses on four policy areas – strategic planning and co-ordination of higher education; educational offerings, student supports and pathways; funding; and information – and includes policy recommendations in each area.

6.1. The labour market and higher education in Virginia

The economy and labour market

Virginia's economy relies heavily on federal spending and is bolstered by a growing professional services industry

With a Gross Domestic Product (GDP) of USD 533 billion and a population of 8.5 million, Virginia is an economy comparable in size to Sweden, with economic output that represents around 2.6% of total GDP in the United States (U.S. Bureau of Economic Analysis, 2019[1]). Virginia's recovery from the recession of 2008-09 has been slow. However, between 2017 and 2019, the economy experienced faster growth in real GDP than in the previous decade, though still a lower rate of growth than for the country as a whole (U.S. Bureau of Economic Analysis, 2019[2]). The state's economy relies heavily on federal government spending, accounting for about one-third of economic activity. In addition, recent economic gains have been concentrated primarily in the northern and central regions of the state. Consequently, Virginia's current economic development policy is focused on diversifying and fostering growth in other sectors of the economy to ensure shared growth in all regions of the state (Northam Administration, 2018[3]).

Virginia has a reputation for business-friendliness and scores highly on a number of national rankings of best states to live in and do business (U.S. News & World Report, 2019[4]; CNBC, 2019[5]). Amazon's decision in 2019 to establish its second headquarters in Virginia is a sign of the state's economic attractiveness. The company's decision rested largely on Virginia's educated workforce and the state's commitment to invest further in building advanced technology skills (VEDP, 2019[6]), as described in Box 6.1. Following a period of accelerated job growth in professional and business services, which includes management and professional, scientific and technical services, this sector now employs the most people in Virginia (U.S. Bureau of Labor Statistics, 2019[7]). As of 2018, the professional and business services sector accounts for about 19% of total employment, followed by the government sector (18%) and the trade, transportation and utilities sector (16%) (U.S. Bureau of Labor Statistics, 2019[8]). Professional, scientific and technical services contribute substantially to Virginia's economy, representing approximately 15% of all establishments and more than 20% of total wages, which is driven largely by computer systems design and related services (VEC, 2019[9]). The education and healthcare services sector has also been growing, while the manufacturing sector has fluctuated between decline and stagnation in the last decade, demonstrating Virginia's shift to a service-based economy (VEC, 2019[9]).

Like many states, however, Virginia is characterised by a distinct rural-urban divide. The state boasts a high-tech economy in the north, which includes professional services supporting the federal government in the area surrounding Washington, DC. Northern Virginia hosts many large technology companies, as well as the largest concentration of data centres in the world. Moreover, the arrival of the new Amazon headquarters in the region is expected to add 25 000 new high-skill jobs within the next 10-20 years, in addition to boosting employment in supporting sectors (VEDP, 2019[6]). The south-western region – formerly reliant on coal and tobacco – is now primarily dominated by agriculture and health services, and an emerging advanced manufacturing sector. The coastal area to the east includes the diverse Hampton Roads region, and is the third most populous region in the state and home to the world's largest naval base. This region specialises in naval shipbuilding and relies heavily on federal defence spending. Despite the ongoing presence of large-scale military employment, parts of the region are heavily distressed, with low labour force participation and low levels of post-secondary educational attainment (Old Dominion University, 2018[10]).

Thus, the economic profile of Virginia's more rural and coastal areas differs widely from the urban centres of Northern Virginia and the capital region. Median household income is about three times higher in Northern Virginia than in the south-western region, and the predominant share of economic growth since 2010 has been concentrated in the metropolitan areas around Richmond, Charlottesville, Blacksburg, and

Northern Virginia (Old Dominion University, 2018[10]). While population growth in the south-central and south-western regions has been declining in the last decade, the population in urban areas of Virginia has continued to grow, with Northern Virginia now representing two-thirds of the total population in the state (UVA Weldon Cooper Center, 2019[11]). In the state overall, out-migration has been larger than in-migration in recent years, but this pattern may shift in coming years, particularly with the continued growth of the technology sector. The proportion of Virginians above the retirement age of 65 (15.4%) is offset by a larger youth population, which forms the basis of the future workforce. The dependency ratio in Virginia is lower than both the US and OECD average. Table 4.1 presents an overview of some key contextual indicators for Virginia.

Table 6.1. Virginia at a glance

	Virginia	United States	Source
Population			
Population estimate	8 517 685	327 167 434	U.S. Census
Dependency ratio (% 65+ over population aged 15-64)	23.3%	24.5%	OECD regional statistics
Percentage of individuals under the age of 18	22.0%	22.4%	U.S. Census
Percentage of individuals aged 65 and over	15.4%	16.0%	U.S. Census
Percentage of Black or African American individuals	19.9%	13.4%	U.S. Census
Percentage of Hispanic or Latino individuals	9.6%	18.3%	U.S. Census
Percentage of Asian individuals	6.9%	5.9%	U.S. Census
Percentage of American Indian or Alaska Native individuals	0.5%	1.3%	U.S. Census
Percentage of White (non-Hispanic) individuals	61.5%	60.4%	U.S. Census
Economy and labour market			
GDP per capita	USD 56 110	USD 57 052	U.S. Bureau of Economic Analysis
Labour force participation rate (out of civilian population aged 16+, November 2019)	66.5%	62.9%	U.S. Bureau of Labor Statistics
Unemployment rate (seasonally adjusted)	2.7%	3.9%	U.S. Bureau of Labor Statistics
Median annual earnings for working-age population aged 25-64	USD 55 000	USD 50 000	American Community Survey
Estimated annual wage needed to cover basic expenses for a full-time working adult	USD 29 474	USD 25 297	MIT Living Wage Calculator
Percentage of population aged 25-64 with an associate's degree or higher	49.6%	42.5%	American Community Survey

Notes: All numbers are for 2018 unless otherwise noted. Racial and ethnic categories are mutually exclusive. MIT Living Wage annual calculations are based on full-time working hours (2 080 hours per year).

StatLink https://doi.org/10.1787/888934135072

Box 6.1. Virginia's investment in advanced technology skills

In 2019, Amazon confirmed that it would establish its second headquarters (HQ2) in Arlington, Virginia. Virginia's proposal to Amazon, spearheaded by the Virginia Economic Development Partnership (VEDP), was based on a package of corporate incentive grants, regional infrastructure expansion, and a commitment to building a highly skilled, technical workforce

The cornerstone of this investment is the Tech Talent Pipeline initiative, which includes state investments of up to USD 1.1 billion to increase the supply of graduates in computer science and closely related fields. For higher education institutions to be eligible for a grant from the state, each institution is required to enter into a memorandum of understanding that sets criteria for eligible degrees, degree production goals, and graduation rates. The initiative also includes a Tech Internship Program, which aims to increase internship opportunities for baccalaureate students, as well as the launch of a new Virginia Tech campus in Northern Virginia (VEDP, 2017[12]).

Today, there are approximately 60 higher education institutions in Virginia that offer computer science degrees. The Tech Talent Pipeline initiative aims to expand and strengthen the capacity of programmes through a performance-based tech talent investment fund, from which higher education institutions can apply for funding for faculty recruitment, state capital investment and enrolment support. While the largest proportion of funds (up to USD 710 million) will go towards supporting bachelor's level education at higher education institutions across the state, funding will also be set aside for master's level programmes at institutions in Northern Virginia. Virginia's community college system has also committed to designing short degree and certificate programmes in technical fields to complement the bachelor's and master's programmes.

A final component of the Tech Talent Pipeline initiative is strengthening STEM (science, technology, engineering and mathematics) and computer science learning in the public primary and secondary schooling system, for which USD 25 million has been earmarked.

Sources: HQNOVA (2017[13]), VEDP (2017[12]).

Virginia has high levels of educational attainment and low unemployment, although regional variations are significant

The labour market in Virginia has tightened in recent years. In November 2019, the unemployment rate in Virginia was 2.7%, significantly lower than that for the United States overall (3.5%) (U.S. Bureau of Labor Statistics, 2019[14]). Furthermore, based on measures of labour underutilisation used by the U.S. Bureau of Labor Statistics, Virginia has significantly lower rates of underemployment in the working population compared to the United States as a whole. Employment growth, combined with negative net domestic migration, has likely contributed to the historically low unemployment level in Virginia, as the size of the labour force has grown at a slower pace than the rate of employment (Old Dominion University, 2018[10]). Rural areas, however, tend to face tougher labour market conditions, due in part to declining industries and fewer new job opportunities. In Wise County, located at the western end of the state, the unemployment rate in November 2019 was 4.2% (not seasonally adjusted), compared to 1.7% in Arlington County in the north and 2.2% in Shenandoah County in the valley region (U.S. Bureau of Labor Statistics, 2019[8]).

The total number of jobs in Virginia increased by a moderate 5.6% from 2013 to 2018, which was below the national growth rate of 7.4% during this period, but positive and stable (Emsi, 2018[15]). Long-term labour market projections suggest an employment growth of approximately 10% by 2026 (VEC, 2019[16]).

Virginia is currently facing shortages of healthcare professionals, educators, and skilled tradespeople (e.g. welders, plumbers, electricians), reflecting a nation-wide trend (Virginia Career Works, 2019[17]). According to projections from the Virginia Employment Commission, a substantial share of job growth in the next five years is expected to occur in the healthcare, social assistance and professional services sectors. Moreover, technological change will affect the pattern of skill demand as jobs with more routine-based tasks gradually disappear (Autor, Levy and Murnane, 2003[18]; Frey and Osborne, 2017[19]). In Virginia, there is some evidence of a growing polarisation of jobs, with job growth concentrated in low-wage and high-wage occupations between 2008 and 2016 (UVA Weldon Cooper Center, 2017[20]). There is also evidence to suggest that the globalisation of labour markets has caused a decline in real earnings among those without a college degree (Autor, 2014[21]).

Educational attainment levels are higher in Virginia than in most other states, with about 50% of the working-age population (aged 25-64) having earned either an associate's degree, a bachelor's degree or a graduate or professional degree, as shown in Figure 6.1. When including post-secondary certificates, approximately 55% of the working-age population has some form of post-secondary credential, which is higher than the US average of 48% (Lumina Foundation, 2019[22]). Educational attainment is a strong predictor of employment, with average earnings generally rising with the level of attainment (OECD, 2018[23]). A relatively large proportion (almost 18%) of working-age adults in Virginia have a graduate or professional degree, contributing to a workforce that is highly educated. At the same time, attainment rates vary substantially by county and region. By region, attainment of an associate's degree or higher among working-age adults ranges from 74% at the highest, to 25% at the lowest (Lumina Foundation, 2019[22]).

Figure 6.1. Levels of educational attainment for Virginia residents aged 25-64, 2018

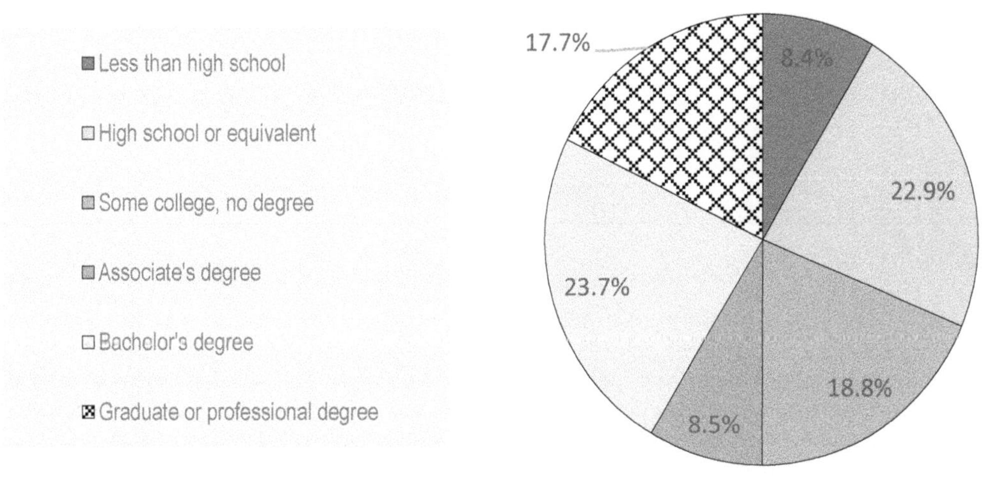

Source: U.S. Census Bureau (2019[24]), *American Community Survey 2018* (database), https://www.census.gov/programs-surveys/acs/data.html.

StatLink https://doi.org/10.1787/888934134027

The rural-urban divide is also evident in patterns of labour force participation. In the south-western region of the state – a population of about 600 000 – the labour force participation rate (LFP) is much lower than the state average, and in some places is less than 50% (VEC, 2019[9]). In Wise County and Lee County, the LFP for the working-age population declined by 22% and 19%, respectively, between 2011 and 2017 (Old Dominion University, 2018[10]). The state-wide labour force participation rate is 65%, just above the national average of 63% (U.S. Census Bureau, 2018[25]). Similar to the rest of the country, the LFP has been in decline since the recession of 2008-09. At the national level, declining labour force participation has largely been attributed to structural changes in the economy, including waning demand for routine-based manual labour (Abraham and Kearney, 2019[26]; U.S. Bureau of Labor Statistics, 2016[27]). Figure 4.2 shows Virginia's labour force participation rate, wage growth, employment and unemployment in a ten-year perspective.

Figure 6.2. Trends in key labour market indicators in Virginia, 2009-19

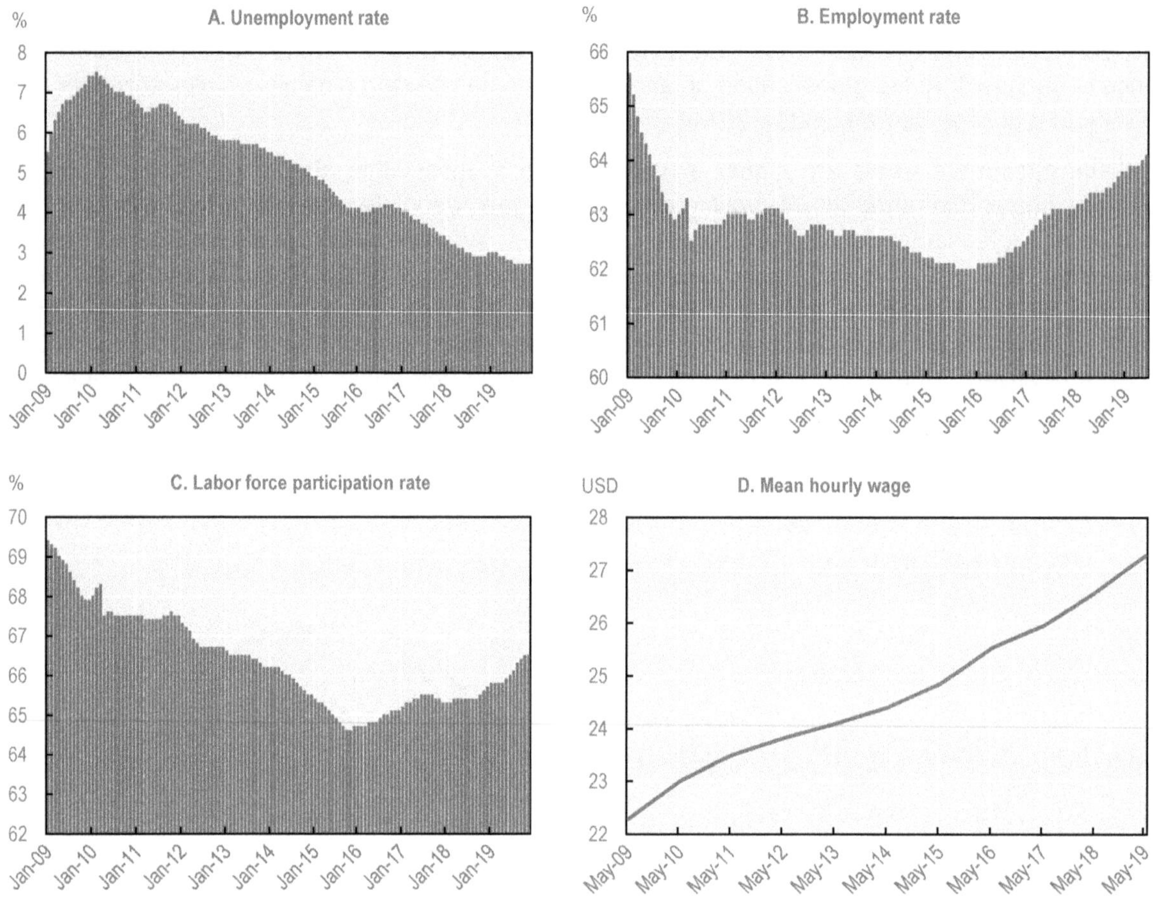

Notes: Data for Panels A, B, and C are seasonally adjusted.. The labour force participation rate is defined as the percentage of people who are either employed or unemployed (but looking for jobs) out of the total civilian non-institutional population, which includes all individuals over the age of 16 who are potentially available for work. The employment rate is the percentage of people who are employed out of the total civilian non-institutional population. The unemployment rate is the percentage of people who are unemployed (but looking for jobs) out of all individuals in the labour force (employed or unemployed but looking for jobs). The mean hourly wage is not adjusted for inflation.

Sources: Panels A, B and C: U.S. Bureau of Labor Statistics (2019[28]), *Labor Force Statistics from the Current Population Survey* (database), https://www.bls.gov/cps/tables.htm; Panel D: U.S. Bureau of Labor Statistics (2019[7]), *Occupation Employment Statistics* (database), https://www.bls.gov/oes/home.htm.

StatLink https://doi.org/10.1787/888934134046

A recent analysis of Virginia's out-of-work population, conducted by the University of Virginia's Weldon Cooper Center for Public Service, defines the population of adults aged 25-64 who are "out of work" as both the unemployed (seeking work) and those outside of the labour force (not seeking work), excluding students, stay-at-home parents, retirees or those with disabilities. In the south-western region of Virginia, the out-of-work proportion of the population is estimated to be 15%, while this proportion is estimated to be as high as 19% in the southern region. In the state as a whole, that proportion is closer to 10% (UVA Weldon Cooper Center, 2018[29]). The Weldon Cooper Center estimates that the majority of those out of work in Virginia are under the age of 34. In fact, 25-34 year-olds are over-represented in the out-of-work population compared to their proportion of the overall population. Females and Black/African Americans are more likely to be out of work than other minority groups. Most of these individuals do not have more than a high school diploma, but a substantial share are defined as having some college but less than a bachelor's degree (UVA Weldon Cooper Center, 2018[29]).

The higher education system

The State Council of Higher Education for Virginia takes a proactive role in achieving state-wide goals for higher education

The State Council of Higher Education for Virginia (SCHEV) is Virginia's co-ordinating body for higher education. Established in 1956, the 13-member State Council makes higher education policy recommendations to the Governor and the General Assembly (Legislature) of Virginia. 12 members of SCHEV are appointed directly by the Governor, with the 13th member as the sitting president of the Virginia Economic Development Partnership. The State Council is supported by a secretariat, headed by a director appointed by Council members.

SCHEV manages state-wide co-ordination and strategic planning for public higher education in Virginia, which includes administering state financial aid programmes, approving new degree programmes, maintaining a comprehensive data system, and providing budget recommendations for higher education. Like many states with a single co-ordinating board for higher education, SCHEV serves both a co-ordinating function for the public system and an administrative function that benefits students and graduates of all higher education institutions in Virginia.

The governance of public higher education institutions in Virginia is a shared responsibility between the General Assembly, Governor, SCHEV and the institutions. At public four-year institutions (including research and comprehensive universities), the members of each institution's governing board—the Board of Visitors—are appointed by the Governor. The Code of Virginia prescribes the composition of the board as well as the board's powers and duties (Virginia General Assembly, 2019[30]). Each board appoints the president or chief executive for its institution.

Public four-year institutions in Virginia enjoy considerable academic, financial and managerial autonomy. The Restructured Higher Education Financial and Administrative Operations Act of 2005 (the Restructuring Act) granted public institutions greater operational and administrative autonomy, reaffirming institutional authority to set their own tuition fees, in exchange for a commitment by institutional boards to meeting state-wide performance goals. SCHEV is responsible for monitoring the progress of such accountability measures, as well as approving new degree programmes, major changes to existing programmes or their discontinuation, and changes to institutional mission statements. Quality assurance more broadly falls under the purview of the regional accrediting body for all public and private degree-granting institutions in the southern states, the Southern Association of Colleges and Schools Commission on Colleges (SACSCOC).

Twenty-three of the state's twenty-four public two-year institutions comprise the Virginia Community College System (VCCS), which was established in 1966. Initially, the system comprised two community colleges and five technical schools, but has grown to a total of 23 community colleges across 40 campuses in the state. As opposed to having a local governing board for each college, all 23 community colleges are governed by the Virginia State Board for Community Colleges and, as such, form part of a unified system with a centralised administration.

There are 15 members of the Virginia State Board for Community Colleges, appointed by the Governor. The State Board selects a system chancellor, who hires the presidents of each college. The State Board approves new degree programmes in applied fields related to career and technical education. New degree programmes in disciplines that are transfer-oriented – for students who intend to transfer to a four-year institution – must be approved by SCHEV.

Higher education policy in Virginia involves multiple agencies and stakeholders, and recent efforts have been made to improve links to workforce development

With the Higher Education Opportunity Act of 2011, also known as the Top Jobs Act, the alignment between higher education and the economic development and workforce objectives for the state became an explicit policy goal. Multiple agencies and stakeholders across both education and workforce policy environments are involved in developing policy for higher education in Virginia.

Appropriations for higher education are approved on a biennial basis by the state Legislature. Matters related to higher education are referred to the Senate Education and Health Committee, the House Committee on Education, and the subcommittees on education and higher education under the Senate Finance Committee and the House Appropriations Committee, respectively. Additionally, as part of the Opportunity Act, the Higher Education Advisory Committee was created to provide recommendations on financial and budgetary matters, including an assessment of whether or not the higher education system is meeting state-wide objectives. The Advisory Committee includes representatives from the executive and legislative branches of government, as well as the presidents of at least five public higher education institutions.

In addition to SCHEV and the Virginia Community College System (VCCS), the Council of Independent Colleges in Virginia (CICV) is an important stakeholder as the representative body for private, not-for-profit colleges. Multiple advisory committees have been set up by SCHEV to represent various stakeholder groups, including the Career College Advisory Board, which represents private, proprietary (for-profit) higher education institutions, and the Private College Advisory Board, which consists of the presidents of private, not-for-profit institutions.

Several members of the SCHEV Council, including the president of the Virginia Economic Development Partnership, represent or engage regularly with the business community in Virginia. Private entities such as the Virginia Chamber of Commerce and the Virginia Business Higher Education Council are frequently consulted in strategic planning processes for higher education and workforce development.

The Virginia Board of Workforce Development is a business-led advisory board that provides policy recommendations on the public workforce development system in Virginia. The Board also includes members of the Governor's cabinet. Recently, the position of Chief Workforce Development Advisor was created to oversee all state, regional and local initiatives for workforce development in Virginia. The position was created at the cabinet level to advise the Governor, along with the Board of Workforce Development, the Secretary of Education, and the Secretary of Commerce and Trade, on matters related to skills development and the quality of the labour force.

In 2016, the Chief Workforce Development Advisor, in co-ordination with the Virginia Board of Workforce Development, established state-level performance metrics for career and technical education (CTE) and workforce training programmes, mainly provided at the post-secondary level by the state's public two-year institutions. As described in Box 6.2, it is the responsibility of the Chief Workforce Development Advisor to develop an integrated workforce system based on better information about workforce supply and demand, in order to meet the needs of the labour market. This also requires understanding the quantity and quality of skills produced in the higher education system.

Workforce development policy at the state level is also the primary vehicle for implementing the federal Workforce Innovation and Opportunity Act of 2014 (WIOA). WIOA-funds are typically distributed through workforce boards at the regional and local levels within the state. In Virginia, there are 15 local workforce development regions, each served by a local workforce board. These workforce boards are intended to serve as the link between the labour market and educational providers, ensuring that regional needs for workforce development are met.

Box 6.2. Developing an integrated workforce system in Virginia

In March 2018, the General Assembly of Virginia passed a bill (HB 1006) to implement a system to better align education and workforce programmes to meet current and projected skills requirements of the labour force. One component of this system has been the development of a workforce dashboard tool to provide information on the supply and demand for workers. Other actions include:

- provide policy advice to the Governor on workforce and workforce development issues in order to create a business-driven system that yields increasing rates of attainment of workforce credentials in demand by business and increasing rates of jobs creation and attainment;
- provide policy direction to local workforce development boards;
- identify current and emerging state-wide workforce needs of the business community;
- advise and oversee the development of a strategic workforce dashboard and tools that will inform the Governor, policy makers, system stakeholders, and the public on issues such as state and regional labour market conditions, the relationship between the supply and demand for workers, workforce programme outcomes, and projected employment growth or decline;
- determine and publish a list of jobs, trades, and professions for which high demand for qualified workers exists or is projected by the Virginia Employment Commission.

Source: Virginia General Assembly (2018[31]).

The post-secondary landscape in Virginia is diverse, but the majority of students are enrolled in public and private, not-for-profit institutions

The post-secondary education landscape in Virginia encompasses private and public higher education institutions, as well as private vocational schools. In 2017, an estimated 45% of 18-24 year-old Virginia residents were enrolled in post-secondary education, which is higher than the US average of 42% (Lumina Foundation, 2018[32]). The majority of students in Virginia are enrolled in public institutions, though this share decreased from 81% in 2003 to 69% in 2018. Out of total enrolments, the share of students enrolled in private (not-for-profit and for-profit) institutions increased during the recession of 2008-09, and has since remained at around the same level. Overall, 94% of students in Virginia are enrolled in public and private, not-for-profit institutions, of which approximately 80% are enrolled in undergraduate (baccalaureate and sub-baccalaureate) programmes. In terms of total headcount, the undergraduate population at Virginia's public and private, not-for-profit institutions was 424 949 in 2018, with about 39% enrolled in public two-year institutions, 41% in public four-year institutions, and the remaining 20% in private, not-for-profit institutions.

Figure 6.3 shows enrolment trends for first-time, full-time students over a 15-year period across different institution types in Virginia. Because many students at public two-year institutions are part-time students, enrolment numbers for full-time equivalent (FTE) students are substantially lower than total headcount numbers. The trend lines show that enrolments at private, for-profit institutions increased rapidly during the recession of 2008-09 and saw a decline after 2012, while enrolments at public four-year and private, not-for-profit institutions have seen a steady increase over time. The figure also shows a sharp decline in enrolment at public two-year institutions since 2011-12. Because of their strong role in workforce training for the local and regional labour market, enrolment in community colleges tend to be counter-cyclical: when employment opportunities increase, enrolments and completion rates at community colleges typically decrease. Much of the growth, and subsequent decline, in enrolment in Virginia's public higher education institutions overall, is attributed to enrolment fluctuation in Virginia's community colleges (SCHEV, 2019[33]).

Figure 6.3. Fall higher education enrolment in Virginia, 2003-18

Total number of first-time, full-time equivalent (FTE) students, by institution type

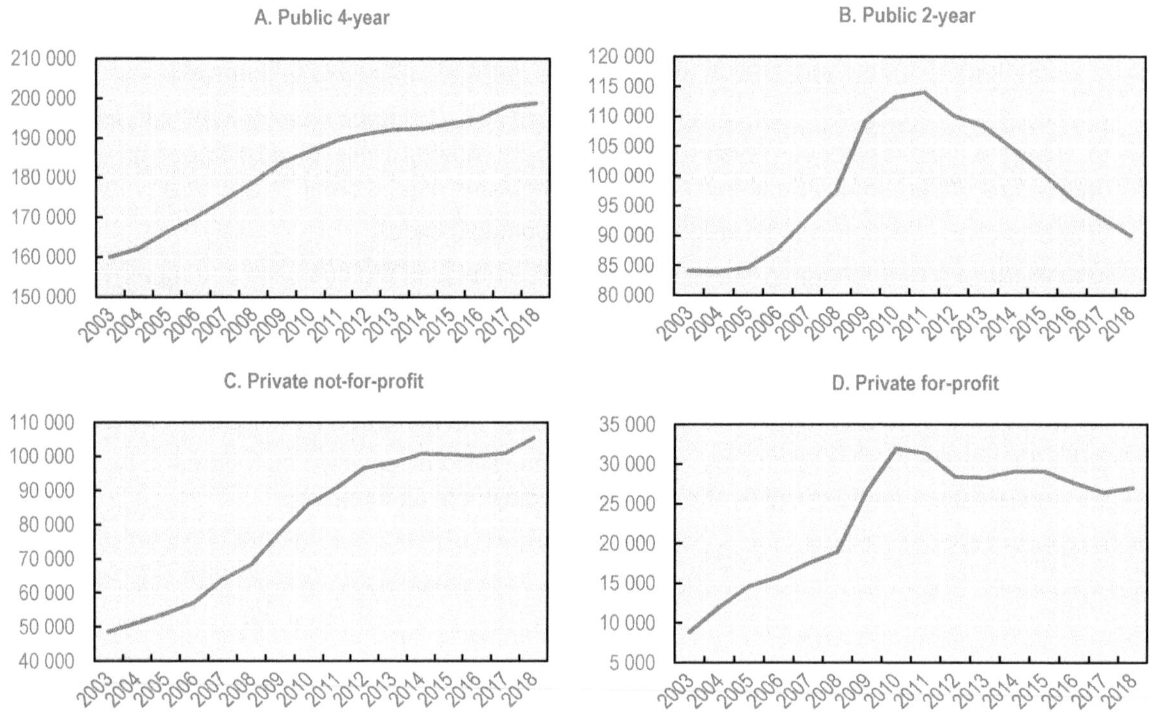

Note: Data for 2018 are provisional.
Source: NCES (2019[34]), *Integrated Postsecondary Education Data System* (database), https://nces.ed.gov/ipeds/use-the-data.

StatLink https://doi.org/10.1787/888934134065

All private and out-of-state higher education institutions are required to obtain approval from SCHEV in order to operate in the state. Private institutions that have been operating for at least 20 years, and have been continuously approved, no longer need to seek approval from SCHEV. Table 6.2 provides an overview of accredited higher education institutions operating in the state.

Table 6.2. Accredited higher education institutions certified to operate in Virginia

	Public	Private	
		Not-for-profit	For-profit
Four-year institutions *(Baccalaureate colleges and universities)*	15	31	9
Two-year institutions *(Junior and community colleges)*	24	0	0
Specialised institutions	1	0	0

Note: Does not include out-of-state higher education institutions operating in Virginia.
Source: SCHEV (2020[35]), *Colleges and Universities*, https://www.schev.edu/index/students-and-parents/explore/virginia-institutions.

StatLink https://doi.org/10.1787/888934135091

Public four-year institutions

Four-year institutions are those that offer at least a bachelor's degree – International Standard Classification of Education (ISCED) Level 6. This category of higher education institutions includes research universities, comprehensive universities and colleges offering post-secondary education from ISCED Level 5 to ISCED Level 8 (associate's degrees, bachelor's degrees, master's degrees and doctoral degrees). The majority of degrees awarded at public four-year institutions are bachelor's degrees, accounting for 70% of all degrees awarded in 2018. Four-year institutions may also award certificates but do so infrequently.

There are 15 public four-year institutions in Virginia, many of which have a strong reputation nation-wide. Some of these institutions, such as the University of Virginia (UVA) and the College of William and Mary (CWM), are highly selective, whereas others, such as Virginia State (VSU), Norfolk State (NSU)[1] and Old Dominion University (ODU) are close to open admissions, enrolling a large share of applicants. George Mason University (GMU) in the northern region of the state has the largest student population overall, with 37 677 students enrolled in 2018, followed by Virginia Tech in the southwest with 34 850 students, and Virginia Commonwealth University (VCU) in the state capital with 31 076 students.

Public two-year institutions

Public two-year institutions offer post-secondary education primarily at ISCED Levels 4 and 5. Two-year institutions award associate's degrees and short- and long-term certificates. The associate's degree normally requires two years of full-time college work and is designed either to prepare individuals for a career, as part of a technical career education programme, or for transfer to a four-year institution in order to pursue a bachelor's degree. Thus, there are two types of associate's degree programmes in Virginia: the technical associate's degree and the transfer associate's degree. The technical associate's degree is offered in applied fields of study such as accounting, law enforcement administration, child care assistance and registered nursing. Transfer-oriented programmes are offered in a wide range of fields of study that aim to provide credits that will count towards earning a bachelor's degree. On average, students enrolled in transfer programmes make up about two-thirds of enrolments at public two-year institutions in Virginia.

Workforce training programmes – also known as career and technical education (CTE) – encompass not only the technical associate's degree but also short-term and long-term certificates. Workforce training programmes are often designed specifically to meet local industry needs. Short-term certificate programmes are typically of a duration of less than one year, and long-term certificate programmes are generally more than one year but less than two years. Some workforce training programmes are credit-bearing, even in fields such as welding, but most are non-credit-bearing. Industry-recognised certifications can also be built into credit-bearing certificates or associate's degree programmes.

Of the 24 public two-year institutions in Virginia, there is one junior college (Richard Bland College) which is part of the College of William and Mary, and 23 community colleges that are part of the Virginia Community College System. The largest community college in terms of student population is Northern Virginia Community College (NOVA), with 50 929 students enrolled in the college in 2018, followed by Tidewater Community College with 20 941 students enrolled in 2018. Overall, enrolment in public two-year institutions has been declining since 2012.

Community colleges in Virginia are located in virtually all regions across the state and on multiple campuses, playing an important role in bringing educational opportunities to the regions of the Commonwealth.

Private four-year institutions

A diversity of not-for-profit and for-profit private higher education institutions operates in Virginia. The largest not-for-profit institution in the state is Liberty University, which, with an undergraduate enrolment of about 46 000 students, is also one of the largest higher education institutions in the United States. The largest for-profit institution is ECPI University, with about 12 000 undergraduate students. Both of these universities offer extensive online education programmes. Many of the 30 other private not-for-profit institutions are located in rural areas and enrol relatively small numbers of students. Excluding Liberty University, the average student population at not-for-profit private institutions was 1 875 in 2018 (2019[36]).

There is no comprehensive overview of private higher education institutions in Virginia, as only institutions that participate in federal or state student aid programmes are required to submit information to public authorities. Table 4.4 provides an overview of public and private, not-for-profit higher education institutions in Virginia that are eligible for federal (Title IV) funding and required to report to SCHEV.

Table 6.3. Profile of public and private not-for-profit higher education institutions in Virginia

	Public four-year institutions	Public two-year institutions[1]	Private not-for-profit four-year institutions[2]
Total student population (headcount, fall enrolment 2018)	220 255	163 945	137 272
Undergraduate students as a percentage of total enrolment (fall enrolment, 2018)	79%	100%	63%
Percentage of undergraduate students who are Pell Grant recipients (2017/18)	27%	34%	45%
Average age of undergraduate students, at entry (first-time college students) in fall 2018	18	19	19
Average age of undergraduate transfer students, at entry (new transfer students) in fall 2018	22	25	25
Total number of post-secondary credentials awarded in 2018	54 317	32 746	32 993
Percentage of certificates awarded, out of total awarded credentials	0.2%	44%	1%
Percentage of associate's degrees awarded, out of total awarded credentials	0.1%	56%	4%
Percentage of bachelor's degrees awarded, out of total awarded credentials	70%	0%	52%
Percentage of professional or master's degrees and above, out of total awarded credentials	27%	0%	40%
Percentage of post-graduate certificates,[3] out of total awarded credentials	3%	0%	3%
First-year retention rate for first-time, full-time undergraduate students (fall 2018)	86%	63%	76%
150% completion rate (full-time, first-time college students)[4]	72%	19%	53%
Average tuition and mandatory fees for in-state undergraduate students (USD, 2019/20 academic year)	USD 13 699	USD 4 620	-
Percentage of undergraduate students receiving state financial assistance and average amount received per student (USD)	20% USD 4 311	21% USD 1 200	-
Percentage of bachelor's degree students graduating with debt in 2017	59%	-	70%
Average student debt for bachelor's degree graduates in 2017 (USD)	USD 28 859	-	USD 32 367

Notes: These figures are based on information from Virginia-based higher education institutions that are eligible for federal (Title IV) funding and that are required to report student-level data to the State Council of Higher Education for Virginia (SCHEV). Graduates of for-profit colleges and universities are not reported as they do not participate in the Tuition Assistance Grant or other forms of state-funded student assistance, and therefore, are not required to submit student-level data to SCHEV. [1] Includes Richard Bland College, which is a public two-year college that is not part of the Virginia Community College System. [2] Includes only institutions that are not required to obtain certification from SCHEV and that are fully accredited by an accrediting agency that is recognised by and has met the criteria for Title IV eligibility of the U.S. Department of Education. [3] Post-graduate certificates normally require 24 credit hours beyond the master's degree. [4] The 150% completion rate refers to the percentage of graduates who completed their degree within one and a half times the normal completion time; that is, 6 years for a four-year degree and 3 years for a two-year degree. The completion rate for four-year institutions is based on the 2012/13 graduate cohort and the completion rate for two-year institutions is based on the 2011/12 graduate cohort.
Source: SCHEV (2019[36]), *Higher Ed Data Dashboard*, http://research.schev.edu/fair/strategicplan3.asp.

StatLink https://doi.org/10.1787/888934135110

6.2. Assessment of labour market outcomes: The alignment between supply and demand of graduate skills in Virginia

Demand for advanced skills

New jobs increasingly require post-secondary education

There is a broad consensus that an increasing proportion of jobs in the United States – and in Virginia – require a post-secondary qualification. A majority of the new jobs created in the years following the recession of 2008-09 have required some form of post-secondary qualification (Carnevale, Smith and Strohl, 2013[37]), which may reflect a growing skill intensity within and between occupations (Autor, Levy and Murnane, 2003[18]; Altonji, Kahn and Speer, 2014[38]; Deming and Kahn, 2018[39]; OECD, 2019[40]). National employment projections for the ten-year period from 2018-28 indicate that 15 of the 20 fastest-growing occupations in the United States require some form of post-secondary education (U.S. Bureau of Labor Statistics, 2019[41]). 10 out of these 15 occupations require at least a bachelor's degree or higher, including physician assistants, nurse practitioners, statisticians and information security analysts. Projections from Georgetown University's Center on Education and the Workforce estimate that by 2020, 35% of all job openings will require at least a bachelor's degree and a further 30% will require an associate's degree or post-secondary certificate (Carnevale, Smith and Strohl, 2013[37]).

The Georgetown Center on Education and the Workforce has estimated further that 68% of all jobs in Virginia will require some post-secondary education or training in 2020 (Carnevale and Smith, 2012[42]). With a relatively high proportion of post-secondary-intensive occupations, Virginia's economy depends on strengthening the supply of middle and advanced skills. Figure 6.4 shows long-term employment projections in Virginia for occupations that typically require some form of post-secondary education or training. As shown, employment of post-secondary graduates in business and financial operations, computer and mathematical occupations, and healthcare practitioner and technical occupations is high in Virginia and expected to continue growing. It should also be noted that these figures may not fully capture the growth in post-secondary-intensive jobs. Occupational projections of this type use an estimate of the minimum educational requirement per occupation and assume that this remains unchanged during the projection period.[2] In addition, projections are based on current industry composition and therefore do not capture new occupations in emerging industries. Thus, projections of this type are likely to underestimate education requirements (Carnevale, Smith and Strohl, 2013[37]).

A skills gap analysis conducted by the National Skills Coalition (NSC) for the period 2014-24 estimated that approximately 45% of jobs in Virginia would require a post-secondary credential of less than four years, corresponding to a "middle skills" requirement (National Skills Coalition, 2017[43]). The NSC analysis maintains that the supply of middle-skill workers in Virginia has not been keeping pace with middle-skill job openings, in part because many middle-skill jobs that previously required a high school diploma now require some form of post-secondary education or training. Education and training for middle-skill jobs can vary from apprenticeships and short-term certificates to associate's degree programmes typically offered by community colleges. Virginia's workforce credential grant programme, which was launched in 2016, has been largely a response to the need to strengthen middle-skill educational opportunities and increase the number of credentialed graduates from programmes in high-demand fields. These fields include information technology, industrial maintenance and mechatronics, and welding (see Section 6.3).

Figure 6.4. Projected employment growth in occupations that typically require some form of post-secondary education, 2016-26

Total number of jobs, based on long-term occupational projections for Virginia

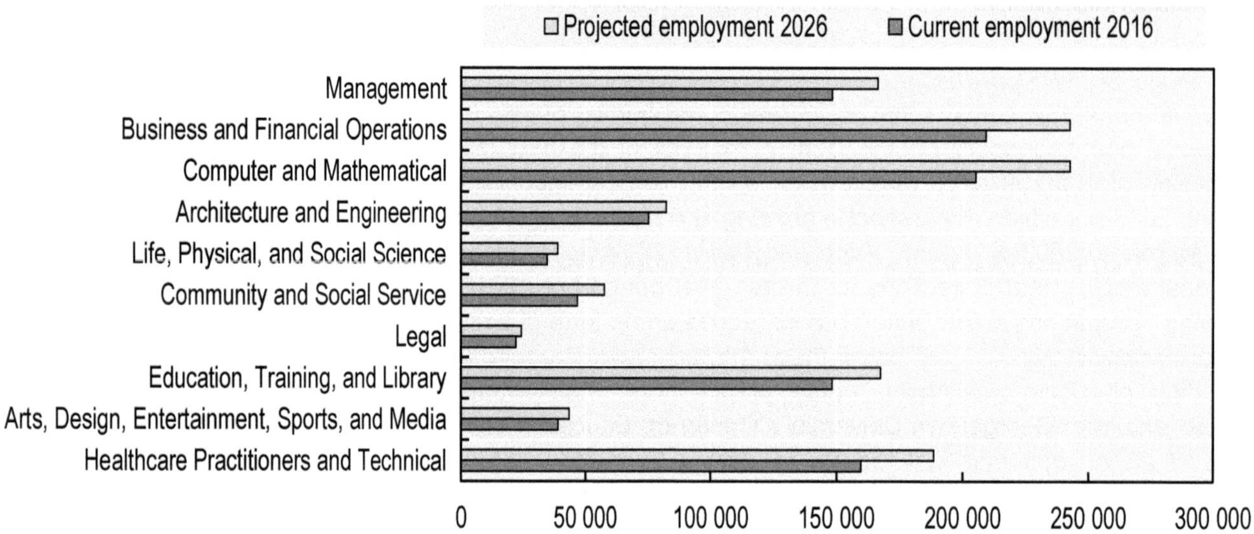

Note: The figure shows major occupational groups according to the US Standard Occupational Classification (SOC) System that usually require some post-secondary education or training (certificate, associate's degree or higher). The educational requirement for each occupation is the minimum level of education needed for entry into an occupation, based on U.S. Bureau of Labor Statistics occupational information.
Source: Adapted from VEC (2019[16]), *Long Term Industry and Occupational Projections, 2016-2026*, https://virginiaworks.com/occupational-projections.

StatLink https://doi.org/10.1787/888934134084

At the same time, the share of "good jobs" held by workers with less than a bachelor's degree is lower in Virginia than in many other states, including Washington, Connecticut and Maryland (Carnevale, Strohl and Ridley, 2017[44]). The Georgetown Center on Education and the Workforce defines good jobs as those with minimum gross annual earnings of USD 35 000 for individuals under the age of 45 and USD 45 000 for those above 45. Based on estimates from 2015, about 60% of good jobs in Virginia are held by workers with at least a bachelor's degree, suggesting a strong advantage for workers with advanced skills. Furthermore, as the technology sector expands, the demand for advanced skills in Virginia is expected to continue to grow. Nearly 150 000 new jobs in STEM-related fields are expected to be added to Virginia's economy in the next five years (Northam Administration, 2019[45]). The arrival of Amazon's new headquarters is expected to add at least 25 000 new jobs, most of which will require advanced skills in information and communication technologies (ICT). A large majority of jobs in other high-growth occupations such as community and social services, as well as healthcare practitioner and technical occupations, will require at least a bachelor's degree.

SCHEV has estimated that there is a need for an additional 1.5 million post-secondary credentials at all levels by 2030 in order to meet the state's post-secondary attainment goals (SCHEV, 2019[46]). In 2019, Virginia's public and private not-for-profit institutions awarded a total of 104 188 degrees, a number that would need to increase annually in order to reach the state's goals. As of 2018, 54% of the working-age population (aged 25-64) in Virginia have a post-secondary credential (degree or certificate) and 49% hold a post-secondary degree. At 51%, the degree attainment level of 25-34 year-olds in Virginia is not much higher than for the working-age population as a whole, creating the risk of inadequate skills supply in the future. Figure 6.5 shows post-secondary attainment levels among 25-34 year-olds in Virginia, including the share of young Virginians with some college but no degree. While the share of those with some college but no degree has been relatively large, it was lower in 2018 than in the previous ten years.

Figure 6.5. Post-secondary educational attainment levels of 25-34 year-olds in Virginia, 2003-18

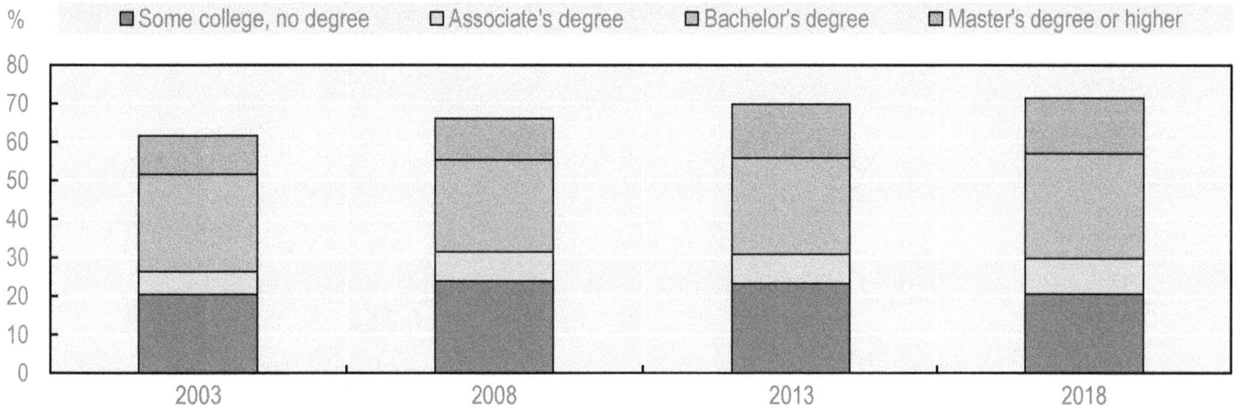

Note: The stacked columns do not sum to 100, because the complement to 100 is given by those with a high school qualification or less.
Source: U.S. Census Bureau (2019[24]), *American Community Survey 2003, 2008, 2013 and 2018* (database), https://www.census.gov/programs-surveys/acs/data.html.

StatLink https://doi.org/10.1787/888934134103

Moreover, there are large attainment gaps by region and sub-population. Figure 6.6 shows average attainment rates across the fifteen local workforce regions in Virginia. In rural areas such as Southwestern Virginia, attainment of at least an associate's degree among the adult population (aged 25-64) is as low as 24.7%, compared to 48.9% state-wide (Lumina Foundation, 2019[22]). Post-secondary enrolment and attainment numbers are also disproportionately lower for Black/African Americans and Hispanics, who constitute an untapped potential in the workforce (Jobs for the Future, 2019[47]; Lumina Foundation, 2019[22]). As the economy increasingly favours individuals with post-secondary education, a lack of qualifications negatively affects an individual's ability to earn a sustainable wage and take part in the economic growth of the state.

Out-migration has been higher than in-migration in Virginia as a whole since 2012-13, particularly among the young adult population. As well as low-income rural areas, this trend has also affected large, high-income areas, such as Fairfax County in Northern Virginia, where many educated Virginians move from other counties for their first jobs, but then frequently move out of state for subsequent work opportunities. In general, out-migration from Fairfax County to other Virginia counties has slowed since the recession of 2008-09, with more Fairfax County residents moving out of state rather than to other Virginia counties. This has also led to slower population and school enrolment growth in counties that have traditionally attracted Virginians from Fairfax County (UVA Weldon Cooper Center, 2019[48]).

Figure 6.6. Higher education attainment in Virginia, 2013-17 average

Proportion of Virginia residents aged 25-64 with an associate's degree or higher level of education, by region

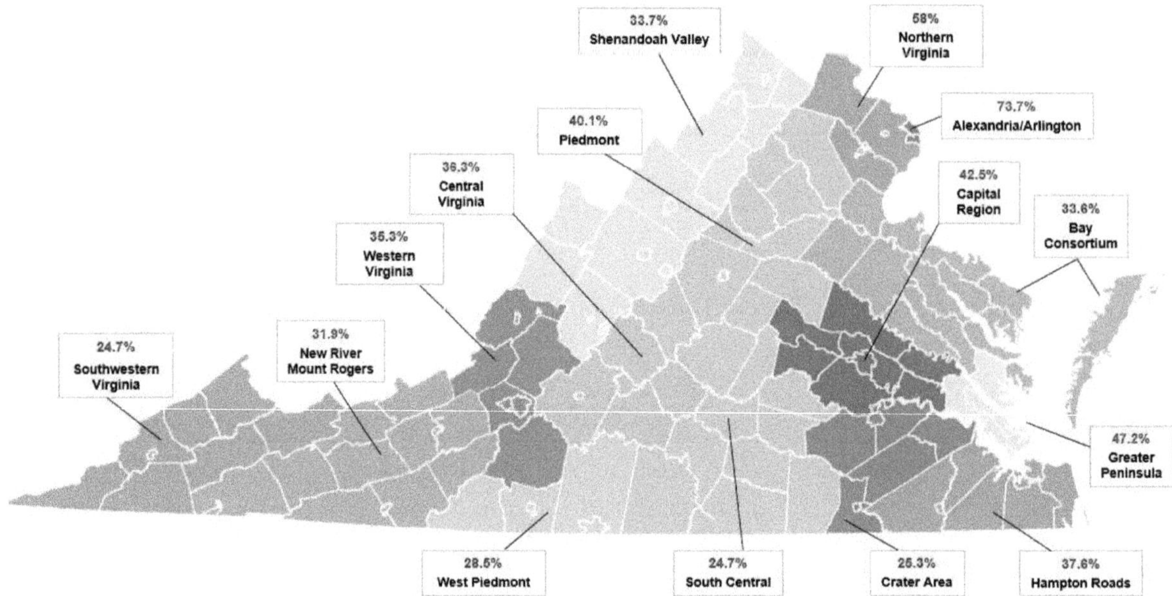

Notes: As shown, there are fifteen workforce regions, or local workforce development areas (LWDAs), in Virginia. Each LWDA is comprised of multiple counties and cities, as defined by the Virginia Employment Commission. The attainment rate for each LWDA shows the average attainment for counties and cities in that region.

Sources: The map is sourced from VEC (n.d.[49]), *Local Workforce Development Areas*, https://virginiaworks.com/Portals/200/Publications/LWDAs/Maps/LWDA%20Regions.pdf. Attainment rates are from US Census Bureau (2018[50]), *2013-17 American Community Survey 5-Year Estimates*, https://www.census.gov/newsroom/press-kits/2018/acs-5year.html, compiled per county in state reports by Lumina Foundation (2019[22]), *A Stronger Nation: Virginia Report 2019*, http://strongernation.luminafoundation.org/report/2020/#page/downloads.

The supply of skills fails to meet demand in certain fields

Available labour market information for Virginia shows there are gaps between supply and demand in several fields. Crucially, there are reported shortages of workers with advanced skills in information and communication technologies (ICT), primary and secondary school teachers, and nurse practitioners, as well as nursing aides and other critical healthcare support workers (Virginia Department of Education, n.d.[51]; VEC, 2019[9]). There are also reported shortages in the skilled trades, reflecting a nation-wide trend.

Virginia's Demand Occupations Taskforce identifies in-demand occupations that require some form of post-secondary education, but less than a master's degree. The taskforce, established by the Virginia Board of Workforce Development, releases a list of high-demand occupations on an annual basis. While the list does not indicate level or intensity of demand across or within occupational groups, it highlights specific job titles that are currently in high demand. Within computer and mathematical occupations for 2018-19, information security analysts, computer network architects, web developers, and statisticians are among the high-demand jobs listed. Within education, training and library occupations, twelve job types are listed as being in high demand, including teacher assistants, pre-school teachers and special education teachers (Virginia Career Works, 2018[52]).

Virginia's Workforce Supply and Demand Dashboard was developed to show potential gaps in workforce supply and demand throughout the state and by region. Demand-side data, based on online job postings in Virginia, are matched with supply-side data on post-secondary graduate credentials obtained in Virginia from the Integrated Postsecondary Education Data System (IPEDS). While there are important limitations to these types of supply-demand models, a simple gap analysis can provide an indication of where misalignment exists between labour market demand and the supply of credentialed workers within the state (see further discussion in Section 6.3.4). Based on the existing data in Virginia's supply and demand model, the dashboard indicates large supply gaps state-wide in healthcare, finance, computers and ICT, nursing, and human services and sales careers. At the middle skills level, large gaps have been identified in clerical and administrative work, healthcare support, and nursing (Virginia Career Works, 2019[17]).

At Virginia's public and private not-for-profit institutions, the number of degrees in data science-related programmes, capturing fields of study such as computer and information sciences, applied mathematics, and management science, nearly doubled between 2008 and 2018. In 2018, almost 31% of bachelor's degrees were awarded in science, technology, engineering, mathematics and health (STEM-H) fields, an increase from about 24% in 1998 (SCHEV, 2019[53]). These fields are important for healthcare support occupations as well, which are increasingly likely to require more technical skills, as advancements in technology permeate the health sector. While the majority of long-term certificates were awarded in STEM-H-related fields in the past, this proportion has diminished in the last ten years, as an increasing number of occupations, particularly in healthcare, now require a minimum of an associate's degree.

Figure 6.7 shows the ten-year trend in credentials awarded in STEM-H fields by Virginia's public and private, not-for-profit institutions. In terms of total numbers, STEM-H credentials are mostly awarded at the associate's and bachelor's degree levels. The greatest number of degrees are awarded at the bachelor's degree level, with degree awards rising steadily over the last ten years. The number of master's degrees awarded in STEM-H fields has increased in recent years, but until recently remained below the number of associate's degrees produced. With growing demand for advanced skills, particularly in ICT-related fields, there will be a need for more advanced degrees at the master's and doctoral levels. The state's new Tech Talent Pipeline initiative aims to add at least 25 000 undergraduate and graduate degrees in computer science and related fields by 2039 (Virginia General Assembly, 2019[54]) (see also Box 6.1).

Figure 6.7. Trends in the production of degrees in STEM-H fields, 2007/08 to 2018/19

Total number of degrees in science, technology, engineering, mathematics and health professions, by education level

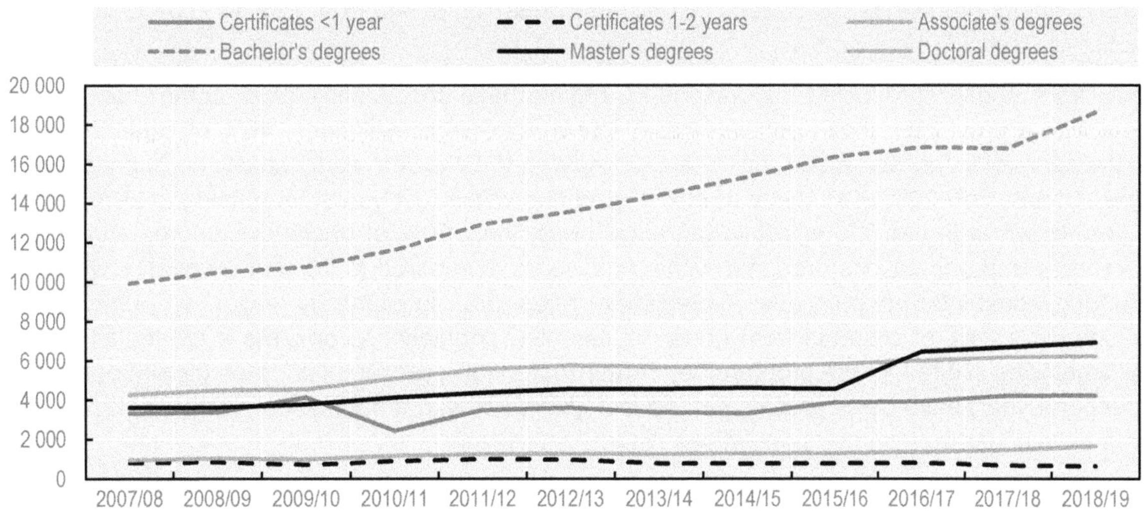

Note: The data are based on degrees conferred by Virginia's public two-year, public four-year, and private not-for-profit four-year institutions. Graduates of for-profit colleges and universities are not reported, as they do not participate in the Tuition Assistance Grant or other forms of state-funded student assistance, and therefore are not required to submit student-level data to SCHEV.
Source: SCHEV (2019[53]), *Virginia Longitudinal Data System 2007-2018* (database), https://vlds.virginia.gov/.

StatLink https://doi.org/10.1787/888934134122

To fill current supply gaps and meet future demand, it is critical that Virginia's higher education system produces enough graduates at both middle and advanced skill levels, particularly given recent out-migration of skilled workers. The need for healthcare and technology workers requires specific attention. Virginia has the fifth highest concentration of technology workers in the United States, with over 206 000 workers in computer and mathematical occupations (U.S. Bureau of Labor Statistics, 2019[71]) and demand for advanced ICT skills has persisted as job growth in computer and mathematical occupations has outpaced workforce supply. Moreover, other industries and occupational sectors increasingly require technical skills in areas such as data science.

Greater demand for specific, ICT-related skills may also be contributing to intensifying interest in micro-credentials, both within and outside the post-secondary environment. Many higher education institutions are responding to this need by offering additional specialisation tracks or certificates in ICT-related fields for degree-seeking students, regardless of their chosen field of study. To date, these types of micro-credentials serve mainly to supplement other degrees or credentials and are valued by employers as such (Gallagher, 2018[55]). However, the continuously evolving demand for ICT skills – in line with rapid advancements in technology – poses a particular challenge for the higher education system in terms of its ability to respond quickly to changing skills needs. With the rise of micro-credentials such as badges and endorsements, measuring skill demand and supply in computer and ICT fields may also become increasingly difficult.

Supply of skilled graduates in the labour market

Retention and completion rates are consistently lower for ethnic minorities and other under-represented groups

Virginia uses a definition of under-represented populations that includes race/ethnicity, federal Pell Grant eligibility (as an indicator of low income), and whether the student is from a city or county in the bottom quintile of bachelor's degree attainment. Using this definition, the proportion of students from under-represented populations in the undergraduate student population at all public institutions and private not-for-profit four-year institutions increased from 56% to 63% between 2007 and 2017. The proportion of students of colour (non-white US citizens or resident aliens) increased from 29% in 2007 to 36% in 2017 (2019[33]).

Students from under-represented populations in Virginia have consistently lower completion rates than students who are not from these populations. At public four-year institutions, 40% of students of colour complete bachelor's degrees within four years, compared to 54% of majority students. At private not-for-profit institutions, only 20% of students of colour graduate within four years, increasing to 29% within five years. As shown in Figure 6.8, at public four-year institutions, 66% of bachelor's degree students from under-represented populations graduate within four years, compared to 73% of graduates who are not from under-represented populations. Completion rates are substantially lower at public two-year institutions: only 24% of students from under-represented populations complete a credential within the normal timeframe allotted for the programme. Furthermore, first-year retention rates (likelihood of transfer to the second year) have been declining in the last six years, with a substantial decrease in retention of students from under-represented populations (SCHEV, 2019[33]).

Figure 6.8. Degree completion rates at public institutions, 2018

Proportion of students completing a higher education programme within its nominal duration (100% completion rate), by socio-economic background

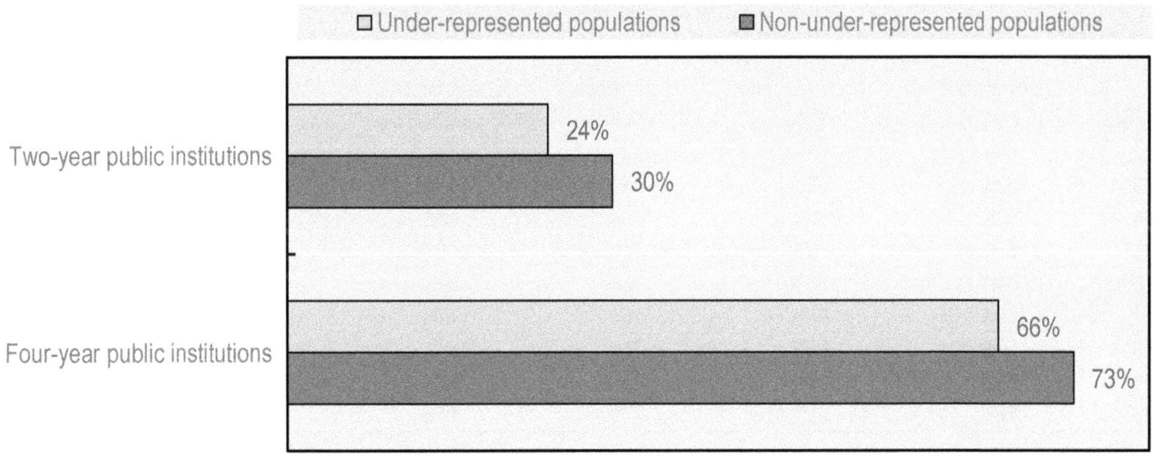

Notes: Includes all full-time, part-time, transfer and first-time college students. Completion rates for four-year institutions based on 2012/13 graduate cohort; completion rates for two-year institutions based on 2014/15 graduate cohort. Under-represented populations in Virginia include racial/ethnic minorities, low-income students (as determined by federal Pell Grant eligibility) and students from a city or county in the bottom quintile of bachelor's degree attainment.
Source: SCHEV (2019[33]), *The Virginia Plan for Higher Education General Assembly Report 2018*, https://www.schev.edu/docs/default-source/about-section/council-files/2019-council-meetings/january-2019/the-virginia-plan-annual-report-2018.pdf.

StatLink https://doi.org/10.1787/888934134141

The likelihood of completion tends to be associated with a student's income and family wealth, as students from higher income backgrounds are likely to have greater access to pre-college preparation. Table 6.4 shows completion rates for different cohorts of bachelor's degree graduates at the public and private four-year institutions by income group. The difference in completion rates between low- and high-income students is substantial; for the 2009/10 cohort at public four-year institutions, 77% of high-income students graduated within six years (150% completion rate), compared to 57% of lower-income students. However, completion rates for students from all income groups are markedly lower at private not-for-profit four-year institutions than for students at public four-year institutions; less than 60% of middle- and high-income students, and only 37% of lower-income students, complete their bachelor's degrees within six years.

Table 6.4. Bachelor's degree completion rates at public and private not-for-profit institutions, by income group

Based on degree completion within six years (150% completion rate) for graduates who entered institution in the designated year

	Public four-year institutions			Private not-for-profit four-year institutions		
	Lower-income	Middle-income	High-income	Lower-income	Middle-income	High-income
2000/01	52%	62%	74%	40%	51%	51%
2001/02	50%	63%	76%	40%	53%	55%
2002/03	52%	63%	76%	40%	50%	55%
2003/04	53%	63%	76%	42%	53%	57%
2004/05	53%	65%	74%	41%	53%	60%
2005/06	54%	65%	75%	39%	49%	54%
2006/07	55%	67%	75%	40%	48%	54%
2007/08	56%	65%	75%	37%	48%	54%
2008/09	56%	66%	73%	35%	48%	55%
2009/10	57%	69%	77%	37%	50%	58%

Note: Includes only full-time students enrolling at the institutions for the first time in fall, spring, or summer of the designated year.
Source: SCHEV (2019[53]), *Virginia Longitudinal Data System 2000-2010* (database), https://vlds.virginia.gov/.

StatLink https://doi.org/10.1787/888934135129

Incomplete qualifications tend to lead to less rewarding labour market outcomes

As seen in Figure 6.8, average completion rates at public two-year institutions are substantially lower than at four-year institutions. Traditionally, community colleges in the United States are responsible for local workforce training and meeting the needs of employers in the region, and enrol students of all backgrounds and levels of academic preparation. Community college students are also more likely to be part-time, older, and from low-income backgrounds, with parents who do not have post-secondary education (JLARC, 2017[56]). As a result, completion rates at community colleges are typically lower than at four-year colleges and universities nation-wide (Levesque, 2018[57]).

Completion rates at Virginia's community colleges have been declining in recent years as a result of a strong economy and a tight labour market that have discouraged students from enrolling in post-secondary education. Indeed, enrolments and completions at public two-year institutions are positively correlated with unemployment rates (SCHEV, 2019[33]). Nonetheless, during the 2008-09 recession and at the peak of student enrolment, the completion rate was 42% for students at public two-year institutions, compared to 70% at public four-year institutions.

Students who earn some college credits but do not obtain a credential (non-completers) risk a lower return on their educational investment because they do not gain the earnings premium associated with holding a completed post-secondary credential, even if they end up earning more with some college credits than they would have with only a high school diploma. Recent studies have shown that non-completers have higher earnings potential compared to those with a high school diploma or less, but that returns for non-completers also vary by field of study (Belfield and Bailey, 2017[58]). Completing credits in some career and technical education (CTE) fields, linked to less credential-intensive sectors, can yield positive wage returns (Bahr, 2019[59]).

While non-completers may do better in the labour market with some college credits as opposed to having just a high school diploma, data from different US states shows their earnings potential in the long term is greatly reduced. Credits from certain fields or programmes may not be valued in the labour market and may thus yield a negative return on investment for an individual who has spent time and money on post-secondary education. For example, the most popular programme-types at Virginia's public two-year institutions are in the broad fields of "general studies" and "liberal arts or liberal studies", which have little immediate relevance to the labour market. Non-completers from these types of programmes are likely to experience greater difficulty in finding well-paid employment.

According to data by the National Student Clearinghouse, 908 882 Virginians have earned some college credit but do not have a degree or certificate (National Student Clearinghouse, 2019[60]). 73% of the "some college, no degree" population were last enrolled at a public two-year institution and 12% were enrolled at a public four-year institution, with the remaining proportion last enrolled at a private institution. The State Council of Higher Education for Virginia estimates that 20% of individuals with some college credit have earned more than 30 credits at the post-secondary level (SCHEV, 2019[46]). The share of those with some college, but no degree, is slightly larger among young adults (22%) than among older cohorts (19%) in Virginia. However, among young adults, the share of those with some college, but no degree, appears to be declining. Findings from the National Student Clearinghouse indicate that potential completers – those with some college and no degree who are likely to return to post-secondary education – tend to remain in the state and return to the same institution type, though not necessarily the same institution. This is an important population to reach in order to improve credential attainment.

Figure 6.9 compares the inflation-adjusted earnings of Virginia residents with either an associate's degree, bachelor's degree, or some college but no degree, which includes individuals who hold a post-secondary certificate. It confirms that having no degree carries a disadvantage in terms of earnings in comparison to associate's degree and bachelor's degree holders, with bachelor's degree holders at a far greater earnings advantage. The earnings of those with some college but no degree have risen slightly between 2013 and 2018 after a long decline, narrowing the gap between those with associate's degrees and those with only some college. Nevertheless, the labour market value of incomplete or non-degree qualifications remains low. The median earnings for these individuals are only slightly above the estimated annual wage needed to cover basic expenses for a full-time working adult in Virginia (MIT, 2019[61]).

Figure 6.9. Median annual earnings for individuals aged 25-64 by higher education level, 2000-18

Pre-tax annual earnings in 2018 USD (adjusted for inflation)

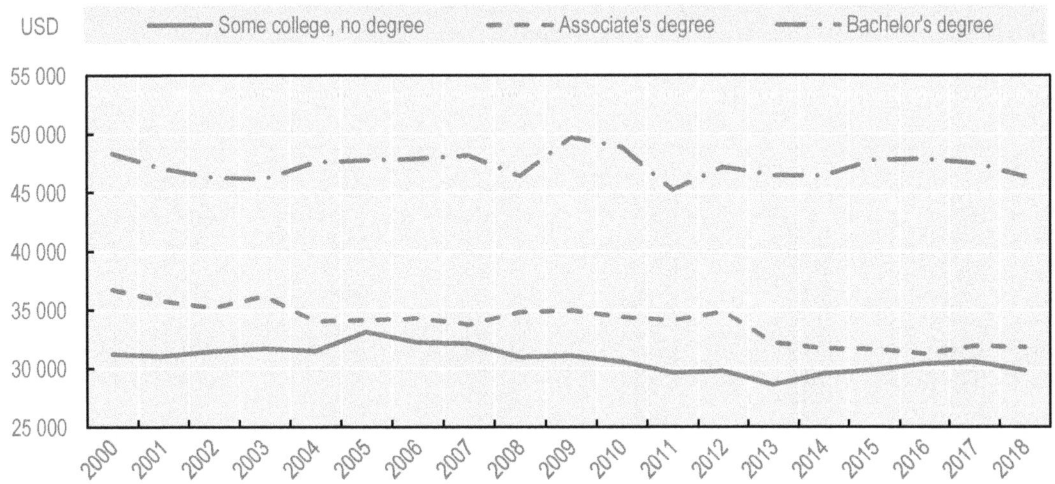

Notes: The estimated median earnings refer to full-time, full-year wage and salary workers, expressed in US dollars adjusted for inflation. The trend line shows a snapshot of median earnings among Virginia residents aged 25-64, at the given educational level, each year.
Source: U.S. Census Bureau (2019[24]), *American Community Survey 2003 to 2018* (database), https://www.census.gov/programs-surveys/acs/data.html.

StatLink https://doi.org/10.1787/888934134160

Variations in labour market outcomes

On average, post-secondary graduates in Virginia enjoy favourable earnings and employment prospects

Most students who pursue post-secondary education do so in search of a meaningful job and a sustainable wage. In 2015, approximately 70% of Americans agreed that it will be more important in the future to have a post-secondary degree or professional certificate in order to obtain a good job (Gallup, 2016[62]). While several factors such as individual choice and local labour market conditions influence the outcomes of graduates in the labour market, graduate earnings and employment outcomes provide an important indication of how graduates are valued in the labour market through the skills they bring to the workplace.

Data from the American Community Survey (ACS) show that individuals aged 25-64 in Virginia with post-secondary education enjoy higher employment rates than those without a post-secondary degree. On average, the likelihood of being employed increases with the level of educational attainment, which in turn improves an individual's earnings potential. Similarly, labour force participation rates generally increase with educational attainment. In Virginia, the labour force participation rate for 25-64 year-olds with post-secondary education is in line with the US average. The rate of labour force participation for individuals aged 25-64 with a bachelor's degree is approximately 87%, compared to the US average of 86%. For individuals with master's and professional degrees, the labour force participation rate in Virginia is 89% and 91% respectively.

There is little variation in labour force participation by ethnic or racial group for post-secondary graduates in Virginia. However, male graduates participate in the labour force at a higher rate than females, with a difference of ten percentage points. Figure 6.10 shows employment rates by gender and educational attainment level for young adults, aged 25-34, in Virginia. While the gender gap is larger for those without post-secondary education, there is also a gap in employment rates between males and females at higher attainment levels, even among young adults. The lower rate of employment for females is often due to barriers to labour market participation such as childcare provision. Overall, however, employment rates rise with the level of educational attainment for both genders.

Figure 6.10. Employment rate of 25-34 year-olds in Virginia, by gender and level of educational attainment, 2018

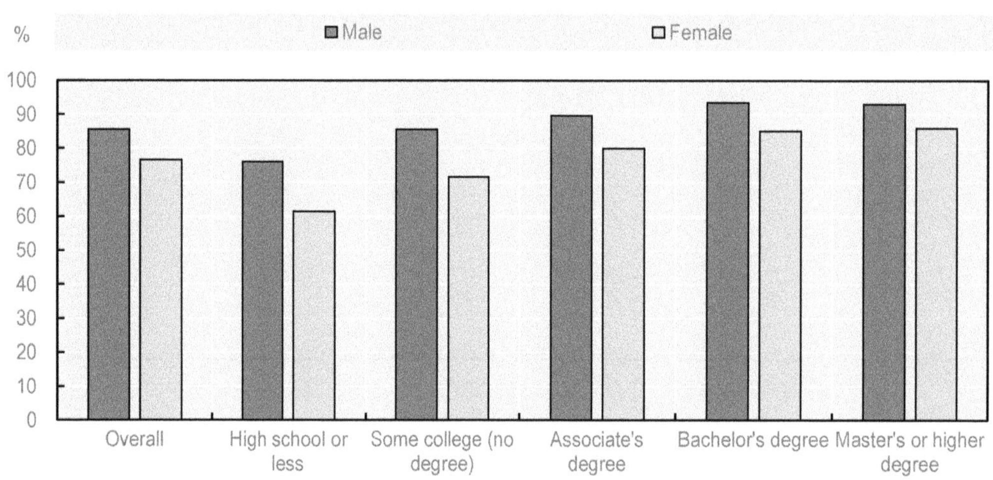

Source: U.S. Census Bureau (2019[24]), *American Community Survey 2018* (database), https://www.census.gov/programs-surveys/acs/data.html.

StatLink https://doi.org/10.1787/888934134179

Employment rates for post-secondary graduates vary somewhat by field of study, with higher employment rates associated with higher earnings. Figure 6.11 shows the employment rates of 25-64 year-olds with bachelor's degrees by field of study in Virginia compared to the US average. With employment rates close to 90%, graduates with degrees in STEM-related fields such as architecture, engineering, computers, statistics and mathematics enjoy the highest employment rates compared to other fields. Several fields enjoy higher rates of employment in Virginia than in the United States on average. In addition to STEM fields, these include the humanities and the arts. However, employment prospects for individuals with a bachelor's degree in education or psychology and social work are markedly lower than in other fields of study and slightly below the US average. Given that educators are in high demand, it is a concern that graduates with degrees in education have trouble obtaining employment in Virginia.

Figure 6.11. Employment and earnings of bachelor's graduates aged 25-64, by key field of study, 2018

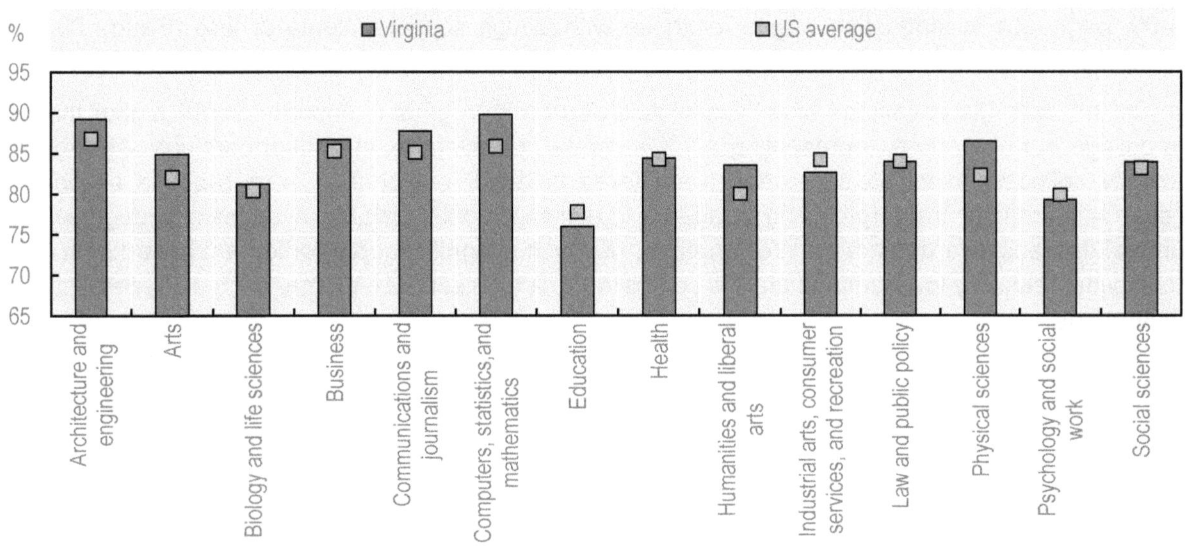

Source: Adapted from U.S. Census Bureau (2019[24]), *American Community Survey 2018* (database), https://www.census.gov/programs-surveys/acs/data.html.

StatLink https://doi.org/10.1787/888934134198

There is limited evidence of over-qualification or underemployment of post-secondary graduates in Virginia. Obtaining accurate and systematic data on the employment outcomes of graduates, however, is challenging (TICAS, 2018[63]). At the national level, graduate employment outcomes are surveyed through the National Association of Colleges and Employers (NACE) First-Destination survey, which provides information on employment outcomes of graduates six months after graduation. However, this survey is primarily focused on whether or not graduates find full-time employment, are seeking continuing education or are still looking for work. It does not attempt to measure whether or not a graduate is employed in an occupation that matches his or her field of study and level of qualification. State-level post-secondary data systems that collect data on earnings through Unemployment Insurance (UI) wage records typically cannot obtain information on the specific occupation of graduates. While UI records often indicate the industry in which an individual is employed, this does not provide enough information to assess qualification or field mismatch.

In order to obtain information on in-field job placements, higher education institutions typically use alumni surveys. However, these data can be unreliable due to low response rates and poorly designed surveys. To inform public policy, a systematic, state-wide review of graduate outcomes would be necessary in order to assess the extent to which graduate skills (both quality and quantity) are meeting employer needs. The General Assembly of Virginia recently granted funding for the development of a graduate outcomes survey which, among other things, aims to collect information on whether or not graduates have secured employment related to their degree. The survey will be developed by the State Council for Higher Education of Virginia, in collaboration with the Virginia Economic Development Partnership.

Earnings data suggest that post-secondary graduates in Virginia are, on average, rewarded for higher skills levels. Figure 6.12 shows that the earnings advantage for individuals with post-secondary education in Virginia is around the same level as, or higher than, the US average at every level of attainment. On average, the earnings advantage for individuals with master's degrees or professional degrees is substantially higher in Virginia than in the United States overall. While there is still an advantage to earning an associate's degree compared to a high school diploma or some college, there is a much higher earnings advantage for graduates with a bachelor's degree or above. Median annual earnings for bachelor's degree holders in Virginia are about 45% higher than for associate's degree holders. This reflects a nation-wide trend, with the earnings premium for bachelor's degree holders rising substantially since the recession of 2008-09, partly due to stagnating wages for those with a high school diploma or less (Baum, 2014[64]; Carnevale, Smith and Strohl, 2013[37]).

However, the earnings advantage of an associate's degree in Virginia is only marginally higher than for some college but no degree, representing a 7% increase, on average, in annual earnings. At Virginia's community colleges, associate's degrees are offered in either a technical track (applied associate's degrees) or a transfer track (providing academic credit that count towards a bachelor's degree). The majority of degrees awarded are transfer-oriented, of which a significant proportion are awarded in fields that may yield relatively low earnings premia compared to a high school diploma, such as general studies and liberal arts.

Figure 6.12. Earnings advantage of post-secondary education compared to upper secondary, by level of attainment, 2018

Upper secondary = 100

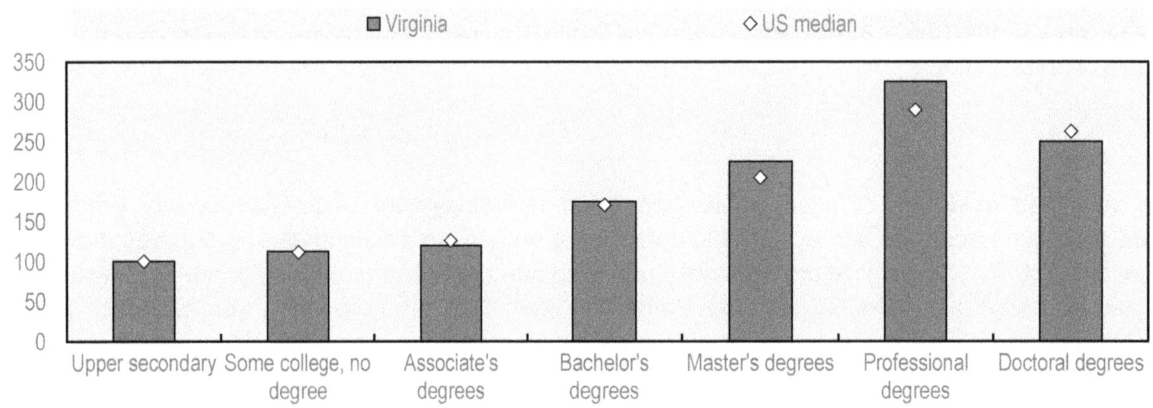

Note: Based on median annual pre-tax earnings of 25-64 year-olds.
Source: U.S. Census Bureau (2019[24]), *American Community Survey 2018* (database), https://www.census.gov/programs-surveys/acs/data.html.

StatLink https://doi.org/10.1787/888934134217

There are notable disparities in graduate earnings and debt levels by field and level of study

Through the Virginia Longitudinal Data System, analysts and policy makers have been able to track the wage outcomes of graduate cohorts from as far back as the 1990s (SCHEV, 2019[65]). Because data on post-secondary degrees and certificates are matched to Unemployment Insurance (UI) wage records from the Virginia Employment Commission, the data include only information on graduates who joined the workforce in Virginia after graduation and thus do not include graduates from Virginia's higher education system who moved out of state. However, it is estimated that about 82% of Virginia bachelor's degree graduates and 88% of associate's degree graduates remain in the state after graduation (SCHEV, 2019[53]).

Recent research has demonstrated that a student's chosen field of study is one of the strongest predictors of future earnings (Carnevale, Cheah and Strohl, 2012[66]; Carnevale et al., 2017[67]; Schneider, 2015[68]; Kim, Tamborini and Sakamoto, 2015[69]). Among Virginia graduates, there is substantial earnings dispersion both within and between fields of study. Figure 6.13 shows the long-term earnings trajectory of the 1992/93 cohort of Virginia graduates by field of study at the bachelor's degree level. STEM field graduates had the highest median earnings five years post-completion (USD 38 346) and enjoyed the steepest earnings trajectory over time compared to other fields of study.

Figure 6.13. Earnings trajectory of Virginia bachelor's degree graduates by field of study, 6-26 years after graduation

Median annual pre-tax earnings in constant USD (adjusted for inflation), based on longitudinal data from 1992/93 cohort of Virginia graduates

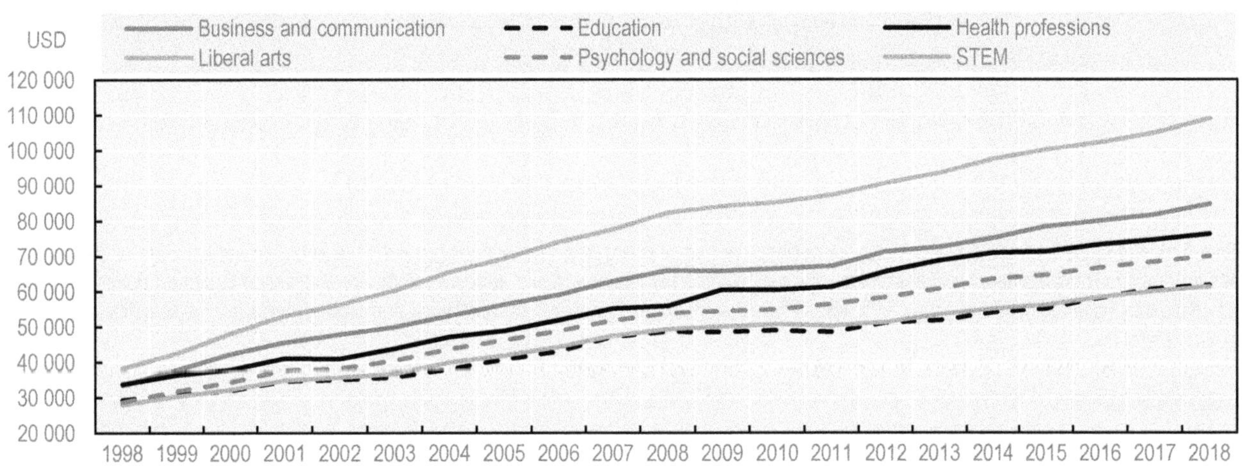

Notes: The data are based on graduates from 4-year bachelor's degree programmes at Virginia's public and private, not-for-profit four-year institutions. Fields of study have been grouped into broader discipline areas. The data include only information on graduates who remained in the state and joined the workforce in Virginia post-graduation. Graduates of for-profit colleges and universities are not reported, as they do not participate in the Tuition Assistance Grant or other forms of state-funded student assistance, and therefore are not required to submit student-level data to SCHEV. Wage values in real dollars. Excludes individuals earning less than 150% of the federal poverty line.
Source: SCHEV (2019[53]), *Virginia Longitudinal Data System* (database), https://research.schev.edu/info/Reports.Guide-to-the-Post-Completion-Wages-of-Graduates.

StatLink https://doi.org/10.1787/888934134236

At the same time, data on Virginia graduates from the 1992/93 cohort also demonstrate wide earnings variation within fields of study. 24 years post-completion (i.e. in 2017), the difference between the highest STEM earners (75th percentile) and the lowest STEM earners (25th percentile) was USD 91 806. By comparison, the difference in median earnings between the highest earning field (STEM) and the lowest earning field (liberal arts) was USD 44 924 (SCHEV, 2019[53]).

Wide earnings dispersion within fields of study is also observed in the working-age population as a whole. Figure 6.14 shows wide earnings dispersion within fields of study at the bachelor's degree level, with the greatest differences within communications and journalism fields, as well as in the social sciences and STEM fields. The smallest dispersion is observed in education and health fields, typically linked to regulated professions. Notwithstanding variation in local labour market conditions, within-field earnings disparities also arise from differences in industry, occupation, and individual skills sets.

Figure 6.14. Distribution of earnings of 25-64 year-old bachelor's graduates, 2018

Median annual earnings in USD, selected fields of study

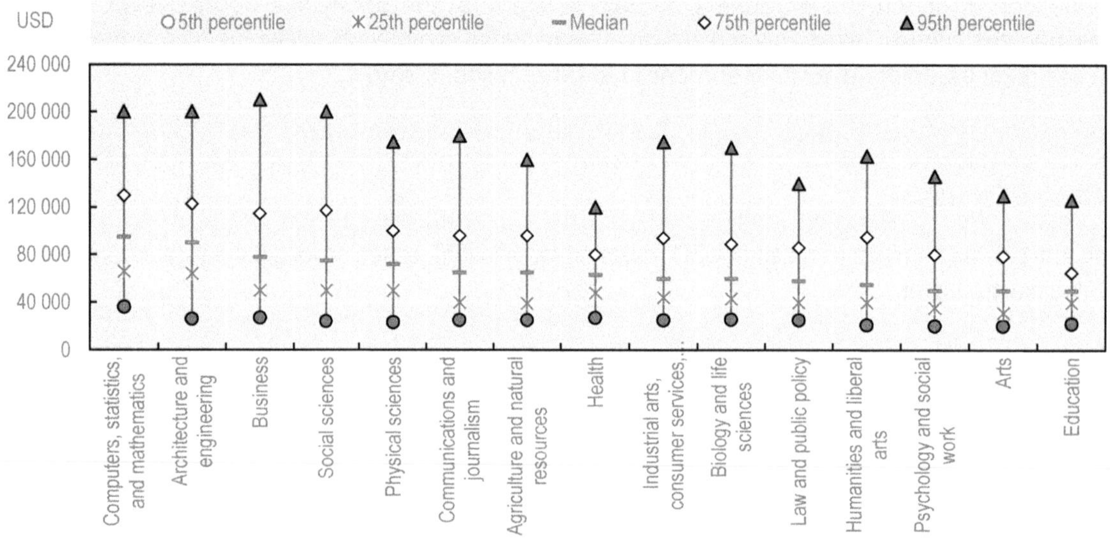

Note: Fields of study are ordered by the annual median earnings of graduates, in descending order. Based on annual earnings of 25-64 year-olds in Virginia. The estimated median earnings refer to full-time full-year wage and salary workers, are expressed in current dollars, and are not seasonally adjusted (BLS definition). The label "industrial arts, consumer services, and recreation" corresponds to "middle skills technology programs and jobs".
Source: Adapted from U.S. Census Bureau (2019[24]), *American Community Survey 2018* (database), https://www.census.gov/programs-surveys/acs/data.html.

StatLink https://doi.org/10.1787/888934134255

Longitudinal data from the 2005/06 cohort of Virginia graduates show clear wage differentials by degree level over a ten-year period. Figure 6.15 illustrates that bachelor's degree graduates enjoy a relatively steep climb in earnings immediately after graduation that continues to rise over time. Graduates with associate-technical degrees start with comparatively high earnings that continue to rise, but at a slower pace than for bachelor's degree graduates. The data also show a substantial earnings gap between associate-technical and associate-transfer graduates that narrows over time. While there is variation by field of study for associate's degree holders, data from multiple cohorts over time have demonstrated that, on average, the earnings of associate-transfer graduates eventually catch up to associate-technical graduates (SCHEV, 2019[33]; Schneider, 2016[70]).

Figure 6.15. Annual earnings of graduates 1-12 years after graduation

Median annual pre-tax earnings of graduates in constant USD (adjusted for inflation), based on longitudinal data from 2005/06 cohort

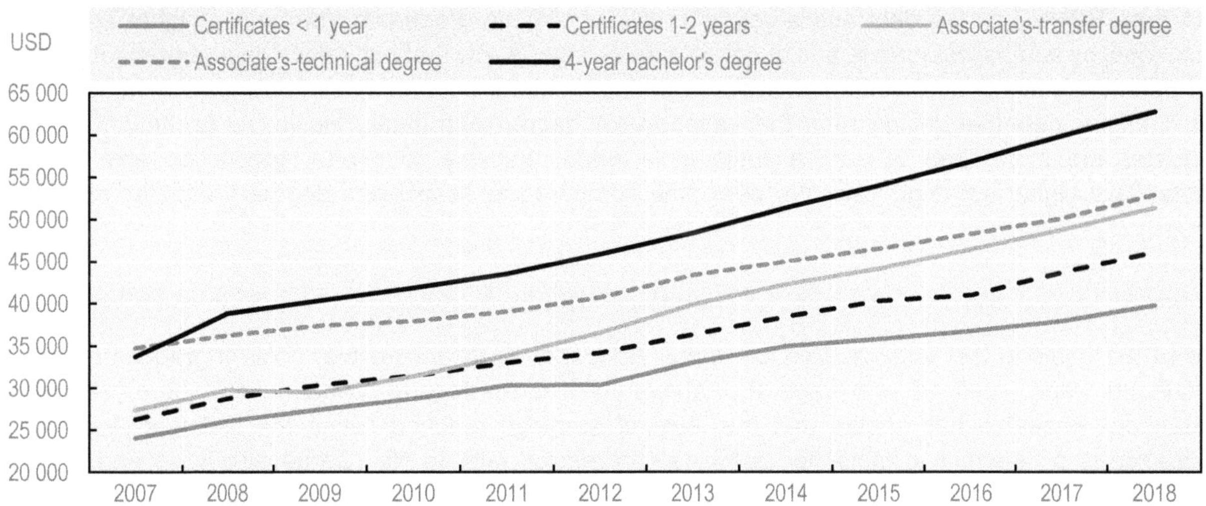

Notes: The graduates are from Virginia's public two-year, public four-year, and private not-for-profit four-year institutions. The data include only information on graduates who remained in the state and joined the workforce in Virginia post-graduation. Graduates of for-profit colleges and universities are not reported, as they do not participate in the Tuition Assistance Grant or other forms of state-funded student assistance, and therefore are not required to submit student-level data to SCHEV. Wage values in real dollars. Excludes individuals earning less than 150% of the federal poverty line.

Source: SCHEV (2019[53]), *Virginia Longitudinal Data System 2007-2018* (database), https://research.schev.edu/info/Reports.Guide-to-the-Post-Completion-Wages-of-Graduates.

StatLink https://doi.org/10.1787/888934134274

In addition to earnings, an important aspect of assessing the returns on investment in post-secondary education is the impact of individual student debt. The cost of higher education in Virginia has been rising steadily since 2002, shifting the cost burden increasingly to students and their families (SCHEV, 2019[71]). According to national data collection of debt levels of bachelor's degree graduates, Virginia ranks 17th out of 50 states for highest average debt levels. In 2018, the average amount of student debt for Virginia graduates was USD 30 363, compared to USD 19 728 in Utah (with the lowest average debt nation-wide) and USD 38 669 in Connecticut (with the highest average debt nation-wide) (TICAS, 2019[72]).

For low-income students in Virginia, tuition and fees as a proportion of family income has been increasing over the past five years. At Virginia's public two-year institutions, tuition and fees are the 8th highest in the country. At public four-year institutions, net tuition revenue per full-time equivalent (FTE) student has increased by 53% since the 2008-09 recession, which in 2018 was USD 9 241, compared to the US average of USD 6 788. Net tuition revenue represented over 60% of total educational revenue in 2018, placing Virginia in the top quartile of states with the highest tuition revenue as a proportion of total educational revenue. In contrast, state educational appropriations per FTE were USD 5 420 in 2018, notably below the US average of USD 7 853 (SHEEO, 2019[73]).

While loan default rates for Virginia graduates are lower than the US average, the proportion of students with debt has been increasing along with the amount of debt each student carries upon graduation. In 2018, approximately 62% of bachelor's degree students in Virginia graduated with debt, compared to 52% ten years earlier (SCHEV, 2019[74]). At the same time, median student debt for bachelor's degree graduates increased by 43% over the ten-year period between 2008 and 2018 (SCHEV, 2019[75]). The increasing student debt burden lowers the return on investment in post-secondary education, and disproportionately affects those from lower-income backgrounds. While bachelor's degree holders are less likely to default on their loans compared to associate's degree and certificate holders, first-generation bachelor's degree graduates are more than twice as likely to default on their loans than students whose parents have attained higher education (TICAS, 2019[72]).

Data from SCHEV on the debt and earnings profile of Virginia graduates from public higher education institutions, by sub-baccalaureate and at baccalaureate level, show that bachelor's degree graduates have a comparatively higher debt burden on average, with a greater proportion of students graduating with debt and a higher debt-to-earnings ratio than associate's degree graduates. However, bachelor's degree graduates are more likely to earn a sustainable wage relatively soon after graduation and enjoy a substantially higher earnings trajectory over time compared to associate's degree graduates (SCHEV, 2019[74]).

Not all post-secondary graduates achieve a sustainable wage three years post-completion

One of the goals of the *Virginia Plan for Higher Education* is to ensure that 75% of graduates earn a sustainable wage – defined as a wage at or above 200% of the federal poverty level – three years after graduation. Research has shown that the level of earnings reached within the first few years after graduation is a determining factor for earnings progression later in life (Carnevale, Rose and Cheah, 2013[76]). A detailed analysis of programme-level wage outcomes of Virginia graduates has shown that the wages of bachelor's degree graduates who earn below the median wage for the state three years post-completion tend to remain below the state-wide median ten years post-completion (Schneider, 2016[70]).

As seen in Figure 6.16, 61% of graduates from transfer-oriented associate's degree programmes achieve a sustainable wage three years post-completion, compared to 81% of graduates from technical programmes. There is also a substantial earnings gap between associate-technical and associate-transfer graduates. While the earnings of graduates with associate's degrees can reach the level of some bachelor's degree graduates over time, the lower end of the earnings distribution is substantially lower. Based on data from recent cohorts, the earnings of associate-transfer graduates at the lower end of the distribution can be less than USD 20 000 per year. While the objective of transfer-oriented programmes is to prepare students for transfer to four-year institutions, only approximately 12-15% of students enrolled in transfer-oriented programmes in any given year actually transfer to a four-year institution. Based on transfer outcomes data, these students are likely to complete a bachelor's degree successfully. However, that still leaves a large proportion of students with relatively poor labour market prospects if they leave post-secondary education with an associate-transfer degree as their highest educational attainment. Given that transfer students make up roughly two-thirds of community college enrolments, this affects a considerable portion of college students.

Overall, despite substantial variation by type of degree and field of study, available data raise concerns about the value of an associate's degree in the labour market. Figure 6.16 shows the proportion of all undergraduates earning a sustainable wage one, two and three years post-completion. It shows that 74% of undergraduates from the latest cohort (graduating in 2015) earned a sustainable wage three years post-completion, just short of the 75% goal in the *Virginia Plan for Higher Education*. This has been attributed to the relatively low wages of graduates from associate-transfer programmes (SCHEV, 2019[33]). The figure also shows that the proportion of graduates achieving a sustainable wage has been declining over the last fifteen years. This may be partially due to the slow recovery of Virginia's economy after the 2008-09 recession.

Figure 6.16. Percentage of graduates earning a sustainable wage after graduation, 1998-2015

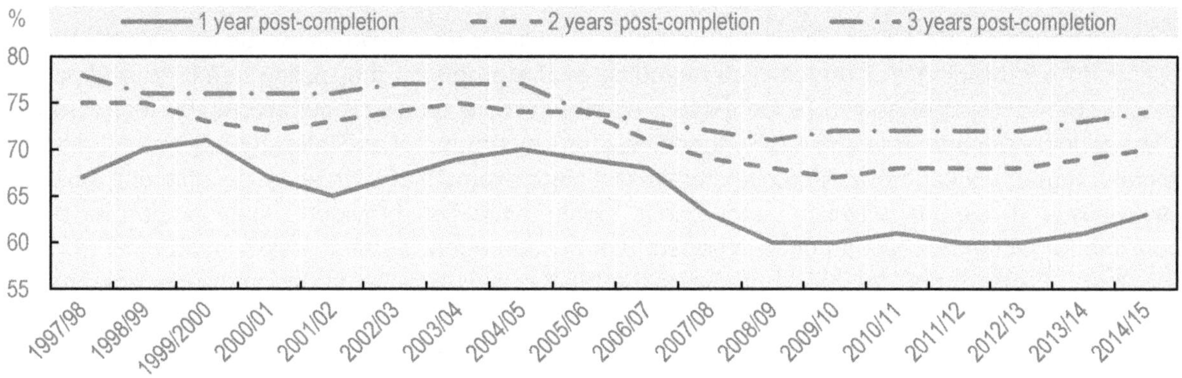

Notes: A sustainable wage is greater than or equal to 200% of the federal poverty level for a single individual. The numbers include all associate's and bachelor's degree graduates from Virginia's public and private not-for-profit institutions.
Source: SCHEV (2019[53]), *Virginia Longitudinal Data System 1998-2015* (database), https://research.schev.edu/info/Reports.Guide-to-the-Post-Completion-Wages-of-Graduates.

StatLink https://doi.org/10.1787/888934134293

6.3. Policies to improve the alignment of the higher education system and the labour market in Virginia

The assessment of the labour market outcomes experienced by higher education graduates and graduate employers in Virginia in the Section 6.2 suggests that, to achieve a good alignment between the supply of middle and advanced skills, and demand for these skills, the Commonwealth needs to:

- **increase higher education attainment** across the state to meet this overall increase in skills demand;
- **enhance, in particular, post-secondary entry and completion rates among under-represented student populations**, whose talent will increasingly be needed to meet skills demand;
- **optimise alignment between skills supply and demand** by encouraging students to obtain credentials in high-demand fields (and potentially – discouraging them from study in low-demand fields).

This section of the chapter provides an assessment of the current policy environment for higher education in Virginia. It identifies current strengths and provides recommendations on where improvements could be made to develop a system that is more likely to lead to a good alignment between skills supply and demand. The analysis has been structured using the policy analysis framework (see Chapter 1), which identifies the main policy levers that policy makers can use to influence the characteristics of higher education systems that affect labour market alignment.

Strategic planning and co-ordination

In the context of this review, strategic planning refers to the stage of policy making through which high-level priorities and goals concerning higher education-workforce alignment are established. These priorities and goals guide more detailed policy design and implementation in specific areas, such as regulation, funding or information provision. Co-ordination refers primarily to co-operation between relevant policy-making bodies in the field of education and workforce development in a given jurisdiction, with a view to establishing a "joined up" strategy and ensuring coherence between policies and programmes for implementation.

Experience from many OECD countries and multiple policy fields has shown the value of strategic planning processes in establishing a common understanding of the problems that policy needs to address and building a shared vision of how to tackle these problems. Where problems cut across the responsibilities of different policy departments and public agencies, inter-departmental and inter-agency co-ordination are necessary. Higher education-workforce alignment is a clear example of such an issue, affecting as it does, the activities and responsibilities of autonomous higher education providers, state authorities directly responsible for higher education policy, other state education agencies and bodies involved in workforce development. Furthermore, the broad nature of the topic means policies in this area affect and serve a wide range of stakeholders – students, graduates, employees or those seeking employment, and employers – whose priorities and views should ideally inform strategy and policy making.

Virginia's strategic plan for higher education has a strong focus on workforce preparation and alignment

Virginia has a well-established, long-term strategy for higher education, which plays a clear role in steering higher education policy making and has a strong focus on the relationship between higher education, employment and economic development. Among SCHEV's legal responsibilities is the task of developing, every six years, a strategic plan for higher education in the Commonwealth that identifies goals for the sector and sets out co-ordinated strategies for achieving these goals. The *Virginia Plan for Higher Education*, adopted by SCHEV in 2014 and subsequently endorsed by the General Assembly, establishes the overall goal for Virginia to respond to growing demand for skills by becoming "the best-educated state by 2030". The *Virginia Plan* establishes explicitly that, by 2030, 60% of the working-age population (aged 25-64) should have obtained an associate's degree or higher, and a further 10% some form of workforce credential,[3] meaning a post-secondary attainment rate of 70% (SCHEV, 2019[33]). To put this in context, in 2017, the proportions of the working-age population in Virginia with degrees and workforce credentials were, respectively, 48.9% and 5%, resulting in an overall attainment rate of around 54%.

As summarised in Box 6.3, the *Virginia Plan* also establishes four overarching goals for higher education in Virginia related to affordable access; student success; effective investment and innovation; and the contribution of the sector to regional and economic development. For each of the four goals, the *Virginia Plan* identifies broad lines of action ("strategies") to guide the more detailed design of state policy and funding initiatives. In addition, the Plan includes six more detailed quantitatively measurable targets to be achieved by 2030, relating to number of degrees awarded, completion rates and attainment among under-represented groups,[4] affordability, tuition and fees, research activity and graduate earnings. The last target specifies that 75% of graduates should "earn sustainable wages three years after graduation", where a "sustainable wage" is defined as earnings at or above 200% of the federal poverty level. In 2016, around 73% of associate's and bachelor's degree graduates from 2012/13 (three years earlier) attained this level of earnings (USD 25 100 per year).

Box 6.3. Goals and strategies of the *Virginia Plan for Higher Education* (2014-20)

"Virginia will be the best-educated state by 2030"

1. Provide affordable access for all:

a) Expand outreach to PK-12 and traditionally underserved populations; b) improve the college readiness of all students; c) cultivate affordable post-secondary education pathways for traditional, non-traditional and returning students; d) align state appropriations, financial aid, tuition and fees so that students have broader access to post-secondary education opportunities, regardless of their ability to pay.

2. Optimize student success for work and life

a) Strengthen curricular options to ensure that graduates are prepared with the competencies necessary for employment and civic engagement; b) provide effective academic and student services infrastructures focused on persistence and completion; c) increase on-time completion of certificates and degrees; d) engage adults and veterans in certificate and degree completion and lifelong learning.

3. Drive change and improvement through innovation and investment

a) Identify and implement public funding strategies to sustain long-term planning and responsiveness; b) cultivate innovations that enrich quality, promote collaboration and improve efficiency; c) foster faculty excellence, scholarship and diversity; d) enhance higher education leadership, governance and accountability.

4. Advance the economic and cultural prosperity of the Commonwealth and its regions

a) Build a competitive, future-ready workforce for all regions; b) become a catalyst for entrepreneurship and a model for business incubation; c) target funding, resources and partnerships to support research and development; d) expand participation and engagement in public service and institutional service to the community; e) demonstrate the impact of higher education on state and regional economic development.

Source: SCHEV (2014[77]).

SCHEV produces an annual report for the General Assembly examining progress in relation to these different goals and quantitative targets and adopts its own "priority initiatives" (SCHEV, 2019[78]) for achieving the goals and strategies of the *Virginia Plan* for each two-year legislative period. At the time of writing, the State Council and SCHEV staff are discussing possible revisions to the *Virginia Plan for Higher Education* and the refinement of priority initiatives, although it is understood that there are unlikely to be changes to the overall goals and headline strategies of the current plan.

At a strategic level, the current goals of the *Virginia Plan* address the three key labour market alignment challenges identified in Section 6.2, through seeking to expand the overall supply of graduates; better serve the needs of under-represented groups most affected by the "leaky pipeline"; and ensure alignment between the programmes students enrol in and the skills requirements of the Virginian economy. In providing such a clear focus and direction, the Plan creates a strong framework within which to design and implement specific policies and programmes to achieve the high-level goals.

The Commonwealth's system of six-year plans for public higher education institutions ensures close articulation between state-wide goals and institutional strategies

As part of the 2005 Restructuring Act (SCHEV, 2019[79]), public higher education institutions in Virginia were granted greater operational and administrative autonomy and, in exchange, required to participate in formalised accountability mechanisms. The Restructuring Act and the subsequent (2011) Higher Education Opportunity Act require all public four-year institutions and the Virginia Community College System to prepare institutional plans with a six-year time horizon, setting out institutional strategies designed to contribute to state-wide higher education goals and, in parallel, to meet quantitative Institutional Performance Standards (IPS) relating to enrolment, progression, transfer and completion.

In their six-year plans, institutions are required by SCHEV to identify specific institutional initiatives that contribute to state-wide goals, prioritise these initiatives and indicate funding needs for each institutional initiative for the coming biennium (see example in Box 6.4). After initial checks by SCHEV staff, plans are formally submitted for review to the six-person Operating Advisory Committee (OpSix), composed of representatives of the executive branch, the General Assembly and SCHEV.[5] OpSix provides (non-binding) feedback on the plans. After OpSix provides feedback on the initiatives, the Governor, the Senate and the House of Delegates independently determine which initiatives they wish to (and can) fund.

Box 6.4. Institutional six-year plans in Virginia: The example of George Mason University (GMU)

Adopted every two years, in each odd-numbered year, at the time of writing, institutions are preparing revised plans for the biennium 2020-22. Alongside information on planned tuition and fees, financial aid and capital investment, institutions submit detailed descriptions of strategies ("initiatives") that contribute to state-wide goals, each costed, with an indication of institutional investment and incremental funding requirement from the state. The initiatives – and thus funding requests to the state – are prioritised then by the Operating Advisory Committee (OpSix).

As an illustration, in its current six-year plan (GMU, 2018[80]), George Mason University, a large doctoral university in Northern Virginia, which has expanded rapidly in recent years, identifies 12 institutional initiatives, of which the top 6 prioritised for 2018-20 were:

1. Provide **affordable access for all students**: Increase student financial aid for both undergraduate and graduate students.
2. **Enrolment growth and degree awards** for Virginia undergraduate and graduate residents.
3. **Student success initiatives** – student experience redesign: Focus on the integration of technologies used by students, faculty and advisors to improve student success.
4. **New and enhanced programs**: New vision for undergraduate education – Mason impact and enhance current programs.
5. **Online Degrees**: Provide some of GMU's leading programs online through the Online Virginia Network partnership.
6. **Accessible Pathways**: Partnering with Northern Virginia Community College (NOVA) to create a two-to-four year transfer model.

Source: Based on information from SCHEV and GMU (2018[80]).

The six-year institutional planning process appears to be an effective way to ensure the engagement of public higher education institutions with the goals of the *Virginia Plan for Higher Education*, as well as for Virginia's public authorities to steer institutional strategy. The development of plans within institutions and subsequent feedback processes from SCHEV and OpSix create space for dialogue and development of a shared understanding of how the state's goals – including those related to workforce alignment – might be achieved. Experience from other advanced higher education systems with institutional performance agreements, such as Denmark, the Netherlands, Ireland or Ontario (Canada), suggests that the planning process itself and related dialogue between institutions and authorities create considerable added value, even before any results of the planning process and implementation are achieved. The data submitted by institutions in their plans is also used by SCHEV to inform its budget planning. The ability for authorities to interact with and influence institutions is a valuable feature of the governance system for higher education in Virginia, where public institutions are considerably more autonomous than their counterparts in US states with centralised governing boards.

While the institutional planning process is positive and appears to be widely accepted by public institutions in Virginia, two main weakness emerge from discussions with stakeholders and reviews conducted within the state. First, limits on state funding mean many institutional initiatives proposed in the plans do not receive additional state funding in practice – thus limiting the scope and potential impact of proposed actions and the incentives provided to institutions to commit to state goals (see Section 6.3). Second, the OECD understands that there is no systematic follow-up of implementation of the initiatives in the state plans beyond self-reporting by institutions in the subsequent planning round. This lack of systematic follow-up is, at least in part, due to limited capacity and resources within SCHEV to evaluate the implementation of institutional initiatives or co-ordinate external evaluations.

Institutional Performance Standards are a way to focus institutional efforts on workforce issues, but current targets could be pushed further and linked funding is limited

The institutional six-year plans are complemented by Institutional Performance Standards (IPS), which include six general education-related performance measures, as well as financial and administrative standards that apply to all public higher education institutions. The education-related performance measures establish standard institutional targets for enrolment, total degree awards, degree awards in STEM-H, awards to under-represented groups and two-year to four-year transfers (Box 6.5). These targets relate directly to identified needs to expand graduate numbers, increase the supply of graduates in STEM-H fields and improve performance among under-represented groups. Institutional performance against the measures is assessed annually by SCHEV to certify institutional performance.

Institutions that meet the established performance standards (financial and administrative compliance and education targets) have been eligible to receive additional funding in some, but not all, budgetary periods. While no funding for performance-related funding of this kind was made available in the last biennium (2015-18), the General Assembly did approve a budget for the current biennium, albeit one limited to a total of USD 13 million for all public institutions in the Commonwealth.

While reports by SCHEV (SCHEV, 2018[81]) highlight that some institutions have failed to meet individual Institutional Performance Standards, whether in terms of administrative and financial compliance or educational performance, such cases appear to be rare. In the current biennium, all institutions were eligible for the award of financial benefits for the financial year 2018 and it is understood that all institutions have been certified as eligible for benefits for 2019 and 2020. If the purpose of the Institutional Performance Standards is indeed to ensure compliance with basic standards, then the current system may adequately fulfil this role. However, if the ambition is to use the system of performance standards to "push" institutions and incentivise even greater efforts to meeting Virginia's labour market needs, then more ambitious targets, even more tailored to the contexts of individual institutions, and a greater allocation of public funding may be required.

Box 6.5. Educational Institutional Performance Standards for public higher education institutions in Virginia

Introduced in the 2005 Restructuring Act and assessed by SCHEV every two years, the institutional performance standards are:

1. Headcount: Institution meets at least 95% of its State Council-approved biennial projections for **in-state undergraduate headcount** enrolment.
2. Degree awards: Institution meets at least 95% of its State Council-approved biennial projections for the number of **in-state associate and bachelor degree awards**.
3. STEM-H degree awards: Institution meets at least 95% of its State Council-approved biennial projections for the number of **in-state STEM-H** (science, technology, engineering, mathematics and health professions) **associate's and bachelor's degree awards**.
4. Progression and retention: Institution meets at least 95% of its State Council-approved biennial projections for the number of in-state, upper level - sophomore level for two-year institutions and junior and senior level for four-year institutions - **program-placed** [enrolled], full-time equivalent students.
5. Degrees for under-represented students: Maintain or increase the number of in-state associate's and bachelor's degrees awarded to students from **under-represented populations**.
6. Two-year transfers: Maintain or increase the number of in-state **two-year transfers** to four-year institutions.

Source: SCHEV (2018[82]).

The goals and activities of the multiple state agencies involved in workforce development are not fully aligned

While SCHEV co-ordinates Virginia's efforts to develop its higher education system, as in other jurisdictions, a range of other state agencies, often working in partnership with non-government actors, are involved in the broader policy field of workforce development in the Commonwealth. Key among these are the state's Public Employment Service, the Virginia Employment Commission (VEC), which works with a network of regional Local Workforce Development Boards (LWDBs) and local job centres; the Virginia Economic Development Partnership (VEDP), which co-ordinates the state's inward investment strategies; and the newly created state regional development board, operating under the banner of GO Virginia, which co-ordinates the activities of devolved councils in nine regions across Virginia (GO Virginia, 2019[83]).

Each of these bodies, understandably, has their own institutional strategy and perspectives on the question of the alignment between higher education and the labour market. Whereas the VEC and the broader workforce system in Virginia focus, to a large extent, on supporting individuals with comparatively low skills to access relevant training (some post-secondary) and employment, the VEDP has focused on marketing Virginia's highly skilled talent pool in its work. The most striking example of this has been the recent successful bid, led by VEDP, to attract Amazon's second headquarters (HQ2) to Northern Virginia. A core component of the state's offer was the promise to boost Virginia's "tech talent pipeline" with at least 25 000 additional bachelor's and master's graduates over the next 20 years (HQNOVA, 2018[84]). GO Virginia, meanwhile, with its state board and nine regional councils, is seeking to mobilise projects to "foster private-sector growth and job creation through state incentives for regional collaboration by business, education, and government" (GO Virginia, 2019[83]). Each GO Virginia regional council has identified priority industry clusters to support through collaborative initiatives, including in the area of skills and workforce development.

The complex landscape of state bodies with a mandate that encompasses workforce development has resulted from various state and federal policies that have added layers of activity over time. For example, Virginia's public workforce system, although co-ordinated by the Virginia Board of Workforce Development (VBWD), in reality involves eight agencies[6] and 25 funding programmes, many of which are mandated by federal law and governed by federal rules (Virginia Career Works, 2017, p. 4[85]). GO Virginia, with its nine regional councils, is a state initiative, but needs to find its place alongside the existing workforce system bodies, education and training agencies, including SCHEV, and the existing dense network of business associations, such as Chambers of Commerce. While the existence of different bodies with distinct but related missions is positive and, by no means, unique to Virginia, it does create risks related to fragmentation and incoherence in strategies and actions. This can reduce focus on key state targets and create unhelpful confusion about messages and responsibilities for employers, educational providers, students and citizens.

Three potential sources of tension stand out in particular in the strategies and focus of the different agencies responsible for workforce development and higher education in Virginia.

First, while Virginia's overarching goals and the *Virginia Plan for Higher Education* stress the need to focus on developing middle and advanced skills, the public workforce system focuses its activities, to a large extent, on those with low skills. This is important work and understandable given the role of the public employment service in helping those sections of society most in need of support to access work. However, the other main goal of the workforce system is to ensure employers can find the skilled workers they need. While a large proportion of demand is for workers with post-secondary qualifications, the interaction between the workforce system and higher education in Virginia appears relatively limited. In the VBWD's latest strategy document, the Virginia Community College System is mentioned as one of the core agencies in the public workforce system because of its role in certain specific programmes (Virginia Career Works, 2017[85]). SCHEV and the rest of the higher education system are not mentioned, despite the goals of the strategy to identify workforce needs and recommend strategies "to better prepare and match trained workers with available and emerging jobs" (Virginia Career Works, 2017, p. 9[85]). There appears to be scope to align the state's workforce and higher education strategies more clearly.

Second, some stakeholders interviewed during the OECD visit to Virginia argued there is a risk that the state's strategy becomes skewed towards promoting credentials in the field of computer science and related fields, at the expense of other areas of high demand, such as health-related occupations, teaching and skilled trades, or valuable non-technology-related degrees. It is true that the Tech Talent Pipeline Initiative that formed part of Virginia's bid for Amazon's HQ2, and related Tech Talent Investment Fund recently adopted by the General Assembly, have attracted a great deal of attention in the state in the last year. At the centre of this initiative are plans to nearly double the number of bachelor's and master's degrees awarded in computer science and closely related fields in Virginia in the period up to 2039, compared to current graduate trends. This will be supported with targeted funding for institutions across the state and for new master's level campuses in Northern Virginia. It is also true that, even with the arrival of Amazon, computer science will only be one of several important high-demand skills fields in Virginia, and that many employed in tech companies do not require computer science qualifications. However, it would be wrong to claim Virginia is focusing exclusively on tech talent. Other policy initiatives are in place to increase the supply of health-related professionals, teachers and workers with workforce credentials in high-demand fields. It will be important, however, for the Tech Talent Pipeline Initiative to be embedded in a holistic view of the Commonwealth's skills needs, as the *Virginia Plan for Higher Education* is revised.

A final potential source of tension in the strategic planning and co-ordination environment for higher education in Virginia is between the largely state-wide focus of SCHEV and the goals of the *Virginia Plan for Higher Education* and the local and regional focus of the public workforce system, GO Virginia and, to some extent, the VEDP. The *Virginia Plan for Higher Education* does include a focus on under-represented population groups and on regional development, but the measures and targets and annual reporting focus almost exclusively on state-wide averages in enrolment, completion and attainment, rather than providing a more differentiated picture of performance across Virginia's diverse regions. A greater regional focus within the *Virginia Plan* could help strengthen coherence with regional workforce and economic development strategies.

Recommendations for strategic planning and co-ordination

1. Review the system of Institutional Performance Standards to: a) introduce more differentiated goals related to skills development in high-demand fields for individual institutions or groups of institutions; and b) consider level of ambition of targets established to ensure that goals "push" institutions, while remaining realistic. In order to create greater incentives for institutions to work towards the targets established, a high-level of performance funding would be beneficial (see also Section 6.3.4).
2. As part of the process to prepare the revised *Virginia Plan for Higher Education* (2020-26), review (potentially through a temporary joint taskforce co-ordinated by SCHEV) state strategies and work programmes with a direct impact on higher education-labour market alignment; identify potential incoherence and overlap; and agree actions to ensure coherence and complementarity in the future. If necessary, recommendations should be made to the General Assembly to modify legislation governing the mandates and activities of key state agencies. The core objective should be to ensure effectiveness, efficiency and readability for target audiences.
3. Explore ways to strengthen co-operation between SCHEV and the Virginia Board of Workforce Development (and other relevant components of the public workforce system), to ensure better alignment between workforce development policy and higher education policy, in terms of messaging, strategy and activities. Part of this should include co-operation to improve the quality and accessibility of data on labour market skills demand in the Commonwealth (see Section 6.3.5).
4. Policy makers (Legislature, executive, state agencies) should seek to ensure Commonwealth policies on skills and workforce development take a balanced and realistic view of the diversity of demand for post-secondary graduates in light of resources and competing skills needs. This includes paying adequate attention to requirements in fields such as education, healthcare and skilled trades, as well as the unquestionable demand in ICT-related occupations.
5. If resources within SCHEV allow, introduce regional measures linked to the goals of the *Virginia Plan for Higher Education* to help ensure actions address the distinct higher education and labour market challenges of different regions and create better links to state agencies whose activities have a strong territorial dimension.

Student supports and pathways

The educational programmes delivered to students in Virginia's autonomous higher education institutions are primarily the responsibility of institutions and their teaching faculty. Interviews with institutional leaders demonstrated a strong commitment in universities and colleges across the Commonwealth to meeting skills demand and ensuring graduates have relevant skills. This is reflected in numerous institutional initiatives to enhance curriculum design, exploit online learning and offer guidance and co-curricular activities to students, many of which are highlighted in the six-year institutional plans discussed above.

However, as in other jurisdictions, public policies are in place in Virginia that influence the programmes offered by institutions and ensure certain quality standards; that create pathways for students between different types of programme and institution; and that seek to ensure students receive guidance and advice to help them move into and through the post-secondary education system. These policies influence the post-secondary educational offerings available, students' ability to progress and transfer, and the level of support available to students and prospective students, and are all relevant in the Commonwealth's efforts to strengthen alignment between higher education and the labour market.

In the absence of a distinct system of higher vocational education, Virginia's higher education system encompasses a wide range of programme types, from workforce credentials lasting less than one year to doctoral degrees. The remainder of this section reviews the policies affecting the numbers, type and format of educational programme provided by higher education institutions in Virginia, as well as the pathways open to students and the guidance and counselling available to them.

SCHEV considers labour market alignment in its upfront approval process for new programmes, but not in ex-post programme productivity reviews

Although public higher education institutions in Virginia enjoy considerable administrative and operational autonomy, they are required to gain approval from SCHEV to create, discontinue or make substantial amendments to degree-level study programmes. SCHEV has responsibility for approving the creation of new programmes, programme closures and substantive changes to existing programmes in public higher education institutions at the associate's degree level and above. Non-degree programmes, such as workforce certificates, do not fall under the system, but public institutions – in most cases the Virginia Community College System – are required to notify SCHEV of the creation of new programmes at the certificate level.

For entirely new degree programmes, the first professional degrees offered in institutions and all modifications to health-related programmes, SCHEV's academic approval policy requires formal approval by the SCHEV Council. For discontinuance of programmes, mergers, spin-offs and modifications, approval can be given at operational level by SCHEV. A "facilitated approval" system exists for four-year institutions, whereby new programmes can be approved by SCHEV rather than having to go to Council, when the institution's own Board of Visitors has approved the programme in question. The basic criteria and evidence requirements for approval under this theoretically "lighter-touch" process remain the same.

A key objective of the programme approval process is to ensure the efficient use of public resources in public higher education institutions by avoiding a potentially wasteful proliferation of publicly subsidised programmes with low enrolment and high staff costs. Institutions are required to demonstrate that there is adequate student demand for new programmes (to ensure sufficient tuition revenue) and that the programmes are not "unnecessarily duplicative" of other programmes in the state. In addition, SCHEV approval policy calls on institutions to provide evidence of the employment demand for graduates from proposed programmes, with explicit requirements to use the Virginia Employment Commission's annual and ten-year labour market projections and examples of relevant job vacancies in the Commonwealth (Box 6.6).

Box 6.6. SCHEV academic approval: Criteria for justifying new programmes

SCHEV's approval process for new academic programmes (associate's degree and above) requires institutions to provide a detailed description of the proposed programme, an in-depth justification of the need for the new programme, an estimation of projected enrolment and detailed information on the cost implications of the programme (including potential calls on state funding). In their justification of the need for the proposed programmes, institutions must demonstrate:

- how the programme responds to current needs in terms of broad developments in the discipline, societal challenges or economic trends;
- evidence of employment demand, based on state and national labour market demand projections (Virginia Employment Commission and Bureau of Labor Statistics) showing demand for graduates from the programme in directly related or closely related occupations, a minimum of 20 job advertisements in related fields, and testimonials from employers;
- evidence of student demand, based on application data, survey data, or other evidence such as correspondence with prospective students;
- evidence that the programme is not "unnecessarily duplicative" of degree programmes at other institutions in Virginia.

Source: SCHEV (2016[86]).

In addition to its upfront approval process, SCHEV is also tasked with reviewing existing undergraduate and postgraduate programmes in public higher education institutions every five years to ensure they are meeting established standards in terms of "productivity"[7]. This is the other main lever the agency can use to regulate directly the programmes provided in public institutions. Regarding the programme productivity review, the Code of Virginia states that SCHEV is required to:

> *"Review and require the discontinuance of any undergraduate or graduate academic program that is (i) nonproductive in terms of the number of degrees granted, the number of students served by the program, the program's effectiveness, and budgetary considerations or (ii) supported by state funds and unnecessarily duplicative of academic programs offered at other public institutions of higher education." (Code of Virginia, 2019[87])*

In practice, for SCHEV, the process involves checking that programmes are meeting expected quantitative standards in terms of enrolment and degree awards according to an established methodology and, after obtaining the opinion of institutions with programmes that fail to meet the established standards, making recommendations to the SCHEV Council on the continued operation of programmes (SCHEV, 2013[88]). Evidence from past rounds of the productivity review process shows that institutions frequently opt to close programmes with low productivity on SCHEV measures, but in some cases provide justification for the continued operation of programmes on the grounds they are central to institutional missions, recently established or unique to the region where the institution is located. SCHEV reports suggest SCHEV staff usually follow institutional positions in their own recommendations to the SCHEV Council (SCHEV, 2014[89]).

Representatives of public higher education institutions in Virginia view SCHEV's current system of upfront programme-level approval as bureaucratic and burdensome. They argue the procedures limit their flexibility to respond in a timely way to changing skills demand in the labour market, noting that it can take up to two years to gain approval for new programmes. Furthermore, several institutional representatives met by the OECD team argued that SCHEV's previous requirement to provide evidence of real current job postings to demonstrate labour market demand was unrealistic in fields where institutions are seeking to anticipate future demand. In response to these critiques, SCHEV staff point to their statutory role in ensuring the relevance and efficiency of Virginia's public higher education system and recent efforts to streamline the approval process. These efforts have included the "facilitated approval" process and updated policy that allows institutions to demonstrate labour market demand for new programmes through any reasonable means.

A balance needs to be found between SCHEV's legal oversight function and legitimate concern to ensure relevant programmes are provided and state resources are well used, and the desire for institutions to adapt their programme offerings flexibly to changing demand from students and employers. SCHEV's requirement for institutions to demonstrate in advance the relationship between planned programmes and official labour market projections and demonstrated economic trends is entirely sensible (as discussed below, there is a case for improving the quality and visibility of these labour market projections). However, institutions' concerns about the need to show current demand in fast-evolving fields and about the time taken to approve new programmes also appear legitimate. These are factors that will need to be taken into account in refining policy in the short to medium term.

It is notable that the ex-post programme productivity reviews do not use the labour market outcomes experienced by programme graduates as a criterion to identify programmes that are performing poorly[8]. The language in the Code of Virginia relating to SCHEV's duties in terms of productivity review, cited above, refers to "program effectiveness" as one of the criteria for discontinuing a programme. While the current SCHEV policy for productivity review focuses on enrolment and graduate data, this language in the legal basis would appear to leave scope for the inclusion of other effectiveness criteria – such as graduate labour market outcomes – in the periodic review. As suggested in the recommendations below, it may be possible to adjust the current balance between upfront and ex-post regulation of programme provision.

Institutional accreditation standards used in Virginia pay no attention to labour market issues, but are outside the direct control of Virginia's law makers

Before turning to other policies that Virginia can and does use to steer the post-secondary educational offerings in the Commonwealth, it is worth noting a relevant policy area where state authorities have little or no real power. In contrast to a majority of national higher education systems in OECD countries, US states have no direct responsibility for the design or implementation of external quality assurance and accreditation systems in higher education. Instead, a general requirement for external accreditation has been mandated by the federal government for institutions receiving federal student aid and implementation of such external accreditation is delegated to regional or sectoral accreditation bodies. As such, the system is effectively a form of self-regulation. Public and private not-for-profit higher education institutions in Virginia are generally accredited by the regional accreditor for the southern states, the Southern Association of Colleges and Schools Commission on Colleges (SACSCOC).

The institutional accreditation standards and processes used by SACSCOC verify a wide range of institutional characteristics and policies, and provide a basic guarantee of academic quality (SACSCOC, 2018[90]). However, the institutional standards make no explicit reference to institutional policies and practices to align skills development with labour market needs and do not examine the real-world labour market outcomes of graduates. Institutional reaffirmation of accreditation is infrequent (every ten years) and although institutions are required to seek approval for "substantive changes" to programmes, the relevant procedures do not take into account labour market relevance of the programmes in question.

Virginia has also used targeted funding to expand provision of non-degree workforce credentials and promote work-based learning in programmes

In addition to their role in programme approval and monitoring, public authorities in Virginia have used two other main policy levers to influence the scale and form of post-secondary educational provision in public institutions. First, as discussed in the previous section, the state-wide and institutional planning process has included efforts to increase degree awards in fields with high labour market demand, including in STEM-H fields. Second, the Commonwealth has used targeted funding programmes to promote certain types of provision designed to equip graduates with labour market-relevant skills. In this latter category, two initiatives stand out in particular: the New Economy Workforce Credential Grant Program and the Commonwealth Innovative Internship Program.

Box 6.7. The New Economy Workforce Credential Grant

In 2016, the General Assembly approved the establishment of the New Economy Workforce Grant Program, as a way to support more Virginians to complete workforce training that leads to a credential (typically a certificate of less than one year) in a high-demand field. The Program covers training provided in public two-year institutions (VCCS and Richard Bland College). In the VCCS, the Grant Program is marketed under the banner of "FastForward". The grant system uses the following performance-based model:

1. Students (who must be Virginia residents) are required to pay one-third of the total cost of the programme upon enrolment, but may use third-party funds, such as non-credit financial aid, training vouchers or employer payment to cover this cost.
2. If the student completes the training, the state provides one-third of the cost of the programme, up to USD 1 500 to institution. If the student does not complete the programme, then the student is required to pay this portion of the total cost.
3. If the student satisfactorily completes the workforce credential after completing the training, the institution receives the remaining one-third of the cost of the programme up to USD 1 500. The combined maximum award to an institution is USD 3 000 for completion of training and a credential.

The General Assembly allocated USD 5 million in 2017, USD 7.5 million 2018 and USD 9.5 million annually for 2019 and 2020. Funds are awarded to institutions on a first-come, first-served basis.

"High-demand fields" are identified in the Virginia Employment Commission's labour market projections and eligible credentials include those related to occupations in transport and material moving (including Commercial Driver's License – CDL), healthcare support, production (including welding and mechatronics), skilled trades and ICT-related professions (such as CISCO networking technician and associate or information systems security project management professional).

SCHEV is responsible for administering the programme, conducting periodic assessments of its performance, collecting student data, and making final decisions on disputes between eligible institutions and grant recipients.

Sources: SCHEV (2019[91]), SCHEV (2019[92]), VCCS (2017[93]).

The Workforce Credential Grant, approved by the General Assembly in 2016, provides funding to public two-year institutions to allow them to offer low-cost opportunities for students to receive training in a high-demand field and obtain an industry-based certification. The state covers up to two-thirds of the cost of the programme, provided the student completes the training and successfully obtains the credential (see Box 6.7 above). As noted in the previous section, the *Virginia Plan for Higher Education* aims for 10% of the working-age population in the state to have a workforce credential by 2030 to complement the targeted 60% with a degree. Moreover, individuals undertaking workforce credential programmes – as opposed to degree programmes at associate's level and above – are not eligible for federal Pell Grants, meaning immediate financial support for gaining these types of credential was limited. As such, the programme seeks both to contribute to the state attainment goal and fill a gap in existing student aid mechanisms.

In 2018, 3 700 individuals enrolled in training under the programme and 2 518 gained a credential, with the largest numbers of awards in the fields of commercial driver's licenses, training related to highway construction, welding and medical care. The average age of students was 35. 92% of students completed their training and 73% obtained a credential. In 2018, SCHEV reports that the average cost to students participating in the program was USD 904, although this does not take account of third-party financial aid received. The average cost to the state of Virginia per credential attained was USD 2 004. Through analysis based on Virginia Longitudinal Data System data for the first student cohorts, SCHEV calculates that individuals who were earning less than USD 20 000 a year before enrolment earned 71% more on completion of the training and 138% more on completion of a credential (SCHEV, 2019[92]). As a result of this success, SCHEV recommended an annual budget increase to USD 13.5 million for 2020.

Alongside the focus on promoting workforce credentials, Virginian authorities have recently introduced a programme to tackle another acknowledged weakness of the current post-secondary education system: a lack of work-based learning opportunities (internships or other forms of practical experience) in degree programmes. Established in 2018, the Innovative Internship Fund and Program aim to expand paid or credit-bearing student internships and other work-based learning opportunities in collaboration with Virginia employers. The programme funds public higher education institutions through a competitive process to develop partnerships with business and the public sector to provide paid internship opportunities for students, and supports a state-wide initiative to improve the "readiness" of students, employers and higher education institutions to participate in internships and other work-based learning opportunities. Building on a successful pilot in 2019 involving Northern Virginia Community College (NOVA) and chipmaker Micron in Northern Virginia, the programme is currently in its second round of implementation.

In the second round of funding, SCHEV received 15 applications requesting slightly more than USD 1 million and awarded nearly USD 330 000 to five universities and colleges by a panel of workforce experts appointed by SCHEV (SCHEV, 2019, p. 245[94]).

Virginia is making efforts to improve pathways between levels of education, although challenges remain

Virginia, like other states, has promoted alternative educational pathways to give students – particularly adult learners and those from under-represented groups – a wider range of options to obtain a bachelor's degree. Two long-established mechanisms, both of which are distinctive features of American higher education in comparison to other OECD systems – are dual enrolment programmes, involving co-operation between high schools and community colleges, and two-year transfer programmes in community colleges, which can allow students to move into the third year of a bachelor's programme at four-year institutions with which transfer agreements exist. In addition to these established pathways, the proliferation of workforce credentials and industry certificates has increased focus on how skills gained in these short programmes can be bundled together and recognised as counting towards credit in high-level qualifications such as applied associate's degrees.

Dual enrolment involves students taking high school courses and community college-level courses in parallel with the expectation that the credits gained will count towards an associate's degree at a community college or a bachelor's degree at a four-year college. A key objective for students is that they save time, and thus money, in gaining a post-secondary qualification. A 2017 report by Virginia's Joint Legislative Audit and Review Commission (JLARC) found that although dual enrolment students who enrol in community college after high school take about one semester less, on average, to earn a post-secondary credential than non-dual enrolment students, most dual enrolment students who transitioned to four-year colleges did not save time (JLARC, 2017[56]). This is most often because credits gained through dual enrolment courses, which are primarily taught in high schools, were not considered of adequate quality to be accepted as transfer credits in four-year colleges. In response to the recommendations of the JLARC report, VCCS reformed the way it oversees dual enrolment programmes and improved information for students on the transferability of dual enrolment courses to community colleges and four-year institutions (JLARC, 2019[95]).

Students entering community college with the aim of reducing the cost of obtaining a bachelor's degree through taking a transfer-oriented associate's degree programme before transitioning into the third year of a bachelor's programme in a four-year college have faced similar problems. Most transfer students who do go on to earn a bachelor's degree – many do not – take longer and earn more (unnecessary) credits than their counterparts who start college in a four-year institution (JLARC, 2017[56]). In its analysis in 2017, JLARC highlighted the large number of transfer agreements between individual community colleges and four-year public institutions, which makes it hard for students to navigate the system and, in particular, to ensure they choose study options in community college that will be accepted for credit accumulation by four-year institutions.

State authorities, including SCHEV, have primarily sought to encourage institutions to facilitate transfer between two-year and four-year colleges through the six-year planning system and Institutional Performance Standards (with one of the targets focusing on transfer). Legislation passed by the General Assembly in 2018 also requires four-year institutions to develop "transfer maps" to improve the legibility of transfer pathways for students (JLARC, 2019[95]). The "Transfer Virginia" initiative, recently launched by the Virginia Community College System aims to simplify the transfer process with clearer pathways and more systematic guidance to students about the study options they should select in order to transition smoothly to specific majors in four-year institutions (VCCS, 2019[96]).

Ultimately, it is entirely legitimate that decisions on whether or not student credits gained in one programme can be accepted towards a credential in second programme rest with academic faculty responsible for ensuring the coherence and quality of the second programme. There is thus a tension between maintaining standards and facilitating student transfer. Recognition of credits and prior learning is a challenge in higher education systems in many OECD member countries. The measures underway in Virginia to create fewer, more coherent pathways, ensure adequate co-operation between staff in two- and four-year institutions, and improve advising and support to students in their study choices are appropriate ways to increase the likelihood of students being able to transfer smoothly.

It is harder to obtain a clear picture of the broader question of the "stackability" of non-credit programmes and credentials, owing to the vast number of industry certifications and other learning elements that could theoretically be combined in a single credential such as a certificate. Ensuring the quality of the different elements and that the combined credential constitutes a meaningful and coherent whole that can be understood and accepted by employers are key challenges. Nevertheless, representatives of community colleges in Virginia told the OECD team that industry credentials are increasingly being embedded in longer programmes (two-year certificates or applied associate's degrees, for example) to provide students with highly relevant qualifications in a combined package.

Guidance and advising services for students in Virginia are often inadequate for the Commonwealth's increasingly diverse student population

Guidance and counselling to help students choose the right study options for them and to cope with entering and completing higher education are an important component in effective and inclusive higher education systems. While the availability of advising services is important for all students, it is particularly relevant for supporting students who are from low-income backgrounds or the first in their family to attend higher education, as well as for older and part-time students, who may be returning to college after time in the workforce. Experience from Virginia and elsewhere shows these groups are most at risk of dropping out of post-secondary education before completing their training and acquiring a credential (JLARC, 2017[56]). If students receive appropriate advice when they are choosing what to study, it is likely to increase their chances of selecting study options that fit well with their capabilities and interests and which they are more likely to complete. Early intervention by career and study counsellors can also help students select study options that lead to good career options, thus benefitting the prospective student and the economy.

Different analyses in Virginia, as well as the OECD team's discussions with stakeholders in Virginia, suggest the number of counsellors per student in both the secondary and post-secondary educational systems is low (SCHEV, 2019[46]). This limits the capacity of existing counsellors to provide high-quality services to help guide students into appropriate higher education options and provide ongoing support within higher education. The OECD does not have access to data on the number of counsellors in secondary education in Virginia (whether dedicated support staff or teaching staff with an advising role). However, at post-secondary level, JLARC reported in 2017 that within Virginia's community colleges, the median number of students to faculty advisers was 55 and the number of students to non-faculty advisers (full-time equivalent) was 250. In three colleges, there were more than 500 students per non-faculty adviser (JLARC, 2017[56]). Given the student profile within community colleges, where there are many first-time, older and low-income students, this level of advising capacity is almost certainly inadequate.

In part as a response to the challenges highlighted by JLARC, VCCS has developed a system-wide policy to identify at-risk community college students who should receive proactive, customised advising services. New students who are identified as being at risk for not completing a credential or degree are now invited to attend orientation before enrolling in courses and to complete a student development course during their first semester. VCCS is also implementing a Navigate software tool – based on national system called iPASS – at each community college to guide students through the "on-boarding", academic planning, and advising processes (JLARC, 2019[95]). Another VCCS initiative – the Great Expectations programme – provides dedicated coaching to students who have experienced foster care as they enter and progress through the community college system (VCCS, n.d.[97]).

Despite these initiatives, the fundamental resourcing challenge for advising services has only partially been tackled. In 2019, JLARC noted that although the General Assembly appropriated USD 5.5 million in the 2019 session to VCCS for general operating support, it did not earmark any funding specifically to expand academic advising capacity (JLARC, 2019[95]).

Recommendations on programmes, pathways and guidance

1. Take steps to simplify and accelerate the initial (ex-ante) programme approval processes used by SCHEV, while introducing stronger monitoring of student and graduate outcomes from approved programmes. One option would be to shift to a system based on "proof of concept", whereby new or substantially reformed programmes are subject to a lighter-touch ex-ante approval process checking alignment with institutional mission and Commonwealth goals, and must then provide evidence of graduation patterns and labour market outcomes after three or five years, depending on programme duration.

   The follow-up of programmes could be integrated into the existing processes for reviewing programme "productivity". This could be done either by interpreting the current language in the Code of Virginia concerning productivity review more broadly, with the concept of "program effectiveness" more explicitly defined to include the labour market performance of graduates; or by revision of the relevant statutes. Programmes with poor outcomes could be discontinued as is currently possible for programmes that do not meet expected productivity targets. Expected outcomes would need to be adapted to the specificities of different programme types, including low earnings in education; higher non-completion in community college programmes and so forth.
2. Through all possible channels, public authorities in Virginia should encourage SACSCOC to include a greater focus on labour market relevance in its accreditation standards and procedures.
3. Continue to use the six-year planning process and related funding (see recommendations on funding) to provide incentives to institutions to implement programmes that embed content and use pedagogical approaches that help students to acquire workforce-relevant skills.
4. Subject to continued positive evaluation of its results, maintain and expand the New Economy Workforce Credential Grant. In public-facing communication, ensure consistency in the branding and description of the programme to provide clear messaging to target populations. This could be through adopting VCCS's FastForward branding for the grant scheme as a whole.
5. Closely evaluate the results of the Innovative Internship Fund and, provided it proves successful, allocate additional resources in future financial years. This initiative appears to respond to a real need to enhance work-based learning opportunities in the Commonwealth, to allow students to gain work-relevant skills.
6. Closely monitor the results achieved by the Transfer Virginia initiative and the lessons learned from other states through involvement of the Aspen Institute. The measures taken to date in Virginia to improve the quality of two-year transfer programmes, particularly by the Virginia Community College System, should lead to enhanced transfer rates and provide four-year institutions with better assurances of graduate quality. If transfer rates do not improve in the next two years, policy makers should remain open to legislative measures.
7. Introduce more explicit requirements for institutional student guidance and success strategies as part of the six-year planning process for institutions and allocate earmarked funding for advising and guidance functions – particularly for the Virginia Community College System.

Funding

In Virginia, as in jurisdictions across the OECD, public funding is arguably the most important tool that law makers and policy makers have at their disposal to help steer and shape the higher education systems under their responsibility. From a labour market alignment perspective – and in Virginia's labour market environment in particular – public funding is necessary to achieve a balance between two main goals. First, the goal of ensuring higher education programmes are of high quality and able to equip students with relevant skills. Second – leaving aside social equity objectives – to ensure higher education is affordable for a sufficient number of citizens to permit an adequate supply of middle and advanced skills for the workforce. Adequate funding (whatever its source) is required to allow institutions to cover the costs of operating high-quality educational programmes, including remuneration of faculty at competitive rates. However, if students are required to cover the full education-related costs of programmes, higher education becomes unaffordable for all but the wealthiest in society.

In Virginia, as in other parts of the United States, public authorities seek to balance this equation by providing operating subsidies to public higher education institutions to allow them to charge lower tuition and fees for in-state students and providing student aid to low and middle-income Virginia residents to further reduce the cost of studying. Student aid provided by the state for Virginian students is in addition to Pell Grants provided by the federal government, which are awarded nationally, using the same criteria for students across the United States. Students from outside Virginia are required to pay the full cost of study in the Commonwealth's public colleges and universities, although they are also eligible for federal student aid. In addition to institutional operating subsidies and student aid, Virginia's law makers have periodically sought to moderate the amount students must pay by placing restrictions on the expenditure of higher education institutions (and thus the costs that must be covered) and on the amount by which institutions can increase the tuition and fees for in-state students (JLARC, 2014[98]).

Achieving the appropriate balance between allowing institutions to obtain the resources they need (as well as determining the level of resources they need) and ensuring affordable higher education for Virginia residents remains one of the key policy challenges in higher education in Virginia.

Basic state operating funding per student has declined, contributing to increased fees and declining affordability in public institutions in Virginia

In a pattern seen in many OECD jurisdictions in recent years, state operating subsidies per student for public higher education institutions in Virginia have declined in real terms in recent years. This trend has been driven by increasing student enrolment, combined with fiscal consolidation in the wake of the 2008-09 financial crisis, which has limited the capacity of Virginia's law makers to maintain spending per student at previous levels.

Figure 6.17. Average funding per FTE student at four-year institutions for education and general programmes, 1992/93 to 2019/20

In 2020 USD (adjusted for inflation)

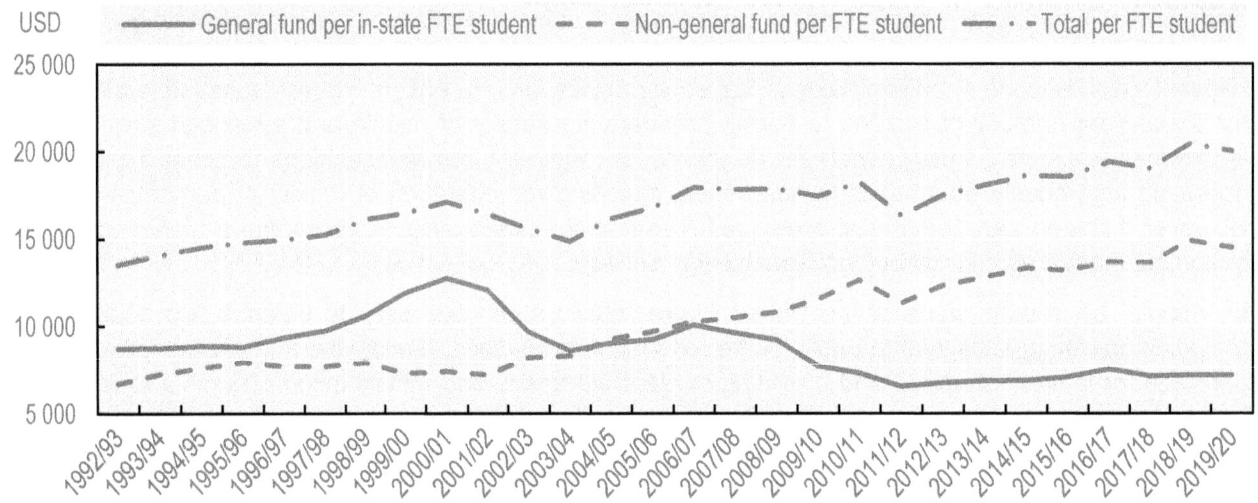

Source: SCHEV (2019[36]), *Higher Ed Data Dashboard*, http://research.schev.edu/fair/strategicplan3.asp.

StatLink https://doi.org/10.1787/888934134312

As illustrated in Figure 6.17, SCHEV calculates that the average state subsidy (General Fund appropriation) per full-time equivalent (FTE) student in public four-year institutions for the 2020 financial year is 41% below its peak in 2001 in constant dollars, despite recent increases in the General Fund subsidies for institutional operating budgets.[9] Data from the national association of State Higher Education Executive Officers (SHEEO) for 2018 place Virginia just 39th of the 50 states in the nation in terms of total state appropriations (of all types, including student aid) to public two-year and four-year higher education institutions. The average appropriation per student in Virginia is USD 5 701, compared to the US average of USD 7 853 (SHEEO, 2019[73]).

In parallel, revenue from tuition and mandatory fees (non-General Fund revenue) has more than doubled in real terms in the last 20 years, with an average annual increase of over 4% in the period between 1993 and 2020. As a result, total funding per FTE student for educational and general activities in four-year institutions has increased by 50% in constant US dollars since the early 1990s.

Box 6.8. State funding for public higher education institutions in Virginia

Different tools, guidelines and processes inform decisions about the level of state subsidies provided to public higher education institutions in Virginia. In practice, the actual level of funding awarded to institutions is always a political decision by the Governor and General Assembly.

- SCHEV calculates the **assumed cost** of operating different types of educational programmes in public higher education institutions using a "**base adequacy model**". This model uses national data on spending levels and pre-determined student-faculty ratios by academic disciplines and level of instruction to provide an estimate of the "education and general" (E&G) operating costs required by each institution. E&G operating costs include faculty and staff compensation, instructional materials and equipment, a basic allocation for research, student and institutional support services, and operations and maintenance of facilities. The model is used purely to calculate resource needs, without consideration of where these resources should come from. The model is widely accepted as providing a transparent and objective means to estimate and benchmark operating costs, although it has been criticised for using outdated salary data and assumptions (JLARC, 2014[98]).
- Since 2004, Virginia has had a **cost-share goal**, according to which the state should aim to meet two-thirds of the cost of education for in-state students, with students responsible for covering the remaining one-third, theoretically from the federally mandated Expected Family Contribution (which may be zero) and federal and state student aid. Cost of education includes core educational services, but excludes mandatory fees for non-educational services and room and board, which represent additional costs of attendance for students. The actual level of funding provided is routinely benchmarked against this target (which has not been met in recent years).
- Taking into account the results of the base adequacy model and the cost-share goal, as well as the availability of public funds, SCHEV makes **budget and policy recommendations** to the Governor and General Assembly each financial year. These recommendations propose budget changes for institutional operating costs (education and general programmes), state student aid and targeted initiatives (SCHEV, 2018[99]). The state's Governor and Legislature are free to accept, reject or amend SCHEV's recommendations. No policy or mechanism current exists to increase institutional operating funds consistently in line with inflation and student enrolment.

Sources: JLARC (2014[100]), SCHEV (2018[99]).

One of the key reasons for the decline in state operating funding is that resources are allocated by the General Assembly through the annual budget process primarily on an incremental basis, rather than through a funding formula that takes into account enrolment or increases in the general cost of living. As highlighted in Box 6.8, Virginia does have in place a sophisticated model for estimating the operating costs of education programmes in its public institutions in light of enrolment numbers. Combined with an aspirational goal that the state should fund two-thirds of the cost of education for in-state students, this model provides a basis for calculating the "desirable" level of state subsidy for each public institution. In practice, however, this level of subsidy has only rarely been achieved since the early 1990s. In the academic year 2019/20, state operating subsidies covered 48% of the cost of education for in-state students – 19 percentage points below the legal target.

As Box 6.8 shows, the corollary of declining state operating subsidies has been increasing student tuition and mandatory education and general fees. Average annual tuition and mandatory education and general fees for in-state students in public four-year institutions in Virginia in 2019/20 were USD 9 274 (on top of which came average mandatory non-E&G fees of USD 4 425 and average room and board of USD 11 000, making a total of USD 24 699). Total average annual fees in public two-year colleges in 2019/20 were USD 4 620. SCHEV estimates that Virginia's doctoral universities (William & Mary, George Mason University, Old Dominion University, University of Virginia, Virginia Commonwealth University and Virginia Tech) had the 7th highest in-state fees in public institutions of the 50 states. Comprehensive universities (such as Norfolk State University) were the fourth most expensive and public two-year institutions were eighth most expensive among their peers across the nation (SCHEV, 2019[71]).

As a rule, Virginia's autonomous higher education institutions have considerable freedom to increase fees as they please, despite their public commitment to promoting affordability (see Section 6.3.1). Virginia is one of only eight states whose co-ordinating board has no direct budget authority. SCHEV reviews and makes recommendations about each institution's budget, but is not authorised to modify institutional budget requests (JLARC, 2014, p. 13[98]). Nevertheless, over the years, Virginia has introduced legislation to encourage public institutions to limit their fee increases. After a number of years of large fee increases, the 2019 General Assembly provided an additional USD 52.5 million in state support to establish the "tuition moderation fund" for public higher education institutions where affordability is a concern. In exchange, public institutions were required to maintain their 2019/20 tuition for in-state undergraduate students at their 2018/19 level. All institutions complied with the requirement (SCHEV, 2019[71]). Virginia's General Assembly had already introduced an annual cap on increases in non-educational mandatory fees (a large proportion of which contribute to inter-collegiate athletics), which have seen very high rates of growth over the last decade. Annual increases in these fees in public higher education institutions are limited to 3% by the state budget legislation (Virginia General Assembly, 2019[101]).

Virginia invests a comparatively high level of resources in financial aid for in-state students, although not always in a targeted way

Given the increases in tuition and fees in recent years, as well as the limited scope for reducing these, financial support to students is an important tool with which Virginia seeks to increase the affordability of higher education and support more of its citizens in obtaining credentials relevant to workforce needs. State policies for student aid aim to increase social equity and support the Commonwealth's goals in terms of skills supply.

Virginia has a number of financial aid programmes, of which the Virginia Student Financial Assistance Program (VSFAP) is by far the largest. The VSFAP provides funding to public higher education institutions, which then allocate resources to students, primarily based on financial need and following state-wide guidelines. These guidelines use a specific definition of "financial need"[10] (the cost of tuition and mandatory fees minus the federally regulated Expected Family Contribution[11]) and a "partnership model" under which all students are expected to contribute a proportion of the cost of tuition and mandatory fees (JLARC, 2014[98]). Awards to students vary considerably between institutions, firstly, because of differences in the cost of fees – and thus the "financial need" calculated for students with the same family income – and, secondly, because institutions have flexibility in the way they award aid, provided they stick to the broad state-wide guidelines.

In 2019/20, Virginia allocated almost USD 250 million of public funds to its student financial aid programmes for students in public institutions. A nation-wide comparison of student aid in 2016/17 showed almost 45 % of all enrolled students in the state received some form of state-sponsored financial aid – the 8th highest rate among all 50 states (SCHEV, 2019, p. 82[102]).

The *Virginia Plan for Higher Education* (see Section 6.3) establishes a target on affordability for 2030, whereby students from low- or middle-income families[12] should receive half of the cost of attendance from a combination of the Expected Family Contribution (EFC) and federal and state grants. The expectation in Virginia is that the remaining half of the cost of attendance should come from institutional aid, loans, and income from work and other sources (SCHEV, 2015[103]). However, SCHEV's most recent report on progress towards state goals shows that the state is some way from meeting this target. As show in Figure 6.18, in 2016/17, federal and state aid, in combination with the EFC, met only one-third of the cost of attendance for low-income students at public four-year institutions in Virginia, and under 40% of the cost of attendance at two-year institutions. The level of coverage of the cost of attendance for middle-income students was slightly higher owing, primarily, to the higher expected family contribution.

Figure 6.18. Student aid and expected family contribution vs. cost of attendance, 2016/17

Average level of unmet financial need for low- and middle-income students in two- and four-year public institutions

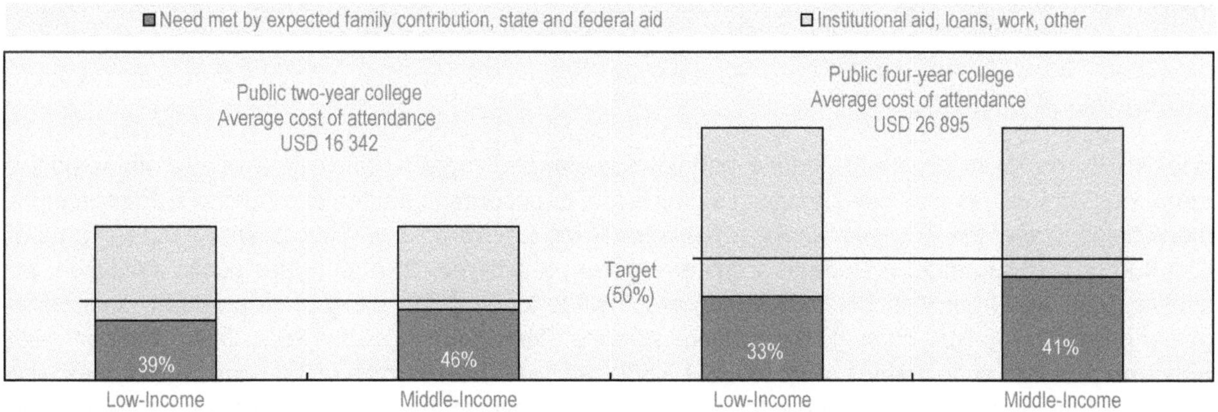

Notes: *Low-income students have household incomes less than 200% of the federal poverty level (below around USD 50 000 per year for a family of four); middle-income students have household incomes of 200-400% of the federal poverty level (between USD 50 000 and USD 100 000). **The average cost of attendance for two-year and four-year public institutions is based on data reported by institutions to the federal government's Federal Student Aid office, using nationally defined standards. The cost of attendance includes tuition and fees; on-campus room and board (or a housing and food allowance for off-campus students); and allowances for books, supplies, transportation, loan fees, and, if applicable, dependent care. Lower average fees and the absence of on-campus room and board explain the lower cost of attendance at two-year institutions. ***The average level of unmet need is the proportion of the average cost of attendance left after taking into account the average amount of federal and state financial aid received by low and middle-income students and the average Expected Family Contribution (EFC) set by federal authorities for students from these income groups.

Sources: SCHEV (2019[36]), *Higher Ed Data Dashboard*, http://research.schev.edu/fair/strategicplan3.asp; SCHEV (2019[33]), *The Virginia Plan for Higher Education - Annual Report 2018*, https://www.schev.edu/docs/default-source/virginia-plan/Reports-and-Updates/the-virginia-plan-annual-report-2018.pdf.

StatLink https://doi.org/10.1787/888934134331

Alongside concerns about the inadequacy of state financial aid budgets in light of growing levels of unmet financial need, current resources are not always targeted effectively to students in public institutions with the greatest financial need. Firstly, the model used to allocate VSFAP resources to individual public higher education institutions uses past enrolment data to estimate the proportion of students from different income groups, rather than data on the current cohort. As enrolment among low-income students has expanded, some institutions have found themselves with growing levels of unmet financial need that are not covered by the allocation model. While VSFAP allocations meet 77% of financial need recognised at the University of Virginia (UVA), they meet only 40% or less at six institutions that have a greater percentage of low- and middle-income students: VCU, Norfolk State, ODU, Virginia State, George Mason, and Mary Washington (SCHEV, 2019[104]).

Secondly, institutions often award aid on a first-come, first-served basis, irrespective of income level, meaning some students from relatively high-income backgrounds receive financial aid because they have "financial need" and applied for aid early. In 2017/18, 24% of VSFAP grants awarded in public four-year institutions, totalling almost USD 12 million were awarded to students with family incomes over 400% of the federal poverty level (SCHEV, 2019, p. 183[94]).

In addition to the VSFAP and other smaller appropriations for financial aid to public higher education institutions, Virginia also allocates public resources to support Commonwealth residents studying in the state's private, not-for-profit institutions. The Virginia Tuition Assistance Grant program (TAG) received USD 71 million of public funding in 2019 (SCHEV, 2019, p. 70[102]), accounting for more than one-fifth of total state spending on student aid. However, unlike the VSFAP and the smaller targeted financial aid funds highlighted below, there is no requirement for TAG funds to be allocated based on financial need or criteria related to workforce skills needs. The programme is thus an untargeted subsidy to private higher education providers.

Virginia has also used student financial aid to incentivise study in certain fields to meet labour market demand

In addition to the main Virginia Student Financial Assistance Program, which is a purely needs-based programme, Virginia has also used financial aid as a tool to encourage students to pursue studies in high-demand fields. Under the *Two-year College Transfer Grant*, for example, which provides a top-up grant of USD 1 000 per year to eligible students transferring from a two-year to a four-year public institution, an additional USD 1 000 per year bonus award is provided to students pursuing undergraduate degrees in engineering, mathematics, nursing, teaching or science. The smaller "*Grow Your Own Teacher*" pilot programme provides scholarships of up to USD 7 500 per year to low-income high school graduates who obtain a teaching qualification in a public four-year college, provided they commit to subsequently teach in high-need public schools in the school divisions in which they graduated from high school (Virginia General Assembly, 2019[105]).

Other examples include the New Economy Workforce Credential Grant Program (FastForward programme), discussed earlier, that covers up to two-thirds of the cost of acquiring workforce credentials in high-demand fields. Although this programme is strongly focused on meeting workforce needs in high-demand and shortage fields and is not needs-based, in practice, a majority of students benefitting from the support are from under-represented population groups. Finally, the Cybersecurity Public Service Grant provides state-matched funding towards grants of up to USD 20 000 per year for bachelor students in cybersecurity, without need-related conditions, if matched funding is provided by an employer.

Elements of performance-related funding have been introduced into the state's overall higher education funding model, but the level of resources attached is limited

Core institutional funding to contribute to basic operating costs and grant aid to reduce costs for individual students are the two main pillars of Virginia's higher education funding model. Although some workforce-related targeting has occurred in the student aid budget (as discussed above), most of the funds invested support the more general workforce-relevant objectives of maintaining quality education and increasing access and attainment. However, the Commonwealth has also experimented with performance-related institutional funding, which seeks to reward institutions for particular initiatives or for attaining state goals, including in terms of workforce development.

Across the two and four-year sector, two main performance-related funding mechanisms have been used, both related to the state and institutional planning processes discussed in Section 6.3.1. First, in their six-year plans, public institutions propose institutional initiatives that contribute to state-wide goals and typically request additional state funding each biennium to implement these strategies. Recommendations on which initiatives to fund are made by the state's Operating Advisory Committee (OpSix), taking into account a prioritisation among initiatives made by institutions themselves. Many initiatives, particularly those related to enrolment, completion, enhancement of learning approaches and student advising and counselling services, contribute to the Commonwealth's high-level skills needs. Overall, however, the level of funding awarded under this upfront targeting mechanism is limited: in 2014, it amounted to a total of USD 16.2 million, equating to less than 2% of state operational support to public institutions (JLARC, 2014[98]). As noted in Section 6.3.1, the lack of systematic evaluation of institutional initiatives means the real "performance" of institutions is not verified and the system relies on the stated intentions of institutions.

Virginia has also made a modest level of appropriations conditional on institutions' achievement of the Institutional Performance Standards (IPS), also discussed in Section 6.3.1. The IPS focus on access and completion, but include a specific target to increase the supply of graduates in STEM-H, a key area of labour market demand. However, here again, the level of funding linked to achievement of the targets is modest (USD 7.2 million in total for 2019 and 2020).

In its 2014 analysis of Virginia's higher education funding system, JLARC argued that the limited level of funding attached to institutional initiatives and Institutional Performance Standards reduced the incentives created by these mechanisms, particularly given the significant shortfalls in state core operational funding (JLARC, 2014[98]). However, evidence from elsewhere in the world suggests relatively modest amounts of additional funding can motivate institutions in their behaviours. In the Netherlands, for example, a relatively small amount of institutional funding was made conditional on development of institutional strategies and achievement of national goals including completion rates and time to degree. Here, while use of standard quantitative targets has been contested, university leaders and public officials believe the marginal funding did incentivise change at institutional level (Evaluatiecommissie Prestatiebekostiging Hoger Onderwijs, 2017[106]). In the United States, including Virginia, where public institutions receive a greater proportion of funding from third parties than in largely public systems like the Netherlands, the level of state funding required to create incentive may be larger.

Within the public two-year college sector in Virginia, the Virginia Community College Board has introduced its own system of performance-related funding to allocate 20% of the educational appropriations it receives from the state budget among the 23 colleges in the Virginia Community College System. The system uses measures of course completion, student retention from one year to the next, and credential acquisition to incentivise colleges to support students in progressing efficiently, while recognising the specific mission of community colleges to educate a wide range of student types, including those who are not seeking credentials (VCCS, 2017[107]).

Although institutions are responsible for setting staff compensation, state funding decisions have a major impact on faculty conditions

A last issue related to higher education funding that was frequently raised during the OECD's visit to Virginia is faculty salaries. In order to maintain and expand high-quality educational offerings in certain high-demand fields – and notably those related to computing – Virginia's public higher education institutions need to be able to attract good teaching faculty. In an increasingly tight labour market, this means being able to offer competitive salaries. However, institutions report difficulties in attracting staff because they cannot meet salary expectations and are competing with other institutions across the nation. SCHEV has identified an inability to attract and retain high-calibre faculty as a major risk for the quality of higher education in Virginia and the achievement of skills pipeline ambitions in fields such as ICT (SCHEV, 2018[99]).

The Governor and General Assembly authorised a 3% increase in general fund appropriations for college and university faculty recruitment and retention for 2019, recognising this concern. However, this increase has been applied across all faculty and staff, rather than being targeted specifically to fields where competition for staff is greatest and salaries are highest. With this in mind, and given the constraints on core institutional funding from limited increases in state appropriates and tuition moderation, SCHEV has invited law makers to consider a targeted salaries fund (SCHEV, 2018[99]).

Recommendations on funding higher education

1. Take steps to ensure the level of Commonwealth funding appropriations for higher education are commensurate with the stated political ambitions to increase higher education attainment and moderate tuition costs to meet labour market demand.
2. Use the current review of higher education funding to rethink Virginia's approach to institutional funding. As part of this, adapt the current cost-share policy to a level of state funding for in-state students that is financially more feasible than the current 67% (perhaps 60%); then work progressively to raise institutional core funding to reach this level. Update the existing base adequacy model with recent data on faculty and staff salaries and use this as part of a more transparent institutional funding model to provide increased and more predictable state resources to institutions.
3. Establish a transparent mechanism for estimating projected need for student financial assistance among students (in workforce credentials, two-year and four-year programmes) in each public higher education institution and use this as a basis for allocating general fund resources for student financial aid to institutions. Financial need should be the primary allocation criterion (to help boost overall attainment), with additional awards for low- and middle-income students in high-demand fields (the model used in the Two-year College Transfer Grant). Clear allocation criteria will also be needed to deal with the (very likely) eventuality that available resources are insufficient to meet projected financial need. Policy makers should consider restricting financial aid eligibility to low- and middle-income students to ensure a better targeting of scarce resources.
4. To support Virginia's overall post-secondary attainment targets and goals for specific skills areas, the General Assembly would be wise to allocate additional general fund resources to student financial aid, to be awarded through the revised methodology suggested above.
5. Consider making a proportion of all financial aid allocations to institutions dependent on students successfully gaining a credential following the basic principles used for the New Economy Workforce Credential Grant.
6. Either: a) revise the objectives of the TAG program to define its purpose as an institutional subsidy to private providers; or b) require funds to be awarded on the basis of students' financial need or enrolment in high-demand fields.
7. Complement the core institutional funding with increased initiative-based funding linked to the institutional six-year plans, and revised and differentiated Institutional Performance Standards (see Section 6.3.2). This should be backed up with enhanced resources for SCHEV to allow more systematic monitoring of the implementation of funded initiatives.
8. Establish a targeted fund to support recruitment of faculty for programmes in high-demand fields, in line with SCHEV's budget and policy recommendations for 2020.

Information

Information about the skills requirements of the labour market, now and in the future, helps educational providers plan and adapt their educational offerings and allows policy makers to ensure they have well-targeted policies in place. At the same time, information about the labour market outcomes of past higher education graduates can provide an indication of the labour market demand for graduates from specific programmes or fields. Such information can help students make informed choices about what to study (although does not guarantee that they will make rational choices) and provides an indication to educators, institutions and policy makers of how well programmes prepare graduates for the workforce. As graduates' labour market outcomes also depend on personal choices, economic and labour market conditions, as well as wage levels in specific sectors, care is always needed in interpreting such data.

Virginia has a comprehensive and well-established longitudinal data system for tracking graduate outcomes

Launched in 2012, Virginia's post-secondary longitudinal data system - Virginia Longitudinal Data System (VLDS) - is recognised as one of the most comprehensive in the United States (SCHEV, 2019[108]; SCHEV, 2019[65]). It centralises data on higher education programmes, students and graduates collected from public higher education institutions and private not-for-profit institutions that receive state funding, notably through the Virginia Tuition Assistance Grant program. The VLDS links this information to data on individual earnings collected by the Virginia Employment Commission to produce information on the earnings over time of graduates from Virginia's universities and colleges who go on to work in the state. This comprehensive set of administrative data provides a valuable resource for policy makers seeking to understand the performance of the higher education system as a whole, as well as the outcomes of under-represented populations and other groups of interest. The breadth of SCHEV's data collection, particularly its financial aid data, is greater than that of similar exercises in most other states. A recent analysis of SCHEV's data system found that while other states, such as Colorado and Minnesota, also report graduate wage information, Virginia's data systems were more comprehensive (SCHEV, 2019[108]).

To complement existing data, SCHEV is supporting a survey of graduates from Virginia higher education institutions, co-ordinated by a team at Virginia Commonwealth University. This will obtain more detailed information on graduates' post-graduation employment trajectories and their engagement in "civic life". This survey, the results of which will be available in 2020, is currently designed to be a one-off activity and to contribute to policy making and potential future communication activities (SCHEV, 2019[94]).

Virginia's data on labour market outcomes could be better exploited to provide easy-to-access information for citizens and students

The Commonwealth has a strong post-secondary data system that merges data across several state agencies. However, from a user perspective, the data collected and stored are not exploited to their full potential. One of the stated objectives of the Virginia Longitudinal Data System is to "provide one-stop access to education and workforce data by policy makers, educators, the public, program directors, researchers, etc." (SCHEV, 2019[65]). However, in a recent survey of policy makers in Virginia, two-thirds of respondents said the "user experience" on SCHEV's own data webpages needed to be improved, with the clarity of tables and graphics receiving the lowest ratings among users (SCHEV, 2019[108]).

Moreover, Virginia does not yet have a clearly established information strategy for prospective and current higher education students and their families seeking information about the likely employment implications for choosing different study options. Ordinary users are currently left to find their way between various national and institutional data sources, which use different measures of quality and workforce success, and sometimes provide contradictory information. Moreover, students in Virginia currently lack easily accessible information on the rates of return on investment in different study programmes. Although there are limits to the impact of high-quality information on labour market outcomes, consolidated information on likely future employment prospects should be part of Virginia's future communication and awareness-raising activities.

Students would benefit from access to reliable data about tuition and fees, average debt levels, earnings and employment outcomes in order to increase their awareness of the expected rates of return on post-secondary education (TICAS, 2019[72]). Although SCHEV has begun to generate information about debt-to-earnings ratios and loan default rates at programme level, these data are not currently available to the public. Increased transparency about the expected return on investment for students before entering post-secondary education is critical in order to inform student choice and ensure that a larger proportion of post-secondary graduates have the opportunity to achieve a sustainable wage.

Co-ordination at the state level could be enhanced to facilitate and improve the use of labour market information for strategic planning in higher education

In addition to collecting information on current employment and earnings, the Virginia Employment Commission (VEC) publishes short and long-term labour market projections following the methodology of national projections produced by the U.S. Bureau of Labor Statistics (BLS). These provide current and projected employment numbers by industry and occupation for Virginia and each of the 15 workforce development areas in the state. The long-term projections estimate changes in employment over a ten-year period, including educational and training requirements for entry into each occupation. SCHEV requires higher education institutions to refer to these labour market projections in their justification of new programme proposals (see Section 6.3).

The occupational projections for Virginia are published on the VEC website (VEC, 2019[109]), but are not presented in a user-friendly form for a wider public of educators or policy makers. Moreover, projections of this kind generally make a conservative assessment of the level of educational attainment needed for each occupation, potentially underestimating current and future demand for post-secondary graduates (see also Section 6.2.1). In addition, information about projected employment demand does not appear to be linked to information about projected supply, for example through national or state post-secondary data systems. A relatively simple gap analysis can be done by matching post-secondary records of credential production by field of study to occupational projections in order to indicate future gaps in supply and demand, provided there is agreement on a suitable way to match field of study to occupation (Wilson, 2014[110]).[13] This can provide a point of departure for further analysis, supplemented with both quantitative and qualitative information from employers and other stakeholders, for example by region or within a particular field.

In some states, gap analyses are conducted systematically at the state level, using diverse methodologies. In Washington, for example, a workforce supply and demand analysis is conducted every two years as a joint agency initiative, using both national and state-level data (WSAC, SBCTC and WTECB, 2018[111]; Hershbein and Hollenbeck, 2015[112]). The Virginia Employment Commission is currently developing a methodology for linking the production of credentialed graduates from Virginia's higher education institutions to projected employment demand by occupation, as well as injecting known in-migration patterns by occupation. Supply and demand analyses may also incorporate real-time data from online job advertisements as a basis for assessing demand for skills and qualifications, allowing for more granular information about skills needs. Using real-time labour market information may therefore become increasingly useful for strategic planning and curriculum development in higher education, thereby improving labour market outcomes over time (Dorrer, 2016[113]). In Virginia, a Workforce Supply and Demand Dashboard was launched within the last three years, showing demand for different occupations based on real-time data from job advertisements (using commercial services from Burning Glass Technologies) and supply based on current graduation patterns (Virginia Career Works, 2019[17]). The dashboard tool shows occupations where there is estimated to be undersupply and oversupply in Virginia based on the available data, along with average salary levels in different occupational clusters. The precise methodology underpinning the dashboard is not entirely transparent; in particular, it is not clear to the average user whether it is a dynamic tool with the data constantly updated or an analysis based on a snapshot at a particular point in time. Moreover, it is unclear if the intended users of the dashboard are primarily workforce development boards or if the tool is intended for a broader group of users within both the higher education and workforce development communities.

While many higher education institutions engage directly with employers and conduct their own labour market analyses to understand skills needs and inform programme and curriculum design, they also rely on public workforce data and labour market information. This underlines the importance of ensuring transparent, consistent and easily accessible information about the labour market and state-wide workforce needs. Virginia's workforce data are presented in multiple places with information that is not entirely consistent across sites. Moreover, it is unclear how the Virginia Career Works Supply and Demand Dashboard relates to information provided by the Virginia Employment Commission and the Virginia Workforce Connection, all of which appear to use different sources of data to measure labour supply and demand. Improving the alignment between higher education and the labour market thus requires co-ordination between agencies – and across traditional policy silos – in the interest of ensuring that Virginia's future skills needs are met. A recent SCHEV Council initiative to identify data needs related to workforce supply and demand could be an important step in the right direction in improving the quality and use of labour market information in higher education.

Recommendations on information

1. Build on existing co-operation between state agencies to design and implement a single online information portal connecting higher education and labour market information **for policy makers and educational institutions**. This enterprise could be overseen by a joint taskforce involving SCHEV, VEC, the Virginia Board of Workforce Development and other relevant stakeholders. It is important that the information be presented in an accessible and logical way and that data be downloadable in an easy-to-use format for further analysis. Existing web resources targeting policy makers and educational institutions should be rationalised or removed once the new portal goes live online. The portal should include a state-wide analysis of skill supply and demand. The recommendations of SCHEV's recent report on using data to inform policy (SCHEV, 2019[108]), and recent Council initiatives on higher education and workforce alignment, may provide additional pointers.
2. Develop a user-friendly web-based information tool **for students and citizens** in Virginia to allow them to learn more about skills demand in the labour market and the employment prospects for graduates from different programmes and fields. A tool provided by the state could be marketed as an objective reference point for impartial information, in contrast to many existing information sources. The public-facing information tool should use a limited number of the most important variables. Key variables to date include: a) high-demand occupations; b) earnings prospects by programme of study; and c) observed rates of return (based on costs of attendance and average earnings and debt levels). International examples that could serve as a source of ideas for different elements of a new informational tool include New Zealand's "Occupation Outlook" (MBIE, 2019[114]), Finland's Occupational Barometer (TEM, 2019[115])and Denmark's comprehensive one-stop portal "The Education Guide" (UVM, 2019[116]).

References

Abraham, K. and M. Kearney (2019), "Explaining the Decline in the U.S. Employment-to-Population Ratio: a Review of the Evidence", *NBER Working Paper No. 24333*, The National Bureau of Economic Research, https://www.nber.org/papers/w24333. [26]

Altonji, J., L. Kahn and J. Speer (2014), "Trends in Earnings Differentials across College Majors and the Changing Task Composition of Jobs", *American Economic Review*, Vol. 104/5, pp. 387-393, http://dx.doi.org/10.1257/aer.104.5.387. [38]

Autor, D. (2014), "Skills, Education, and the Rise of Earnings Inequality among the Other 99 Percent", *Science*, Vol. 344/6186, pp. 843-851, http://dx.doi.org/10.1126/science.1251868. [21]

Autor, D., F. Levy and R. Murnane (2003), "The Skill Content of Technical Change", *Quarterly Journal of Economics*, https://economics.mit.edu/files/11574. [18]

Bahr, P. (2019), "The Labor Market Returns to a Community College Education for Noncompleting Students", *The Journal of Higher Education*, Vol. 90/2, pp. 210-243, http://dx.doi.org/10.1080/00221546.2018.1486656. [59]

Baum, S. (2014), *Higher Education Earnings Premium: Value, Variation, and Trends*, Urban Institute, https://files.eric.ed.gov/fulltext/ED544781.pdf (accessed on 20 May 2019). [64]

Belfield, C. and T. Bailey (2017), "The Labor Market Returns to Sub-Baccalaureate College: A Review", *CAPSEE Working Paper*, Center for analysis of postsecondary education and employment, https://ccrc.tc.columbia.edu/media/k2/attachments/labor-market-returns-sub-baccalaureate-college-review.pdf. [58]

Carnevale, A., B. Cheah and J. Strohl (2012), *Hard Times: College Majors, Unemployment and Earnings: Not All College Degrees Are Created Equal*, Georgetown University, https://repository.library.georgetown.edu/bitstream/handle/10822/559308/Unemployment.Final.update1.pdf?sequence=1&isAllowed=y (accessed on 20 May 2019). [66]

Carnevale, A. et al. (2017), *Major Matters Most. The Economic Value of Bachelor's Degrees from The University of Texas System*, Georgetown University, https://vtechworks.lib.vt.edu/bitstream/handle/10919/86951/UTSystemMajorsMatter.pdf?sequence=1&isAllowed=y (accessed on 20 May 2019). [67]

Carnevale, A., S. Rose and B. Cheah (2013), *The College Payoff: Education, Occupation, Lifetime Earnings*, Georgetown University, https://1gyhoq479ufd3yna29x7ubjn-wpengine.netdna-ssl.com/wp-content/uploads/collegepayoff-completed.pdf (accessed on 20 May 2019). [76]

Carnevale, A. and N. Smith (2012), *A Decade Behind: Breaking out of the Low-Skill Trap in the Southern Economy*, https://1gyhoq479ufd3yna29x7ubjn-wpengine.netdna-ssl.com/wp-content/uploads/2014/11/DecadeBehind.FullReport.073112.pdf. [42]

Carnevale, A., N. Smith and J. Strohl (2013), *Recovery: Job Growth and Education Requirements through 2020*, Georgetown University Center on Education and the Workforce, Washington, DC, https://1gyhoq479ufd3yna29x7ubjn-wpengine.netdna-ssl.com/wp-content/uploads/2014/11/Recovery2020.FR_.Web_.pdf (accessed on 10 May 2019). [37]

Carnevale, A., J. Strohl and N. Ridley (2017), *Good Jobs That Pay Without a BA: A State-by-State Analysis*, https://1gyhoq479ufd3yna29x7ubjn-wpengine.netdna-ssl.com/wp-content/uploads/Good-Jobs-States.pdf. [44]

CNBC (2019), *America's Top States for Business in 2019*, https://www.cnbc.com/2019/07/10/americas-top-states-for-business-2019.html (accessed on 2 August 2019). [5]

Code of Virginia (2019), *§ 23.1-203. Duties of Council*, Code of Virginia, https://law.lis.virginia.gov/vacode/title23.1/chapter2/section23.1-203/ (accessed on 21 September 2019). [87]

Deming, D. and L. Kahn (2018), *Skill Requirements across Firms and Labor Markets: Evidence from Job Postings for Professionals*, University of Chicago, https://www.journals.uchicago.edu/doi/pdfplus/10.1086/694106 (accessed on 16 May 2019). [39]

Dorrer, J. (2016), "Using real-time labor market information to achieve better labor market outcomes", *Lumina Issue Papers*, Lumina Foundation, https://www.luminafoundation.org/files/resources/using-real-time-labor-market-information-full.pdf. [113]

Emsi (2018), *Virginia: Economy Overview*, http://www.economicmodeling.com. [15]

Evaluatiecommissie Prestatiebekostiging Hoger Onderwijs (2017), *Van afvinken naar aanvonken - Rapport over de evaluatie van de prestatiebekostiging hoger onderwijs (Report on the evaluation of the higher education performance-based funding)*, Evaluatiecommissie Prestatiebekostiging Hoger Onderwijs (Evaluation committee on higher education performance funding), https://www.rijksoverheid.nl/documenten/rapporten/2017/03/20/van-afvinken-naar-aanvonken (accessed on 13 March 2020). [106]

Frey, C. and M. Osborne (2017), "The future of employment: How susceptible are jobs to computerisation?", *Technological Forecasting and Social Change*, Vol. 114, pp. 254-280, http://dx.doi.org/10.1016/J.TECHFORE.2016.08.019. [19]

Gallagher, S. (2018), *Educational Credentials Come of Age: A Survey on the Use and Value of Educational Credentials in Hiring*, Northeastern University, Center for the Future of Higher Education and Talent Strategy, https://www.northeastern.edu/cfhets/wp-content/uploads/2018/12/Educational_Credentials_Come_of_Age_2018.pdf (accessed on 20 July 2019). [55]

Gallup (2016), *The 2015 Gallup-Lumina Foundation Study of the American Public's Opinion on Higher Education*, https://www.gallup.com/services/190583/americans-value-postsecondary-education-report.aspx. [62]

GMU (2018), *George Mason University 2018 Six-year Plan*, George Mason University, Fairfax, https://www.schev.edu/docs/default-source/institution-section/6-year-plans/gmu/2018/gmu-2018-six-year-plan-part-ii.pdf (accessed on 19 September 2019). [80]

GO Virginia (2019), *GO Virginia*, Virginia Initiative for Growth and Opportunity, https://govirginia.org/ (accessed on 20 September 2019). [83]

Goldman, C. et al. (2015), *Using Workforce Information for Degree Program Planning in Texas*, RAND Corporation, https://doi.org/10.7249/RR1011. [117]

Hershbein, B. and K. Hollenbeck (2015), *Refining Workforce Education Supply and Demand Analysis: Final Report*, W.E. Upjohn Institute for Employment Research, https://research.upjohn.org/cgi/viewcontent.cgi?article=1034&context=up_technicalreports. [112]

HQNOVA (2018), *Tech-Talent Pipeline Initiative*, Virginia Economic Development Partnership, Richmond, https://hqnova.com/assets/pdfs/NOVA_Higher-Ed.pdf (accessed on 16 September 2019). [84]

HQNOVA (2017), *Virginia's Amazon Proposal*, https://hqnova.com/info.html#va-proposal (accessed on 14 September 2019). [13]

JLARC (2019), *JLARC Impacts - Actions taken on report recommendations 2015-2018*, Joint Legislative Audit and Review Commission, Richmond, http://jlarc.virginia.gov/pdfs/reports/Rpt517-3.pdf (accessed on 21 September 2019). [95]

JLARC (2017), *Operations and Performance of the Virginia Community College System*, Joint Legislative Audit and Review Commission, Richmond, http://jlarc.virginia.gov (accessed on 2 July 2019). [56]

JLARC (2014), *Addressing the Cost of Public Higher Education in Virginia*, Joint Legislative Audit Review Commission, Richmond, http://jlarc.virginia.gov (accessed on 4 September 2019). [98]

JLARC (2014), *Addressing the Cost of Public Higher Education in Virginia*, Joint Legislative Audit Review Commission, Richmond, http://jlarc.virginia.gov (accessed on 4 September 2019). [100]

Jobs for the Future (2019), *Making Higher Education Policy Work for the Untapped Workforce*, Jobs for the Future, https://www.jff.org/resources/policy-work-untapped-workforce-brief/. [47]

Kim, C., C. Tamborini and A. Sakamoto (2015), "Field of Study in College and Lifetime Earnings in the United States", *Sociology of Education*, Vol. 88/4, pp. 320-339, http://dx.doi.org/10.1177/0038040715602132. [69]

Levesque, E. (2018), *Improving community college completion rates by addressing structural and motivational barriers*, Brown Center on Education Policy, Washington DC, https://www.brookings.edu/research/community-college-completion-rates-structural-and-motivational-barriers/ (accessed on 11 February 2019). [57]

Lumina Foundation (2019), *A Stronger Nation: Virginia Report 2019*, http://blob:http://strongernation.luminafoundation.org/3d08f981-8b2b-4cff-857a-d5fb67b04ec0. [22]

Lumina Foundation (2018), *A Stronger Nation*, https://www.luminafoundation.org/resources/a-stronger-nation-report (accessed on 19 June 2019). [32]

MBIE (2019), *Occupation Outlook*, Ministry of Business, Innovation and Employment, https://occupationoutlook.mbie.govt.nz/ (accessed on 25 September 2019). [114]

MIT (2019), *MIT Living Wage Calculator*, http://livingwage.mit.edu/states/51 (accessed on 10 August 2019). [61]

National Skills Coalition (2017), *Middle Skill Jobs State by State: Virginia's Forgotten Middle*, https://www.nationalskillscoalition.org/resources/publications/2017-middle-skills-fact-sheets/file/Virginia-MiddleSkills.pdf. [43]

National Student Clearinghouse (2019), *Some College, No Degree: A 2019 Snapshot for the Nation and 50 States*, https://nscresearchcenter.org/some-college-no-degree-2019/. [60]

NCES (2019), *Integrated Postsecondary Education Data System (database)*, National Center for Education Statistics, https://nces.ed.gov/ipeds/use-the-data (accessed on 18 January 2020). [34]

Northam Administration (2019), *Establishment of the Virginia STEM Education Commission*, https://www.governor.virginia.gov/media/governorvirginiagov/executive-actions/EO-36-Establishment-of-the-Virginia-Stem-Education-Commission.pdf (accessed on 26 August 2019). [45]

Northam Administration (2018), *A Comprehensive Economic Development Policy for the Commonwealth*, https://www.vus.virginia.gov/media/governorvirginiagov/governor-of-virginia/pdf/A-Comprehensive-Economic-Development-Policy-for-the-Commonwealth.pdf. [3]

OECD (2019), *OECD Skills Outlook 2019 : Thriving in a Digital World*, OECD Publishing, Paris, https://dx.doi.org/10.1787/df80bc12-en. [40]

OECD (2018), *Education at a Glance 2018: OECD Indicators*, OECD Publishing, Paris, https://doi.org/10.1787/eag-2018-en. [23]

Old Dominion University (2018), *2018 State of the Commonwealth Report*, https://www.ceapodu.com/wp-content/uploads/2018/12/2018SOC-Report.pdf. [10]

SACSCOC (2018), *Resource Manual for The Principles of Accreditation: Foundations for Quality Enhancement*, Southern Association of Colleges and Schools Commission on Colleges, Atlanta, http://www.sacscoc.org (accessed on 1 July 2019). [90]

SCHEV (2020), *Colleges and Universities*, https://www.schev.edu/index/students-and-parents/explore/virginia-institutions. [35]

SCHEV (2019), *2019-20 Tuition and Fees: Tuition and Fees at Virginia State-Supported Colleges and Universities*, State Council of Higher Education for Virginia, https://schev.edu/docs/default-source/Reports-and-Studies/Tuition-and-Fees/201920tuitionandfeereportacc.pdf. [71]

SCHEV (2019), *Agenda Book - July 16, 2019*, State Council of Higher Education for Virginia, Richmond, https://www.schev.edu/docs/default-source/about-section/council-files/2019-council-meetings/july-council-files/agenda-book-(for-posting-on-sitefinity).pdf (accessed on 14 September 2019). [102]

SCHEV (2019), *Agenda Book - September 16-17, 2019*, State Council of Higher Education for Virginia, Richmond, https://www.schev.edu/docs/default-source/about-section/council-files/2019-council-meetings/september-2019/rev-agenda-book-pdf-(w-page-numbers-for-posting).pdf (accessed on 21 September 2019). [94]

SCHEV (2019), *Higher Ed Data Dashboard*, https://research.schev.edu/fair/strategicplan3.asp (accessed on 8 April 2020). [36]

SCHEV (2019), *History of the Virginia Longitudinal Data System*, http://research.schev.edu//info/Articles.The-Virginia-Longitudinal-Data-System.ashx (accessed on 20 August 2019). [65]

SCHEV (2019), *Median Graduate Debt, 10 Year Trends*, https://research.schev.edu//studentdebt/DebtProfile_SL021.asp. [75]

SCHEV (2019), *New Economy Workforce Credential Grant*, https://www.schev.edu/index/institutional/grants/workforce-credential-grant (accessed on 21 September 2019). [91]

SCHEV (2019), *Outcomes of Virginia Graduates: An Emerging Picture*, https://www.schev.edu/docs/default-source/about-section/council-files/2019-council-meetings/may-2019/undergrad-outcomes-of-virginia-public-institutions_final_may-19.pdf (accessed on 26 August 2019). [74]

SCHEV (2019), *Restructuring Act of 2005*, https://www.schev.edu/index/institutional/planning-and-performance/restructuring (accessed on 19 September 2019). [79]

SCHEV (2019), *Review of Financial Aid Funding Formulas and Awarding Practices State Council of Higher Education for Virginia*, State Council of Higher Education for Virginia, Richmond, https://www.schev.edu/docs/default-source/Reports-and-Studies/2019/financialaidreport102019.pdf (accessed on 10 November 2019). [104]

SCHEV (2019), *Strategic Plan - Initiatives*, https://www.schev.edu/index/statewide-strategic-plan/initiatives (accessed on 19 September 2019). [78]

SCHEV (2019), *The Cost of Doing Nothing: An Urgent Call to Increase Educational Attainment in the Commonwealth*, State Council of Higher Education for Virginia, Richmond, http://www.schev.edu (accessed on 27 June 2019). [46]

SCHEV (2019), *The New Economy Workforce Credential Grant - Annual Report for 2018*, State Council of Higher Education for Virginia, Richmond, https://www.schev.edu/docs/default-source/Reports-and-Studies/2019/workforcereport2018.pdf (accessed on 21 September 2019). [92]

SCHEV (2019), *The Virginia Plan for Higher Education - Annual Report 2018*, State Council of Higher Education for Virginia, Richmond, https://www.schev.edu/docs/default-source/virginia-plan/Reports-and-Updates/the-virginia-plan-annual-report-2018.pdf (accessed on 27 June 2019). [33]

SCHEV (2019), *Using Data to Inform Policy - Report of Council's Ad Hoc Committee on Data and Policy*, State Council of Higher Education for Virginia, Richmond, https://schev.edu/docs/default-source/Reports-and-Studies/2019/reportadhoccommitteeondataandpolicy.pdf (accessed on 15 September 2019). [108]

SCHEV (2019), *Virginia Longitudinal Data System*, https://vlds.virginia.gov/ (accessed on 1 July 2019). [53]

SCHEV (2018), *Agenda Book - September 17-18, 2018*, State Council of Higher Education for Virginia, Richmond, https://www.schev.edu/docs/default-source/about-section/council-files/2018-council-meetings/september/agenda-book-w-pg-links-(for-posting).pdf (accessed on 19 September 2019). [81]

SCHEV (2018), *FY 2020 Budget and Policy Recommendations for Higher Education in Virginia*, State Council of Higher Education for Virginia, Richmond, https://www.schev.edu/docs/default-source/Reports-and-Studies/2018-reports/fy2020budget-recommendations11918.pdf (accessed on 29 June 2019). [99]

SCHEV (2018), *Resources and Planning Committee #C3-Action on Measures of Institutional Performance - Meeting of September 17, 2018*, State Council of Higher Education for Virginia, Richmond. [82]

SCHEV (2016), *State-Level Requirements for Approval of Various Academic Program Actions at Public Institutions*, State Council of Higher Education for Virginia, Richmond, https://www.schev.edu/docs/default-source/institution-section/GuidancePolicy/academic-approval-policies/2016-academic-approval-policy.pdf (accessed on 1 July 2019). [86]

SCHEV (2015), *The Virginia Plan for Higher Education - Measures and Targets - Additional Information*, State Council of Higher Education for Virginia, Richmond, https://www.schev.edu/docs/default-source/virginia-plan/measuresandtargetsadditionalinformation07212015.pdf (accessed on 23 September 2019). [103]

SCHEV (2014), *Agenda Book - July 21-22, 2014*, State Council of Higher Education for Virginia, Richmond, https://www.schev.edu/docs/default-source/about-section/2014-council-meetings/july2014/072114agendabook.pdf (accessed on 21 September 2019). [89]

SCHEV (2014), *Framework of the Statewide Strategic Plan for Higher Education (As Adopted by the State Council of Higher Education for Virginia on September 16 and October 28)*, https://www.schev.edu/docs/default-source/about-section/council-files/2014-council-meetings/nov2014/framework-statewidestrategicplanforhighered-2014-10-28.pdf (accessed on 30 June 2019). [77]

SCHEV (2013), *Virginia Public Higher Education Policy on Program Productivity*, State Council of Higher Education for Virginia, Richmond, https://www.schev.edu/docs/default-source/institution-section/GuidancePolicy/policies-and-guidelines/programproductivitypolicyrevisedoct2013.pdf (accessed on 21 September 2019). [88]

Schneider, M. (2016), *Degrees of Value: Differences in the Wages of Graduates From Virginia's Colleges and Universities*, American Institutes for Research, Washington, D.C., https://www.air.org/system/files/downloads/report/Differences-in-Wages-Graduates-Virginia-Colleges-Universities-September-2016.pdf (accessed on 1 July 2019). [70]

Schneider, M. (2015), *Higher Education Pays: But a Lot More for Some Graduates Than for Others*, College Measures, https://www.air.org/sites/default/files/Higher_Education_Pays_Sep_13.pdf (accessed on 20 May 2019). [68]

SHEEO (2019), *SHEF: FY 2018 State Higher Education Finance*, State Higher Education Executive Officers Association, http://www.sheeo.org/shef (accessed on 30 July 2019). [73]

TEM (2019), *Ammattibarometri - Occupational Barometer*, Ministry of Economic Affairs and Employment, https://www.ammattibarometri.fi/?kieli=en (accessed on 25 September 2019). [115]

TICAS (2019), *Student Debt and the Class of 2018*, The Institute for College Access and Success, https://ticas.org/interactive-map/. (accessed on 23 October 2019). [72]

TICAS (2018), *Of metrics and markets: Measuring post-college employment success*, The Institute for College Access and Success, https://ticas.org/accountability/metrics-and-markets/. [63]

U.S. Bureau of Economic Analysis (2019), *Gross Domestic Product by State: Fourth Quarter and Annual 2018*, https://www.bea.gov/news/2019/gross-domestic-product-state-fourth-quarter-and-annual-2018 (accessed on 31 May 2019). [1]

U.S. Bureau of Economic Analysis (2019), *Regional BEARFacts: Virginia*, https://apps.bea.gov/regional/bearfacts/pdf.cfm?fips=51000&areatype=51000&geotype=3 (accessed on 11 March 2020). [2]

U.S. Bureau of Labor Statistics (2019), *Fastest growing occupations: 20 occupations with the highest percent change of employment between 2016-26*, https://www.bls.gov/ooh/fastest-growing.htm (accessed on 23 August 2019). [41]

U.S. Bureau of Labor Statistics (2019), *Labor force statistics from the current population survey*, https://www.bls.gov/cps/ (accessed on 12 March 2020). [28]

U.S. Bureau of Labor Statistics (2019), *Mid-Atlantic Information Office; Virginia*, https://www.bls.gov/regions/mid-atlantic/virginia.htm (accessed on 4 August 2019). [14]

U.S. Bureau of Labor Statistics (2019), *Occupation Employment Statistics*, https://www.bls.gov/oes/home.htm (accessed on 26 August 2019). [7]

U.S. Bureau of Labor Statistics (2019), *State and Metro Area Employment, Hours and Earnings*, https://www.bls.gov/sae/data/home.htm (accessed on 8 August 2019). [8]

U.S. Bureau of Labor Statistics (2016), *Labor force participation: what has happened since the peak?*, Monthly Labor Review, https://www.bls.gov/opub/mlr/2016/article/pdf/labor-force-participation-what-has-happened-since-the-peak.pdf. [27]

U.S. Census Bureau (2019), *American Community Survey 2018 (database)*, https://www.census.gov/programs-surveys/acs/data.html (accessed on 18 January 2020). [24]

U.S. Census Bureau (2018), *American Community Survey 2013-2017 5-year Data Release.* [50]

U.S. Census Bureau (2018), *QuickFacts: Virginia*, https://www.census.gov/quickfacts/fact/table/VA,US/PST045218 (accessed on 4 August 2019). [25]

U.S. News & World Report (2019), *Best States Rankings*, https://www.usnews.com/news/best-states/rankings (accessed on 4 August 2019). [4]

UVA Weldon Cooper Center (2019), *Observed and total population for the U.S. and the States*, https://demographics.coopercenter.org/national-population-projections (accessed on 6 August 2019). [11]

UVA Weldon Cooper Center (2019), *Out-migration from Virginia continues for the fifth consecutive year, pushing population growth below national levels*, http://statchatva.org/2019/01/28/out-migration-from-virginia-continues-for-the-fifth-consecutive-year-pushing-population-growth-below-national-levels/ (accessed on 4 December 2019). [48]

UVA Weldon Cooper Center (2018), *Who is out of work in Virginia?*, Demographics Research Group, https://demographics.coopercenter.org/sites/demographics/files/FullReport_VBWD_OWW_UVACooperCtr.pdf. [29]

UVA Weldon Cooper Center (2017), *Job polarization in Virginia means fewer middle-wage jobs*, http://statchatva.org/2017/06/06/job-polarization-in-virginia-means-fewer-middle-wage-jobs/ (accessed on 16 August 2019). [20]

UVM (2019), *About UddannelsesGuiden*, Børne- og Undervisningsministeriet, https://www.ug.dk/programmes/aboutugdk (accessed on 25 September 2019). [116]

VCCS (2019), *Transfer Virginia launches*, http://www.vccs.edu/vccsblog_post/transfer-virginia-launches-goal-is-to-ensure-that-students-are-able-to-make-the-jump-from-community-college-to-the-states-four-year-universities-more-efficiently/ (accessed on 21 September 2019). [96]

VCCS (2017), *FastForward - Credentials Available*, Virginia Community College System, https://www.fastforwardva.org/credentials-available/ (accessed on 21 September 2019). [93]

VCCS (2017), *VCCS E&G Outcomes-Based Funding Model*, Virginia Community College System, Richmond, https://www.ccleague.org/sites/default/files/images/overview_vccs_outcomes_based_funding_model.pdf (accessed on 19 February 2020). [107]

VCCS (n.d.), *Great Expectations | Promising futures for Virginia foster youths - Virginia Community College System*, http://greatexpectations.vccs.edu/ (accessed on 6 May 2020). [97]

VEC (2019), *2016-2026 Industry and Occupational Projections*, Virginia Employment Commission, https://virginiaworks.com/occupational-projections/page79862/1/size79862/12/page80257/1/size80257/12?page79862=2&size79862=12&page80257=1&size80257=12&page81630=1&size81630=12 (accessed on 9 August 2019). [16]

VEC (2019), *Statewide Economic Analysis Report*, Virginia Employment Commission, https://virginiaworks.com/Portals/200/Publications/LMI%20Publications/Statewide%20Economic%20Analysis/PDF/SEA%202019.pdf (accessed on 3 January 2020). [9]

VEC (2019), *Virginia Labor Market Information Long and Short-Term Occupational Projections*, Virginia Employment Commission, https://virginiaworks.com/occupational-projections?page79862=1&size79862=12&page80257=1&size80257=12&page81630=1&size81630=12#Long-Term-Occupational-Virginia-2016-2026-Projections-2536 (accessed on 25 September 2019). [109]

VEC (n.d.), *Local Workforce Development Areas (LWDAs)*, Virginia Employment Commission, https://virginiaworks.com/Portals/200/Publications/LWDAs/Maps/LWDA%20Regions.pdf (accessed on 22 January 2020). [49]

VEDP (2019), *Virginia Economic Review (First Quarter)*, Virginia Economic Development Partnership, https://issuu.com/vedpvirginia/docs/vedp_q2_v11spreads?fr=sZWRIZDEyMDc5Mg (accessed on 2 August 2019). [6]

VEDP (2017), *Amazon HQ2 Submission: Partnership Proposal*, Virginia Economic Development Partnership, https://issuu.com/teamsubjectmatter/docs/nova_r1_proposal_full_doc_single_pa?e=35488011/65733964. [12]

Virginia Career Works (2019), *Workforce Supply and Demand Dashboard*, Virginia Board of Workforce Development, https://virginiacareerworks.com/dashboards/ (accessed on 2 July 2019). [17]

Virginia Career Works (2018), *2018-2019 Virginia Demand Occupations List*, https://virginiacareerworks.com/wp-content/uploads/2018-2019-Virginia-Demand-Occupations-List-FINAL.pdf (accessed on 8 July 2019). [52]

Virginia Career Works (2017), *Virginia Board of Workforce Development - Strategic Plan 2017-2019*, Virginia Board of Workforce Development, Richmond, https://virginiacareerworks.com/wp-content/uploads/VBWD-Strategic-Plan-2017-2019.pdf (accessed on 15 September 2019). [85]

Virginia Department of Education (n.d.), *Education workforce data and reports*, http://www.doe.virginia.gov/teaching/workforce_data/index.shtml (accessed on 14 September 2019). [51]

Virginia General Assembly (2019), *Budget Bill - HB1700 (Chapter 854) Item 4-2.01 b Nongeneral Fund Revenues.*, https://budget.lis.virginia.gov/item/2019/1/HB1700/Chapter/4/4-2.01/ (accessed on 12 November 2019). [101]

Virginia General Assembly (2019), *Budget Bill - HB1700 (Chapter 854) Item 141 (SCHEV) Higher Education Student Financial Assistance.*, https://budget.lis.virginia.gov/item/2019/1/HB1700/Chapter/1/141/ (accessed on 24 September 2019). [105]

Virginia General Assembly (2019), *HB 2490: Tech Talent Investment Program and Fund*, https://lis.virginia.gov/cgi-bin/legp604.exe?191+sum+HB2490 (accessed on 4 December 2019). [54]

Virginia General Assembly (2019), *Title 23.1. Institutions of Higher Education; Other Educational and Cultural Institutions*, https://law.lis.virginia.gov/vacode/title23.1/ (accessed on 12 August 2019). [30]

Virginia General Assembly (2018), *§ 2.2-2472. Powers and duties of the Board; Virginia Workforce System created.*, https://law.lis.virginia.gov/vacode/title2.2/chapter24/section2.2-2472/ (accessed on 12 August 2019). [31]

Wilson, B. (2014), *How many more skilled workers do we need? Using supply and demand reports for state workforce planning*, National Skills Coalition, State workforce and education alignment project, https://www.nationalskillscoalition.org/resources/publications/file/how-many-more-skilled-workers.pdf. [110]

WSAC, SBCTC and WTECB (2018), *A Skilled and Educated Workforce 2017 Update: An analysis of postsecondary education, workforce preparation, and employer demand in Washington*, Washington Student Achievement Council/State Board for Community and Technical Colleges/ Workforce Training and Education Coordinating Board / Workforce Training and Education Coordinating Board, Olympia, https://wsac.wa.gov/sites/default/files/2017.ASkilledAndEducatedWorkforce.pdf (accessed on 31 May 2019). [111]

Notes

[1] Virginia State and Norfolk State are also Historically Black Universities.

[2] The minimum educational requirement for entry into an occupation is based on the U.S. Bureau of Labor Statistics (BLS) education and training classification system, which also underlies the Occupational Information Network (O*NET). Occupational employment projections provide a general overview of estimated replacement needs and employment growth per occupation. However, there are limitations to using the educational and training requirements for projections of future education or skills needs. Occupational employment projections are based on current industry composition and thus do not adequately capture new occupations in emerging industries. They also assume that education requirements per occupation remain unchanged during the projection period. As employer demand for post-secondary qualifications and skills has been rising at a rapid pace in the last decade, estimates of projected educational requirements based on occupational outlooks are likely to be conservative. See (Carnevale, Smith and Strohl, 2013[37]) for a more detailed discussion of the limitations of BLS estimates of education requirements.

[3] A post-secondary certificate, industry certification, state licensure or apprenticeship.

[4] Under-represented groups are defined as non-White populations; Pell Grant recipients; those aged 25 or older and those from a Virginia locality with low undergraduate attainment rates (most of which are rural).

[5] Operating Advisory Committee (OpSix) comprises the Secretaries of Finance and Education, the Director of SCHEV, a representative of the Department of Planning and Budget, and the Chairs of the House Appropriations and Senate Finance Committees.

[6] Department for the Blind and Vision Impaired, Department for Aging and Rehabilitation Services, Department of Education, Department of Labor and Industry, Department of Social Services, Virginia Community College System, Virginia Economic Development Partnership, Virginia Employment Commission.

[7] For associate's degrees in the Virginia Community College System, this task is delegated to the VCCS Board.

[8] The employment outcomes of graduates are considered when determining whether programmes identified as performing poorly in terms of student numbers and graduation rates should nevertheless be allowed to continue.

[9] General fund appropriations for educational and general Programs (the primary operating funds for colleges and universities) increased 11.2% between FY 2018 and FY 2020.

[10] Financial need is more generally calculated in the United States by subtracting the Expected Family Contribution from the total cost of attendance, including room and board, as well as books and equipment.

[11] The EPC is calculated based on family income by the federal government for each student applying for federal aid and, for low-income families, may be zero.

[12] Low-, middle- and high-income levels are defined in relation to the federally defined poverty level. Low-income students have household incomes less than 200% of the federal poverty level (below around USD 50 000 per year for a family of four); middle-income students have household incomes of 200-400% of the federal poverty level (between USD 50 000 and USD 100 000); and high-income students have household incomes exceeding 400% of the federal poverty level (over USD 100 000).

[13] There are important limitations to supply-demand analyses linking post-secondary credential production with occupational demand. There is not always a one-to-one relationship between fields of study and occupations or jobs, particularly in fields such as the social sciences, humanities, and liberal arts. Furthermore, a graduate with a credential in a particular field of study may have the skills and competencies required for multiple occupations. This kind of flexibility in the labour market is generally desirable. In addition, degree completions may capture workers who upgrade skills for their current jobs but are not available to fill new openings, and not all degree completers will enter the labour market. Still, supply-demand models and gap analyses can provide an indication of where there is likely to be considerable misalignment between labour market demand and the supply of credentialed graduates. To inform policy, however, these models should be supplemented with other qualitative and quantitative information, including estimates of net migration of skilled workers in the labour market. See for example (Goldman et al., 2015[117]) for a discussion of various supply-demand models and data sources, and additional guidance on using workforce information for programme planning in higher education.

7 Washington

This chapter provides an overview of the labour market and higher education system in the state of Washington, an assessment of the labour market outcomes of graduates, and a discussion of state policies that contribute to aligning higher education and the labour market. The policy discussion focuses on five policy areas – strategic planning and co-ordination of higher education; funding; educational offerings; student supports and pathways; and information – and includes policy recommendations in each area.

7.1. The labour market and higher education in Washington

The economy and labour market

Washington's innovation-driven economy is growing rapidly, but income gaps are widening

Washington has enjoyed the highest annual economic growth rate of any state in the United States in the last two years, with 5.7% growth in real Gross Domestic Product (GDP) in 2018 and 4.7% growth in 2017. The compound annual growth rate for real GDP in Washington for the ten-year period from 2008 to 2018 was 2.9%, compared to an annual growth rate for the United States of 1.8% (U.S. Bureau of Economic Analysis, 2019[1]). The strong performance of the information services sector has largely driven the overall economic growth of the state, a pattern that is expected to continue in the short- to medium-term. Indeed, Washington is home to two of the world's largest companies – Amazon and Microsoft – as well as a host of other technology companies specialising in information services such as software, big data and cloud computing (ESD, 2019[2]).

With a population of about 7.5 million and a GDP of USD 563 billion in 2018, Washington's economic output accounts for about 3% of total GDP for the United States (U.S. Bureau of Economic Analysis, 2019[1]). The top industries in Washington, each contributing a sizeable share of the state's GDP, are finance; insurance and real estate; information; professional and business services; and government. Highest projected growth towards 2026 is expected in the information and professional and business services sectors. The high level of economic growth in Washington has contributed to growth in employment and wages, with higher personal income growth in Washington compared to the US average. In 2017, average annual wages grew by 5%, primarily driven by wage growth in the retail trade and information services sectors (ESD, 2019[2]).

At the same time, income inequality in Washington has increased substantially in the last three decades. The difference in hourly wages between the top and bottom 10% of earners in 1980 was approximately USD 26 per hour, compared to USD 43 per hour in 2018, adjusted for inflation (Keating, 2019[3]). Nation-wide, the gap in hourly wages between the top and bottom 10% of earners in 2018 was USD 37. Thus, while personal income growth has been rising in Washington, it has benefitted more individuals at the higher end of the income scale. Personal income levels also vary widely across the state. In 2017, per capita personal income for the state was USD 57 896. In King County – which includes Washington's biggest city, Seattle – per capita personal income in 2017 was USD 83 383, compared to USD 35 587 in Franklin county, with the lowest per capita income in the state (OFM, 2019[4]).

The regions of Washington each have distinct economic profiles. With a relatively large government sector and dominant healthcare and retail trade industries, the south-western region has enjoyed substantial growth in personal income and GDP in the last five years. The north-eastern region has a strong agricultural economy and growing healthcare and tourism industries. The Olympic region to the west, formerly reliant on the timber industry, faces challenges with slow job growth and high unemployment, as does the south-central region, which has the highest unemployment rate in the state. Indeed, many regions outside the areas surrounding the Puget Sound (which include the cities of Seattle, Tacoma and Olympia) face similar challenges in terms of relatively high unemployment and lower educational attainment levels. In addition, it is estimated that 280 000 residents of Washington's rural areas do not have access to broadband internet, which can have a negative impact on productivity (Washington Roundtable, 2018[5]).

Though educational attainment rates vary widely across the state, Washington's workforce is well-educated. The higher education attainment rate (associate's degree or above) is 48% for 25-64 year-olds (Figure 7.1). With the inclusion of post-secondary certificates, the proportion of the working-age population with some form of post-secondary credential rises to 56%, which is substantially higher than the US average of 48% (Lumina Foundation, 2019[6]). Compared to many other states, a relatively large share of Washington adults have either a workforce-relevant certificate (8%) or an associate's degree (11%). However, the proportion of African Americans, Hispanics and Native Americans with a post-secondary credential is lagging behind that of Whites and Asians.

Figure 7.1. Levels of educational attainment for Washington residents aged 25-64, 2018

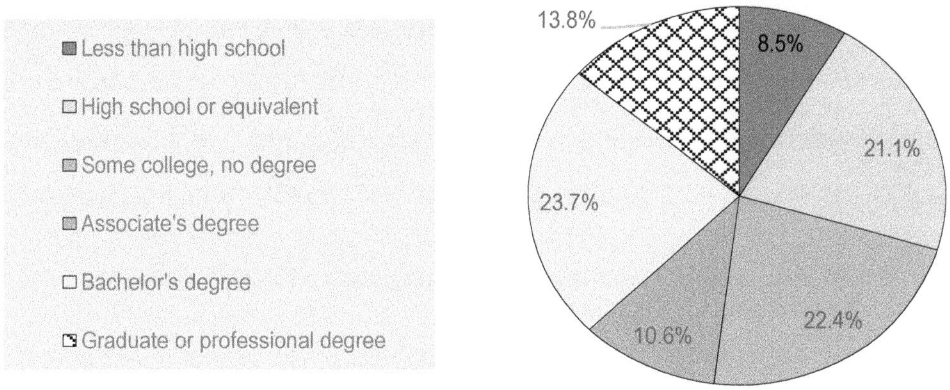

Source: U.S. Census Bureau (2019[7]), *American Community Survey 2018* (database), https://www.census.gov/programs-surveys/acs/data.html.

StatLink https://doi.org/10.1787/888934134350

The state's population has experienced tremendous growth in the last decade. Washington has benefitted from substantial net in-migration of workers from other states, attracting more than 10 000 workers with at least some post-secondary education between 2011 and 2015 (WSAC, SBCTC and WTECB, 2018[8]). Of these, about 15% had a certificate or associate's degree, 30% had a bachelor's degree and 55% had a graduate or professional degree. In a national context, these figures place Washington fourth in overall net in-migration of workers with more than upper secondary education, and third for those with bachelor's degrees and above (WSAC, SBCTC and WTECB, 2018[8]). In addition, Washington attracts many skilled workers from other countries (WTECB, 2011[9]).

Furthermore, the proportion of Washington residents above the retirement age of 65 (15%) is offset by a larger youth population, which forms the basis of the future workforce. At 22%, the dependency ratio in Washington is slightly lower than both the US and OECD average. Table 7.1 presents an overview of some key contextual indicators for Washington.

Table 7.1. Washington at a glance

	Washington	United States	Source
Population			
Population estimate	7 535 591	327 167 434	U.S. Census
Dependency ratio (% 65+ over population aged 15-64)	23.4%	24.5%	OECD Regional statistics
Percentage of individuals under the age of 18	22.1%	22.4%	U.S. Census
Percentage of individuals aged 65 and over	15.4%	16.0%	U.S. Census
Percentage of Black or African American individuals	4.3%	13.4%	U.S. Census
Percentage of Hispanic or Latino individuals	12.9%	18.3%	U.S. Census
Percentage of Asian individuals	9.3%	5.9%	U.S. Census
Percentage of American Indian or Alaska Native individuals	1.9%	1.3%	U.S. Census
Percentage of White (non-Hispanic) individuals	68%	60.4%	U.S. Census

	Washington	United States	Source
Economy and labour market			
Real GDP per capita	USD 68 007	USD 57 052	U.S. Bureau of Economic Analysis
Labour force participation rate (out of civilian population aged 16+)	64.3%	62.9%	U.S. Bureau of Labor Statistics (LAUS)
Unemployment rate (seasonally adjusted)	4.6%	3.9%	U.S. Bureau of Labor Statistics (LAUS)
Median annual earnings for working-age population aged 25-64 (USD)	USD 60 000	USD 50 000	American Community Survey
Estimated annual wage needed to cover basic expenses for a full-time working adult (USD)	USD 27 664	USD 25 297	MIT Living Wage Calculator
Percentage of population aged 25-64 with an associate's degree or higher	47%	42.5%	American Community Survey

Notes: All numbers are for 2018 unless otherwise noted. Racial and ethnic categories are mutually exclusive. MIT Living Wage annual calculations are based on full-time working hours (2 080 hours per year).

StatLink https://doi.org/10.1787/888934135148

Despite a relatively high unemployment rate, labour shortages persist in several sectors across the state

The largest sectors of employment in Washington are government; professional and business services; and leisure and hospitality. Employment growth has been observed in every industry in Washington, except for mining and logging, with growth above the state average for the majority of industries in the last two years (ESD, 2019[2]). Furthermore, employment in the information services and professional and business services sectors continues to grow at a rapid pace, in line with patterns of wage growth and economic output. Wage growth, as measured in average hourly earnings, slowed after the recession of 2008-09, but has strengthened since 2015. Job growth has increased since the end of the recession and the number of high-wage jobs added to the economy has more than doubled since the early 2000s, primarily in information services, healthcare, aerospace and computer systems design (ESD, 2019[2]).

Despite strong employment and wage growth, however, the unemployment rate in Washington is higher than the US average. At 4.6% in June 2019, the unemployment rate in Washington ranked 45th out of 50 states (plus the District of Columbia) in the United States (U.S. Bureau of Labor Statistics, 2019[10]). This varies widely between regions and counties. In 2016, the unemployment rate in the south-central region was 7.2%, compared to 6.7% in the south-western region and 6.6% in the Olympic region (Washington Roundtable, 2018[5]). Based on unemployment insurance (UI) data, unemployment state-wide is concentrated primarily in the manufacturing and construction industries. State-wide, the unemployment rate is down from a ten-year high in early 2010. Figure 7.2 provides an overview of key labour market indicators in Washington.

Based on both current and projected employment patterns, labour shortages have been identified in several major occupational groups. At the middle-skills level, gaps in workforce supply and demand have been identified in service occupations, business, management and sales, as well as computer and information sciences. At the advanced skills level, there are large gaps in computer and mathematical occupations and in education professions (WSAC, SBCTC and WTECB, 2018[8]). In the ten-year period between 2016 and 2026, employment in computer and mathematical occupations has been projected to grow at a faster rate than other major occupational groups (ESD, 2019[2]). Gaps in skill demand and supply are examined further in Section 7.2.

Figure 7.2. Trends in key labour market indicators in Washington, 2009-19

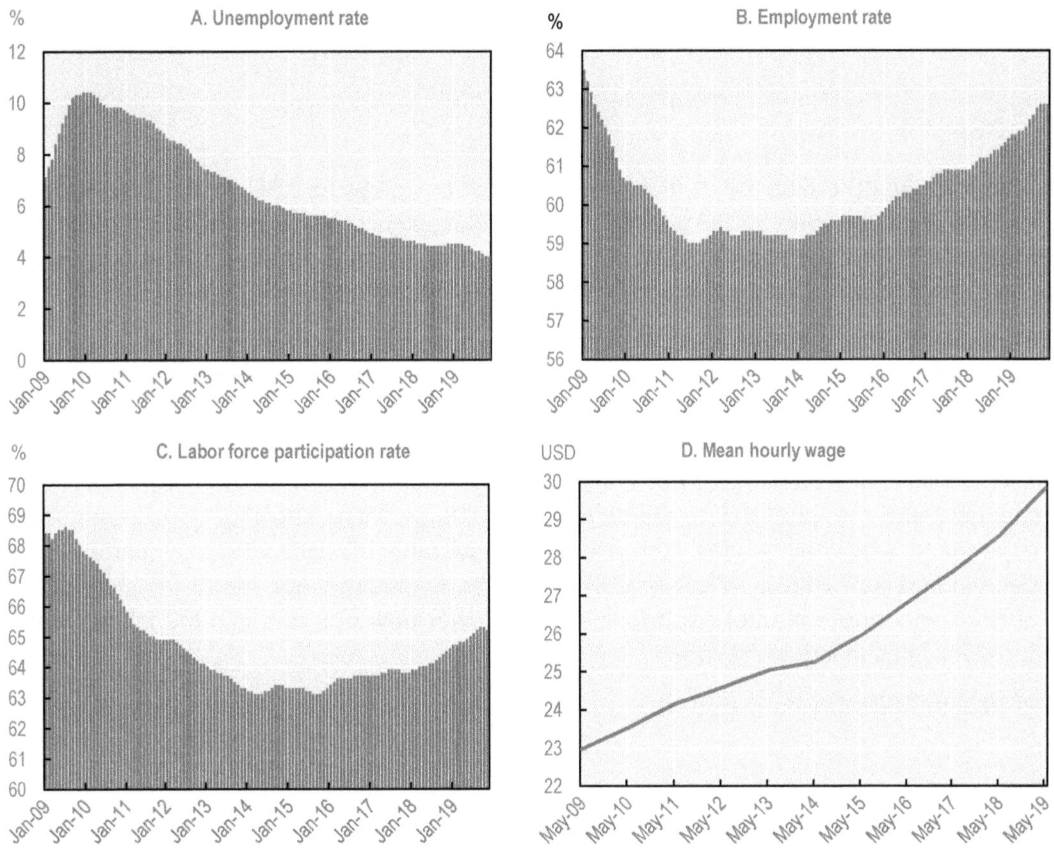

Notes: Data in panels A, B and C are seasonally adjusted. The labour force participation rate is defined as the percentage of people who are either employed or unemployed (but looking for jobs) out of the total civilian non-institutional population, which includes all individuals over the age of 16 who are potentially available for work. The employment rate is the percentage of people who are employed out of the total civilian non-institutional population. The unemployment rate is the percentage of people who are unemployed (but looking for jobs) out of all individuals in the labour force (employed or unemployed but looking for jobs). The mean hourly wage is not adjusted for inflation.

Sources: Panels A, B and C: U.S. Bureau of Labor Force (2020[11]), *U.S. Bureau of Labor Force Statistics from the Current Population Survey* (database), https://www.bls.gov/cps/tables.htm. Panel D: U.S. Bureau of Labor Statistics (2019[10]), *U.S. Bureau of Labor Statistics, Occupation Employment Statistics* (database), https://www.bls.gov/oes/home.htm.

StatLink https://doi.org/10.1787/888934134369

The share of households with job-related earnings and the proportion of the labour force with a full-time job remain below pre-recession levels (ESD, 2019[2]). The labour force participation rate state-wide was 64.3% in June 2019, just above the national average of 63%(Table 7.1) . Similar to the rest of the country, the labour force participation has been in decline since the recession. At the national level, declining labour force participation has been largely attributed to structural changes in the economy, including waning demand for routine-based manual labour (Abraham and Kearney, 2019[12]; U.S. Bureau of Labor Statistics, 2016[13]). In Washington, however, the labour force participation rate appears to be on the rise, as depicted in Figure 7.2.

Earnings in Washington are higher, on average, than in the United States overall. In the period between 1990 and 2017, wage growth has increased but disproportionately favoured the top 10% of earners (ESD, 2019[2]). Washington is also one of 29 states that has raised the minimum wage above the federal minimum, with a minimum wage in 2018 of USD 11.50 per hour. In 2014, the Seattle City Council approved an increase in the minimum wage to USD 15 per hour to be phased in over time, which was the highest minimum wage for any city in the United States when it was approved. The City Council invited researchers to evaluate the effects of the new policy, and several studies have been carried out by the University of Washington, as outlined in Box 7.1.

Box 7.1. The Seattle Minimum Wage Study

Seattle's minimum wage ordinance to increase the minimum wage to USD 15 per hour took effect in April 2015. The increase was to be phased in over time, with small businesses implementing the minimum wage for its employees by 2021. The rate at which it increases depends on the size of the business and whether or not they contribute to employees' health care.

A group of researchers at the University of Washington has studied the effects of the minimum wage increases on various employment outcomes. Minimum wage increases may have different effects on different types of workers. One of the study's recent findings is that, based on a group of 14 000 low-paid workers in Seattle who earned less than the new minimum wage before it was implemented, experienced workers saw gains from the minimum wage increases, while non-experienced workers saw no change (Jardim et al., 2018[14]; Jardim et al., 2018[15]). More specifically, workers with above median experience saw their wages increase by an average of USD 251 per quarter, while less experienced workers saw little to no average change. The minimum wage increases also reduced the number of low-wage labour market opportunities, with fewer new entrants into the labour market and reduced turnover rates in low-wage jobs.

Source: University of Washington (n.d.[16]).

The higher education system

In a system with broad institutional autonomy, the Washington Student Achievement Council is responsible for strategic oversight of higher education in the state

The Washington Student Achievement Council (WSAC) serves as a co-ordinating body for higher education in Washington. Its predecessor, the Washington Higher Education Coordinating Board (HECB), was created by the Washington State Legislature in 1985 and abolished by the Legislature in 2012. A fundamental change with the establishment of WSAC in 2012 was the removal of programme approval authority. The agency has responsibility for strategic oversight and compliance; authorisation of private and out-of-state degree-granting institutions; as well as the administration of state financial aid, college access programmes, approval of veteran's benefits, and transfer agreements.

In the bill proposing the creation of WSAC, the legislation states: "It is the intent of the legislature to create the student achievement council to provide the focus and propose the goals for increasing educational attainment including improving student transitions from secondary to post-secondary education and training and between and among post-secondary institutions. Due to the large and growing gap between education requirements and achievement, it is the intent of the legislature to focus on increased educational attainment as a key priority and to closely track progress towards meeting this statewide objective" (Washington Legislature, 2012, pp. 2-3[17]). Thus, WSAC is responsible for establishing state-wide goals for educational attainment and collaborates with its partner agencies to develop strategies and policy recommendations to present to the Legislature in order to advance the state's post-secondary attainment goals. However, the agency does not have institutional budget authority. WSAC is overseen by an executive director and five citizens (one of whom must be a student) appointed by the Governor, and one representative each from the four-year public institutions, two-year public colleges, K-12 school system, and independent higher education institutions.

The State Board for Community and Technical Colleges (SBCTC) is a key collaborative partner with WSAC in the post-secondary landscape, advocating for policies and budget recommendations that will make progress towards the state's attainment goals. The SBCTC serves as the governing board responsible for co-ordinating and directing the state's system of 34 community and technical colleges. Individual colleges receive their state funding through the SBCTC, and allocations are determined by a general funding formula. The SBCTC is overseen by a board consisting of nine members, appointed by the Governor.

In Washington, public four-year colleges and universities enjoy a substantial level of autonomy. In general, they are responsible for programme approval, staffing, admissions and quality assurance. The Degree-Granting Institutions Act of 1979 requires that all private and out-of-state institutions obtain authorisation from WSAC to operate in the state, unless they are exempt or participating in the State Authorization Reciprocity Agreement. Authorised institutions must renew their approval every two years. The governance of public four-year institutions in Washington is shared between the Governor, WSAC and the institutions. The members of each institution's governing board – the Board of Regents or the Board of Trustees – are appointed by the Governor, in accordance with the Revised Codes of Washington.

Agencies and stakeholders across education and workforce policy environments in Washington partner together to reach state-wide goals

In addition to the WSAC and the SBCTC, the main stakeholders in higher education policy include representative bodies of the different higher education providers. The Independent Colleges of Washington (ICW) is the representative body of ten private, not-for-profit institutions, and the Council of Presidents represents public baccalaureate institutions. WSAC also convenes advisory committees for informing policy recommendations and strategy, involving students, faculty and citizens, as well as stakeholders from business and industry.

WSAC collaborates with partner agencies, such as the Workforce Training and Education Coordinating Board (WTECB), the science, technology, engineering and mathematics (STEM) Education Innovation Alliance, and the Washington State Apprenticeship and Training Council, to develop strategies to meet state-wide goals. The WTECB is a state agency collaborating with labour, business and government leaders, aiming to link higher education to Washington's workers and industry needs. The WTECB serves as the state's Board of Vocational Education and develops policies about how Career and Technical Education (CTE) is delivered across the state. It also monitors the state's workforce system and oversees private career schools. Workforce development policy at the state level is also the primary vehicle for implementing the federal Workforce Innovation and Opportunity Act of 2014 (WIOA). The programme is administered by Washington State Employment Security Department, and overseen at the regional and local level by 12 regional Workforce Development Councils across the state.

The STEM Education Innovation Alliance is an organisation established by the Legislature in 2013, focused on improving STEM (science, technology, engineering and mathematics) education in Washington. It brings together leaders from business, non-profit and government organisations, and advises WSAC on how to better align its strategies with the STEM framework for education and accountability developed by the alliance.

The primary responsibility for establishing policies for steering the public higher education system in Washington rests with the Legislature, based on recommendations from executive agencies and non-profit partners. Washington's state Legislature plays a prominent role in supporting the alignment between higher education and labour market needs. In 2019, the Legislature passed a monumental bill to increase state investments to enhance and facilitate labour market alignment. Key initiatives are outlined in Box 7.2 and discussed further in Section 7.3.

Box 7.2. The Washington Education Investment Act

The goal of the Washington Education Investment Act (House Bill 2158), which passed in April 2019, is to implement a system to enhance investment in career-connected learning and workforce education, and to improve access to post-secondary education. Notably, the legislation establishes the Workforce Education Investment Account in the state treasury, primarily to support higher education programmes and financial aid programmes, and creates the Workforce Education Investment Accountability and Oversight Board. The Board provides guidance and recommendations to the Legislature on what workforce education priorities should be funded, and monitors how these funds are increasing student success and career readiness.

Key initiatives include:

- creation of the Washington College Grant Program, which extends the eligibility criteria and the maximum college grant for full tuition and partial tuition scholarships;
- targeted investments in high-demand fields, such as computer sciences, engineering, health care, and information technology;
- expansion of the Guided Pathways Program to better align education in community and technical colleges (CTCs) to the labour market;
- creation of a state-wide, career connected learning system (Career Connect Washington), an initiative launched by the Governor and advanced by a broad spectrum of state partners, facilitating connections between industry and education.

Source: Washington Legislature (2019[18]).

Washington's higher education landscape is characterised by a diversity of institutions, including a large number of community and technical colleges

The institutional landscape in Washington includes a wide range of private and public higher education institutions. As of 2018, 85% of students in Washington were enrolled in public institutions, 12% were enrolled in private, not-for-profit institutions, and the remaining 3% in private, for-profit institutions. The proportion of students enrolled in each type of institution has remained relatively constant since 2003 (NCES, 2019[19]).

Figure 7.3 shows enrolment trends for all first-time, full-time students over a 15-year period across different institution types in Washington. Because many students at public two-year institutions are part-time students, enrolment numbers for full-time equivalent (FTE) students are substantially lower than total headcount numbers. The trend lines show that enrolments at all four types of institutions increased during the recession of 2008-09, and though the rate of growth has declined since then, enrolment numbers have remained higher than pre-recession levels. Enrolments at public four-year institutions have continued to grow post-recession, while enrolments at public two-year institutions declined sharply after the recession but have gradually been increasing. As a proportion of the population, however, the share of individuals enrolled in post-secondary education is substantially lower in Washington compared to other states. In 2017, only 34% of 18-24 year-olds in Washington were enrolled in post-secondary education, compared to the US average of 42% (Lumina Foundation, 2018[20]). This will be discussed further in Section 7.2.

Figure 7.3. Fall higher education enrolment in Washington, 2003-18

Total number of first-time, full-time equivalent (FTE) students, by institution type

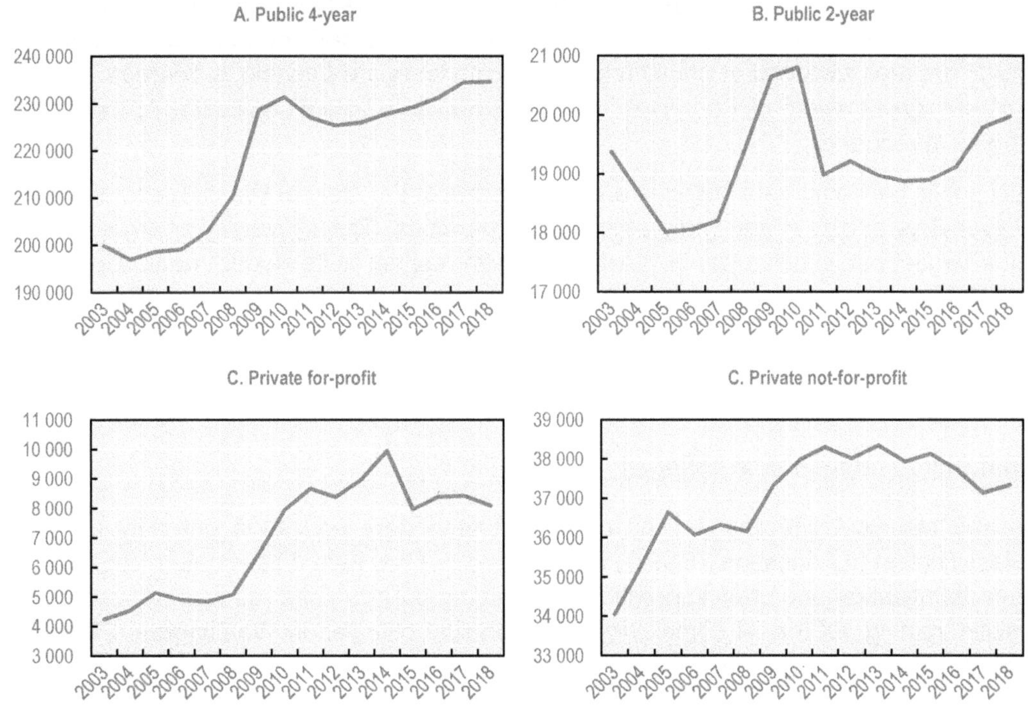

Note: Data for 2018 is provisional.
Source: NCES (2019[19]), *Integrated Post-secondary Education Data System* (database), https://nces.ed.gov/ipeds/use-the-data.

StatLink https://doi.org/10.1787/888934134388

Table 7.2 provides an overview of the higher education institutions operating in the state. The Degree-Granting Institutions Act of 1979 requires that all private and out-of-state institutions obtain authorisation from WSAC to operate in the state, unless they are exempt or participating in the State Authorization Reciprocity Agreement (SARA). Authorised institutions must renew their approval every two years. Table 4.4 provides a profile of public higher education institutions in the state.

Table 7.2. Accredited higher education institutions certified to operate in Washington

	Public	Private (exempt)	
		Not-for-profit	*For-profit*
Four-year baccalaureate colleges and universities	6	16	2
Community and technical colleges	34		
Associate's colleges	5		
Baccalaureate colleges	29		
Religious institutions (seminaries and church-related colleges)		54	

Note: Does not include out-of-state higher education institutions operating in Washington.
Sources: WSAC (2020[21]), *Colleges and institutions in Washington*, https://wsac.wa.gov; NCES (2019[19]), *Integrated Post-secondary Education Data System* (database), https://nces.ed.gov/ipeds/use-the-data.

StatLink https://doi.org/10.1787/888934135167

Public baccalaureate colleges and universities

Four-year institutions are those that offer at least a bachelor's degree. This category of higher education institutions includes research universities, comprehensive universities and colleges that offer post-secondary education (associate's degrees, bachelor's degrees, master's degrees and doctoral degrees). The majority of degrees awarded at public four-year institutions are bachelor's degrees, accounting for about 75% of all degrees awarded. Four-year institutions may also award certificates at lower qualification levels, but do so infrequently.

There are six public baccalaureate colleges and universities in the state of Washington, of which two are research universities and four are comprehensive universities. The University of Washington-Seattle campus is the largest public university in Washington with respect to its student population. In fall 2018, the University of Washington enrolled 43 980 full-time equivalent (FTE) students. The second biggest public university is Washington State University, where 28 552 FTE students were enrolled in fall 2018. Western Washington University has the third biggest student population, with 15 216 FTE students enrolled in fall 2018.

Community and technical colleges

Community and technical colleges (CTCs) offer post-secondary education primarily at International Standard Classification of Education (ISCED) levels 4 and 5. They award associate's degrees and short- and long-term certificates, and offer apprenticeship training programmes, as well as worker re-training and basic skills training. Of the 34 community and technical colleges in Washington, 29 colleges also offer applied bachelor's degrees (ISCED level 6).

The associate's degree normally requires two years of full-time college work and is designed either to prepare individuals for a career, as part of a technical career education programme, or to pursue a bachelor's degree. About 39% of public baccalaureate graduates in Washington started at a community or technical college (SBCTC, 2019[22]). There are three types of associate's degree programmes in Washington: the technical associate's degree, the transfer associate's degree, and the transfer technical associate's degree. The technical associate's degree is offered in more applied fields of study such as accounting, law enforcement administration, child care assistance and registered nursing. The transfer associate's degree is offered in a wide range of fields of study and provides bachelor credit for students to transfer to a four-year college. The transfer-technical associate's degree prepares students to pursue education toward an applied bachelor's degree. On average, transfer students make up about 40% of enrolment in community and technical colleges in Washington.

About 46% of students in community and technical colleges are enrolled in workforce training programmes, also known as Career and Technical Education (CTE), which encompass not only the technical associate's degree but also professional-technical certificates. Workforce training programmes are often designed specifically to meet local industry needs. Short-term certificate programmes typically last from six months to one year, but they are usually designed to build on top of each other and lead to a longer-term certificate.

An open admissions policy is in place in the public two-year sector. In the 2018/19 academic year, the total student population of community and technical colleges was 362 862 (or 169 652 in FTE), which represents about 58% of all students enrolled in public higher education institutions. The largest community college in terms of student population is Bellevue College, with 27 706 (or 12 107 FTE) students enrolled in 2018, followed by Spokane Community College, with 21 929 students enrolled in 2018. Overall, enrolment in technical and community colleges has been declining since 2010.

Private four-year institutions

There is no comprehensive overview of private higher education institutions in Washington, as only institutions that participate in federal or state student aid programmes are required to submit information to public authorities. Most students enrolled in private baccalaureate institutions are enrolled in one of the colleges of the Independent Colleges of Washington (ICW). On average, ICW's colleges award 20% of the baccalaureate degrees awarded in the state. The largest private, not-for-profit institution is Gonzaga University, which enrolled 6 501 students in fall 2018. The largest for-profit institution is Charter College, with 2 853 students enrolled in fall 2018. Most of the for-profit and not-for-profit private institutions enrol a relatively small proportion of students in Washington. Of the 6 private four-year for-profit institutions that provide data to the Integrated Post-secondary Education Data System (IPEDS), 4 enrolled less than 100 students in FTE in fall 2018. And 8 of the 19 four-year non-for-profit enrolled less than 1 000 FTE students in fall 2018.

Table 7.3. Profile of public higher education institutions in Washington

	Public four-year institutions	Public two-year institutions
Total student population (total headcount, fall enrolment)	112 273	362 862
Undergraduate students as a percentage of total enrolment (fall enrolment)	89.9%	100%
Percentage of part-time students	31.0%	52%
Percentage of undergraduate students who are Black/African American	4.2%	8%
Percentage of undergraduate students who are Hispanic/Latino	12.9%	18%
Percentage of undergraduate students who are White	49.1%	60%
Percentage of undergraduate students who are Pell Grant recipients	26.0%	m
Total number of undergraduate credentials awarded (at two-year institutions, this includes certificates, associate's degrees, and applied bachelor's degrees)	25 373	59 181
150% completion rate (full-time, undergraduate students)	53.6%	m
Average tuition and mandatory fees for in-state undergraduate students (USD, 2018/19 academic year)	m	USD 4 027

Note: Data are from the 2018/19 academic year.
Sources: SBCTC (n.d.[23]), *Washington State Board for Community and Technical Colleges*, https://www.sbctc.edu; ERDC (2019[24]), *Statewide Public Four-Year Dashboard*, https://erdc.wa.gov/data-dashboards.

StatLink https://doi.org/10.1787/888934135186

7.2. Assessment of labour market outcomes: The alignment between supply and demand of graduate skills in Washington

Alignment of supply and demand

Responding to shortages in medium- and high-skill occupations is a widespread concern and a focus of state efforts

Across OECD countries, technological change and globalisation have profoundly affected the nature of jobs performed by workers and, in turn, the skills demanded by employers. As routine tasks have become easier to offshore or automate, the number of routine-based jobs traditionally held by workers with lower education levels has fallen. By contrast, the demand for workers with high levels of skills who can perform non-routine tasks and adapt to changing work environments has increased (OECD, 2019[25]; OECD, 2017[26]), consequently increasing the demand for post-secondary educated workers.

Nationally, estimates have suggested that by 2020 approximately 35% of all job openings will require at least a bachelor 's degree and about 30% at least some college or an associate's degree (Carnevale, Smith and Strohl, 2013[27]). Employment projections conducted in Washington for the period 2020-25 are in line with these national estimates. About 66% of all job openings in Washington over this period are projected to require at a least one year or more of post-secondary training. Of these, about half will require "mid-level skills". The state defines mid-level skills as those conveyed by apprenticeships, one year or more of post-secondary education, a training certification or an associate's degree (WSAC, SBCTC and WTECB, 2018[8]).

To understand the extent to which the state is prepared to meet the demand for post-secondary educated workers, state agencies have developed projections of supply and demand at different skill levels, and across the state's occupational sectors. These projections are available on a public dashboard maintained by the SBCTC and are published in the "Skilled and Educated Workforce" summary report every other year. The latest edition of this report suggests that the demand for workers with some post-secondary education is expected to exceed the supply of graduates at this level by approximately 10 000 workers annually between 2020 and 2025. The annual gap is expected to be 7 000 at the bachelor's level over the same period. The gap is smaller at the graduate level, but significant in certain fields such as computer science (WSAC, SBCTC and WTECB, 2018[8]).

Washington's supply and demand analysis also permits the identification of "high demand fields". These fields are occupational groupings mapped to broad fields of study. Occupational groups are considered to be in high demand when the gap between the supply of graduates and projected annual openings is equal to or exceeds 15% of the total number of projected annual openings. As seen in Figure 7.4, eight fields were in high demand at the mid-skill level, and seven at the bachelor's level, in 2017. Key fields in high demand across all levels (including the graduate level) include human and protective services, educators, and computer and information science.

It is important to note that these projections have some limitations: new and emerging industries may not be captured, degree completions may capture workers who upgrade skills in their current jobs but are not available to fill new openings, and data lacks on whether workers in fact have the right level of skills for their jobs. Supply data, which combine past degree completion and current graduate labour force participation patterns, may also not fully reflect new dynamics in higher education enrolments and completions. However, these projections offer a useful picture of where the main gaps exist.

The state can help address the gap between the supply and the demand for post-secondary educated workers in several ways, including producing graduates in the state of Washington or recruiting workers with post-secondary education from other states or countries.

Figure 7.4. Projected gaps in the supply and demand of post-secondary graduates

Total expected number of graduates and job openings between 2020 and 2025, by level of qualification required

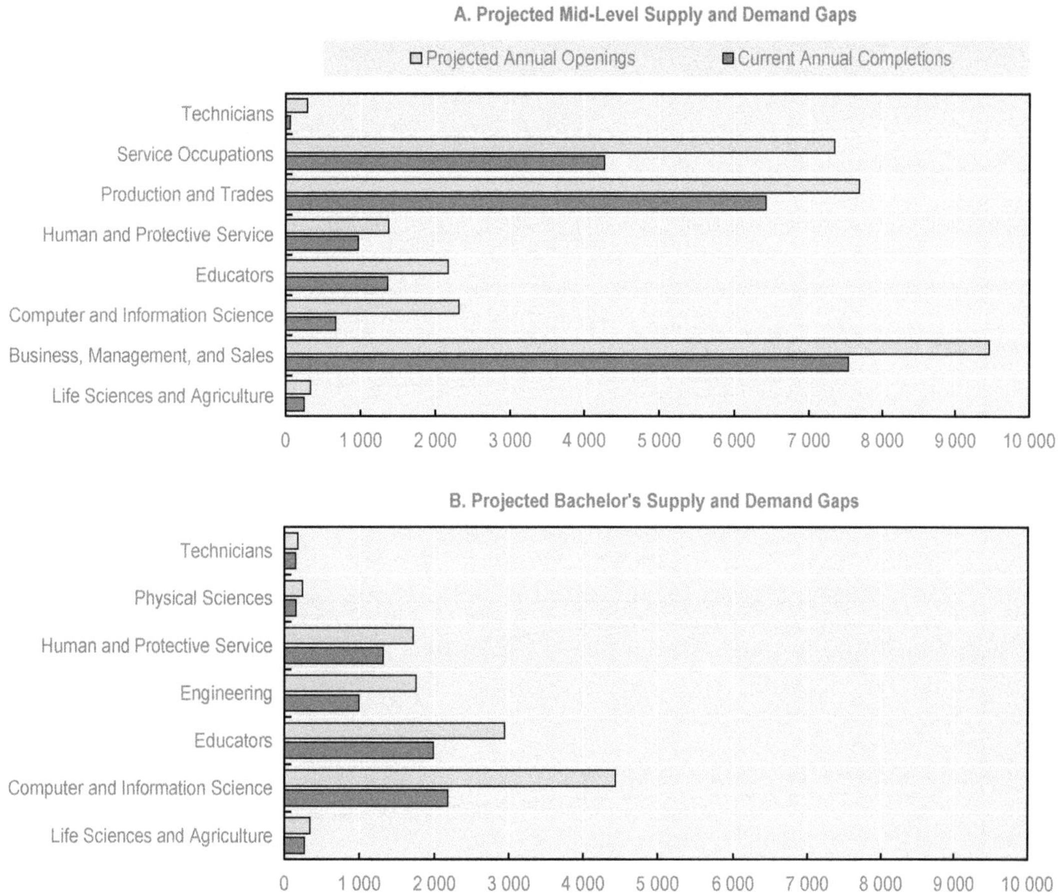

Source: WSAC, SBCTC and WTECB (2018[8]), *A Skilled and Educated Workforce, 2017 Update* (figures 6 and 7), https://wsac.wa.gov/sites/default/files/2017.ASkilledAndEducatedWorkforce.pdf.

StatLink https://doi.org/10.1787/888934134407

The production of post-secondary credentials in Washington in response to labour market demand has been strong. There have been steady increases in the number of post-secondary degrees completed in computer science, engineering, and other STEM and health fields, particularly at the bachelor's level. In 2017, 28% of bachelor's degrees awarded at Washington's public and private institutions were in STEM subjects, up from 22% in 2012 (Washington State STEM Education Innovation Alliance, 2019[28]). At the bachelor's level, most of the growth in credentials awarded by public institutions has taken place in STEM or other in-demand fields, as shown in the top panel of Figure 7.5.

At the sub-baccalaureate level, there has been an increase in the credentials awarded by public colleges in information technology and STEM subjects, but a decrease in nursing and other healthcare-related fields (see bottom panel). The differences in expected returns may play a role: holders of a sub-baccalaureate credential (i.e. apprenticeship, long or short certificate or associate's degree) in computer science have median close to USD 75 000 annually. By contrast, a graduate in the health sector could expect around USD 42 000 with an associate degree or a long-term certificate, and about USD 38 000 with a short-term certificate (WSAC, SBCTC and WTECB, 2018, p. 8[8]). In that sector, the lower interest of students in sub-baccalaureate credentials may also result from a job market favouring applicants with bachelor's degrees, especially for high-demand professions such as registered nurses.

Figure 7.5. Trends in the production of degrees in high-demand fields, 2007/08 to 2016/17

Degrees and certificates awarded annually by public four-year institutions (Panel A) and public two-year institutions (Panel B), selected fields

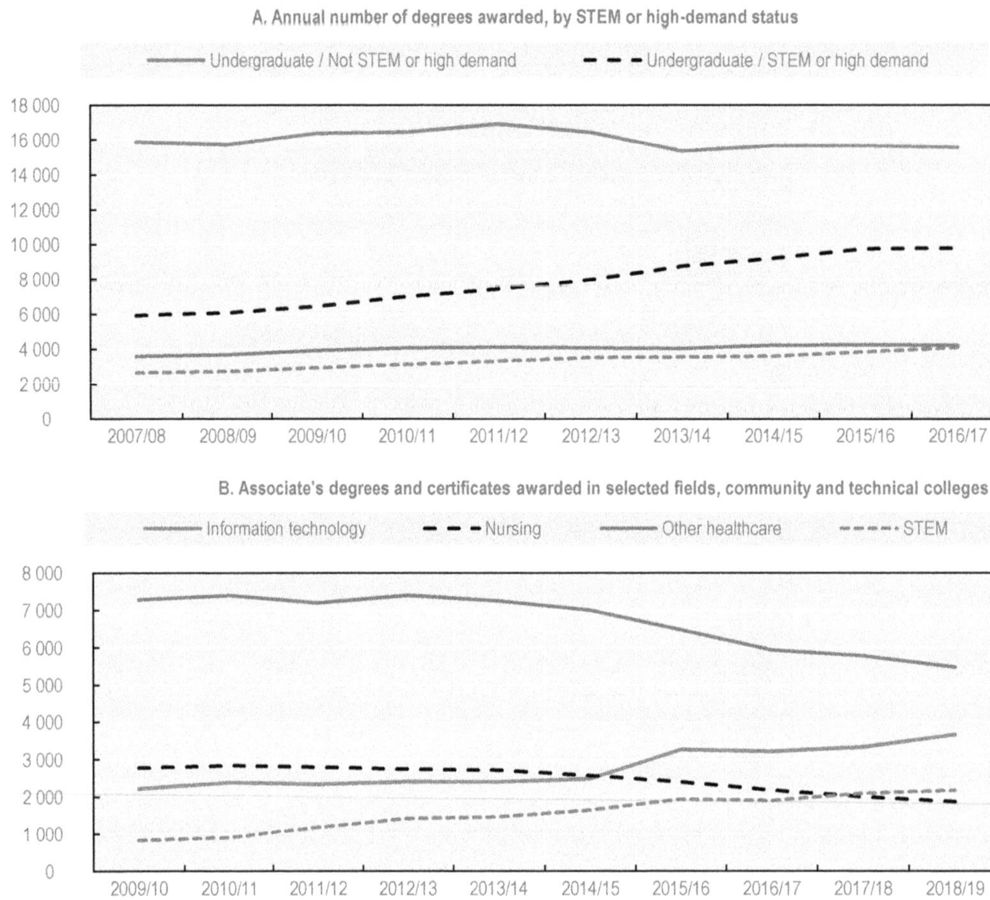

Note: High employer demand programmes are identified by the institutions, in consultation with the Workforce Training and Education Coordinating Board and the Washington Student Achievement Council, based on the needs of the state.
Sources: A) Adapted from ERDC (2019[29]) *Higher Education Outcomes Dashboard*, https://erdc.wa.gov/data-dashboards; B) Adapted from SBCTC (n.d.[23]), *Washington State Board for Community and Technical Colleges*, https://www.sbctc.edu.

StatLink https://doi.org/10.1787/888934134426

Net in-migration from other states is another response to Washington's shortage of qualified workers. Between 2011 and 2015, Washington benefitted from high net in-migration of workers from other states, attracting more than 10 000 workers with at least one year of post-secondary education, of which about 15% had a certificate or associate's degree, 30% had a bachelor's degree and 55% had a graduate or professional degree. These figures place Washington fourth in overall net in-migration of workers with more than upper secondary education, and third for those with bachelor's degrees and above (WSAC, SBCTC and WTECB, 2018[8]).

Immigration rates from abroad are also important. While recent data is not available, a 2011 report from Washington's Workforce Training and Education Coordinating Board indicates that in 2010, Washington had the eighth highest number of H-1B visa petitions in 2010 out of all states. The H-1B visa provides entry to foreign workers employed temporarily in a specialty occupation or field. Federal legislation sets the annual caps, although a number of exceptions apply. Washington's information technology sector is a large user of H-1B visas to hire skilled workers: in 2010, Microsoft employed 20% of Washington's H-

1B workers and Amazon employed another 9% (WTECB, 2011[9]). Washington also recruits talent from abroad to be educated in Washington institutions. The share of international students completing post-secondary credentials in Washington has grown substantially, from 4.3% to 6.4% of total degrees awarded between 2012 and 2016 (WSAC, 2019[30]). As shown in Figure 7.15, this group also tends to choose fields such as engineering and mathematics, which correspond to a key range of high-demand occupations.

Immigration offers a way to meet employer needs that cannot be met by the domestic supply, but these flows are subject to uncertainties, from changes in immigration policy to competition among states and countries for skilled labour. The domestic production of skills is therefore the main channel for Washington state to meet its labour market needs, while ensuring Washingtonians can enjoy the benefits of the state's economic growth. However, despite significant state efforts to boost attainment, particularly in high-demand fields such as STEM and health, both labour and skills shortages persist. Labour market shortages depict a situation where an insufficient number of graduates are available to fill available jobs, whereas skills shortages happen when there are enough graduates, but their skills do not match employer needs (LMIC, 2018[31]). Understanding the potential drivers of these shortages can help identify relevant policies and actions that could be considered by state authorities. Two aspects are discussed below: the constraints in the supply of higher education, and the constraints with respect to student demand.

As we will discuss in Section 7.3, Washington institutions are generally responsive and adjust their programmes to changes in student demand, for instance through the development of course concentrations, minors and new programmes to facilitate the acquisition of specific skills that students view as enhancing their employability. However, several types of challenges exist with respect to institutional supply. First, in certain STEM and health fields, a conjunction of factors may constrain the supply of study spaces. The shortage of qualified faculty in fields where the salaries offered in industrial or clinical settings are much higher than those offered by post-secondary institutions is one challenge. The limited number of work-based opportunities for students in fields where a practicum or other type of supervised work is a graduation requirement, such as in many health programmes, is another frequently cited barrier. In addition, the cost of providing certain high-demand programmes requiring special equipment, while seldom discussed during OECD interviews, can also affect the provision of programmes in fields such as engineering or health.

While no quantitative evidence is available on the scope of unmet student demand, stakeholders have reported cases of students waiting to enter in-demand classes by taking other, potentially unrelated credits, until the course they aim to enrol in is made available. As discussed in the policy section, the state has taken steps to address these constraints, through the infusion of funding for in-demand faculty salaries and for infrastructure in in-demand fields to expand capacity. Additional steps that will be discussed in the policy section (Section 7.3), such as expanding the engagement of employers in providing work-based learning opportunities, could further help alleviate these supply constraints.

Student demand constitutes the second part of the equation and appears to be the main driver behind the insufficient supply of graduates in high-demand fields. The factors that underpin insufficient student demand to meet labour market needs are diverse and vary by field of study. In certain cases, the lack of attractiveness of certain sectors or occupations, due to pay or job conditions or other reasons, appears to be a key challenge. In Washington, the low earnings of in-demand professions in the social service sector, such as education or human and protective services, compared to the earnings of other post-secondary graduates, may deter students from these professions. With respect to teaching, this is consistent with nation-wide issues: while American teachers at lower secondary levels have higher starting salaries than on average across OECD countries with available data, a larger share of teachers than on average in OECD countries report increasing teacher salaries as a key priority (OECD, 2018[32]).

In certain fields with high earnings, low student demand appears to have other contributing factors. The low take-up of apprenticeship may result from the lack of emphasis and time spent on career and technical education (CTE) in high school and the complexity of CTE pathways (Office of the Washington State Auditor, 2017[33]). The limited role of apprenticeship in the United States, compared to countries such as Germany or Switzerland, may create a self-reinforcing dynamic: few students who pursue an academic route choose apprenticeship, and apprenticeship is in turn viewed as a less desirable option. In recognition of this issue, the Career Connect Washington initiative described in Section 7.3 of this chapter supports the expansion of apprenticeship, including through a communication strategy to improve perceptions of apprenticeship as a sound pathway to good-paying jobs. The initiative also highlights the value of apprenticeships as a route to occupations beyond the trades, such as healthcare and information technology, and as a track combining practical experience and classroom learning that can be part of a higher education pathway to associate's or bachelor's degrees.

In high-earning fields that require programmes of study at the associate's, bachelor's or advanced graduate levels, a first challenge resides in Washington's particularly high and fast-growing demand. While still below 5% of total employment, employment in information and communications technology (ICT)-related sectors is already twice as large in Washington as it is in the United States on average. It is projected to be one of the three fastest growing sectors in the state, whereas it will decline slightly on average in the United States (ESD, 2019[2]). Filling jobs in the information technology sector, and in other advanced STEM-related occupations, appears limited by the total pool of students who are willing and able to pursue these fields in the state. As discussed later, women and under-represented minorities tend to access fields of study such as computer science or engineering at relatively low rates.

Skills shortages, on the other hand, call for a better alignment of post-secondary programmes with employer needs. According to Washington employer representatives met during the OECD visit, the amount of time needed to complete a post-secondary programme results in an insufficient number of qualified candidates and candidates whose skills may not be adequately responsive to rapidly changing job needs. Employers' reported needs for advanced, diverse and updated skillsets within short timeframes challenge the traditional model of higher education. This calls for an increased focus on new ways to embed labour market relevance in post-secondary programmes, including through innovation in the educational offer and stronger partnerships between post-secondary education and labour market stakeholders. The extent to which the Washington system supports these approaches is discussed in Section 7.3.

Overall post-secondary attainment rates are high, but college participation is significantly lower than in leading states

Attaining a post-secondary qualification is no longer the only way to obtain skills, yet it remains a key mechanism to obtain the combination of knowledge, skills and attitudes valued in the labour market. Employer feedback indicates a continued reliance on a completed qualification, while also searching for alternative, often complementary, approaches to assess and hire people for certain skills or profiles (Gallagher, 2018[34]). Boosting the post-secondary education attainment rate can thus play an important role in raising the skill levels in the workforce generally, in addition to addressing specific occupational shortages, as discussed previously.

The state's workforce is well-educated, with a higher education attainment rate of 48% for the population aged 25-64. However, as seen in Figure 7.6, rates of attainment also vary widely across the state, with an attainment rate of 24% in Yakima compared to 63% in Whitman County.

Figure 7.6. Higher education attainment in Washington, 2013-17 average

Proportion of Washington residents aged 25-64 with an associate's degree or higher level of education, by county

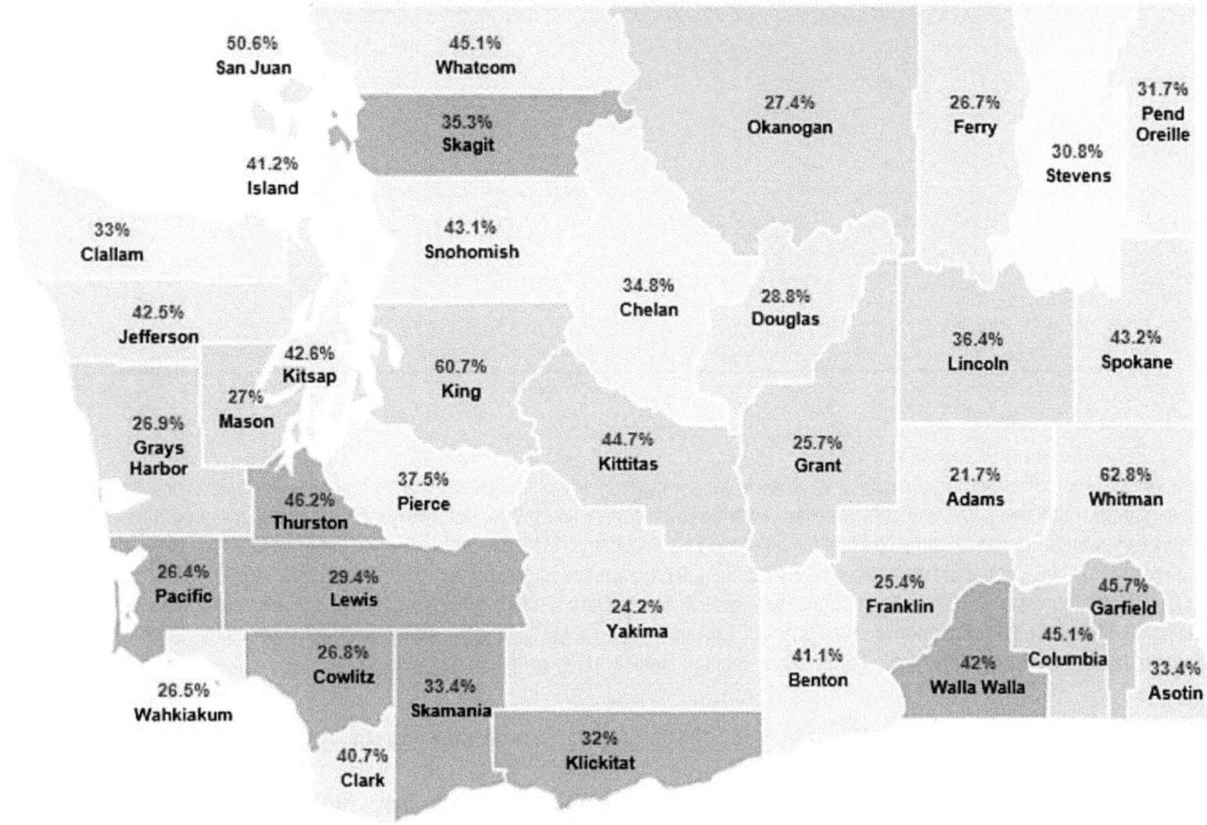

Sources: Map: Adapted from WSAC (n.d.[35]), *County Maps*, https://wsac.wa.gov/college-bound. Attainment rates: U.S. Census Bureau (2018[36]), *American Community Survey 5-Year Estimates (2013-17)*, https://www.census.gov/newsroom/press-kits/2018/acs-5year.html; compiled per county in state reports by Lumina Foundation (2019[6]), *A Stronger Nation: Washington Report 2019*, http://strongernation.luminafoundation.org/report/2020/#page/downloads.

Current higher education enrolment patterns suggest it will be difficult to reach the state's target of 70% post-secondary attainment of the population aged 25-44 in 2023. The share of 18-24 year-olds enrolled in degree-granting post-secondary institutions in Washington is low, at 36.7%, compared to 42.5% on average in the United States. Washington state operates programmes such as Running Start that enable youth to complete an associate's degree at the same time as they complete high school, which may lead some individuals to identify themselves as "not enrolled" if they have previously completed a post-secondary credential. However, when excluding individuals who have at least an associate's degree, the difference in reported enrolment rates is even larger, at 34.4% in Washington compared to 41.7% in the United States (U.S. Census Bureau, 2019[7])

When looking at a broader age group, Washington's college-going rate is well below those of states with similarly high attainment rates, at 11.5% of 18-57 year-olds, compared to 19.2% for example in Massachusetts, or 14.7% in Virginia (Lumina Foundation, 2018[20]). In the public post-secondary sector, enrolment growth over the past decade has been modest and concentrated in the four-year institutions, where enrolments grew by about 18% compared to 2007. Enrolments in two-year institutions have stayed the same, only spiking just after the recession of 2008-09. As seen in Figure 7.7, other pathways such as apprenticeship plummeted during the recession and have now only returned to 2007 levels.

Figure 7.7. Annual enrolment in public post-secondary institutions and apprenticeships, 2007-19

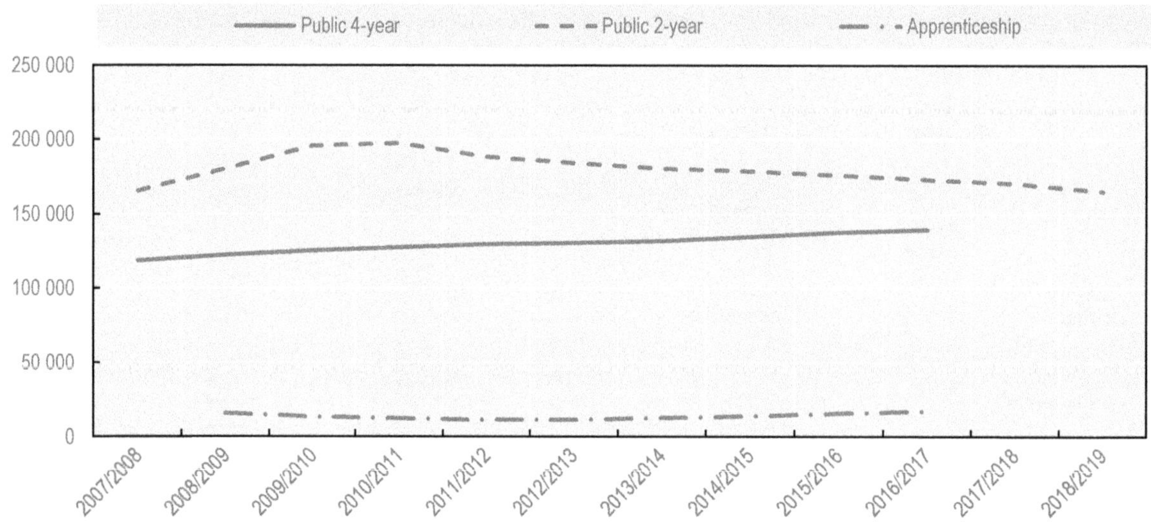

Notes: The data are displayed on a single chart to allow for comparison at system level. Data for four-year institutions and apprenticeships refer to annual enrolments (all students enrolled regardless of course load).Data for two-year institutions (all programmes excluding apprenticeships) refer to annual enrolments of full-time equivalent students. More students take part-time loads at two-year public colleges. For reference, total headcount at public two-year institutions (all programmes excluding apprenticeships) was 348 224 in 2018/19.

Sources: Public four-year: ERDC (n.d.[37]), *Education Research and Data Center*, https://erdc.wa.gov. Public two-year: SBCTC (n.d.[23]), *Washington State Board for Community and Technical Colleges*, https://www.sbctc.edu. Apprenticeship: Washington State Department of Labor and Industries (n.d.[38]), *Washington State Department of Labor and Industries*, https://www.lni.wa.gov.

StatLink https://doi.org/10.1787/888934134445

Low enrolments appear to result both from stagnant rates of transition from high school to post-secondary education, and from a lack of progress in the participation of adults in post-secondary education. In 2016, 62% of the 2016 high school graduates had enrolled in post-secondary education a year later, a rate that has remained stable over the past decade. The share of students over the age of 30 enrolled in public four-year institutions has declined slightly since 2007/08, from about 16% of all enrolments to 13.6% in 2016/17. The same trend can be observed in community colleges, where the share of students over the age of 30 went from 29.5% to 26.8% between 2007/08 and 2018/19 (ERDC, 2019[24]; SBCTC, 2019[39]).

These trends suggest that more needs to be done to increase students' awareness of the various post-secondary pathways available to them, and their motivation to participate. Recent research across the state's nine educational service districts sheds light on some of the barriers which may limit student participation in post-secondary education (WICHE/WSAC, 2017[40]). These include challenges at the point of transition between high school and post-secondary education, such as uneven access to dual-credit programmes, and the practical limitations facing students who may be interested in Career and Technical Education courses while meeting the graduation requirements, which are largely based on academically-oriented courses. Low completion rates constitute the second aspect of the "leaky pipeline", which results in lower attainment rates and missed opportunities for students and the Washington economy. Of students who completed high school in 2009, 54% had obtained no degree in 2019, a proportion that is only slightly lower than in 2005 when it was 57% (ERDC, 2019[41]). Low completion rates are of particular concern among under-represented populations. Multiple reasons underpin the slow progress on this front, from insufficient academic preparation, to difficulty in navigating the post-secondary environment, cost constraints (including the opportunity cost of not working), and personal constraints such as work and family. For both access and completion, particular challenges face under-represented populations, which warrant a specific focus, as further discussed in this section.

Ensuring graduates have transferable and durable skills is increasingly important

In addition to increasing the state's overall higher education attainment rate, it is important to understand the types of skills needed in the economy to support students' choices of study fields and ensure they develop skills relevant to the labour market throughout their higher education programmes. As the tasks demanded of workers undergo rapid changes across and within occupations, it becomes increasingly important to understand the skills that employers demand and whether higher education institutions are able to provide these skills effectively.

Analysis conducted by Washington's Employment Security Department combines employment projections by occupation and information on skills demand from online job postings to convert employment projections into "hard skills" projections (ESD, 2019, p. 121[2]). This analysis aims to support the connection between education and training with tactual skills demanded by employers, rather than with generic occupational definitions. The analysis reveals that the top six skills based on projected openings in the state and across the twelve Workforce Development Areas include: food preparation, bilingual, forklifts, mathematics, quality assurance and freight+, representing together more than 15% of job openings.

While ICT jobs still represent a small share of current and projected openings, the skills projected to experience the most growth across the state all pertain to ICT. Ranked by a combined average of projected annual growth rates over 2016-26 and total average annual openings, the top 10 growing skills are Java, JavaScript, C#, C/C++, web services, Linux, agile software development, Python and big data. The analysis further reveals that ICT skills are also widely demanded outside of ICT occupations. The report finds that out of a total of 633 occupations converted to skills state-wide, ICT skills are present in 583 occupations. For 238 of these occupations, ICT skills comprise more than one-quarter of total numbers and for 86, they comprise more than one-half of total numbers (ESD, 2019[2]).

Table 7.4 highlights the top 15 occupations outside of the ICT sector with the largest demand for ICT skills. Feedback from stakeholders met during the OECD team's visit corroborated the widespread demand for digital skills across industry sectors, noting, for example, in the Yakima Valley the increasing requirement for workers in the agriculture sector to be able to operate new machines that require a degree of computer literacy (e.g. programming of drones). Further, the acquisition of certain skills that are not primarily ICT-related, such as quality assurance of lean manufacturing, may also require ICT skills (ESD, 2019[2]).

Online job postings data offer promising ways to better understand labour market changes, but include a number of caveats. In particular, employer behaviours and intentions are an important factor. Research has shown that skills explicitly named in job postings may not necessarily be the only skills required, and are often those which are typically uncommon in the occupation or hard to find in general.

As technologies and work practices are changing fast, specific skills, including those that are ICT-related and in high demand today, may quickly become obsolete. Various meta-cognitive, cognitive and socio-emotional skills may thus become more important to help workers continuously learn and adapt to new technologies and new working methods. In Washington, a recent survey, as part of a study of the Washington Student Achievement Council and the Western Interstate Commission on Higher Education, asked employers about their skills needs and hiring experiences. Based on responses from 190 employers across all counties, socio-emotional skills (or, "soft skills"), particularly better communication, interpersonal skills and work habits, were among the most frequently cited as needed and lacking in graduates from all educational levels (WICHE/WSAC, 2017[40]).

Table 7.4. Top 15 occupations not primarily computer related with largest shares of computer skill requirements

	Occupation	Share of skills that are ICT
271022	Fashion Designers	0.849
492095	Electrical and Electronics Repairers, Powerhouse, Substation and Relay	0.814
271014	Multimedia Artists and Animators	0.807
193011	Economists	0.776
439111	Statistical Assistants	0.773
191029	Biological Scientists, All Other	0.766
254011	Archivists	0.760
271013	Fine Artists, including Painters, Sculptors, and Illustrators	0.752
152011	Actuaries	0.736
271024	Graphic Designers	0.728
131161	Market Research Analysts and Marketing Specialists	0.724
271021	Commercial and Industrial Designers	0.716
152041	Statisticians	0.700
152031	Operations Research Analysts	0.689

Notes: Washington state, Q2 2017 occupational estimations (June 2014 to May 2017 sample, skills/occupations matrices). Each included occupation's vector of skill numbers was normalized (i.e. scaled) to totals of one.
Source: ESD (2019[2]), *2018 Labor Market and Economic Report*, https://esd.wa.gov/labormarketinfo/report-library.

StatLink https://doi.org/10.1787/888934135205

A range of factors may explain the strong demand for both ICT and socio-emotional skills in Washington. Regarding ICT, rapid changes in technology and prerequisites (e.g. quantitative reasoning capability) to acquire these skills may constrain the supply of individuals with these skills. While post-secondary programs in computer science provide these skills, they may not be widely accessible to students in other fields. The gap in socio-emotional skills may be influenced by other factors. These may include challenges in reliably identifying and measuring social and emotional skills; although research is growing in this area, and an international survey of social and emotional skills is under development (OECD, 2019[42]). Another issue relates to how socio-emotional skills may be taught at the post-secondary level and in the workplace. The recent work of the National Commission for Social, Emotional and Academic Development provides various recommendations for embedding these skills through K-12 levels of education, and more broadly in the lives of youth. At the post-secondary level, stakeholders met in Washington indicated that developing social and emotional skills for the world of work is best done in work-based learning experiences, as further discussed in Section 7.3.

Returns by level and field of study

Pursuing post-secondary education provides individuals with a wide range of benefits, which go well beyond labour market outcomes. International evidence shows that having completed post-secondary education is associated with higher levels of skills and better employment, as well as better health and increased civic participation (OECD, 2013[43]; OECD, 2016[44]). Obtaining good jobs and rewarding careers is of key importance to students who choose to pursue post-secondary education (NSSE, 2018[45]). As discussed in Chapter 2, a large body of research shows that the type of post-secondary programme pursued has a strong impact on labour market outcomes, alongside factors such as graduates' occupation and demographic characteristics, and broader economic conditions. The next section focuses on the link between levels and fields of study and employment and earnings in Washington.

Higher levels of study generally yield higher employment and earnings in Washington, though apprenticeships provide strong returns to graduates

In Washington, as elsewhere in the United States and across the OECD, the likelihood of participating in the labour force and being employed increases with each level of education. In 2018, 75.2% of Washingtonians aged 25-34 with a high school diploma were employed in 2018, notably above the US average (71.6%). This figure was 77.5% for those with some college but no degree, 79.9% for associate's degree holders, and 87% for bachelor's degree holders. This places Washington around the US average for bachelor's degree holders, but well below it for individuals who have completed some post-secondary courses but no degree (79.1%), or who have earned an associate's degree (84.1%) (U.S. Census Bureau, 2019[7]).

Completing higher education also brings, on average, significant earnings benefits. Generally, the wage premium associated with completing post-secondary education increases with each level of education. At the undergraduate level, for people aged 25-34, the differences in median earnings between graduates with an associate's or a bachelor's degree are important, more so in Washington than on average in the United States. The annual wage premium for completing an associate's degree compared to a high school diploma in Washington was USD 4 000 in 2018, whereas it was USD 7 900 on average in the United States. By contrast, the annual wage premium for completing a bachelor's degree compared to a high school diploma reached USD 24 000, compared to USD 20 000 on average in the United States (U.S. Census Bureau, 2019[7]); see Chapter 3).

The state of Washington collects and publishes various types of data on graduate outcomes, as summarised in Table 7.6. The Washington State Education Research and Data Center (ERDC) provides several dashboards that allow for comparisons of student outcomes several years after they complete post-secondary education. The High School Graduate Outcomes dashboard provides information on high school graduates for 2-12 years after they completed high school. These data, provided in Figure 7.8, show the advantage of students at higher levels of study, but also show that the earnings of students who have completed an apprenticeship can be superior to those of graduates with advanced degrees. Despite this earning advantage, there were just below 20 000 active apprentices in 2019, of which close to 85% were in construction trades (WSATC, 2019[46]).

Earnings differences between associate's and bachelor's degree holders tends to grow over time. Data from the High School Graduate Outcomes dashboard suggests that, four years after high school graduation, graduates with a bachelor's degree earned on average 21% more than their peers with an associate's degree, who had already been in the workforce for one or two years. 12 years after high school graduation, bachelor's degree holders earned 32% more than associate's degree holders (ERDC, 2019[41]).

Figure 7.8. Annual earnings of graduates 1 to 12 years after high school graduation

Median pre-tax earnings of upper secondary graduates, in 2015 USD (adjusted for inflation)

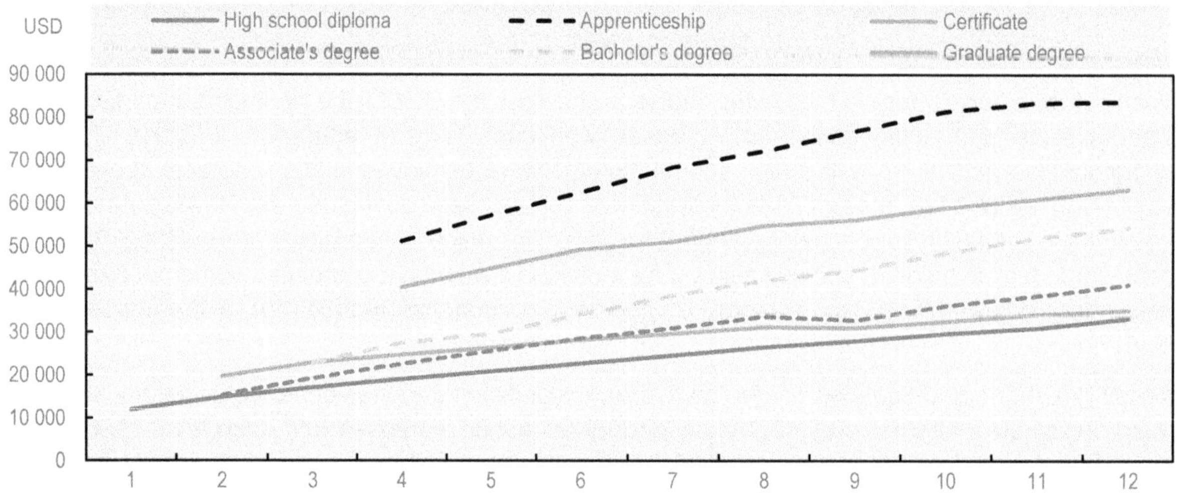

Source: Adapted from ERDC (2019[41]), *High School Graduate Outcomes Dashboard*, https://erdc.wa.gov/data-dashboards/high-school-graduate-outcomes.

StatLink https://doi.org/10.1787/888934134464

These patterns are, for the most part, in line with those observed in the United States as a whole, where the premium for completing post-secondary education has grown significantly since the 1980s, particularly at higher levels of study (Oreopoulos and Petronijevic, 2013[47]; Baum, 2014[48]). Several factors underpin this evolution. Part of it results from global skill-biased technological change and specific features of the United States' labour market, tax and social systems, discussed in Chapter 2. Part of it results from the specificities of the innovation-driven Washington economy, where the need for advanced skills exacerbates the higher returns observed for higher levels of study.

At the other side of the spectrum, however, the higher-than-average median wages of upper secondary graduates in Washington dampen the premium associated with shorter programmes such as certificates and associates. For the 25-34 year-old population, the median annual earnings of upper secondary graduates was USD 36 000 compared to USD 31 000 on average in the United States in 2018 (U.S. Census Bureau, 2019[7]). This may be a transitory phenomenon linked to Washington's booming post-recession economy, which has led to a surge in jobs requiring upper secondary education, for instance in construction. These higher earnings of upper secondary graduates may be a factor behind the challenge in increasing the college-going rate in Washington.

Factors such as labour market concentration may also be at play. Where employers have larger market power, the demand for skills has been found to increase, particularly for social, emotional and organisational skills, with a larger effect on low-skilled occupations (Hershbein and Macaluso, 2018[49]). This is of particular relevance in Washington, which is home to large employers across a variety of economic sectors, ranging from aerospace to agriculture/food manufacturing and information technology. In addition, while firms employing more than 500 people represent 0.5% of all firms in the state, they represented close to half of all employment in the state in 2015, and experienced strong employment growth between 2010 and 2015 (US SBA Office of Advocacy, 2018[50]).

The high earnings of graduates from apprenticeship programmes are particularly striking. They may relate to ongoing changes in the nature of apprenticeship pathways in the state, which are gradually moving from mostly traditional construction trades to trades in high-earning sectors, such as ICT, aerospace and health (WSATC, 2019[46]). On the one hand, this high premium for labour market relevant programmes with direct applicability in high-demand occupations aligns with research in other states (Schneider, 2015[51]). On the other hand, international research suggests that returns to job-specific training can be high in the initial years of a career, but decline over time as the skills learnt in specific training may not be well adapted to changing tasks (Hanushek et al., 2017[52]). The data shown above suggest that the while the earnings of apprenticeship graduates flatten 10 years after high school graduation, they remain notably higher than for post-secondary certificates and degrees.

The cost of higher education and debt burden is relatively low in Washington

Assessing the cost of higher education is the other part of the equation to understand to what extent post-secondary education is worth the investment. In this area, Washington performs relatively well compared to other states, in two respects. First, Washington resorts less to tuition fees to fund higher education than on average in the country, with net tuition representing a little over 40% of total educational revenue in 2018 compared to 46.6% on average in the United States. The increase in the net tuition revenue per full-time equivalent student has been small (1.7%) over the past five years, compared to an increase of 10.2% on average across the United States. This is in a context where total educational revenue per full-time equivalent student, while still below the US average, is rising significantly thanks to state investments (+8.3% since the recession, compared to a US average of +6.4% (SHEEO, 2019[53])).

Second, Washington is a state with comparatively low debt burdens. In 2018, graduates had an average debt load of USD 23 524, placing the state 44th in the distribution which ranged from USD 38 669to USD 19 728. About; 48% of students graduate with debt, compared to a range from 76% to 36% in other states (TICAS, 2019[54]). Large investments in student aid over the past decade, and particularly through the 2019 Washington budget, discussed later in this chapter, are helping to reduce the upfront cost of attending higher education.

However, a recent study on student financial aid in Washington suggests that the share of the post-secondary-related costs covered by student aid, and the form of that aid (e.g. grant, subsidised and unsubsidised loans), vary substantially according to the type of programme pursued. Two key findings from this study are that students in shorter and less expensive courses of study, such as associate's degrees, often face an "unmet need" (costs not covered by financial aid from all sources) that is greater than that faced by students pursuing bachelor's degrees, and that all students incur some debt, including non-completers (ERDC, 2018[55]). In addition, while the debt loads of students pursuing a bachelor degree are unsurprisingly higher than those pursuing shorter credentials, the difference is relatively small and may be insufficient to notably enhance the return on investment for students in shorter degrees. To better understand the financial barriers faced by specific student groups, information on debt loads disaggregated by demographic characteristics such as race and ethnicity would be helpful, as outlined in the chapter's recommendations on information (Section 7.5).

Graduates in STEM fields enjoy particularly high labour market returns in Washington

Employment rates vary by field of study, with a spread of over 10 percentage points. Fields of study with higher employment rates also tend to be associated with higher earnings. While these patterns are consistent with the US average, they are more pronounced in Washington with respect to low-earning fields. As Figure 7.9 (Panel A) shows, in 2018, graduates from industrial arts, consumer services and recreation (a diverse category ranging from middle-skills technology programmes to art/entertainment to nutrition or retailing) and health had employment rates close to 80%, which is notably lower than the national average. Graduates from programmes that command high earnings, such as architecture and engineering, computer science, mathematics and statistics, or business, but also communications and journalism, enjoyed employment rates very close to 85%, consistent with the national average.

As shown in Panel B of Figure 7.9, differences in earnings by fields of study are significant, and greater in Washington than in the US on average. For the population aged 25-64, the earning advantage of a bachelor's graduate compared to an upper secondary graduate (the higher education premium) ranges from 18.4% for education graduates to 136.8% for architecture and engineering graduates on average in the United States. In Washington, the earning premium ranges from 12.6% in education to 154.5% in computers, statistics and mathematics. The earning premium for architecture and engineering and health are notably higher than in the three other states involved in this OECD study (U.S. Census Bureau, 2019[7]).

Figure 7.9. Employment and earnings of bachelor's graduates aged 25-64, by key field of study, 2018

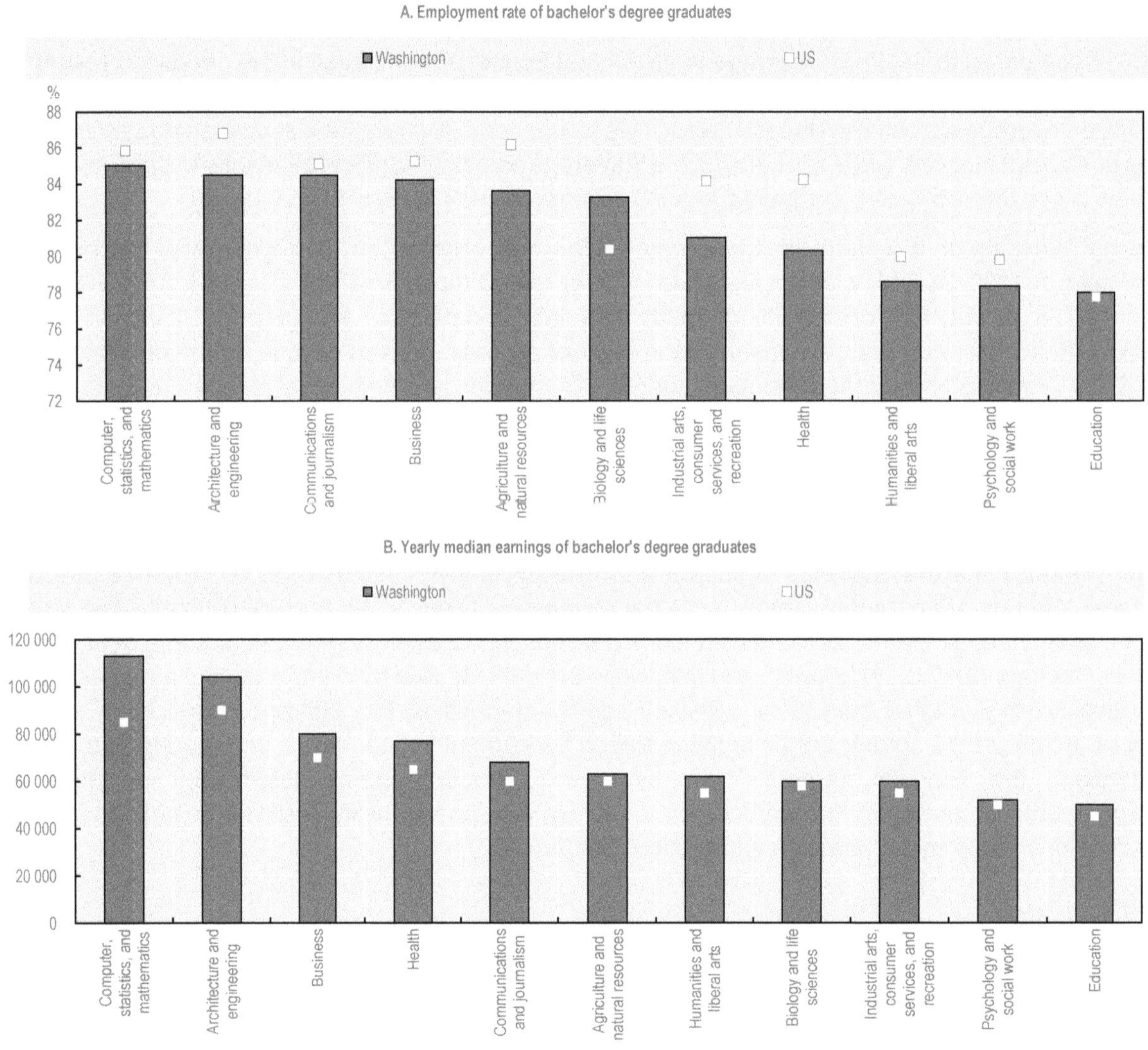

Note: The estimated median annual pre-tax earnings refer to full-time full-year wage and salary workers, are expressed in current USD, and are not seasonally adjusted (U.S. Bureau of Labor Statistics definition).
Source: Adapted from U.S. Census Bureau (2019[7]), *American Community Survey 2018* (database), https://www.census.gov/programs-surveys/acs/data.html.

StatLink https://doi.org/10.1787/888934134483

Data from Washington's Earnings for Graduates dashboard permit the exploration of graduates' earnings by field of study nine years after graduation. These data suggest that earnings grow in the first few years after graduation in all fields, but the extent of this growth varies across fields and levels of study. For instance, at the bachelor's level, graduates from computer science, engineering, and humanities see an increase in their earnings of 79%, 63% and 73%, respectively, between their first and ninth year after graduation (ERDC, 2019[41]). However, due to low starting salaries, humanities graduates still earn about half the median wage of engineering graduates nine years after graduation. By contrast, for fields of study leading to regulated occupations in sectors such as health and education, earnings grow much less over time. Between the first and the ninth year after graduation, earnings increase by 25.6% in health professions and related programmes, and by 41.2% in education. However, it is important to keep in mind that health graduates enjoy higher starting salaries than education graduates, as shown in Figure 7.10.

Figure 7.10. Earnings trajectory of bachelor's graduates, selected fields

Median annual pre-tax earnings of upper secondary graduates 1 to 9 years after degree award, 2015 USD (adjusted for inflation)

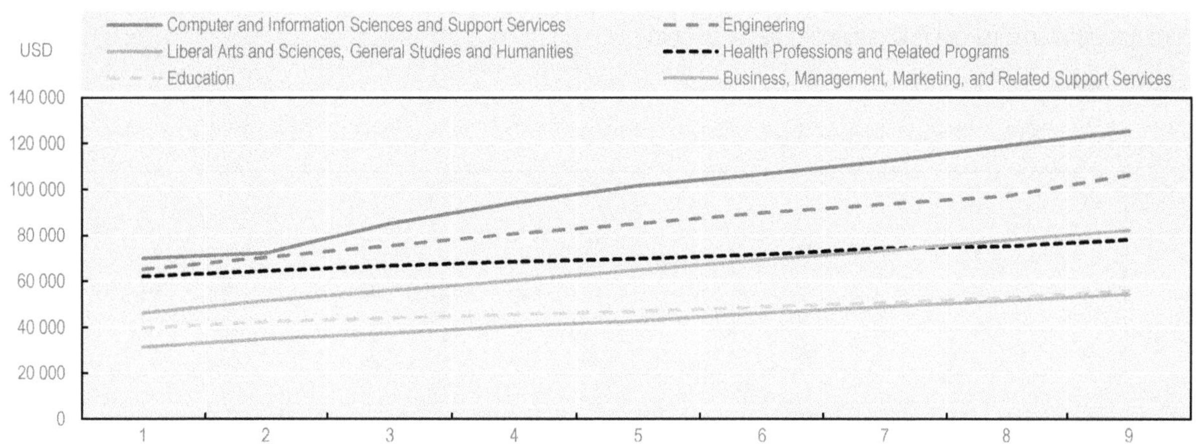

Notes: Earnings are adjusted to Q4 2015 using the Chain-Weight Implicit Price Deflator (IPD) for Personal Consumption Expenditures. Earnings data are displayed for individuals who work all four quarters in a calendar year, and whose annual earnings are at least USD 14 000 (nominal dollars).
Source: Adapted from ERDC (2019[41]), *Higher Education Outcomes Dashboard*, https://erdc.wa.gov/data-dashboards.

StatLink https://doi.org/10.1787/888934134502

These fields of study differences are consistent with national patterns, and are underpinned by a range of factors. One key factor relates to the occupational choices of graduates; in many cases, a college major conditions graduates' future occupations, and occupations are in turn strong determinants of earnings (Altonji, Blom and Meghir, 2012[56]; Carnevale et al., 2017[57]). The earning differentials between fields also appear to have grown over the past twenty years, as technological change has increased the market value of abstract tasks and decreased that of routine tasks (Altonji, Kahn and Speer, 2014[58]). Research suggests that these changes have particularly benefitted occupations in STEM and, more broadly, fields of study that emphasise quantitative skills, including business, economics and finance (Schneider, 2015[51]; Hershbein and Kearney, 2014[59]). While national, these findings are of particular relevance to Washington's economy.

The economic and policy environment in the United States and Washington state also contributes to earning differentials by field. In general, income dispersion is greater in the United States than in many

OECD countries. Wage-setting mechanisms in some sectors underpin the problem of "high-demand low-earning" majors such as education or human services. During the OECD visit, representatives of post-secondary institutions explained their challenge as employers of faculty in certain high-demand fields such as nursing, as they have to compete with the wages practicing nurses can earn in a clinical setting.

Within-field variation is wide in Washington, and greater in general fields of study without direct linkage to highly standardised/regulated occupations

Graduates from the same field of study can also experience very different labour market outcomes (Urban Institute, 2019[60]). Washington data show such within-field dispersion as in Figure 7.11. Compared to other states in this study, the within-field dispersion is particularly large (U.S. Census Bureau, 2019[7]). Large spreads are seen in fields of study with loose connections to occupations, such as business and social sciences, but also in computer science and engineering, which suggests that there is great diversity in the types of occupations in which these graduates work. The dispersion is less important in education or health.

Figure 7.11. Distribution of earnings of 25-64 year-old bachelor's graduates, 2018

Median annual earnings in USD, selected fields of study

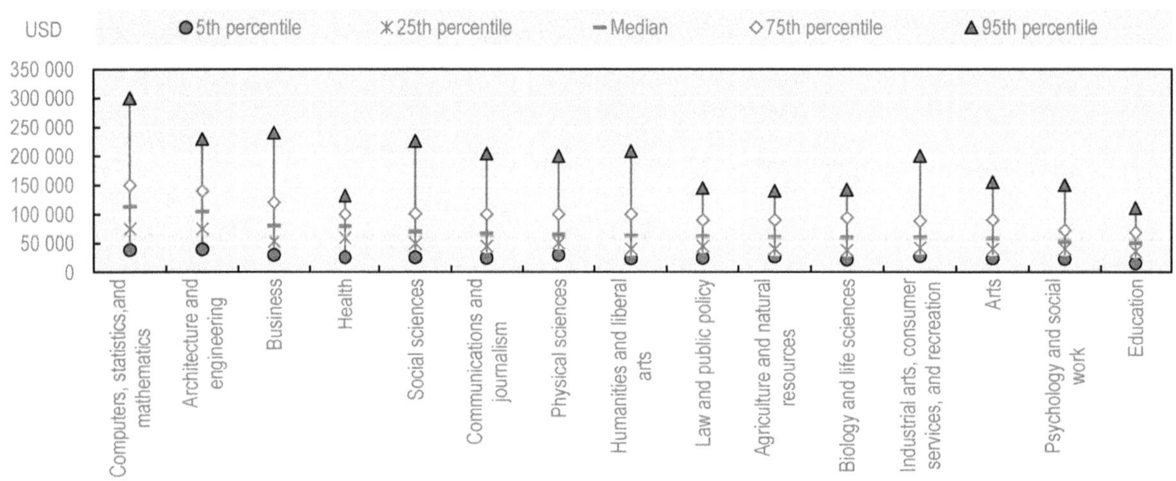

Notes: The estimated median earnings refer to full-time, full-year wage and salary workers, are expressed in current dollars, and are not seasonally adjusted (U.S. Bureau of Labor Statistics definition). The label "industrial arts, consumer services, and recreation" from the Census corresponds to "middle skills technology programs and jobs".
Source: Adapted from U.S. Census Bureau (2019[7]), *American Community Survey 2018* (database), https://www.census.gov/programs-surveys/acs/data.html.

StatLink https://doi.org/10.1787/888934134521

Differences in earnings within fields of study result from a host of different factors. Part of these differences may be due to the wide array of occupations that graduates may work in, which are very often not related to their major (Schanzenbach, Nunn and Nantz, 2017[61]). These variations in occupations are to be expected particularly in general fields of study, which are not closely connected to a clearly defined occupational path. These variations may also be linked to the type of company graduates work for and the tasks they perform. The question of whether graduates are employed in jobs that require the level of skills acquired in post-secondary education is particularly crucial. While there is no Washington-specific data on this topic, international and US-wide evidence suggests that over-qualified graduates earn less than their well-matched peers, and that the wage penalty increases for graduates who are both over-qualified and working outside of their study field (see Chapter 2).

Variation in earnings within fields of study may also result from differences in the quality of the education and skills obtained by graduates, from the self-selection of students with different social networks and skill-base in certain fields, or from employers' perception of graduates' education and skills. During the OECD visit, employer representatives reported the institution attended as an important signal of quality. Some graduates may also have complemented their qualification by acquiring supplemental credentials. Indeed, stakeholders met during the visit noted that students in general fields of study such as social sciences and humanities were often keenly aware of the need to obtain certain technical skills. Stakeholders reported that students' interest in enhancing their skills profile to make it more attractive to employers played a strong role in moving institutions towards new offerings, such as minors or course concentrations in particular subjects (data science was frequently mentioned, for example).

Returns by demographic groups

The previous section has shown that variations in graduate earnings are particularly wide by level and field of study in Washington. This section explores how social inequalities tend to map themselves onto these different labour market outcomes, resulting in a distribution of students by level and field of study that is skewed by gender, income, race and ethnicity. This, in turn, results in lower economic gains from completing post-secondary education for under-represented students compared to other graduates.

There are notable ethnic, racial and gender gaps in outcomes

In Washington, as across the country, post-secondary education graduates enjoy employment and earnings premia compared to high school graduates across all racial and ethnic groups. However, higher education does not eliminate the employment and income gaps that exist in the broader American population, but instead may reinforce them (Carnevale and Strohl, 2013[62]). Research suggests that in countries with a high premium for education, such as the United States, low social mobility is common because educational attainment is passed on through generations (Autor, 2014[63]). Further, the ability of the American educational system to promote social mobility has faded in recent decades; educational achievement at both school and post-secondary levels is increasingly associated with family income (Reardon, 2011[64]; Bailey and Dynarski, 2011[65]).

In Washington, Hispanic and Black/African American graduates aged 25-34 with a bachelor's degree have slightly higher labour force participation and employment rates than White graduates, whereas the reverse is true on average in the United States. For instance, the employment rate of White bachelor's degree holders was 87.5% in Washington compared to a US average of 89.3%, while the figure was 89.3% versus 87.6% for Hispanics, and 93.6% versus 88% for Black/African Americans (U.S. Census Bureau, 2019[7]).

With respect to annual median earnings, White graduates with a bachelor's degree earn more than Hispanic and Black/African American graduates. While in line with national patterns, the difference is more pronounced in Washington, due to higher-than-average earnings of White graduates. As a result, in 2018, there was an earnings gap of USD 10 000 between White and Hispanic workers, compared to USD 4 300 on average in the United States, and a gap of USD 15 000 between White and Black/African Americans, compared to a US average of USD 10 000 (U.S. Census Bureau, 2019[7]), see Chapter 3).

Information presented in Figure 7.12 shows the outcomes of Washington high school graduates two to twelve years after they have completed high school, and distinguishes median earnings of graduates with the three most awarded types of credentials in Washington: certificates, associate's degrees and bachelor's degrees. The data suggest that the variation in earnings by ethnic and racial group tends to decrease 12 years after completion for associate's degree graduates, but persists for both certificate and bachelor's graduates, where the gap in fact tends to grow over time.

Figure 7.12. Annual earnings in Washington by racial and ethnic groups and level of study, 2017

Median pre-tax earnings in 2015 USD (adjusted for inflation), 2 to 12 years after high school graduation

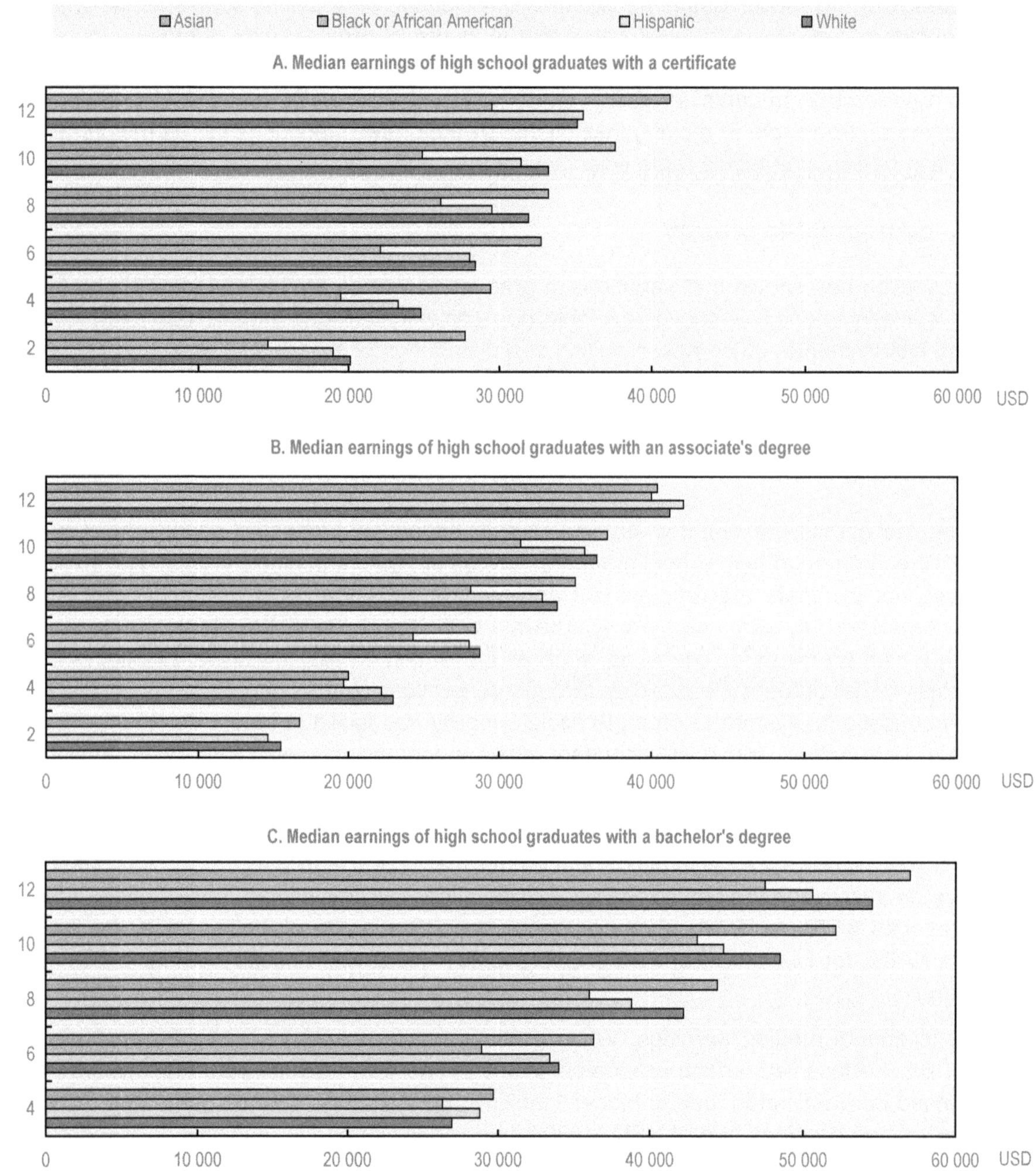

Source: Adapted from ERDC (2019[41]), *High School Graduate Outcomes Dashboard*, https://erdc.wa.gov/data-dashboards/high-school-graduate-outcomes.

StatLink https://doi.org/10.1787/888934134540

Gender differences are important in Washington. In 2018, 82.4% of women aged 25-34 with a bachelor's degree were employed in Washington, a figure lower than the three other states participating in this review and about two percentage points below the national average (84.6%). Since the employment rates of men aged 25-34 with a bachelor's degree are slightly higher in Washington than on average in the United States, at 91.8% versus 91.2%, this translates into a participation gap of 9.4 percentage points, compared to an US average of 6.6 percentage points. The gender gap in earning for the same group is also more pronounced in Washington than on average in the United States, with an USD 17 000 earnings gap between men and women, compared to a gap of USD 10 000 on average in the United States (U.S. Census Bureau, 2019[71]); see Chapter 3).

Washington data suggest that the gender gap in median earnings exists across the main types of post-secondary credentials awarded in the state. It is greatest at the certificate level on average but tends to converge over time, as the gender gap increases for associate's and bachelor's degree holders. This is consistent with previous findings for racial and ethnic gaps: equity gaps are generally greater at higher levels of education and earnings. Yet, while women who hold a certificate earn less than men, it is the only post-secondary credential where women have a greater premium for completing post-secondary education than men (ERDC, 2018[66]). This is likely due to the low earnings of women with a high school diploma, and relatively high earnings of men whose highest attainment is upper secondary education.

Figure 7.13. Earnings differences by gender and level of study

Panel A: Median annual pre-tax earnings in 2015 USD (adjusted for inflation), 2 to 12 years after high school graduation. Panel B: Median annual earnings gap between men and women, in percentage of women's earnings.

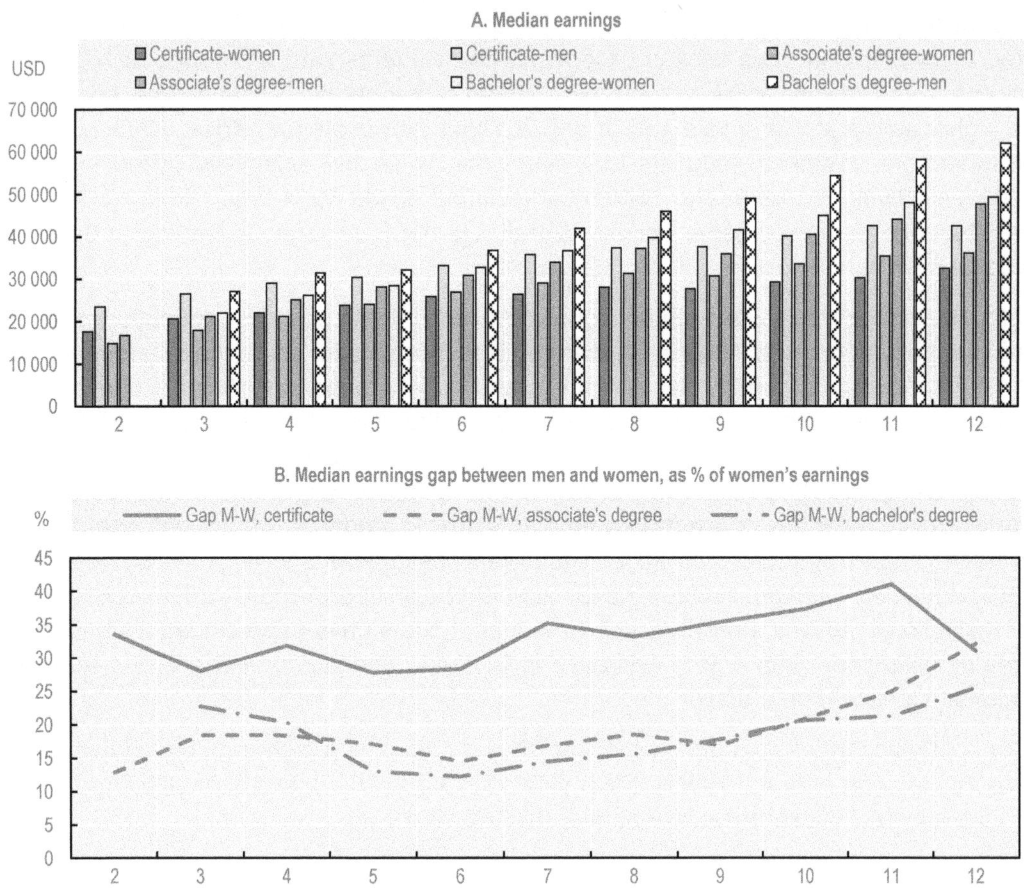

Source: Adapted from ERDC (2019[41]), *High School Graduate Outcomes Dashboard*, https://erdc.wa.gov/data-dashboards/high-school-graduate-outcomes.

StatLink https://doi.org/10.1787/888934134559

General differences in labour market outcomes by race and ethnicity in the American working-age population result from a variety of factors, including individuals' educational attainment, occupation and industry, geographic location, as well as discrimination (U.S. Bureau of Labor Statistics, 2019[67]). Among individuals with post-secondary education, many of these factors apply, in addition to key differences in the nature of higher education pursued, namely the level, field and institution of study, as discussed in the next section. Research on the alignment between qualifications and employment also shows that over-qualification is more prevalent among Black/African American and Hispanic graduates than among the general college-educated population (Rose, 2017[68]).

Various challenges help explain gender gaps. Broad issues may contribute to the gender gap in participation and employment, including the shortage of childcare across the state, a problem identified as a barrier to education participation (WICHE/WSAC, 2017[40]). Earnings differences, on the other hand, appear largely driven by the field of study chosen by women in higher education, despite equivalent academic preparedness for high-earning fields at high school level, for example in math and science. However, the smaller gaps among younger generations suggest improvements are underway.

Low participation in programmes leading to high-demand high-paying occupations among under-represented groups contributes to poorer labour market outcomes

Access to higher education in the United States has increased significantly since the 1960s across all racial and ethnic groups (NCES, 2017[69]). However, greater access overall has also been associated with increased polarisation of student populations according to income, race and ethnicity in different types of institutions. Students who are Black or African American, Hispanic or low-income are more concentrated than before in open-access colleges, while students who are White or high-income are increasingly concentrated in selective schools, which have higher per-student spending, completion rates, and lead to higher earnings (Carnevale and Strohl, 2013[62]; Carnevale and Rose, 2003[70]; Chetty et al., 2017[71]). Furthermore, research suggests that over time, while the selectivity of top institutions has increased, the selectivity of middle- and bottom-tier institutions has decreased (Hoxby, 2009[72]). Under-represented students thus enjoy better access overall, but not to institutions leading to the best labour market outcomes.

In Washington, the share of racial and ethnic groups enrolled in post-secondary education reflects roughly their share of the population, with Whites representing a slightly smaller share than their population share (Figure 7.14). Among each of the four largest ethnic and racial groups, only Asian students attend four-year institutions in larger numbers than they do two-year institutions, while roughly half of White students attend four-year institutions. The reverse is true for Hispanic and Black and African-American student groups, in which a majority attend two-year institutions. Enrolment changes in the past five years suggest that enrolment growth is largely concentrated among Hispanic students, whose enrolments in two-year institutions have jumped by more than 20% in four-year institutions and 40% in two-year institutions. White and Black/African American students have experienced an approximately 20% decline in enrolment at two-year institutions. While a smaller group, American Indians have experienced a significant decline in both types of institutions, with a 36% decrease in four-year institutions and a 22% decrease in two-year institutions (not shown on graph).

The share of apprenticeship enrolments, which, as shown earlier, is a high-earning pathway, shows that the large majority of apprentices are White (76% in 2011, 73% in 2015), and a small but growing minority is Hispanic (8.8% to 10.7% over the same period) (WSAC, 2019[30]).

Figure 7.14. Enrolment by race and ethnicity in public institutions, 2015

Total number of students (Panel A) and percentage change compared to 2011 (Panel B)

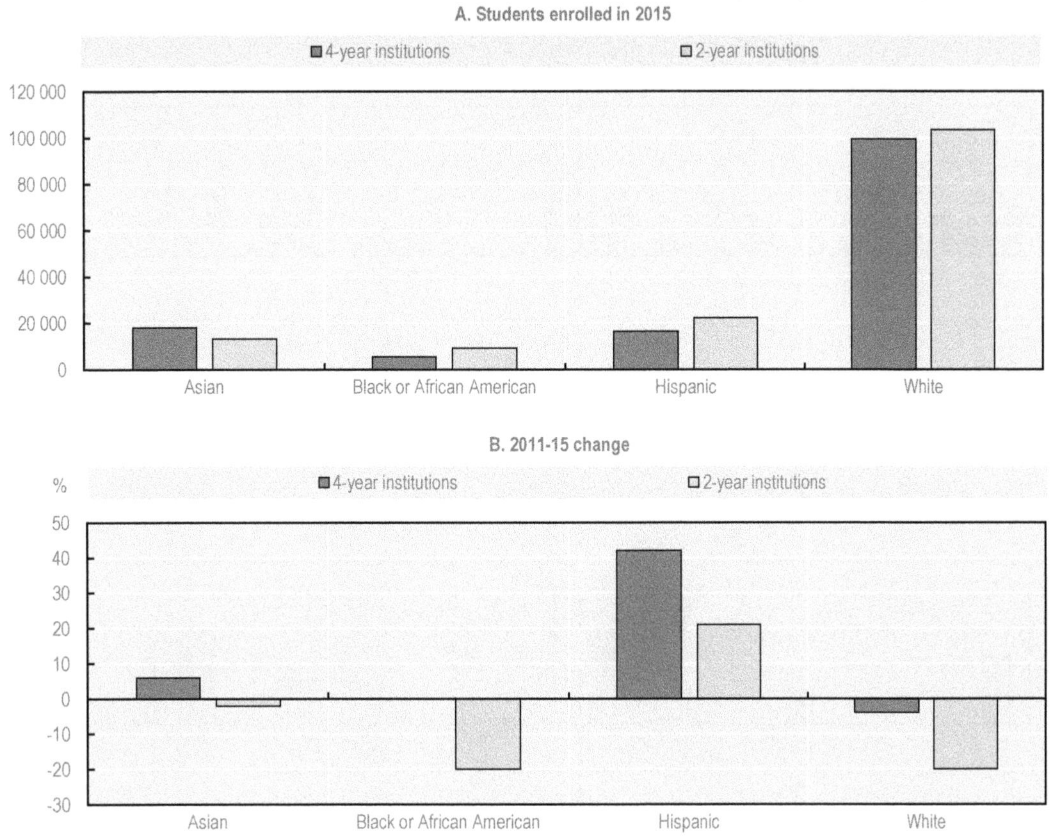

Note: These data capture only first-time, full-time fall enrolment, and are thus likely to undercount enrolments of part-time students.
Source: Adapted from WSAC (2017[73]), *Progress on Postsecondary Enrolments*, https://wsac.wa.gov/roadmap/access.

StatLink https://doi.org/10.1787/888934134578

Students from under-represented groups also tend to be over-represented in for-profit private institutions. These institutions combine poorer labour market outcomes than other types of institutions, in some cases negative returns, greater shares of students who carry debt, and larger debt loads than in other post-secondary sectors (NCES, 2018[74]; Chakrabarti and Jiang, 2018[75]; Cellini and Turner, 2018[76]). While, in Washington, the share of students enrolled in for-profit institutions is small and declining (2.5% in 2015), it is worth noting that there are larger shares of under-represented students in these institutions: in 2017, 3.6% of Hispanics, 3.7% of Black/African Americans and 11.3% of American Indians or Alaska Natives were enrolled in a for-profit institution in 2017. By contrast, 1.3% of Asians and 2.5% of White students enrolled in these institutions.

Graduates' fields of study play a key role in determining graduates' occupations and earnings, as discussed in the previous section. Using data from the Integrated Post-secondary Education System permits the identification of the share of post-secondary degrees awarded in select fields for various ethnic and racial groups and for both genders in select fields of study. Figure 7.15 shows data for both public and private institutions, and two- and four-year institutions.

Figure 7.15. Degrees awarded in select fields of study by race, ethnicity and gender, 2016-17

Degrees awarded by all post-secondary institutions in Washington, in selected fields, as a share of all degrees awarded to the given racial/ethnic group.

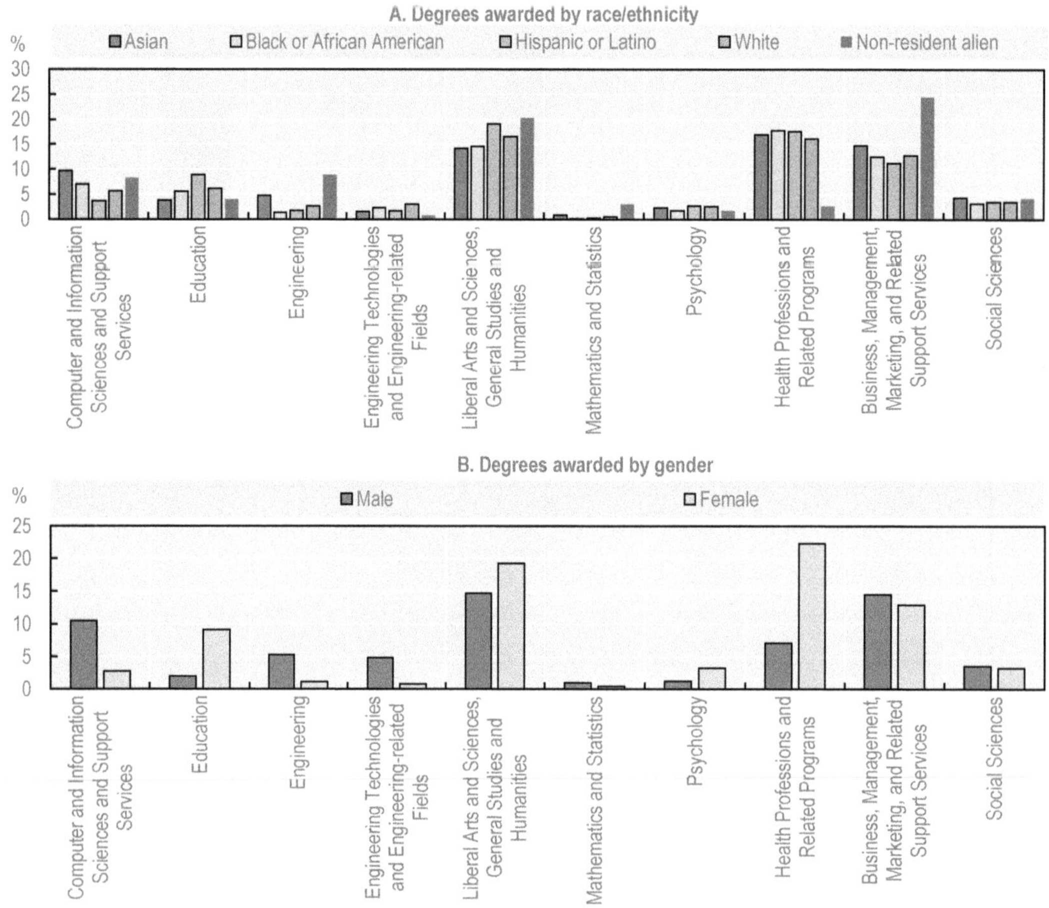

Notes: All students (including non-certificate-seeking students, full-time and part-time), first major only. Health professions and related programmes include 35 different types of programmes, including optometry, public health, medicine, dentistry and veterinary medicine.
Source: NCES (2019[19]), *Integrated Post-secondary Education Data System* (database), https://nces.ed.gov/ipeds/use-the-data.

StatLink https://doi.org/10.1787/888934134597

Figure 7.15 shows that both liberal arts and sciences and health professions and related fields account for between 14% and 20% of awarded degrees for all racial and ethnic groups (except for non-resident alien graduates). Between 10% and 15% of degrees awarded across all groups are in business and related fields (with the exception of international students, for whom 25% of degrees awarded are in business). However, differences can be seen in some fields that command very different earnings. Around 8% of all degrees awarded to Asian and non-resident alien students are in computer and information sciences, a much higher share than for other groups. Similar patterns across groups are observed in engineering. The education field presents the opposite picture: Hispanic, Black or African American and White students tend to choose education more than Asian or international students. The difference by gender, shown in Panel B, shows similar patterns: a larger share of degrees awarded to men are in computer science, engineering and business, whereas greater numbers of women choose health professions, education and liberal arts and science.

Various factors contribute to under-represented students' lower access to high-earning fields of study. Some relate to students' subjective choices and preferences, which are shaped by multiple factors including family and peer influences, and their knowledge – or lack thereof – of the outcomes of different types and fields of study (Baker et al., 2017[77]). Research also shows that high-achieving, low-income students are less likely to apply to selective institutions than their peers, despite the availability of financial aid to help them cover costs. This research also suggests that well-targeted, inexpensive interventions, including semi-customised information and simplified application processes can help (Hoxby and Turner, 2013[78]; Hoxby and Avery, 2014[79]). This highlights the importance of well-targeted student supports, as discussed in Section 7.3. Another major challenge is that of student preparedness, which is poorer among under-represented groups.

Low preparedness for higher levels of study and higher debt loads dampen the value of post-secondary education for under-represented groups

Under-represented racial and ethnic minorities not only face poorer labour market outcomes, but they also face particular barriers to accessing quality higher education and to completing the programmes in which they enrol. Regarding general access to higher education in Washington, substantial progress has been made. From 2005-15, the share of students enrolling in post-secondary education in their first year after graduation has improved, from 22% to 31% for Black or African American students, and from 15% to 22% among Hispanics. That share has also improved among White students from 31% to 36%, and among Asian students from 40% to 53%. It has remained low among American Indians or Alaska Natives (16% to 19%) (ERDC, 2019[41]). This progress suggests that Washington's efforts to remove barriers to access for all, including by improving student aid, are showing results. However, as shown in the previous section, significant efforts are required to help these students access high-earning fields and selective institutions.

Under-represented minorities have low completion rates, which prevents them from benefitting from the employment and earning premia resulting from a completed credential. Washington's *Ten-Year Roadmap* (the state's guiding policy in higher education) dashboard provides completion rates, measured for full-time, first-year freshmen at four-year institutions. While a main drawback of these figures is that they do not take into account transfer students, they allow for comparisons by student group.

In 2015, the completion rate was 68.3% on average for all four-year public institutions, ranging from 72.2% in private not-for-profit institutions, 68.6% in public institutions, and 26.6% in for-profit institutions. Looking at ethnic and racial groups, the rate for all four-year institutions ranged from 49.6% for American Indian students, 50.7% for Black or African American students, 58.9% for Hispanic students, 69.8% for White students and 77.9% for Asian students. The completion rate for Hispanic and Black or African American students at for-profit four-year institutions was respectively 18.6% and 16.7% (WSAC, 2019[30]).

Low academic achievement is a major factor underpinning low access rates (in particular to high-earning fields of study and selective institutions), low completion rates, and overall low returns on investment once the costs of education and debt loads are taken into account (Webber, 2016[80]). In STEM subjects, the state of Washington shows that low-income students and minorities perform below other groups as early as the 3rd grade, with disparities increasing throughout the educational pipeline (Figure 7.16).

Student debt affects all student groups, however it has very different consequences depending on students' earnings potential and ability to obtain supports to make payments when they need. Research suggests that the growth in default rates has been concentrated among specific groups. These include non-completers as well as graduates with short-term credentials and from institutions with low per-student resources and higher shares of low-income and African American students (Addo, Houle and Simon, 2016[81]; Looney and Yannelis, 2015[82]).

Figure 7.16. STEM performance of children, 2019

Percentage of students meeting the math standard on Washington's Smarter Balanced Assessment, 3rd, 5th, and 8th grade

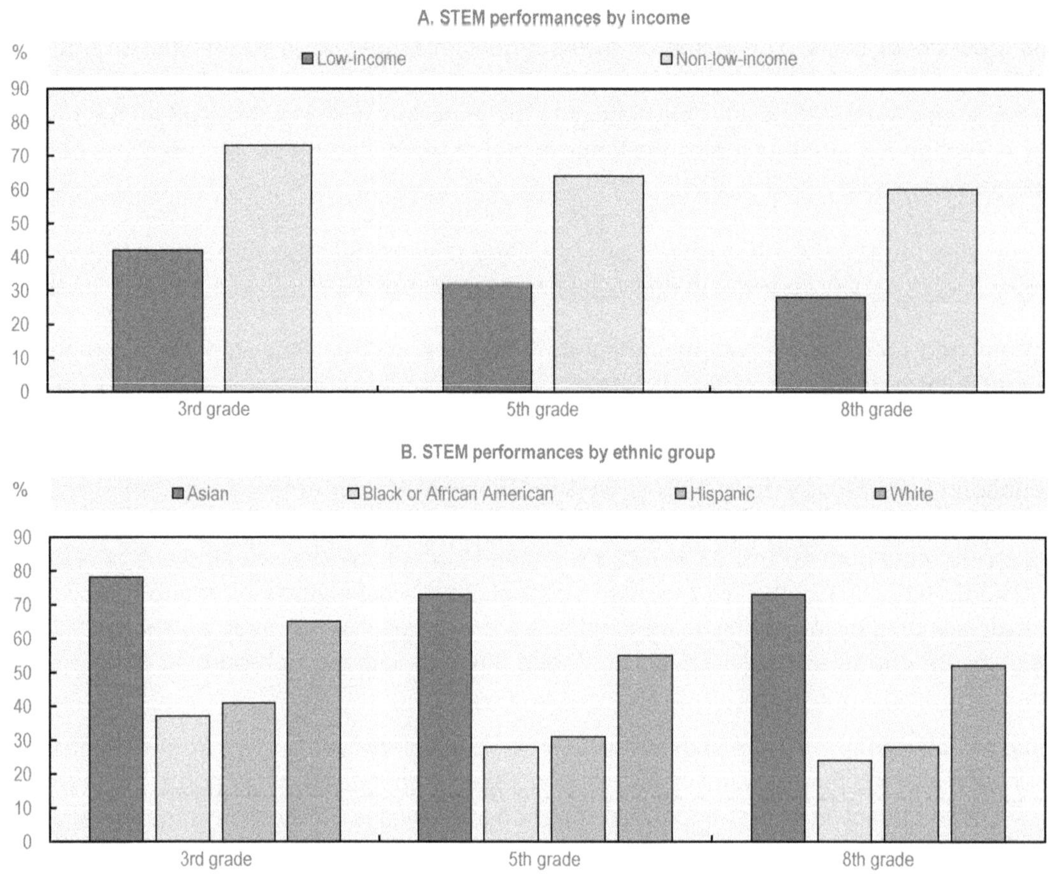

Notes: The scores for this test fall on a continuous scale from approximately 2 000 to 3 000 and it changes across grade levels. Based on their score, students fall into one of four categories of performance called achievement level and they are considered to meet the standards if they perform at levels 3 and 4.
Source: Adapted from Washington STEM (n.d.[83]), *Talent Supply and Demand Dashboard*, https://stem.wa.gov.

StatLink https://doi.org/10.1787/888934134616

With respect to gender gaps in accessing high-earning fields, preparedness is not a main problem. The majority of women enrol in post-secondary education, and complete at higher rates than men, at 70.6% on average in four-year institutions, compared to 65.5% (WSAC, 2019[30]). They also display equivalent academic ability, but tend to opt out from high-earning fields such as STEM as they go through the educational system. This finding echoes that of international research which shows ongoing challenges of self-concept and self-efficacy for young girls in mathematics (OECD, 2016[84]). As a result, a focus early on in education on girls' interest in a broader range of subjects, including mathematics and science, appears to be a key mechanism to help women access fields of study leading to high-earning careers. A broader range of supports beyond the educational system, such as childcare, is also needed to ensure women can access, and progress in, demanding careers.

7.3. Policies to improve the alignment of the higher education system and the labour market in Washington

The assessment of labour market outcomes in the previous section suggests that Washington faces three main challenges: an insufficient higher education attainment rate to address key labour market shortages, wider earnings differences by fields of study than the national average, and challenges for under-represented populations to reap the benefits of the state's booming economy.

To respond to these challenges, the state would benefit from focusing on the following five policy areas to improve the alignment of higher education and the labour market:

- **strategic planning and co-ordination** to support alignment between higher education and workforce needs;
- **funding of higher education** to address issues of access, equity and attainment;
- **educational offerings** responsive to labour market needs;
- **student supports and pathways** to promote completion and good labour market outcomes;
- **targeted information for students, educators and policy makers** about educational opportunities and labour market needs to support student choices and guide institutional practices and policy.

This section of the chapter identifies current strengths and areas for improvement in each of these five policy areas, and provides recommendations to help improve the alignment of higher education and the labour market in Washington.

Strategic planning and co-ordination

In Washington's decentralised higher education system, state authorities set broad policy targets

Washington's guiding policy in higher education is the 2013 *Ten-Year Roadmap*, a strategic document produced through a broad stakeholder consultation process across the state, and grounded in legislation (Revised Codes of Washington 28B.77.001). The Roadmap guides state-wide efforts for ten years, focusing on increasing educational attainment in the state, at both secondary and post-secondary levels.

The Roadmap includes two attainment targets to be achieved by 2023: all adults aged 25-44 in Washington should have a high school diploma or equivalent, and at least 70% of Washington adults aged 25-44 should have a post-secondary credential. While no explicit targets relate to the alignment of higher education and the labour market, the Roadmap includes a clear focus on preparing students for the labour market and meeting employer needs. To support progress toward the Roadmap's goals, the Washington Student Achievement Council (WSAC) adopts strategic frameworks on a biennial basis. These two-year plans outline key challenges and makes policy and funding recommendations to the Governor and the Legislature to advance toward the two attainment goals, as outlined in Box 7.3. WSAC is responsible for publishing information on state-wide progress made to achieve the Roadmap goals, made available publicly through a Roadmap dashboard (WSAC, 2019[30]).

Box 7.3. The *2013 Roadmap* Actions and Four Challenges of the *2019-21 Strategic Action Plan*

Washington has identified twelve actions in three areas – ensure access, enhance learning, and prepare for future challenges – to support the attainment targets set for 2023. The actions are listed in order by priority within each of the three objectives.

Ensure access:

- Ensure cost is not a barrier for low-income students.
- Make college affordable.
- Ensure all high school graduates are career and college ready.
- Coordinate and expand dual-credit and dual-enrolment programmes.
- Increase support for all current and prospective students.

Enhance learning:

- Align post-secondary programs with employment opportunities.
- Provide greater access to work-based learning opportunities.
- Encourage adults to earn a post-secondary credential.
- Leverage technology to improve student outcomes.

Prepare for future challenges:

- Respond to student, employer, and community needs.
- Increase awareness of post-secondary opportunities.
- Help students and families save for post-secondary education.

The *2019-2021 Strategic Action Plan* outlines four challenge areas requiring priority actions to meet the goals of the Roadmap:

- Address affordability: Offer multiple pathways that are accessible to students regardless of financial means.
- Close opportunity gaps: Confront barriers with support for students under-represented in educational success.
- Support regional leaders: Address regional workforce shortages and support efforts to accelerate attainment.
- Reengage adult learners: Build a framework to help adults complete post-secondary credentials.

Sources: WSAC (2013[85]; 2019[86]).

As outlined earlier in the chapter, WSAC regularly convenes secondary and post-secondary institutions and stakeholders to seek input on higher education policy. In particular, representatives from public four-year institutions, public two-year institutions, independent not-for-profit institutions and schools (K-12 level) are members of the Council. WSAC also supports the planning of higher education by working with other state agencies to generate information about labour market needs. In particular, WSAC collaborates with the SBCTC and WTECB to analyse labour market projections and the current higher education supply to identify potential gaps. This work is published through biennial "A Skilled and Educated Workforce" reports that inform the Legislature and stakeholders on sectors facing a need for increased higher education supply.

WSAC has relatively limited policy levers to steer the actions of higher education institutions toward meeting state-wide goals compared to other states in this study. For instance, unlike Virginia and Ohio, WSAC does not have a process of institutional plans that set out how institutions can meet goals that are both specific to their mission and relevant to state-wide policy (see Chapter 3). Unlike the state co-ordinating boards in the three other participating states, WSAC has no role in approving new programmes proposed by four-year public institutions. In the two-year sector, the State Board for Community and Technical Colleges provides general oversight of the college system, allocates state operating and capital funds, and oversees policy development for this sector. The Council also has a role in higher education consumer protection; it approves new degree-granting post-secondary institutions consistent with statutory criteria, and establishes minimum criteria to assess whether students who attend proprietary institutions of higher education shall be eligible for state financial aid.

Washington's decentralised model of higher education presents certain advantages from the perspective of fostering labour market relevant higher education. Government typically sets broad directions and provides funding, while leaving substantial room for all stakeholders at state and local levels to participate in improving the system's labour market alignment. Various stakeholders, including institutions, employers, intermediary organisations and others, fill this space by developing innovative solutions to specific problems, such as STEM shortages or low post-secondary participation among under-represented groups. These innovative solutions are often the product of partnerships between stakeholders.

Collaborative partnerships help align higher education and the labour market

In this governance context, partnerships are a primary channel through which stakeholders work to improve the alignment of post-secondary education with labour market needs. For instance, institutions often work together on a regional or local basis to create pathways that are relevant to the particular needs of the area. This type of approach was particularly evident in smaller communities visited by the OECD team, where strong relationships were in place between "feeder" community colleges and their regional university to facilitate the transfer of students. Efforts to prepare students for transfer appeared to be an important factor motivating collaboration, which can be explained by the large and growing share of transfer degrees granted in the state: 67% of all associate degrees granted by public community colleges in 2017/18 were transfer degrees, up from 62% in 2013/14. In addition, the fast development of "major-related program" transfer degrees, which are more closely aligned to bachelor's programmes than the more generic "direct transfer agreements" (DTA) degrees, is likely to require increased collaboration between two-year and four-year institutions to ensure the alignment of the curriculum.

Washington institutions met during the OECD visit also highlighted various types of partnerships with employers. These often involved joint work on the design and delivery of programmes, with the goal of equipping students with specific skills required by employers, often through the development of targeted programmes (e.g. Microsoft Project Management Certificate). Another example is the creation of an inter-disciplinary innovation hub at Eastern Washington University in partnership with the energy corporation Avista, outlined in Box 7.4.

Box 7.4. Eastern Washington University and Avista Development partnership

The new Catalyst Building in Spokane's University District is planned as part of the partnership between Eastern Washington University (EWU) and Avista Development. This building will feature Eastern Washington University as the primary tenant, opening the doors for EWU to become an innovation hub connecting students to the regional business community.

As the main tenant, EWU will move three programmes from its College of Science, Technology, Engineering and Mathematics (CSTEM) currently offered in Cheney to the Spokane location, namely its computer science, electrical engineering and visual communication design (VCD) programmes. This move will add 50 faculty members and an additional 1 000 students to Spokane, bringing a total of 4 000 EWU students to the Spokane University District. By bringing together students in engineering, computer science and graphic design, this initiative will also promote the development of inter-disciplinary learning and skills among students.

Source: InsideEWU (2018[87]).

WSAC regularly partners with a range of organisations on education and workforce issues, such as the Seattle Metropolitan Chamber of Commerce and the Washington Roundtable. These two industry associations represent leading employers in the state, and work to advance student success and alignment of education and the workforce through affiliate organisations, the Chamber's Alliance for Education and the Roundtable's Partnership for Learning.

In addition, several public-private partnerships have developed over the past decade, often as a result of Governor-led initiatives, to address system-wide issues with respect to aligning educational opportunities with the needs of the labour market. The STEM Education Innovation Alliance, created in 2013 and reporting directly to the office of the Governor, brings together leaders from labour, education, government, and non-profit organisations to monitor and publicise developments in STEM education. In particular, the Alliance produces an annual STEM Education Report Card, which provides information on the preparedness of Washington students in STEM disciplines from pre-school to K-12, the supply of graduates in STEM compared to the labour market demand for these graduates, and equity gaps facing under-represented groups in STEM education. The Alliance provides annual recommendations for action to the state Legislature (Washington State STEM Education Innovation Alliance, 2019[28]).

Career Connect Washington (CCW), established in the 2019 Washington Education Investment Act, constitutes a recent example of a public-private partnership that focuses on connecting youth under 29 to jobs by providing career-connected learning opportunities. CCW aims to address the "programme-rich system-poor" nature of the Washington system, through incentivising local-level partnerships among stakeholders to scale up career-connected learning opportunities available to youth. Among its main components, the programme includes a competitive grant programme available for employers and educators to develop regional networks and create or expand programmes that incorporate work-based learning. CCW also provides funding to develop a range of new registered apprenticeships in non-traditional fields such as information technology, health care, and advanced manufacturing, as well as construction. This initiative is further described in Box 7.6.

Two other notable public-private partnerships, the relatively recent Washington State Opportunity Scholarship and long-standing Mathematics, Engineering, Science Achievement (MESA) programme focus on promoting interest in STEM fields, particularly among under-represented groups. These initiatives are largely composed of student supports, and are described in Box 7.8. Finally, a Future of Work Task Force was created through legislation in 2018 to explore how the state should respond to the changing nature of the labour market. Composed of representatives from business, labour and the

Legislature, the Task Force's purpose is to provide recommendations to the Legislature and Governor on how to help workers and employers across the state thrive in a context characterised by rapid technological change, environmental and security issues, and global interdependence. The Task Force has been asked to review a series of mechanisms that are directly relevant to post-secondary education. These include the development of collaborative applied research between institutions and businesses, a focus on the labour market relevance of teaching and learning, and the development of a skills development pipeline that allows all Washingtonians to engage in lifelong learning through portable and cost-efficient credentials (Papadakis, 2018[88]). While such effort is promising, its results will need to be co-ordinated with other initiatives underway.

At the local level, many non-profit organisations lead collaborative efforts to address economic and social barriers to participating and completing post-secondary education. For instance, the United Way of Thurston County launched an Education to Financial Stability Task Force in 2019 with a range of public, private and other non-profit partners to advance a legislative and policy agenda to remove barriers to education for young people, in a county that faces a combination of skills gaps and high levels of poverty.

The lack of a well-identified co-ordination and accountability mechanism limits the state's progress

However, decentralised decision-making has the drawback of increasing the responsibility of each actor in the system to take action and to co-operate effectively with others. This does not always occur in the absence of a clear line of accountability, and can limit effectiveness in meeting key objectives such as increasing post-secondary attainment or improving the quality and labour market relevance of higher education (Payne and Roberts, 2008[89]; McGuinness, 2016[90]). In Washington, limited co-ordination may be a contributing factor to several challenges, including overall insufficient participation in post-secondary education, limited student mobility across the system and re-entry of adults into the system, and gaps in the rapid deployment of new or expanded post-secondary opportunities to meet labour market needs.

First, part of the skills shortages observed in Washington may result from inefficiencies in the state's "skills pipeline", from K-12 to post-secondary education. Career and technical education (CTE) in particular is an area where misalignment between the actions of different stakeholders can undermine the goal of strengthening and expanding labour market relevant pathways for students who may not pursue bachelor's level education. A recent State Auditor's report on CTE highlighted four areas of focus to improve the quality and take-up of these opportunities. One is to improve student and family awareness of CTE options. All others focus on improving co-ordination between stakeholders, namely between state agencies, between educational institutions at the secondary and post-secondary level, and between institutions and employers (Office of the Washington State Auditor, 2017[33]).

Mechanisms exist that could facilitate student preparation and transition between secondary and post-secondary institutions, such as dual credits. However, these mechanisms are not systematically in place and are not always well co-ordinated with the regular operations of high schools. In a regional educational assessment from 2017, dual credit options were found to be unevenly distributed across the state. Moreover, in schools that offer dual credit, stakeholders reported that the focus of staff and resources on dual credit and academic preparation could take away from other programming (WICHE/WSAC, 2017[40]). Competing policy objectives are thus apparent: in a constrained resource environment, efforts to boost students' access to college through intensive academic preparation may detract from ensuring an equal focus on the quality of alternative pathways after high school.

Co-ordination between higher education institutions and employers was another key challenge noted during the OECD visit. Institutions reported difficulty in securing meaningful and sustained employer engagement on colleges' advisory boards. The challenge in engaging employers is further indicated by the low employer response rate to a recent ad hoc survey conducted as part of Washington's research on regional needs assessment. The survey was sent to 5 128 employers across the state and 190 responses were received, at a 4% response rate (WICHE/WSAC, 2017[40]). This contrasts with experiences of other countries, such as Australia or the United Kingdom, that secure high response rates to annual surveys with a focus on employers' skills needs, which in turn is an important tool to shape post-secondary policy and supply (see Chapter 3). Examples of employers actively sharing information about their skills needs in Washington, such as through the Health Workforce Sentinel Network, appeared promising but infrequent. This topic is further discussed in Section 7.3.

Limited co-ordination can also create heightened competition between institutions, which may undermine the educational supply, in quantity or quality, in some areas of the state. Distance to institutions is a major factor affecting decisions to attend college and the choice of programme, particularly among first-generation and disadvantaged students (Garza and Fullerton, 2018[91]; Turley, 2009[92]). Stakeholders met throughout the OECD visit in central and eastern Washington expressed concerns about institutional competition for limited funding, and the approach to distributing this funding. A problem raised by some stakeholders focused on the mechanism through which institutions advocate for funding. This approach, which appears to rely mostly on direct communication between institutions and state legislators, or (in some cases) through collective communication via umbrella bodies for each sub-sector, was perceived to provide a recurring advantage to high-ranking institutions compared to regional institutions serving local labour market needs and with larger shares of disadvantaged students. As will be further discussed, despite a shift of state funding towards colleges and regional institutions, the overall decreasing funding levels continue to pose challenges for institutions that cannot rely on high levels of tuition. The combination of lower institutional revenue and higher shares of disadvantaged students can exacerbate inequities.

Some countries have implemented mechanisms to help government steer the provision of higher education. These tools are often utilised to help balance competing priorities, such as the geographic accessibility of a range of quality post-secondary options, along with the promotion of excellence in teaching and research. These tools range from institutional self-assessments to mutually agreed metrics to which funding consequences are attached. Ireland provides an example of an approach based on dialogue between government and institutions. This approach, which involves the definition of "compacts" between government and each institution, is described in Box 3.3 in Chapter 3.

Recommendations for strategic planning and co-ordination

1. Monitor progress against the state-wide metrics set out in the Career Connect Washington initiative. The definition of career-connected initiatives should be clear, standardised and used by all stakeholders. Reporting of these metrics should be state-wide and regional.
2. Request public higher education institutions and employers benefitting from state support to report on the supply of labour market relevant education and career-connected learning to identify and address gaps. Institutions could report on the share of students engaged in career-connected learning, by level and field of education and student demographics.
3. Employers who benefit from tax credits and over a certain revenue size could report on their contribution to labour market relevant education and career-connected learning. Metrics of interest include, for example: the number of career-connected learning opportunities provided to students; the share of workers by age group and demographic benefitting from company support in undertaking up-skilling activities; and ways in which the company may be engaged in skills advisory councils of local higher education institutions or otherwise engaging with higher education institutions on skills needs.
4. Consider the development of a large-scale employer survey that requests information on a periodic basis about skills gaps and recruitment challenges, satisfaction with graduate skills, employee training, practices to support labour market relevant education provision, and practices that would help government and others engage with employers. Best practices and international experience in employer survey administration to generate good response rates from diverse employer groups should be considered (e.g. United Kingdom and Australia employer skills surveys, see Chapter 3).This would complement the proposed graduate outcomes survey (see recommendations on information).
5. Enhance employer representation on key planning bodies. This includes representation from employers of various business sizes, sectors and geographic areas on the WSAC Board and the CCW networks.
6. Consider establishing a process to assist the Washington State Legislature in assessing the extent to which the post-secondary system supports state-wide, regional and local labour market needs. This process could take the form of compacts, in which public higher education institutions outline institutional missions and highlight progress towards: i) the institution's stated mission; ii) state-wide objectives such as those stated in the WSAC Roadmap and Strategic Action Plan, the *2019 Workforce and Education Investment Act*, and the Career Connect Washington initiative; and iii) regional and local needs.
7. Continue to improve existing data systems to complement the institutional agreements/compacts with a set of metrics pertaining to the institution. This would include information on participation and completion, career-connected practices and outcomes, and labour market outcomes. A number of metrics of interest that are currently missing are included in recommendations on information.

Funding

Recent state investments are promising steps to improve post-secondary participation and graduate outcomes and meet labour market needs

Funding to support institutions and intermediary organisations

Post-secondary education funding in Washington has two key strengths: a strong commitment to accessibility, which helps remove financial barriers to participation, and a growing focus on providing work-based learning opportunities to students, a practice which has been shown to improve students' transition to the workplace (Comyn and Brewer, 2018[93]).

Annual state appropriations to institutions represent the main category of expenditure in post-secondary education, ahead of student financial assistance. In 2019, the state of Washington spent about USD 2 billion annually on public higher education institutions in 2019, a 17% increase since 2000. As shown in Chapter 3, state appropriations in Washington have fallen more than in other states after the recession of 2008-09, but have increased more than in other states in recent years. Total state funding in 2019 was close to, but not yet reaching, pre-crisis levels. At the same time, significant tuition increases since 2009 have allowed total funding levels to remain stable and even grow over time, most notably in the four-year sector. This regular funding through annual appropriations is not connected to labour market needs.

In addition to regular funding, institutions receive ad hoc investments that respond to particular needs. The Workforce Education Investment Act (WEIA) 2019, contains a series of provisions that infuse funding to institutions, specifically to address labour market needs. For instance, it commits over USD 40 million over two years to increase high-demand programme faculty salaries, including but not limited to nursing educators, other health-related professions, information technology, computer science, and trades, including welding. These investments have the benefit of being rapid responses to critical issues, but can run the risk of not addressing broader funding challenges discussed in the next section.

The state of Washington also channels funds to stakeholders whose work can contribute to a better alignment of the educational supply and labour market needs. Funding has been provided to various public-private partnerships that aim to alleviate the shortage of STEM graduates and increase the engagement of under-represented students in these fields. The endorsement and funding of the Career Connect Washington initiative is a prominent example of such an approach, which recognises that aligning the supply and demand of skills relies in part on the actions of diverse stakeholders at the local level. The creation and funding of regional networks, led by organisations such as regional workforce boards, chambers of commerce or educational service districts, may help expand the quantity of career-connected opportunities available and help raise interest in career and technical education.

Student financial aid

Investments in student aid have been substantial and growing. In 2015, Washington was one of only four states, alongside California, New Jersey and Wyoming, that spent more than USD 4 000 per low-income student, exceeding the federal expenditure on Pell Grants for their state (Eaton et al., 2019[94]). This focus on supporting low-income students is likely to be a main contributor to Washington's good position with respect to student debt, as one of the ten states with lowest student debt (TICAS, 2018[95]). The State Need Grant (SNG), which preceded the Washington College Grant until 2019, represented an investment of USD 324 million in 2018, a 138% increase since 2003 (Bania, Burley and Pennucci, 2013[96]). Despite this investment, an important share of eligible students on income criteria were not receiving the award due to funding constraints.

The recent Washington Education Investment Act (WEIA), passed in 2019, addresses the SNG's limitations by converting it into the new Washington College Grant, described in Box 7.5. The Washington

College Grant expands eligibility to students, for instance by supporting those in registered apprenticeships, and by raising the income eligibility threshold to cover students from middle-income families in addition to low-income students. The Grant also increases the maximum award to cover full tuition and fees. To address the previous backlog of eligible students due to funding constraints, the Grant becomes an entitlement programme starting in academic year 2020/21, which means that all eligible students are guaranteed to receive funding.

Box 7.5. The Washington College Grant

The Washington College Grant, introduced in 2019 through the Washington Education Workforce Investment Act, replaces the State Need Grant as Washington's main state financial aid programme. As the state's most extensive financial aid programme, the State Need Grant served over 70 000 low-income students each year. However, funding limitations have meant that not all eligible students received grants (at the time the grant was introduced, an estimated 18 000 eligible students could not be served.)

The 2019/20 academic year serves as a transition year to implement the Washington College Grant. Grant funding will not yet be guaranteed, but with increased funding, the programme will serve an additional one-third of the remaining unserved students, so approximately 6 000 additional students. In addition, the maximum award amounts for public colleges and universities will increase to cover full tuition and fees.

Starting in the academic year 2020-21, key features of the Washington College Grant will include:

- **Planned investments:** USD 199 million will be allocated over the 2020-2021 biennium to the Washington College Grant. This will fund: the backlog of eligible students who did not receive a grant previously due to funding limitations; the increase of the maximum award to cover full tuition and fees; grants and expansion to apprenticeship programs; and the expansion of the income eligibility threshold. Starting in the academic year 2020/21, grant funding will be guaranteed for all eligible students. General funds would be used should the funds planned in the WEIA be insufficient.
- **Income eligibility:** all students at or below median family income (MFI), which is currently USD 91 766 for a family of four, will be eligible. Students with family incomes up to 55% of the MFI will qualify for full awards (the maximum set for their institution type), while students with family incomes between 56% and 100% MFI will qualify for prorated partial awards. Previously, students qualified for the State Need Grant if their family income was at or below 70% of the state's MFI, which is USD 61 500 for a family of four.
- **Programme eligibility:** all students in eligible institutions, which include public two- and four-year colleges and universities, and many accredited private/independent colleges, universities and career schools. The grant can be used towards bachelor's and associate's degrees, vocational certificates, and registered apprenticeships. Students enrolled full-time or part-time are both eligible.
- **Maximum awards:** the grant will cover full tuition and fees at any approved/eligible in-state public college or university, and comparable amount towards tuition and other education-related costs at an approved private college or career training programme.

Source: WSAC (n.d.[97]); information provided by the Washington Student Achievement Council to the OECD team on 30 September 2019.

To support the large investments committed through the WEIA, Washington has developed an innovative funding approach calling on the contribution of large firms in need of highly-skilled workers. While most revenues supporting WEIA expenditure will come from the state's general fund, a surcharge to the business and operations tax will be applied to certain industries including advanced computing businesses, representing about 21% of the total funding. The funding provided through the surcharge will be deposited in a dedicated Workforce Education Investment Account, rather than in the general state fund, and will be overseen by the Workforce Education Investment Accountability and Oversight Board. This approach aims to ensure the funds are used as intended and will allow for progress to be tracked against a set of relevant metrics. However, the creation of this new entity will require strong co-ordination with the existing bodies that play a role in the realms of secondary and post-secondary education as well as employment, including WSAC, SBCTC, WTECB, the Department of Labour and Industries' Apprenticeship and Training Council (ATC), and the Office of the Superintendent of Public Instruction (OSPI).

Washington is also investing in specific programmes targeting students facing significant economic challenges. Examples of recent policy initiatives include the assistance for college students programme (2SHB 1893). In this effort, WSAC is working with partners in the Department of Social and Health Services and SBCTC to implement a multi-pronged strategy to increase basic needs supports for college students. This includes increasing college students' access to emergency assistance through a new grant pilot programme to community and technical colleges; increasing college students' eligibility for the US Department of Agriculture's Supplemental Nutrition Assistance Programme (USDA SNAP) (known as Basic Food programme in Washington), increasing college students' access to SNAP benefits via electronic benefits transfer (EBT) card use on campus, through USDA waivers and support of campus USDA applications, and increasing communication with all college students receiving financial aid about possible eligibility for public benefits and steps to apply.

Another example is the Homeless College Students pilot programme (2SSB 5800). Implemented by WSAC and SBCTC, the pilot programme includes funding to six community and technical colleges to create programmes to support homeless and housing-insecure students, and conducts a needs assessment for food and housing insecurity across participating colleges. This is expected to provide participating institutions and the state authorities with key data for future improvements and policy development. This programme is complement by a state-wide learning community on homelessness in post-secondary education for pilot institutions and volunteer colleges over 2019-21. The learning community aims to provide resources and technical assistance, connect institutions with agencies and community-based organisations, facilitate the co-ordination of efforts, and support the development of legislative recommendations.

State funding to institutions could be used more effectively to boost quality at community colleges and encourage labour market relevance across all fields

Funding levels

Washington's post-secondary education funding landscape also faces important challenges. Low per-student funding in the two-year sector is a particular challenge, given that community college students are more often low-income and less academically prepared than students in the four-year sector (Musu-Gillette et al., 2017[98]; AACC, 2019[99]). Another challenge relates to the allocation of public funding: the main channels through which the state funds post-secondary education, namely annual institutional appropriations and the Washington College Grant, do not take into account students' labour market outcomes. While this policy choice may not create issues for a large part of institutions and students, risks exist for students who face poor outcomes and yet incur important costs to attend post-secondary education.

Total funding levels have slightly increased over the past two decades. In 2019, state funds per full-time equivalent student in public post-secondary education, including both four-year and two-year institutions, were slightly above the 2000 level (USD 8 569 versus USD 8 316 in constant 2019 dollars). As Figure 7.17 shows, state investments directed to community colleges have stayed stable, but they have significantly decreased for four-year institutions. Four-year institutions have, however, been able to compensate through much greater rises in tuition fees, thus achieving a total revenue per full-time equivalent student that is twice as large on average among four-year institutions compared to community colleges.

Figure 7.17. Per-student expenditure, state appropriations and tuition fees, 2000-19

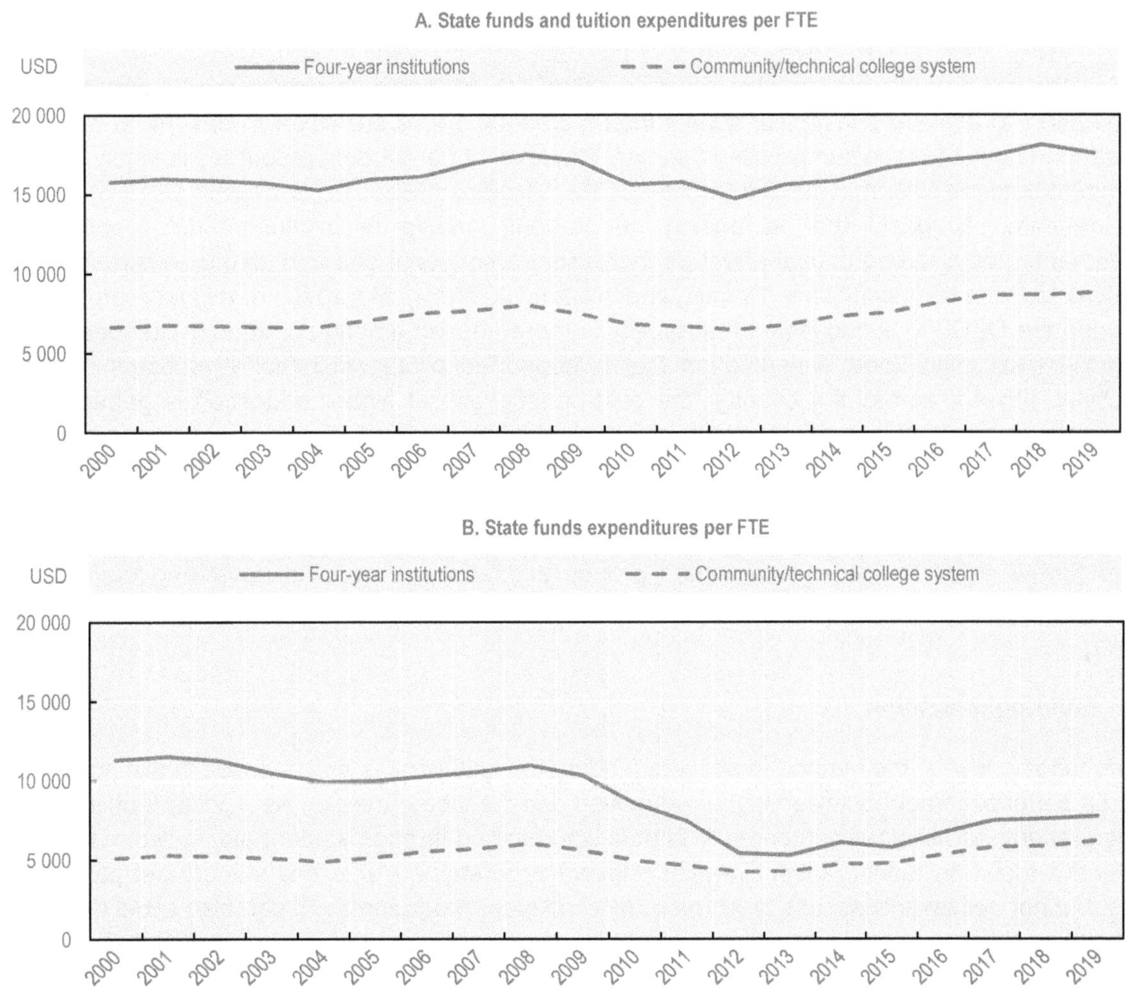

Notes: Actual state-funded FTE, in 2019 constant dollars. State funds include Stimulus FY 2010, Opportunity Express in 2011, Opportunity Pathways since 2011.
Source: Adapted from the Legislation Evaluation and Accountability Programme (LEAP) Office (2020[100]), *Washington State Fiscal Information*, http://fiscal.wa.gov/OtherResources.aspx.

StatLink https://doi.org/10.1787/888934134635

Overall, and despite tuition increases, expenditure by student in Washington remains lower than on average in the United States. While total educational revenue per full-time equivalent student in public higher education has increased by 8.3% in Washington since the recession, versus a US average of 6.4%, it remains below average at USD 12 403 in 2018 constant dollars, versus USD 14 556 on average in the United States. Despite experiencing strong economic growth in recent years, Washington spends less on higher education per capita than the national average. This is noteworthy when compared to other states with large public higher education sectors, higher-than-average participation rates, and innovation-driven economies such as New York or California (SHEEO, 2019[53]).

The 2019 WEIA recognises the particular challenges faced by community colleges, which have limited ways to raise funds through either tuition or private donations. The legislation provides an infusion of funding to support regular operating costs as well as employee compensation, programme enhancements, student services and general quality enhancements (close to USD 28 million over fiscal years 2019-21). It also provides USD 32 million over 2019-21 to support the implementation of the Guided Pathways programme, a promising programme that aims to help students identify their career goals and design their educational pathway accordingly. The programme is discussed in the student support section of the chapter.

However, the scale of this new funding, which the SBCTC will distribute among the 34 public colleges, may fall short to achieve substantial quality improvements. There are several reasons to continue to increase funding in the community college sector. The level of per-student resources is highly correlated with student outcomes (Carnevale and Strohl, 2013[62]; Goolsbee, Hubbard and Ganz, 2019[101]). Further, recent research suggests that increasing per-student funding to institutions to support quality improvements has a strong causal effect on increasing enrolments and completion, whereas lowering tuition was found to be insignificant (Deming and Walters, 2017[102]). Moreover, employer representatives met during the OECD visit suggested that quality is more uneven among community colleges than it is among four-year institutions, a perception that is supported by recent national research on college productivity. Indeed, across the country, the cost-benefit ratio of higher education is generally lower among open-access colleges compared to selective institutions, but it is also more inconsistent, even after controlling for students' aptitudes upon entry (Hoxby, 2018[103]). Third, community colleges constitute an existing infrastructure for labour market relevant education that is worth leveraging (Goolsbee, Hubbard and Ganz, 2019[101]). Community colleges have good territorial coverage, are often an entry point to further study for under-represented groups and adults in need of up-skilling than four-year institutions, and tend to deliver better outcomes than private for-profit institutions (Cellini and Turner, 2018[76]).

Funding allocation

Besides funding levels, the method to allocate funding to institutions is an important public policy tool to support a better alignment between higher education and the labour market. As a policy tool, institutional funding presents advantages compared to channelling funding through student aid, in two main ways. It can place a focus on funding labour market relevant programmes, whereas student aid can increase access, but not necessarily access to labour market relevant programmes. It can also avoid the risk that institutions increase tuition fees or decrease institutional aid as a result of increases in state financial aid (Goolsbee, Hubbard and Ganz, 2019[101]).

In Washington, appropriations to both two- and four-year institutions are made through a base-plus method. A formula also applies to two-year institutions. In the four-year sector, appropriations are made directly by the Legislature to four-year institutions. In the two-year sector, funding is appropriated to the SBCTC, which then allocates funding to community and technical colleges through a funding formula.

Despite a strong focus on the provision of career-connected learning in the state, there is no linkage between regular state appropriations to institutions and labour market outcomes. This can be a challenge, as some high-demand fields can be costly to deliver. Institutions with more constrained resources and who are rewarded by metrics other than labour market outcomes (e.g. enrolments or completions) may have limited offerings of higher-cost, higher-earning programmes, such as healthcare or information technology (Holzer, 2015[104]). The link between public funding and performance has developed in a range of countries, with states like Ohio, Tennessee and Texas having models that attach a substantial share of institutional funding to meeting key metrics, including labour market outcomes (Minaya and Scott-Clayton, 2017[105]; Dougherty and Reddy, 2013[106]). Examples of such models are presented in Chapter 3 of the report.

In Washington, performance funding is in place in the college sector through the Student Achievement Initiative (SAI) established in 2007. Through the SAI, the SBCTC allocates about 5% of state funding based on performance metrics linked to credential completion and student retention. A recent evaluation found that the model has not improved overall completion rates, but has increased the production of short-term certificates in the years following the implementation of the SAI. This unintended effect suggests that institutions are responsive to performance funding schemes, and that there may be other factors at play that drive completion and retention, such as the need for sufficient resources and capacity to improve student success (Hillman, Tandberg and Fryar, 2015[107]). These findings have two implications that merit closer attention: first, the SAI may need to be accompanied with additional investments in the quality of student learning and student supports. Second, there is value in considering a broader range of outcome metrics than just completion and retention. These could include labour market outcomes (both upon graduation and over time), job stability, and measures that take into account the lower earnings of "social service" jobs such as those in the public sector (Minaya and Scott-Clayton, 2017[105]).

No performance funding applies in the four-year sector. While labour market outcomes of graduates from four-year institutions are generally good, the assessment provided in this chapter shows wide variation by field of study. A first step in encouraging focus on labour market relevance for all students may consist of providing more easily accessible information on earnings by programmes (see recommendations for information). Another step could be requesting institutions to provide information on their efforts to expand career-connected learning (see recommendations for strategic planning and co-ordination).

A large amount of public funds is also channelled through student financial aid. The main goal of student aid is to improve accessibility to higher education and to allow students to choose the types of institutions, levels and fields of study that suit best their preferences and abilities. However, given the growing amount of public funds utilised for student aid, caution should be exercised to ensure that the greater number of students who may choose to go to higher education are protected against the risk of poor quality programmes that could leave students with a combination of debt and low earnings. While the risk of accumulating debt is relatively low, given that much of Washington's student aid approach is based on grants, it is still a concern, particularly among vulnerable students, given the indirect costs of higher education (among others, living, transportation, childcare and lost wages).

Recommendations on funding

1. Continue efforts to increase annual funding to community and technical colleges to: (i) invest in quality instruction and continue scaling up funding for Guided Pathways and other evidence-based practices to improve students' completion of high-quality, labour market relevant credentials; (ii) continue raising faculty salaries in particular in shortage fields; and (iii) invest in faculty professional development to strengthen teaching of labour market relevant skills. Increased state funding should be accompanied by reporting of colleges on graduate labour market outcomes, in line with recommendation 7 in strategic planning and co-ordination.
2. Consider the inclusion of labour market related metrics in the Student Achievement Initiative. These could include employment and earnings, as well as employment in social service occupations, and unemployment rates, alongside current retention and completions metrics.
3. Consider establishing state "rapid response" funding to institutions to address short-term labour market needs, including supporting the development of career-connected learning opportunities. These funds should be allocated based on local/regional labour market needs and institutional strengths. The proposed institutional compacts (recommendation 6 in strategic planning and co-ordination) could facilitate decisions on how these funds should be allocated.
4. Consider establishing accountability requirements for institutions with large shares of Washington College Grant-supported students (over a threshold to be determined by the state). These institutions could be required to disclose information on debt load and labour market outcomes for graduates. Thresholds could be determined that would motivate ineligibility for institutions that fall under a certain standard of debt-to-outcome ratio.
5. Consider financial incentives for completion targeted to students identified as at risk of dropping out, combined with academic supports and counselling (see also recommendations on student supports).
6. Simplify the various state and federal financial supports available to disadvantaged adults, from social benefits to work-related benefits under the Workforce Investment and Opportunity Act to help adults participate in post-secondary education, in line with the state's Adult Reengagement initiative (see also recommendations on student supports).

Educational offerings

Washington's post-secondary education system is comprehensive, and institutions pay increasing attention to labour market relevance

State initiatives

Ensuring a sufficient supply of post-secondary programmes across the state and improving access and completion rates are both key to helping the state meet its labour market needs. As discussed previously, the state and employers have several options to ensure sufficient numbers of post-secondary graduates are available to fill jobs in the economy. They can produce graduates through Washington institutions, or attract graduates from other states or countries. The different routes to supplying graduates have drawbacks and benefits, as highlighted in Table 7.5. Taking into consideration the goal to provide good employment opportunities to Washingtonians and the volatility of migration flows, boosting the domestic production of graduates is a policy priority in Washington.

Table 7.5. Three ways to increase the supply of graduate skills

	Post-secondary graduates from Washington institutions	Post-secondary graduates from other states	Post-secondary graduates from other countries
Benefits	• The state is able to influence the quantity and quality of graduate skills through policy. • Employers are familiar with the skills of Washington graduates. • Employers can provide input into the design of Washington's programmes to ensure alignment. • Washington graduates can take advantage of quality jobs produced in the state.	• No cost to the state for the education of post-secondary educated workers. • Diversity of the post-secondary educated workforce.	• No cost to the state for the education of post-secondary educated workers. • Diversity of the post-secondary educated workforce.
Drawbacks	• Challenge in increasing the number of post-secondary students overall, particularly in high-demand fields. • Need to leverage all populations, which can require costly outreach and supports.	• Volatility of the supply of out-of-state graduates given competition across states to attract talent. • Uncertainty about the skills of graduates from other states.	• Volatility of the supply given international competition to attract talent. • Volatility of the supply due to federal role in determining the number and profile of skilled migrants. • Uncertainty about the skills of graduates from other countries.

Washington generally has a large range of post-secondary opportunities available to students. While stakeholders met during the OECD visit noted some shortages of study spaces during the OECD visit, these appeared to be well identified and limited to specific in-demand fields, such as nursing, computer science and education. In these fields, stakeholders identified faculty shortages as an important issue, due to the competitive salaries that qualified professionals can obtain in industry or clinical settings. In some programmes, nursing again in particular, the shortage of clinical positions for students to complete required programme components also limits the capacity to meet student demand. In other cases, study at a certain level is not possible in all areas of the state. For example, stakeholders reported that education doctorates are often not available in regional public institutions, despite being in high-demand among place-bound individuals.

These challenges appeared to be taken into account by state policy, with targeted infusion of funding to increase faculty salaries, and new approaches to develop learning opportunities outside of traditional post-secondary programmes, including through online delivery and community-based learning. For instance, the Professional Educator Standards Board (PESB) has received public funding to develop alternative routes to certification targeting non-teaching staff in the educational system and individuals outside of the sector who want to change careers. These alternative routes are partnerships between approved teacher preparation programmes, school districts and other organisations that aim to provide shorter and more affordable routes to certification and could contribute to alleviating teacher shortages.

Besides ensuring a sufficient supply of higher education, co-ordinating boards in some states use the process of approving new programmes for which public institutions require funding to assess whether the proposed programmes will help address current and future labour market needs, as discussed in Chapter 3. In Washington, the Higher Education Coordination Board in place from 1985 to 2012 had the authority to review new programme funding proposals submitted by institutions to the Legislature. However, some stakeholders have described this exercise as limited to reducing overlaps in offerings, which resulted in unnecessary delays in programme approvals. This function was discontinued when WSAC was created.

However, Washington's current policy focus on career-connected learning presents an opportunity to boost the development of labour market relevant programmes, within and outside of post-secondary education. In 2016, Washington was one of six states competitively selected to receive funding as part of the National Governors' Association (NGA) Policy Academy on Scaling Work-Based Learning. The Policy Academy, supported by funding from the Siemens Foundation, has focused on assisting states in scaling high-quality, work-based learning programmes for youth and young adults in STEM-intensive industries such as advanced manufacturing, healthcare, information technology, and energy. Washington continues to participate in the Policy Academy, now in its third phase, as a mentor state. The state's participation in this initiative was an important catalyst in developing Career Connect Washington, an initiative to significantly expand the number of youth who participate in career exploration, career preparation and career launch programmes. The initiative also aims to induce career-oriented thinking earlier in a young person's pathway and to change the negative perceptions associated with vocational routes (Box 7.6).

Apprenticeship is a model of particular interest in Washington. The state is engaged in expansion strategies, including through making apprentices eligible for the Washington College Grant and making funding available to institutions and stakeholders through Career Connect Washington (Box 7.6). The state's goal is to double enrolments from about 20 000 active apprenticeships in 2018, and to diversify both the profiles of apprentices and the sectors where apprenticeship can be pursued. A much-cited example of a well-functioning programme is Apprenti, also described in Box 7.6. Stakeholders repeatedly described the programme as meeting industry needs within a compressed timeframe, while providing a significant earning boost to participants.

Box 7.6. Improving labour market relevance of post-secondary pathways in Washington

Career Connect Washington

The Career Connect Washington programme aims to significantly expand the scale of career-connected learning opportunities in the state through a system-wide approach. The programme stems from work conducted between 2017 and 2019 by the Career Connect Task Force, convened by the Governor and composed of leaders from business, labour, government, non-profit organisations and educational institutions. The Task Force was charged with reviewing existing career-connected learning opportunities in the state and recommending approaches to expand their provision. These opportunities include the following, at both secondary and post-secondary level:

- career exploration programmes, such as career fairs or courses proposing work-based problem solving;
- career preparation programmes, which include short internships or concentration of vocational courses in secondary education ("Career and Technical Education (CTE) concentrators");
- career launch programmes, such as registered apprenticeship and programmes requiring work-based learning in two- and four-year institutions.

The Task Force identified the existence of many quality career-connected learning opportunities in the state, but also the need to expand their scale significantly through a system-wide approach. As a result, the Career Connect Washington (CCW) was created and obtained funding through the Washington Workforce Education Investment Act 2019.The Act calls for:

- cross-sector co-ordination through a cross-agency work group across the state;
- resources to K-12 and higher education partners to support enrolment in career launch and registered apprenticeship programmes, as well as other career-connected learning opportunities;
- regional leadership and co-ordination to facilitate connections between industry and education;
- creation of a grant programme tailored to the local needs of students and employers, and designed for students to receive dual credit; this includes supporting career-connected learning programme intermediaries working within and across regions.

The programme aims to achieve ambitious targets, including that 100% of high school students in the class of 2030 participate in career exploration or career preparation activities, and that 60% of the class of 2030 participate in a career launch programme. The initiative aims to track participation metrics by sub-group (e.g. region, industry and demographic).

The programme is supported by close to USD 40 million in 2019-21. The funding supports the creation of new career-connected learning opportunities through competitive funding allocated to programme intermediaries, regional networks and education district co-ordinators; increased enrolment in existing career-connected programmes; supports for low-income students and those in underserved areas to participate, including for transportation; as well as start-up and capital funding.

As part of CCW, funding has been allocated to the development of new registered apprenticeships in non-traditional fields such as information technology (USD 2 million), health care (USD 1.6 million), and advanced manufacturing. In addition, USD 1.5 million has been dedicated for a regional pre-apprenticeship pathways pilot programme in the Marysville School District, USD 0.9 million for expansion of state apprenticeship staffing, and USD 0.7 million for controls apprenticeship pathways in the South Kitsap School District.

Apprenti

Apprenti is an initiative of the Washington Technology Industry Association (WTIA) created to address the technology talent shortage in Washington State, particularly in the Greater Seattle Area. With a first cohort starting in 2017, the programme now operates nationally at around 50 companies (many of which are major employers) and expects to produce more than 700 graduates in 2019. The Apprenti model aims to help under-represented groups, including minorities, women and veterans, gain training, certification and placement in the tech industry. The model involves a competency assessment and a series of features distinguishing it from traditional internships, which are common in the United States.

	Apprenti Registered Apprenticeship	Internship
Term	12 months plus training period	3-6 months
Employment status	Protected class with contracted duration	At will
External oversight	Registration (state or federal labour agencies)	Educational institution or none
Resulting credential	National, portable certification of occupational competence	None
Compensation	Training wage at least 60% of fully-qualified regular employees; raise to at least 70% after 6 months, then at will	Stipend or unpaid
Benefits provided	Health, dental, vision, retirement, life insurance	Usually none
Education provided	8-22 weeks of full-time practical skill instruction	Experiential learning

The programme reports positive results: 75% of completers were hired by the company they had an apprenticeship with, or by another company in the industry. Participants in the first cohort are reported to have experienced significant income growth; the median income of entrants was USD 28 000 annually, the starting salary in the Apprenti programme was USD 45 000 during training, rising to USD 51 000 after 6 months. Apprenti graduates hired full-time are reported to earn at least USD 75 000.

Sources: Apprenti (n.d.[108]), Career Connect Washington (2019[109]), Washington Legislature (2019[18]).

Institutional initiatives

Representatives from public institutions met during the OECD visit were actively working to develop new ways for students to acquire labour market relevant skills. They reported doing so through various means, from the creation of new minors and certificates that aim to be "add-ons" complementing programmes, to the development of new degree types and better linkages between post-secondary education and alternative pathways such as apprenticeship.

In recent years, CTCs have worked to develop new types of programmes responding to both student and labour market needs. The growing provision of applied bachelor degree programmes (referred to as AB or Bachelor of Applied Science (BAS) programmes) is an example of this. Currently, 27 out of the 34 public CTCs in the state offer these types of degrees. While enrolments in these programmes represent less than 3% of total enrolments, their growth has been substantial over the past decade, from less than 100 in 2007 to close to 3 500 full-time equivalent students in 2017, with good earning outcomes (SBCTC, 2017[110]).

In the four-year sector, institutions respond to growing student demand for stackable credentials with a large number of minors and short certificates of 15 credits (five classes), in areas as diverse as data science, professional writing or global leadership. Both sectors reported various partnership approaches to support the development of collaborative programmes. In less densely populated areas of the state with fewer institutions, both universities and colleges reported collaborating to deliver new and/or in-demand programmes. An example provided was the physician assistant programme delivered in partnership between the Pacific Northwest University and Heritage University.

> *Expanding teaching practices that convey labour market relevant skills and stronger employer engagement is needed*

Embedding labour market relevance across all study programmes

Despite the strengths of its system, Washington's efforts to improve the labour market relevance of post-secondary education have limitations. While institutions met during the OECD visit acknowledged the importance of offering labour market relevant education, the extent to which such focus translated in academic content and teaching practices appeared to vary widely by institution, programme, course and faculty member. In addition, the creation of new credentials meeting employer needs appeared challenging, given employers' expectations for rapid provision of labour market relevant skills on the one hand, and the complex programme design and approval processes in higher education on the other.

The US model of higher education has a long-standing tradition of utilising methods such as problem-based learning that have been shown to encourage the acquisition of transferable social and behavioural skills valued in today's labour market, such as critical thinking, team work and problem solving (Hoidn and Kärkkäinen, 2014[111]). At the national level, the 2018 Faculty Survey of Student Engagement showed that approximately two-thirds of the 13 000 professors who responded designed upper-level courses so that students solve complex real-world problems (TCHE, 2019[112]). However, information on teaching methods and student engagement in post-secondary education is not available across Washington, which makes it difficult to assess the prevalence of these practices.

In the two-year sector, the focus on conveying employability skills was prominent in the "professional/technical" stream, which enrolled about 32% of students across Washington's 34 colleges in 2018/19 (SBCTC, 2019[39]). In the "academic transfer" stream (about 50% of students) and all other programmes where students take on average a much lighter course load, the extent to which students were able to develop labour market relevant skills was less clear. In the four-year sector, stakeholders emphasised the key role of work-based learning in equipping students with labour market relevant skills. However, while work-based learning is a core component of applied and professional fields and was often facilitated by faculty's connections with industry, these opportunities appeared to be less widespread in general fields of study such as science, business, social sciences and humanities.

Several barriers were reported to stand in the way of expanding practices, both in the classroom and more broadly in post-secondary education, that support the development of labour market relevant skills. One barrier often cited by stakeholders was the limited resources and staff in career centres, as well as inconsistent engagement of teaching faculty with career centres. In several cases, the partnership between career centres and teaching staff was mentioned as a key success factor to connect students with work-based learning opportunities, as faculty members have greater awareness of specific labour market pathways for their students and in some fields, also have industry connections.

From the faculty perspective, the lack of time to engage in activities such as helping students find work-based learning opportunities or redesigning the curriculum was a main barrier. Particularly in the four-year sector, stakeholders also reported a lack of incentives for faculty to spend time on these activities, given the greater professional rewards associated with research. Faculty preparedness was also an issue: some faculty may not have received adequate training and professional development on the ways in which to incorporate labour market relevance in their teaching and to maintain updated knowledge.

Despite these limitations, several methods were mentioned during the OECD visit on how to engage faculty in teaching practices that focus on conveying labour market relevant skills, particularly in the college sector. These ranged from a deliberate focus on teaching methods as a criteria for hiring faculty members, to connecting faculty with institution-wide efforts focused on employability. Efforts to address faculty continuing education needs were also mentioned: the SBCTC requires faculty in the professional and technical stream to update their skills on a regular basis to maintain their status as certified faculty.

The Guided Pathways model is also promising. The programme helps students choose courses that form a coherent and realistic labour market pathway, and according to stakeholders can also provide a framework for faculty to adjust course content to students' skills needs and career goals. Scaling these efforts remains a challenge, although innovative practices exist. The use of an employability lens to assess the relevance of course content provides one interesting example developed by Quality Assurance (QA) Commons, and described in Box 7.7.

Box 7.7. Quality Assurance (QA) Commons Essential Employability Qualities

Created in 2016, the goal of QA Commons is to provide "an innovative certification process that aims to ensure today's graduates enter the workforce prepared for the responsibilities they will be expected to face". Based on research and a pilot project with 27 colleges and universities, QA Commons has identified a set of nine skills expected to be required across fields of study and occupations, as well as a process to help programmes if they provide those skills to students. The nine skills are described as:

- people skills: collaboration, teamwork and cultural competence;
- problem-solving abilities: inquiry, critical thinking and creativity;
- professional strengths: effective communication, work ethic and technological agility.

The process to obtain the certification that a given programme conveys essential employability qualities (EEQ certification) focuses on five aspects, reviewing whether the programme:

- develops skills in a work-based context, such as through a capstone project;
- co-ordinates its activities with the institution's career services;
- creates meaningful relationships with employers;
- engages with students to make sure they feel they are being prepared well;
- reports how its graduates fare in the labour market.

Various institutions across multiple states have engaged in this process. Kentucky, for example, has put forward 20 programmes across two-year institutions and the state flagship university.

Source: TCHE (2019[112]).

Developing new credentials through stronger partnerships with employers

Employers continue to rely on post-secondary credentials as a proxy for a certain level of knowledge and skills acquired by graduates. A recent survey suggests that 48% of employers surveyed view educational credentials compared to other job qualifications as more important than five years ago, whereas only 23% viewed them as less important (Gallagher, 2018[34]). This view was expressed in Washington as well; business associations emphasised a preference for bachelor's degrees from flagship institutions as an important quality signal. On the other hand, employers and students, including adult learners, are seeking new ways of acquiring skills quickly, as shown by the rapid development of alternative and micro-credentials, as well as company-designed training and assessment (TCHE, 2019[112]).

However, higher education institutions face challenges in developing micro-credentials, and in integrating them with their traditional degree offer. Stakeholders in Washington raised the time-consuming and complex process of designing and securing programme approval. This challenge was often dealt with in innovative ways, for instance through the development of minors and the use of the "corporate education" arm of institutions. Other stakeholders discussed how an open dialogue with the regional accrediting body, the Northwest Commission on Colleges and Universities, and the increased focus of the body on the missions and profiles of institutions, has helped with securing accreditation for new programmes.

As previously noted, effectively engaging employers in the design of post-secondary programmes is an ongoing challenge. National research shows that the trend of company-designed training and assessment is concentrated among large national firms, whereas the overall share of employers providing tuition benefits has decreased in the past five years, from 56% to 51% providing tuition benefits for undergraduate study, and 52% to 49% providing benefits for graduate study (TCHE, 2019[112]). Among those employers who invest in training, their engagement with higher education is mixed.

In Washington, this collaboration was described as highly contingent on the existence of a trusted local college. Employer representatives met during the OECD visit reported strategies of large employers that focused on recruiting students into company training programmes through competency-based assessments. The reported goals were diverse: to identify high-potential hires, diversify the profiles of employees, and shrink the time required to hire. Different goals and approaches prevail in higher education, which can complicate partnerships between employers and institutions. Practices exist however, such as the use of intermediary organisations that can help employers and institutions collaborate, to improve the engagement of employers in institutional efforts and help institutions understand and respond to employer needs.

Recommendations for educational offering

1. Monitor the results of the Career Connect Washington initiative and the extent to which it helps more students across levels and fields of study obtain work-based experience and develop labour market relevant skills. The type of work-based learning should be defined so as to ensure the experiences are high quality; and the institutions, fields and demographics of CCW participants should be monitored to ensure equitable access to these opportunities.
2. Expand the Work Study programme to 2009 levels, even if the financial aid component is no longer necessary for Washington College Grant recipients, as a key way to provide work experience to low-income students. The programme should maintain its focus on low-income and under-represented groups, and guidelines should be developed to ensure the work opportunities provided through the programme help students obtain valuable skills for their future career.
3. As part of CCW, continue to expand innovative apprenticeship models such as Apprenti to new fields of study and explore ways to develop relevant pre-apprenticeship programmes to ensure students with lower preparedness can access these programmes.
4. Continue efforts to develop new labour market relevant learning pathways. This could include pilot projects with professional regulatory bodies to identify alternative routes to certification that facilitate career changes and alleviation of labour shortages, and pilots with employers and groups of employers to collaborate on the design of new (or redesign of current) learning opportunities that meet labour market needs, including micro-credentials. The state, in partnership with professional regulatory bodies and employers, should continue efforts to recognise quality credentials and include them in national initiatives, such as the Credential Engine (see also recommendations on information).
5. The state should work with institutions to incentivise a greater focus of faculty on ensuring all students can acquire labour market relevant skills regardless of their programme of study. Several approaches could be considered, such as: (i) targeted funding to encourage staff professional development plans in public institutions and "release time" for faculty to work in industry and other work contexts; (ii) targeted funding to encourage the provision of work-based learning opportunities in less professionally-oriented fields of study; and (iii) grants or refundable tax credits to small and medium-sized enterprises to help them provide paid internships and other high-quality work-based learning opportunities, with a particular focus on under-represented students. This could also include incentives for industry professionals to teach at higher education institutions in fields where there is typically less industry engagement.

Student supports and pathways

Washington's student supports play an important role in raising participation and success rates among under-represented groups

Supporting student learning is fundamental to the higher education mission, and in turn is critical to promote good labour market outcomes. High-impact teaching and learning practices can help improve academic performance (Kuh, 2008[113]). Some of these practices, such as the provision of work-based learning discussed in previous section, are directly tied to improving the labour market relevance of higher education, and the employment and earnings prospects of students.

In addition to teaching and learning practices, student supports can also improve student performance and outcomes. These encompass a range of services that help students choose, access and complete post-secondary qualifications. Student supports can be financial and non-financial, including academic and career counselling, mechanisms to facilitate student mobility such as credit transfer, and information (discussed in the next section of this chapter). Student supports are particularly important in a country like the United States, given the large numbers of incoming students who are not academically ready for college-level instruction, a problem that is prevalent nationally (Chen and Simone, 2016[114]). The stakeholder workshop held in Washington as part of the project further confirmed the importance of student supports; respondents to the pre-workshop survey identified student supports, both financial and non-financial, as well as pathways into and across higher education programmes, as key areas where system-wide action would be particularly effective.

Washington has made significant investments in the affordability of post-secondary education through the Washington College Grant, as discussed earlier. Under the previous State Need Grant, a large number of students were eligible but did not obtain it due to funding constraints: in 2012/13, this was the case for about 32 000 students, out of 106 000 who were eligible (Bania, Burley and Pennucci, 2013[96]). Thus, the move towards an entitlement state aid programme is likely to have a positive impact on enrolment in future years, given the unmet demand observed in the state. The expansion of eligibility to apprentices may also contribute to rising enrolments. Some other state-wide programmes help alleviate the cost barrier to post-secondary education, with a specific focus on helping low-income students access in-demand, high-earning fields of study (see Box 7.8).

Addressing other indirect costs of attending higher education, such as childcare, is a significant concern in Washington, as noted earlier in this chapter. The state's childcare grants programme, created in 1999, aims to help institutions provide their students with access to affordable, accessible and quality childcare opportunities. The programme is small and currently only available at the six public four-year institutions, which each receive USD 75 000 per year in state funding to provide grants to students, using a model requiring that the state grant be matched at least dollar-for-dollar by the participating institution's administration or student government association.

Box 7.8. Helping low-income and minority students access high-demand, high-earning fields of study

Washington STEM

Washington STEM is a state-wide, independent non-profit organisation comprised of STEM experts whose role is to identify and foster innovative STEM programs and partnerships. Washington seeks smart and scalable solutions that lead to opportunities for students underserved and under-represented in STEM fields. Washington STEM supports policy making through advocacy, identifies areas of focus on which it collects data (such as early math achievement), and supports regional STEM networks. These 11 regional STEM networks bring educators, business leaders, STEM professionals, and community leaders together to build student success and connect them with STEM career opportunities in their communities.

The Washington State Opportunity Scholarship (WSOS)

The WSOS was created in 2011 to address needs in sectors including aerospace, engineering, technology and health care and rising tuition costs at Washington institutions. The programme consists of scholarships for low- and middle-income students to pursue these fields of study at the baccalaureate level and in Career and Technical Education programmes; funds are provided by industry and philanthropic organisations and are matched dollar-for-dollar by the state. This initiative has served close to 20 000 students and outcomes are promising: 61% of students served are women, 64% are students of colour and 65% are first-generation college students. While the average family income of the most recently awarded cohort of baccalaureate scholars was just over USD 41 000 at the time of acceptance into WSOS, the average salary of recent WSOS graduates employed full-time was USD 62 297. Almost 95% of WSOS Baccalaureate graduates are employed or in graduate school, and most (81%) live in Washington state.

Washington Mathematics, Engineering, Science Achievement (MESA)

Washington's MESA programme aims to improve diversity and retention with an emphasis on traditionally under-represented students in STEM fields, including African Americans, Native Americans, Hispanic/Latinos, Pacific Islanders, and women. This programme is one of eleven state programmes co-ordinated by a national body. It benefits from industry sponsorship to fund various supports in schools, community colleges and engineering programmes. These supports are diverse, including teacher training, academic tutoring/counselling, internships, field trips, and recognition events to support both student access and retention into STEM.

Sources: Washington MESA (n.d.[115]), Washington State Opportunity Scholarship (n.d.[116]), Washington STEM (n.d.[83]).

A large body of research provides insight into the types of student supports that promote student success in post-secondary education. A range of studies using randomised controlled trials find strong positive impacts on student retention and completion of intensive and multi-faceted students supports, which include individual advising and coaching, alongside information and financial supports. By contrast, supports focused only on information or financial incentives are not found to be effective (Angrist, Lang and Oreopoulos, 2009[117]; Bettinger et al., 2012[118]; Bettinger and Baker, 2014[119]; Carrell and Sacerdote, 2017[120]). Some of this research suggests effective supports can reduce the cost per degree, given that the cost of the intervention is compensated by the increase in degrees produced (Scrivener et al., 2015[121]).

Washington is a leading state in developing Guided Pathways, an evidence-based model that aims to redesign the experience of college students from start to end. The approach involves four main components. First, institutions develop easily accessible, student-facing maps of college pathways (e.g. courses required to complete a programme, transfer to a four-year institution, time to completion, etc.). Second, students obtain advice in their choice of pathways and help in developing an academic plan, whether they have a goal in mind or are undecided. They obtain support, such as academic advising to stay on the pathway. Finally, pathways are designed with relevant learning outcomes to be achieved to support further study or employment in a chosen area (Bailey, 2017[122]). By providing funding for the expansion of Guided Pathways programmes to all colleges, Washington is taking a step towards a more systematic student support system, which could help with retention and transfer.

Transfer pathways, primarily between two-year and four-year institutions, also have the potential to increase access and completion of post-secondary education and, in turn, to improve students' labour market outcomes. About half of Washington students who earn a bachelor's degree in the state's public four-year institutions, and one-quarter of those obtaining a bachelor's degree in the private not-for-profit institutions, have transferred from a two-year institution. Washington is a leader in this area; a recent national study found that a little more than half of students who have transferred earned a bachelor's degree within six years of having started at a community college, placing Washington second out of all states (Shapiro et al., 2017[123]).

State authorities attribute this success to the existence of collaborative bodies that bring the public and private sectors together, the Joint Transfer Council and the Intercollege Relations Commission, and to state-wide transfer associate's degree agreements. The development of major-specific transfer degrees, particularly in areas of high demand, is a promising step to help students identify areas of interest and prepare for success in four-year institutions. An example of these pathways are the ten "major related programs" (MRP), in biology, business, computer science, construction management, math education, music, nursing and pre-nursing, engineering and engineering technology. While major-specific transfer degrees are recent and still compose a small share of all transfer degrees, early findings suggest that students who complete these degrees often complete a bachelor's degree as effectively as non-transfer students (that is, with a comparable number of median credits). These programmes are regularly reviewed to assess their relevance and student take-up (WSAC, 2019[124]).

Ensuring good outcomes for more students requires well-targeted and more effective student supports and pathways

The state's efforts to support student access and success in higher education have shown results, but more remains to be done. All population groups have seen increases in their attainment rate since 2013, with the largest increase among Hispanics (+6 percentage points), followed by Black/African Americans (+8 percentage points), Asians (+5 percentage points) and Whites (+3 percentage points) (WSAC, 2019[30]). However, gaps remains wide: in 2017, 25% of Hispanics and 39% of Black/African Americans aged 25-44 had a degree, compared to 51% of Whites and 71% of Asians.

Improving student supports and pathways can help improve access and completion rates, and opportunities exist in Washington to expand and improve them, and to increase students' use of these supports. In particular, the design of comprehensive supports provided systematically should be pursued, as evidence shows that multi-faceted supports provided at strategic junctures or on a continuous basis tend to be more effective than interventions of one type and at a single point in time. Efforts should also continue to increase supports' take-up among vulnerable groups. Broadly available services, such as career services, are not always being taken advantage of. While there are no Washington-specific data, the 2018 annual report of the Survey of Student Engagement suggests that only about half of seniors utilised career resources, even though those who did found them helpful in gaining confidence in their career plans. The survey also found that participation in an internship or field experience was less frequent among students of colour (NSSE, 2018[45]).

Transfer pathways could also be improved. Despite the good results of transfer students in Washington discussed earlier, more students could take advantage of transfer opportunities. Indeed, the increase in annual enrolment in public four-year institutions over the past decade is largely a result of the growth of direct-entry students (+26.7% between 2007/08 and 2016/17). By contrast, the enrolment growth of transfer students has been around 10.1% over the same period (ERDC, 2019[24]). Increasing students' use of transfer pathways may be particularly important among under-represented groups. National research indeed suggests that income levels make a difference in student participation in transfer pathways. Low-income students are less likely to transfer to a four-year institution, and if they do, less likely to attain a bachelor's degree, compared to their high-income peers. This is despite the fact that both groups are as likely to attain a pre-transfer certificate or an associate's degree, suggesting that the opportunity gap grows as student progress along their educational pathway (Shapiro et al., 2017[123]).

To improve the design and use of student supports, more needs to be known about the specific barriers facing particular groups with low educational attainment. In addition to minorities, women, and low-income students, more should be known about adults who have either no post-secondary credential or attended some college but dropped out. Adults in that situation who are between the ages of 25 and 44 represent together close to one million adults in Washington (WSAC, 2018[125]). They face particular challenges in obtaining a post-secondary credential, and in fact, over the past decade, the share of students over 30 at public four-year institutions and over 25 at community colleges has declined slightly, from about 16% to 13.6% and 43.3% to 40%, respectively (ERDC, 2019[24]; SBCTC, 2019[39]). In addition, despite the existence of a policy supporting the award of academic credit for prior learning, a recent state report on the subject suggests a slight decrease in the credits recognised, in large part due to decreased veteran enrolment in community colleges, who were the main recipients of this approach (WSAC, 2018[126]).

The recent launch of Washington's Adult Reengagement Framework, alongside efforts to foster the recognition of prior learning since 2012, are promising steps. The Framework proposes a multi-pronged approach, leveraging the state's expanded financial aid, a dedicated information portal, and engaging multiple stakeholders in reaching out and addressing the barriers faced by adult learners. In this effort, it will be important to take account of the wide variability of learner needs and work with institutions on how they can best support adult learner success. Similarly, the state's prior learning recognition approach should continue to be monitored, in particular with respect to institutional progress in recognising learning acquired through new pathways, including alternative credentials.

Box 7.9. Innovative student pathways: Central Washington University's FlexITrade Degree Pathway

Working together with local post-secondary institutions, labour unions, and the construction industry, Central Washington University's Information Technology and Administrative Management (ITAM) department designed a pathway to complete a Bachelor of Applied Science (BAS) with a specialisation in project management for individuals who have completed a registered apprenticeship programme in the construction trades.

The FlexITrade pathway is designed to streamline the path to complete a bachelor's degree by enabling skilled workers to transition into management and other opportunities. It is expected to benefit trade organisations in recruiting and retaining skilled workers, and employers by offering project management skills along with essential soft skills highly desired in most organisations working in the construction trades, as well as other industries.

Key features of the programme include:

- performance-based, flexibly-paced courses available fully online;
- high-touch advising from a dedicated faculty mentor;
- modular, alternative credentials designed for immediate career advancement;
- opportunities for prior learning assessment incorporating professional and on-the-job learning.

The FlexITrade pathway was designed through an extensive collaborative process to help create a bridge between two separate systems: trade apprenticeships and higher education. The programme was designed in collaboration with community and technical college partners and with input from a steering committee with representation from the electrical, construction, and plumbers/pipefitters trade unions, the construction industry, the Washington State Lieutenant Governor's office, and trade advocacy organisations. The programme was designed using seed funding of USD 130 000 provided via legislative allocation.

The performance-based, flexibly-paced option for study in the Information Technology and Administrative Management (ITAM) programme began in 2014. It has served over 120 students as of Spring 2019. The full FlexITrade programme was designed in 2018/19, with a goal for implementation in 2020.

Source: Information provided by Central Washington University to the OECD, June 2019.

The expansion of student supports may best be achieved through system-wide investments, especially in community colleges, as discussed in the funding section of the chapter. With respect to transfer pathways, efforts to further expand and simplify articulation agreements, as well as better communicating them to prospective students, are important strategies. Better understanding the institutional incentives to develop transfer agreements should be part of this effort. As institutions have the authority to establish entry standards and decide when to accept credits, unexpected barriers may exist. For instance, some stakeholders met during the OECD visit noted that accepting transfer students can be a challenge for four-year institutions because of their increased reliance on tuition fees as part of their total funding. Further, while creating transfer pathways can involve substantial benefits for students and employers, the collaborative work involved for institutional partners is significant.

Another challenge lies in effectively expanding transfer pathways in an environment where students' learning experiences become more complex. One example of building pathways between apprenticeship and a four-year institution is promising in this area (see Box 7.9). Washington is also working with Credential Engine, a national non-profit organisation building a national registry of credentials, to better understand the increasingly diverse landscape of educational credentials. The state aims to include approximately 3 800 Washington credentials currently included in the state's Career Bridge website in the Credential Engine national registry. This initiative places Washington among the first states to populate this growing registry of degrees, certificates, licenses, apprenticeships and micro-credentials. Further expanding the credentials included in such registry could benefit both students and institutions, including by facilitating the development of credit transfer and credential recognition agreements.

Recommendations for student supports and pathways

1. Scale up Guided Pathways programme to serve all first-year students at community and technical colleges, and monitor student take-up by programme and demographic group.
2. Undertake a study of under-represented students in high school and in the first year of post-secondary education. The study would help gain a better understanding of student motivations for pursuing post-secondary education and particular fields of study, as well as the barriers they face in completing higher education. It would further help identify where gaps exist between student needs and available supports.
3. Develop a state-wide mapping of supports currently available to post-secondary students, including those directly linked to post-secondary attendance and broader social benefits (including various supports related to health, childcare, etc. with a particular focus on ensuring their availability is assessed on a regional and local basis).
4. Develop evidence-based nudging programmes targeted to under-represented groups, and monitor their take-up and impact in the state. This could include pilot programmes targeting high school students in low-income schools through a combination of information and help with applications for college and student aid. Using information on first-year students' income and academic records, identify students most at risk of dropping out and consider piloting a programme that enrols them automatically in career and study counselling.
5. Dedicate or enhance existing state funding to expand and improve pathways from secondary to post-secondary education, across post-secondary institutions and programmes, and between post-secondary education and other learning programmes. This could include targeted funding to train and equip high school guidance counsellors with: (i) knowledge of different study and career choices, including alternative pathways such as apprenticeships, dual enrolment and state initiatives to facilitate transitions (e.g. Running Start, High School and Beyond, Guided Pathways); and (ii) skills to communicate effectively with different types of students, particularly students from low-income and under-represented group.
6. Continue to improve state efforts on credit transfer. These could include:

(i) monitoring the take-up of credit transfer opportunities by under-represented groups;

(ii) targeted funding to develop standardised, state-wide articulation agreements between two-year and four-year institutions (e.g. all transfer degrees from two-year public institutions are recognised in their entirety by four-year institutions, except in cases justified by the four-year institution);

(iii) targeted funding to expand the opportunities for credit transfer to include community colleges' professional and technical programmes and, more broadly, Career and Technical Education (CTE) courses that offer a good return on investment, including dual credit articulation agreements (as recommended in the 2017 State Auditor's report); to help recognise high-quality CTE opportunities, develop a process to involve employers in helping set industry standards, as recommended in a previous OECD review of vocational education and training in the United States (Kuczera and Field, 2013[127]).

(iv) create a centralised database of all credit transfer opportunities into post-secondary education (building on the Ready, Set, Grad website), across post-secondary programmes, and between post-secondary programmes and quality CTE and alternative credentials.

Information

Washington has developed multiple informational tools to provide data and guidance on post-secondary education and workforce needs

In order to support the different needs of students and other stakeholder groups, Washington has developed many digital tools to provide information on post-secondary opportunities, career pathways and the labour market. In addition to informational tools to help students plan their careers and provide guidance on study choice, there are multiple dashboards that match education and workforce data to provide information about skills gaps across the state.

Student-level data on post-secondary enrolments, progress and completions at public four-year institutions is collected through Washington's Public Centralized Higher Education Enrollment System (PCHEES), an entity organised under the state's Office of Financial Management (OFM). The SBCTC collects information about educational and labour market outcomes of graduates from Washington's community and technical colleges, and the Independent Colleges of Washington (ICW) collects information about graduates from private, not-for-profit four-year institutions.

The ERDC maintains two public-facing dashboards on the outcomes of post-secondary graduates. Information on student enrolments, progress and completions at public four-year institutions is provided by institution, field of study, and specific sub-groups in a comprehensive dashboard that was created in collaboration with the six public universities and colleges. Data on earnings outcomes of Washington graduates were included in a new dashboard in 2017, matching Unemployment Insurance (UI) wage records to education data from the PCHEES and SBCTC. The Earnings for Graduates dashboard provides median earnings of graduate cohorts from 2007/08 onwards by award type, field of study and institution. Data are available by degree type at both the sub-baccalaureate and baccalaureate levels for graduates of public two-year and four-year institutions. Earnings data is also available from industry councils and apprenticeship committees for completers of apprenticeship programmes. More detailed information on earnings and employment outcomes for graduates of the community and technical colleges are presented in a different dashboard maintained by SBCTC.

SBCTC is responsible for maintaining a dashboard to provide information on patterns of workforce demand and supply state-wide and by region. It also includes median earnings by occupational or career cluster and identifies gaps by sub-baccalaureate and baccalaureate qualification level. In parallel, WSAC provides, through its Roadmap dashboard, predicted supply and demand gaps using employment projections from Washington's Employment Security Department. Typically, employment projections at state-level rely on the U.S. Bureau of Labor Statistics (BLS) ten-year Occupational Outlook forecast, which includes the minimum level of education and training required for entry into an occupation. In order to provide an indication of future gaps in skill supply and demand, diverse methodologies can be used (Wilson, 2014[128]; Hershbein and Hollenbeck, 2015[129]). Washington's Roadmap dashboard includes projections for occupations at both middle and advanced skill levels based on empirical analysis and multiple sources of data, as seen in Table 7.6.

Table 7.6. Overview of digital sites or platforms linking information about post-secondary education with information about the labour market in Washington

Website or platform	Information provided	Data sources	Co-ordinator
WSAC Roadmap dashboard	Current and future skills gaps	• American Community Survey • IPEDS • BLS employment projections • ESD long-term employment projections	Washington Student Achievement Council (WSAC)
Washington state workforce supply and demand dashboard	Current skills gaps, primarily at middle-skills level	• IPEDS • Burning Glass Technologies	Washington State Board for Community and Technical Colleges (SBCTC)
Washington's STEM Talent supply and demand dashboard	STEM awareness, K-12 achievement and preparedness, STEM post-secondary degree completions, supply/demand gaps	• IPEDS • College Board • OSPI Report Card • Washington STEM Survey • American Community Survey	Washington Student Achievement Council (WSAC); Education Research and Data Center (ERDC)
ERDC earnings for graduates dashboard	Earnings of graduates who have received certificates or degrees from public colleges, universities and apprenticeship programmes in Washington	• UI wage records • PCHEES • SBCTC	Education Research and Data Center (ERDC)
ERDC public four-year dashboard	Student enrolment, progress and degree production for graduates of public four-year institutions in Washington	• PCHEES	Education Research and Data Center (ERDC)
SBCTC dashboard for community and technical colleges	Student and course enrolment, demographics, student progress, completions; Labour market outcomes for professional-technical programmes, apprenticeships and transfer students	• SBCTC data warehouse • UI wage records	Washington State Board for Community and Technical Colleges (SBCTC)
Washington Career Bridge	Average earnings and employment outlook and educational requirements provided per career. Includes information on job trends and educational programmes, primarily targeted towards middle-skill workers. In addition, a credential inventory is under development to include a registry of degrees, certificates, licenses, apprenticeships and micro-credentials.	-	Workforce Training and Education Coordinating Board
Adult re-engagement portal	Information to recruit, retain and graduate adults who have some college credit, but no credential. Information includes career options, occupations, jobs data and post-secondary programmes leading to relevant credentials.	-	Washington Student Achievement Council (WSAC)

Several new initiatives are under development in Washington to improve the quality and availability of information about post-secondary education. The Adult Reengagement Initiative, highlighted previously, targets adult learners to support them in returning to post-secondary education and completing a credential. The initiative includes a planned information portal (College and Career Compass) with targeted outreach, particularly to under-represented populations, providing information related to career options and post-secondary programmes leading to relevant credentials. Another recent initiative from the Workforce Training and Coordinating Board is a collaboration with the national Credential Engine, discussed in the previous section. .Table 7.6 provides an overview of informational tools currently in use that have been developed or initiated by a state agency.

At the same time, untargeted information and insufficient data can be a hindrance to reaching the state's post-secondary attainment goals and improving labour market outcomes

Governments across the OECD recognise that career guidance and the collection of labour market information can help learners enter post-secondary programmes that match their interests, aptitudes and abilities, and lead to promising employment and earning outcomes. To this end, many have invested heavily in building linked education and employment information systems, and platforms displaying the information they yield. Two particular challenges in Washington are insufficient data to provide a detailed picture of graduate labour market outcomes, and ensuring that data on labour market outcomes is available to students and families in a way that effectively supports their choices.

At the state level, Unemployment Insurance (UI) wage records typically indicate the industry in which an individual is employed, but they do not provide information on the specific occupation of graduates. Thus, it is difficult to assess whether or not a graduate is employed in an occupation that matches his or her field of study. In order to obtain more detailed information on in-field job placements, higher education institutions typically use alumni surveys. However, these data can be unreliable due to low response rates and poorly designed surveys. In the past, the Workforce Training and Education Coordinating Board has periodically surveyed Washington employers in order to obtain information about possible skills gaps, hiring and training practices. However, the last survey of this kind was conducted in 2012 and other industry-specific employer surveys are currently conducted on an ad hoc basis. WSAC also conducted an employer survey for its regional educational needs assessment in 2017 (WICHE/WSAC, 2017[40]), but there are no plans to carry out this survey on a systematic basis. Other countries, such as Australia and the United Kingdom, conduct regular surveys of employers regarding their skills needs and satisfaction with graduates, which could be considered in Washington. Australia in particular offers an interesting example by linking their graduate and employer surveys (see Box 3.14 in Chapter 3).

Furthermore, because of rising student debt levels and growing public concern over the cost of higher education, reporting accurate information on student debt alongside earnings data is critical. Indeed, some studies suggest that a significant share of students do not fully understand the costs of higher education or how much debt they are accumulating (Akers and Chingos, 2014[130]). Particularly, young people who are the first ones in their family to enrol in post-secondary education are likely to lack information about the returns on their education. For first-generation students, the costs of attending higher education are more salient than future benefits. It is typically more difficult for first-generation students to find information about the benefits of post-secondary education attendance and field of study choice within the students' primary social network (Bleemer and Zafar, 2018[131]).

The most recent survey of state post-secondary data systems conducted by the State Higher Education Executive Officers (SHEEO) Association shows that many states provide coverage of both public and private, not-for-profit higher education institutions in their post-secondary data systems. In Washington, data on post-secondary graduates is only collected for public two-year and four-year institutions. Additionally, earnings data on Washington graduates is not available by sub-population or region/locality.

Disaggregating earnings data by characteristics such as gender and race or ethnicity would allow policy makers to better understand and monitor the labour market outcomes of under-represented populations. Moreover, making this information available at programme level would allow students and other stakeholders to more accurately assess the costs and benefits of choosing their programme of study.

Finally, Washington's multiple dashboard tools require users to consult several different sites for information about student population and enrolments, institutional characteristics, and graduate outcomes. In addition, SBCTC's workforce supply and demand dashboard identifies skills gaps at sub-baccalaureate and baccalaureate levels. At the same time, the WSAC Roadmap dashboard provides projections for future skills gaps. Furthermore, it is unclear if the intended users of SBCTC's dashboard are primarily workforce development councils and students at community and technical colleges, or if it is intended for a broader group of users within both the higher education and workforce development communities. While workforce dashboards were initially created as part of the workforce development system aimed at middle-skill workers, they can also serve as tools to improve the link between workforce development and higher education policy by strengthening and expanding their use.

There are a number of websites that are targeted to students and their families to provide guidance on opportunities and pathways in post-secondary education. These include sites such as "Ready, Set, Grad" and 12th year initiatives to help high school students navigate applications for financial aid and other educational choices. However, educational information is often disconnected from information on the labour market. Providing easy access to layered information about the costs and benefits of educational choices through single websites and/or mobile applications is a way to help students make better choices. Because the tailoring of information is crucial to ensure that it reaches students in a manner in which they can easily access and absorb it (Lavecchia, Liu and Oreopoulos, 2015[132]), creating a single, public-facing tool can contribute to improve the accessibility and user-friendliness of labour market information and post-secondary opportunities.

Recommendations on information

1. Improve the availability of key data by sub-population. For instance, data on median earnings and average student debt should be made available at the individual programme level, rather than only by major field of study. It should be possible to disaggregate earnings data by sub-population and locality, in a similar way as is currently done with data on post-secondary enrolments and completions. To protect student privacy and avoid the potential for identifiable individual data with small samples, aggregate wage data could be provided for combined cohorts at programme level. In addition, consider ways to expand coverage of labour market outcomes data to include information about graduates from private, not-for-profit institutions and making this information available to the public in the same place, for example by further developing the dashboards maintained by ERDC.
2. Explore the development of a state-wide graduate outcomes survey to capture in-field job placement rates and assess the signalling value of post-secondary qualifications. The survey could cover a range of areas, including whether or not graduates are matched to jobs related to their field of study or level of qualification, and the extent to which graduates are using the skills acquired from post-secondary education. A state-wide graduate outcomes survey would standardise information about graduate experiences, including in-field job placements and skills use, rather than relying on information from individual higher education institutions on an ad hoc basis. Such an approach would support higher education strategic planning and complement the actions proposed in Recommendation 1, in particular through the proposed employer survey. In the longer term, the graduate outcomes survey could be combined with

an employer survey to gain a better understanding of the quality of graduate skills, as is current practice in Australia and the United Kingdom (see Chapter 3).

3. Consider creating a single skills supply and demand dashboard for Washington that consolidates information from the SBCTC workforce supply and demand dashboard and the WSAC Roadmap dashboard. The SBCTC dashboard and the WSAC Roadmap dashboard rely on different data sources and are targeted towards different users. If a single skills supply and demand dashboard is created for both middle- and advanced skill levels, this could include both current and projected skills gaps, drawing from the data sources that are currently used in two different dashboards. In addition, using real-time labour market information about skill demand, granular level data about top skills requirements could be extracted by occupation or field. A single skills supply and demand dashboard for the state should also identify skill gaps by region, as is currently done in the SBCTC workforce supply and demand dashboard.
4. Review and consider consolidating existing informational tools and portals into a single information platform with signposts helping specific user groups identify the information they need. Information should be designed so as to clearly respond to the needs of different users. The platform should provide links to existing dashboards and efforts should be made to ensure that the metrics used in each dashboard are transparent and clearly defined. To the extent possible, the metrics should be harmonised such that consistent definitions are used throughout the state for both post-secondary and workforce data systems. Better understanding how individuals use labour market and learning information could help in designing an integrated tool. The Labour Market Information Council of Canada (see Box 3.12 in Chapter 3) may offer useful insights in this area.

References

AACC (2019), *Fact Sheet 2019*, American Association of Community Colleges, http://www.aacc.nche.edu (accessed on 19 July 2019). [99]

Abraham, K. and M. Kearney (2019), "Explaining the Decline in the U.S. Employment-to-Population Ratio: a Review of the Evidence", *NBER Working Paper No. 24333*, The National Bureau of Economic Research, https://www.nber.org/papers/w24333. [12]

Addo, F., J. Houle and D. Simon (2016), "Young, Black, and (Still) in the Red: Parental Wealth, Race, and Student Loan Debt", *Race and social problems*, Vol. 8/1, p. 64, https://www.ncbi.nlm.nih.gov/pmc/articles/PMC6049093/ (accessed on 12 August 2019). [81]

Akers, E. and M. Chingos (2014), *Are College Students Borrowing Blindly?*, Brooking Institution, https://www.brookings.edu/wp-content/uploads/2016/06/Are-College-Students-Borrowing-Blindly_Dec-2014.pdf. [130]

Altonji, J., E. Blom and C. Meghir (2012), "Heterogeneity in Human Capital Investments: High School Curriculum, College Major, and Careers", *Annual Review of Economics*, Vol. 4, pp. 185-223, http://dx.doi.org/10.1146/annurev-economics-080511-110908. [56]

Altonji, J., L. Kahn and J. Speer (2014), "Trends in Earnings Differentials across College Majors and the Changing Task Composition of Jobs", *American Economic Review*, Vol. 104/5, pp. 387-393, http://dx.doi.org/10.1257/aer.104.5.387. [58]

Angrist, J., D. Lang and P. Oreopoulos (2009), "Incentives and Services for College Achievement: Evidence from a Randomized Trial", *American Economic Journal: Applied Economics*, Vol. 1/1, pp. 136-163, http://dx.doi.org/10.1257/app.1.1.136. [117]

Apprenti (n.d.), *Apprenti: Paving the path for talent in tech*, https://apprenticareers.org/who-we-are/ (accessed on 16 April 2020). [108]

Autor, D. (2014), "Skills, Education, and the Rise of Earnings Inequality among the Other 99 Percent", *Science*, Vol. 344/6186, pp. 843-851, http://dx.doi.org/10.1126/science.1251868. [63]

Bailey, M. and S. Dynarski (2011), "Inequality in Postsecondary Education", in Duncan, G. and R. Murnane (eds.), *Whither Opportunity? Rising Inequality, Schools, and Children's Life Chances*, Russell Sage Foundation, New York. [65]

Bailey, T. (2017), "Guided Pathways at Community Colleges: From Theory to Practice", *Diversity and Democracy*, Vol. 20/4, https://www.aacu.org/diversitydemocracy/2017/fall/bailey (accessed on 28 August 2019). [122]

Baker, R. et al. (2017), *The Effect of Labor Market Information on Community College Students Major Choice*, http://conference.iza.org/conference_files/EcoEdu_2016/marinescu_i1517.pdf. [77]

Bania, N., M. Burley and A. Pennucci (2013), "The Effectiveness of Washington's State Need Grant Program: Final Evaluation Report", No. Doc. No. 14-01-2301, Washington State Institute for Public Policy, Olympia, http://www.wsipp.wa.gov (accessed on 6 August 2019). [96]

Baum, S. (2014), *Higher Education Earnings Premium: Value, Variation, and Trends*, Urban Institute, https://files.eric.ed.gov/fulltext/ED544781.pdf (accessed on 20 May 2019). [48]

Bettinger, E. and R. Baker (2014), "The Effects of Student Coaching: An Evaluation of a Randomized Experiment in Student Advising", *Educational Evaluation and Policy Analysis*, Vol. 36/1, pp. 3-19, http://dx.doi.org/10.3102/0162373713500523. [119]

Bettinger, E. et al. (2012), "The Role of Application Assistance and Information in College Decisions: Results from the H&R Block FAFSA Experiment*", *The Quarterly Journal of Economics*, pp. 1205-1242, http://dx.doi.org/10.1093/qje/qjs017. [118]

Bleemer, Z. and B. Zafar (2018), "Intended college attendance: Evidence from an experiment on college returns and costs", *Journal of Public Economics*, Vol. 157, https://doi.org/10.1016/j.jpubeco.2017.11.002. [131]

Career Connect Washington (2019), *Career Connect Washington: 2019 Progress Report to the Legislature*, https://careerconnectwa.org/wp-content/uploads/2019/08/CCW-Report-to-the-Legislature-sept.-2019.pdf. [109]

Carnevale, A. et al. (2017), *Major Matters Most. The Economic Value of Bachelor's Degrees from The University of Texas System*, Georgetown University, https://vtechworks.lib.vt.edu/bitstream/handle/10919/86951/UTSystemMajorsMatter.pdf?sequence=1&isAllowed=y (accessed on 20 May 2019). [57]

Carnevale, A. and S. Rose (2003), *Socioeconomic Status, Race/Ethnicity, and Selective College Admissions.*, The Century Foundation, New York, https://eric.ed.gov/?id=ED482419 (accessed on 26 July 2019). [70]

Carnevale, A., N. Smith and J. Strohl (2013), *Recovery: Job Growth and Education Requirements through 2020*, Georgetown University Center on Education and the Workforce, Washington, DC, https://1gyhoq479ufd3yna29x7ubjn-wpengine.netdna-ssl.com/wp-content/uploads/2014/11/Recovery2020.FR_.Web_.pdf (accessed on 10 May 2019). [27]

Carnevale, A. and J. Strohl (2013), *Separate and Unequal: How Higher Education Reinforces the Intergenerational Reproduction of White Racial Privilege*, Georgetown Public Policy Institute; Center on Education and the Workforce, Washington DC, https://cew.georgetown.edu/wp-content/uploads/SeparateUnequal.FR_.pdf (accessed on 22 July 2019). [62]

Carrell, S. and B. Sacerdote (2017), "Why Do College-Going Interventions Work?", *American Economic Journal: Applied Economics*, Vol. 9/3, pp. 124-151, http://dx.doi.org/10.1257/app.20150530. [120]

Cellini, S. and N. Turner (2018), "Gainfully Employed? Assessing the Employment and Earnings of For-Profit College Students Using Administrative Data", *NBER Working Paper No. 24333*, http://www.nber.org/papers/w22287 (accessed on 30 August 2018). [76]

Chakrabarti, R. and M. Jiang (2018), *Education's Role in Earnings, Employment, and Economic Mobility*, Federal Reserve Bank of New York, New York, https://libertystreeteconomics.newyorkfed.org/2018/09/educations-role-in-earnings-employment-and-economic-mobility.html (accessed on 25 July 2019). [75]

Chen, X. and S. Simone (2016), *Remedial Coursetaking at U.S. Public 2- and 4-Year Institutions: Scope, Experience, and Outcomes – Statistical Analysis Report*, National Center for Education Statistics, Institute of Education Sciences, U.S. Department of Education, https://nces.ed.gov/pubs2016/2016405.pdf (accessed on 28 August 2019). [114]

Chetty, R. et al. (2017), "Mobility Report Cards: The Role of Colleges in Intergenerational Mobility", *NBER Working Paper No. 23618*, No. 23618, National Bureau of Economic Research, https://opportunityinsights.org/paper/mobilityreportcards/ (accessed on 26 July 2019). [71]

Comyn, P. and L. Brewer (2018), *Does work-based learning facilitate transitions to decent work?*, International Labour Office, Geneva, http://www.ilo.org/publns (accessed on 28 August 2019). [93]

Deming, D. and C. Walters (2017), *The Impact of Price Caps and Spending Cuts on U.S. Postsecondary Attainment*, Harvard University, UC Berkeley, NBER, https://scholar.harvard.edu/files/ddeming/files/DW_Aug2017.pdf (accessed on 28 August 2019). [102]

Dougherty, K. and V. Reddy (2013), "Performance Funding for Higher Education: What Are the Mechanisms? What Are the Impacts?", Community College Research Center, Teacher's College, Columbia University, https://ccrc.tc.columbia.edu/publications/performance-funding-mechanisms-impacts.html (accessed on 7 August 2019). [106]

Eaton, C. et al. (2019), "The Organizational Ecology of College Affordability: Research Activity, State Grant Aid Policies, and Student Debt at U.S. Public Universities", *Socius: Sociological Research for a Dynamic World*, Vol. 5, pp. 1-19, http://dx.doi.org/10.1177/2378023119862409. [94]

ERDC (2019), *High School Graduate Outcomes Dashboard*, Washington State Education Research and Data Center, Olympia, https://erdc.wa.gov/data-dashboards/high-school-graduate-outcomes (accessed on 18 July 2019). [41]

ERDC (2019), *Higher Education Outcomes Dashboard*, Washington State Education Research and Data Center, https://erdc.wa.gov/data-dashboards (accessed on 8 April 2020). [29]

ERDC (2019), *Statewide Public Four-Year Dashboard*, Washington State Education Research and Data Center, https://erdc.wa.gov/data-dashboards/public-four-year-dashboard#about-dashboard (accessed on 19 July 2019). [24]

ERDC (2018), *The Earnings Premium of Washington Higher Education: Gender Deficit in Earnings among Washington College Graduates*, Washington State Education Research and Data Center, Olympia, https://erdc.wa.gov/publications/economic-returns/earnings-premium-washington-higher-education-gender-deficit-earnings (accessed on 25 July 2019). [66]

ERDC (2018), *Unmet Need among Financially Needy College Students in the State of Washington*, Washington State Education Research and Data Center, Olympia, https://erdc.wa.gov/publications/student-outcomes/unmet-need-among-financially-needy-college-students-state-washington (accessed on 30 July 2019). [55]

ERDC (n.d.), *Education Research and Data Center*, https://erdc.wa.gov/ (accessed on 9 April 2020). [37]

ESD (2019), *2018 Labor Market and Economic Report*, Employment Security Department Washington State, Olympia, https://esdorchardstorage.blob.core.windows.net/esdwa/Default/ESDWAGOV/labor-market-info/Libraries/Economic-reports/Annual-Report/2018%20Labor%20Market%20and%20Economic%20Report.pdf (accessed on 8 July 2019). [2]

Gallagher, S. (2018), *Educational Credentials Come of Age: A Survey on the Use and Value of Educational Credentials in Hiring*, Northeastern University, Center for the Future of Higher Education and Talent Strategy, https://www.northeastern.edu/cfhets/wp-content/uploads/2018/12/Educational_Credentials_Come_of_Age_2018.pdf (accessed on 20 July 2019). [34]

Garza, A. and A. Fullerton (2018), "Staying Close or Going Away: How Distance to College Impacts the Educational Attainment and Academic Performance of First-generation College Students", *Sociological Perspectives*, Vol. 61/1, pp. 164-185, http://dx.doi.org/10.1177/0731121417711413. [91]

Goolsbee, A., G. Hubbard and A. Ganz (2019), "A Policy Agenda to Develop Human Capital for the Modern Economy", in Kearney, M. and A. Ganz (eds.), *Expanding Economic Opportunity for More Americans: Bipartisan Policies to Increase Work, Wage and Skills*, https://www.aspeninstitute.org/longform/expanding-economic-opportunity-for-more-americans/a-policy-agenda-to-develop-human-capital-for-the-modern-economy/ (accessed on 12 August 2019). [101]

Hanushek, E. et al. (2017), "General Education, Vocational Education, and Labor-Market Outcomes over the Lifecycle", *The Journal of Human Resources*, Vol. 52/1, pp. 52-87, http://dx.doi.org/10.3368/jhr.52.1.0415-7074R. [52]

Hershbein, B. and K. Hollenbeck (2015), *Refining Workforce Education Supply and Demand Analysis: Final Report*, W.E. Upjohn Institute for Employment Research, https://research.upjohn.org/cgi/viewcontent.cgi?article=1034&context=up_technicalreports. [129]

Hershbein, B. and M. Kearney (2014), *Major Decisions: What Graduates Earn Over Their Lifetimes*, The Hamilton Project, https://www.financialbuildingblocks.com/assets/What%20Graduates%20Earn%20Over%20Their%20Lifetimes.pdf (accessed on 20 May 2019). [59]

Hershbein, B. and C. Macaluso (2018), *Labor Market Concentration and the Demand for Skills*, http://conference.iza.org/conference_files/DATA_2018/macaluso_c26795.pdf (accessed on 21 May 2019). [49]

Hillman, N., D. Tandberg and A. Fryar (2015), "Evaluating the Impacts of "New" Performance Funding in Higher Education", *Educational Evaluation and Policy Analysis*, Vol. 37/4, pp. 501-519, http://dx.doi.org/10.3102/0162373714560224. [107]

Hoidn, S. and K. Kärkkäinen (2014), "Promoting Skills for Innovation in Higher Education: A Literature Review on the Effectiveness of Problem-based Learning and of Teaching Behaviours", *OECD Education Working Papers*, No. 100, OECD, Paris, https://doi.org/10.1787/19939019. [111]

Holzer, H. (2015), "Higher Education and Workforce Policy: Creating More Skilled Workers (and Jobs for Them to Fill)", *Economic Studies*, The Brookings Institution, Washington DC, https://www.brookings.edu/wp-content/uploads/2016/06/higher_ed_jobs_policy_holzer.pdf (accessed on 12 August 2019). [104]

Hoxby, C. (2018), "The Productivity of U.S. Postsecondary Institutions", in Hoxby, C. and K. Stange (eds.), *Productivity in Higher Education*, National Bureau of Economic Research/University of Chicago Press, https://www.nber.org/chapters/c13875.pdf (accessed on 7 August 2019). [103]

Hoxby, C. (2009), "The Changing Selectivity of American Colleges", *Journal of Economic Perspectives*, Vol. 23:4, pp. 95-118, https://pubs.aeaweb.org/doi/pdfplus/10.1257/jep.23.4.95 (accessed on 26 July 2019). [72]

Hoxby, C. and C. Avery (2014), "The Missing "One-Offs": The Hidden Supply of High-Achieving, Low-Income Students", *Brookings Paper on Economic Activity, Spring 2013*, The Brookings Institution, https://www.brookings.edu/wp-content/uploads/2016/07/2013a_hoxby.pdf (accessed on 1 September 2019). [79]

Hoxby, C. and S. Turner (2013), "Expanding College Opportunities for High-Achieving, Low Income Students", No. 12-014, Stanford University, https://siepr.stanford.edu/sites/default/files/publications/12-014paper_6.pdf. [78]

InsideEWU (2018), *New building, partnership a catalyst for EWU growth in Spokane*, https://inside.ewu.edu/. [87]

Jardim, E. et al. (2018), "Minimum Wage Increases and Individual Employment Trajectories", *NBER Working Paper No. 25182*, National Bureau of Economic Research, https://www.nber.org/papers/w25182. [14]

Jardim, E. et al. (2018), "Minimum Wage Increases, Wages, and Low-Wage Employment: Evidence from Seattle", *NBER Working Paper No. 23532*, National Bureau of Economic Research, https://www.nber.org/papers/w23532. [15]

Keating, A. (2019), *The growth of economic inequality in Washington*, Economic Opportunity Institute, http://www.opportunityinstitute.org/research/post/economic-inequality-2019/ (accessed on 30 August 2019). [3]

Kuczera, M. and S. Field (2013), "A Skills beyond School Review of the United States", *OECD Reviews of Vocational Education and Training*, OECD Publishing, Paris, https://www.oecd-ilibrary.org/docserver/9789264202153-en.pdf?expires=1561390375&id=id&accname=ocid84004878&checksum=E75EE5A7013C24152714E0164041745D (accessed on 24 June 2019). [127]

Kuh, G. (2008), *High-Impact Educational Practices: What They Are, Who has Access to Them, and Why They Matter*, Association of American Colleges and Universities, Washington DC, https://provost.tufts.edu/celt/files/High-Impact-Ed-Practices1.pdf (accessed on 29 August 2019). [113]

Lavecchia, A., H. Liu and P. Oreopoulos (2015), "Behavioral Economics of Education: Progress and Possibilities", *NBER Working Paper No. 20609*, http://www.nber.org/papers/w20609. [132]

Legislation Evaluation and Accountability Programme (LEAP) Office (2020), *Washington State Fiscal Information*, http://fiscal.wa.gov/default.aspx (accessed on 28 February 2020). [100]

LMIC (2018), *What's in a Name? Labour Shortages, Skills Shortages, and Skills Mismatches*, Labour Market Information Council, https://lmic-cimt.ca/wp-content/uploads/2018/10/LMI-Insights-No.-3.pdf (accessed on 2 August 2019). [31]

Looney, A. and C. Yannelis (2015), "A crisis in student loans? How changes in the characteristics of borrowers and in the institutions they attended contributed to rising loan defaults", *Brookings Papers on Economic Activity*, No. 2, The Brookings Institution, Washington DC, https://www.brookings.edu/bpea-articles/a-crisis-in-student-loans-how-changes-in-the-characteristics-of-borrowers-and-in-the-institutions-they-attended-contributed-to-rising-loan-defaults/ (accessed on 12 August 2019). [82]

Lumina Foundation (2019), *A Stronger Nation: Washington Report 2019*, http://blob:http://strongernation.luminafoundation.org/7f19044b-3524-491d-9c9c-0111133c43ab. [6]

Lumina Foundation (2018), *A Stronger Nation*, https://www.luminafoundation.org/resources/a-stronger-nation-report (accessed on 19 June 2019). [20]

McGuinness, A. (2016), *State Policy Leadership for the Future: History of state coordination and governance and alternatives for the future*, Education Commission of the States, Denver, https://www.ecs.org/wp-content/uploads/051616-State-Policy-Leadership-for-the-Future-KL-final4-1.pdf (accessed on 10 September 2019). [90]

Minaya, V. and J. Scott-Clayton (2017), "Labor Market Outcomes and Postsecondary Accountability: Are Imperfect Metrics Better than None?", in Hoxby, C. and K. Stange (eds.), *Productivity in Higher Education*, National Bureau of Economic Research/University of Chicago Press, https://www.nber.org/chapters/c13876.pdf (accessed on 7 August 2019). [105]

Musu-Gillette, L. et al. (2017), *Status and Trends in the Education of Racial and Ethnic Groups 2017*, National Center for Education Statistics/American Institutes for Research, https://nces.ed.gov/pubs2017/2017051.pdf (accessed on 19 July 2019). [98]

NCES (2019), *Integrated Postsecondary Education Data System (database)*, National Center for Education Statistics, https://nces.ed.gov/ipeds/use-the-data (accessed on 18 January 2020). [19]

NCES (2018), "Loans for Undergraduate Students", in *The Condition of Education*, National Center for Education Statistics, https://nces.ed.gov/programs/coe/indicator_cub.asp (accessed on 24 July 2019). [74]

NCES (2017), *Digest of Education Statistics, 2017, Table 303.20 Percentage of recent high school completers enrolled in college by race/ethnicity: 1960 through 2016*, https://nces.ed.gov/programs/digest/d17/tables/dt17_302.20.asp (accessed on 26 July 2019). [69]

NSSE (2018), *Survey Findings on the Quality of Undergraduate Education Engagement Insights - National Survey of Student Engagement, Annual Results 2018*, Center for Postsecondary Research, Indiana University, http://nsse.indiana.edu/pdf/NSSE_Annual_Results_2018.pdf (accessed on 29 August 2019). [45]

OECD (2019), *OECD Skills Outlook 2019 : Thriving in a Digital World*, OECD Publishing, Paris, https://dx.doi.org/10.1787/df80bc12-en. [25]

OECD (2019), *OECD Study on Social and Emotional Skills*, http://www.oecd.org/education/ceri/social-emotional-skills-study/ (accessed on 4 September 2019). [42]

OECD (2018), *TALIS 2018 Results: Teachers and School Leaders as Lifelong Learners - Volume I*, OECD Publishing, Paris, https://www.oecd-ilibrary.org/docserver/1d0bc92a-en.pdf?expires=1568054859&id=id&accname=ocid84004878&checksum=0DC4BCF15B37C0F8CAEC24A2BF81DBCB (accessed on 9 September 2019). [32]

OECD (2017), *OECD Skills Outlook 2017: Skills and Global Value Chains*, OECD Publishing, Paris, https://dx.doi.org/10.1787/9789264273351-en. [26]

OECD (2016), *PISA 2015 Results (Volume I): Excellence and Equity in Education*, PISA, OECD Publishing, Paris, https://dx.doi.org/10.1787/9789264266490-en. [84]

OECD (2016), *Skills Matter: Further Results from the Survey of Adult Skills*, OECD Publishing, Paris, https://doi.org/10.1787/9789264258051-en (accessed on 21 August 2018). [44]

OECD (2013), *OECD Skills Outlook 2013 First Results from the Survey of Adult Skills*, https://www.oecd.org/skills/piaac/Skills%20volume%201%20(eng)--full%20v12--eBook%20(04%2011%202013).pdf (accessed on 28 September 2017). [43]

Office of the Washington State Auditor (2017), *Performance Audit: Leading Practices for the State's Secondary Career and Technical Education Programs*, http://www.sao.wa.gov. (accessed on 2 August 2019). [33]

OFM (2019), *Per capita personal income by county 1980-2017*, Washington State Office of Financial Management, https://www.ofm.wa.gov/washington-data-research/statewide-data/washington-trends/economic-trends/washington-and-us-capita-personal-income/capita-personal-income-county (accessed on 5 March 2020). [4]

Oreopoulos, P. and U. Petronijevic (2013), "Making College Worth It: A Review of Research on the Returns to Higher Education", *NBER Working Paper No. 19053*, National Bureau of Economic Research, Cambridge, http://www.nber.org/papers/w19053 (accessed on 2 September 2019). [47]

Papadakis, E. (2018), *Washington's Future of Work Task Force: An Orientation*, Workforce Training and Education Coordinating Board, http://www.wtb.wa.gov/Documents/FOWOrientation.pdf (accessed on 9 September 2019). [88]

Payne, A. and J. Roberts (2008), "Government Oversight of Organizations Engaged in Multiple Activities: Does Centralized Governance Encourage Quantity or Quality?", McMaster University; University of Toronto, https://www.researchgate.net/profile/Joanne_Roberts2/publication/4822358_Government_Oversight_of_organizations_Engaged_in_Multiple_Activities_Does_Centralized_Governance_Encourage_Quantity_or_Quality/links/0c960529519499d966000000/Government-Oversight-of- (accessed on 10 September 2019). [89]

Reardon, S. (2011), "The Widening Academic Achievement Gap Between the Rich and the Poor: New Evidence and Possible Explanations", in Duncan, G. and R. Murnane (eds.), *Whither Opportunity? Rising Inequality, Schools, and Children's Life Chances*, Russell Sage Foundation, New York, https://cepa.stanford.edu/sites/default/files/reardon%20whither%20opportunity%20-%20chapter%205.pdf (accessed on 22 July 2019). [64]

Rose, S. (2017), *Mismatch: How Many Workers with a Bachelor's Degree Are Overqualified for Their Jobs?*, Urban Institute , Washington, http://www.urban.org/sites/default/files/publication/87951/college_mismatch_final.pdf (accessed on 21 May 2019). [68]

SBCTC (2019), *Community and Technical Colleges at a Glance*, https://www.sbctc.edu/resources/documents/about/facts-pubs/community-and-technical-colleges-at-a-glance.pdf. [22]

SBCTC (2019), *Enrollment Data Dashboard*, Washington State Board for Community and Technical Colleges, Olympia, https://www.sbctc.edu/colleges-staff/research/data-public/enrollment-data-dashboard.aspx (accessed on 18 July 2019). [39]

SBCTC (2017), "Program growth and graduate employment outcomes of Washington's applied baccalaureate degrees", *Research report*, No. 17-4, SBCTC, https://www.sbctc.edu/resources/documents/colleges-staff/research/bachelor-applied-science-research/17-4-applied-baccalaureate-program-growth-employment-outcomes-8-23-17.pdf (accessed on 19 July 2019). [110]

SBCTC (n.d.), *Washington State Board for Community and Technical Colleges*, https://www.sbctc.edu/ (accessed on 8 April 2020). [23]

Schanzenbach, D., R. Nunn and G. Nantz (2017), *Putting Your Major to Work: Career Paths after College*, The Hamilton Project, https://www.brookings.edu/wp-content/uploads/2017/05/es_20170511_putting_major_to_work_career_paths_after_college.pdf (accessed on 20 May 2019). [61]

Schneider, M. (2015), *Higher Education Pays: But a Lot More for Some Graduates Than for Others*, College Measures, https://www.air.org/sites/default/files/Higher_Education_Pays_Sep_13.pdf (accessed on 20 May 2019). [51]

Scrivener, S. et al. (2015), *Doubling Graduation Rates*, MDRC, New York, https://files.eric.ed.gov/fulltext/ED558511.pdf (accessed on 28 August 2019). [121]

Shapiro, D. et al. (2017), "Tracking Transfer: Measures of Effectiveness in Helping Community College Students to Complete Bachelor's Degrees", *Signature Report*, No. 13, National Student Clearinghouse Research Center, Herndon, VA, https://nscresearchcenter.org/wp-content/uploads/SignatureReport13_corrected.pdf (accessed on 28 August 2019). [123]

SHEEO (2019), *SHEF: FY 2018 State Higher Education Finance*, State Higher Education Executive Officers Association, http://www.sheeo.org/shef (accessed on 30 July 2019). [53]

TCHE (2019), *Career-Ready Education: Beyond the skills gap, tools and tactics for an evolving economy*, The Chronicle of Higher Education, https://store.chronicle.com/products/career-ready-education (accessed on 2 August 2019). [112]

TICAS (2019), *Student Debt and the Class of 2018*, The Institute for College Access and Success, https://ticas.org/interactive-map/. (accessed on 23 October 2019). [54]

TICAS (2018), *Student Debt and the Class of 2017*, The Institute for College Access & Success, Washington DC, https://ticas.org/sites/default/files/pub_files/classof2017.pdf (accessed on 12 August 2019). [95]

Turley, R. (2009), "College Proximity: Mapping Access to Opportunity", *Sociology of Education*, Vol. 82/2, pp. 126-146, http://dx.doi.org/10.1177/003804070908200202. [92]

U.S. Bureau of Economic Analysis (2019), *Regional BEARFacts: Washington*, https://apps.bea.gov/regional/bearfacts/action.cfm (accessed on 2 September 2019). [1]

U.S. Bureau of Labor Statistics (2020), *Labor Force Statistics from the Current Population Survey*, https://www.bls.gov/cps/ (accessed on 12 March 2020). [11]

U.S. Bureau of Labor Statistics (2019), *Labor force characteristics by race and ethnicity, 2017*, http://www.bls.gov/cps/documentation.htm. (accessed on 24 July 2019). [67]

U.S. Bureau of Labor Statistics (2019), *Occupation Employment Statistics*, https://www.bls.gov/oes/home.htm (accessed on 26 August 2019). [10]

U.S. Bureau of Labor Statistics (2016), *Labor force participation: what has happened since the peak?*, Monthly Labor Review, https://www.bls.gov/opub/mlr/2016/article/pdf/labor-force-participation-what-has-happened-since-the-peak.pdf. [13]

U.S. Census Bureau (2019), *American Community Survey 2018 (database)*, https://www.census.gov/programs-surveys/acs/data.html (accessed on 18 January 2020). [7]

U.S. Census Bureau (2018), *American Community Survey 2013-2017 5-year Data Release*. [36]

University of Washington (n.d.), *The Minimum Wage Study*, https://evans.uw.edu/policy-impact/minimum-wage-study (accessed on 4 March 2020). [16]

Urban Institute (2019), *Variation in Earnings*, http://collegeaffordability.urban.org/after-college/variation-in-earnings/#/ (accessed on 31 August 2019). [60]

US SBA Office of Advocacy (2018), *Washington Small Business Economic Profiles for 2018*, US Small Business Administration Office of Advocacy, https://www.sba.gov/sites/default/files/advocacy/2018-Small-Business-Profiles-WA.pdf (accessed on 4 September 2019). [50]

Washington Legislature (2019), *Washington Education Investment Act*, https://app.leg.wa.gov/billsummary?BillNumber=2158&Initiative=false&Year=2019 (accessed on 7 August 2019). [18]

Washington Legislature (2012), *House Bill 2483: Higher Education Coordination*, http://lawfilesext.leg.wa.gov/biennium/2011-12/Pdf/Bills/Session%20Laws/House/2483-S2.SL.pdf?cite=2012%20c%20229%20%C2%A7%201. (accessed on 7 March 2020). [17]

Washington MESA (n.d.), *Washington MESA*, https://www.washingtonmesa.org/ (accessed on 8 April 2020). [115]

Washington Roundtable (2018), *Unlocking Washington's Full Potential*, https://www.waroundtable.com/wp-content/uploads/2018/01/UnlockingthePotentialWA.pdf. [5]

Washington State Department of Labor and Industries (n.d.), *Washington State Department of Labor and Industries*, https://www.lni.wa.gov/ (accessed on 9 April 2020). [38]

Washington State Opportunity Scholarship (n.d.), *Washington State Opportunity Scholarship*, https://www.waopportunityscholarship.org/ (accessed on 8 April 2020). [116]

Washington State STEM Education Innovation Alliance (2019), *2019 STEM Education Report Card*, https://stem.wa.gov. (accessed on 17 July 2019). [28]

Washington STEM (n.d.), *Washington STEM*, https://washingtonstem.org/about/ (accessed on 8 April 2020). [83]

Webber, D. (2016), "Are college costs worth it? How ability, major, and debt affect the returns to schooling", *Economics of Education Review*, Vol. 53, pp. 296-310, http://dx.doi.org/10.1016/j.econedurev.2016.04.007. [80]

WICHE/WSAC (2017), *Washington State Regional Educational Needs Assessment*, Western Interstate Commission for Higher Education/ Washington Student Achievement Council, https://www.wsac.wa.gov/sites/default/files/2017.12.08.regional.education.needs.assessment.pdf (accessed on 17 July 2019). [40]

Wilson, B. (2014), *How many more skilled workers do we need? Using supply and demand reports for state workforce planning*, National Skills Coalition, State workforce and education alignment project, https://www.nationalskillscoalition.org/resources/publications/file/how-many-more-skilled-workers.pdf. [128]

WSAC (2020), *Colleges and institutions in Washington*, https://wsac.wa.gov/colleges-and-institutions-washington (accessed on 8 April 2020). [21]

WSAC (2019), *2019 Transfer Report: Measuring statewide transfer degree effectiveness*, https://www.sbctc.edu/colleges-staff/research/data-public/transfers-dashboard.aspx (accessed on 24 June 2019). [124]

WSAC (2019), *2019-2021 Strategic Action Plan*, Washington Student Achievement Council, https://wsac.wa.gov/sites/default/files/2019-21.12.17.SAP.pdf (accessed on 5 May 2020). [86]

WSAC (2019), *Roadmap Overview and Key Measures Dashboard*, Washington Student Achievement Council, https://wsac.wa.gov/roadmap/overview#dashboard-overview (accessed on 24 July 2019). [30]

WSAC (2018), *2018 Academic Credit for Prior Learning (ACPL) Report Update*, Washington Student Achievement Council, Olympia, https://www.wsac.wa.gov/sites/default/files/2018.ACPL.Report.Update.pdf (accessed on 29 August 2019). [126]

WSAC (2018), *Adult Reengagement*, Washington Student Achievement Council, Olympia, https://www.wsac.wa.gov/sites/default/files/2018.11.27.ARF.Brief.pdf (accessed on 29 August 2019). [125]

WSAC (2017), *Progress on Postsecondary Enrollments*, https://wsac.wa.gov/roadmap/access (accessed on 9 April 2020). [73]

WSAC (2013), *The 2013 Roadmap*, Washington Student Achievement Council, Olympia, https://www.wsac.wa.gov/the-2013-roadmap (accessed on 15 July 2019). [85]

WSAC (n.d.), *Statewide College Bound Scholarship Sign-Up Map and Data - County Maps*, Washington Student Achievement Council, https://wsac.wa.gov/college-bound (accessed on 6 May 2020). [35]

WSAC (n.d.), *The New Washington College Grant*, Washington Student Achievement Council, https://wsac.wa.gov/wcg (accessed on 12 March 2020). [97]

WSAC, SBCTC and WTECB (2018), *A Skilled and Educated Workforce 2017 Update: An analysis of postsecondary education, workforce preparation, and employer demand in Washington*, Washington Student Achievement Council/State Board for Community and Technical Colleges/ Workforce Training and Education Coordinating Board / Workforce Training and Education Coordinating Board, Olympia, https://wsac.wa.gov/sites/default/files/2017.ASkilledAndEducatedWorkforce.pdf (accessed on 31 May 2019). [8]

WSATC (2019), *Apprenticeship Quarterly Report - First Quarter 2019*, Washington State Department of Labour & Industries, Washington State Apprenticeship & Training Council, http://www.Lni.wa.gov/TradesLicensing/Apprenticeship (accessed on 4 September 2019). [46]

WTECB (2011), *H-1B Workers in Washington*, Workforce Training and Education Coordinating Board, http://www.wtb.wa.gov/Documents/H1B_2011_Report.pdf (accessed on 9 September 2019). [9]

Annex A. Fact-finding visits to Ohio, Texas, Virginia, Washington and Washington, DC

This review was based upon desk-based research and fact-finding visits to the jurisdictions involved in the review. During fact-finding visits, OECD staff conducted interviews and workshops with public officials; higher education leaders and staff; and key stakeholders, including employers, professional associations, economic development organisations and other intermediary bodies.

Between April and October 2019, the OECD team visited the four participating states holding interviews with key officials and stakeholders, as well as a stakeholder workshop in each state. Based upon guidance from the OECD team, each state co-ordinator identified and invited a range of stakeholder organisations to the interviews and workshop held in the state.

Table A.1. Principal state co-ordinators and representatives of state higher education agencies

Ohio	Texas	Virginia	Washington
Ohio Department of Higher Education (ODHE)	Texas Higher Education Coordinating Board (THECB)	State Council of Higher Education for Virginia (SCHEV)	Washington Student Achievement Council (WSAC)
Cheryl Rice Vice Chancellor, Higher Education Workforce Alignment	**David Gardner** Deputy Commissioner/Chief Academic Officer **Ginger L. Gossman** Senior Director, Innovation and Policy Development **Jenna Cullinane Hege** Deputy Assistant Commissioner for Strategic Planning	**Peter A. Blake** Director **Alan Edwards** Director of Policy Studies	**Michael P. Meotti** Executive Director **Isaac Kwakye** Director of Research **Daryl Monear** Associate Director

Organisations participating in OECD interviews and workshops

Ohio

The fact-finding visit to Ohio was conducted from 30 September to 8 October, 2019. Interviews took place in Athens, Bowling Green, Cincinnati, Columbus and Elyria from 30 September to 7 October, and the workshop was held in Columbus on 8 October.

Table A.2. Organisations participating in OECD interviews and workshop in Ohio

AICUO (Association of Independent Colleges and Universities of Ohio)
APEG (Appalachian Partnership for Economic Growth)
Art Academy of Cincinnati
Ashland University
Aultman College
Bluffton University
Bowling Green State University

Buckeye Hills Regional Council
Capital University
Cincinnati State Technical and Community College
Clark State Community College
Cleveland State University
Columbus College of Art & Design
Columbus State Community College
Cuyahoga Community College/Tri-C
Defiance College
Denison University
Franklin University
Governor's Office
Governor's Office of Workforce Transformation
Governor's Office of Appalachia
Higher Learning Commission
Hiram College
Hocking College
InnovateOhio
IUC (Inter-University Council of Ohio)
Lake Erie College
Lakeland CC
Lorain CCC
Lourdes University
Mercy College
Miami Regional University
Muskingum University
NFIB (National Federation of Independent Business)
Northwest State
OACC (Ohio Association of Community Colleges)
Ohio Business Roundtable
Ohio Chamber of Commerce
Ohio Christian University
Ohio Council of Retail Merchants
Ohio Department of Education
Ohio Department of Higher Education
Ohio Department of Job and Family Services
Ohio Education Research Center
Ohio Farm Bureau
Ohio House of Representatives
Ohio Manufacturers Association
Ohio Mid-Eastern Government Association (Omega District)
Ohio Senate
Ohio State University
Ohio University
Ohio Wesleyan University
Otterbein University
Owens Community College
P20 Council
Shawnee State University
Sinclair Community College
Southern State Community College
Stark State College
Terra State Community College

Tiffin University
University of Akron
University of Cincinnati Blue Ash Campus
University of Findlay
University of Toledo
Ursuline College
Washington State Community College

Texas

The fact-finding visit to Texas took place from 16-24 September, 2019. Interviews were conducted in Austin, Houston, Dallas-Fort Worth and El Paso from 16-23 September, and the workshop was held in Austin on 24 September.

Table A.3. Organisations participating in OECD interviews and workshop in Texas

Accenture
Amazon
Apple
Austin Community College
BBVA Compass America
Biehl International
Borderplex Alliance
CEA Group
Certain Affinity
City of Austin
Civitas Learning
Collin County Community College District
Communities Foundation of Texas
Council of Public University Presidents and Chancellors
Dallas Chamber of Commerce
Dallas County Community College District
Dallas County Promise
Dell
DFW Regional Workforce Leadership Council
Doctors Hospital at Renaissance
Dow Chemical
EcoTourism, Alamo Economic Development Board
Educate TX
El Paso Community College
El Paso Community Foundation
El Paso Electric Company
Enterprise Rental Car
Federal Reserve Bank of Dallas
Fluor Corporation
Fort Bliss Military Base
Greater Houston Partnership
Greater Texas Foundation
Hidalgo County
House Higher Education Committee

Hunt Companies
IBM
Independent Colleges and Universities of Texas
JP Morgan Chase
La Unión Del Pueblo Entero
Lamar University
LBJ School of Public Affairs
Lockheed Martin Aeronautics Company
Lone Star College
Lower Rio Grande Valley Development Council
McAllen Economic Development Corporation
Mission Economic Development Corporation
National Oilwell Varco
Navarro College
North Central Texas College
North Texas Community College Consortium
Office of the Governor of Texas
Project Arriba
RGV Focus
RGV Partnership
S&B Engineers and Constructors
Sam Houston State University
Senate Higher Education Committee
Shell Companies
South Texas College
Southern Methodist University
Starr County Industrial Foundation
Tarleton State University
Tarrant County College
Tenet Healthcare
Texas 2036
Texas A&M System
Texas A&M University
Texas Association of Community Colleges
Texas Association of Manufacturers
Texas Business Leadership Council
Texas Department of Transportation
Texas Education Agency
Texas Instruments
Texas Lutheran University
Texas Restaurant Association
Texas State Technical Colleges
Texas Southmost College
Texas State Technical College
Texas State Technical College, Harlingen
Texas State Technical College, North Texas
Texas State Technical College System
Texas Tech University Health Science Center
Texas Wesleyan University

Texas Women's University
Texas Workforce Commission
Texas Workforce Investment Council
T-Mobile Call Center
Trellis Company
United Way of Greater Houston
United Ways of Texas
United Way of South Texas
United Way of Southern Cameron County
University of Houston
University of Texas at Arlington
University of Texas at Austin
University of Texas at El Paso
University of Texas at Rio Grande Valley
University of Texas at Rio Grande Valley, School of Engineering
University of Texas at Rio Grande Valley, School of Medicine
University of Texas MD Anderson Cancer Center
U.S. Department of Labor, Dallas Regional Office
UT System
Valley Baptist Medical Center
Wal-Mart
Wayland Baptist University
WestStar Bank
Workforce Solutions Borderplex
Workforce Solutions Cameron
Workforce Solutions Houston-Galveston
Workforce Solutions Lower Rio Grande Valley

Virginia

The fact-finding visit to Virginia took place from 13-22 May, 2019. Interviews were conducted in Fairfax, Richmond, Norfolk, Staunton and Roanoke from 13-21 May, and the workshop was held in Richmond on 22 May.

Table A.4. Organisations participating in OECD interviews and workshop in Virginia

Amazon Web Services
Blue Ridge Community College
Cameron Foundation of Petersburg
Community College Workforce Alliance
Council of Independent Colleges in Virginia
ECPI University
Ferrum College
George Mason University
Growth and Opportunity for Virginia
Hampton Roads Economic Development Alliance
Hampton Roads Workforce Council
Harvest Foundation
House Appropriations Committee

James Madison University
John Tyler Community College
Liberty University
Mary Baldwin University
McGuireWoods Consulting
Micron Technologies
MITRE Corporation
Newport News Shipbuilding
Norfolk State University
Northern Virginia Community College
Northern Virginia Technology Council
NoVa Workforce Research Center
Office of the Governor of Virginia
Old Dominion University
Radford University
Reynolds Community College
Roanoke College
Roanoke Regional Partnership
Senate Finance Committee
SCHEV Council Members
Shenandoah University
Shenandoah Valley Partnership
State Board for Community Colleges
Tidewater Community College
Tidewater Consortium for Higher Education
University of Richmond
University of Virginia
University of Virginia, College at Wise
University-based Economic Developers
Valleys Innovation Council
Virginia Board of Workforce Development
Virginia Business-Higher Education Council
Virginia Career Works Piedmont Region
Virginia Chamber of Commerce
Virginia Chief Workforce Development Advisor
Virginia Commonwealth University
Virginia Community College System
Virginia Deputy Secretary of Commerce and Trade
Virginia Deputy Secretary of Education
Virginia Director of Planning and Budget
Virginia Economic Development Partnership
Virginia Employment Commission
Virginia House Appropriations Committee
Virginia House Education Committee
Virginia Secretary of Education
Virginia Secretary of Finance
Virginia Senate Finance Committee
Virginia Small Business Association
Virginia State University

Virginia Tech Carilion School of Medicine
Virginia Wesleyan University

Washington

The fact-finding visit to Washington was conducted from 29 April to 7 May, 2019. Interviews took place in Olympia, Seattle, Spokane and Yakima from 29 April to 6 May, and the workshop was held in Seattle on 7 May.

Table A.5. Organisations participating in OECD interviews and workshop in Washington

Association of Washington Business
Career Connect Washington
Council of Presidents
Eastern Washington University
Evergreen State College
Greater Seattle Partners
Heritage University
House College and Workforce Development Committee
Independent Colleges of Washington
Kaiser Permanente
Microsoft
Northwest Career Colleges Federation
Office of Superintendent of Public Instruction
Office of the Governor of Washington
Olympic Consortium Workforce Development Council
Pacific Northwest University
Seattle Metropolitan Chamber of Commerce
Seattle University
Senate Democratic Caucus
Senate Higher Education & Workforce Development Committee
Society of Professional Engineers in Aerospace
South Central Workforce Council
South Puget Sound Community College
Spokane Community College
Spokane STEM Network
Spokane Workforce Council
State Board for Community and Technical Colleges
STEM Education Innovation Alliance
University of Washington
Washington Department of Labor and Industries
Washington Economic Development Association
Washington Education and Research Data Center
Washington Employment Security Department
Washington Roundtable
Washington State Labor Council
Washington State Opportunity Scholarship
Washington State University, Health Sciences
Washington STEM

Washington Technology Industry Association
Western Washington University
Workforce Development Council of Seattle-King County
Workforce Training and Education Coordinating Board
Yakima County Development Association
Yakima Valley College

Washington, DC

The fact-finding visit to Washington, DC took place on 9-10 May, 2019.

Table A.6. Organisations participating in OECD interviews in Washington, DC

American Enterprise Institute
Center for American Progress
Georgetown University Center on Education and the Workforce
Jobs for the Future
National Skills Coalition
New America
The Century Foundation
The Institute for College Access & Success (TICAS)
U.S. Department of Education, Office of Planning, Evaluation and Policy Development
U.S. Department of Education, Office of Postsecondary Education

Pre-workshop stakeholder surveys

Stakeholders attending the workshops in each state were invited to respond to a short survey in advance of the workshop. Participants were asked about their views on how graduates are doing in the labour market, whether they have the skills required to meet labour market needs, and what policy makers and other stakeholders could do to improve the alignment of higher education and the labour market.

The survey included 19 questions on the following topics:

- general perception of the value of higher education;
- perception of skills needed in the labour market at present and in future;
- perception of graduates' skills;
- drivers of graduates' employment and earnings;
- the role of government, institutions, employers and other stakeholders in aligning higher education and the labour market.

The objective of the survey was to encourage workshop participants to reflect on some of the key issues being examined in the OECD review of labour market relevance and outcomes in higher education. Some key findings from the survey were presented during the workshops. The survey was not a statistical data collection.

A sample of questions and key findings for each of the main topics is presented below.

Perception of skills needed in the labour market at present and in future

Sample question: To what extent do you think these skills will change in importance to employers over the next 5-10 years? Please rate each skill according to how much you think it will change in importance to employers in the next 5-10 years.

	1 Decrease in importance	2 Decrease slightly in importance	3 Stay the same as now	4 Increase slightly in importance	5 Increase considerably in importance	Don't know
Subject matter knowledge						
General computer literacy						
Advanced computer skills						
Critical thinking (e.g. the process of conceptualizing, analyzing, and/or synthesizing information)						
Complex problem-solving						
Written and oral communication						
Professional and personal integrity (e.g. abiding by ethical standards and norms of privacy, honesty and respect)						
Leadership/management						
Entrepreneurship						
Cooperation and teamwork						
Self-motivation and initiative						
Active listening, empathy and other interpersonal skills						
Resilience (e.g. adaptability; capacity to recover quickly from difficulties)						
Conscientiousness (e.g. attention to detail, self-discipline and timeliness, persistence)						
Creativity and innovative thinking						
Numeracy and quantitative reasoning						

Results (N=100)

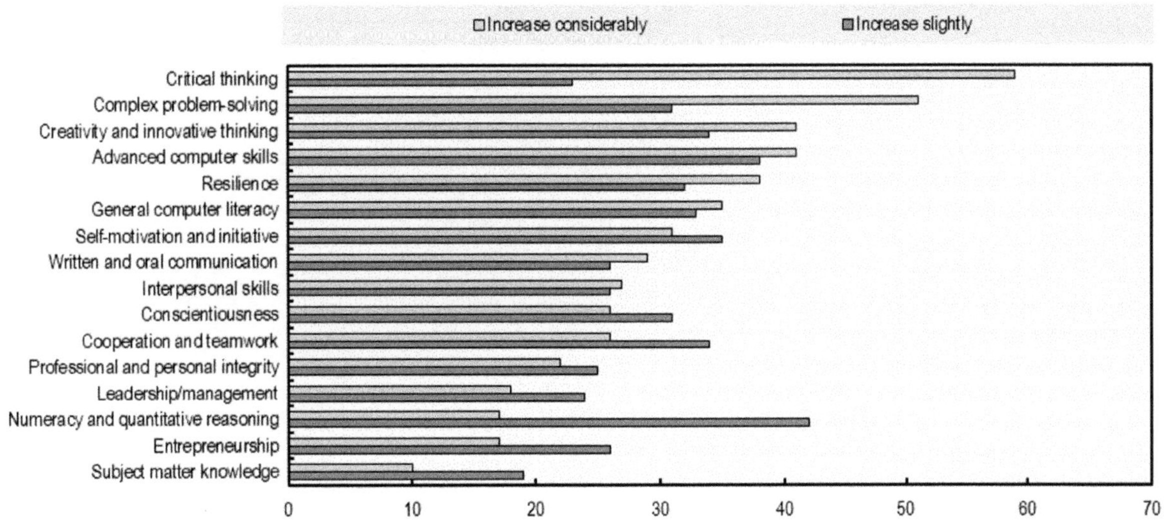

Perception of graduates' skills

Sample question: Please read the following statements and indicate the extent to which you agree or disagree.

	Strongly agree	Agree	Neither agree nor disagree	Disagree	Strongly disagree
Recent graduates generally have good subject matter knowledge (e.g. knowledge of accounting, economics, biology, anthropology, etc.)					
Recent graduates generally have good cognitive skills (e.g. critical thinking, problem-solving, oral and written communication, numeracy skills)					
Recent graduates generally have good social and emotional skills (e.g. conscientiousness, resilience, cooperation, active listening, empathy)					

Results (N=100)

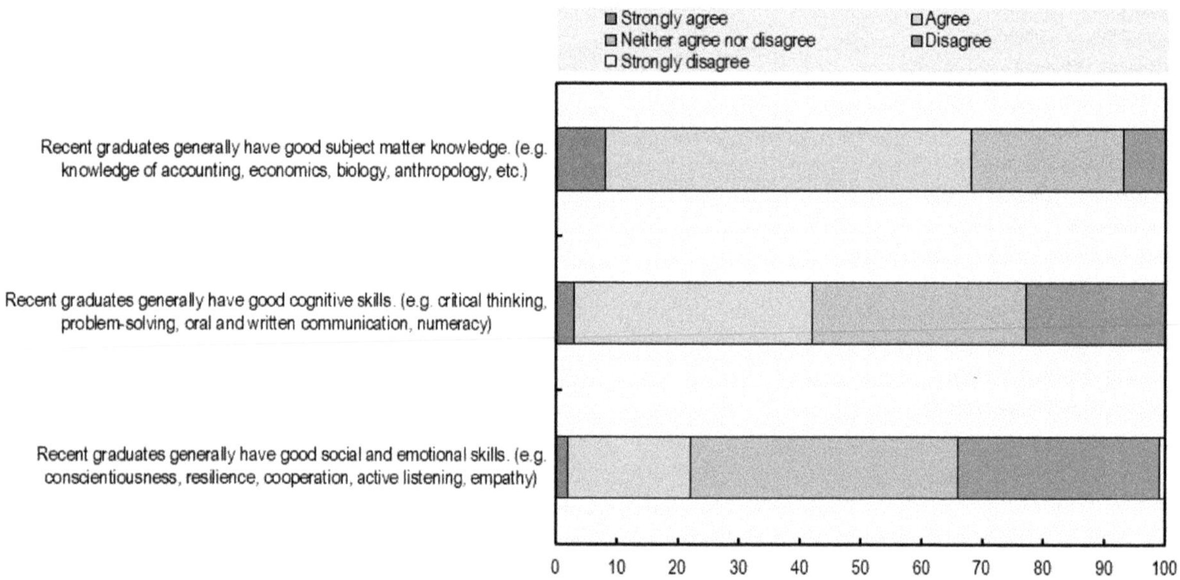

Drivers of graduates' employment and earnings

Sample question: Multiple factors influence graduate success in the labor market. Please rate the following factors in terms of how important you think they are for predicting success in the labor market (approx. 5 years after graduation). N= 98

	1 Not important	2	3	4	5 Very important
The kind of higher education graduates have obtained (e.g. level, institution, field of study)					
Skill- or competency-based certificates or supplementary credentials					
Work experience (e.g. internships, capstone projects and other work-based and experiential learning)					
Other student characteristics (e.g. socio-economic background, abilities, extracurricular activities)					
The local and regional economic context (e.g. economic structure and performance, industry composition)					
Wider global trends affecting regional and local labor market (e.g. technological change, international trade patterns)					
State policy in higher education					
State policy in other domains (e.g. employment, tax)					
Federal policies (in any area)					
Actions taken by non-governmental coordinating bodies					
Other: (please specify__________)					

Results (N=98)

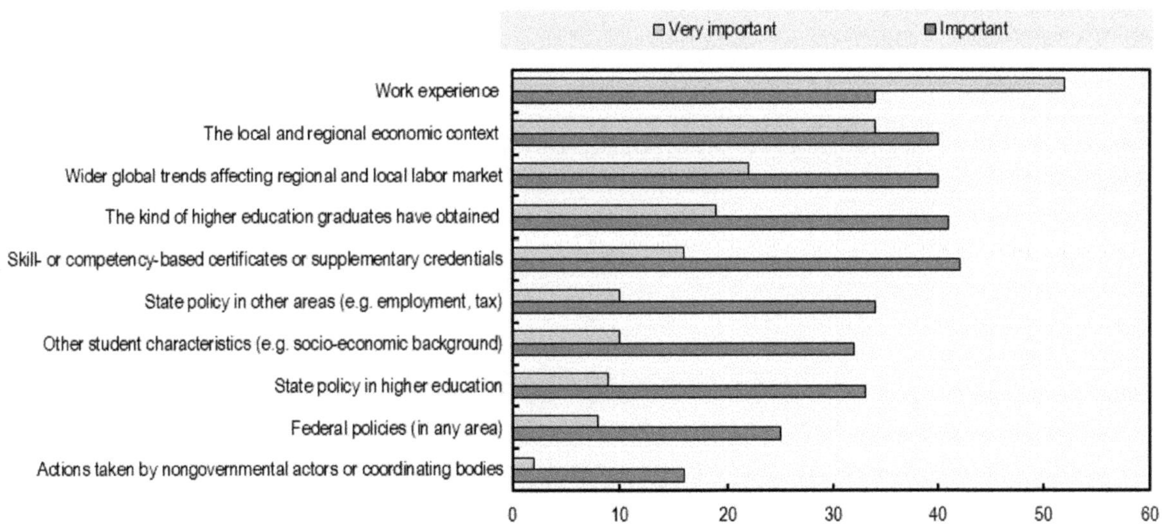

The role of government, institutions, employers and other stakeholders in aligning higher education and the labour market

Sample question: Please rate the following types of policy action (which could be taken by public authorities or non-governmental bodies in cooperation with government) in terms of how effective you think they would be in improving the alignment between higher education and the labor market.

	1 Not at all effective	2	3	4	5 Very effective
Strategic planning and forecast mechanisms to help higher education providers to strategically plan the programs offered and ensure that these respond to labor market needs – both current and projected.					
Policies promoting the **quality and diversity of higher education provision**, including content and delivery of particular programs and curricula.					
Policies to develop **pathways into and between programs and institutions** to accommodate learners at different stages of their working lives.					
Academic staff policies that encourage faculty to cultivate labor market-relevant skills in their students.					
Policies to provide **financial support to students** to help them develop labor-market relevant skills and complete a credential.					
Policies to provide **non-financial support to students** (e.g. academic, career counselling) to help them develop labor-market relevant skills and complete a credential.					
Policies to promote the **provision of information and guidance** for students and graduates about their choice of institution, field of study and occupation					
Quality assurance and accreditation processes that contribute to good quality educational credentials that are trusted by employers					
Public funding to higher education institutions that takes into account the (current and projected) career prospects of graduates to encourage the provision of labor market-relevant higher education					
Signalling mechanisms to help employers understand the skills that graduates from different programs should possess and to help graduates convey the skills they have obtained in higher education					

Results (N=98)

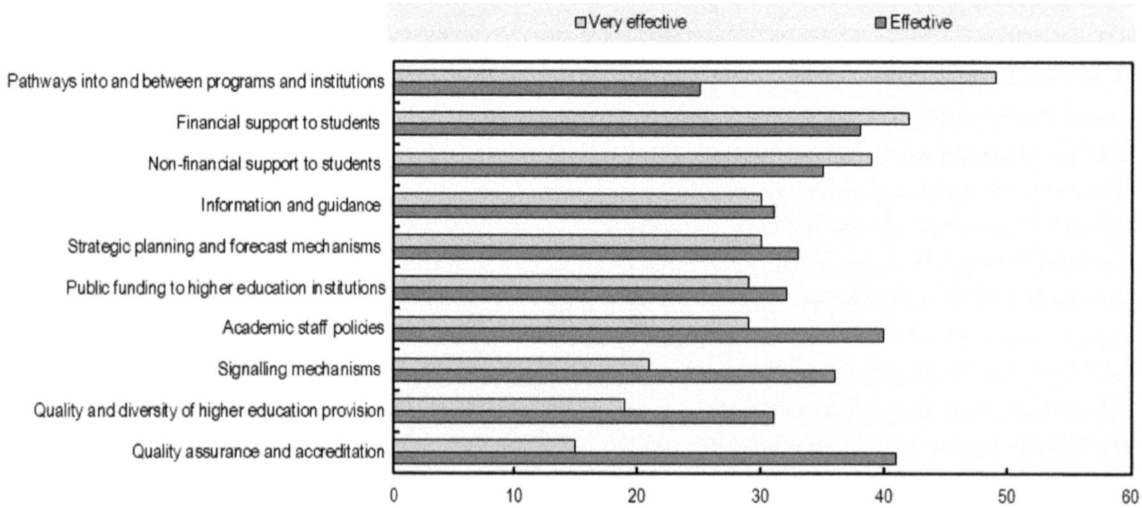

Sample question: Please read the following statements and indicate the extent to which you agree or disagree.

	Strongly agree	Agree	Neither agree nor disagree	Disagree	Strongly disagree
The state government should take on a larger role in influencing the behavior of higher education institutions.					
Employers should take on a larger role in engaging with higher education institutions and communicating skills needs.					
Professional or industry associations should take on a larger role in engaging with higher education institutions and communicating skills needs.					
Higher education institutions should increase their efforts to ensure that program and curriculum design are better aligned with the needs of the labor market.					

Results (N=99)

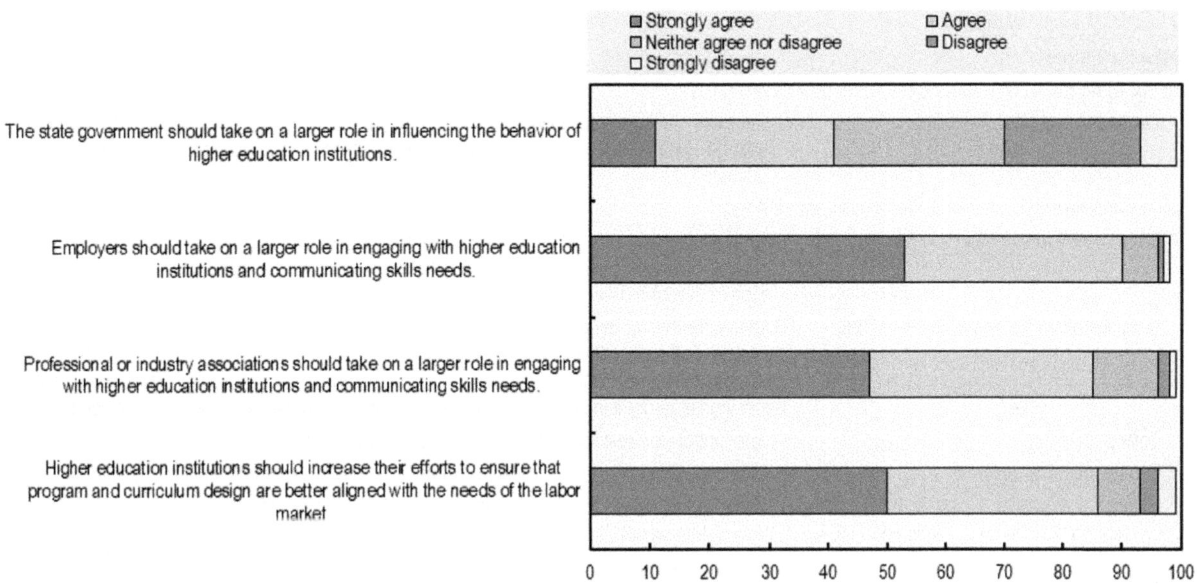

Annex B. Comparative tables: Data sources and definitions

The following table includes data sources and definitions used in the two comparative tables included in Chapter 3, namely:

- Table 3.1. Economy, population and higher education in Ohio, Texas, Virginia and Washington
- Table 3.2. Scorecard: Labour market outcomes of higher education graduates, 25-34 year-olds

Table B.1. Sources and definitions for overview and scorecard indicators, 2018

	Indicator	Definitions
Overview indicators		
Source for Indicator 1: U.S. Bureau of Economic Analysis (2019[1])		
1	Per capita real GDP, in USD	The state GDP per capita is expressed in real US dollars, using chained 2012 dollars. The indicator was retrieved from the Bureau of Economic Analysis Interactive Data Tables (SAGDP10N).
Source for Indicators 2 to 11: U.S. Census Bureau (2019[2])		
2	Employment rate, 25-64 (%)	Persons were considered employed if they worked at least one hour for pay or profit during the week preceding the survey, worked at least 15 hours as "unpaid family workers," or had a job from which they were temporarily absent (e.g., because of illness or vacation time).
3	Annual median earnings, 25-64, in USD	Annual median earnings are computed based on individuals' total pre-tax wage and salary income. Full-time, full-year workers are included and the self-employed are included for the purpose of international comparisons. This differs from American Community Survey (ACS) earnings data used in Chapters 4 to 7, where self-employment earnings are excluded.
4	Total population	Total population resident in the state/country of reference, all ages
5	Total population under 18	Total population resident in the state/country of reference, persons under 18 years-old
6	Higher education attainment rate, associate's degrees (%), 25-34 and 35-64	Share of individuals resident in the state/country of reference in each age group whose highest educational qualification is an associate's degree
7	Higher education attainment rate, bachelor's degrees (%), 25-34 and 25-64	Share of individuals resident in the state/country of reference in each age group whose highest educational qualification is an associate's degree
8	Higher education attainment rate, associate's degrees and above (%), 25-34 and 25-64	Share of individuals resident in the state/country of reference in each age group who hold an associate's degree or above
9	Degree holders who migrated to the state within the past year as a share of all degree holders (%)	Degree holders who migrated to the state within the past year refer to graduates holding an associate's degree or above who took residence in the state within the past year, whether they arrived from another state or country. This indicator is computed by dividing the number of degree holders who migrated in the state in a given year by the total number of degree holders in the state during that year.
10	Share of employed bachelor's graduates by birthplace, 25-64 (%), in the state, out-of-state or outside of the United States	Share of bachelor's graduates resident in the state/country of reference with at least one hour of paid employment in the week preceding the survey, by place of birth
11	Share of the population enrolled in post-secondary education (undergraduate level) (%), 18-24 and 25-44	Share of the population resident in the state/country of reference in each age group who reported being enrolled in college (first, second, third or fourth year) in the 3 months before the survey was taken
Source for Indicators 12 to 15: NCES (2019[3])		
12	12-month enrolment by post-secondary sector as a share of total enrolment,	12-month enrolment refers to full-time equivalent students who enrolled from July 1 of one year through June 30 of the next. Total enrolment refers to all full-time equivalent enrolment

	2017/18, (%), public four-year institutions, public two-year institutions, private non-profit institutions, private for-profit institutions	in post-secondary education, both public and private, at all levels of education. Enrolment data cover all post-secondary institutions (degree-granting and non-degree-granting). In this indicator, the category "public four-year institutions" also include public institutions that only provide graduate-level education. For both public four-year and two-year institutions, the share of institutions that only provide graduate-level education or only provide non-degree programmes (such as certificates) is below 3%.
13	Completion rate within 150% of the nominal duration, by type of institution	Share of degree/certificate-seeking post-secondary students in a given cohort who completed their programme within 150% of the nominal time (e.g. four years for a bachelor's degree and two years for an associate's degree). Calculations are based on the adjusted entry cohort, i.e. the cohort excluding students removed for the following reasons: death, permanent disability or entry into service in armed forces, foreign aid missions, or church missions. The indicator presents completion rates for 2018, thus referring to the cohort of students entering post-secondary education in 2012 in four-year institutions and the cohort entering post-secondary education in 2015 for two-year institutions.
14	150% completion rate in public 4-year institutions, by race/ethnicity	Share of degree/certificate-seeking post-secondary students in a given cohort who completed their programme within 150% of the nominal time for three racial and ethnic groups: White, Black/African American and Hispanic/Latino. Racial and ethnic categories are mutually exclusive. Calculations are based on the adjusted entry cohort, i.e. the cohort excluding students removed for the following reasons: death, permanent disability or entry into service in armed forces, foreign aid missions, or church missions.
Source for Indicators 15 to 17: SHEEO (2019[4]). See tables 4 and 6 in SHEF: FY2018 State Higher Education Finance report. The indicators refer only to public higher education institutions.		
15	Total educational revenue per full-time equivalent enrolment (public and private sources) in USD	Full-time equivalent (FTE) enrolment is a measure of enrolment in which each unit of measurement is equal to one student enrolled full-time for one academic year, based on all credit hours (including summer sessions). The SHEF data capture FTE enrolment in public institutions of higher education from those credit or contact hours associated with courses that apply to a degree or certificate, excluding non-credit continuing education, adult education, and extension courses.
16	Educational appropriations per full-time equivalent enrolment (public sources only), in USD	This indicator is a measure of state and local support available for public higher education operating expenses. They exclude spending for research, agriculture-related programmes, and medical education.
17	Net tuition revenue as a share of total education revenue (public post-secondary institutions)	Net tuition revenue is the total amount of tuition and fees minus state financial aid, institutional tuition waivers or discounts, and medical student tuition and fees. This includes revenue tuition and fees from in-state and out-of-state students as well as undergraduate and graduate students. While net tuition revenue reflects the share of instructional support received from students and their families, it does not consider many factors that contribute to a student's net price and does not directly measure tuition rate increases. Total education revenue is the sum of educational appropriations and net tuition revenue. In some states, a portion of tuition revenue is used to fund capital debt service and similar non-operational activities. These sums are excluded from the total educational revenue, which measures the amount of revenue available to public institutions to support instruction.
Source for Indicators 18 and 19: TICAS (2019[5]). Indicators cover undergraduate students only, and loans from both public and private sources. The data were provided voluntarily by approximately half of all public and non-profit bachelor's degree-granting four-year institutions, representing more than 70% of graduates.		
18	Percentage of bachelor's degree graduates (public and private non-profit) with debt (%)	Share of graduates from public four-year and non-profit four-year institutions who graduated in 2018 with debt
19	Average debt of bachelor's degree graduates with loans (USD)	Average debt of students from public four-year and private non-profit four-year institutions who graduated in 2018 with student loans
Source for Indicator 20: NCES (2019[3]).		
20	Degrees/certificates conferred in selected fields of study as a share of the total, all levels	The four fields of study used for this indicator aggregate several fields of study from the Classification of Instructional Programmes (CIP) 2010. They are similar but not identical to International Standard Classification of Education (ISCED) fields of study. The four fields include the following CIP codes: • Education: 13 - Education • Information and Communications Technology: 10 - Communications Technologies/Technicians and Support Services; 11 - Computer and Information Sciences and Support Services • Business and Law: 22 - Legal Professions and Studies; 52 - Business, Management, Marketing, and Related Support Services • Arts and Humanities: 16 - Foreign Languages, Literatures, and Linguistics; 23 - English

		Language and Literature/Letters; 24 - Liberal Arts and Sciences, General Studies and Humanities; 25 - Library Science; 38 - Philosophy and Religious Studies; 39 - Theology and Religious Vocations; 50 - Visual and Performing Arts; 54 – History.

Scorecard Indicators

Sources:

US data: All indicators have been computed using data from the 2018 American Community Survey (2019[2]).

International data: Indicators have been computed using the OECD database (2020[6]). The reference year is 2018 or the latest year available. The employment rate by educational attainment (indicator 1) and employment rate by gender (indicator 3) are based on 2017 for Chile, while employment by field of study (indicator 2) is calculated using 2017 information for Chile and the United States. For annual median earnings by educational attainment (indicator 5) and by field of study (indicator 6), data are from 2017 for most OECD countries. Data from 2016 are used for Australia, Canada, Finland, Luxembourg, Mexico, Poland and Spain; 2015 for the Czech Republic, France and Italy; and 2014 for Lithuania.

1	Employment rate by educational attainment (%)	Ratio of the employed population aged 25-34 to the total population in that age group. Persons were considered employed if they worked at least one hour for pay or profit during the week preceding the survey, worked at least 15 hours as "unpaid family workers," or had a job from which they were temporarily absent (e.g., because of illness or vacation time). Educational attainment levels include: • Upper secondary education, which corresponds to ISCED Level 3. • Some college, no degree" includes individuals who started but did not complete a post-secondary qualification and individuals who completed post-secondary qualifications shorter than associate's degrees, such as certificates. This category is not tracked in international data collections. • Associate's degree corresponds to ISCED Level 5. • Bachelor's degree corresponds to ISCED Level 6. For fields of study used in Indicator 2, see Table B.2. International comparisons of employment and earnings by field of study. Race and ethnicity: White, Black/African American, and Hispanic/Latino. The racial and ethnic categories are mutually exclusive.
2	Employment rate of bachelor's degree holders by selected fields of study (%)	
3	Employment rate by gender, bachelor's degree holders (%)	
4	Employment rate by race and ethnicity, bachelor's degree holders (%)	
5	Annual median earnings (full-time full-year workers) by educational attainment (USD)	Annual median earnings are computed based on individuals' total pre-tax wage and salary income. Full-time, full-year workers are included and the self-employed are included for the purpose of international comparisons. This differs from ACS earnings data used in Chapters 4 to 7, where self-employment earnings are excluded. Earnings indicators for the US states and US average and maximum are reported in absolute and in relative terms. As earnings have not been adjusted based on different costs of living in the four states, absolute figures have to be interpreted with caution, and in light of the context indicators (Table 2.1, Chapter 3). Annual median earnings for OECD countries are computed based on individuals' total pre-tax wage and salary income, with the exception of Ireland, Latvia, Luxembourg, Mexico and Turkey, which consider earnings net of income tax. Full-time, full-year workers are included. Earnings indicators are reported only in relative terms. See Annex 3 of OECD Education at a Glance (2019[7]) for detailed information about the sources for each country. For educational attainment, fields of study, and race and ethnicity: see above.
6	Annual median earnings (full-time full-year workers) of bachelor's degree holders by selected fields of study (USD)	
7	Annual median earnings (full-time full-year workers) by gender, bachelor's degree holders (USD)	
8	Annual median earnings (full-time full-year workers) by race and ethnicity, bachelor's degree holders (USD)	
9	Share of the population with a degree (associate's and above) earning above the median wage for the 25-64 year-old population (all earners) (%)	The share is calculated based on individuals' total pre-tax wage and salary income. It includes all earners, namely individuals working full-time and full-year as well as people working part-time and part-year and the self-employed, to allow for international comparisons with indicators on median earnings from the OECD database (2020[6]). This indicator reflects the effects of degree attainment, as well as other factors such as work experience and earnings, and should be interpreted with caution.

Scorecard Indicators 2 and 6 report employment and earnings comparisons by field of study between the four US states, the US average and international jurisdictions. For the US states and the US average, Census codes used in the American Community Survey were used. For international jurisdictions, the International Standard Classification of Education (ISCED) was used. The correspondence between these classifications used in this report is outlined in Table B.2.

Table B.2. International comparisons of employment and earnings by field of study

Employment rate by selected fields of study (Scorecard Indicators 2 and 6, Table 3.2, Chapter 3)	
ISCED 2011, when applicable	**American Community Survey (Census codes)**
01 - Education	23 - Education Administration and Teaching
ISCED does not include a "STEM" aggregate. The OECD aggregate, also used in the OECD's annual *Education at a Glance* publication, includes the following ISCED fields of study: - 05 Natural sciences, Mathematics and Statistics - 06 Information and Communications Technologies - 07 Engineering, Manufacturing and Construction	Science, Technology, Engineering and Mathematics (STEM): 14 – Architecture 20 – Communication Technologies 21 – Computer and Information Sciences 24 – Engineering 25 – Engineering Technologies 36 – Biology and Life Sciences 37 – Mathematics and Statistics 38 – Military Technologies 50 – Physical Sciences 51 – Nuclear, Industrial Radiology, and Biological Technologies 56 – Construction Services 57 – Electrical and Mechanic Repairs and Technologies
06 - Information and Communications Technology	20 – Communication Technologies 21 – Computer and Information Sciences
04 - Business, Administration and Law	32 – Law 62 – General Business
02 - Arts and Humanities	15 – Area, Ethnic, and Civilization Studies 26 – Linguistics and Foreign Languages 33 – English Language, Literature, and Composition 34 – Liberal Arts and Humanities 35 – Library Science 48 – Philosophy and Religious Studies 49 – Theology and Religious Vocations 60 – Fine Arts 64 – History

Sources: Degrees conferred by selected fields of study: UNESCO Institute for Statistics (2015[8]), *International Standard Classification of Education, Fields of Education and Training 2013 (ISCED-F 2013), Detailed field descriptions*, http://uis.unesco.org/sites/default/files/documents/international-standard-classification-of-education-fields-of-education-and-training-2013-detailed-field-descriptions-2015-en.pdf; U.S. Census Bureau (2019[2]), American Community Survey 2018 (database), https://www.census.gov/programs-surveys/acs/data.html.

References

NCES (2019), *Integrated Postsecondary Education Data System (database)*, National Center for Education Statistics, https://nces.ed.gov/ipeds/use-the-data (accessed on 18 January 2020). [3]

OECD (2020), *OECD Education Statistics*, https://doi.org/10.1787/edu-data-en. [6]

OECD (2019), *Education at a Glance 2019: OECD Indicators*, OECD Publishing, Paris, https://www.oecd-ilibrary.org/docserver/f8d7880d-en.pdf?expires=1568316502&id=id&accname=ocid84004878&checksum=FEF13445781E06CE49671ADC97573E5B (accessed on 12 September 2019). [7]

SHEEO (2019), *SHEF: FY 2018 State Higher Education Finance*, State Higher Education Executive Officers Association, http://www.sheeo.org/shef (accessed on 30 July 2019). [4]

TICAS (2019), *Student Debt and the Class of 2018*, The Institute for College Access and Success, https://ticas.org/interactive-map/. (accessed on 23 October 2019). [5]

U.S. Bureau of Economic Analysis (2019), *Interactive Data Tables (database)*, https://apps.bea.gov/itable/iTable.cfm?ReqID=70&step=1 (accessed on 17 April 2020). [1]

U.S. Census Bureau (2019), *American Community Survey 2018 (database)*, https://www.census.gov/programs-surveys/acs/data.html (accessed on 18 January 2020). [2]

UNESCO Institute for Statistics (2015), *International Standard Classification of Education Fields of education and training 2013 (ISCED-F 2013)-Detailed field descriptions*, http://dx.doi.org/10.15220/978-92-9189-179-5-en. [8]

www.ingramcontent.com/pod-product-compliance
Ingram Content Group UK Ltd.
Pitfield, Milton Keynes, MK11 3LW, UK
UKHW051456290926
15471UKWH00008B/1235

9 789264 728738